Strategizing Management Accounting

The theory and practice of management accounting should be seen within the context of varieties of global capitalism, to appreciate its role as a 'calculative technology of capitalism' which is practised on factory floors, corporate boards, computer networks, spreadsheets, and so forth. This new textbook is the first to introduce the field from a rounded social science perspective.

Strategizing Management Accounting offers a theoretical discussion on management accounting's strategic orientation by accommodating two interrelated lines of analyses, from historical and contemporary perspectives. The book illustrates how 'new management accounting' has evolved into the form in which it exists today in its neoliberal context and how those new management accounting practices have become manifestos for the managers, as calculative technologies of decision making, performance management, control, corporate governance, as well global governance, and development within various forms of organizations across the globe. Each chapter draws on Foucauldian analysis of biopolitics explaining how neoliberal market logic informs a set of strategies and mechanisms through which the various social entities and discourses are made governable by considering them as biopolitical entities of global governance.

Written by two recognized accounting experts, this book is vital reading for all students of management accounting and will also be a useful supplementary resource for those wanting to understand and research accounting's vital role in contemporary society.

Chandana Alawattage is Professor/Chair in Accounting at University of Aberdeen Business School, UK.

Danture Wickramasinghe is Professor/Chair in Management Accounting at Adam Smith Business School, University of Glasgow, UK.

'Another landmark book by the authors. It is essential and provocative reading for any social scientist, whether an established researcher or a postgraduate aspiring to become one, wishing to understand the history of management accounting knowledge and practices from the emergence of modernity in the seventeenth century until today.'

– Trevor Hopper, Professor Emeritus of Management Accounting,
University of Sussex, UK

'The authors of this book have tackled management accounting as a social science. It is a contemporary massive literature review which explores many important themes regarding management accounting technologies and practice. It is theoretically informed and provides many alternate theoretical lenses so accounting researchers, educators and students can use this book to explain management accounting in contemporary times. Particularly I like the final chapters that explored the neoliberal governability in a global sense and important issues such as biopolitical security including global financial scandals, systematic financial risks, corruption, environment and sustainability, development and poverty, etc. I highly recommend this book.'

– James Guthrie, Distinguished Professor of Accounting,
Macquarie University, Australia

Strategizing Management Accounting

Liberal Origins and Neoliberal Trends

Chandana Alawattage and
Danture Wickramasinghe

LONDON AND NEW YORK

First published 2019
by Routledge
2 Park Square, Milton Park, Abingdon, Oxon OX14 4RN

and by Routledge
711 Third Avenue, New York, NY 10017

Routledge is an imprint of the Taylor & Francis Group, an informa business

© 2019 Chandana Alawattage and Danture Wickramasinghe

The right of Chandana Alawattage and Danture Wickramasinghe to be identified as authors of this work has been asserted by them in accordance with sections 77 and 78 of the Copyright, Designs and Patents Act 1988.

All rights reserved. No part of this book may be reprinted or reproduced or utilised in any form or by any electronic, mechanical, or other means, now known or hereafter invented, including photocopying and recording, or in any information storage or retrieval system, without permission in writing from the publishers.

Trademark notice: Product or corporate names may be trademarks or registered trademarks, and are used only for identification and explanation without intent to infringe.

British Library Cataloguing-in-Publication Data
A catalogue record for this book is available from the British Library

Library of Congress Cataloging-in-Publication Data
A catalog record for this book has been requested

ISBN: 978-1-138-78354-6 (hbk)
ISBN: 978-1-138-78355-3 (pbk)
ISBN: 978-1-315-76863-2 (ebk)

Typeset in Bembo
by Swales & Willis Ltd, Exeter, Devon, UK
Printed and bound by CPI Group (UK) Ltd, Croydon CR0 4YY

To our families

Contents

Preface: Learning management accounting as a social science	xv
Introduction	xv
From vocationalism to liberal education	xvii
Learning management accounting: the vocational tradition	xviii
Learning management accounting as a social science	xxi
Contextualizing	xxiv
Historicizing	xxiv
Theorizing	xxvi
Epistemic dynamics	xxvii
Market dynamics	xxvii
Techno-organizational dynamics	xxviii
Organization of the text	xxviii
Acknowledgements	xxxii

PART I
Liberal origins   1

1   Old spirit of capitalism: the political–economic context of
management accounting   3

1.1	*Contextualizing the old logic of management accounting: pillars of analysis*	3
1.2	*Political base of traditional management accounting: modernity, modernism, and*	
	capitalism	5
1.3	*Governmentality: political changes of modernity and management accounting*	6
	1.3.1 Biopolitical accounting: accounting for population and economy	9
	1.3.2 Social medicine as a case of population accounting	9
	1.3.3 Disciplinary accounting: micro-management of individual bodies	11
	Disciplining space	12
	Disciplining time	13
	Disciplined bodies	14
1.4	*Capitalism: ideology and economic structure of management accounting*	16
	1.4.1 Liberal markets	17
	1.4.2 Accumulative markets	18
	1.4.3 Free labour and socialized capital	19

viii   *Contents*

1.5	*Summary and conclusions*	20
	Assignments	22

2   Old spirit of capitalism: the institutional context of management accounting   **24**

2.1	*Introduction*	24
2.2	*Socializing capital: the invention of corporation*	25
	2.2.1 Transcending capital	26
	2.2.2 The logic of capital and its calculative mode of operation	27
	2.2.3 Management accounting as a tool of calculative justification	27
	2.2.4 Management accounting as a tool of calculative structuring	28
2.3	*Capitalizing production: the invention of the factory*	30
	2.3.1 Production systems before the invention of factory systems	30
	2.3.2 The factory system	33
	Mechanization of production	34
	Rationalization of work	34
	Regimentation of labour	36
	Cost accounting	38
2.4	*Managerial hierarchy*	40
	2.4.1 Disciplinary logic of managerial hierarchy	40
	2.4.2 Structural logic of managerial hierarchy: specialization	40
	2.4.3 Democratic logic of managerial hierarchy	41
	2.4.4 Logic of economic coordination: hierarchy vs markets	42
2.5	*Summary and conclusions*	43
	Assignments	44

3   The practicist epistemology of management accounting   **46**

3.1	*Introduction*	46
3.2	*Reflective practice: practicist epistemology of management accounting*	48
	3.2.1 Management accounting as a reflective practice	49
	3.2.2 Intra-organizational epistemic practices	50
	3.2.3 Extra-organizational epistemic practices	50
	3.2.4 Practicist epistemology as actor–networks	52
3.3	*Pedagogical reproduction*	55
	3.3.1 Pedagogy as a symbolic system	55
	3.3.2 Pedagogical reproduction at work: deconstructing the CIMA qualification structure	56
	3.3.3 Becoming an accountant as the embodiment of the field	61
3.4	*Summary and conclusions*	66
	Assignments	67

4   The scientific epistemology of management accounting   **69**

4.1	*Introduction*	69
4.2	*Academic theorization and the professional practice*	70

Contents ix

4.3	*Mainstream vs critical theorizations*	72
4.4	*Rationalist justification of management accounting knowledge*	72
4.5	*Economic rationality of management accounting*	74
	4.5.1 Economic logic of managerial decision making	75
	4.5.2 The economic rationality of management control	79
4.6	*Systems rationality of management accounting*	81
	4.6.1 Cybernetics and management control	82
	4.6.2 Structural functionalism and management control	86
	Structural functionalism in classical definition of management control	86
	Simons' levers of control and structural functionalism	87
4.7	*Empiricist epistemology of management accounting*	89
	4.7.1 Testing contingencies	89
	4.7.2 Case studying the practice	93
4.8	*Summary and conclusions*	94
	Assignments	95

PART II
Neoliberal trends

97

5 Neoliberalization of management accounting

99

5.1	*A point of departure*	99
5.2	*Neoliberal transformations*	101
5.3	*Neoliberal effect*	103
5.4	*Neoliberal market logic*	104
	5.4.1 Techno-managerial reconstruction of neoliberal markets	107
	5.4.2 Market as a heterotopia	109
5.5	*Neoliberal political logic*	110
5.6	*Neoliberal reconstructions in management accounting*	111
	5.6.1 Strategizing the firm	112
	5.6.2 Strategizing the state and civil society	113
	5.6.3 Strategizing the biopolitical issues	113
5.7	*Summary and conclusions*	114
	Assignments	116

6 Strategizing the firm: strategic discourses of competitive positioning

118

6.1	*Introduction*	118
6.2	*Reinventing the strategic terrain*	119
	6.2.1 Mapping the strategic terrain for strategy prescriptions	120
	6.2.2 Neoliberal implications of portfolio planning models	123
6.3	*Strategizing economics: Porter's strategy discourses*	123
	6.3.1 Structure-conduct-performance model	124

x *Contents*

	6.3.2	Competitive advantage: from factor endowment to competitive positioning	126
	6.3.3	Competitive strategy: towards generic market strategies	128
	6.3.4	Strategic analyses	129
6.4		*Biopolitics of Porterian strategy discourses*	131
	6.4.1	Competitiveness as a biopolitical problem	132
	6.4.2	Epistemological politics of competitiveness	133
6.5		*Summary and conclusions*	137
		Assignments	138

7 Strategizing the firm: strategic discourses of organizational reconfiguration **140**

7.1		*Introduction*	140
7.2		*Post-bureaucratic discourses: reinventing bureaucracy*	141
	7.2.1	Job redesign movement: Taylorism humanized	143
	7.2.2	Management by objectives: participation in decision making and domesticating industrial relations	144
	7.2.3	The post-bureaucratic ideal: the interactive type	145
7.3		*Postmodern discourses: the emergence of a new cultural and informational social order*	147
	7.3.1	Signification of simulacra and the movement from production to reproduction	148
	7.3.2	Entrepreneurialization of labour	150
	7.3.3	Immaterialization of labour	152
	7.3.4	Management by themes	154
7.4		*Strategic critique of performance management: Kaplanian influences*	155
	7.4.1	Strategic linking and balancing: reinvention of performance management	156
		Critiquing the traditional	156
		Discoursing the new simulacrum: strategic performance management systems	157
		The BSC promotes top executive ideology as strategy	160
		The BSC's reconceptualization of the shareholder as the strategic ultimatum	161
		Causal and finality relations in the BSC	162
7.5		*Summary and conclusions*	164
		Assignments	164

8 Strategizing the firm: strategic reconfiguration of the production systems – flexibility and quality **167**

8.1		*Introduction*	167
8.2		*Manufacturing flexibility*	168
	8.2.1	Flexible consumption	169
	8.2.2	Flexible machines	170

	8.2.3	Flexible labour	172
	8.2.4	Flexible manufacturing systems	173
		System flexibilities	174
		Accounting in FMS	176
	8.2.5	Flexible specialization and integration	177
	8.2.6	Flexible accumulation	179
8.3	*Producing quality and leaning the production*		181
	8.3.1	Quality as a new managerial paradigm	182
	8.3.2	Economic justification of TQM: cost minimization logic of zero-defect rate and continuous improvements	183
	8.3.3	Quality-based discourses of organizational transformation	186
		Incorporating quality into top management discourses and leadership	186
		Japanization of the organizational processes	186
8.4	*TQM and JIT as disciplinary and biopolitical regime*		189
	8.4.1	Disciplinary politics of TQM/JIT	189
	8.4.2	Biopolitics of TQM/JIT	190
8.5	*Summary and conclusions*		191
	Assignments		192

9 Strategizing cost management

9.1	*Introduction*		194
9.2	*The old spirit of cost management*		195
9.3	*Problematizing the old spirit*		199
9.4	*New cost management: a surveillance assemblage*		203
9.5	*Cost management as a holistic programme*		208
	9.5.1	Cost controls beyond the shop-floor: new vistas for cost management	208
		1 The beyond budgeting movement	210
		2 Cost management innovations in operations management	211
		ERP effect	212
		The Japanese effect	213
	9.5.2	Cost management in the new terrain of decision making: the theory of constraints and throughput accounting	214
	9.5.3	Bundling: the hybridization effect	216
		Bundling	216
		Hybridization	217
	9.5.4	Strategizing the cost object	218
9.6	*Summary and conclusions: neoliberal implications*		221
	Assignments		222

10 Strategizing interfirm relations

10.1	*Introduction*		224
10.2	*Interfirm relations, supply chains, and heterarchy*		225

xii *Contents*

	10.2.1 Reorganization of accountability relations	227
	10.2.2 Organization for diversity: basis of heterarchy	229
10.3	*New vistas of management accounting in interfirm relations*	231
10.4	*Open-book accounting and distributed intelligence*	235
	10.4.1 Target costing in interfirm relations	238
	10.4.2 Functional analysis in interfirm relations	238
	10.4.3 The BSC in interfirm relations	239
	10.4.4 Value chain accounting in interfirm relations	239
	10.4.5 Category management in interfirm relations	240
	10.4.6 Total cost of ownership in interfirm relations	240
10.5	*Trust and power issues in interfirm relations*	240
	10.5.1 Trust as a social reality	241
	10.5.2 Trust as a basis for designing system interfirm relations	242
	10.5.3 Power as an alternative to trust	243
10.6	*Summary and conclusions*	244
	Assignments	245

11 Strategizing the state and NPM agenda — 247

11.1	*Setting the scene*	247
11.2	*Neoliberalism and the state transformation*	249
	11.2.1 The state is re-engineered	251
	11.2.2 Rightward orientation of state bureaucracy	253
	11.2.3 Elevation of the penal scheme	254
11.3	*NPM ideals*	255
	11.3.1 NPM as a deterministic embracement	256
	11.3.2 NPM as a critical encounter	258
11.4	*Specific practices of NPM accounting (NPMA)*	260
	11.4.1 Cost management	260
	11.4.2 Strategic planning and performance measurements	262
	11.4.3 New forms of budgeting	263
	11.4.4 New form of accountability	264
11.5	*Summary and conclusions*	266
	Assignments	268

12 Strategizing civil society as a management accounting entity — 270

12.1	*Introduction*	270
12.2	*Civil society: meaning and transformation*	271
	12.2.1 Meaning	271
	12.2.2 Transformation: the case of developing countries	273
12.3	*Biopolitics of civil society*	276
12.4	*The process of strategizing*	281
	12.4.1 Corporatizing civil society entities	283
	12.4.2 Incorporating ideological and discursive resources	284
	12.4.3 Constructing entrepreneurial selves	286

Contents xiii

	12.4.4 Adopting multiple evaluative criteria	287
12.5	*Summary and conclusions: linking civil society accountability to management accounting*	289
	Assignments	290

13 Neoliberalization of corporate governance — 292

13.1	*Setting the scene*	292
13.2	*Neoclassical origin of corporate governance ideas and its neoliberal extensions*	294
	13.2.1 Neoliberal extensions	297
13.3	*Corporate governance transformations: a biopolitical view*	299
	13.3.1 Corporate governance, security, and global governmentality	300
	13.3.2 Neoliberal corporate governance as a form of soft regulation	303
13.4	*Neoliberal corporate governance in practice*	304
	13.4.1 Neoliberalization of legitimacy	307
	13.4.2 Neoliberalization of accountability	307
	Individualizing accountability in corporate governance	308
	Socializing accountability in corporate governance	308
	Biopolitical accountability	309
13.5	*Management accounting and corporate governance*	310
13.6	*Summary and conclusions*	312
	Assignments	313

14 Greening the firm: environmental management accounting — 315

14.1	*Introduction*	315
14.2	*Sustainability: the basic concept and its components*	316
14.3	*Sustainability's neoliberal political logic*	318
	14.3.1 Rationalizing the oxymoron	320
14.4	*Management accounting's rationalization of sustainability*	321
	14.4.1 Corporate accountability and sustainability	322
	14.4.2 Strategizing sustainability	324
	14.4.3 Envisioning sustainability	325
	14.4.4 Sustainability as postulate of strategic positioning	327
14.5	*Operationalizing sustainability*	328
	14.5.1 Sustainability in capital investment decisions	328
	14.5.2 Sustainable value chain analysis and competitive position analysis	329
	14.5.3 Sustainable balanced scorecards	330
	Privileging financial over sustainability	333
	14.5.4 Cost accounting for sustainability	333
	Use of ABC in sustainability costing	333
	Lifecycle costing (LCC) and whole life costing (WLC)	335
	14.5.5 Environmental management systems	337
14.6	*Summary and conclusions*	338
	Assignments	340

xiv *Contents*

15 Strategizing development — 342

15.1 *Introduction* — 342

15.2 *Development and accounting: the connection* — 344

15.3 *Developmentality and governmentality* — 347

    15.3.1 Development discourse and its textual ramifications — 347

    15.3.2 The development machine — 349

    15.3.3 Developmentality, governmentality, and calculative practices — 350

15.4 *Accountingization of development: the case of World Bank Development Reporting* — 351

    15.4.1 Calculating (under)development: the problematization phase — 352

    15.4.2 Managing the underdeveloped and professionalization of development — 357

15.5 *Developmentalization of accounting: the case of microfinance* — 363

    15.5.1 Microfinance as a 'Holy Grail' of rural development — 363

    15.5.2 Microfinance and accounting — 363

    15.5.3 Writing back to the World Bank: microfinance in the financial market — 364

15.6 *Summary and conclusions* — 365

    Assignments — 366

References — 368

Index — 394

Preface

Learning management accounting as a social science

> What professional men should carry away with them from a University, is not [only] professional knowledge, but [also] that which should direct the use of their professional knowledge, and bring the light of general culture to illuminate the technicalities of a special pursuit.
>
> (John Stuart Mill 1867, parenthesis ours)

Introduction

The central theme of this textbook, as its title manifests, is 'strategizing' management accounting. By the term strategizing, we mean two things here:

1. The way in which management accounting has recently incorporated various notions of strategy and strategic management to redefine and extend its scope. In that sense, strategizing is something that happened to management accounting - how it has changed from conventional management accounting to strategic management accounting. In understanding this change *in* management accounting, as we will further explain later in this preface, we will locate management accounting in its epistemic dynamics, market dynamics, and techno-managerial dynamics. In locating management accounting in these dynamics, we then carry out three interrelated analytical tasks – historicizing, contextualizing, and theorizing.
2. Something that management accounting, together with other managerial disciplines and discourses, has done, and is doing, to many other organizational, social, and political entities. So, strategizing here is an act that management accounting performs upon others. Here the attention is on the way in which management accounting has been instrumental in transforming other social entities such as economic enterprises, markets, states, civil societies, and even individuals into strategic entities. This means that, in this book, we are conceptualizing an overarching stream of changes in a wide spectrum of social institutions. In a broader sense, we call this change 'neoliberalization' and we see the notion of 'strategizing' – transforming social entities and actors into social entities which consciously or subconsciously guide their behaviour and performance on the basis of a set of strategic imperatives emanating from neoliberal markets – as a central theme. Yet again, in understanding the role that management accounting plays in this regard, we locate both management accounting and the relevant social entities in their epistemic, market, and techno-managerial dynamics.

xvi   *Preface*

So, this text runs on these two rails; and in driving our thought process on these rails, we need to expand our 'learning approach' to management accounting. As we will further explain in this preface, conventionally management accounting has been learnt and taught as a 'vocational subject'. While appreciating this approach, we reckon that this is not sufficient to properly engage with the notion of strategizing in the two dimensions we mentioned earlier. Hence, we need to extend this

Table 0.1 Two paradigms of accounting education

Comparative dimensions	Vocational approach to accounting education (vocationalism)	Social science approach to accounting education (liberalism)
Purpose	To create a productive and efficient accountant capable of (a) following professional rules, standards, principles, and ethics and (b) productively and efficiently deploying professional knowledge and skills in a given organizational setting.	To prepare ourselves to live responsible, productive, and creative lives in a dramatically changing world recognizing, appreciating, and respecting the cultural, ethical, and political diversity of our world.
Learning orientation	Predominantly skill-oriented (how to do) and job specific.	Predominantly knowledge-oriented to make individuals capable of exercising their reflective capacity and freedom of thinking and speech.
Learning methods	Learning through practical exercises, case studies, managerial simulations, and on-the-job training.	Learning through wider reading, research, and engagement in polyphonic dialogues and debates.
Epistemic features	Unification of knowledge: searching for a 'universally applicable' set of principles, concepts, and standards.	Divergence and diversification of knowledge: polyphonic and pluralistic nature of knowledge is acknowledged and appreciated.
Role perspective of the student	Insider view: often assume the role of the professional practitioner. So, the classroom is to be converted into a 'training ground' where the prospective professionals learn their future job. Aim is to learn how to do.	Outsider view: looks at the accounting profession from an outside academic angle. Aim is to see accounting practice at a distance locating it in its context and to explain, justify, and critique the practice for its betterment.
Role of theory	Theory is understood in terms of a set of generalizable propositions and rules. And the efficacy of the theory is judged on the basis of its applicability in the practice.	Theory is understood as a sensitizing device that provides the people with an alternative way of understanding, interpreting, explaining, critiquing, and justifying the practice.
Institutional boundaries	Concentrates mainly on the 'organizational' and 'managerial' roles and implications of management accounting.	Attention is moved beyond the managerial and organizational implications to wider socio-political and cultural implications.
Underlying political ideology	Capitalist – shareholder value maximization. Neoclassical economics as the root discipline.	Polyphonic – represents different political ideologies and theoretical logics. Takes an interdisciplinary approach.

vocationalism into an approach in which we learn management accounting as a social science. This preface outlines the way in which we aim to mobilize these two approaches in framing this book.

From vocationalism to liberal education

Accounting education is a paradox in universities (see Table 0.1). On the one hand, as John Stuart Mill argues (see the opening quote), universities, especially those liberal universities, appreciate and promote the ethos of what we generally call 'liberal education': a form of education which moves much beyond the 'vocationalism' of creating a skilled and productive worker. Liberal education appreciates that there is a fundamental difference between education and job training. Liberal education takes, as one of its primary purposes, the creation of a 'good citizen' with a wider cultural, political, social, and scientific understanding and appreciation. For the Association of American Colleges and Universities (AACU):

> [l]iberal education is one that prepares us to live responsible, productive, and creative lives in a dramatically changing world. It is an education that fosters a well-grounded intellectual resilience, a disposition toward lifelong learning, and an acceptance of responsibility for the ethical consequences of our ideas and actions. Liberal education requires that we understand the foundations of knowledge and inquiry about nature, culture and society; that we master core skills of perception, analysis, and expression; that we cultivate a respect for truth; that we recognize the importance of historical and cultural context; and that we explore connections among formal learning, citizenship, and service to our communities.
>
> ... Liberal learning is not confined to particular fields of study. What matters in liberal education is substantial content, rigorous methodology and an active engagement with the societal, ethical, and practical implications of our learning. The spirit and value of liberal learning are equally relevant to all forms of higher education and to all students.
>
> ... liberal learning is global and pluralistic. It embraces the diversity of ideas and experiences that characterize the social, natural, and intellectual world. To acknowledge such diversity in all its forms is both an intellectual commitment and a social responsibility, for nothing less will equip us to understand our world and to pursue fruitful lives.
>
> (www.aacu.org/About/statements/liberal_learning.cfm)

On the other hand, accounting education, in contrast to other social sciences such as sociology, politics, anthropology, etc. has a peculiar historical root. It began as a 'vocation' in the accounting professional institutions and then moved into the universities. In this transition from the profession to universities, accounting education carried forward much of its professional and vocational features of job training. Hence, accounting education in universities, by and large, embraces the ethos of what we generally call a 'vocational or professional approach' to accounting education. In such a vocational approach, the emphasis is on constructing a productive and efficient accountant capable of 'properly' following the rules, principles, standards, calculative procedures, and ethical protocols established by the profession.

As you will understand, while appreciating the necessity for vocational elements of accounting education, this textbook promotes a social science approach to management accounting and, within that overall aim, the purpose of this preface is to:

Figure 0.1 Ingredients of vocationalism in management accounting

(a) provide a broader comparison between vocational and social science approaches to learning management accounting
(b) explain the fundamental building blocks of our 'social science approach' to accounting education and
(c) explain the epistemic logic of the textbook by articulating how chapters in the book bind together.

Learning management accounting: the vocational tradition

How should we approach management accounting as a field of study? The most popular approach is vocationalism – to study management accounting as a vocational, professional, and managerial practice. This is the approach many followed in their early years of university accounting programmes as well as in passing professional examinations such as those of the Chartered Institute of Management Accountants (CIMA). In this vocational tradition, management accounting is defined, taught, and learnt as a set of calculative tools, principles, and concepts that help accountants and other corporate managers to make effective and efficient decisions. As such, management accounting is often, in a way correctly, conceived of as a body of knowledge that managers deploy in managing economic enterprises. Its primary sites of deployment are large private-sector corporations, though its applications in public and non-profit-sector organizations are on the rise. Hence, it is conceived and taught as a subject which directly frames managerial actions. In this sense, CIMA (2005, 18) defines management accounting as:

> [t]he application of the principles of accounting and financial management to create, protect, preserve and increase value for the stakeholders of for-profit and not-for-profit enterprises in the public and private sectors.

Thus, management accounting's usefulness is understood in terms of its role in corporate value creation. Its efficacy is judged by its capacity to enhance the corporate competencies and resources through which corporate value is protected and increased. In this vocational sense, management accounting is a *body of knowledge* to be applied and practised in various forms of organizations with a view to creating value. It is organized in the forms of various principles, concepts, calculative tools, and procedures. As is evident in popular management accounting texts and professional curricula, this body of knowledge is broadly categorized into three interrelated areas: product costing tools and techniques; decision-making tools and techniques; and performance management tools and techniques. Typically, university courses in the early years cover these vocational elements of management accounting and you master the application of those techniques in different managerial scenarios.

Vocationalism in management accounting is defined by a set of boundary-setting parameters (see Figure 0.1). First, is its concentration on the *technical competence*, which is one's capacity to carry out required analytical tasks and calculations needed to understand, explain, and communicate managerial realities and to solve managerial problems. Thus, for example, management accountants should be competent in calculating the 'correct' costs of a product, activity, or any other 'cost object' such as a department, division, market segment, or a customer. Similarly, they should be able to ascertain, by deploying the correct calculative techniques and procedures, the profit and other financial as well as non-financial impacts of various short- and long-term decisions. They should be competent in devising appropriate performance management systems and deploying them effectively ensure that people achieve the set organizational objectives and goals. They should also be competent in understanding and explaining the managerial rationalities of their decisions and actions. After all, they should be competent enough to support corporate managers in their operational and strategic decisions by providing appropriate and correct calculations and analysis.

The wisdom for the technical competence is often derived from practice – the inventions in the corporate and consultancy practices. Such practical inventions are then often supplemented by rigorous statistical and mathematical concepts and tools (such as regression analysis, linear programming, and other management science techniques), software packages (such as Enterprise Resource Planning) as well as institutionally specific procedures and protocols. Also, there has always been a stream of contributions derived from neoclassical economics and other mainstream branches of management such as operations management (e.g. concepts of quality costing and management, inventory management, and supply chain management). The competence of deploying such principles and techniques, and carrying out necessary calculations and analysis, has then been translated into a set of 'transferable skills' that can be incorporated into classroom teaching exercises and case studies. Real-world corporate scenarios

xx *Preface*

are thus abstracted, summarized, and written into management accounting cases so that the real world is simulated (partially with their own limitations) within the undergraduate, masters, and professional learning environments. So, teaching management accounting as a vocation has been about transfer of this technical competency to students, prospective professionals, and professionals seeking continuous professional development. This can happen through both off-the-job and on-the-job learning. Technical competency includes not only calculative competencies but also problem-solving skills, interpersonal skills, and communication skills.[1]

Second, vocationalism in management accounting pays attention to what we may call *managerial interpretations*. Management accounting is more than a mere set of calculative tools. It is a 'science' of *professional interpretations*: understanding, appreciating, and communicating the managerial implications of what management accounting calculations reveal. For example, it involves interpreting what a certain set of calculations (e.g. financial ratios) reveals about the corporate strategy or operational plans. Such interpretations needs management accountants' attention on: (a) the fundamental assumptions under which management accounting calculations are carried out; (b) the particular strengths and limitations of management accounting tools, calculations, and also data used for such calculations; (c) the particular assumptions made of the business scenario, especially of the market conditions, future forecasts, and their sensitivities; and (d) the behavioural, organizational, political, and environmental implications of alternative managerial actions and decisions.

The third parameter is the *organizational system*. Conventional understanding of management accounting is defined within, and in relation to, organizational systems, especially as a subsystem of the management control system (MCS). So, application of management accounting is structured and managed as an element of the organization's managerial functions. Hence, in its vocational perspective, implications of management accounting are mainly seen in 'managerial' and 'organizational' terms. Its place and role are understood in relation to: (a) the organization's operational planning, control, and decision-making processes and (b) the organization's strategic planning and control systems. Even the *behavioural implications*, which constitute the fourth parameter of the conventional definition of management accounting, are understood within the organizational boundaries.

Management accounting, even in its conventional mode of teaching and learning, does include a set of behavioural or psychological considerations. In its evolution during the last few decades or so, it has paid attention to the *behavioural implications* of adopting various management accounting techniques and tools. For example, there are well-acknowledged attempts to understand and explain how various modes of budgeting and performance management can influence employee motivation and satisfaction (see Mia 1988, 1989). Quite often we can see, in university and professional management accounting examinations, that there is at least a part of budgeting, performance management, or variance analysis questions demanding a brief discussion on their behavioural implications. Such behavioural implications of management accounting are often understood in terms of theories of human motivation; how such motivational theories explain the systems of corporate performance measurement and reward systems.

These parameters are boundary setting. They define not only its scope but also the approaches we traditionally take to teach and learn management accounting. Taken together they have characterized management accounting as a *functionalist discipline* – a body of knowledge which conceptualizes economic enterprises as functional wholes with a unified social purpose of capital accumulation; and, hence, a body of knowledge that takes the contribution to corporate wealth creation as its ultimate objective (see CIMA definition quoted earlier). Management accounting, as a sub-function of management, is there to enhance the organization's ability to do so. Its *raison d'être* is defined in its usefulness in contributing to corporate profit maximization. In this vocational sense, it has become a technology of profit maximization: it has been seen as something 'belonging' and 'useful' to corporate management, and its usefulness is understood and explained within the organizational parameters of profit maximization. It is taught and learnt only with the expectation that its students will become effective managers capable of preserving, protecting, and increasing corporate wealth. In other words, it is still taught mainly as a 'professional' discipline: a body of knowledge through which managers are to be disciplined to think and calculate in order to maximize corporate wealth.

This means that the vocational mode of learning can only give us a professional perspective: to see corporate realities from the perspective of people who are within, and managing, corporations; to judge the corporate realities only in relation to the creation of corporate wealth. Of course, this perspective, and hence the traditional mode of learning and teaching management accounting, are quite useful in making 'effective' functionalist managers. And such managers are, of course, necessary to make sure that world is efficient, effective, and progressive in economic terms. It provides the necessary ideology, tools, and principles to become an effective agent of capital and, hence, to speed up the corporate capital accumulation process. And, after all, this approach trains us to think as accountants. In that sense, as the CIMA definition explains, this approach is necessary as a technology to preserve, protect, and create corporate wealth.

The vocationalism in management accounting is very well grounded as a separate discipline of professional learning, within and outside universities, through numerous volumes of management accounting textbooks, handbooks, and other pedagogical materials such as case studies. Hence, our intention here is not to contribute to that stock of knowledge. However, in its current mode of vocationalism in management accounting, contrary to Mill's good old ideal we quoted at the beginning of this preface, our students by and large carry only a professional knowledge, not the light of general culture to illuminate the technicalities of a special pursuit. So, our attempt here is to raise management accounting to a different level: learning and teaching management accounting as a social science. Nevertheless, this does not mean that we are trying to replace vocational and managerial modes of teaching management accounting. Instead, what we are trying to do here is to supplement it: with a few polemic intentions, to offer a chance to direct the use of professional knowledge, and to bring the light of general culture and politics to illuminate the technicalities of a special pursuit.

Learning management accounting as a social science

Outside university and professional classrooms, there has long been a growing recognition of management accounting as a social science. Since the mid-1970s when the critical accounting research started to lay its foundation through the launching of critical journals like *Accounting, Organizations and Society* (AOS), *Accounting, Auditing and Accountability Journal* (AAAJ), and *Critical Perspectives on Accounting* (CPA), there has xxii *Preface*

been a remarkable growth in sociological and political perspectives and interpretations of accounting phenomena. It is not an exaggeration to say that critical management accounting research has long been very much sociological and political. Accounting research has drawn from various political and sociological perspectives and theories to explore and understand management accounting technologies and practices as sociological and political phenomena. Classic examples for laying such a sociological foundation for accounting are Hopwood and Miller's (1994) seminal text *Accounting as Social and Institutional Practice* and Tinker's (1985) *Paper Prophets: A Social Critique of Accounting*.

Even before the beginning of these sociological and political perspectives, accounting research did have certain social science approaches. It drew on neoclassical economics, especially agency theory and transaction cost theory, to conceptualize the management accounting phenomenon. In fact, critical accounting research initially came out as a critic of these neoclassical economic theorizations of accounting. Having offered theoretical, ideological and methodological alternatives to conventional the neoclassical economic theorization of management accounting, these critical stances then moved on to their own theoretical debates constructing a very rich set of theoretical and methodological sub-camps, ranging from orthodox Marxism (e.g. Bryer 1994, 1999, 2000a, 2000b, 2006; Hopper and Armstrong 1991) to institutional theorists (e.g. Abrahamsson and Gerdin 2006; Burns and Baldvinsdottir 2005; Hopper and Major 2007; Lukka 2007; Modell 2001, 2003; Scapens 2006, 1994; Scapens and Macintosh 1996), actor-network theorists (e.g. Alcouffe et al. 2008; Arnaboldi and Azzone 2010; Colwyn Jones and Dugdale 2002; Cuganesan 2008; Justesen and Mouritsen 2011), Foucauldians (e.g. Hopper and Macintosh 1993; Hoskin and Macve 1986, 1988), and those who draw on post-Foucauldian French philosophers such as Bourdieu (e.g. Alawattage 2011; Cooper 2002; Cooper et al. 2011) and Boltanski (e.g. Annisette and Trivedi 2013; Ramirez 2013). They have been busy offering alternative sociological and political-economic perspectives and interpretations on management accounting in general, its capitalist history, and its various technological tools and methods in particular.

However, surprisingly, much of these attempts at seeing management accounting as a social science have remained outside the university lecture and tutorial rooms. They have not been sufficiently translated into a coherent pedagogical scheme so that management accounting can be presented to our students as a social science. There are of course some notable edited collections (e.g. Ashton et al. 1995; Bhimani 2006; Bromwich and Hopwood 1986; Hopper et al. 2007) and book-length essays (e.g. Macintosh and Quattrone 2010) which attempt to bring together various dimensions of social and political research in management accounting. Of course, they composite a good set of *supplementary* reading for, and are often in the recommended reading lists of, advanced management accounting courses. However, they would hardly culminate in a coherent pedagogical scheme for promoting management accounting as a social science within university lecture and tutorial rooms.

Perhaps the only exemption is our previous text *Management Accounting Change: Approaches and Perspectives* (Wickramasinghe and Alawattage 2007). We experimented in that book by bringing management accounting change to the forefront and contextualizing it in a broader socio-historical narrative of capitalism, a pedagogical framework to delineate management accounting as a collective project in social science. As Vollmer (2009, 141–142) commented on this text:

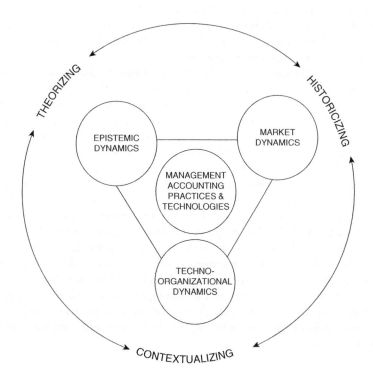

Figure 0.2 Building blocks of our social science approach

> The release of 'Management accounting change: Approaches and perspectives' (Wickramasinghe & Alawattage, 2007) is significant not only because it offers an alternative to classic texts in instructing management accounting students, but also because it covers some distance towards projecting management accounting as a regular social science associated with a distinct set of problems and research interests shared by a collective of scholars ... the book by Wickramasinghe and Alawattage clearly presents the most ambitious attempt to date at comprehensively delineating management accounting as a collective project in social science, a project set to grow towards some state of maturity.

In this book, we try to extend this agenda of projecting management accounting as a social science, by extending the thematic coverage as well as reorganizing the themes focusing more on the recent changes in management accounting. In doing so, we will try to address some issues that Vollmer (2009) and others kindly and keenly pointed out regarding our previous text. For example, quite correctly, Vollmer accuses our socio-historical narrative of being biased towards Anglo-American business organizations and our failure to make this inherent bias more explicit. We acknowledge that we are of course guilty of this accusation and try our best to rectify this (and some other issues) in this new book, although we ourselves are not fully satisfied about the degree to which we could incorporate 'non-Western' contexts and historicities within the epistemic and thematic boundaries we set for ourselves in

xxiv *Preface*

making the project of writing this text possible and manageable. However, as you will see, although there is a certain degree of overlap, this book is not a new edition to our previous book but a new text which tries to theorize liberal origins and neoliberal transformations of management accounting.

This book has a broader focus. Its subject matter is the *interconnections* between ideological, institutional, and technological changes in global capitalism. In that way, it tries to theorize and explain the connections between the historical dynamics of capitalism and management accounting practices. This means that its approach is dialectical: it tries to understand and explain management accounting vis-à-vis evolutionary dynamics in varieties of global capitalism. As such, in this text, management accounting will receive a cultural political-economic treatment.

In contrast to the traditional and mainstream vocational approach we discussed earlier, our social science approach is built upon a particular conceptual framework (see Figure 0.2). This scheme includes two interconnected layers of analysis, which can only be separated for the purposes of simplification and understanding. First, there are the analytical processes and strategies of contextualizing, historicizing, and theorizing. Second, there are epistemic dynamics, market dynamics, and techno-organizational dynamics. These are the elements from which the evolution of management accounting practices and technologies stem. Taken together, throughout this book, we theorize, contextualize, and historicize management accounting practices and technologies in relation to their epistemic, market, and techno-organizational dynamics.

Contextualizing

As we have already noted, we will explain the meanings of and rationales for management accounting practices vis-à-vis the evolutionary dynamics in varieties of global capitalism. As such, management accounting is primarily understood as a 'technology of capitalism', one which materializes and grounds the 'spirits of capitalism' (old and new) within: factory floors; corporate boards; computer networks; managerial reports and spreadsheets; policy initiatives of government and other trans-governmental organizations such as the OECD, World Bank and IMF; and above all, within epistemic communities and professional and academic curricula. In other words, we will not simply attempt to explain and describe emerging management accounting technologies and paradigms on their own. Instead, we will explain them by locating them within the global dynamics of capitalism in order to see how they co-evolve. This means that, in reference to extant literature in management accounting and related fields, we are attributing certain political functionalities and rationalities to management accounting: we will explain how management accounting plays certain political functions in reproducing the global capitalism today. Accordingly, management accounting must be understood not only within its immediate managerial and/or organizational context but also by placing it within its wider cultural-political contexts.

Historicizing

This runs alongside the notion of contextualizing. Contextualizing management accounting within its broader socio-cultural and political context is done through bracketing various management accounting practices and technologies within historical narratives of capitalism. This means that historical change becomes one of the

Table 0.2 Theoretical logics of management accounting

Theoretical logics	Theoretical sources	Main analytical foci
Efficiency logic	Neoclassical economics, especially agency theory and transactions cost theory.	Production and operational optimization; performance contracting; corporate governance; management accounting history.
Systems logic	Systems theory, cybernetics, and classical organizational theory.	Organizational configurations; organizational control structures; management control systems; environmental interactions of organizations; external control of organizations; sustainability.
Contingency logic	Open systems theory, contingency theory, and population ecology.	Organizational control structures; management control systems; environmental interactions of organizations; external control of organizations; sustainability.
Class logic	Marxist and post-Marxist political economy.	Class dynamics at the point of production; management control and deskilling; control structures, organizational control, and state dynamics; management accounting history; role of management accounting in development and underdevelopment; macro–micro connections in management accounting practices.
Disciplinary logic	Foucauldian notions power, knowledge, discipline, and governmentality.	Management accounting as a disciplinary practice; history of management accounting; discourses and management accounting; development discourses and accounting; governance, state, and management accounting.
Political logic	Critical theory of Habermas; post-Marxists such as Laclau and Mouffe.	Democracy and accounting; sustainability; accountability; corporate governance.
Institutional logic	Sociological institutionalism (old and new).	Diffusion, convergence, and divergence of management accounting technologies; management accounting change; macro–micro connection of management accounting practices; institutionalization and deinstitutionalization of management accounting.
Network logic	Actor-network theory and sociology of translation.	Management accounting change; diffusion of management accounting technologies.
Logic of practice	Bourdieu's theory of practice, reflexive sociology. and forms of capital.	Management accounting as a field; management accounting as a practice; accounting education; accounting profession; calculative reproduction of social structures.
Logic of logics	Institutional logic perspective and Boltanski and Thévenot's sociology of worth.	Management accounting change; ideological construction of management accounting practices.

xxvi *Preface*

organizing principles of our text. We see management accounting change not simply as a historical fact but as a pedagogically superior point of reference to explore and understand management accounting. As we once noted, 'as a learning methodology, change can broaden our understanding of management accounting. It leads us to realize that management accounting is a social science rather than a mere set of technical tools available for practice' (Wickramasinghe and Alawattage 2007, 10–11). In other words, while we try to understand and explain the rationales of management accounting by placing it within its wider political context (i.e. capitalism), we appreciate that capitalism is not a historically static phenomenon. Instead, capitalism evolves producing varieties of capitalism and it is this historical evolution of capitalism that necessitates new management accounting techniques and practices. Hence, we try to understand and explain the transformation of management accounting from modern to postmodern, from mechanistic to post-mechanistic, from conventional to strategic, and so on by paralleling it with the episodic changes taking place in Western capitalism. In doing so, we locate management accounting first within the parameters of the 'old spirit of capitalism' in order to understand the way in which liberal economic democratic principles of early capitalism gave rise to conventional modes of management accounting. Then we locate management accounting within the parameters of 'new spirits of capitalism' in order to explain how the contemporary 'neoliberal' form of capitalism has resulted in the invention of a series of new management accounting tools and practices that we now commonly understand as strategic management accounting, environmental management accounting, and so on.

Theorizing

This text is a massive literature review. It reviews a large amount of seminal literature that explains management accounting technologies and practices. In so doing, it pays special attention to the alternative theoretical lenses that accounting researchers use to explain management accounting phenomena. Even a cursory reading of seminal management accounting literature clearly shows the role that various social theories play in this regard. Accounting scholars indeed have had a long multidisciplinary tradition of drawing on various social theories to make economic, political, and sociological senses of management accounting practices. Since the early 1970s, they have drawn on, for example, neoclassical economic theories, Marxism, post and neo-Marxism, and many other classical and contemporary German and French philosophical traditions. These theoretical frameworks provide alternative 'logics' of seeing management accounting practices (see Table 0.2 for a synoptic view of popular theories used in management accounting research). It has become almost impossible to write a serious academic piece (such as a journal paper or a PhD thesis), especially in the critical accounting field, without the use of such a theoretical framework. Such theories have become 'sensitizing devices': a set of conceptual frameworks which management accounting scholars use to analyse, understand, and explain empirically observed management accounting practices.

So, theorizing involves drawing on such social theories to explain the management accounting phenomena. We do this throughout this text. Depending on their appropriateness to the particular issue that we are dealing with, we draw on a multitude of theoretical frameworks. We also try to illustrate how a particular management accounting issue can be explained differently if we draw on different theories.

These theoretical logics have also become 'higher order principles' of justification (Boltanski and Thévenot 2006): one's opinions, explanations, and arguments are justified (and critiqued) by drawing from such theoretical frameworks. Also, it should be noted, such theoretical frameworks are divisive (though not necessarily in a 'bad' way). They offer competing ontological assumptions (i.e. about reality – what is reality and how reality can be recognized) and epistemological assumptions (i.e. about knowledge – what is knowledge and how should knowledge be constructed) that divide accounting scholars into different schools of thought or 'academic tribes'. They also manifest the polyphonic nature of management accounting academia and highlight, as in the case of any other social science, the contested nature of management accounting as a field of social science. This means that, as in the case of any other social science, management accounting academics are divided into different camps and tribes based on such theoretical logics that they appreciate and draw on. It is this polyphonic division in the field which makes it an interesting site of dialogue, critique, and justifications. Academia progresses through the debates between them.

Epistemic dynamics

We understand that the developments in management accounting are connected with a particular set of epistemic practices and discourses. They include, *inter alia*: management consultants and their discourses; mainstream and popular knowledge dissemination centres such as Harvard Business School and their flagship publication outlets such as *Harvard Business Review*; global development agencies such as the OECD and World Bank who actively promote the diffusion of Western management and accounting innovations to the peripheral nations; and also various professional accounting bodies such as CIMA, whose examinations, curriculum, and qualification schemes operate as powerful epistemic means of disseminating new management accounting techniques. These epistemic practices are discursive. They are instrumental in discovering and promoting a 'new spirit of capitalism' (Boltanski and Chiapello 2007) and disseminating them to corporate training rooms; university classrooms; professional curriculum, handbooks, and exam papers; and the factory floors and corporate board rooms. And, after all, they are instrumental in making sure that the 'new spirit of capitalism' is to be included in the development policies and technology assistance packages for less developed countries. In carrying out the three analytical tasks we mentioned here (i.e. contextualizing, historicizing, and theorizing), we read about epistemic dynamics – the way in which various epistemic institutions engage in changing management accounting practices.

Market dynamics

Markets and their competitive dynamics should not anymore be considered as mere exogenous factors or places where firms simply valorize the surplus value that they create in factories. Instead, they have become 'strategic spaces' that firms actively seek to create, manage, and appropriate. Markets are the spaces within which 'competition' is invented and put into operation by firms; they are the spaces within which the firms put their strategic tools and thinking into practice. Especially in the contemporary neoliberal world, the market has become the point of reference against which organizations now need to reconfigure their ideologies, structures, relations, and practices. This means that, in a political-economic sense, market dynamics need to be taken as one of the key sources of management accounting change. Much of the

xxviii *Preface*

change that we have experienced in the last few decades has much to do with the changes taking place in the markets. They are globalized, digitalized, virtualized, neoliberalized, and framed and governed by new regulatory mechanisms. Such changes taking place in the market sphere, then, have influenced management accounting by bringing new analytical and managerial challenges. For example, with the increasing managerial emphasis placed upon analysing, understanding, and strategizing the markets, management accounting is now faced with new tasks of analysing the profitability of customer and market segments. So, in carrying out the three analytical tasks of contextualizing, historicizing, and theorizing management accounting, we also need to give due attention to market dynamics – the way in which changing market conditions have brought about new management accounting rationalities, technologies, and practices.

Techno-organizational dynamics

Along with epistemic and market dynamics, economic enterprises continuously and constantly reinvent their organizational and technological apparatuses. Managing technological and organizational change has become a fundamental concern of corporate management. Organizational changes in terms of their visions, missions, strategies, as well as their structures and operational processes are deemed to be essential elements of ensuring organizational success. During the last few decades, factories have been transforming from places of mass production to ones of lean and flexible production; their technological infrastructures are changing from mechanization to digitalization; their information infrastructures are moving from offline systems to online, real-time, and cloud-based systems; their technical capacities to capture, store, and analyse data are increasing at a massive speed while simultaneously multiplying the 'information risks' so dangerous in such IT infrastructures; their workers are changing from deskilled workers to 'digeratis'; corporate hierarchies are in the process of reforming into networks; and so on. In a nutshell, organizations are transforming themselves into what nobody exactly knows. And, management accounting changes are also being driven by such techno-organizational dynamics. So, we need to read them carefully and locate management accounting within them in contextualizing, historicizing, and theorizing the management accounting changes.

Organization of the text

As it should be clear from our discussions so far, our aim is to explain management accounting changes by contextualizing, historicizing, and theorizing. To that end, our empirical attention is very much on epistemic, market, and techno-organizational dynamics. However, this does not mean that we ignore technical and procedural aspects of management accounting such as budgeting, activity-based costing (ABC), balanced scorecards (BSC), enterprise resources planning (ERP), target costing, and so on. After all, management accounting techniques and practices are not marginal to the project of teaching management accounting as a social science. They indeed constitute the core of management accounting. Our attempt is to understand and explain various management accounting practices and techniques within such epistemic, market, and techno-organizational dynamics. In that sense, throughout this text, we will be looking for alternative sociological and political interpretations and explanations of the emergence and evolution of various management accounting techniques and practices. However, we are not organizing the chapters of this text based on such techniques and practices as most of the existing management accounting texts do. That is because our aim here is not simply to 'teach' or 'talk' about such techniques and practices on their own. Instead, as we have already mentioned, our aim is to contextualize, historicize, and theorize them. To that end, we have organized the chapters around some evolutionary themes of capitalism so that we can locate management accounting techniques and practices within the evolutionary dynamics of capitalism. We reckon that this is an important epistemic strategy because, after all, management accounting emerged and evolved as a technology of capitalism and modernity (see Hopper and Armstrong 1991; Johnson and Kaplan 1987a, 1987b; Loft 1995).

Accordingly, the text is divided into two main parts: liberal origins and neoliberal trends. Part I – Liberal origins – sets the historical and epistemological foundation of conventional management accounting. It articulates the historical and epistemological context in which management accounting originally evolved into a professional practice in 'modern' organizations and into a specific body of knowledge that frames organizational practices. This part is populated by four chapters, the first two of which deal with the *political and institutional context* of management accounting, while the third and fourth deal with the *epistemic context*.

Chapter 1: Old spirit of capitalism: the political-economic context of management accounting. In this chapter, we trace the evolution of management accounting along the emergence of capitalism and modernity. Here we explain the political role of management accounting by locating it within the political apparatuses of modernity and capitalism. Using Foucauldian notions of governmentality, disciplinary politics, and biopolitics, we first explain how and why management accounting can be related to the 'old spirit of capitalism' as a disciplinary technology. Second, we extend this discussion to connect management accounting with the ideological and structural elements of capitalism, especially liberal markets, accumulative markets, free labour, and socialized capital.

Chapter 2: Old spirit of capitalism: the institutional context of management accounting. The aim of this chapter is to explain how the 'old spirit of capitalism' was organized and the role that management accounting played therein. Here our attention is on the spheres of 'organizing' capitalism – the firm or the corporation, the factory, and the managerial hierarchy.

Chapter 3: The practicist epistemology of management accounting. Management accounting exists as a practice in the capitalist organizations in an organizational specific manner. Management accounting also exists as a 'body of knowledge' within and beyond such individual corporations in an epistemic plane. This chapter turns towards this epistemic existence of management accounting to explain how management accounting is organized as a 'body of knowledge'. The dialectical connection between management accounting as a practice and management accounting as a body of knowledge is explained here with a view to articulate how management accounting knowledge is constructed through reflective practices, pedagogical reproduction, and embodiment of the field by professional accountants.

Chapter 4: The scientific epistemology of management accounting. While Chapter 3 deals with the professionalization of management accounting knowledge, this chapter

xxx *Preface*

explains the 'scientification' of management accounting. Here, taking neoclassical economics and verities of systems theories as examples, we explain the roles that academic theorization and scientific epistemology play in establishing the techno-managerial and economic rationalities of management accounting.

Part II, Neoliberal trends, which constitutes the majority of the book, considers current transformations taking place in management accounting. Here we draw on contemporary global market dynamics, epistemic dynamics, and techno-organizational dynamics to shed some light on the way in which management accounting has redefined its scope, techniques, and processes to accommodate changing strategic imperatives emanating from globalized markets, neoliberal epistemic institutions, and the techno-managerial changes that have taken place during the last few decades. More specifically, the chapters in this section provide a biopolitical explanation for the emergence and popularization of various 'new' management accounting techniques and practices that accounting scholars broadly categorize under the labels of 'strategic management accounting' and 'postmodern' or 'post-bureaucratic' or 'post-Fordist' management regimes. The part is populated with the following chapters:

Chapter 5: Neoliberalization of management accounting. This chapter provides a conceptual outline of neoliberal transformations. Here we articulate how neoliberal transformations have created a new biopolitical regime of governmentality in which 'biopolitical circulation' (vis-à-vis disciplinary confinement) of things and construction of entrepreneurial selves have become the defining moments. We explain how this neoliberal turn has created a new set of market and strategic imperatives demanding that firms and their management accounting function take a new strategic form.

Chapter 6: Strategizing the firm: strategic discourses of competitive positioning. This chapter constitutes the first of the set of chapters that articulate various dimensions of 'strategizing' the firm and its management accounting function. It explains how the firm itself has become the core managerial element that must be positioned in a competitive structure: as a totality, as an image, as a brand, as a portfolio of strategic business units, and so on. Here we pay special attention to the recent invention of management technologies that have reconceptualized the market/industry as a 'strategic terrain' and strategic management as the overarching organizational function that aims at 'positioning' the firm and its offerings in this competitive terrain to achieve a sustainable competitive advantage. We also explain the neoliberal implications of this strategic trajectory of the firm.

Chapter 7: Strategizing the firm: strategic discourses of organizational reconfiguration. This chapter explains the way in which post-bureaucratic discourses, postmodern discourses, and strategic performance management discourses have reformed the structural and processual configuration of the firm.

Chapter 8: Strategizing the firm: strategic reconfiguration of the production systems – flexibility and quality. Regarding the internal configuration of the firm and its production systems, neoliberal transformation has brought about three interrelated key success factors or strategic imperatives: flexibility, quality, and cost-efficiency. This chapter concentrates on the managerial discourses that aim at enhancing flexibility and quality.

Preface xxxi

Chapter 9: Strategizing cost management. This chapter then concentrates on the third critical success factor – cost-efficiency – and explains the neoliberal logics, tools, and techniques for dealing with this strategic imperative.

Chapter 10: Strategizing interfirm relations. Critical success factors of flexibility, quality, and cost-efficiency cannot be realized simply through the internal reconfiguration of the firm. They demand careful attempts at coordinating activities across many organizations, especially across the supply chain. This chapter deals with the managerial elements of strategizing interfirm relationships.

Chapters 11 and 12 deal with the ways in which the strategy discourses have moved beyond the boundaries of for-profit organizations into the realms of polity and society. Accordingly, Chapter 11 explains how new public management discourses have reconfigured the administrative apparatuses of the state. Chapter 12 looks at the way in which these neoliberal discourses affect the organization and direction of civil society towards neoliberal market logic.

One of the key elements of neoliberal governmentality is the signification of biopolitical security issues such as global financial scandals and systemic risks, corruption, environmental unsustainability, poverty, etc. As a result, there is an ever increasing necessity to coordinate attempts across the economy, society, and polity to address such biopolitical issues. The way in which these biopolitical issues have influenced the neoliberal reconstruction of management accounting is dealt with in the last three chapters of the book.

Chapter 13: Neoliberalization of corporate governance. This chapter deals with the way in which recent political and managerial discourses have reconfigured the corporate governance apparatuses.

Chapter 14: Greening the firm: environmental management accounting. In this chapter, we articulate how the field of management accounting has responded to the global sustainability agenda.

Chapter 15: Strategizing development. Here we discuss how management accounting technologies have been mobilized to address issues of poverty and development in the peripheral nations.

Note

1 It is interesting to see that the majority of white papers (e.g. *Bedford Report* and *AICPA Future Issues Paper*, see http://aaahq.org/aecc/history/appB.htm) and academic literature (Montano et al. 2001) is concerned about the lack of attention existing accounting pedagogies have given to the development of communication, interpersonal, and problem-solving skills. Thus, recent and current attempts to develop the accounting education have largely been in the line of 'inventing' methods to enhance the ways of imparting these transferable skills to students.

Acknowledgements

This book is a product of the help and blessings of a number of people. From the inception, Professor Trevor Hopper's (University of Sussex) encouragement was stimulating. Our research with Professor Cameron Graham (Schulich School of Business, Canada) also provided some interesting insight for shaping this book. Professor James Guthrie (Macquarie University, Australia) and Professor Lee Parker (RMIT University Australia) provided us with invaluable moral support. Then students at University of Glasgow and Aberdeen who took our management accounting courses provided formal and ad hoc comments collectively and individually on the early versions of some of the chapters. We were glad to see that the students were excited to know that there is politics and socio-cultural dynamics (which they had inadvertently ignored in their previous courses) behind the accounting numbers.

We wish to acknowledge the professional and friendly support given by Terry Clague and Mathew Ranscombe at Routledge and their understanding of the pains of putting this book together. While producing it, we received much encouragement and support from the staff in the production process at Routledge.Our families lived with this book for several years. We are grateful for their forbearance and encouragements during this time which was far too long for all of us. Our wives, Lalanie and Shamanie, should have the credit for providing the stimulating academic and social environment in which the book materialized. It was delightful to have our children Imesha, Sajan and Kasun, Jessi, Manoj, Sherina 'disturb' the daily writing process.

Part I

Liberal origins

1 Old spirit of capitalism

The political-economic context of management accounting

1.1 Contextualizing the old logic of management accounting: pillars of analysis

Learning management accounting as a social science entails moving beyond its techno-managerial contents to see it as a socio-cultural and political phenomenon. For this purpose, it needs to be located within its wider context. In a broader sense, capitalism is management accounting's political economic context; it is the political system in which management accounting is located. Hence, the connection between management accounting and capitalism is one of the key themes that we need to pay our attention to here. At the outset, this connection is dialectical. On the one hand, it was the birth of capitalism that gave rise to management accounting. In different ways, early developments in industrial capitalism in late nineteenth and early twentieth centuries necessitated management accounting. Its subsequent neoliberal developments since the 1980s underlie the recent evolutions in management accounting into what is now coming to be known as strategic management accounting. On the other hand, management accounting is one of the key technologies that facilitates the functioning and growth of capitalism. Management accounting, as a mundane set of organizational practices, provides calculative techniques and practices to materialize the ideology of capital accumulation. It is this dialectical connection between capitalism and management accounting which will provide our focal attention in understanding management accounting as a socio-political phenomenon.

During the recent past, we have seen a historical rupture in capitalism. Sociologists and organizational theorists call this rupture a 'new spirit of capitalism' (Boltanski and Chiapello 2007; Du Gay and Morgan 2014). They see capitalism entering a new phase of development encompassing: political-economic logics of neoliberalism; market dynamics of globalization; and technological shifts of digitalization, networking, and virtualization. As a corollary to this, we also see certain changes in management accounting practices and techniques. A wide spectrum of 'new' management accounting techniques and practices ranging from Activity-Based Costing (ABC) and Balanced Scorecards (BSC) to 'big data analytics' are now in circulation. However, the focus of this chapter is neither the new spirit of capitalism nor the 'new' management accounting. Instead, the focus here is on the 'old spirit of capitalism' and the traditional mode of management accounting. This is because, we believe, the old provides the comparative basis to understand and explain the new, which we will be doing in the second part of this book.

We conceptualize the management accounting 'context' in three interrelated analytical pillars: political-economic, institutional, and epistemic (see Figure 1.1). The political-economic context refers to the wider systemic apparatuses that frame micro-organizational

4 Liberal origins

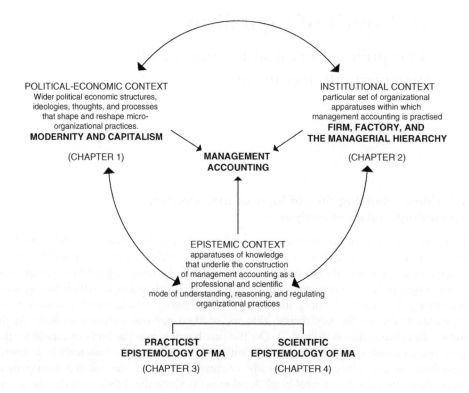

Figure 1.1 Contextualizing management accounting: the old logic

practices. *Modernity* and *industrial capitalism* designate the political economic system with which traditional management accounting originated and evolved. Despite their theoretical differences, accounting scholars in general agree that the origin and development of management accounting is directly related to the evolution of modern industrial capitalism (e.g. Hopper and Armstrong 1991; Johnson and Kaplan 1987a, 1987b; Kaplan 1984; Loft 1995). As such, management accounting embraces a particular political economic and historical logic pertaining to modernity and industrial capitalism. This chapter explores this political–economic and historical logic of management accounting.

The institutional context refers to a much narrower scope: the particular set of 'organizational apparatuses' within which management accounting is practised. We see three interrelated organizational apparatuses constituting the institutional context: (1) the factory-based organization of labour, (2) the managerial hierarchy or bureaucracy, and (3) the organization of capital into firms. As such, we take *factory, bureaucracy*, and the *firm* as the major elements of the institutional context of conventional management accounting. Chapter 2 articulates how these elements contextualized management accounting.

Epistemic context refers to the *apparatuses of knowledge* that underlie the construction of management accounting as a professional and scientific mode of understanding, reasoning, and regulating organizational practices. There are two distinct but interrelated apparatuses here. First is the professional apparatus which we call 'practist epistemology' of management accounting and will be discussed in Chapter 3. The second is what we call 'scientific epistemology' of management accounting, which will be dealt with in Chapter 4.

This chapter is organized as follows:

1. Section 1.2 introduces the concepts of modernity, modernism, and capitalism. While explaining their meaning, this section articulates how their emergence and growth are related to the development of human sciences or 'disciplines', including management accounting, and how such disciplines constitute the basis of control and regulation in modern societies.
2. Section 1.3 takes this discussion into a deeper level to explain modernity as a transformation in the mode of government. This transformation was from sovereignty to governmentality. Hence Foucault's notion of 'governmentality' is central to this discussion. Macro and micro dimensions of governmentality are discussed in two distinct but interrelated terms: biopolitical accounting and disciplinary accounting.
3. Section 1.4 brings us to capitalism. Capitalism is discussed as the ideological and structural context of management accounting. Liberal economic democracy was the political ideology of modernity. Hence attention is paid to how it transformed economic relationships and structures into a capitalistic social order where accumulation of capital became the dominating principle of organizing social relations. The notion of 'freedom' is discussed here in terms of free markets, free labour, and socialized capital. The role of accounting is discussed with special attention being given to the return on capital employed as the accounting signature of capitalism.
4. Finally, Section 1.5 summarizes and concludes the chapter with an overall discussion on the accounting implications of modernity and capitalism.

1.2 Political base of traditional management accounting: modernity, modernism, and capitalism

Capitalism, modernism, and modernity are interrelated concepts that accounting academics use to explain the origin and evolution of management accounting. Indeed, these concepts are complex, debatable, and hence difficult to define. However, for the purpose of contextualizing management accounting, we define *capitalism* as a social order in which freedom in (and through) the market, the socialized private ownership of capital, and the perpetual accumulation of private capital are the dominating principles of organizing social relations. *Modernity*, on the other hand, is the historical phase during which this social order was established in the Western world. *Modernism*, on the other hand, refers to the political-economic thought and the cultural movement that characterized the period of modernity. Modernity is the historical phase or trajectory; modernism is the political cultural thought behind that historicity; and capitalism is the economic, structural, and organizational manifestation of that thought.

The age of modernity is the epoch that began with the Enlightenment, the philosophical movement which dominated the world of ideas in Europe in the eighteenth century. This was the period where *rationalism* started to become a political phenomenon and a dominating social movement. Philosophers like René Descartes and Immanuel Kant introduced the idea that it is through rational reasoning that humans can establish a foundation of universal truth. People like Isaac Newton then championed the idea that *science* should be the *modus operandi* of this rational reasoning. Political leaders of modernity then connected this scientific rational reasoning with the idea of *social progresses* to transform governments. Progressive social transformation based on scientific rational reasoning then became a political imperative. Political and philosophical notions such as

6 *Liberal origins*

liberty, progress, reason, equality, tolerance, fraternity, and so on, became important normative elements of the cultural-political and economic landscape. This was indeed an ideological and political movement against the abuses of power by sovereign states. And it was a movement that questioned religious orthodoxy. It is this ideological and political repositioning of the West based on a notion of progress through scientific *reasoning*, individual *freedom*, and *equality* which we broadly call modernism. These modernist developments in political thought fed into not only dramatic political transformations such as French and American democratic revolutions but also into a whole trajectory of overarching and long-lasting socio-economic transformations such as industrialization, urbanization, colonization, human sciences, educational establishments, and changes in occupations and property ownership. After all, modernity and modernism were 'great transformations' (cf. Polanyi 1944) that changed the political and economic landscape of the Western, and consequently, non-Western civilizations.

Scientific reasoning (vis-à-vis religious reasoning) thus became politically and culturally acceptable and significant. It became the basis of providing meaning for human actions. Human agency and freedom were connected with the capacity to rationalize these actions through scientific reasoning. This provided the political cultural impetus for the growth of a diverse set of human sciences, including accounting. Such human sciences not only brought up specific schemas of scientific reasoning but also made the 'disciplinary knowledge' the dominating apparatus of power in modern societies (Foucault 1995). People were controlled, disciplined, and regulated through an emerging set of disciplines which penetrated every aspect of social being. This was indeed the formation of a new form of government where human sciences played governing roles. This was a new rationality or mentality of government which also brought up management accounting as a technology of government.

1.3 Governmentality: political changes of modernity and management accounting

Governmentality is the term that Foucault, a well-known French philosopher and historian, uses to describe this new rationality of government. Governmentality differs from the pre-modern sovereign forms of government (i.e. sovereignty) due to the nature of the power on which it is based. Governmentality runs on two notions of power: biopower (or biopolitics) and disciplinary power. In governmentality, people are governed not so much by the exercise of the sovereign power of the state but by the diffused and distributed use of biopower and disciplinary power.

These two modes of modern power are, in many ways, different from the sovereign or royal power that any agent of sovereignty (such as king, queen, prince, magistrate, sheriff, etc.) exercised. Sovereign power was centralized in the state (i.e. the sovereign) and was often passionate, violent, and repressive. Its deployment was deductive and took physical form, such as banning, exclusion, repression, torture, or execution. And it was commanding and demanding: it commanded and demanded a sacrifice from the subject to save the throne. It was based on the pre-modern political thought that 'the state exists only for itself and in relation to itself, whatever obedience it may owe to the other systems like nature or God' (Foucault 2008, 4). In this pre-modern logic of the sovereign state, the population was merely a source of power for the sovereign and the state had the power to command a sacrifice from the population for the security of the state. The state existed for itself and people existed for its protection (so went the old saying 'save the king/queen').

Modernity was the period in which the political state began to radically depart from this *raison d'état*. It brought the welfare of the population to the centre of the government. The state no longer existed for itself but for the welfare of the population. As Foucault (2000, 216–217) argues:

> [p]opulation comes to appear above all else as the ultimate end of government. In contrast to sovereignty, government has as its purpose not the act of government itself, but the welfare of the population, the improvement of its condition, the increase of its wealth, longevity, health, and so on; and the means the government uses to attain these ends are themselves all, in some sense, immanent to the population; it is the population itself on which government will act either directly, through large-scale campaigns, or indirectly, through techniques that will make possible, without the full awareness of the people, the stimulation of birth rates, the directing of the flow of population into certain regions or activities, and so on. The population now represents more the end of government than the power of the sovereign; the population is the subject of needs, of aspirations, but it is also the object in the hands of the government.

Biopower and disciplinary power constitute those techniques that a modern state deploys to construct the population as a collective body, to regulate it, and to ensure its welfare. Their mode of operation is corrective, rather than punitive. They operate through normalizing the human body and mind within society itself, rather than criminalizing, physically punishing, and excluding the deviant bodies from society. The sovereign laws of the state still do have a role to play, however. Disciplinary knowledge constitutes the pervasive mode of power and plays a greater role in the operationalization of the modern form of government – governmentality. Disciplines such as statistics, medicine, psychiatry, political economy, and accounting enable and enact these forms of power. Thus, knowledge is power: disciplines create a particular set of knowledge-power nexuses in which governmentality is enacted.

Disciplinary knowledge, and hence disciplinary power, constitutes disciplinary principles, disciplinary techniques, and disciplinary practices. They are the devices of control, regulation, and normalization. For example, medicine, as a discipline, constitutes a diverse range of disciplinary principles, techniques, and practices through which individuals, as patients, are examined, monitored, regulated, and controlled. Within the disciplinary contexts that medicine creates, individuals become *objects* – the patients – to be examined and known, to be monitored, and to be regulated using a particular set of disciplinary principles, techniques, and practices that medicine, as a discipline, prescribes. Another set of individuals, doctors, nurses, and other medical practitioners, then become *subjects* – those who embody, carry, and exercise the power of the discipline. In the same vein, management accounting also constitutes a set of disciplinary techniques and practices. These place individuals and groups within a series of subject-object nexuses by, for example, transforming them into employees, subordinates, cost objects, cost centres, profit centres, accountants, managers, and so on. Thus, disciplines inscribe individuals into series of power relations, i.e. relations among people (and things) posited as relations between subjects and objects. Foucault calls these processes of transforming individuals into subjects and objects 'subjectivation' and

8 *Liberal origins*

'objectivation'. Disciplinary technologies, like accounting, enable the exercise of power by creating knowledge-power relations that make subjectivation and objectivation possible.

One of the key features of this 'disciplinary regime of government' (i.e. governmentality) is that both the objects and subjects are governed by the disciplinary apparatuses to which they are subjected. In the process of taking care of patients by being a doctor or a nurse, for example, an individual is equally subject to the principles, techniques, and processes of medicine. The subject becomes an object qua being a subject. Thus, in the final analysis, though they embed, carry, and wield the power of the discipline (of which they also become objects), it is not the subjects who ultimately control and discipline the objects. Instead, it is the discipline which regulates both the object and the subject. The key point is that the power is with the discipline, not the individual per se, although individuals by being a subject of disciplinary power may enjoy the exercise of that disciplinary power and construct their own subjectivity and agency. Management accounting is such a powerful discipline. It enables and enacts a particular set of subject-object relations in the form of labour and capital, subordinate and manager, cost objects and cost controllers, decision scenarios and decision makers, and so on. Governing now takes place within such subject-object relations created by a wider spectrum of disciplines. These subject-object relations are now distributed across every organization in society. They diffuse and decentralize the function of government to form what we now call governmentality. As such, government, in the form of governmentality, now operates within a multitude of political-economic spaces, such as factories, offices, banks, hospitals, schools, universities, and so on.

Governmentality as a mode of government is not overtly punitive. Instead, it is corrective and intended to be 'careful': driven towards the 'care' and the 'welfare' of the population and individuals. Governmentality involves a double manoeuvre: simultaneous centrifugal and centripetal forces of biopower and disciplinary power. Disciplinary power is centripetal and operates as the 'anatomico-politics of the human body' confining the individual within micro-institutional apparatuses of power. Biopolitics is centrifugal and operates in the opposite direction, circulating individuals within macro apparatuses of power to construct a collective social body (i.e. population/economy). Disciplinary power is confining, biopower is circulating; disciplinary power is individualizing, biopower is totalizing. It is their co-existence and subtle interconnection that create the governmentality in which 'power took possession of life', says Foucault (2003, 253, parentheses ours):

> To say that power took possession of life in the nineteenth century, or to say that power at least takes life under its care in the nineteenth century, is to say that it has, thanks to the play of technologies of discipline [i.e. disciplinary power] on the one hand and technologies of regulation [i.e. biopolitics] on the other, succeeded in covering the whole surface that lies ... between body and population ... We are, then, in a power that has taken control of ... the body as one pole and the population as the other.

This means that governmentality simultaneously creates two modes of accounting: biopolitical accounting (i.e. accounting for population) and disciplinary accounting (i.e. accounting for individual bodies).

The political-economic context 9

1.3.1 Biopolitical accounting: accounting for population and economy

Biopolitical accounting involves constructing the collective social body of population and economy as accounting entities. Technologies such as social medicine, statistics,[1] political economy, and so on (which Foucault broadly calls 'technologies of regulation') play an important role here. Population becomes a distinct social body through the biopolitical accounts, statistics, and narratives that these disciplines create. Population is accounted for as a political problem, as a problem that is simultaneously scientific and political, as a social body that simultaneously presents as a biological problem and a problem of power (see Foucault 2003, 245). Collectively, these disciplines create a numerical profile and a political narrative of the population. They profile and narrate the population in terms of its pathological traits, such as health, wealth, and literacy. It is the management of these pathological traits which then becomes the focus of government.

How was this collective social body brought about historically? For Foucault, two important historical trajectories are important here: (1) the evolution of economic thought, especially mercantilism and liberalism at the early stage of capitalistic development, and (2) the formation of 'social medicine'. At the end of the sixteenth and beginning of the seventeenth centuries, mercantilism was the dominating political and economic thought in Europe. Mercantilism was a political practice that aimed to regulate international monetary currents, the corresponding flows of goods, and above all, the productive activities of the population. It was premised on the understanding that commercial exchange was essential to enable the financing and maintenance of armies and other apparatuses of the sovereign state. And the state's capacity to engage in commercial exchanges was dependent on the productive capacity of the population. Hence a healthy and productive population was considered to be an essential element of maintaining strong state apparatuses. This resulted in European nations taking a serious political interest in the regulation of the 'pathological traits of the population', especially its health, wealth, and the education. In that sense, rationality of government started to gain a new meaning – accounting and managing the pathological traits of the population. A healthy, wealthy, educated, and law abiding population became the administrative rationality towards a prosperous nation.

1.3.2 Social medicine as a case of population accounting

Initially, population accounting was limited to the evaluation of the active strength of the population. Birth rate and mortality tables started to become popular tools of accounting for the health and growth of the population. However, this was without any organized intervention to improve the health of and increase the growth in the population. Accounting of the population was merely taking a stock of the population in terms of its size, birth, and mortality rates, so that its future projection could be understood. It was the subsequent formation of social medicine that exemplified the modernist attempt to govern the health of the population. For Foucault, the formation of social medicine into a technology of governmentality took place in three stages (see Foucault 2000, 134–156):

1. *State medicine* was initially programmed in Germany and refers to the concept and programme of 'medical police' (*Medizinischepolizei*). This brought up (a) a system of systematic recording and reporting of sicknesses and epidemics based on the

10   Liberal origins

information gathered from the hospitals and doctors of different towns and regions; (b) standardization of medical practices and medical knowledge in order to 'normalize' the conduct of medical practitioners; (c) an administrative organization for overseeing the activity of medical practitioners; and (d) the creation of medical officers, appointed by government, who would take responsibility for a region.

2. *Urban medicine* emerged initially in the French urban centres. Though its concern was on the general health of the population, it was not a medicinal practice directly working on the bodies of the patients. This brought up different health phenomena to be governed and managed: insalubrity and 'public health' (*hygiene publique*). Their focus was on the state of things and places (such as cemeteries, ossuaries, slaughterhouses, and so on) rather than on the people themselves. Urban medicine was directed at the state of the 'things' and environment insofar as they affected health. Public health, as a technology of governmentality, was the politico-scientific control of the environment for the purposes of managing a pathological trait of the population (see Foucault 2000, 151). In this case, social medicine was driven towards the standardization and normalization of city spaces, as spaces related to the health of the population.

3. *Labour force medicine* emerged in England where the formation of the working class was faster and more intensive due to rapid industrial development. English urban city spaces were divided into rich and poor areas in the belief that cohabitation between rich and poor in an undifferentiated urban environment constituted a health and political hazard for the city and its population in general (see Foucault 2000, 152). Backed by legal enforcement in terms of the Poor Law and the Health Service Legislations, and an accompanying institutional and administrative infrastructure to implement such legislature, the English system of social medicine manifested as three coexisting medical systems: a welfare medical system designed for the poorest people; an administrative medical system responsible for general problems such as vaccination, epidemics, and so on; and a private medical system benefitting those who could afford it (see Foucault 2000, 155–156). Yet, alone, it embraced a biopolitical system in which (a) meticulous accounting and reporting on epidemics and diseases were maintained; (b) a set of biopolitical interventions was put in place through vaccinations and other inspection regimes; and (c) the localization and destruction of unhealthy and insalubrious dens of iniquity was carried out.

These developments in social medicine resemble early inventions in the form of a comprehensive 'responsibility accounting system'. Doctors and other medical practitioners appeared as administrators with clearly defined structures, processes, practices, and technologies to make themselves responsible and accountable for the health of different segments of the population. This was not simply medicine, but social medicine as accountability, a political tool of governmentality. This is the way in which medicine, as a discipline, was mobilized to form a particular set of accountability structures and practices in order to account for and manage a pathological trait of the population.

The outcomes were: the perpetual political intervention in the management of the health of the population; the production of a diverse set of health statistics; and the differentiation, classification, profiling, assessment, and regulation of the population on the basis of these health statistics. This was population accounting par excellence. It provided a basis for evaluating the efficacy of the actions of the political authority in terms of their impact on the welfare of the population. For accounting students, this is a

The political-economic context   11

classic way to understand the manner in which accountability systems and practices were created beyond the boundaries of 'accountancy', by people other than 'accountants', as was the case when engineers like Frederick W. Taylor invented standard costing. Indeed, these social medicine inventions exemplify how modern accountability structures and practices evolve. This logic of governmentality is not only limited to the management of health but also extends well to other pathological traits such as wealth, education, lawfulness, and so on. A cursory reading of news today can tell you how significant these biopolitical accounts are in modern democracies.[2] Disciplines do not simply exist in the form of pure knowledge. Instead, they are always embedded within a set of accountability structures and practices that they themselves create. And it is those accountability structures and practices that enable and enact governmentality. Thus, it is not difficult to see how other disciplines, such as public administration, education administration, policy economics, development economics, and also accounting, relate to governmentality. One way or the other, they all are related to the management of, and accounting for, different pathological traits of the population. They all collectively construct a statistical social body which we call the population and economy, or the nation. They all create different forms of accountability structures and practices and define the forms of power-knowledge nexus, subject-object relations, within the multitude of institutional sites ranging from hospitals to factories, offices, universities, and schools.

1.3.3 Disciplinary accounting: micro-management of individual bodies

Governmentality is not only macro and biopolitical. It is simultaneously micro-organizational and anatomico-political. Population is managed not purely as a singular social body but through individualizing and normalizing bodies within a multitude of micro-institutional settings. Disciplines such as social medicine and accounting are deployed on the mind and the body of the individual within micro-institutional settings. Biopolitics needs to be supplemented by the anatomico-politics of the human body.

Government is diffused and multiplied within a myriad of institutions ranging from prisons to hospitals and factories. As Foucault (1995, 228) claims, 'prisons resemble factories, schools, barracks, hospitals, which all resemble prisons'. They are the micro sites in which governance is now taking place. We are governed not by an overarching totalizing state per se. Instead, we live in a 'disciplinary society' where a dispersed spectrum of organizations is in operation to govern us as disciplinary objects and subjects. We are governed, in differentiating organizational settings, for example, within the object-subject nexus of: employees and managers, cost objects and cost controllers, patients and doctors, students and teachers, benefit-seekers and assessors, prisoners and guards, customers and marketers, etc. Those organizations have differently internalized the processes of government: surveillance, control, discipline, punishment, normalization, and so on. Organizational disciplines and disciplinary practices, management accounting being one of them, configure these organizations into micro sites of governmentality. It is through such disciplines that governmentality is perpetually reproduced in every realm of human life.

The configuration of organizations into micro sites of governmentality includes the deployment of a set of organizational principles and practices that normalize and correct human behaviour and performance. Foucault (1995) broadly classifies these principles and practices into three main categories:[3] disciplining space, disciplining time, and disciplined bodies.

12   *Liberal origins*

Disciplining space

Modern organizations are disciplinary and disciplined spaces. First, they are the social spaces in which disciplines are in play to discipline human conduct. Human disciplines, including management accounting, are used to understand, conceptualize, design, monitor, and regulate behaviour in organizations. In this sense, modern organizations are disciplinary spaces. Second, and, in addition, modern organizations are also social spaces structured by disciplinary principles and technologies. Modern organizations are conceptualized, designed, configured, and organized into what they are by disciplines such as management, accounting, industrial engineering, law, as well as architecture. It is this social and technical structuring of the space that makes the disciplines capable of disciplining. In other words, the possibility of subjugating humans through disciplines into governable subjects and objects is realized through the micro-structuring of the social spaces. Such disciplined spaces make anatomico-politics of the human body possible.

According to Foucault (1995; see also Hopper and Macintosh 1993), disciplining the space involves the distribution of heterogeneous individuals over carefully designed spatial arrangements. In modern societies, individuals' productive functions and identities are spatially distributed, arranged, and designated. This begins with *general confinement* – the emergence of special purpose self-enclosed locations to contain individuals in a monotonous disciplinary state. Schools, factories, hospitals, universities, military barracks, prisons all represent such special purpose enclosures/confinements. People receive different productive functions and identities by being attached to these enclosures, for example, as patients-doctors, students-teacher, and labourers-managers. These enclosures are designed to carry out a monotonous set of activities in a specified and standardized manner by a set of disciplined bodies.

Nevertheless, the general confinement, in itself, is insufficient to enact an effective disciplinary regime. It needs to be supplemented and intensified through a further set of spatial principles: partitioning, functionally useful serialization, and ranking or hierarchization.

Partitioning involves the further division of general enclosures into as many self-contained 'cells' or locations as there are elements or bodies to be distributed (Hopper and Macintosh 1993, 193). Examples include further division of a factory (i.e. the general enclosure) into machine centres, offices, cost centres, and so on. Thus, each and every individual in the general enclosure is distributed to an identifiable and observable productive space. Reciprocally, each productive space-time location owns and occupies an individual. The space-time locations (e.g. a particular machine centre in the second shift of the day) become productive, and the individual becomes useful because of this connection between the individual and the individualized space. Each space-time location is to be defined in terms of its productive functions and outputs. An example is a machine centre defined in terms of its hourly production targets. It is in relation to these productive attributes of the space that it become possible to know, master, and make the individual useful. For example, machine operators occupying the machine are observed, measured, evaluated, and corrected in relation to the hourly targets of that machine centre. This is isolating individuals and mapping them along individualized productive cells so that they are visible and governable in terms of the productive attributes of those cells. In a factory setting, employees will be governed in terms of the number of units produced, amount of time and resources spent, and the contribution made to the company's profit by the particular productive cell they occupy. Such

The political-economic context   13

attributes are deemed to be objective measures because they are determined not by the heterogeneity and subjectivity of the individuals who occupy the productive cells but by the 'scientific' and 'objective' specifications of the productive cells. In this way, partitioning places a heterogeneous mass of humans on a homogeneous social order in which individuals, by being individualized in individualized space-time locations, become homogeneous categories (e.g. grade A or category A labour in an assembly line).

Yet alone, such partitioned and individualized productive spaces would not be useful on their own. They need to be assembled in a *serialized* manner to form a disciplinary grid. While being divided, distributed, and compartmentalized, they should also form an assemblage, a totality: a profitable company, an efficient factory, a well-functioning hospital, etc. The functional logic of this serializing, for example, could be the logic of the 'value-chain', if we use Michael Porter's strategic management terminology. Or it could be the engineering logic of 'line balancing and optimization' or 'throughput accounting' in an assembly line. In either way, serializing individualized productive cells is one of the essential disciplinary principles in the detailed configuration of generic enclosures. It is attempted through various managerial, engineering, or technical principles pertaining to different disciplines. Serialization transforms individualized space-time locations into a set of productive processes and relations. Such processes and relations are also *hierarchical*. They are arranged in accordance with their relative *rankings*, not only to facilitate hierarchical surveillance and control but also to facilitate the circulation of individuals up, down, and across the disciplinary grid.

This disciplinary structuring of spaces through general enclosure, partitioning, serializing, and ranking is material, engineering, and architectural to the extent that it constitutes distribution and spatializing of physical objects like buildings, corridors, CCTV cameras, walls, fences, rooms, workstations, machines, and furniture. More importantly, it is also social and behavioural to the extent that it involves creating social relations between human and non-human social actors. It is managerial and capitalist as well, because such structuring constitutes techno-managerial and financial logics of production and accumulation. This is where disciplines like management accounting play a significant role in disciplining the spaces. They offer conceptual schemas to design, differentiate, connect, and rank them. They also offer calculative techniques to measure, communicate, and control their performance. Examples are cascading BSCs, functionally linked operational and master budgets and variance analysis, DuPont frameworks of financial analysis, ABC/Activity Based Management (ABM), etc. They offer conceptual frameworks through which enclosed, partitioned, serialized, ranked, and individualized productive spaces are given financial meanings – perhaps the only meanings that ultimately make sense in a capitalistic world.

Disciplining time

Disciplining space works through inserting individuals into enclosed, serialized, ranked, and functional spaces. Nevertheless, to make space-time locations productive, bodies that they enclose within need to perform efficiently. This is the *efficient body principle* – making sure that individual bodies are made to perform efficiently. According to Foucault, this works through *disciplining the time*. This means that an efficiently performing body is produced by positioning it against the time. In this sense, the efficient body embodies three interrelated dimensions of time-defined performance:

14   *Liberal origins*

1. **The regularity of the performance**. An efficient body is predictable: it performs the functionalities of the productive cell in a time-regular fashion, i.e. according to a *timetable*. Hence, timetabling is the disciplinary practice that ensures regularity of performance. It can take so many different forms in so far as the performance of the body is scheduled against time and space. Examples include budgeting, production scheduling, ERP, school time tables, doctors' ward visit schedules, and so on. Timetabling routinizes the body in a time-space spectrum – the body is expected to move in a particular predictable pattern across time and space. Most of the management accounting inventions, of course, involve elements of refining and advancing the 'time-tabling' functionality of organizational activities to better suit changing techno-managerial conditions.

2. **Efficacy with which the body articulates the productive machinery**. This is achieved through rigorous prescription of how the body and its parts should connect to, and move with, the specified tools and equipment: shovel, machine, pen, typewriter, keyboard, joystick, gun, or whatever. The body and its parts are given specific motions and their sequence, ranges, and durations. This was what the Scientific Management Movement, pioneered by Frederick W. Taylor, achieved during the late nineteenth and early twentieth centuries. Time and motion studies were used to develop a set of working methods and standards to prescribe not only the way in which a particular work activity should be performed with a specified set of tools and equipment but also the standard times within which the activities should be completed. These standards then became the basis for 'incentive payment schemes' – a particular disciplinary regime in which only 'above-average efficiency' would be rewarded and incentivized.

3. **The efficient body should make exhaustive use of time**. Idling is not accepted and is to be mitigated through the proper use of disciplinary techniques and practices, namely *dressage* or *corrective training*. Corrective training makes the individual accept ideologically that idling is a sin, or an economic dishonesty, or a 'moral hazard' if we use the terminology of agency theory. Not only that, corrective training properly incorporates the body into a body-machine system by making the individual capable of following the orders that the productive machinery imposes upon them. The productive machinery seeks the obedience of, and reflective reactions from, the efficient body through a series of signals. Dressage makes the individuals capable of reacting to these signals and places him or her within a world of signals, each with its unique responses and moral imperative (see Hopper and Macintosh 1993, 196). Such signalling of the productive system could be various: the sound of a bell ringing or a whistle calling workers to start their shift; an adverse cost variance in a standard costing system seeking managerial explanations and actions; a slight increment in a defective rate displayed in a quality assurance system demanding managerial attention; a movement in stock prices on the stock-market monitoring screens demanding attention from market analysts; a time lag indicator of an order processing system that calls for prompt action from a manager; or an alarm in a hospital ward calling for the quick and appropriate deployment of medical attention on a patient.

Disciplined bodies

Successful enforcement of enclosure and efficient body principles demands another set of disciplinary measures and practices to ensure the (a) visibility of individual conduct at a distance, (b) inner drive of individuals to meet the demands placed upon them by the

The political-economic context   15

productive machine, and (c) continuous and progressive assessment of the bodies to check and maintain their fitness with the productive machinery. These are achieved through the following, respectively:

(a) Systems of *hierarchical surveillance*, as a special kind of 'looking on' or 'disciplinary gaze', were invented to enhance the visibility of individual conduct at a distance. Ever enlarging and dispersing productive spaces (e.g. larger factories, geographically wide-spread network of production facilities, and distanced political entities such as colonies) made the direct supervision and control rather difficult, if not impossible. Indirect modes of seeing at a distance thus became an economic and political necessity. One of the essential elements of any effective control system is surveillance. This has to be maintained despite the totality of the production system becoming too great and, despite the distance between the top and the bottom, owner and the worker, capital and the labour, centre and the periphery having become greater than ever. The solution was to invent a pyramid-like administrative hierarchy. These comprise series of multiple and intersecting managerial modes of observations capable of seeing without been seen. This is serialized, ranked, and hierarchical surveillance. The 'seeing' in such hierarchies is in the form of information integrated into the methods of production, supervision, and control. Sequentially and hierarchically arranged managerial positions (i.e. observational points in the hierarchy) relay the 'seeing' from bottom to top, from periphery to centre, from worker to the owner, from labour to capital, making everybody in the hierarchy visible to the higher levels at a distance.

(b) Systems of hierarchical surveillance create a necessary chain of connection and informational arrays and, thereby, makes seeing, knowing, and controlling at a distance ever stronger. However, in order not to make it an overly imposing punitive system, an inner motivational drive within individuals needs to be created. To this end, the conduct of the individual and their outcomes should be linked to a system of rewards (and punishments). One of the fundamental functions of the newly added layers of management during the early periods of modernity was to invent and maintain systems of reward and punishments that linked individual conduct with the accumulative goals of the organization. This is what Foucault (1995) calls *normalizing sanctions*. This was radical and revolutionary because this normalized the system of rewards and punishments within spaces hitherto not covered by the general laws of the state. As a result, organizations like factories, schools, hospitals, and so on became their own miniature legal systems, relatively independent and separated from the state but capable of exercising their own judgements, punishments, and rewards on individuals. In that sense, normalizing sanctions within institutional spaces beyond the juridical processes of sovereign state were indeed an extension of the government into the 'normal' spaces of socio-economic life, but with a new disciplin-ary logic (i.e. governmentality): discipline and punishment (i.e. sanctioning) now took place within these 'normal' private social spaces.

(c) The subjugation of individuals to these miniature legal systems was perpetual and progressive. They continuously and progressively assessed individuals to maintain their fitness with the ever-evolving productive machinery. This was where the disciplinary practice of *examination* became a political practice. Initially originating in educational institutions and military establishments, examination evolved into a major technique of exercising disciplinary power during the late seventeenth century (Foucault 1995; Hopper and Macintosh 1993; Hoskin and Macve 1986,

16   *Liberal origins*

1988). As a disciplinary practice, examination became ritualistic, frequent, regular, and often took on a 'scientific' bearing to subjugate individuals into perpetual corrective processes of observation, assessment, recording, reporting, comparison, appreciation, rewarding, warning, and punishment.

Examinations, depending on the organizational setting in which they are deployed, can take so many different forms ranging from the ritualistic daily 'check ups' of patients by medical practitioners, to 'walking around inspections' by line supervisors, to periodic performance evaluation meetings by specialist managers. In any case, examination involves the deployment of disciplinary knowledge to:

(a) *Know and reveal* the otherwise hidden elements of one's behaviour or individuality and

(b) *Compare* that revelation with already established norms and averages so that the individual is placed in a comparative spectrum for correction and normalization.

Examination is a process in which 'power seeing' is combined with 'knowledge seeing' to transform productive spaces like factories, hospitals, and schools into 'examinatories of objects'. Social relations therein are formalized into a series of connections between examiners and examined, both of whom are then subjugated to the processes of examination themselves. Workers and managers, patients and doctors, students and teachers, all become objects of this examination. Workers, patients, and students alike become the object by being the bodies to be examined and known. Managers, doctors, teachers, and the like would still be subjugated and objectified, qua being a subject, by the same examination process. The conduct of the examination, and the examiners, should also be disciplined by the same disciplinary knowledge. Examination is a fundamental technique of deploying knowledge as a tool of knowing, control, domination, and disciplining.

Examination is 'progressive' in the sense that it accumulates. More than an end in itself, examination provides the beginning and the base for progressive accumulation of knowledge, hence a greater capacity to discipline, and a greater potential of production and accumulation of wealth. It creates not only a perpetual, detailed, and archived knowledge but also the necessary data to compile national databases for biopolitical accounting of the population. Hence individuals can simultaneously be known and disciplined as individuals and be related to the population as a data point: examination connects the micro with the macro, biopolitics with disciplinary politics.

1.4 Capitalism: ideology and economic structure of management accounting

So far, discussion in this chapter has explained how Western society was transformed into a disciplinary society – a society which is governed by the disciplinary apparatuses of governmentality. We saw how management accounting can be interpreted as a technology of governmentality. However, it is important to understand that neither biopolitical nor anatomico-political disciplining take place for their own sake. Governmentality has a political ideology, a moral philosophy, and an economic structure. It is capitalism that provides political ideology, moral philosophy, and gives economic structure to modern societies. Capitalism transforms the modern disciplinary society into a society of capital accumulation. There is indeed a dialectical connection between

The political-economic context   17

governmentality and capitalism. Capitalism provides the structural logic – capital accumulation – to a disciplinary society. Governmentality provides a superior form of government to make capital accumulation more efficient than ever before. Foucault (1995, 220–221) articulates this connection as follows:

> If the economic take-off of the West began with the techniques that made possible the accumulation of capital, it might perhaps be said that the methods for administering the accumulation of men [sic] made possible a political take-off in relation to the traditional, ritual, costly, violent forms of power, which soon fell into disuse and were superseded by a subtle, calculated technology of subjection. In fact, the two processes – the accumulation of men and the accumulation of capital – cannot be separated; it would not have been possible to solve the problem of the accumulation of men without the growth of an apparatus of production capable of both sustaining them and using them; conversely, the techniques that made the cumulative multiplicity of men useful accelerated the accumulation of capital.

1.4.1 Liberal markets

Capitalism propagated *liberal economic democracy* as its moral philosophy. Liberal economic democracy promulgated the idea that social agents should be free to act on their own accord for social progress to take place. This freedom was to be realized in two distinct but interrelated domains: political and economic. In the political domain, this freedom was to be exercised through the system of universal franchise and parliamentary systems of representative democracy. Freedom in the economic domain was signified by three interrelated concepts: *free markets, free labour,* and *socialized capital.* This was indeed an outcome of the modernist developments in political thought that we discussed in the previous sections. The modernist political movement was to enlighten and emancipate individuals from the religious dogma and abusive sovereign power. So, the notion of freedom that modernism and capitalism collectively embraced was the freedom of the individual from the sovereignty. In that sense, liberal economic democracy embraced a political economic system where the role and presence of the state in the social and economic life of the masses were to be kept at a minimum.

Given this liberalist desire for minimum presence by the sovereign state in the economic affairs of the people, what should govern the conduct of the people? The free market was the liberal answer. Liberalism offered a governing supremacy to the market and assumed that the market can and should govern economic activities. Market was understood as a social space where the individual should be allowed to exercise their free choice and economic rationality. Hence it was understood as a social mechanism capable of liberating individuals from the pre-modern abusive sovereign modes of power. Hence, according to this liberalist morality, market was not simply a place where economic transactions took place but the ideal mechanism through which economic activities of the people should be governed and coordinated. This means that the market should be conceptualized as a governing mechanism, a command centre, which offers a particular set of signals (i.e. price signals) to which economic agents such as producers, consumers, and labourers would rationally and freely respond. The market was considered to be a morally superior mechanism of governance because it provided the opportunity for 'free choice'. And, therefore, it was assumed to be a 'natural system of liberty' independent of political

18   *Liberal origins*

authority. Moreover, liberalist claimed that the price mechanism would result not only in individual freedom and economic rationality but also in socially optimal outcomes.

In the context of markets, the liberal notion of freedom is indeed the freedom to compete and the right to free and fair competition. Adam Smith (2012 [1776]), a prominent liberalist, claimed that in a capitalist society,

> [e]very man, as long as he does not violate the laws of justice, is left perfectly free to pursue his own interest his own way, and to bring both his industry and capital into competition with those of any other man, or order of men.

What should they be competing for? For accumulation of their private capital, was the liberal economic answer. Thus, capitalism attributed an overarching economic purpose to freedom – accumulation of capital. The efficacy with which social agents exercised market freedom was to be judged by the rate at which they accumulated their individual capital, which is now known as the return on capital employed.

Once profit motive entered the equation of liberalism, and once freedom could be exercised within the competitive parameters of the market with profit motives, liberalism became calculative, and freedom in the market became a series of calculated actions. The social agents that liberalism propagated should be calculative, capable of assessing the accumulative potential (i.e. profitability) of their actions in light of the competitive parameters of the market. This means that the freedom that modernity and capitalism offered to individuals could be enjoyed to the extent that the individual was equipped with a sufficient degree of accounting literacy to assess the cumulative potential of their actions. This was where accounting became crucial in capitalism.[4] The cumulative mentality and morality of liberal capitalism were operationalized and symbolized through accounting. Accounting thus became the 'sign' or 'signature' of capitalism (see Bryer 2000a; Chiapello 2007).

1.4.2 Accumulative markets

However, the market is neither a capitalistic invention nor something that uniquely signifies the existence of capitalism. Markets predate capitalism. However, there is a fundamental difference in the capitalist and pre-capitalist forms of market transactions. Pre-capitalist markets constituted only 'simple circulation' or the 'direct form of the circulation of commodities'. According to Marx (1990 [1867], 248), this took the form of commodity-money-commodity (C-M-C), which was 'the transformation of commodities into money and the reconversion of money into commodities: selling in order to buy', for instance 'in the case of the peasant who sells corn and with the money thus set free buys clothes' (Marx 1990 [1867], 20). In this form of simple or commodity circulation, market transactions do not result in capital accumulation but only a consumption surplus.

Capitalism brought the 'circulation of capital' into the market, which took the form M-C-M, the transformation of money into commodities, and the reconversion of commodities into money: buying in order to sell (Marx 1990 [1867], 248). This was one of the aspects that made capitalism different from pre-capitalist social systems. The capitalist market brought the notion of capital and its accumulation into being. This circulation of capital resulted in the accumulation of capital when it took the form M-C-M*, where $M^*=M+\Delta M$, i.e. the original amount of money invested in the market plus an increment. As capital was the money thrown into the sphere of circulation for the purpose of it being recovered with a surplus (see, Chiapello 2007, 279), this increment over the original capital became the 'surplus value', as Marx called it. In this 'circulation of capital', the market constituted the social sphere in which the accumulation of capital was made possible, a process which Marx called the 'valorization' of surplus value. And, in this form of capitalist markets, accumulation of capital became an end in itself: 'the circulation of money as capital is an end in itself, for the valorization of value takes place only within this constantly renewed movement. The movement of capital is therefore limitless' (Marx 1990 [1867], 253). As Bryer 2000a, 2000b) argues, the rate of return on capital has thus become the accounting signature of capitalism: accounting provides the signatory manifestation of the capitalist ethic of accumulation by making it possible to calculate the return on capital employed – the relative rate at which the accumulation takes place during a given period of time.

1.4.3 Free labour and socialized capital

Although the surplus value or profit is valorized in the market, it is created elsewhere, often in the factory. This is where free labour entered the equation of capitalism (and liberalism) as one of its fundamental requirements. In pre-capitalist modes of production, labour was not necessarily free. Labourers (e.g. peasants, slaves, indentured labour, and caste labour) were bonded to a particular land, a master, or an occupation by a set of archaic social bonds. For capitalism to emerge and operate, labour had to be freed from such bonds and made available to be bought by the capitalist in the market as a commodity. This was the commodification of labour. Thus, the notion of free labour, according to Marx (1990 [1867], 270–271), constituted certain necessary conditions:

1. It was the labour power (rather than the labour or the labourer) that appeared in the market for sale. The labour power was the capacity of the labourer to produce a use-value of any kind. The labour power to so appear in the market as a commodity, its possessor must have it at his/her disposal. S/he must be the free proprietor of his/her own labour capacity, hence of his/her person.
2. For labour power to appear in the market as a commodity, its seller, the labourer, and its buyer, the capitalist, both should enter into relations with each other on a footing of equality as owners of commodities, the only difference been their role in the market: one was a seller and the other was the buyer. They both should be equal in the eyes of the law, parties to a market contract or transaction.
3. For this to be the case, labour power needed to be sold only for a limited period of time, because if the labourer were to sell his labour power in a lump, once and for all, then he would be selling him/herself, converting him/herself from a free man into a slave. In a capitalist system, such selling or buying of oneself cannot and shouldn't be permitted (hence anti-slavery laws!). Instead only the labour power was to be traded. The labourer should be able to constantly treat and trade his/her labour power as his/her own property.
4. The labourer should be 'free' from the possession of any other means of subsistence other than selling his/her own labour power. S/he should be free from all the other objects needed for realization of his/her own labour power. Thus s/he was compelled to offer his/her labour power in the market

20   *Liberal origins*

This is the notion of freedom or liberation that a labourer should enjoy in capitalism: s/he has been freed so that the accumulative markets can function. Nevertheless, in a liberalist sense, the market in itself is a better system of governance than feudal aristocracy or even 'labour-camp socialism' (Ivanova et al. 2000).

Capitalist developments during modernity were a double manoeuvre. While it created a force of 'free labour' available to be traded in the market as a commodity, it also created forces of 'free capital'. This was indeed pooled or 'socialized capital' made up of small divisible units, tradable on their own as a commodity for an expected rate of return on investment. Examples are the bonds, debentures, stocks and shares which started to become popular with the invention of joint stock companies. During the period of modernity, there emerged a series of political, legal, and economic transformations and technological inventions that ultimately resulted in fully grown markets, institutions, and instruments of free capital.[5] The key here was the divisibility, tradability, and transferability of capital in the market so that a commercial freedom was created. Individuals could invest in and socialize capital in equal terms to pursue a competitive rate of return. It was this socialization of capital, inter alia, that created two fundamental conditions of widespread capitalism: the mentality of rate of return on investment and the separation of ownership from management of economic enterprises. The capital came into being on its own, in the form of the 'firm' or the 'corporation', as an entity independently managed by a class of managers separated from the investors. Thus, the management of the capital was separated from its ownership. In this process, as Bryer and others vividly explain, double-entry bookkeeping and other technologies of accounting played a crucial role. Though there were certain fundamental differences in their arguments in terms of the specific timing of historical happenings, theoretical underpinnings and interpretations, and particular accounting technologies and meanings that they emphasized, both accounting and sociology scholars (e.g. Marx, Sombart, Weber, Bryer, and Chiapello) agree, one way or the other, that it was accounting which signified the socialization of capital in terms of various accounting devices and measures, whether they be return on capital employed, double-entry bookkeeping, profit and loss account, or the balance sheet. We will be discussing this socialization of capital in more detail in the next chapter.

1.5   Summary and conclusions

Prototypical contents that we study in many undergraduate, postgraduate, and professional accounting courses tell us that management accounting is a techno-managerial or professional practice, deployed primarily for the purposes of enhancing the effectiveness and the efficiency of the operational and strategic decisions that managers make. We don't necessarily disagree with this view but emphasize the necessity of understanding the wider set of political-economic and historical logics behind the evolution of management accounting. Management accounting needs to be understood not only as a managerial tool but also as a socio-political phenomenon evolving with the changing political-economic context. It has a set of political-economic rationales and roles to play. Its evolution has been related to the historical dynamics of the political state and economy.

Origin and evolution of management accounting was related to the radical socio-political, economic, and technological transformations manifested by what we now interconnectedly label as modernity, modernism, and capitalism. For the purpose of this chapter, we defined modernity as the historicity that manifested the great transformation since the Renaissance; modernism as the political cultural thought behind that historicity; and capitalism as the economic, structural, and organizational manifestation of that thought and historicity. Modernity was the process, modernism was the political thought behind the process, and capitalism was the political–economic outcome.

These notions have been explained through many different angles across different disciplinary boundaries. In sociology and other associated disciplines, for example, there are quite different analyses focusing on their economic, political, social, and cultural dimensions (see Braham et al. 1992; Hall and Gieben 1993; Hall et al. 1992). However, for the purposes of relating them to management accounting, our focus was mainly on two specific dimensions: (1) the transformation of the form of government from sovereignty to governmentality, and (2) the constitution of capitalism. We related both of these to accounting technologies.

The state underwent a dramatic change in the period of modernity, encompassing a new rationality or mentality of government. Governmentality is the term Foucault used to explain this new form of government where power took on a different form and purpose. Population became its purpose and disciplinary knowledge became its form. Government was diffused and dispersed into myriad organizational settings including hospitals, schools, factories, and prisons. Governmentality was enacted and enabled within such institutional settings through subjectivation and objectivation. Individuals became subjects and objects of disciplinary knowledge that these organizations enacted and enabled. Management accounting was one of the disciplinary practices that subjectivated and objectivated individuals, for example, as cost controllers and cost objects, and as managers and subordinates.

In contrast to the pre-modern form of sovereignty, governmentality was not punitive but corrective; driven towards the care and welfare of the population and individuals through disciplining, correction, and regulation. It involved a double manoeuvre of power: biopower and disciplinary power. Biopower was centrifugal and directed towards constructing the collective social body that we call population and economy. Hence it constituted accounting for population: measuring, assessing, and managing the population as a singular collective body in terms of its pathological traits such as health and wealth. Disciplinary power was centripetal and operated as the anatomico–politics of the human body confining it within disciplinary institutions. Such anatomico–politics of the human body operated through a particular set of disciplinary principles and practices which Foucault broadly classifies into three distinct categories: disciplining space, disciplining time, and disciplined bodies. Management accounting constitutes such disciplinary functionalities, as Hopper and Macintosh (1993) vividly illustrate in their seminal case study.

While governmentality provided the context for management accounting to emerge and evolve as a disciplinary practice, capitalism provided the political ideology and economic structure that enabled and effected management accounting as a technology of capital accumulation. Capitalism brought capital accumulation as a normative element of social actions to the centre of disciplinary society. Capitalism and modernity initially emerged as a social movement of enlightenment and emancipation, especially against the dominating and abusive power structures of the pre-modern sovereign states. Thus, capitalism embraced a certain form of freedom which was captured in what we now call liberal economic democracy. In this political doctrine, liberty was to be exercised in two interrelated domains: political and economic. While representative democracy with universal franchise embraced the

22 Liberal origins

political liberty, economic freedom was constituted in free markets, free labour, and free (i.e. socialized) capital.

Markets in a capitalistic sense played a dual role: liberating and accumulating. Capitalism and liberalism provided a governing supremacy to the markets and assumed that the market should and can govern the economic activities, minimizing the presence of the sovereign state. This is the liberating function of markets, making the individual economic activities free from sovereign or aristocratic interventions. The cumulative role is associated with the invention of the 'circulation of capital' which, in turn, necessitated free labour and socialized capital and created the capitalist mentality of return on capital employed – the ultimate accounting signature of capitalism.

Assignments

These assignments are meant to extend your knowledge beyond what you understand from this chapter. These are not simply revision questions. The content covered in this chapter is necessary but will not be sufficient in attempting these tasks. Therefore, you are required to do some extra reading in attempting these tasks.

1. **Thematic essay:**
   'Management accounting is a disciplinary technology'.
   Write an essay, of approximately 3,000 words, on the above theme articulating how accounting can be related to governmentality as a rationality of government in modern societies.
2. **Poster:**
   Draw a poster illustrating accounting as a technology of accumulation. Pay special attention to the connection between liberal economic democracy, capitalism, the capitalist mentality of return on capital employed, and accounting.
3. **Presentation:**
   Prepare a set of PowerPoint slides, together with notes if necessary, for a 30-minute presentation on the following theme:
   'In capitalism, management accounting plays a dual role: disciplining and accumulation'.
4. **Extended bibliography:**
   Write an extended bibliography on the use of Foucault's concept in accounting research. For this, you need to do a literature survey of major accounting journals and edited books where critical accounting research is published. Organize the bibliography into a table in the following format.

Bibliographic info	Nature of the paper/book chapter (e.g. conceptual/theoretical, empirical, a response to a previous publication)	Major arguments, conclusions, and contributions

5. **Literature review:**
   Management accounting history has been a highly debated issue in critical accounting academia. Johnson and Kaplan's (1987a) *Relevance Lost: The Rise and Fall of Management Accounting* provided a neoclassical economic-based explanation of management accounting history. Since then there has been a strong set of Marxist and Foucauldian

critiques on their thesis providing alternative theoretical interpretations on the history of management accounting.

Write a review essay articulating the major differences in these three camps of explaining management accounting history.

Notes

1 It is interesting to note here that the original meaning of the term 'statistics', as it emerged during the period of modernity, was that it is the science of the state or statists.
2 See Rose (1991) and Miller (2001) for seminal discussions on how this form of democracy, which Rose and Miller call 'governing by numbers', operates.
3 See Hopper and Macintosh (1993) for an splendid case study of how these disciplinary principles and practices are in use in a large, complex, multinational firm. We drew heavily on their paper in writing this section.
4 For a detailed discussion on the genealogy of the term 'capitalism', the different meaning attached to it, and the connection between accounting history and the history of capitalism, see Bryer (2000a, 2000b); Chiapello (2007).
5 See Bryer (2000a, 2000b, 1993a, 1993b) and Chiapello (2007) for detailed analyses of the historicity of capital formation and the role that accounting played therein.

2 Old spirit of capitalism
The institutional context of management accounting

2.1 Introduction

In the previous chapter, we mentioned that the context of the traditional form of management accounting constitutes three interrelated elements: political-economic, institutional, and epistemic. Chapter 1 dealt with the political-economic context identifying modernity, modernism, and capitalism as major political and historical pillars on which the traditional mode of management accounting stands. We explained how modernity resulted in a new form of government – governmentality – and how governmentality provided the basis for the emergence of disciplinary institutions and disciplinary technologies. This led us to understand management accounting as a disciplinary practice involving two interrelated political dynamics: biopolitics and anatomico-politics. We also discussed how capitalism and its underlying political philosophy – liberal economic democracy – provided not only the political ideology of capital accumulation but also the structural conditions – free market, free labour, and socialized capital – to transform disciplinary institutions and technologies into a system of capital accumulation. In light of this accumulative mentality, return on capital employed became the accounting signifier of capitalism, making accounting a necessary technology of capitalism.

In this chapter, we turn to the second element – the institutional context. Some of its features have already been discussed in the previous chapter, especially when we dealt with anatomico-politics. We discussed how certain disciplinary principles and practices were put in place for disciplining space, time, and body. This deployment of disciplinary principles and practices is manifested in the diffusion of government, in the form of governmentality, into myriad forms of organizations. Thus, we could conceptualize management accounting as a set of disciplinary technologies and practices. By being so, it helped the institutionalization of governmentality within organizations. Hence, Foucauldian analysis of management accounting as a set of disciplinary technologies and practices provided a particular view of the institutional context of management accounting. However, in this chapter our focus is different. Here, we concentrate on three interrelated concepts: the firm, the factory, and the managerial hierarchy. These are the key elements related to the *socialization of capital*. Therefore, our attention here is more on how the capital is socialized and how management accounting relates to this.

The chapter is organized into three main sections.

1. Section 2.2 deals with the notion of the firm (or more formally the corporation) as a form of socialized capital. As already mentioned in the previous chapter, the notion of the *socialization of capital* is defined here as the economic political

formation of capital into divisible and tradable units so that they can openly be traded in the capital markets. The emergence of corporations was a critical historical event in this regard. In contrast to pre-corporate forms of pooling capital, such as partnerships and mutual trusts, the corporate form of socialization made the sharing of ownership possible on the basis of market relations, not requiring mutual trust, personal relations, or any other non-market form of social bonding. Accordingly, this section discusses the history and the political-economic outcomes of the socialization of capital in corporations and the accounting implications thereof.

2. Section 2.3 takes you to the notion of the factory, which is the institutional form in which the *capitalization of production* takes place. What we mean by capitalization of production is the technological, managerial, and political processes through which the 'ownership and control' of the labour process shifts from labour to capital. As a prelude to this, this section first discusses the nature of production relations before the invention of the factory system. Then it moves on to discuss the particular transformations that made the capitalization of production possible: mechanization of production, rationalization of work, regimentation of labour, and cost accounting.

3. Section 2.4 discusses the third element of the institutional context, the *managerial hierarchy*. Here we conceptualize the managerial hierarchy as the capitalist invention that connects and creates an intimacy between capital and labour. In making this connection, the managerial hierarchy embeds certain disciplinary logic, structural logic, democratic logic, and a logic of economic coordination.

4. Finally, Section 2.5 concludes the chapter with a summary.

2.2 Socializing capital: the invention of corporation

The growth of capitalism was indeed a matter of how capital[1] was organized into 'firms' or 'corporations'. The term firm has been popular among economists while the term corporation is more managerial and legalistic. Its origins can be traced back to the 1600s when the first commercial corporation, the East India Trading Company, was established by Royal Charter by Queen Elizabeth I (see Robins 2006, 218). This was followed by many other Royal Charters, including the Dutch East India Company. These chartered companies were the progenitors of modern corporations. And they were indeed colonial. They were institutional inventions driven by certain political and commercial necessities of colonial mercantilism.

Mercantilism represented a particular political-economic ideology where foreign trade was considered to be one of the key determinants of the nation's power over others. It represented an economic ideology that zero-sum colonial control of land was the foundation of economic and political power. It drew nations towards the development of naval powers, colonial expansion, and monopolizing colonial trade routes. Colonial trading became the most enriching avenue for the European nations. However, trade missions had always been risky due to 'turbulence in the sea', including naval wars and pirating. Financing colonial expeditions and trade ventures demanded a large amount of initial capital outlays, making it too big and too risky to be borne by one or just a few merchants. Thus, there was a perfect political-economic necessity for socializing capital on large scale: to pool the necessary capital and to mitigate the risk by diversifying the investment among as many potential investors as possible. The answer was the institutional form of what we now call the corporation. Nevertheless, mercantilism was a policy which promoted neither the free market nor free competition. Instead, it operated through monopolizing trade

26   Liberal origins

routes so that the sovereign state, through its charters, had an absolute power over colonial trade. The initial chartering of corporations was a means of offering monopoly powers over colonial trade routes. In this sense, the invention of corporations had a dual role, political and commercial, entwined into one. Corporations at this colonial time would essentially act on the government's behalf, although with private investment and appropriation of profits. They were closely connected to the military and colonial policy of the European Empires, indeed becoming the commercial and military apparatuses of the colonial state as well as the missionary apparatuses of the colonial Church (see Robins 2006).

Since then, corporations have evolved remarkably into their current forms through various capital market, administrative/legal, and techno-managerial inventions and reformations. The monopoly charters of colonial corporations are long gone. Their legal and administrative characters were changed through a series of inventions and reformations of company law; for example in the UK, through the Joint Stock Companies Act 1844, the Limited Liability Act 1855, the Joint Stock Companies Act 1856, and the Companies Act 2006. There have been parallel developments in stock markets and their affiliated institutional and technological infrastructures. Collectively, they have all made corporations rather open, making it possible, at least theoretically, for anyone to take part in socialized capital. Capital thus exists, in its most socializable form, as a commodity to be traded in the capital market, divided into its ultimate unit – a 'share'. And the success of capitalism is measured, monitored, and judged on the basis of how these 'shares' perform in the capital market individually and collectively, which mass media and market data companies now telecast in real time. This means that the socialization of capital has become a fundamental doctrine of modern capitalist democracies.

2.2.1 Transcending capital

A corporation or firm is an 'entity' into which capital is legalized, formalized, and organized so that capital can stand, on its own, independent of its owners and other social entities such as the state, families, communities, the church, and so on. This is one of the fundamental features that differentiates capitalism from any other social order: capital has its own independent and transcending existence. When capital is legalized and organized into corporations, it has a legal personality so that it can engage in economic transactions on its own for its own accumulation and enlargement. It can recruit its own set of managers to manage its affairs, independent of its owners. At the point of its invention in the early seventeenth century, this was indeed a radical transformation in the organization of capital. Unlike the traditional partnership forms in which a few personally related and mutually trusting investors pooled their resources to set up a business that they themselves ran as well as owned, corporations separated ownership from management.[2] Capital thus gained its own logic of existence and growth. Capital has evolved into a set of organic, self-realizing, and competing social entities capable of coordinating, controlling, governing, facilitating, empowering, developing, as well as disturbing, destructing, and exploiting the lives of all other beings, including the natural environment.

The focal point here is the transcendence that capital has gained in the modern world. Despite the common managerial and legal discourses that firms are owned by its shareholders, and hence, they are subordinate to the interests of the shareholders, it is not difficult to understand the opposite. Once the capital has been consolidated into large corporate entities, and once its shareholding is diversified and dispersed across a large number of small investors, each of whom has no consolidated power over the firm, it is

The institutional context   27

the firm that has the upper hand in dominating corporate relationships. It is the capital existing as corporations that would be 'buying' the shareholders' money (i.e. people's savings or earnings above consumption levels) in the open market, by issuing shares when necessary, to further consolidate its power. Thus, when it is consolidated into a corporation, it is the capital with which everyone else, either as investors, labourers, managers, governments, customers, and so on, needs to be associated in order to satisfy whatever needs they have. Thus existence, happiness, and the progress of everyone and everything else has become rather dependent on these entities of socialized capital – corporations.

2.2.2 The logic of capital and its calculative mode of operation

It is true that corporations can and should bring benefits to others (e.g. employment, goods and services, technological developments, tax revenues, education and training, social welfare), but their existential logic is their own accumulation. Capitalism, as a political ideology, repeatedly tells us that the welfare of everyone else depends on the capacity of capital to reproduce and accumulate itself. The accumulative power of capital has been projected as the holy source of energy for everyone and everything else, and hence everyone should be directed towards capital accumulation. This is not just theory or ideology, this is the discourse that shapes and reshapes the minds of policy makers, managers, and employees within corporate training rooms, MBA classrooms, Harvard case studies, and the majority of business school curricula. This is the idea of dependency that capitalism has discursively constructed. The logic of development in modern capitalism is capital accumulation itself. Hence, as mainstream accounting and finance textbooks often teach us, the ultimate objective of each and every activity carried out, and every person operating within corporate hierarchies (and outside), is to maximize shareholders' wealth, which is indeed not their privately held consumables but the capital they have already invested, alienated, and socialized in the form of corporations. Hence, capital accumulation effectively means nowadays the 'corporate growth' through perpetual reinvestment.

   With this existential and developmental logic of capital, its mode of operation is calculative: it accumulates itself-by enabling calculations. Capital, in its corporate form of existence, is self-reflective and self-scrutinizing in order to measure and assess the progress that it makes on its own self-accumulation. This is where management accounting, performing two interrelated functions for capital – justification and structuring – becomes critical as a technology of capital accumulation.

2.2.3 Management accounting as a tool of calculative justification

Capital accumulation needs a persistent and continuous process of justification. Justification is the act of rationalizing social actions and social positions. It involves the acts of arriving at agreements on social actions and positions. Such acts then involve the establishment and mobilization of 'higher order principles' or 'legitimate orders' that will sustain justification (Boltanski and Thévenot 2006). In capitalism, capital accumulation is the dominating higher order principle, though other principles such as customer satisfaction, employee satisfaction and welfare, sustainability, and ethics also play a supplementary role. Thus, justification in corporations is primarily an act of rationalizing the individual and collective actions and positions on the basis of their contribution to corporate profits. This is what corporate decision making involves:

28   Liberal origins

selection and justification of courses of actions and positions on the basis of the profitability of those actions and positions.

Nevertheless, in the modern world, one essential epistemic condition of justification is the necessity of numerical illustration of the rationality upon which the decisions are made. The connection of a particular social action, decision, or position to the accumulation of capital needs to be demonstrated through an accepted mode of calculation of inputs, processes, and outputs. Hence, modern corporations need calculative technologies. Management accounting is one of these. Presenting itself as an 'applied economic science', management accounting offers the analytical tools to perform calculative rationalization of social actions on the basis of their contribution to capital accumulation. It helps corporate management offer solutions to the problem of capital accumulation presented to them as basic economic problems of what, in what quantities, how and for whom the corporation should be producing. This is what management accounting does in the process of analysing alternative managerial courses of action in terms of cost-volume-profit analysis, limiting factor analysis, enterprise resource planning, capital investment decisions, and so on – to make decisions regarding what, how, and for whom the company should be producing within a set of market and capital constraints. It offers a set of managerial tools to determine and communicate alternative courses of action but all in relation to capital accumulation. In this way, management accounting presents the normativity of capital accumulation as the dominant rationality in making socio-political and economic choices. As such, management accounting is a calculative technology of capitalism, a technology through which the capitalist ideology of accumulation is mobilized as a criterion of justification within corporate boards, meeting rooms, spreadsheets, annual reports, incentive schemes, and so on.

2.2.4 Management accounting as a tool of calculative structuring

Structuring is the act of organizing social spaces into structures and processes of domination and control so that people and things are related to each other to create a machinery of capital accumulation. This is the act of creating an 'organization structure' showing the division of labour into specialized divisions and departments. This rather generic managerial function often falls within management accounting. However, management accounting performs a special role in this regard by offering the necessary calculative technologies for the integration and coordination of otherwise divided and distributed organizational units. It offers the financial logic to see the connections between the organizational sub-units and, thereby, creating a financial totality, as often represented by the profit and loss account and balance sheet (or the 'master budgets' in an ex-ante basis of decision making). This is done mainly through technologies and practices of 'responsibility accounting'. According to the principles of responsibility accounting, every unit and department would become a cost centre, revenue centre, profit centre, or an investment centre creating a 'financial hierarchy' within the managerial hierarchy. This hierarchy, either expressed in terms of a hierarchy of financial ratios in the DuPont system of financial analysis, or as a cascading array of BSCs, or as a stream of functional budgets integrated into master budgets (see Figure 2.1), is a *dominating structure*, meaning that it facilitates hierarchical control and surveillance based on financial performance. As such, the calculative logic of capital accumulation is supplanted upon the techno-managerial logics of division of labour and specialization. Figure 2.1 illustrates how three instances of management accounting – the DuPont system of ratio analysis, functional budgeting, and BSCs – supplant capitalism's accumulative logic over the organization's techno-managerial hierarchy. All these management accounting techniques, one way or the other, direct various managerial elements towards the return on capital employed, which is the rate at which capital is accumulated, the accounting signature of capitalism (Bryer 2000a, 2000b; Chiapello 2007).

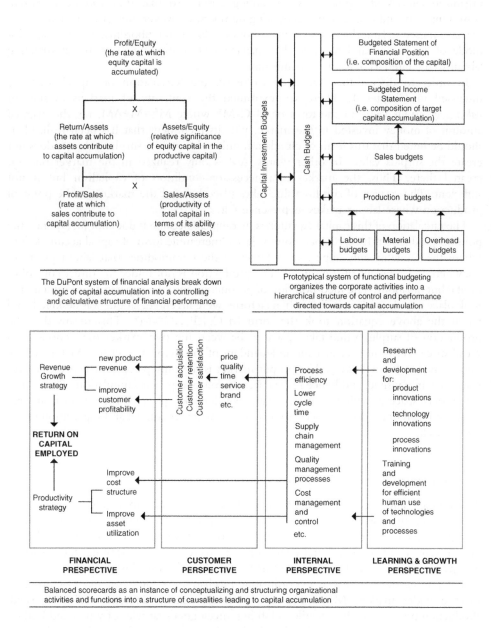

Figure 2.1 Driven towards capital accumulation: management accounting instances of structuring corporations into mechanisms of capital accumulation

30   *Liberal origins*

2.3 Capitalizing production: the invention of the factory

The discussion so far has concentrated on the transcendence of capital, the dominating presence of its accumulation as a political ideology, and how capital is socialized and organized into corporations. In doing so, we discussed how management accounting plays a role in the calculative justification and structuring of the social actions and positions and how management accounting spells out the corporations – the socialized, legalized, and organized entities of capital – as accounting entities so that they can be cognized, communicated, and managed by accounting numbers. However, one critical element that we have missed so far is the way in which labour is present and subordinated in the capitalist mode of production and the role that management accounting plays in subordinating labour to the interests of capital accumulation.

In order to discuss this, we need to revisit the 'circulation of capital' that we discussed in Chapter 1. There we explained the centrality of markets as sites of *valorizing* surplus value in the form of M-C-M* where M*=M+ΔM, i.e. the original amount of money invested in the market plus its increment that has been realized. It should be noted that this form of circulation only valorizes the surplus value: it does not create the surplus value. In other words, ΔM is only realized in the market but not created there. Thus, the market is a necessary condition of capitalism but is not sufficient. The *creation* of surplus value takes place beyond the market, at the point of production where labour makes its presence felt.

The circulation of this capital equation is incomplete because it does not incorporate the point of production. It represents more or less a 'mercantile form of capital accumulation' where the capitalist only appears as a buyer of the commodities that labour produces elsewhere independent of the capital. The production is not under the direct control of capital but of labour. The incorporation of production into the apparatuses of capital only took place in industrial capitalism when factories were invented, labour was deskilled, and when the above equation took the form M-C...P...C*-M*. This means that the production of surplus value takes place in between the two market transactions; in a social space (i.e. P) in between and independent of the factor market (i.e. M-C) and the output market (i.e. C*-M*). The output market is the only place in which the surplus value becomes visible, and hence realizable, in terms of capital accumulation. The factory is the social space in which creation of surplus value takes place. It is different from pre-capitalist forms of production because it is under the direct control and supervision of the capital itself.

2.3.1 Production systems before the invention of factory systems

The political and accounting significance of the factory becomes much clearer if we understand it in comparison to its predecessors, especially pre-capitalist craft production. In a pre-capitalist world, the point P in the above equation of circulation would have been taken by either agricultural estates or craft manufacturers operating under *putting-out systems*, these being the most relevant for the discussion in this chapter.

The putting-out system was a coordinating mechanism of 'domestic manufacturing' to meet a wider market. Manufacturing was fundamentally domestic and craft-based. Production processes such as textiles, clothing, metal goods, articles of wood and leather, and many more were performed in hundreds of household units by employing domestic family labour. The skills of manufacturing were transferred from one generation to the next on an ancestry basis and were often a speciality of a given kinship group or a guild (similar to castes in certain South Asian contexts). These domestic production units were often organized along family relations and family control, or on a gang-basis with a gang leader, often called the master craftsman. These diverse units of production were coordinated by wealthy entrepreneurs and their agents through a kind of quasi-market mechanism where the entrepreneurs provided the fixed capital, raw materials, and much of the working capital, and controlled the sale of the finished products (Littler 1982). The recruitment and control of labour and the supervision of work processes were, however, totally in the hands of the master craftsman. He was a kind of contractor of production from the entrepreneurs and received a lump sum for the completed work. Hence, this system was also called 'internal contracting'. His net income consisted of the difference between this lump sum and the wages he paid to his labour gang plus other working capital he might have accrued. Littler (1982, 64–65) describes this system:

> As Hobsbawm points out, 'capitalism in its early stages expands, and to some extent operates, not so much by directly subordinating large bodies of workers to employers, but by sub-contracting exploitation and management' (Hobsbawm 1964, 297). Thus, the immediate employer of many workers was not the large capitalist, but an intermediate, internal contractor who had a contractual relationship with the overarching employer, and in turn was an employer of labour himself. The employer provided the fixed capital, supplied the raw materials and much of the working capital and controlled the sale of the finished product. The contractor hired and fired, supervised the work process and received a lump sum from the employer for completed work. The contractor's income consisted of the difference between the wages he paid to his employees or gang (plus the cost of any working capital he might provide) and the payments from the employer ... In addition, the contractor was sometimes responsible for his own financial control and much of his own purchasing.

Within this system of subcontracting, the mode of control was rather ritualistic and constituted a strong belief in traditions. There were clear skill hierarchies within work groups. For example, in the flint-glass industry, the basic work-team was called a 'chair'. It consisted of a 'gaffer', a 'servitor', a 'footworker', and a 'boy' or 'taker-in'. Early in the nineteenth century, the 'chair' was a subcontracted work-group, and the gaffer enjoyed virtually unlimited power over the underhands (Littler 1982, 67–68). Promotion in the skill hierarchy was a matter of length of attachment to the master craftsman. The length and the nature of the service in these attachments were established social norms represented as rituals and traditions.

According to the Marxist theory of production, production entails two types of social relations: 'relations *of* production' and 'relations *in* production'. Totality of these two forms of relations constitutes the 'mode of production'. The set of relations within which surplus labour is expropriated from labour is termed 'relations *of* production' (Burawoy 1979). Obviously, these are 'relations of economic ownership or property relations', and they are defined as 'the basis of general relations of dominance and subordination, both within and beyond the sphere of production' (Littler 1982, 20). In other words, relations of production determine the way in which the surplus value is appropriated and distributed among labourers, capitalists, and other stakeholders. These are mainly the market and legal relations which come into play within the factor and output markets.

32   *Liberal origins*

Relations *in* production, on the other hand, are the relational aspects of the labour process itself. They are the 'set of relations into which men and women enter as they confront nature, as they transform raw materials into objects of their imagination' (Burawoy 1979, 15). These are mainly the relations that people enter into and maintain at the point of production – in the factory, farm, offices, and so on – when people transform inputs into outputs. The combination of these two types of relations entails the basic control structure of production: how surplus is created and how it is appropriated; the way in which the cake is produced and the way in which the cake is shared and consumed.

In a system of craft production, relations *in* production entailed 'skilled' labour. The term 'skill' has to be understood in its specificity here. As Littler (1982) explains, this term can be conceptualized in three different ways:

1. Skill as job learning time. In this sense, a skilled worker is one who has received a specialized professional or technical training for a given period of time (e.g. an apprenticeship for a given period to qualify as a skilled worker or professional).
2. Skill as social status. This is the social legitimation of certain jobs and professions as skilled.
3. Skill as job autonomy. This refers to the worker's capacity to do a job from start to finish without interference or intervention from the employer.

It is the third conception of skill – job autonomy – which is relevant here. In this sense, when workers are 'skilled' (i.e. are granted the autonomy to make decisions pertaining to the design and carrying out of the job as a whole), they themselves control the production process. Craftsmen enjoyed such job autonomy and hence were deemed to be skilled. For example, Blackburn and Mann (1979, 292) concluded that:

> A relatively skilled person was one of trust, where the worker was granted a sphere of competence within which decisions, whether routine or complex, could be taken by the worker himself. This guaranteed autonomy (skill) is the essence of traditional craft production within which the workers themselves control the production process … It is social, not technical. The centre of the technique is not complexity, but autonomy and freedom.

This means the labour process in craft production constituted simple techniques and tools, together with a simple technical division of labour. A group of workers, which was often organized under a master craftsman, carried out a whole job and produced a marketable output. There was a set of clear hierarchical relations within such a worker-group in terms of skill hierarchies at least between the master craftsman and others. The overall system of internal contracting and the overarching relationships between subcontractors and capitalists provided the framework for relations of production – the relationship within which capitalists and intermediary internal contractors appropriated the surplus value from production.

Any mode of production and control inherently contains contradictions which provide the impetus for change (see Cooper et al. 2005). This was so with the craft production and its associated social relations structured by internal contracting. By 1900, in Britain and the USA, craft production and internal contract systems were largely in demise due to the development of such internal contradictions into a crisis in the production system itself. Craft production was dominated by the intermediate subcontractors who had discretionary power over the control of production techniques and labour. It was this power itself that provided the impetus for its demise, as the exercise of that power contradicted the interests of both the subordinated labourers and the overarching capitalists. At the bottom end, the subordinated workers reacted against the petty tyrannies of their master craftsmen. At the top end, the power of internal contractors undermined and threatened the capitalist control over production and made the production system relatively inflexible to the growing needs of the capitalists to meet expanding market demands. As a result, the internal contractor was squeezed from both ends and the system of internal contracting began to degrade. However, a system of production would not disappear unless a superior mode of production was available to replace it. By the beginning of the twentieth century, capitalism had begun to discover a superior system of production – the *factory* and the technology of *mass production*.

2.3.2 The factory system

The factory was the capitalistic social space par excellence. In a technological sense, it involved the mechanization of production using either manual, steam, or electric-powered machineries so that large-scale production, and the economies of scale, were technologically possible. However, the factory was much more than this mere technological transformation of production. It was indeed the cumulative manifestation of a whole gamut of social, political, economic, as well as technological transformations that took place during the historical phase of modernity, industrial capitalism, and the industrial revolution. For example, Josiah Wedgwood, the famous potter from Staffordshire, was among the pioneers developing English factory production during the industrial revolution. His success story was, on the one hand, a series of innovations in superior product designs. What was most remarkable, on the other hand, however, was his success in transforming a traditional 'pot-bank' to a 'factory' where the discipline of the workers, the minute division of labour, the systematization of production, and a system to record and monitor at a distance the actual performance of individuals, were achieved to ensure mass production of high-quality ceramics at a lower cost, which brought him huge profits. However, it was not an easy task. He had centuries of local tradition to oppose him. The potters had enjoyed their independence too long to take kindly to the rules which Wedgwood attempted to enforce – the punctuality, the constant attendance, the fixed hours, the scrupulous standards of care and cleanliness, the avoidance of waste, the ban on drinking. They did not surrender easily. The stoppages for a wake or a fair or a three-day drinking spree were an accepted part of the potter's life – and they proved the most difficult to uproot. When they did work, they worked by rule of thumb. Their methods of production were careless and uneconomical. Their working arrangements were arbitrary, slipshod, and unscientific, for they regarded the dirt, the inefficiency, and the waste, which their methods involved, as the natural companions to pot-making (see McKendrick 1961, 1970).

This Wedgwood example provides a vivid description of the complexity of the transformation that the invention of the factory brought about. In a broader sense, for the purpose of further discussion, this transformation can be discussed under the following interrelated themes:

34   *Liberal origins*

- mechanization of production
- rationalization of work
- regimentation of labour
- cost accounting.

Mechanization of production

Perhaps the most obvious feature of the factory system was the mechanization of production. This was rather different from the use of simple or even mechanical tools by men and women to produce a particular good or a service. Mechanization involved reinvention of production processes so that it was not the men and women who did the production but the machines. The machines were no longer tools to help workers exercise their craftsmanship in production. Instead, the machines became the central force of production: the things that produce; and men and women became the tools of the machinery. The role of men and women (and also children in the early stages of the factory system, and even today in some developing country factories) in production was transformed into helping the machines to do the production. Thus, for the first time in human civilization, men and women (i.e. labour) were subordinated to the tools of the production and the production process itself.[3] In a pre-capitalist craft system, production was something embodied by the labour, inseparably connected to the body of the worker. Mechanization took this away from the human body and gave it to the machines, not only because doing so was much more efficient and less painstaking for the human body but also because it made labour more controllable and subordinated to the interests of capital. Once such production machines were put in place, it was capital not labour which dictated the process of production.

As such, the mechanization of production was political in the sense that the production process was no more owned or dominated by the skill of the craftsmen: production became by and large independent of the skill of the men and women. This was indeed the technological dimension of *capitalizing production*. Mechanization is the first of the interrelated transformations through which capital started to own, control, and dominate the labour process, which is the mundane set of mechanical activities and movements that create production.

Rationalization of work

Mechanization is only one of the transformations that helped capitalize production. And it initiated a set of other changes that were need for the capitalization of production. Closely related to the mechanization of production, there were certain managerial innovations that (a) deskilled[4] the labour force and (b) separated the concept and planning of work. These changes were driven by the capitalist need for a system of control where managers could dictate to the workers the precise manner in which work was to be performed. This was achieved during the early decades of the twentieth century by *systematization, fragmentation*, and *standardization* of jobs, the collective outcome of which was the *rationalization of work*. The Scientific Management Movement initiated by Frederick W. Taylor in the last decade of the nineteenth century provided the crucial methodological base for this rationalization.

Systematization refers to the process of 'gathering together all of the traditional knowledge which in the past has been possessed by the workmen and then ... classifying, tabulating and reducing this knowledge to rules, laws, and formulae'[5] (Taylor 1967

[1911], 36). This 'gathering of all traditional knowledge' was done by what later came to be known as work study, which included the time and motion study. That means it became the managers' responsibility to study the work 'scientifically', and specify the motions to be followed and time to be taken to do a given task or job. This innovative approach to gather traditional knowledge helped not only the transfer of such knowledge to management but also the discovery of new methods, which hitherto had been unknown. As Braverman (1998 [1974], 78) argues, this process:

> [d]isassociated the labour process from the skills of the workers (hence it is deskilled). The labour process is to be rendered independent of craft, tradition, and the workers' knowledge. Henceforth, it is to depend not at all upon the abilities of the workers, but entirely upon the practice of management.

Job fragmentation refers to breaking apart labour processes into a sequentially linked set of small 'jobs' and 'tasks' so that an unskilled worker with little or no training can perform such tasks to set standards. Job fragmentation not only helped deskill labour but also eliminated 'collective labour' by replacing it with 'individualized labour' (see Figure 2.2). Workers were rendered relatively independent from one other and less interdependent and interactive. They were attached individually to the machinery and the work they individually performed rather than to each other. Thus, production relations became predominantly technical rather than social. It was each segmented element of the job which was interdependent and collective rather than the workers performing that segment.

Standardization refers to the process of prescribing, for each job, the 'standard method' and 'performance levels' in terms of time and quantities. Indeed, standardization facilitated the linking of remuneration to the actual performance of the individual workers and effectively removed the labour management activities (hiring, firing, and payments) from the master craftsmen. Taken together, Taylorist ideas on labour rationalization led to a deskilled workforce and the divorce of planning and doing.[6]

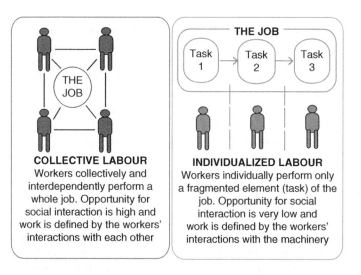

Figure 2.2 Collective labour vs individualized labour

36 Liberal origins

It was the Ford Motor Company which provided the best experimental grounds for the principles of Scientific Management and began to complete the project of transition to mass production. Henry Ford was one of the few businessmen who strongly felt the limits and burdens of traditional craft production in meeting the ever-increasing demand for his products, especially for his famous Model T. He also understood the value of the principles of Scientific Management and readily applied them in his factory settings. He indeed carried Scientific Management a further step forward by introducing flow-line (assembly-line) technology and a new labour control regime which revolved around the 'five-dollar day'. Ford's transition from craft to assembly-line production systems was a slow but steady movement. By 1903, car manufacturing at Ford's still relied upon 'jack-of-all-trades' workmen who physically had to move around the factory from one car in-the-making to another, while the car in-the-making was wholly stationary in the same workstation throughout its transformation from a bare frame to a finished product. By 1908, conditions had been changed dramatically. Assemblers were stationary in their workstations doing a limited set of unskilled jobs, while the car in-the-making was moving from one work-station to another on an assembly line to be finished at the end. Stock runners were set aside to perform various jobs that required their physical movement around the factory (see Sward 1948, 32). By 1914, this system culminated in the endless-chain conveyor which could reduce the assembly time to one-tenth of what was formerly needed. By 1925, Ford could produce almost as many cars in a single day as had been produced in an entire year (Braverman 1998 [1974], 101).

In addition to the rationalization of labour and production, mass production has another side. That is the assumption of mass markets for products, or, in other words, the assumption that the supply will find its own demand. Thus, the only challenge for capitalists is to find means and ways of speeding up production while reducing the average cost. Hence, mass production is obviously a managerial philosophy which drives the organization to forever enhance production efficiency, for which, it is assumed, there is no demand constraint.

Regimentation of labour

Mechanization and rationalization of production never went smoothly. As we already mentioned in the case of Joshua Wedgwood's pottery factory, resistance was inevitable as these changes demanded radical alterations to the lifestyles of the labourers. The monotony of doing a 'brainless' small piece of work repetitively for long hours was indeed stressful and brought no meaning into their lives. The result for the Ford Motor Company, for example, was that, despite all these remarkable achievements in speeding up the production process, it faced a 'crisis of labour'. The new work methods and technology proved to be increasingly unpopular among workers, and the result was a remarkably high labour turnover.[7] The 'five-dollar day' – the payment of five dollars a day for an eight-hour day – was the solution Ford came up with. This was so much above the prevailing rate that it halted the outflow of labour. However, it was a bargain, and to qualify for the 'five-dollar day' certain conditions had to be met: six months' continuous employment; aged over twenty-one; satisfactory personal habits both at work and at home (cleanliness and prudence); and no consumption of alcohol or tobacco. Furthermore, Ford set up a new department – the Sociological Department – to check these conditions with the workers and to advance the Ford Philosophy which constituted the core of labour regimentation in the Ford Motor Company in the early twentieth century (see Figure 2.3). This meant that regimentation of the labourer had to be done on and off the factory floor, mobilizing not only managerial techniques of systematization, fragmentation, and standardization of jobs but also other social and religious forms of regimentation and discipline, including racial and ethnic stereotyping. Such regimentation was not only aligning the body of the worker with the machine for a specified period of time every day but also confining him or her to believe in a particular work ethic and the political ideology of capitalism.

THE PHILOSOPHY OF FORD

On work

Too much good fellowship may indeed be a bad thing, for it may lead to one man trying to cover up the faults of another. That Is bad for both men. When we are at work we ought to be at work. When we are at play we ought to be at play. There is no use trying to mix the two. The sole object ought to be to get the work done and to get paid for it. When the work is done, then the play can come, but not before.

And workmen

We do not have piece work. Some of the men are paid by the day and some are paid by the hour, but in practically every case there is a required standard output below which a man is not expected to fall. Were it otherwise, neither the workman nor ourselves would know whether or not wages were being earned. There must be a fixed day's work before a real wage can be paid. Watchmen are paid for presence. Workmen are paid for work.

And charity

Charity is no substitute for reform. Poverty is not cured by charity it is only relieved. To cure it the cause of the trouble must be located and then removed. Nothing does more to abolish poverty than work. Every man who works is helping to drive poverty away.

On mechanics

We have found ways to cut down corrosion and to limit deterioration by electrolysis, ways to prevent rust. The new chromium-plating process which we are sing on airplane parts, for example, makes this metal practically indestructible in so far as the influence of weathered conditions on it is concerned. Rust-proof metals are being developed, we are finding ways to preserve wood, means of strengthening and preserving steel.

The point is, if there is enough thinking done along this line, there is no reason why we could not do the same with the human body. There is no law against it. The great problem is to get people in the mental attitude where they are willing to try to do it, willing to use the facts after we get them. There is a certain amount of mental inertia to be overcome in the promotion of any new thing. A few individuals may be quickly educated, but it takes time for society to move, to consent to the adoption of the new way.

And morality

Rightness in mechanics, rightness in morals are basically the same thing and cannot rest apart.

And living

Just as a clean factory, clean tools, accurate gauges, and precise methods of manufacture produce a smooth-working, efficient machine, so clear thinking, clean living, square dealing make of an industrial or domestic life a successful one, smooth-running and helpful to everyone concerned. It has always been surprising to me that so few people realise this great fact.

On alcohol

The coming of prohibition has put more of the workman's money into savings banks and into his wife's pocketbook. He has more leisure to spend with his family. The family life is healthier. Workmen go out of doors, go on picnics, have time to see their children and play with them. They have time to see more, do more – and, incidentally, they buy more. This stimulates business and increases prosperity, and in the general economic circle the money passes through industry again and back into the workman's pocket. It is a truism that what benefits one is bound to benefit all, and labor is coming to see the truth of this more every day.

And tobacco

Anything that interferes with our ability to think clearly, lead healthy, normal lives, and do our work well will ultimately be discarded, either as an economic handicap or from a desire for better personal health.

Tobacco is a narcotic which is exacting a heavy toll from our present generation. No one smokes in the Ford industries. Tobacco is not a good thing for industry nor for the individual.

If you study the history of almost any criminal, you will find that he is an inveterate cigarette smoker. Boys, through cigarettes, train with bad company. They go with other smokers to the post rooms and saloons. The cigarette drags them down.

On Christianity, America and the Jews

For the present, then, the question is wholly in the Jews' hands. If they are as wise as they claim to be, they will labour to make Jews American, instead of labouring to make America Jewish. The genius of the United States of America is Christian in the broadest sense, and its destiny is to remain Christian. This carries no sectarian meaning with it, but relates to a basic principle which differs from other principles in that it provides for liberty with morality, and pledges society to a code of relations based on fundamental Christian conceptions of human rights and duties

---

Figure 2.3 The philosophy of labour regimentation at Ford

Source: based on Beynon (1975, 26–27).

38 *Liberal origins*

Cost accounting

Capitalization of production also meant that that various manufacturing processes hitherto carried out by subcontractors and craftsmen outside the organizations were absorbed into the processes internal to the corporation. Unlike mercantile capital, socialized corporate capital, which had internalized production, would not now buy the finished products of which the value was 'fairly' and readily determined by market transactions. Instead, corporations would buy the raw materials, labour, and other inputs and process them into output, of which the value now had to be calculated internally to make sure that they, after all, contributed to the accumulation of capital. This is where cost accounting became a fundamental necessity of corporatized capital, to ascertain the economic values of inputs, processes, and outputs. That means, with the absence of market mechanisms (as it was absorbed into the corporate hierarchy), capital was left with no objective indicators about the 'value' of the production which was now being capitalized. The emergent solution was the subjective estimation of 'cost' of production. Cost accounting was the mechanism by which this was done. Johnson and Kaplan (1987a, 7), in their classic *Relevance Lost*, explain:

> The emergence ... of such organizations created a new demand for accounting information. As conversion processes that formerly were supplied at a price through market exchanges became performed within organizations, a demand arose for measures to determine the 'price' of output from internal operations. Lacking price information on the conversion processes occurring within their organizations, owners devised measures to summarize the efficiency by which labour and material were converted to finished products, measures that also served to motivate and evaluate the managers who supervised the conversion process.

Started with rudimentary estimations of prime costs associated with direct labour and direct materials, cost accounting systems soon evolved into those with specific techniques and procedures to allocate company-wide expenses (so-called overheads) to cost centres and cost units. These overhead absorption techniques, indeed, allowed large corporations to set competitive and more prudent prices and helped overcome financial difficulties during recessionary periods (see, for example, the Wedgwood case in Hopwood 1987). The contribution of cost accounting to the capitalization of production was, however, much more than assisting with the estimation of costs and setting prudent prices. Cost accounting was instrumental in the following ways:

1. It helped reconfigure organizations along manageable domains by rhetorically dividing the organization into profit centres, service centres, cost centres, and costs units, etc., according to which cost and revenue estimations are carried out to ascertain relative performance. Cost accounting thus complemented properties of bureaucracy by inserting economic objectives into the administrative apparatuses and provided economic tangibles to further the functional division of labour within organizations.
2. Cost accounting provided capitalists with a powerful instrument to observe labour in economic terms. It provided a set of new calculative measures through which labour processes (which were hitherto 'black boxes' for capitalists and their agents) could be observed at a distance and replaced many supervisory and personal observations (Hopper and Armstrong 1991; Hopwood 1987). Reflecting

The institutional context 39

upon the installation of cost accounting systems in Wedgwood, for example, Hopwood (1987, 218) wrote:

[o]bservations could now be conducted indirectly. No longer did he [Josiah Wedgwood] have to rely solely on the lookout for 'unhandiness', scolding those individuals who did not follow his instructions ... Such personal observation and supervision could start to be complemented by the exercising of control at a distance, both in time and space.

3. Especially through budgeting and standard costing, cost and management accounting helped create a new regime of control where every individual within the organization was made accountable and governable by economic numbers. For example, Miller and O'Leary (1987, 242) point out the:

[p]ossibility of a knowledge of every individual within the enterprise was established. A visibility and an allocation or responsibility could be attached to the individual. The person's activities were at last rendered knowable according to prescribed standards and deviations from the norm. Standard costing and budgeting made possible a pinpointing of responsibilities for preventing inefficiencies at the level of every individual from whom they derived. The human element of production, and most importantly the individual person, could now be known according to their contribution to the efficiency of the enterprise.

4. Also related to the previous point, cost and management accounting helped create a doctrine of control which has now come to be known as 'management by exception'. That is, managers would regularly be informed of the actual performance of individuals and departments against the standards, so that managerial actions would be directed only to 'exceptional' deviations from standards, thereby saving time, effort, and resources. This further helped the reduction of direct supervisory efforts and enhanced 'control at a distance'.

In this way, coupled with mechanization of production, rationalization of work, and regimentation of labour, the emergence of cost and management accounting techniques was behind the capitalization of production (i.e. bringing the mundane processes of production under the direct control of the capital itself) within the socialized forms of capital (i.e. corporations). The context of this was monopoly capitalism, where large monopolistic corporations enjoyed an ever expanding consumer market and, hence, were not constrained by limited demand in the output markets. They struggled against labour constraints and resistance, however. The underlying purpose of this capitalization of production was to provide a stable and superordinate mechanism for the purpose of rationalization of labour to pursue the interests of capital accumulation. The outcome was a mode of production characterized by (a) the separation of conception and planning of work from production itself; (b) highly fragmented, mechanized, and deskilled jobs for which there existed specific performance expectations in terms of standards and targets; (c) systems of accounting for every transaction and event taking place within and across the boundary of the organization so that the 'values' of corporate inputs, processes, and outputs could be accurately estimated; and (d) a system of control through

40 *Liberal origins*

which capital now owned and dictated the mundane physical actions and movements that constitute the labour process.

2.4 Managerial hierarchy

Administrative hierarchies are not recent or modern inventions. The hierarchical arrangement of authority has had a very long history dating back to the Roman Empire and Catholic Church, or perhaps even before that. The structuring of military forces and other administrative wings of sovereign states had always been hierarchical. However, the use of such formal hierarchy in the management of 'private' economic activities was modern, especially in the context of forming corporations as socialized entities of private capital. In corporate entities, managerial hierarchy represented, accumulated, ordered, and placed the things, peoples, and relations in between the socialized capital and the capitalized labour. In other words, the series of hierarchically arranged managerial relationships that the corporations brought in to structure its systems of surveillance, discipline, and control of labour for the purpose of capital accumulation. It connected and created an intimacy between capital and labour. Indeed, it is through managerial hierarchy that socialized capital gained its institutional capacity to exploit and accumulate capital through capitalizing production.

2.4.1 Disciplinary logic of managerial hierarchy

In the sense of biopolitics and anatomico-politics of modernity (see Chapter 1), managerial hierarchies emerged to provide the institutional infrastructure within which partitioning, functionally useful serialization, and ranking/hierarchization could take place. Or, to put it another way, the emergence of disciplinary practices and principles of general enclosure, partitioning, functionally useful serialization, and hierarchical ranking brought up managerial hierarchies as the internal structure of socialized capital so that control at a distance (for the purpose of capital accumulation) through a system of hierarchical surveillance was made possible. In this sense, managerial hierarchy could be conceptualized as a necessary disciplinary apparatus of modern disciplinary enclosures such as economic corporations, hospital, schools, prisons, and so on. Thus, corporations, simultaneously being entities of socialized capital and disciplinary enclosures, incorporated certain disciplinary principles and practices, often institutionalized into the hierarchical arrangement of its management, but with the aim of capital accumulation. Nevertheless, as a structural element of socialized capital, managerial hierarchy needs to be understood and explained more widely than this disciplinary logic. There are certain structural and democratic logics behind managerial hierarchies.

2.4.2 Structural logic of managerial hierarchy: specialization

The period of modernity and industrial revolution was indeed a period of great differentiation, division, and specialization. There emerged a series of 'faculties of knowledge' and 'industrial specializations' due to the developments and diversification in human sciences and the industry. Fragmentation and diversification of economic and industrial sciences into its sub-disciplines such as mechanical engineering, manufacturing, management, marketing, accounting, and so on was critical for the way in which the internal structures of corporations evolved. The evolution of corporate structures reflected these epistemic differentiations as well as market and industrial segmentations.

Behind these differentiations and segmentations, there was also a particular economic logic, the possibility of economizing on the basis of division of labour and specialization. In a managerial sense, corporate hierarchy constituted the structural parameters within which (a) division of work and (b) delegation of authority took place. While putting people and things into a (vertical) hierarchical arrangement, managerial hierarchy conceptualized, divided, and distributed the activities necessary to achieve the corporate objectives into functional and divisional categories, creating opportunities for functional and divisional specializations, and, thereby, possibilities for continuous technological and managerial innovations. The economic benefits of specialization were made visible and translated into profits within corporate hierarchies.

The corollary to this logic of specialization and the division of work was that the delegation of authority started to receive a different rationality. Authority is the power that a person wields because of the social position that s/he holds. For Weber (1978 [1968], 215), there are three distinct types of authority: charismatic, traditional, and rational. Charismatic and traditional authority were the bases of pre-modern social hierarchies, especially of the aristocracy. Charismatic authority derived from extraordinary grace and the magnetism of the ruler's personality, as in the case of religious leadership. It was traditional authority which was more associated with the craft and other feudal modes of production, where lineage, primogeniture, and kinship were the governing principles of access to command and authority. In contrast, rational legitimate precepts became the defining characteristic of bureaucracy, which was the form of social ordering that corporations brought in. The legitimate rationality to assume authority by a person in such bureaucracies was the congruence between the knowledge and expertise (often manifested in terms of measurable criteria of qualifications, experience, and performance) that the particular person held and those that were required by the particular position in the hierarchy. Specialism and expertise thus became the bases upon which the social relations of domination and control were to be determined.

2.4.3 Democratic logic of managerial hierarchy

Accordingly, capital received a particular operational structure within corporations: a vertical and horizontal grid of positions of authority, power, social status, and economic compensation. This was an institutional grid within which a whole new managerial class was established and defined. This was a connecting array of positions between the capital and working class that also manifested itself as a ladder of social mobility. In this social grid, rational legitimacy to command (i.e. authority) derived from the general obedience of organizational members to an 'objective set of rules and structures', which dictates an 'impersonal' order of things and people (Weber 1978 [1968]). Thus, on the one hand, there was a set of rules that organizational members collectively believed to be necessary to achieve social objectives attached to economic enterprises. On the other, there was a hierarchy in which people could mobilize themselves if they followed the set rules and guidelines and if they strived to achieve the necessary credentials (performance, qualifications, experience, and seniority, etc.) prescribed for the higher positions in the hierarchy. As Clegg (1990, 38) points out, 'At the base of bureaucracy are its members' beliefs in the legitimacy of its existence, its protocols, its personnel and its policies'. Hence, bureaucracy was a technically and politically superior form of organization (vis-à-vis its predecessor aristocracy) that, to a certain degree, could manufacture the consent of the workers

42   Liberal origins

to the interests of capital through the 'rational' chances of upward mobility within the hierarchy. As Weber expresses it: 'Each man becomes a little cog in the machine and aware of this, his one preoccupation is whether he can become a bigger cog' (quoted in Clegg 1990, 30).

Nevertheless, especially because the possibility of becoming a bigger cog was rather remote and less probable when there were thousands of fellow workers competing for the same opportunity, the managerial challenge was to sustain the idea in the individual cognition that everyone has a 'fair and rational' chance of getting this opportunity. This capitalist rationality and fairness should be based on the individual *performance*, which was the contribution that the individual made to the accumulation of corporate capital directly or indirectly, rather than on any other forms of social connections such as family connections, race, ethnicity, caste, and so on, as it was in pre-capitalist forms of social ordering. Hence the distribution of the limited opportunity of upward social mobility in the managerial hierarchy among competing workers should be based on their objectively measured performance. This was where management accounting's performance measurement and evaluation technologies became a technology of corporate democracy, as far as they were effectively deployed with that rationality.

2.4.4 Logic of economic coordination: hierarchy vs markets

For proponents of transaction cost economics (e.g. Williamson, Chandler, Johnson, and Kaplan), managerial hierarchy is an alternative to market as a mechanism of coordinating economic activities. While markets are the invisible hand of coordinating economic transactions, hierarchies constitute the visible hand. Transaction cost economics deals with the issue of why managerial hierarchies (visible hands) should coordinate economic transactions when the markets (invisible hands) are assumed to be the perfect mechanism of doing so (see Chandler 1977; Johnson and Kaplan 1987; Kaplan 1984; Williamson 1975). According to these institutional economists, then, these two mechanisms co-exist because (a) transactions differ in respect to their key characteristics of frequency, uncertainty, and asset specificity; (b) markets and hierarchies have different problem-solving and control apparatuses in terms of administrative controls, incentive intensity, autonomous adaptation, and coordinated adaptation; and hence (c) a specific institutional arrangement is chosen to coordinate and govern a specific type of transaction because that combination offers the most economic means of doing so. Whether a given institutional arrangement (i.e. market vs hierarchy) is more economical than another to coordinate a specific type of transaction is explained in terms of the 'transaction costs' associated with each institutional arrangement. Thus, for example, it is argued that a firm has a role to play in the economic system if transactions can be organized within the firm at less cost than if the same transactions were carried out through the market (Williamson 1988, 65).

According to this logic, corporate hierarchies emerge and exist when their coordination of transactions can accumulate capital better than market coordination. In other words, corporate capitalism is superior to its predecessor, mercantile form of capitalism, because corporate capitalism is more efficient and effective in terms of its capacity to accumulate. However, to gain that coordinating superiority, the hierarchy should be capable of making economically rational decisions, and that rationality should stem from the calculative structuring of the decision-making processes within the hierarchy. In other words, decision making within the hierarchy should be formalized and rationalized through (a) particular authority structures which specify who can and should make certain decisions under what conditions and criteria; (b) a particular accountability structure through which such decision makers are held accountable to the decisions that they make; (c) a particular decision-support structure that provides the necessary informational, knowledge, and expert support for such decision making; and (d) a particular reward structure through which individual effort, performance, and risk taking are optimized in terms of capital accumulation. In this sense, managerial hierarchy is a decision-making, accountability, and reward structure put in place to make sure that every decision made in the corporation is governed through a rationalized and formalized set of decision-processes leading to the accumulation of corporate capital. This is where accountability in general, and management accounting in particular, become a critical element of the managerial hierarchy; they underlie all four conditions of rationalization and formalization discussed here.

2.5 Summary and conclusions

While modernity and capitalism provided the broader political-economic and historical context for the emergence and growth of management accounting, the corporation, the factory, and the managerial hierarchy constitute its immediate institutional context. Each these concepts, nevertheless, needs to be understood in the context of the capitalist ethos of capital accumulation, because it is their affiliation with the notion of capital accumulation that makes them capitalistic.

Corporation refers to the particular socialized form that capital started to assume from the beginning of the seventeenth century, when the first set of corporations was established by Royal Charters to fund and monopolize colonial trade ventures. Since then corporations have seen a remarkable growth and evolved into organic, self-realizing, competing, and independent social entities into which capital is socialized and organized. Hence, corporations constitute the most evolved form of socialized capital. In this form, capital is transcending and dominating. It is also self-reflective and self-scrutinizing, creating a space for management accounting to play a critical role in socializing capital by being a technology for justification and structuring. In this context, management accounting becomes a symbolic system, one that performs the interrelated functions of cognitions, communication, and domination.

The factory is the capitalist invention to 'capitalize production'. The factory system of production indeed represents a historical rupture in the production systems, especially when it is compared with its predecessor, the craft-based putting-out system. The evolution of factory systems was underlined by four distinct but interrelated historical processes: mechanization of production, rationalization of work, regimentation of labour, and cost accounting. The cumulative effect of these processes was a mode of production characterized by (a) separation of conception and planning of work from production; (b) highly fragmented, mechanized, and deskilled jobs for which there exist specific performance expectations in terms of standards and targets; (c) systems of accounting for every transaction and event taking place within and across the boundary of the organization so that the 'values' of corporate inputs, processes, and outputs can be accurately estimated; and (d) a system of control through which capital now owns and dictates the mundane physical actions and movements that constitute the labour process.

Managerial hierarchy connects and creates an intimacy between capital and labour. Indeed, it was through the set of hierarchized relations within corporations that socialized capital gained its capacity to capitalize production, to exploit labour, and to

44   *Liberal origins*

accumulate capital. The political and managerial rationale of managerial hierarchy needs to be understood in terms of its disciplinary logic, structural logics, democratic logic, and the logic of economic coordination and governance.

Assignments

These assignments are meant to extend your knowledge beyond what you understand from this chapter. These are not simply revision questions. The content covered in this chapter is necessary but will not be sufficient in attempting these tasks. Therefore, you are required to do some extra reading in attempting these tasks.

1. **Thematic essay:**
   'Socialization of capital and capitalization of production were the most fundamental historical changes underlying the emergence and growth of management accounting'. Write an essay, of approximately 3,000 words, on the above theme articulating the role that management accounting plays in the above two political-economic and historical processes.
2. **Poster:**
   Draw a poster illustrating the 'institutional context' of traditional management accounting. You need to pay special attention to how the corporation, factory and managerial hierarchy constitute the institutional context and how management accounting is implicated in these institutional elements.
3. **Presentation:**
   Prepare a set of PowerPoint slides, together with notes if necessary, for a 30-minute presentation on the following theme:
   'Managerial hierarchy connects and creates an intimacy between capital and labour'.
4. **Extended bibliography:**
   Write an extended bibliography on the use of the Marxist labour process theory in explaining management accounting and control. For this, you need to do a literature survey of major accounting journals and edited books where critical accounting research is published. Organize the bibliography into a table in the following format.

Bibliographic info	Nature of the paper/book chapter (e.g. conceptual/theoretical, empirical, a response to a previous publication)	Major arguments, conclusions, and contributions

5. **Literature review:**
   Write a review paper, circa 2,000 words, summarizing the main arguments that Eve Chiapello offers on 'Accounting and the birth of the notion of capitalism' (see Chiapello (2007) 'Accounting and the birth of the notion of capitalism'. *Critical Perspectives on Accounting* 18(3), 263–296).

Notes

1 It should be noted that the terminology of capital is multi-layered. At the macro level capital can mean the total system, as Marx named his classic *Das Capital* to mean the capitalist system. In that sense, capital is the political economic totality that capitalist society brings about. It can also mean capital as a class, the ruling class of society. As we are using the

term capital in this section, capital can mean the institutional forms into which the total capital is divided and distributed for its competitive operationalization. In that sense it means the corporation or the firm, which is the institutional form that particular competing unit of capital would take. This is the form it takes after socialization. Yet again the term capital can take on rather micro-technical meanings as well, as in micro-economic theory and accounting. This is where the term capital is used to mean a 'factor of production', or a type of resource, or balance sheet item. It is in this micro-technical sense that capital is often categorized as fixed, variable, equity, debt, working capital, etc. Then, in the sociological literature of Bourdieu, capital can take various forms: economic capital, social capital, and symbolic capital. For him, capital can be anything that helps further accumulation of capital in either of these forms, by being translated between those forms (Bourdieu 1986).

2 Due to the pervasive use of double-entry bookkeeping rules, especially the entity concept and the use of a capital account, even when a firm is not legally incorporated into a corporation to gain a legal personality, it still has an independent accounting personality. Thus, accounting plays a central role in the separation of ownership from management.

3 For Marx, this was 'alienation'. See also Charlie Chaplin's, *Modern Times: Factory Work* for a contemporary visual critique of the way in which men and women are subordinated to the machines in the factory system of production.

4 As we explained in the previous section, the term 'skill' here means the worker's capacity and autonomy to do a whole job. Hence deskilling refers to the process of taking this 'job autonomy' away from the worker, mainly through division of work into such minute elements that even an untrained or unskilled worker could carry it out.

5 This is the first principle of Taylor's Scientific Management.

6 This is the second principle of Taylor's Scientific Management. It reads as 'all possible brain work should be removed from the shop and centred in the planning and laying-out department' (Taylor 1964 [1911], 98–99). Thus, in effect, the 'ownership of work' no longer belongs to labour but capital, and labour is to be reduced to a brainless series of body movements tuned to the motions of the machines. This is the exact point of which Charlie Chaplin's *Modern Times: Factory Work* offers a visual critique.

7 Sward (1948, 48–49) states: 'So great was labour's distaste for the new machine system that toward the close of 1913 every time the company [Ford's] wanted to add 100 men to its factory personnel, it was necessary to hire 963'.

3 The practicist epistemology of management accounting

3.1 Introduction

As we discussed in the previous two chapters, the context of conventional management accounting can be seen in three interrelated dimensions. First is the *political-economic context* which broadly captures the way in which the growth of modernity, modernism, and capitalism necessitated management accounting as a calculative technology and a practice. In that respect, management accounting evolved in parallel with the emergence of governmentality, the liberal economic democracy of modernism, and the accumulative mentality of capitalism. Second is the *institutional context* which captures the immediate institutional setting of the firm (i.e. the socialized capital); the factory (i.e. the capitalized mode of production); and the managerial hierarchy that connects and creates an intimacy between capital and labour. Now in this chapter our attention is on the third element: the *epistemic context*.

What do we mean by epistemic context? This is indeed a tricky question. In answering this, we first need to be clear about the distinction and the connection between *management accounting as a practice* and *management accounting as a body of knowledge*. Management accounting exists, on the one hand, as a body of knowledge constituting a particular set of theories, principles, techniques, procedures, protocols, and rules. As accounting students, you are first exposed to this existence of management accounting in course syllabi, exam papers, textbooks, journal papers, lecture rooms, training sessions, instructional manuals, case studies, Microsoft Excel analytical tools, simulation packages, and so on. These are the textual artefacts in which management accounting exists as a pedagogical practice. Such textual artefacts provide *ostensive definitions* of management accounting. On the other hand, management accounting also exists as a set of practices institutionalized and embedded in the routines, rules, and processes of corporate decision making, performance evaluation, and control. It is what managers 'actually' do as part of the operational and strategic activities of their organizations. It constitutes a set of calculative reasoning that the managers carry out in their 'real' organizational contexts. In that sense, management accounting constitutes the way in which management accountants and other managers deploy the body of knowledge, and the particular set of calculative rationalities, which we call management accounting. It is these practices that offer diverse *performative definitions* of management accounting.

There is a dialectical connection between these dual existences of management accounting: each reproduces the other. The corporate practice of management accounting provides (a) the practical or empirical basis upon which management accounting knowledge is constructed and (b) the empirical sites in which the emerging management accounting concepts, principles, and techniques are tested for their practicalities. However, for management accounting to be adopted commonly by a wide spectrum of organizational entities as one of their fundamental sets of calculative practices and rationalities, it needs to be based on certain scientific rationalities. In other words, it needs to be articulated into a coherent body of knowledge with relevant theoretical, conceptual, scientific, and institutional elements. This means that management accounting needs to be a theoretically and scientifically 'informed practice': a practice constituted by a coherent theoretical, conceptual, scientific, and institutional foundation. Figure 3.1 depicts this dialectical connection.

So, what we mean by the epistemic context is the apparatuses which construct this dialectical connection between knowledge and practice. It is the context within which management accounting is epistemologically legitimated as a valid body of knowledge that the practising managers can draw on to rationalize their practices. For the purpose of this chapter, we identify three distinct but interrelated epistemological apparatuses: reflective practice, pedagogical reproduction, and academic theorization. The epistemology of management accounting rests on these three processes (see Figure 3.2).

This chapter takes on the first two elements – reflective practice and pedagogic reproduction – while the next chapter deals with the third element, academic theorization. Accordingly, this chapter is structured into two main sections. Section 3.2 will elaborate on management accounting as a reflective practice, with special attention to its intra- and extra-organizational elements. Here our attention is on the intra- and

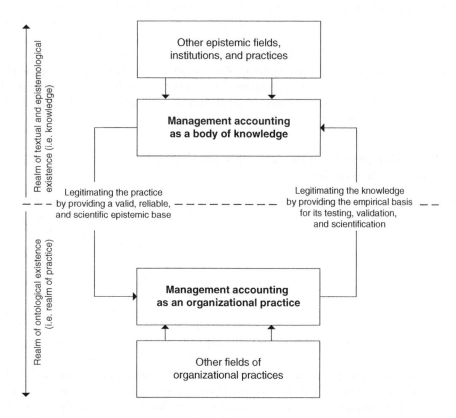

Figure 3.1 Management accounting as an informed practice

48 *Liberal origins*

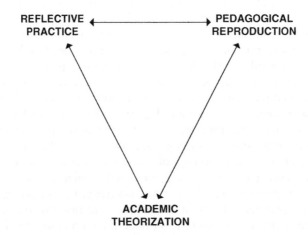

Figure 3.2 Epistemological elements of management accounting

extra-organizational practices that inductively construct management accounting knowledge. This section also provides a discussion on how certain 'actor-networks' play a critical role in producing management accounting knowledge. Section 3.3 then takes your attention to accounting pedagogy as a mode of diffusing and reproducing management accounting practices. In this section, we draw on Bourdieu's reflexive sociology and CIMA's Qualification Structure to explain and illustrate how accounting pedagogy operates as a 'symbolic system'. We further extend this discussion to explain how professional practitioners internalize the practice through 'embodiment' of the logics of the field in different forms of embodiment and capital. Finally, the chapter concludes with a summary.

3.2 Reflective practice: practicist epistemology of management accounting

Management accounting, like other professionalized knowledge, embeds a 'practicist epistemology' (Calvert-Minor 2012; Kinsella 2009; Raelin 2007). Here we use the term *epistemology* to mean the social and institutional processes that conceive and produce what we take to be knowledge, in this case knowledge that is labelled as management accounting. In other words, epistemology deals with the way in which knowledge is conceived and produced. By the term *practicist* epistemology, what we mean is a particular type of epistemology in which knowledge is conceived and constructed inductively, bottom–up, from practice to theory. In this case, the 'epistemic agency', which is the socio-political and institutional capacity to define what should constitute good or generally acceptable knowledge, lies with professional practitioners, the informed manager, or the skilled worker (vis-à-vis theorist, academic, or philosopher) and the epistemic practices that they have established within their work environment. This means that there are two interrelated elements in the practicist epistemology: (a) *intellectual capacity of practitioners* (individually and collectively) to reflect upon their practices and (b) *epistemic structures, networks, and practices*

Practicist epistemology 49

that they have put in place to translate and organize their experiences into transferable and generalizable knowledge.

3.2.1 Management accounting as a reflective practice

Knowledge stems from practitioners' experiences, their practical experimentations and innovations, and their pressing need to solve the problems that they endlessly encounter in their operational environment. In that sense, management accounting is a reflexive practice. The manager who deploys management accounting is a reflexive practitioner. As mentioned earlier, this reflexivity, on the one hand, refers to the intellectual and cognitive capacity of the practitioners to critically assess the situation that they are in: the problems they encounter; the suitability of the tools and techniques that they have to handle the situation; the reliability and validity of the information that they are presented with; the relative efficacy of the solutions that they can bring in; their capacity to implement their decisions; and so on. Indeed, this cognitive and intellectual capacity of individuals is a necessary element but, in itself, is not sufficient.

Reflection is more than a state of mind. It is a set of institutionalized practices that enact and enable the practitioners to translate their practices, experiences, subjective reflections, and 'substantive rationalities' (Weber 1978 [1968]) into transferable knowledge. In other words, practitioners' cognitive capacity would help them to gain a tacit knowledge of what and how things are to be done. However, such tacit learning would not automatically become an independently existing body of 'professional knowledge' capable of framing and disciplining the actions and thoughts across organizations. In the practicist epistemology, in between the individual tacit knowledge and professional knowledge and making the necessary bridge between them, there exists a diverse set of epistemic processes and practices that translate the avocation into a profession. The distinction that Moore (1970) (see also, Schon 1991, 22) makes between avocation and profession is important here. For him, an avocation is the antithesis to a profession; it is based upon customary activities and modified by the trial and error of individual practice. In contrast, a profession involves generation and application of general principles to specific problems. In this sense, practicist epistemology involves various epistemic practices and processes that generate general principles to be deployed in diverse operational and managerial settings.

Such epistemic processes and practices are diverse. They often take place inseparably intertwined with operational practices. However, one way or the other, they involve textualizing the practice. This means that the practice needs to be documented – conceptualized, storied, and stored – so that they become general principles to be learnt and practised across different times and spaces. The textualization of practice is the core of empiricist epistemology and offers the fundamental basis for the construction of professional knowledge. One of the key processes through which this textualization take place is the standardization of practices. Since the emergence of the Scientific Management Movement in the late nineteenth century, standardization has become a fundamental managerial activity. In a generic sense, standardization includes careful observation and documentation of good practices so that a specific set of inputs, methods, and outputs can be prescribed as the norms, standards, or best practices to be followed. Standards or norms so derived then become the means through which the 'technical rationalities' of the professional work are expressed. It is those standards, norms, or good practices, once textualized, which become the professional knowledge. Epistemic practices associated with this textualization can broadly be categorized as intra-organizational and extra-organizational epistemic practices.

50   *Liberal origins*

3.2.2 Intra-organizational epistemic practices

Standardization and textualization often take place within organizations in the form of rules and regulation manuals, procedural manuals, instructional manuals, training manuals, guidebooks, technical and administrative protocols, codes of conducts, and various other forms of bureaucratic recording of practices. All these indeed collectively represent an organizational memory – a storage of practical know-how – which the individual in the organization can appropriately access. In a management accounting sense, these include various organizational texts which document and prescribe, for example, the way in which costing of a particular activity or a product is to be carried out; recording of a particular transaction in the costing system should be done; a particular set of calculations needed for a particular decision is to be performed; or performance of a particular cost, profit, or investment centre is to be assessed. Management accounting knowledge is thereby institutionalized into behavioural codes, rules, and norms.

3.2.3 Extra-organizational epistemic practices

The knowledge that such intra-organizational practices creates often crosses organizational boundaries to make them generalizable and deployable in other organizational settings. The institutionalization of accounting as a profession provides the necessary institutional infrastructure to compile, diffuse, and generalize organizational-specific practices in a formal and publicly accessible manner. Professionalization of accounting lifted the intra-organizational production of knowledge to a trans-organizational level, meaning that accounting became a body of knowledge that exists at a level over and above individual organizational practices. The organization of professional practitioners into a coherent professional body created a set of epistemic forums where knowledge could easily be translated into communal knowledge. These epistemic forums provided a common textual space in which the individual experiences could be storied, narrated, and generalized for others to be adapted and adopted. Such forums then made management accounting knowledge isomorphic across various organizational settings. Examples of such epistemic forums include:

- **Professional magazines and journals**: Practitioners publish their professional experimentations, research, experiences, expert knowledge, as well as professional opinions on current practices and trends in professional magazines and journals. *The Accountant*, one of the oldest accounting magazines in the world, for example, explains its epistemic role as follows:

  Established in 1874, The Accountant is one of the oldest and most prestigious trade magazines in the world. Today The Accountant offers a comprehensive range of briefing services across topics including regulation, legislation and education for those working in the accounting profession. It reports news globally, surveys leading and emerging accounting bodies around the world, provides commentary from senior industry figures and profiles key business and industry leaders. ACCA members may also include reading The Accountant towards their CPD qualification, if it has provided knowledge or skills relevant to their role or aspirations.

  (www.theaccountant-online.com/static/aboutus/)

Another popular example is the *Harvard Business Review*, which has been a very influential professional outlet of diffusing North American managerial discourses. They operate as a medium of textualizing, accumulating, constructing, communicating, and sharing professional knowledge. Being accredited forums of the professional associations, prestigious universities, and consulting houses, they bear strong epistemic powers to impose certain ideas and technologies as professional knowledge and, hence, generally acceptable knowledge.

- **Official publications of professional associations**: These include various white papers, standards, discussion papers, research monographs sponsored by professional associations, and surveys published by the relevant professional associations. Examples include CIMA official terminology, CIMA topic gateway series publications, and CIMA terminology of Islamic Banking.
- **Management consulting services**: Consultants play a significant role in the diffusion and dissemination of professional practices. Their functionality and status as advisors and experts provide them with the opportunity not only to carefully study the actual organizational practices but also to form 'actor-networks' through which new managerial ideas and technologies are produced and diffused. The invention and popularization of ABC is an excellent example of this (see Section 3.2.4 below).
- **Action research**: Closely related to the role of consultants, one of the key epistemic processes is what we often call 'action research' (see Reason and Bradbury 2013). This is a mode of researching the diverse practices across different organizational settings with the aim of identifying the generalizable propositions in such diverse practices and then designing managerial models and frameworks based on these findings. Examples of this include the research that Robert Kapan and his colleagues carried out in relation to the invention and popularization of BSC and ABC.

Populated by such epistemic practices, practicist epistemology has a normative and prescriptive orientation. Its aim is to generate generalizable methods, models, and frameworks. It assumes that the problems and conditions managers come across in different organizational settings are not so different that generalizable ideas and models cannot be developed to manage them. As such, the standardization of managerial practices across different organizational sites is not only possible but also desirable because that makes the management of organizations economically more efficient and effective. As Moore (1970, 56) argues:

> If every professional problem were in all respects unique, solutions would be at best accidental, and therefore have nothing to do with expert knowledge. What we are suggesting, on the contrary, is that there are sufficient uniformities in problems and in devices for solving them to qualify the solvers as professionals ... Professionals apply very general principles, standardized knowledge, to concrete problems

Practicist epistemology also holds that these general principles and standardized knowledge should stem from practice itself. Hence it is inductive: it induces the general principles and standards from the practice itself. Its methods of improvement are incremental and find their way through respective cycles of problems and solutions. The validity of such general principles and standards rests:

52 *Liberal origins*

1. First, with we may call the 'internal validity' or 'technical rationality'. This is the *organizational efficacy* of such general principles, models, and frameworks. In this sense knowledge is validated and legitimated as useful based on its applicability in different organizational settings and its capacity to solve the managerial problems to which it is applied.
2. Second, with what we may call the 'external validity' or 'scientific rationality'. This refers to their congruence with higher order theoretical and conceptual propositions deduced from the theoretical and scientific academic domains. In the case of management accounting, such scientific domains include the sciences such as economics, industrial sociology, psychology, and so on. We will further elaborate this aspect in the next chapter.

3.2.4 Practicist epistemology as actor-networks

In popular literature, the innovation of management accounting knowledge is often projected as heroic acts of a few great inventors such as Robert Kaplan. We cannot indeed underestimate the influence that they had, and continue to have, on the trajectory of management accounting knowledge. They indeed made a significant contribution to the body of knowledge which we appreciate now as management accounting. However, we should also emphasize the importance of the *epistemic networks*. A group of sociologists who had long been studying the sociology of science and technology (e.g. Callon 1991; Latour 1987, 2005; Law 1991; Law and Hassard 1999) use the theoretical concept of 'actor-network' to explain the way in which scientific ideas and technological artefacts come into being. Their focus has been on epistemic systems as networks which bind together human and non-human actors to form seamless webs of connections (Hughes 1988; Jones and Dugdale 2002).

The notion of actor-network is a complex idea. It is quite hard to pinpoint its meaning, because, perhaps, it does not, or cannot, have a precise ostensive meaning independent of the context within which it is used. As Latour (2005, 131) describes, 'network is a concept, not a thing out there. It is a tool to help describe something, not what is being described'. However, for the purpose of understanding the way practicist epistemology works, we define it as a heterogonous alliance of human and non-human actors which enables those actors to spread ideas and technologies. It is not simply a network of actors but an actor-network that enrols, enables, and controls allies in the spread of ideas and technologies. The focus is not primarily on the actors that constitute the network but the network that enables the actors. Actors like Kaplan, capable of spreading out the ideas and technologies of ABC and BSC, for example, arise out of such heterogeneous networks. Actors' capacity to invent and spread ideas and technologies is defined by their enrolment in the actor-network. In other words, actors and networks mutually form and reform each other (see Jones and Dugdale 2002, 123).

An actor-network consists of *actors* and *intermediaries*. Actors are the ones who seek to mobilize, consolidate, or transform the network they are associated with. They can be both human and non-human. A management accounting technique or method such as ABC, in itself, becomes an actor because it seeks to create a set of professionals capable of mobilizing, consolidating, or transforming a network in which they are enrolled. Such non-human actors act upon the other human and non-human actors. As Callon (1991, 134) puts it, an intermediary is 'anything (or anyone) passing between actors which defines their relationship between them'. Four main types of intermediaries are identified: texts or literary inscriptions; technical artefacts; human beings defined in terms of their skills, knowledge, and know-how; and money.

If we look at the practicist epistemology from an actor-network perspective, what we see is the way in which the elements of practicist epistemology (such as professional magazines and journals, consultants, action researchers, professional bodies and their official publications, corporations and their internal documents, and so on) are (re) assembled into actor-networks to invent and spread management accounting knowledge. It is not the individual actors that occupy the central point in the invention and spread of ideas and technologies but the actor-network that they continuously reassemble. Individual actors recreate and reproduce the networks in which they are enrolled. The invention and spread of ideas and technologies then take place through reassembling the actor-network. They do that by circulating and associating intermediaries; by enrolling (and losing) allies in their network; and by subscribing to intermediaries such as accounting techniques, documents, journal and magazine articles, and computer software.

Coupling Actor-Network Theory (ANT) with Giddens' (1990) analysis of *The Consequences of Modernity*, Jones and Dugdale (2002) provide an interesting analysis of the invention and popularization of ABC. Seeing from ANT, they conceptualize ABC as a socio-technical system. As such, ABC was perpetually reproduced by an ever-evolving actor-network. This actor-network evolved by associating and disassociating actors and intermediaries over different times and spaces. It is these associations and disassociations which eventually brought ABC to what it is now: a disembedded global expert system. As a global expert system, it exists by being inscribed into a host of texts: hundreds of academic and professional articles, case studies, simulation packages, student textbooks, training manuals, course curricula, exam papers, marketing materials of consultants and software developers, and software packages.

Jones and Dugdale (2002) trace the evolution of ABC by following the associations and disassociations that its actor-network, especially those of its most prominent actor Robert Kaplan, made over different times and spaces. Such associations and disassociations certainly included human actors: Kaplan's research and consulting colleagues, readers of their publications, collaborating corporate managers, corporate clients, and students. They also included the non-human actors: research and consultancy projects and programmes, Harvard University, the American Accounting Association (AAA); traditional management accounting techniques such as absorption costing made outdated by ABC; concurrent managerial and academic themes such as post-industrial manufacturing, computer aided manufacturing, advanced manufacturing technologies, just-in-time, total quality management, declining American competitiveness, and Japanese management; and micro-managerial issues such as improving quality and productivity while reducing the operational costs of their consulting clients and case-study companies. The making and remaking of ABC was the trajectory of these associations and disassociations.

Seen from the Giddens' conception of the 'consequences of modernity', they conceptualize ABC as an 'expert system'. As an expert system ABC calculates modernity's most potent 'symbolic token' – money. According to Giddens, expert systems disembed social relations. They lift social relations out from their local setting and abstract them to a global level by subjecting them to standardized definitions and measurements. This disembedding then makes it possible to know the activities going on in dispersed local contexts at a distance as a result of the definitions and measurements that the expert systems offer. For example, ABC's standardized definitions and measurements of cost drivers make it possible for managers (e.g. at head office) to know

54 *Liberal origins*

the volumes and costs of their distant, dispersed, local activities. Then this standardized abstracted knowledge is mobilized as the basis for acting upon the local context – planning and controlling local social relations. This is known as re-embedding the local social relations within the abstract global level. While the local comes to be better known and effectively managed, an expert knowledge system is created and reproduced in these processes of disembedding and re-embedding.

Jones' and Dugdale's theorization of ABC highlights a particular neoliberal trend in the practicist epistemology, which we will be discussing further in the forthcoming chapters. However, for the time being, it is important to discuss three main aspects that Jones and Dugdale (2002, see especially 156–157) emphasize in their paper. First, are the associations that the epistemic actor-networks in the field of management make with the changes in the modes of production and market systems. Such actor-networks persistently and persuasively emphasize a 'universal fact' that a new context has arrived. As such, the 'old' management wisdom is discoursed as dangerously outdated because it leads the corporations to fail. For example, in the popular management accounting literature, Western corporations are often juxtaposed alongside the Japanese and other Eastern corporations to highlight the failure of the old Western modes of management. This is projected as a universal 'fact', attributing it to the situations faced by a wide range of diverse organizations including financial services firms, hospitals, and universities. The diverse problems they face are narrated into a singular managerial rhetoric and narrative of 'lack of strategic orientation' creating an organizational market for new 'strategic management tools'. This is the profitable economic space in which consulting houses, software developers, professionals, and academics construct their epistemic actor-networks. Second, is the change in the locus of production of management accounting knowledge. In the ABC actor-network, neither the academic apparatuses of authenticating knowledge (such as peer-reviewed journals) nor the professional associations played a salient role. Instead, it was management consultancy that had a pivotal role, even translating the academics (e.g. at Harvard) into consultants. Third, is the role of computer software in *black-boxing*[1] management accounting knowledge. In the case of ABC, the development of ERP software, into which ABC can effectively be integrated, played a significant role. This was possible by the very close association between the consultancy houses and the hardware and software suppliers. Professional knowledge thus became something that could easily be disassociated form the professionals – the carnal body on which the knowledge was once inseparably located – and black-boxed as a 'technology' that could be produced, marketed, and distributed by computer programmers and consulting houses. The accounting academics and professionals thus simply became 'opinion leaders' and 'happy customers' cited in their marketing materials. As Scarbrough (1996, as cited in Jones and Dugdale 2002, 157) argues, this manifests:

> [a]n epochal shift in the societal appropriation of knowledge ... [and] a seismic shift in knowledge production towards distributed social networks and market mechanisms.

And in this epochal shift:

> [e]xpertise is increasingly being bought and sold outside the professional arena and claims to truth are being tested in the same way as any other product – by customers in the market place.

3.3 Pedagogical reproduction

In its very generic sense, pedagogy refers to the methods and processes of disseminating professional knowledge within teaching/learning and training environments. It constitutes (a) a particular set of epistemic processes such as lecturing, training, examinations, and accreditations, and (b) a set of epistemic tools such as syllabi, textbooks, exam papers, classroom teaching materials, revision kits, case studies, videos as well as interactive and simulation software. However, in exploring the epistemic implications of pedagogy, we need to interpret it more widely than just trying to understand it in terms of its processes and tools. We need to capture the ways in which it disembeds and re-embeds the practices as professional knowledge. Thus 'professional pedagogy' needs to be understood as a site of reproduction. In essence, the pedagogical processes and technical tools we mentioned earlier are epistemological elements through which a particular practice is reproduced (rather than represented) outside that particularity. In that sense, they create an abstract linguistic or textual reality. It is not the term 'representation' which would be more suitable in explaining this because the textualization of the practice should not be taken simply as a 'faithful' and 'mirror-like' representation. Instead, it is a 'reproduction' which constitutes pedagogical reinvention of contents, intents, definitions, logics, critiques, and justifications, especially to suit the peculiarities of the pedagogical setting in which the practice is to be discussed and discoursed. Pedagogy does not only 'teach' the practice but it also recreates the professional field. In other words, the outcomes of professional pedagogy are much more complex than simply 'representing' and discoursing the 'reality of the practice' as technical knowledge.

3.3.1 Pedagogy as a symbolic system

Perhaps a better way to conceptualize the pedagogy is as a 'symbolic system'. According to Bourdieu (1979), symbolic systems simultaneously perform three interrelated but distinct functions: *cognition, communication*, and *domination*. In the first two functions (cognition and communication), symbolic systems become instruments of knowledge and communication that exert a symbolic power: a power to construct reality as a gnoseological order (i.e. an order constructed upon knowledge and epistemic concepts). In other words, it is through symbolic systems that we create cognitive images of things and communicate them. In a way, this is not remarkably different from the Giddens' idea of 'expert system', one which disembeds and re-embeds local relations and practices. In either case, we see professional pedagogy as a system that connects the epistemological or symbolic context with the practice. In this sense, accounting pedagogy offers a system of thoughts, first, to disembed, cognize, and communicate, and second, to re-embed and dominate the practice. The task of the pedagogy is, therefore, to construct a gnoseological order through which the practice is to be cognized, communicated, and dominated. In this way, professional knowledge and pedagogy become a transcendental system operating over and above practice, reforming and reproducing it.

This happens because, as a symbolic system, professional pedagogy has the power to impose legitimate meanings upon things, people, and their relations. This, for Bourdieu, constitutes 'symbolic power' (Bourdieu 1979; Bourdieu and Passeron 1990). Pedagogical tools such as professional syllabi, course manuals, and textbooks abstract and disembed certain social relations, practices, and technologies as management accounting practices and techniques. Placing certain practices and techniques in management accounting

56 *Liberal origins*

textbooks and syllabi defines them specifically as elements of management accounting and offers them a particular epistemic identity as management accounting tools and practices. Thus, a dispersed and localized set of calculative practices and tools receive a higher order meaning and an epistemic identity. Such practices and technologies are then standardized, systematized, organized, accredited, and translated into a gnoseological order; one that is composed of concepts, principles, theories, and other epistemic forms in which knowledge exists; and one that orders the things, relations, and people according to such concepts, principles, and theories. As management accounting students, practitioners, and academics, we see certain things (which could be something totally different from others in different fields such as engineering) as management accounting because we have been subjected to that particular gnoseological order that accounting pedagogy has created. For example, when they appear in industrial engineering textbooks and course syllabi, ERP and other inventory management systems are industrial management tools for those who were brought up in that particular gnoseological order. But when they appear in management accounting textbooks and syllabi, they receive a management accounting identity and meaning. Reciprocally, we become management accounting students, practitioners, and academics because we see, cognize, and appreciate things from that gnoseological order. And, as a necessary institutional condition, one to become a management accounting student, practitioner, or academic, s/he should gain the necessary knowledge, skills, and attitudes to see the world in that order. This is the pedagogic imposition of meaning and hence constitutes 'symbolic power and symbolic violence' – an arbitrary imposition of subjective meanings as objective ones.

As is often seen in management accounting professional curricula and popular textbooks, we are made to cognize and communicate corporate practices using a threefold categorization: costing, decision making, and control. As we often see in management control systems textbooks and course curricula, for many decades the control dynamics within corporations were to be seen through the dichotomies of operational, managerial, and strategic controls. In the same vein, shareholder wealth or profit maximization was to be appreciated as the ultimate objective of the firm. For many decades now, accounting students and trainee managers have been asked to consider that environmental and social issues pertaining to corporate activities cannot, and perhaps should not, be taken into account because they are 'externalities'. This is again a pedagogical imposition of meanings. And these arbitrarily imposed meanings are considered legitimate because they are imposed by the epistemic power of being associated with the professional pedagogy, because they are accredited and institutionalized meanings.

3.3.2 Pedagogical reproduction at work: deconstructing the CIMA qualification structure

We now deconstruct[2] CIMA's qualification structure and syllabus to further exemplify the symbolic power of accounting pedagogy to impose meaning and reproduce the practice. CIMA produces a unique set of epistemic agents – 'chartered management accountants' and, hence, holds an epistemic power pertaining to the professional pedagogy of management accounting. Indeed, it dictates what this particular epistemic agent should consist of. The legitimacy of this power to define stems from, as its Director of Education spells out, the way it has organized its professional pedagogy:

CIMA now designs its qualifications in what we believe to be a unique way. Based on rigorous international primary research with all of our key stakeholders and involving the participation of over 6,000 individuals and organisations – members, students, employers (both existing and potential), CIMA tuition partners, universities and our examiner and marker team – we have designed a professional finance training and development solution that is second to none.

(CIMA 2008, 2)

The same document also defines what is meant by being a 'chartered management accountant' (CMA):

[someone w]ho combine[s] management and finance skills in a unique way and who fully understand[s] the businesses they are working in. While we respect and learn lessons from the past, through this qualification we prepare our future members to be focused on the future: driving value; managing performance; understanding how organisations are best led and inspired; and helping to sustain vibrant business[es] and government. We provide a strong grounding in international accounting and financial reporting which is comparable to that offered by all of our competitors. In addition we offer strategic risk management, business strategy and much more.

(CIMA 2008, 2)

These are strong 'institutional statements' which define the scope, content, and intentions of the field of management accounting. Such statements make and articulate connections that redefine the field in terms of what it considers as the necessary elements of management accounting knowledge and practices. What we see in these statements is a pedagogic action which culminates in a 'strategic act': an act that tries to establish and/or sustain a 'pedagogic authority' superior to other competing professional bodies in the field. The core of this act is making a new or refined connection between two pedagogical elements: (a) the curriculum and the qualification structure, and (b) its outcome, the 'expert body' that it produces – the CMA. The pedagogic authority stems from the connection between the two as well as the particular epistemic qualities attributed to each of them. The first element is legitimated by connecting it to a broader actor-network (or a practicist epistemology) bearing scientific, professional, and pedagogical credentials. The second element is legitimated by its functionality (i.e. driving value, managing performance, understanding organizations, and so on). In both elements, these pedagogic actions recreate and redefine meanings that we attribute to management accounting, management accountants, and management accounting education.

Professional pedagogy thus gains a legitimate purpose: reproduction of 'embodied', or corporeally located, professional knowledge. This holds the corporeal, the entity through which the professional knowledge should ultimately be enabled and enacted, as the central element of the professional pedagogy. This is the embodiment of knowledge into individual bodies so that they can be accredited as professionals – as CMA or chartered *global* management accountants (CGMA), as they are redefined in the 2015 qualification structure. To this end, professional knowledge is organized into an epistemic factory: a particular input-throughput-output system in which the potential, hence selective, bodies are processed in order to transform them into expert bodies. This is done through (a) dividing and classifying professional knowledge into specific units of teaching/learning and assessments, and (b) organizing them into a hierarchical

58   *Liberal origins*

and sequential order that specifies the roadmap or the epistemic processes through which bodies are processed for accreditation. The outcome of this is a 'pedagogical system' which (re)defines what is counted as management accounting and what it involves in becoming a management accountant.

The CIMA 2015 qualification structure brings in a refined notion of 'competencies' to pedagogically redefine the CMA. On the basis of the 'professional competencies' that they are expected to have and functionalities that they are expected to perform, a CMA is defined as a professional who 'does accounting and finance work in the context of the business to influence people and lead within the organization'. This description of management accountants is based on four interrelated competency components: core accounting and finance skills; business acumen; people skills; and leadership skills. All these competencies are to be underpinned by ethics, integrity, and professionalism (CIMA 2014, 6–7).

These competencies are further refined into a set of managerial functions – decide, monitor, and implement – which are then associated with the levels of management – strategic, management, and operational – in order to constitute a hierarchical order of knowledge, competencies, and qualifications (see Table 3.1). This hierarchical arrangement is an important element of professional pedagogy because it establishes a sequential and progressive path for individual bodies to pass along. Hierarchization compartmentalizes and connects the knowledge into a vertical order of social and professional achievements. And it offers the social actors a competitive structure to demonstrate knowledge and competencies. Demonstrating a higher degree of knowledge and competencies offers greater opportunities for individuals to accumulate capital in all its forms: economic capital, social capital, and cultural/symbolic capital. Thus, it transforms professional pedagogy into a 'field', a contested terrain in which social actors compete for capital accumulation in their different forms (see Section 3.3.3).

Professional pedagogy also defines and arranges knowledge and competencies into a horizontal order, into a spectrum of areas in which professionals can become specialized. Traditionally, the criteria for this horizontal ordering have been either (a) internal divisions in the profession (e.g. financial accounting, management accounting, management control, auditing, taxation, corporate law, public-sector accounting) or (b) interdisciplinarity or interdependency of functional management (such as accounting and finance, HRM, operations, and so on). The CIMA qualification structure redefines this horizontal ordering according to what they call enterprise pillar, performance pillar, and financial pillar (see Table 3.1). These pillars loosely resemble strategy making and planning; implementation; and financial reporting. More than a specialization, they now designated particular areas of knowledge where CMAs should display their professional competencies in deciding, monitoring, and implementation.

Examination is one of the defining elements of professional knowledge. Examinations offer official recognition of the knowledge and competencies that individuals hold and which designate them as experts. As Marx once noted, 'the examination is nothing but the bureaucratic baptism of knowledge, the official recognition of the transubstantiation of profane knowledge into sacred knowledge' (quoted in Bourdieu and Passeron 1990, 141). The vertical and horizontal ordering of knowledge creates a bureaucratic as well as epistemic structure to implementing the pedagogical acts of examinations, accreditations, teaching, and learning. It involves division, distribution, and mapping of knowledge components along a set of categorizing variables (e.g. pillars and levels) so that individual units of teaching/learning and assessment are identified and mapped in relation to other knowledge components. So, unitized and

Table 3.1 Vertical and horizontal ordering of management accounting knowledge and competencies

	E3	P3	F3
STRATEGIC (DECIDE)	*Strategic Management*	*Risk Management*	*Financial Strategy*
MAKES STRATEGIC DECISIONS PROVIDES OVERALL CONTEXT FOR EFFECTIVE IMPLEMENTATION OF STRATEGY	A Interacting with the organization's environment B Evaluating strategic position and strategic options C Leading change D Implementing strategy E The role of information systems in organizational strategy	A Identification, classification and evaluation of risk B Responses to strategic risk C Internal controls to manage risk D Managing risk associated with cash flows E Managing risks associated with capital investment decisions	A Formulation of financial strategy B Financing and dividend decisions C Corporate finance
	E2	P2	F2
MANAGEMENT (MONITOR)	*Project and Relationship Management*	*Advanced Management Accounting*	*Advanced Financial Reporting*
MONITOR IMPLEMENTATION OF STRATEGY ENSURE CORRECTIVE ACTION IS TAKEN	A Introduction to strategic management and assessing the global environment B The human aspects of the organization C Managing relationships D Managing change through projects	A Cost planning and analysis for completive advantage B Control and performance management of responsibility centres C Long-term decision making D Management control and risk	A Sources of long-term finance B Financial of reporting C Analysis of financial performance and position

(*Continued*)

Table 3.1 (Continued)

OPERATIONAL (IMPLEMENT)	E1 *Organizational Management*	P1 *Management Accounting*	F1 *Financial Reporting and Taxation*
IMPLEMENT STRATEGY REPORT ON IMPLEMENTATION OF STRATEGY	A Introduction to organizations B Managing finance function C Managing technology and information D Operations management E Marketing F Managing human resources	A Cost accounting systems B Budgeting C Short-term decision making D Dealing with risk and uncertainty	A Regulatory environment for financial reporting and corporate governance B Financial accounting and reporting C Management of working capital, cash, and sources of short-term finance D Fundamentals of business taxation
	ENTERPRISE PILLAR	*PERFORMANCE PILLAR*	*FINANCIAL PILLAR*
	Articulate a vision	Ground the vision in reality	Report attainment of the vision
	How do we develop strategy?	How do we ensure our strategy is realistic?	How do we prepare financial statements?
	How do we plan for its effective implementation?	How do we monitor activity to ensure strategy is being implemented effectively?	How do we interpret financial statements to understand our performance and to help us make decisions?

Source: CIMA (2014, 8–9).

Practicist epistemology 61

ordered knowledge then needs to be supplemented by a specific set of learning outcomes to make the teaching/learning and examination as objective and standardized as possible across different localities. This standardization of knowledge through learning outcomes is necessary to meet the demand for a universal definition of how the students in different learning/teaching and examination settings can demonstrate their knowledge to be accredited. CIMA thus predefines and standardizes a particular set of 'pedagogic acts' that professional trainees should be able to perform at different levels of the pedagogical hierarchy (see Table 3.2). In this way, becoming a management accountant has been translated into a specific set of pedagogical acts.

3.3.3 Becoming an accountant as the embodiment of the field

Professional pedagogy of accounting is much more than examinations. And becoming an accountant involves much more than passing exams. Every professional accreditation system involves on-the-job training and continuing professional development (CPD) components, with which professionals experience and internalize professional practice. Thus, becoming an accountant involves the 'embodiment' of the practice by experiencing and socializing. In this regard it is important to see the profession as a 'field', which is a theoretical concept central to Bourdieu's reflexive sociology. Seeing from this perspective, a field is an institutionalized social hierarchy with dominant and subordinate positions based on types and amount of capital (Swartz 1997, 123). Higher positions in the field are desirable because they are associated with greater stakes, interests, and capacity to accumulate capital. Also, a field is a conflictual social setting, or a 'field of struggle', where social actors compete with others to occupy dominant positions so that they can claim a higher stake in the field. Every field has its own 'structural logic' and 'rules of the game' which define which type of capital and practices are instrumental in reaching dominant positions and gaining a higher stake. This means that every field has its own self-defining stakes and interests, which are irreducible to the stakes and interests specific to other fields (Bourdieu 1993, 72). Stakes, interests, and the rules of the game in the field of professional accountancy, for example, are rather different from those of the accounting academia. Hence social actors in different fields struggle for different stakes in different manners. It is the 'logic of the field' that spells out what is appropriate and hence rewarding in a particular field. The accounting profession (which is indeed not a unified singular field but a

Table 3.2 Defining pedagogic acts of management accounting

Level	Learning objective: the pedagogic act	The pedagogic command (i.e. examination rubric)
5	Evaluate	Advise, evaluate, recommend
4	Analyse	Analyse, categorize, compare and contrast, construct, discuss, interpret, prioritize, produce
3	Apply	Apply, calculate, demonstrate, prepare, reconcile, solve, tabulate
2	Comprehend	Describe, distinguish, explain, identify, illustrate
1	Know	List, state, define

Source: adapted from CIMA (2014, 10–11).

62 *Liberal origins*

collection of fragmented but closely related fields or subfields) does have unique 'filed logics' for the accounting students to experience, socialize, and internalize. We would never be able to tell or teach students these in a textbook, but they are something that they 'learn' in their particular ways as their professional life unfolds.

One's success in the field depends on the extent to which one masters the 'logic of the field' or the extent to which one develops a 'feel for the game'. As Bourdieu (1998, 80) explains, 'having a feel for the game is having the game under the skin; it is to master in a practical way the future of the game; it is to have a sense of the history of the game'. The type of work, work outcomes, and knowledge appreciated and rewarded; things that you need to learn and master; the way you should dress and behave; the way you should interact with your superiors, colleagues, and subordinates; the type of relations that you need to develop and maintain; the type of relations that you should not appreciate and get involved with; and even where one should sit in a meeting or conference room, are some mundane examples of how the logics of the field would manifest themselves. They would all be more or less different in different fields. Developing a feel for the game thus involves the development of an acumen of the field practices, relations, and the way field hierarchy is manifested in day-to-day social encounters.

This is where accounting pedagogy becomes a practice of 'embodiment'. Embodiment means the ways in which social actors internalize the structural and practical logics of the field and develop a feel for the game. This embodiment, according to Bourdieu, can take place in different forms: illusio, habitus, doxa, and bodily hexis (see Figure 3.3). These are the modes of reproducing the objective social structures within the cognitive schemata of the socialized body, and the medium through which the socialized body is facilitated to produce actions according to the logic of the field (see Alawattage 2011). Social fields such as the accounting profession are arbitrary, socially constructed realities rather than things of nature. Often unaware of this, individuals invest in the game (i.e. the field), get caught up in it, take it seriously, and believe it is worth playing (see Free and Macintosh 2009, 7). This belief that this particular field is where one should invest one's time is called *illusio* (not necessarily an illusion). It is a sort of social calculation or rationalization that drives social agents towards a particular field: the calculation or rationalization that a professional accounting student, for example, would have relied on to decide whether accounting is the profession where s/he can develop a lucrative career and, hence, a better future.

Being the inhabitants of a particular field struggling and competing to play the game of the field appropriately, individuals embody general dispositions, inclinations, attitudes, and values of the field. Once embodied, they become more or less the permanent and durable dispositions of the individual. These durable dispositions are called *habitus*. Becoming 'somebody' (vis-à-vis 'nobody') in a particular field demands the embodiment of the field dispositions, making them a more or less permanent disposition of the individual him/herself. In other words, an individual learns to see and value things in the way that s/he is 'expected' to see and value them in a particular field. For example, as an accountant, this means seeing and valuing things predominantly in financial terms – in terms of financially measurable debits and credits, assets and liabilities, profits and losses, costs and benefits, etc. This may, reciprocally, also include an inclination not to see, not to place any trust in, or not to 'consider' many important things which are not financially measurable. An accountant is a distinct social actor who has embodied the general dispositions, inclinations, and values of a particular field (i.e. accountancy). Habitus, on the one hand, originates from

Practicist epistemology   63

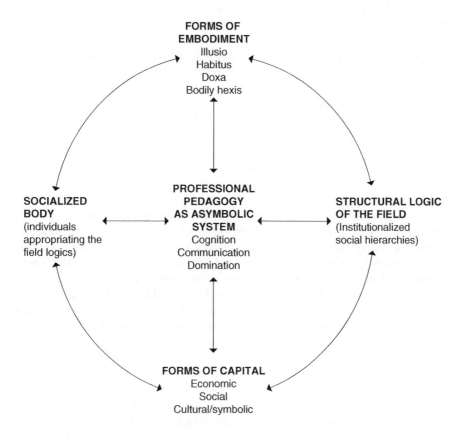

Figure 3.3 Key concepts of Bourdieu's reflexive sociology

the field, belongs to the field, and hence represents the structural logic of the field. On the other hand, it simultaneously exists in the individual bodies and manifests the logics of the field through the individual bodies. Thus, an accountant is only an accountant to the extent s/he manifests the logics of accountancy; and accountancy exists as a field to the extent that the individual bodies, which we call accountants, manifest the structural logics of accountancy. Habitus lies in between individual bodies and the field, transposing each onto the other.

This transposition of habitus onto the body is corporeal as well as mental and cognitive. Hence, the embodiment of field logic can, and should, also be 'carnal' (bodily); manifested in certain physical attributes of the human body. Examples are the way a person holds and uses cutlery during a meal, and the recognizable posture and bearing of a person who has spent lots of time in the military. Such physical manifestations of field logics are called *bodily hexis*, which Bourdieu (1990, 69–70) defines as a 'political mythology realized, embodied, turned into a permanent disposition, a durable way of standing, speaking, walking, and thereby feeling and thinking'.

Every field has a dominant vision and orthodoxy which are generally accepted as self-evidently 'correct' and 'right'. This is what Bourdieu call *doxa*. It constitutes a set of core beliefs and fundamental principles. As Bourdieu (1998, 57) puts it, 'doxa is a particular point

64 *Liberal origins*

of view, the point of view of the dominant, which presents and imposes itself as a universal point of view'. In relation to the accounting profession, for example, the views that market capitalism is the most efficient mode of economic coordination, that market value is the fair value, and that the ultimate corporate responsibility and accountability is towards its shareholders, are views portrayed by the dominant one, the capitalist. These are strongly presented and imposed as a self-evident, correct, right, and hence, universal point of view. Accounting pedagogy, implicitly and explicitly, popularizes this doxa as the dominating vision, as the one that accountants should collectively embrace. Nevertheless, doxa is not a historically static element of the field logic; it evolves with the field. As such, a change in the doxic viewpoint manifests itself in the evolution of the field. For example, increasingly popularizing notions of multiple stakeholder accountability and sustainability manifest certain changes in the doxic viewpoints of the accounting profession and, as such, they now make increasing appearances in the pedagogical elements of accountancy.

Such embodiments provide the individual with a corporeal and cognitive capacity to appropriate field logic and accumulate different forms of capital. As such, one's capacity to act and outperform others in the field is a matter of the way that s/he has embodied the field logics and, accordingly, the type and amount of capital that s/he possesses or has access to. Here, following Bourdieu, we define capital in a broader sense to mean much more than economic or material capital. It should include cultural and social capital as well, because social actors mobilize not only economic or material capital but also social and cultural capital when they play the game in their field. While economic capital is institutionalized in the form of property rights, cultural and social capital take somewhat subjective and complex forms. For example, cultural capital can exist in three different states: (a) the embodied state (i.e. in the form of long-lasting dispositions of the mind and body); (b) the objectified state of tangible cultural products, such as uniforms and other dress codes, pictures, books, cars, phones, and other techno-cultural items; and (c) the institutionalized state, such as accreditations and qualifications (Bourdieu 1986). Similarly, social capital represents durable networks of institutionalized relationships of mutual acquaintances and recognition, which provides individual social actors with a 'credential' that helps them to exploit and dominate the social relationships in a particular field of power (Bourdieu 1986, 248–249). One's social progress and mobility are often explained by the accumulation of all these types of capital, often by exchanging one type with another, in circulation.

There are quite a few accounting studies which theorize the accounting phenomena from the lenses of Bourdieusian notions of 'reflexive sociology' (e.g. Alawattage 2011; Baxter and Chua 2008; Cooper 2002; Cooper et al. 2005; Free and Macintosh 2009; Hamilton and Ó hÓgartaigh 2009; Oakes et al. 1998; Shenkin and Coulson 2007). An interesting paper to highlight at this point is the one by Baxter and Chua (2008). Their study is based on the life of Ralph Smith, the Chief Financial Officer (CFO) of OzRetail – a leading Australian retailer. Their analytical attention was on the field logics of being (and becoming) the CFO. In this study they vividly explain how Smith mobilizes various forms of capital, and his habitus and bodily hexis, to dominate the daily practices in the field. They quote Smith to provide examples for the way he mobilizes symbolic capital (first class air travel and company car in this instance):

> For instance, I had a hell of a fight with the Managing Director about where we fly on aeroplanes. Personally, I don't give a damn where I fly on an aeroplane. If I'm paying, I'll fly in the cargo hole. But if I'm travelling interstate as the second most

expensive officer in the company and a guy who works 60 hour weeks, sits on umpteen boards and has a rather high profile in the business community – well every two weeks there's been an article on Mr Smith of some description in the last twelve months. But, you know, I ride in the front of the aeroplane and I expect my people, who earn a third of what I do or something like that, to say, well that's where we expect the bugger to ride.

I think company cars are absolutely critical. I think if I drove around in a beat up [Ford] Falcon that would be stupid of me. I mean, the MD says, 'Oh, we should give all the Mercs [Mercedes] back'. I said, 'Well, you're not getting mine, it's part of my package'.

(Baxter and Chua 2008, 218)

This means that Smith is acutely aware of the way that symbolic capital such as first class air travel and a company car helps to impose his dominant position in the field hierarchy. Not only that, he also has a strong 'feel for the game', for example, regarding how he should position himself physically in the meetings:

If I want to control a meeting I never sit at the head of the meeting ... It's partly creating a feeling that there is not a structure at the meeting, yet everyone knows there is. It's partly enabling you to sit at the table to eyeball certain people. For instance, I never sit on the same side of the table as [the Chief Accountant] ... because on occasions I want to squash him quickly ... You take him out of the meeting, if you have to, for a while. And the other one I always try to sit opposite is [the Treasurer] because I can shut her up! Try to! I think it is important where you sit in a meeting.

(Baxter and Chua 2008, 220)

Baxter and Chua exemplify how a particular individual mobilizes the logics of the field to appropriate a dominating position in the field. In so doing the individual embodies field logic in the forms of habitus and bodily hexis and deploys the capital so accumulated to position himself appropriately in that position. This exemplifies the way that the practicist epistemology is realized as a process of embodiment. Here is a final quote from Baxter and Chua which vividly articulate this:

Each working day our CFO rises early in the morning, showers, puts on his dark blue suit, chooses a tie to reflect his mood and then has a quick breakfast of coffee and cereal at the kitchen table. He leaves his comfortable suburban house before his family has risen from their beds. Driving in his Mercedes along the same route of local roads, freeways and city streets, he reaches his office by 7.30am. He grabs another cup of coffee and reviews the messages and mail that his assistant has left for him from the previous day. He makes a couple of phone calls and then prepares for his first meeting of the day in his position as the CFO. He has been working in the field of accounting for over 30 years and effortlessly engages in the routines of an accomplished accounting practitioner, living up to the expectations of the position whilst, at the same time, bringing something of his own style to his day to day work. At the end of each day he silently notes that some things went well and others didn't go quite according to plan. His practical knowledge continues to grow, form and re-form every day – usually in subtle and imperceptible ways, but sometimes it is changed or challenged quite markedly. Tomorrow he will do it all again, and the day after that, and the day after that.

(Baxter and Chua 2008, 228)

3.4 Summary and conclusions

This the first of the two chapters that discuss the epistemic context of management accounting. Holding a dialectical connection between them, management accounting exists in two distinct forms: as a body of knowledge and as a set of practices. The epistemic context refers to the apparatuses which construct the dialectical connection between knowledge and practice. It is the context that makes each of them reproduce the other. Such apparatuses can broadly be classified into three interrelated epistemological processes or pillars: reflective practice, pedagogical reproduction, and academic theorization. The first two constitute the practicist epistemology of management accounting and have been the focus of this chapter. The third one constitutes the scientific epistemology of management accounting and will be discussed in the next chapter.

We used the term epistemology here to mean the social and institutional processes that conceive and produce what we take to be knowledge, in this case the knowledge that is taken to be management accounting. Practicist epistemology then means a particular type of epistemology in which knowledge is conceived and constructed inductively, bottom-up, from practice to theory. In a practicist epistemology, the socio-political and institutional capacity to define what should constitute generally acceptable knowledge (i.e. epistemic agency) lies with (a) reflective capacity of the professional practitioner, informed manager, or skilled worker, and (b) the epistemic practices that they have established in their working environments and professional settings.

Management accounting can be seen as a reflexive practice to the extent that its knowledge stems from practitioners' experiences, their practical experimentations and innovations, and their pressing need to solve the problems that they encounter in their day-to-day operational settings. Hence the management accountant is a reflexive practitioner. However, reflection is more than a state of mind. It is institutional. It constitutes the institutional arrangements put in place to enable practitioners to translate their practices, experiences, subjective reflections, and substantive rationalities into transferable knowledge. Such institutional arrangements can broadly be divided into intra-organizational epistemic practices and extra-organizational epistemic practices.

Practicist epistemology can also be seen as an actor-network. This is especially important in understanding how new management accounting techniques such as ABC and BSC are innovated and diffused. According to ANT, this takes place by associating and disassociating actors and intermediaries over different times and spaces. When coupled with Giddens' idea of expert systems, epistemic actor-networks disembed social relations and practices from their local settings and abstract them to a global level by subjecting them to standardized definitions and measurements that expert systems offer. When such standardized definitions and measurements are used to plan and control local relations, the local is re-embedded with the global but with a different meaning. Jones and Dugdale's (2002) ANT-based analysis of ABC highlights a particular trend in the practicist epistemology where neither the accounting academics nor the professional institutions hold a dominating epistemic role in the production and diffusion of management accounting knowledge. Instead it is the consulting houses and software developers who now play the defining role in the practicist epistemology.

The professional pedagogy needs to be understood as a site of reproduction. Pedagogical processes and technical tools are epistemological elements through which a particular practice is reproduced outside that particularity. They create an abstract linguistic or textual reality. In that sense they become symbolic systems which simultaneously perform three interrelated functions: cognition, communication, and domination. In performing these functions, accounting pedagogy exerts a symbolic power, the power to impose meanings. In this chapter, as an example, we deconstructed CIMA's qualification structure and syllabus to demonstrate the multiple ways that this imposition of meaning, and therefore the reproduction of practice, take place through accounting pedagogy.

Finally, accounting pedagogy also involves certain elements to embody practice. In understanding this embodiment of practice, we need to conceptualize the accountancy profession as a field. We used Bourdieu's reflexive sociology to articulate (a) how this embodiment take place and (b) how the accounting profession can be understood as a 'field' where professional practitioners mobilize different forms of embodiment and different forms of capital to appropriate structural and practical logics of the field.

Assignments

These assignments are meant to extend your knowledge beyond what you understand from this chapter. These are not simply revision questions. The content covered in this chapter is necessary but will not be sufficient in attempting these tasks. Therefore, you are required to do some extra reading in attempting these tasks.

1. **Thematic essay:**
   'Management accounting, as a body of knowledge, evolves through a dialectical confrontation between the theory and the practice'.Write an essay, of approximately 3,000 words, on the above theme articulating the dialectical connection between the theoretical and practical realms of management accounting.
2. **Poster:**
   Draw a poster illustrating the 'epistemic context' of traditional management accounting. You need to pay special attention to reflective, pedagogic, and scientific elements of the accounting pedagogy. You may also need to read the next chapter in developing a comprehensive view in your poster.
3. **Presentation:**
   Prepare a set of PowerPoint slides, together with notes if necessary, for a 30-minute presentation on the following theme:'The practicist epistemology of accounting is an actor–network'.
4. **Extended bibliography:**
   Write an extended bibliography on the use of (a) actor–network theory and (b) Bourdieu's reflexive sociology in explaining the accounting epistemology and pedagogy. For this, you need to do a literature survey in major accounting journals and edited books where critical accounting research is published. Organize the bibliography into a table in the following format.

Bibliographic info	Nature of the paper/book chapter (e.g. conceptual/theoretical, empirical, a response to a previous publication)	Major arguments, conclusions, and contributions

68   *Liberal origins*

5. **Literature review:**
   Drawing on relevant Bourdieusian theoretical notions, develop a theoretical review (circa 3,000 words) of your own experiences of being an accounting student. Use Baxter and Chua (2008)'s paper as the basis for your analysis (i.e. think of the way they use Smith's experiences to illustrate how to become and then being a CFO). And think of the following points in attempting this task:

   - How do you define the 'field' of accounting?
   - What attracted you to this particular field, and how do you rationalize your choice of being a player in this field?
   - What sort of professional attributes do you think you need to become an accountant? How did you come to know that you require these attributes?
   - How do you experience the competition or the game in the field? What strategies do you see people using to play the game? How do you relate these strategies to specific types of capital and forms of embodiment?

Notes

1 'Black box' is a metaphor that Latour introduced to explain science in action. He borrowed it from cybernetics to denote a particular operational context where technical instructions that are so complicated and need to be repeated all the time have a black box drawn around them. This allows the black box to function only by giving it input and output instructions. Its inner operational logic dos not need to be known. It is just there so that users need only to specify the input and/or output data.

2 Here we use the term 'deconstruction' as a method of critical analysis which tries to explore the internal meanings and workings of the conceptual system. Hence, there is no any intention or necessity to demean or criticize the intentions, rhetoric, and activities of CIMA. Instead, we indeed appreciate the content therein but try to provide a theoretical analysis as to how they can be seen differently from the point of view of sociology of professional pedagogy. We are using here both the 2010 Qualification Structure and Syllabus (published in 2008) and the 2015 Professional Qualification Syllabus (published in 2014). The change from 2010 to 2015 is evolutionary rather than revolutionary but signifies some important 'additions' to the issues, themes, and topics with which a management accountant now has to be increasingly concerned.

4 The scientific epistemology of management accounting

4.1 Introduction

As we discussed in the previous chapter, the epistemic context of management accounting constitutes the apparatuses which construct a dialectical connection between knowledge and practice. We discussed it as the context within which management accounting is legitimated as a valid body of knowledge that the practising managers can draw upon to frame their managerial practices. We identified three distinct but interrelated epistemological elements relevant in this regard: reflective practice, pedagogical reproduction, and academic theorization. In the previous chapter we discussed the first two elements and this chapter concentrates on the last one – academic theorization, which we may also call scientific epistemology.

The chapter is organized as follows.

1. Section 4.2 briefly explains the component of professional knowledge and outlines the role that scientific epistemology or academic theorization plays in the construction and justification of professional knowledge. Here our attention is on explaining the key components of professional knowledge, their hierarchical arrangement, and their connection with theory and academia, and the way in which scientific rationalities and justifications are provided in the field of management accounting.
2. As a prelude to the rest of the chapter, in Section 4.3 our focal attention is on the fundamental differences between mainstream and critical theorization in accounting and explaining the different socio-political and technical roles they play.
3. In this chapter, we broadly differentiate between two modes of scientification: rationalist and empiricist. Section 4.4 deals with the rationalist justification of management accounting knowledge. Under this rationalist mode of scientification we identify two major theoretical strands: economic and systems rationality of management accounting practices. Section 4.5 deals with economic rationality and Section 4.6 discusses systems rationality.
4. Empiricist epistemology is the subject matter that we cover in Section 4.7. Here we identify two distinct modes of providing empirical support for scientific and theoretical rationalizations: empirical testing and case studies. Using contingency theory-based research as an example, in Section 4.7.1 we discuss the main features of the empirical testing of theoretical propositions of management control systems. Section 4.7.2 then articulates the way case studies are used in constructing and justifying management accounting knowledge.
5. Section 4.8 finally concludes the chapter with a summary.

4.2 Academic theorization and the professional practice

Professional knowledge is composed of three basic components: (a) the discipline or basic science component; (a) the applied science or engineering component; and (3) the skill or attitudinal component (see Schein 1972). As shown in Figure 4.1, these components can be hierarchically ordered. The discipline or basic science component at the top is abstract, theoretical, and delineates the general principles. The skill and attitudinal component at the bottom is directly related to concrete problem solving. And applied science or engineering component in the middle links the other two by offering prescriptive and analytical models for more concrete problem solving.

The two lower components constitute the professional competencies that practicist epistemology deals with. The skill or attitudinal component refers to the mastery with which professional practitioners carry out their work. This is associated with practitioners' training and experience and manifests their capacity to diagnose problems, analyse them, and then offer solutions. This is indeed the corporeal and the cognitive and, hence, represents the embodied elements of professional knowledge. They exist in the bodies of the individual practitioners: as their knowledge, as their skills, and as their mental dispositions. The applied science or engineering component, on the other hand, refers to the technical models and frameworks which practitioners use to conceptualize, design, plan, implement, and control organizational processes and activities. They are the core elements of the 'expert systems'. They operate as the medium through which the practice is abstracted for the purpose of cognition, analysis, communication, and control. For example, budgeting systems, systems of standard costing and variance analysis, BSC, costing methods, ERP models, inventory control models, investment decision

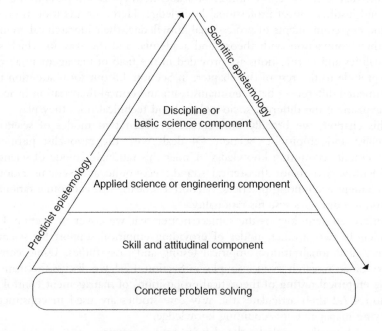

Figure 4.1 Components of professional knowledge

techniques, and other decision-making and control techniques (which you learn in typical management accounting courses) represent such applied science or engineering components of management accounting. They are indeed the 'conceptual tools' that practitioners use in deploying the skill and attitudinal components of their professional knowledge. As such, professional skill also involves the familiarity and mastery of these conceptual tools: the practitioners' expert ability to deploy these tools in problem solving.

These two components manifest the *technical rationality* and the *practicist epistemology* which we discussed in the previous chapter. Technical rationality refers to their instrumentality in more concrete problem solving and, therefore, the achievement of organizational objectives. This means that a particular set of skills, attitudinal, and applied science components are rational to the extent that they are technically capable of solving more concrete organizational problems. In the case of management accounting, the technical rationality implies the instrumentality of these knowledge components in solving the managerial problems of, for example, determining the product mix for the maximum or target amount of profit, determining cost minimizing inventory levels, estimating the 'true' cost of a cost object, setting appropriate performance targets for managers and employees, and so on. The third element – the discipline or basic science component – on the other hand, holds a *scientific rationality* and *scientific epistemology* which we discuss in this chapter.

In contrast to practicist epistemology, scientific epistemology is often deductive and works from top to bottom – from abstract theoretical concepts to applied science models and skill and attitudinal components. Its purpose is to offer a *theoretical basis* for professional knowledge. It does so by connecting them to certain higher order theoretical propositions of relevant 'sciences' or disciplines such as economics, psychology, and management. In that way it tries to establish that the applied engineering, skills, and attitudinal components of professional knowledge do have a 'scientific' or 'disciplinary' basis. Hence scientific epistemology is a project to theorize the practice with a view to offering theoretical justifications and explanations to professional practices so that they are legitimated as *generally acceptable*. As we discussed in the previous chapter, in modern societies, general acceptability stems not from divine or any other source of transcendental wisdom, but from the scientific justifications. Thus, scientific epistemology offers theoretical/scientific rationality for the professional prescriptions regarding how organizations and organizational actors should make decisions and conduct their organizational affairs. Such theorizations involve finding the underlying structures, patterns, motives, and rationales behind the individual and collective behaviour in organizations and markets. This then also involves modelling and programming organizational processes and dynamics in order to determine the optimum decision conditions and to predict likely behaviours under given conditions. For example, neoclassical economics' theorizations of organizational control often argue that social agents are by nature risk-averse and work-averse, and that their decision conditions are characterized by information asymmetry and the possibilities of hidden actions. Then such conditions would lead to the agency problem manifesting as a gross economic inefficiency that needs to be mitigated through truth-inducing performance contracts (see Section 4.3). Then based on such assumptions, predictive and optimization models (i.e. applied science or engineering components) are developed for practitioners to use in concrete organizational scenarios of 'agency problems'. This is justifying management accounting models by connecting them to a higher order scientific knowledge of economics.

72 *Liberal origins*

As such, *scientific rationality* means whether a particular element of knowledge can be justified by reference to a certain set of higher order principles or theoretical propositions of *scientific disciplines*. This is, for example, connecting medical practice to medical sciences, law to jurisprudence, engineering to engineering sciences and physics, and accounting to economics and management sciences, etc. This is the epistemological justification of practice 'from above'.

4.3 Mainstream vs critical theorizations

Academic theorization of management accounting can broadly be divided into two streams: mainstream vs critical. It should be noted that our attention in this chapter is predominantly on the *mainstream* theorization of management accounting, not on critical theorization. It is the mainstream theorizations, especially economics and systems theory-based theorizations, which underlie the institutional legitimation of management accounting as a technology of, and for, corporate capitalism, hence our attention on mainstream theorization. Nevertheless, differentiation between mainstream and critical theorization is important here. Table 4.1 summarizes these differences.

Accordingly, it is not difficult to understand that it is mainstream theorization that undertakes the job of providing the scientific justification for management accounting knowledge as it is applied as a 'technology of capitalism'. This is the scientification of professional knowledge so that the latter is justified rather than critiqued. This, however, does not mean that there are no 'critiques' in the mainstream theorization. Critiques do play a role even in mainstream theorization. However, that critique is not political; instead it is functional. For example, Johnson and Kaplan, in justifying and popularizing ABC and BSC, did offered a severe critique on the traditional mode of management accounting (Johnson and Kaplan 1987a, 1987b). However, that critique is more or less about losing relevance or the incapacity of traditional costing and budgeting techniques to strategize and optimize organizational activities in the light of changing market and techno-managerial conditions. In its final analysis, such functional critiques are also directed towards the enhancement of the capitalistic functionality of management accounting and the justification of management accounting as a corporate technology. It does so by explaining management accounting technologies and practices on the basis of certain theoretical and scientific propositions drawn from other basic sciences. There are two distinct but interrelated modes of scientification here: *rationalist* and *empiricist*.

4.4 Rationalist justification of management accounting knowledge

The rationalist approach to construct and justify knowledge is based upon the premises that (a) the knowledge of a particular subject matter is underwritten by rational insight and deductive reasoning; (b) the knowledge of a particular subject matter is *innate* (i.e. determined by nature rather than by particular course of experience); and (c) the concepts or ideas which constitute our capacity to conceptualize particular subject matters are innate (see Longworth 2009, 68–69). In an overall sense, therefore, the rationalist approach to construct and justify knowledge involves 'logical reasoning' to delineate the 'natural' propositions that can explain and describe the particular subject. In the case of management accounting, this involves delineating the natural laws and

Table 4.1 Mainstream vs critical theorization of management accounting practices

Comparative dimension	Mainstream	Critical
Purpose	Regulation: the status quo is considered to be more or less satisfactory and hence only needs improvements. Or the status quo is in a disequilibrium and hence needs adjustments to bring it to equilibrium (its optimum level).	Radical change: the status quo is considered to be unsatisfactory in terms of ethical, political, and/or moral grounds, hence a political critique and a radical change is sought.
The conception of ideal type	The ideal type scenario is conceptualized in terms of economic and techno-managerial efficiency. The notion of equilibrium is the main analytical device through which efficiency is to be established. Improvements and system adjustments are necessary to bring the system to equilibrium.	The ideal type is conceptualized in terms of the balance of power and wealth distribution between classes, genders, racial groups, professional groups, and any other social categorizations including the contradictions between the market economy, political state, and civil society. Structural and ideological changes as well as changes in institutional practices are sought to bring a balance to the power and wealth distribution and to establish moral and political justice.
Political standing	The researcher/scientist tries to be politically neutral assuming that organizational activities in the sphere of private capital are (and should be) apolitical. Hence, knowledge is justified by manifesting them as necessarily apolitical and scientifically objective.	The researcher/scientist is explicitly taking a political view (i.e. often taking the side of the underdog) on the status of affairs and actively seeking to affect a political/critical voice on the status quo. The established knowledge is questioned and problematized by revealing their inherent political partialities/discriminations and the impossibility of being politically (and scientifically) neutral.
Ontology and epistemology	An objective functional structure or a mechanism is assumed to be out there determining the individual, organizational, and market behaviour (ontology). Hence, it is imperative to research and understand the propositions and parameters of that structure or mechanism in order to control and regulate it. The way to understand and reveal such parameters and propositions is to first hypothesize and then empirically test them. Predictive models can be developed accordingly (epistemology).	Reality is socially constructed and multiple. Changing political, economic, cultural, and historical conditions and institutions underlies the individual, collective, and organizational behaviours (ontology). Hence, the attention of the researcher/ scientist needs to be on the socio-cultural and political processes/institutions/networks through which the social construction of reality take place. The researcher/scientist him/ herself is a part of this setting and hence cannot be totally independent from it. Social transformation comes from the enhancement of the capacity of the individual and collective social actors to reflect upon their situation, understand it, and then mobilize their agency to transform the status quo (epistemology).

(*Continued*)

74 *Liberal origins*

Table 4.1 (Cont).

Comparative dimension	Mainstream	Critical
Analytical mode	Equilibrium analysis with a view to establishing the conditions under which optimum or equilibrium status can be established. Modelling and measurements to establish the system parameters under which the maximum technical and economic efficiencies can be achieved.	Interpretive: driven towards providing alternative theoretical and political interpretations of the phenomenon at hand. Enhancing potential for emancipation and social justice through reflective critical understanding and activism.
Popular social sciences/ theoretical fields	Neoclassical economics, management science, systems theory, industrial psychology.	Political economics, sociology, political science, anthropology, social theory.
Management accounting implications	Establishing calculative techniques and procedures necessary to determine the equilibrium/optimum level. Management accounting as a calculative technology of system optimization and reaching economic equilibrium.	Understanding and explaining why and how management accounting technologies would act differently under various cultural-political, economic, and historical conditions. Management accounting as a political technology of power struggles, exploitation, and domination.

propositions underlying, for example, market dynamics, organizational dynamics, managerial decision-making processes, and control practices. The nature of such logical reasoning is that the reasoning is to be based on certain 'higher order principles' which have already been established elsewhere as scientifically true or theoretically valid. In other words, a particular knowledge is established as scientifically valid and theoretically acceptable by associating that knowledge with certain scientific and theoretical propositions established in basic sciences. Theoretical and scientific propositions of *neoclassical economics* and *systems sciences* have been very influential in the construction and justification of management accounting knowledge. This means that management accounting knowledge carries two interrelated scientific and theoretical rationalities: (a) economic rationality and (b) systems rationality, which we will be discussing the next two sections.

4.5 Economic rationality of management accounting

The economic rationalization of management accounting means the use of economic theories to justify and explain management accounting phenomena. In other words, it involves providing an economic logic and meaning to management accounting technologies and practices.

There has been an interesting connection between accounting, as a professional practice, and economics, as a social science: between the numbers that accounting produces and the theories that economics produces. Perhaps one of the classic examples that illustrates this epistemic connection between accounting and economics is in the writings of Ronald H. Coase, the Nobel Prize Laureate in Economics in 1991. Coase introduced the notion of transaction costs to explain the nature and the limit of the firm (Coase 1937, 1988a, 1988b, 1988c, 1992, 2000) and laid the foundation for what has now come to be known as transaction cost economics. In a paper written in the *Journal of Accounting and Economics*, describing the background and objectives of a series of papers he writes on the connection between accounting and economics, Coase (1990) explains how his research is aimed at (a) encouraging the use of accounting numbers in economic theorization, on the one hand, and (b) improving the theory and practice of accounting by drawing on economic theories, on the other. He argues:

> Understanding cost accounting and opportunity costs within a firm was tied to understanding the organization of firms. The theory of the accounting system is part of the theory of the firm. Like a similar request made fifty years ago, the paper concludes with a call for interdisciplinary studies between economics and accounting.
>
> (Coase 1990, 3)

Economics holds a particular world view and encompasses a wide range of theoretical propositions on the behaviours of individuals, firms, and markets, and the macro economy. Economic rationalization of management accounting involves bringing these economic theories to interpret, explain, and justify management accounting techniques and practices.

The economic rationalization of social phenomena begins with the notion of scarcity – the limited availability of resources to meet unlimited human needs – which is considered to be a natural and fundamental condition of human life. Hence the most rational thing to do as human beings is to maximize the efficiency with which we use economic resources. Everything is to be rationalized, legitimated, accepted, and rejected on the basis of their efficiency or inefficiencies. This efficiency logic has even become a system of beliefs in which being inefficient is often considered a 'moral sin' (Nelson 2001).

Accordingly, human societies have set up certain social mechanisms to make sure that scarce resources are used efficiently. And they continue to reinvent such mechanisms to make them even more efficient than they have ever been. Firms and markets are the mechanisms through which we coordinate the efficient use of scarce resources. Therefore, more than anything else, they are 'economic spaces' structured and managed to make sure that resources are used efficiently. Economic efficiency stems from the adherence to certain economic ideologies, laws, and propositions that they dictate. And management accounting is a particular technology that demonstrates these economic ideologies, laws, and propositions. We can discuss this economic logic of management accounting under two broader headings:

1. Economic rationality of managerial decision making.
2. Economic rationality of management control.

4.5.1 Economic logic of managerial decision making

According to the branch or theory of economics which we call 'transaction cost economics' (TCE) or 'transaction cost theory' (TCT), markets and hierarchies (and their hybrid forms[1]) are alternative institutional arrangements for coordinating economic transactions. Certain transactions would be executed in markets based on market

76   *Liberal origins*

signals while others are executed within corporate hierarchies based on various institutional arrangements such as production planning and transfer pricing. In an ideal economic scenario, a large number of relatively small producers independently carry out the production in response to market signals and, therefore, markets operate as the coordinating mechanism of production and exchange. A hierarchy, on the other hand, absorbs these individual producers as labourers and suppliers of other production factors and coordinates their input through a set of institutional arrangements of economic decision making. The decision as to which institutional arrangement should coordinate a given type of transaction depends on the 'transaction costs' related to each institutional arrangement. The choice will be based on the 'logic of transaction cost minimization', which can be summarized as follows:

1. Transactions differ in their attributes: their frequency, complexity, and asset specificity.
2. Markets and hierarchies differ in their incentive and control instrumentality. The market is stronger in 'incentive intensity'. Hierarchies, on the other hand, are stronger in 'administrative controls' than markets (see Williamson 1991a, 1991b; Williamson and Winter 1988).
3. The decision as to which institutional arrangement should govern a particular set of transactions is evolutionary and based on the potential of each governance structure to economize on transaction costs. Market, hierarchy, and hybrid forms bear different problem-solving and control capacities. Because of these discriminatory features, transactions should be aligned discriminately with coordinating mechanisms. Some may be better left to market mechanisms, while others may be better off with hierarchies or hybrid forms.
4. However, this 'discriminatory alignment' between transactions and governance structures should allow for economic agents' behavioural limitations of bounded rationality and opportunistic behaviour. Behavioural conditions of bounded rationality and opportunistic behaviour then make 'comprehensive contracts' unfeasible. Therefore, institutional arrangements to coordinate economic activities would be effective if they provided for adaptive and sequential decision making so that optimum efficiencies are achieved through 'adaptation' to the ever changing contractual circumstances due to bounded rationality and opportunistic behaviour (Williamson 1991a, 1991b, 2005).

Thus, firms (vis-à-vis markets) become more efficient mechanisms of economic decision making if they can provide a particular set of institutional arrangements to facilitate adaptive and sequential decision making leading to a lower transaction cost (see Williamson and Winter 1988).

Nevertheless, to make firms capable of coordinating economic activities more efficiently than the markets, they need to be appropriately structured and equipped with necessary calculative technologies. This is where the economic rationality of management accounting stems from management accounting as a technology that improves the efficacy of hierarchically coordinated economic decision making. Economic rationality of management accounting needs to be understood here as two interrelated functionalities: structuring and calculating.

1. **Structuring**: This includes *organizing* the firm into a coherent structure of decision making so that every operational decision is made with a unifying economic logic:

making a contribution to the firm's aggregate profit, which is the ultimate efficiency criteria in a capitalist firm. The outcome is a diversified and distributed, but coherent, structure of decision centres and processes covering all operational decisions that the firm must make in running its business. This is done through the notion of *responsibility accounting* which rests upon the concept of *responsibility centres* – particular localities (or a totality) to which managers are assigned as the responsible decision makers and controllers. Accordingly, the organization is divided into a series of hierarchically arranged responsibility centres: investment, profit, revenue, and cost centres. The structuring of the organization into responsibility centres is, in its first instance, determined not by the accounting considerations but by other techno-managerial considerations. For example, departments and faculties in a university, wards in a hospital, production cells in an automotive factory, departments in a bank, are not primarily decided on the basis of accounting criteria but techno-managerial necessities. Nevertheless, accounting transforms such techno-managerial considerations into monetary calculations of costs, revenues, profits, and return on investments. Accounting's role is to replicate the production and administrative rationalities and processes in monetary terms on papers and computer screens so that they are visible, understandable, and governable, and hence, directed towards the economic rationality of efficiency/profits.

2. **Calculating**: This includes assessing the costs and profitability of products, methods, and markets so that the fundamental economic problems of what, how, and to whom to produce can be answered on the basis of profit criteria. Management accounting offers 'applied science models' for this. The fundamental economic question of *what* is answered in organizational settings, for example, by deploying limiting factor analysis, where the profit-maximizing product mixes are determined through the calculation of contribution per limiting factor. In this technique, the economic notion of scarcity is translated into what management accountants call limiting factors. And the notion of economic efficiency is programmed into cost, revenue, and profit functions. Managers may even use more sophisticated techniques such as linear programming when the decision scenario becomes rather complicated with multiple limiting factors. Similar techniques are also used to choose between different technologies of production (i.e. answering the problem of *how*), yet again on the basis of the profits that the production by alternative technologies can make. This profit logic is extended to long-term capital investment decision scenarios where decision parameters such as cost of capital, internal rate of return, payback periods, and investment risks are deployed as calculative rationalities. Management accounting technologies such as market and customer profitability analysis are now increasingly used in answering the problem of *to whom*.

The accounting-based *structuring* and *calculations* configure the firm into a hierarchical structure of accounting calculations. It is within this calculative structure that the economic notion of efficiency is operationalized. Figure 4.2 summarizes this accounting structuring of the firm and illustrates how economics provides the theoretical (and theoretically normative) basis for the techniques that we often collectively call management accounting. The figure contains two interconnected panels containing long-run investment decisions and short-run operational decision scenarios. The top panel demonstrates how economic theory of investment provides the theoretical basis for the set of techniques that we call capital investment decision techniques in management

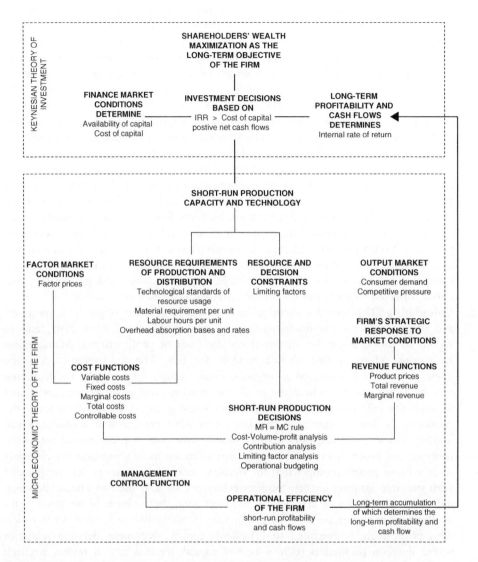

Figure 4.2 The firm (hierarchy) as a calculative structure of economic efficiency – profit

accounting. There you can see the way in which accounting calculations operationalize the notion of long-term economic efficiency – the maximization of shareholders' wealth.

The lower panel illustrates the way in which accounting calculations structure the firm to operationalize the economic notion of short-term profit maximization. According to the neoclassical economic orthodoxy, the optimum production decisions are reached when the marginal revenue (MR) is equal to marginal cost (MC), the point at which the profit is maximized. This is, however, simplified and made operational with the notions of budgeted or target profits. This simplification is necessary because of the nature of the accounting information available in corporate settings. As such, management accounting techniques such as cost-volume-profit (CVP) analysis, limiting factor analysis, and operational budgeting have thus become important corporate management tools of profit planning. These techniques involve making decisions pertaining to production mixes, production methods, and distribution/marketing strategies, and such decisions are made subject to the constraints imposed by the scarcity of resources and output market conditions.

Although such decisions are, after all, made on the basis of the decision criteria directed towards profits and the maximization of shareholders' wealth, they are indeed techno-managerial decisions regarding the production, marketing, and distribution of the products. Management accounting calculations are indeed a quantification of the financial impact – the bottom line – of such techno-managerial considerations. In other words, these financial calculations are the *capitalistic test* of the techno-managerial decisions. Techno-managerial efficiency would become an economic criterion only through translating it into measures of profitability, which is what management accounting does.

4.5.2 The economic rationality of management control

Our discussion on economic rationality so far has not pay proper attention to the way in which *human nature* interferes with economic efficiency. In other words, it has not considered the conflicting interests that different social actors bring to the organizational processes. It assumes a perfect goal congruency between the parties to economic activities. It assumes that the mere presence of calculative technologies would maximize economic efficiency. It only hinted that there is a need for a control function. The contract theory (i.e. agency theory) takes this issue of conflicting interests into account and offers a theoretical justification as to why management control becomes an economic imperative within hierarchical arrangements of economic decision making and coordination. Contract theory is often used in rationalizing management accounting as a technology of control which is necessary to mitigate certain economic inefficiencies arising from conflicting interests of social actors.

Agency theory's world view is that the social actors in organizations have conflicting interests and that each actor will pursue his or her own self-interests (see Baiman 2006, 20). When this conflicting self-interested behaviour is coupled with the difficulties in monitoring individual behaviour due to information asymmetry, there is the possibility of the agency problem. Hence, in group scenarios such as organizations, there is an inherent necessity for control mechanisms to mitigate the inefficiencies arising from the agency problem. The economic rationalization is that the control function of management accounting is based upon this inefficiency logic associated with the agency problem.

The agency problem, as an economic concept, provides a particular conception of the innate conditions of human beings and their economic outcomes. In the context of contract theory, it comprises the following assumptions or properties about the 'nature' of human actions (see Figure 4.3):

1. Work-averse, risk-averse, self-interested individuals and, hence, the possibility of conflicting interests among the members of a group, especially between principals and agents.
2. The possibility of hidden information.
3. The possibility of hidden actions.
4. The possibility of economic inefficiencies arising from the above three conditions.

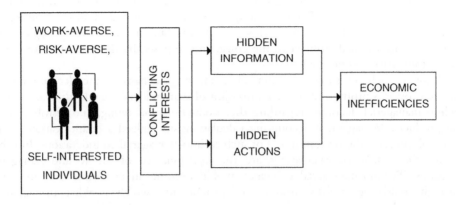

Figure 4.3 Elements of the agency problem

The notion of self-interest has paradoxical connotations in economic theory. On the one hand, self-interest is taken as a necessary and reliable force for promoting the interests of society in many areas. For example, Adam Smith (Smith 2012 [1776], section I.ii2: 26–27) famously asserted that 'it is not from the benevolence of the butcher, the brewer, or the baker, that we expect our dinner, but from their regard to their own interest'. So, self-interest serves an important social function. It is not simply a destructive phenomenon that destroys the collectivism and harmony but a socio-psychological force that leads individuals to reach their self-interest in a competitive manner. To realize one's self-interest, s/he should engage in production and exchange that have values to others. Hence, it is self-interest which drives individuals to engage in value-creating economic activities. On the other hand, economists still argue, it is the basis for certain dysfunctional organizational phenomena, especially the possibility of hidden information, hidden actions, and, hence, economic inefficiencies. Nevertheless, even in this second connotation, the fundamental problem to be mitigated is not the self-interest itself, but the other dysfunctional possibilities arising from self-interest.

Contract theory assumes that work is inherently a function of disutility for agents; they incur dissatisfaction from doing the work they are hired to do. Therefore, all else being equal, the agent would prefer to make as little effort as possible (see Baiman 1990, 2006). So, agents are assumed to be work-averse and risk-averse. Given these work and risk aversions, there is a natural tendency for the agent's interest (i.e. do as little as possible unless there is a good economic incentive to do otherwise) to conflict with that of the principal (to earn the maximum return from the agent).

Information asymmetry is the possibility that the agent has private information to which the principal cannot costlessly gain access. This includes information about the critical variables which constitute performance contracts. For example, information about the production function (i.e. the relationship between the input, effort, and output), utility function (i.e. agent's risk and reward preferences), and agents outside the opportunity utility (i.e. the agent's labour market conditions) is crucial to designing an optimum performance contract. When this hidden information is coupled with risk and work aversion, the problem of hidden action (i.e. the moral hazard problem) is a possibility.

The possibility that the principal cannot observe the agent's actions means that the performance contracts can be devised only on the basis of imperfect indicators (i.e. performance measurements) of the agent's actions and outcomes. The principal is not able to contract the agent directly on the basis of the amount of effort or risk that s/he exerts on the work. Instead, the only possibility for the principal is to devise a *truth-inducing compensation contract* (Baiman 1990, 2006). It is only through such compensation contracts that the principal can try to elicit the private information from the agent and to induce him/her to implement the actions that are compatible with the principal's interests.

Contract theory compels us to see the role of management accounting in terms of such truth-inducing compensation contracts: management accounting as a technical means through which such contracts are put in place to mitigate the inefficiencies resulting from conflicting interests, hidden information, and hidden actions. Hence, the economic rationality of management accounting is to:

- reduce the information symmetry
- mitigate the possibility of hidden actions
- align the agents' interests with the interests of the principal and thereby
- mitigate the economic inefficiencies arising from the agents' innate tendency to avert risk and effort.

These are to be achieved through various forms of performance contracts aimed at an optimum trade-off between three variables: *production efficiency, risk sharing,* and *information rent* (see Baiman 1990, 2006). In management accounting terms, such contracts are various forms of performance management and control systems. Examples include: quality and production control; budgeting systems; BSC; ABM; variance investigation systems; cost allocation systems; the DuPont-system of investment analysis; and transfer pricing systems. Despite various technical differences between such diverse systems of performance contracting, there is one common thread that unites them all: they all are aimed at aligning the self-interests of the agents with the corporate objectives. This alignment requires:

1. Standardizing *production efficiency* through planning, standard setting, and benchmarking.
2. Establishing systems of *risk and reward sharing* between the agents and the principal through appropriate incentive payments.
3. Establishing systems of *information renting*. That is to run monitoring and recording systems so that the principal is kept consistently and accurately aware of the agent's performance in terms of his/her system inputs, processes, and outcomes.

In summary, the role of management accounting, according to contract theory, is to configure the organization into a series of truth-inducing compensation contracts. And they can exist in many different forms ranging from conventional budgetary contracts to BSCs. In this sense, the essential building blocks of any organization are performance contracts. Organizations are written into them and exist upon them.

4.6 Systems rationality of management accounting

More than economic rationalization, perhaps it is the systems theory-based rationalization that provides a scientific rationality for management accounting and control.

82   *Liberal origins*

Systems theory was instrumental in bringing the theoretical advancements in science and engineering to reconceptualize economic organizations as cybernetic and socio-technical systems. According to general systems theory (GST), with or without human interventions, things can be ordered into productive systems. Systems exhibit *order, pattern, purpose,* and *consistency* of them over time. The purpose of GST is to study the laws according to which this ordering of things into systems takes place. Hence its attention is on the 'system dynamics' that provide order, pattern, and purpose to things that can be conceptualized as systems. Organizations are conceptualized as such systems and various organizational elements, such as management control, as their subsystems.

The word system does not refer to existing things in the real world as they are. Instead, it is rather a way of organizing our thoughts about real-world phenomena. As such, the notion of system is more of an epistemological device – something that frames our thinking and understanding of the real-world phenomena. It is the thinker who thinks of things as systems because those things contain properties of the theoretical construct that we call a system. In other words, systems do not exist in the real world independent of systems of thoughts. For example, organizations or management control are what they are on their own. Nevertheless, they become systems in our thoughts as soon as we deploy the system concepts to explain them. Hence systems are systems thinking and systems thinking offers a particular rationality about the nature of things: the way they are constituted, the way they interconnected, the way they grow and die, and the way they are controlled and regulated.

When it comes to the conceptualization of management accounting and control through systems concepts, two distinct but interrelated theoretical logics have been influential:

- cybernetic conception of systems
- structural functionalism.

4.6.1 Cybernetics and management control

The term cybernetics has a history dating back to Norbert Wiener (1988, [1948]) when he used the term to denote a field of study covering the science of control and communication in animals, men, and machines. Since then it has submerged into the wider field of GST to denote a field of studying how systems regulate themselves, reproduce themselves, and evolve and learn (see Berry et al. 2005, 8). The initial impetus for the application of cybernetics in management control and organizational theory was provided by Stafford Beer with his two seminal works *Decision and Control* (1994, [1966]) and *Brain of the Firm* (1972). Checkland's seminal work *Systems Thinking, Systems Practice* (1999, [1981]) further extended cybernetics to the 'soft systems' approach.

Since the early 1970s, cybernetics was drawn on to theorize management and accounting control. For example, Lowe's (1971) paper 'On the idea of a management control system' used certain notions of cybernetic controls to explain management control. Similarly, Ansari's (1979) paper on 'Towards an open system approach to budgeting' attempted to juxtapose the open system approach with cybernetics. However, it was Otley and Berry's (1980) paper 'Control, organisation and accounting' which played a seminal role in popularizing cybernetics in the field of management accounting. They drew on the notion of cybernetics to emphasize the inseparability of control and communication and emphasized the assertion that 'control can only exist when knowledge of outcomes is available' (Otley and Berry 1980, 236).

Cybernetic rationalization of management control conceptualizes management control more or less as a closed loop technical system consisting of the following elements (see Figure 4.4):

1. **The system to be controlled**: This needs to be conceptualized as a particular configuration of inputs, processes, and outputs. Hence, controls can be directed either at inputs, processes, or outputs, resulting in three modes of controls: feedback control (i.e. output-driven controls), concurrent control (i.e. process-driven controls), and feed-forward control (i.e. input-driven controls).

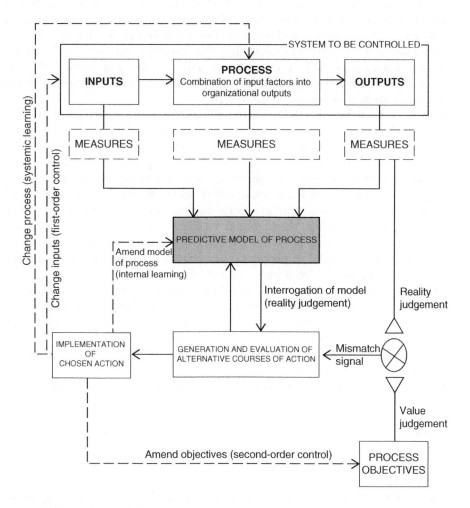

Figure 4.4 Cybernetic model of management control
Source: adapted from Otley and Berry (1980, 236).

84 *Liberal origins*

2. **The predictive model**: The predictive model plays a central role in the cybernetic conception of control. The notion of *prediction* used in cybernetics modelling needs to be understood with a wider meaning. Predictive model here is an epistemic device. It is a conceptual framework through which we understand, measure, monitor, and regulate the system that we want to control. Accordingly, a predictive model establishes the way we want to look at the operational system, measure it, and regulate it. For example, a system of BSCs constitutes such a predictive model. Once established, it facilitates (and compels) the managers to see operational processes in terms of the dimensions and measures that it put in place to measure performance. Such a predictive model builds in the cybernetics controls element of *detector* – the act of detecting the actual status by measuring the system inputs, processes, and outputs, but only within the parameters that the predictive model put in place. For example, conventional performance measurement systems were criticized for their inability to measure beyond the financial indicators, a limitation that the BSC aimed at overcoming by conceptualizing non-financial measures as well. Nevertheless, even a BSC can measure the system performance only within the parameters and indicators that it put into place. 'To the extent that such a model is non-existent or defective, then control is impossible and attempted control actions may well be counter-productive' (Otley and Berry 1980, 236). After all, it is through such predictive models that the likely outcomes of various alternative courses of action can be assessed.

3. **Measures**: as defined by the predictive model, there are predefined measures to detect and monitor the status of the system to be controlled. Such measurements often encapsulate three generic dimensions: *effectiveness* (the extent to which a system achieves its intended transformation), *efficiency* (the extent to which the system achieves its intended transformation with minimum use of resources), and *efficacy* (the extent to which the system contributes to the purpose of a higher order system of which it is a subsystem). As controls are to be directed at inputs, processes, and outcomes, there should be measures pertaining to all of them creating a complex system of feed-forward, concurrent, and feedback controls. Such measures provide the necessary data upon which the managers can make 'reality judgements' and 'interrogate the model'.

4. **Systems objectives**: these are the benchmarks against which the measured status quo of the system needs to be compared for making 'value judgements'. Such objectives are related to system inputs, processes, and outputs. Such value judgements involve judgements regarding the desirability of the system status and are triggered by the mismatches between the objectives and the actual measures. They would then trigger corrective actions.

5. **Choices of relevant alternative actions available to the controllers**: In a cybernetic conception of control actions, the controllers may direct the corrective actions towards any one of or a combination of: (a) changing the inputs (first-order control); (b) amending the objectives (second-order control); (c) changing the process (systemic learning); and/or (d) amending the predictive model (internal learning).

This initial cybernetic model of management control has been revisited, critiqued, and extended towards a wider framework of management control systems. Hofstede (1981), for example, developed a typology of management control in which both cybernetic and non-cybernetic attributes of management control are recognized. His typology is based on four fundamental questions as to whether a cybernetic control environment presents: (a) whether objectives are unambiguous, (b) whether outputs are measurable, (c) whether effects of interventions are known, and (d) whether activity is repetitive. If the answers for all these questions are yes in a particular control situation, then it is a perfectly cybernetic condition where control can be programmed and routinized. If not, different control situations exist. Accordingly, Hofstede offers a typology of management control based on cybernetic vs non-cybernetic characteristics (see Table 4.2):

Table 4.2 Hofstede's control typology

Control type	Whether the objectives are unambiguous, or if not, whether the ambiguity can be resolved	Whether the outputs are measurable, or if not, acceptable surrogate measures can be found	Whether the effects of interventions are known	Whether the activity is repetitive	Cybernetic vs non-cybernetic features
Routine	Yes	Yes	Yes	Yes	Perfect cybernetic system and hence control is routinized.
Expert	Yes	Yes	Yes	No	Cybernetic control but with control entrusted to experts (i.e. personnel having prior experience of such activities)
Trial and error	Yes	Yes	No	No	Cybernetic, but the control methods are learnt through trial and error
Intuitive	Yes	No but acceptable surrogate measures can be found	No	No	Non-cybernetic. Management control as an art rather than a science.
Judgmental	Yes, or any ambiguities of objectives can be resolved	No	No	No	Non-cybernetic. Control becomes a matter of subjective judgements.
Political	No	No	No	No	Non-cybernetic. Here the control is always political control which depends on power structures, negotiation processes, distribution of resources, and compromising between conflicting interests and values.

Source: based on Hofstede (1981).

86   *Liberal origins*

4.6.2 *Structural functionalism and management control*

Structural functionalism is the philosophical tradition behind the system theory. It is a particular philosophical and sociological tradition which uses biological analogy to explain sociological phenomena (see Burrell and Morgan 1979). While cybernetics equates social entities to machines, structural functionalism equates them to biological beings. As such, social entities are understood and explained in terms of the social *functions* they perform. Accordingly, social phenomena such as society, culture, organizations, social groups, technologies, and also accounting, should be regarded as a complex whole, in their own terms, and understood in terms of (a) the *relationships* between their various parts and with their ecological surrounding and (b) the *functional roles* that they perform within such relationships to maintain a productive totality.

The notion of 'social structure' emanates from this conception of relationships between various social elements. A social structure is an established network of relationships, or a totality, among various social elements. For structural functionalists, the maintenance and reproduction of such social structures is the functional purpose of any constituting elements of the structure – hence *structural functionalism*. The functionality of a system is understood in terms of how it establishes and maintains a *system equilibrium* by meeting its *functional imperatives*. As Talcott Parson (Parsons and Smelser 2005, 16 [1959]; see also Burrell and Morgan 1979) puts it, 'any social system is subject to four independent functional imperatives or "problems" which must be met adequately if equilibrium and/or continuing existence of the system is to be maintained'. These four functional imperatives constitute the key elements of Parson's famous AGIL scheme of structural functionalism:

1. *Adaptation* (A): establishing a viable and continuing fit between the system and its environment.
2. *Goal attainment* (G): defining the goals of the system; mobilizing and managing the resources and effort to attain goals.
3. *Integration* (I): establishing control; inhibiting deviancy from the expected system behaviour; maintaining coordination between subsystems; avoiding serious disturbances.
4. *Latency* or pattern maintenance (L): Holding the effort, energy, and performance of the social actors and subsystems at expected levels through motivation and leadership.

Structural functionalism in classical definition of management control

Theoretical developments in the area of management control, especially performance management, have been clear manifestations of structural functionalism (e.g. Ferreira and Otley 2009; Otley 1999; Simons 1995). Management control is often defined as the *processes* that are carried out with the aim of (a) setting appropriate organizational objectives and then (b) monitoring and regulating the actual performance of the organization to make sure that those objectives are achieved. To this end, the organization is configured into a coherent *structure* of *unit entities*: not only divisions, departments, teams, and individuals but also conceptual systems of management control, operational control, and strategic planning. Then they should be unified by a *set of relations* created through the delegation of objectives, authorities, responsibilities, and accountabilities as well as information flows. The continuity and growth of the organization is the functional purpose of management controls. And this continuity is maintained through the *processes of the organizational life* of accountants, other managers, employees, and regulators. Such processes, according to Ferreira and Otley (2009), for example, involve analysis, planning, measurement, control, rewarding, as well as supporting and facilitating organizational learning and change. They are all driven towards the sustenance and growth of the organization through efficient and effective achievement of the goals and objectives imposed upon the organization by its environment.

As a more or less generally accepted wisdom in the field of management control, there are three distinct but interrelated *organizational processes and systems* to ascertain this structural continuity and environmental adaptation. They are *operational control, management control*, and *strategic planning*. They are put in place to address different 'functional imperatives' that systems theory describes. For example, we can see certain correspondence between the accounting conceptualization of organizational control and the propositions of structural functionalism of Parson (see Table 4.3). This idea of functionally differentiated systems to deal with different functional imperatives has long been celebrated by management accounting researchers. And a majority of management control systems textbooks (e.g. Anthony et al. 2014; Emmanuel et al. 2004; Merchant and Van der Stede 2007) is designed around this classification of, and distinction between, operational control, management control, and strategic planning.

Simons' levers of control and structural functionalism

Robert Simons' (1995) strategic control framework – the levers of control (LOC) – provides a splendid example of how structural functionalism underlies the theorization of management control systems. Given the competitive and turbulent nature of the organizational environment nowadays, Simons identifies four distinct 'strategic system imperatives' that organizations need to concentrate on (see Figure 4.5): (a) defining the core values; (b) avoiding risks by delineating the acceptable domain of activities;

Table 4.3 Parson's structural functionalism and classical theory of management control systems

Control function/ hierarchy	Functional imperatives addressed	Calculative practices through which the functional imperatives are met
Strategic planning	Adaptation (A): establishing a viable relationship between the system and its external environment.	SWOT analysis, industry analysis, market analysis, value chain analysis, capital investment decisions, corporate planning.
Management control	Goal attainment (G): define goals of the system and mobilize and manage resources and efforts. Integration (I): inhibiting deviancy and maintaining coordination between different operational units, avoiding serious system disturbances.	Budgeting, standard costing and variance analysis, financial statement analysis, BSC, transfer pricing, performance management.
Operational control	Latency or pattern maintenance (L): programming and routinization of tasks; providing the necessary motivation for the people and units.	Production scheduling, inventory management, quality control, internal checks and balances, record keeping (of production, sales, expenditures, employee performance).

88 *Liberal origins*

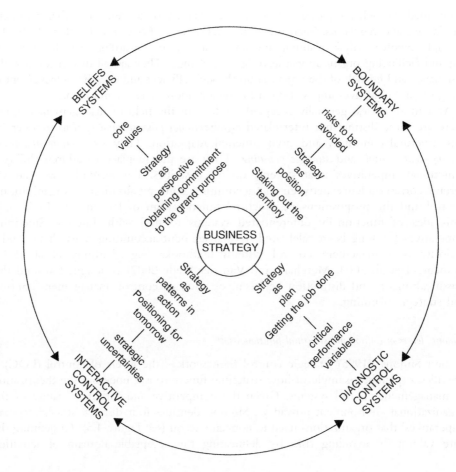

Figure 4.5 Simons' Levers of Control Framework
Source: adapted from Simons (1995, 159).

(c) managing critical performance variables and implanting intended strategies; and (d) managing strategic uncertainties and adapting to competitive environments. The success of the organizational system then depends on the extent to which these strategic imperatives are met. Hence corporate strategies and control systems should be directed towards these strategic imperatives.

Accordingly, the notion of strategy needs to be dynamically defined in relation to these imperatives. The structural function of strategy, in its multiple forms, is to define how the organization is going to address these strategic imperatives. And the structural functionality of management control systems, which are the LOCs in Simons' framework, is to implement and control these strategic definitions. Thus, there would be four distinct strategic definitions and four distinct LOCs to manage them:

1. *Strategy as perspective* and *belief systems* to define and manage the core values.
2. *Strategy as position* and *boundary systems* to delineate the acceptable domain of activities in terms of strategic risks to be taken and avoided.

3. *Strategy as plan* and *diagnostic control systems* to define and manage critical performance variables.
4. *Strategy as pattern* and *interactive control systems* to manage strategic uncertainties and to adapt to the complete environment.

Thus, Simons' LOC framework offers a structural-functionalist logic of management control and strategy. It conceptualizes an organization as a social system aiming at establishing a dynamic equilibrium among competing functional imperatives. Finding a dynamic equilibrium among these competing imperatives is the strategic act which needs to be realized through different LOCs. Each of these LOCs is there to perform a different dimension of strategy in order to meet each of those strategic imperatives. Thus, for management accounting scholars such as Simons, organization is an integration of functionally differentiated systems (i.e. LOCs) put in place to address different functional imperatives.

4.7 Empiricist epistemology of management accounting

Nevertheless, it should be noted that economic and systems rationalities of management accounting knowledge do not arise purely from logical reasoning. They are often verified by empirical testing and illustration. This is where the empiricism, as a philosophical stance of constructing and justification of knowledge, comes into play. Empiricism holds that for knowledge to be to valid and acceptable, it should be possible to verify or falsify on the basis of empirical observations and experimentations. Thus, logical reasoning in the construction of management accounting knowledge is often coupled with testing and illustrations for their empirical grounding. We call this aspect of management accounting epistemology its *empiricist elements*. It is through these empiricist elements that the knowledge derived from logical reasoning is tested and illustrated within particular empirical contexts.

We see two modes of the empirical grounding of management accounting knowledge, each of which is based on different methodological propositions. The first is the hypothetico-deductive 'testing' of certain theoretical propositions or hypotheses, which often take the form of testing certain contingent relationships between organizational variables. The second is the 'case studies' that offer narratives or stories as to how certain economic and systems rationalities are in play in real organizational settings.

4.7.1 Testing contingencies

Contingency theory-based rationalization of management accounting knowledge provides one of the best sets of examples as to how empiricist epistemology works. In line with the development of the notion of open system, researchers started to investigate the contingent variables upon which the nature and effectiveness of organizations' structural elements depended. This theoretical concern first became popular in 1960s in the field of organizational theory, especially in relation to the academic debates on the issues of effectiveness and efficiency of different forms of organizational structures. In a broader sense, the fundamental focus of contingency theory-based accounting literature is to identify the ways in which the external or contextual conditions of the organizations differ and how such differences influence the internal configuration of the organizations. One of the key examples in this regard is Burns' and Stalker's (1961)

90   *Liberal origins*

conceptualization of two contingent forms of organizational structures which perform better in different environmental contexts. Thompson (1967), Perrow (1970), Lawrence and Lorsch (1986), and Galbraith (1973) are some other examples of early studies that emphasize the contingent nature of organizations and their structures. Such studies culminated in the understanding that:

1. There is no best way to organize any system; under different conditions or circumstances (such as variations in strategy, size, technological unpredictability, or environmental uncertainty), differences in organizational structural arrangements and control systems can be observed (see Galbraith 1973; Pfeffer 1997).
2. Not all ways of organizing are equally effective. This is what is sometimes known as the 'consonance hypothesis', meaning that those organizations that have organizational structures and control systems that more closely match or fit with the requirements of the context will be more effective than those that do not (Pfeffer 1982).
3. Organizations adapt and change their structures by moving away from the mismatch between the organizational structure and its context. Because the system effectiveness is a matter of contingency match with the contextual factors, the basic impetus for system changes stems from the changes in those contingency variables that define the context. In this sense, the evolution of various organizational apparatuses such as management accounting needs to be understood as a means through which various misfits arising due to environmental contingencies are managed.

A contingency is a relatively permanent, unavoidable, and changing business circumstance or condition (rather than something which arises from an emergency) that a business needs to respond to in a systematic manner. It has to be acknowledged and dealt with by managers rather than avoided (Clegg et al. 2005). Hence, they represent a fundamental force that drives the structural changes in organizations and their control systems. For example, an external environment such as hostile competition and its underlying uncertainty are contingencies (rather than emergencies) that a firm must deal with, continuously as a design fundamental, especially in designing organizational structures and management control systems. In other words, unlike emergencies, dealing with contingencies requires them to be incorporated at the point of system design. Such designs should be flexible enough to progress through the evolving systemic mismatches that take place due to changes in such contingencies.

The main *contingency factors* (or *structural contingencies*) which have been subject to investigation in management accounting literature are: environment, technology, size and structure, and culture (see Figure 4.6). These are understood to be the factors that *contingently determine* the form and efficiency of the organizational structure. The structure is then characterized and explained by *structural dimensions* such as organizational form, differentiation, bureaucratization, and administrative components. These are the defining characteristics according to which one form of organization structure would be compared and contrasted with another form. Contingency theory focuses on the interrelationships between structural contingencies and structural forms as characterized by structural dimensions, and how these interrelationships influence organizational effectiveness. In that sense, for contingency theorists, and also for system theorists, organizational efficiency stems from the optimality of the system dynamics but, in contrast to system theorists, such system dynamics need to be understood in terms of the fit between the structural contingencies and structural dimensions.

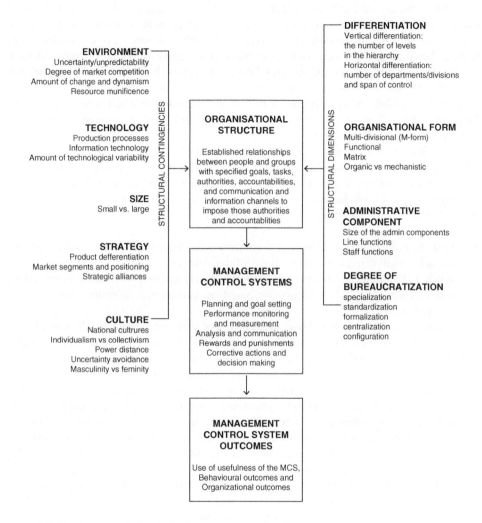

Figure 4.6 Contingency relationships of management control

The epistemic implication of this contingency logic of management control is a form of empiricism where these theoretically and rationally presumed contingencies are to be 'tested' within different real-world scenarios. The aim of such testing is still to identify certain generalizable system rationalities/dynamics but through empirically particular settings. The notion of empirically particular settings takes a specific meaning here. It involves the *possible* (i.e. contingent) status that the contingent variables can take (e.g. environment being stable or unstable, organizational size being small or large, technology being small-batch production vs large-batch and mass production vs process production). Thus, as defined by the contingent variables taken into account in defining such possibilities, any given management control systems could be situated in one of the many possibilities or contingencies. Given such multiple possibilities, then the epistemic aim is to identify which structural (or behavioural) forms of control

92   Liberal origins

would be effective and efficient under each of those possibilities. This is done through empirical investigation as to which form of management control systems would commonly prevail under different situations. In other words, this is established by testing the 'management control system outcomes' against different situations defined by structural contingencies and structural dimensions which we depicted in Figure 4.6. As such, we see a series of management accounting and control research trying to empirically establish the connections between (a) different 'structural contingencies' and 'structural dimensions' of the MCS, on the one hand, and (b) management control system outcomes, on the other.

There has been a stream of accounting research that tries to establish the way in which MCS outcomes would contingently vary according to the variability in the environmental context (e.g. Brownell 1981, 1982, 1983; Chapman 1997; Chenhall and Brownell 1988; Govindarajan 1984; Hopwood 1972; Khandwalla 1972; Otley and Berry 1980). Their epistemological approach has been:

1. First, to construct taxonomies of the external environment on the basis of selected variables that can characterize and differentiate one type of environment from another. Examples are Burns' and Stalker's (1961) taxonomy of stable vs uncertain; and Khandwalla's (1977) taxonomy based on turbulence, hostility, diversity, and complexity.

2. Second, to hypothesize how organizational structures and MCS would vary according to such taxonomical differences in the environment. For example, Burns and Stalkers' rationalization was that a *stable* environment would lead to a *mechanistic* structure of organization and control, while in an *uncertain* environment an *organic* structure of organization and control would be more effective. Lawrence and Lorsch (1967) examined the impact of uncertainty on the differentiation (differences in functional departments) and integration (collaboration between departments) of an organization. They found that better-performing organizations under uncertainty are highly differentiated as well as highly integrated while similar organizations in stable conditions are less differentiated and less integrated. Hage and Aiken (1970, 1971) found a strong association between environmental uncertainty and participation in decision making. Chandler (1962) found that market diversification leads to divisionalized forms of organizations. And Child (1972) confirmed that firms operating in more hostile environments adopted more centralized and tightly controlled organizational structures.

3. As such, the knowledge that this epistemology creates is a conditional knowledge that a particular type of control system, or particular set of MCS outcomes, would be more prevalent in a particular taxonomy of the environment.

This generic epistemological template has been widely used for other contingency variables (i.e. structural contingencies) as well. Similar taxonomies of technology, organization size and structure, strategy, and culture are constructed in order to identify how MCS outcomes would vary with them. The idea is to empirically identify particular 'situations' (as defined by the taxonomical differences in those structural contingencies) and to empirically verify which MCS types and outcomes are more prevalent, and hence presumably more effective in each of those situations (see Chenhall 1997, 2003; Kalagnanam and Lindsay 1999).

Scientific epistemology   93

4.7.2 Case studying the practice

The second mode of empiricist epistemology popular in management accounting is case studies. During the last few decades, case studies have become a popular mode of constructing and justifying management accounting knowledge, especially due to their inherent capacity to provide 'rich accounts' of real organizational practices. Establishing the detailed nature of management accounting practices has been one of the key aims of popularizing case studies (see Cooper et al. 1983; Llewellyn 1992; Scapens 1990, 1992). Case studies have been especially useful in providing insightful accounts regarding the idiosyncrasies or organization-specific particularities in management accounting practices. In other words, while certain theoretical and empirical generalizations were possible through case studies to the extent that the case-specific data replicates the empirical findings and theoretical rationalizations elsewhere, they have been very useful in explaining the subtle differences in practices: to understand the rationalities behind how and why practices are different (and isomorphic) across different organizational settings. They have also been especially useful in offering certain 'lessons' of implementing management accounting technologies in specific contexts. After all, case studies are powerful epistemological devices because of their capacity to explore and explain the 'substantive rationalities' (Weber 1978 [1968]) underlying the diverse practices. Substantive rationality means here how organizational actors, in their own way, rationalize their social actions, relations, and their outcomes often beyond the 'technical rationalities' imposed upon them by bureaucratic and formal systems. In other words, case studies have the capacity to show how and why things happen in real practice beyond (and within) the a priori formal and theoretical rationalities. Scapens (1990, 265), for example, argues that:

> Case studies offer us the possibility of understanding the nature of management accounting in practice; both in terms of the techniques, procedures, systems, etc. which are used and the way in which they are used. In undertaking case studies, we need to be careful to distinguish the formal accounting systems which senior managers believe are used and the ways in which they are actually used. Case studies which examine only formal accounting systems run the risk of failing to understand how these systems are embedded within the day-to-day practices of accountants and managers.

Fieldwork is one of the key methodological elements of the types of case studies that we are talking about here, those which can bring both formal and informal dynamics of management accounting practices. It involves the triangulation of research methods such as: in-depth interviews with the key social actors in the particular organizational setting; participant and non-participant observations of the practices; study of the documents that the social actors in the particular setting produced and used; and archival records and other research pertaining to the particular research site and the issue at hand. Such methods then make it possible to have a 'closer look' at the organizational practices, historicity, as well as perceptions and opinions of the social actors involved in such practices and historicity.

Though the differences among them are not necessarily very clear-cut, Scapens (1990) provides a useful classification of case studies in management accounting:

1. **Descriptive case studies**. These are studies which aim at providing rich 'descriptions' of the accounting systems, procedures, and techniques currently in use in the

94 *Liberal origins*

case organization(s). The focal attention of this type of case studies is more on the formal and bureaucratic aspects of the accounting systems. They try to provide an exact picture of the practice, trying to be non-interpretive, non-normative, and non-judgemental as much as possible.

2. **Illustrative case studies**. Here the attention is slightly different from those of descriptive studies in that the primary aim here is to 'illustrate' how useful or productive a particular method, procedure, technique, or system can be in practice. The focal attention here is to illustrate how a particular act should be done or a particular problem should be solved. Hence, there is an implied normative judgement regarding the superiority of the method or techniques efficacy which the case study is going to illustrate. Innovative practices in the field often attract the attention of these types of studies. However, it should be noted that illustrative case studies can also take a different form in which what is being illustrated is not the efficacy of a particular management accounting technique or procedure but the validity of theoretical propositions of a particular theoretical framework. For example, a case study which illustrates the validity of neoclassical economic understanding of management control or the usefulness of Simons' LOC framework in explaining the control dynamics in a particular organization.

3. **Experimental case studies**. These are the studies through which a new accounting procedure or technique is 'tested' in real-life scenarios. The opportunities for these types of case studies are presented for academics especially in the context of action research and other consulting environments (which we discussed in the previous chapter – practicist epistemology).

4. **Exploratory case studies**. These are case studies aimed at exploring the possibilities for further development of knowledge. The focus is therefore on identifying the potential practices upon which tentative theoretical, technical, and methodological propositions can be built for further studies.

5. **Explanatory case studies**. These are the studies where we can often see theoretical interpretations and explanations of the practices. Focal attention is to provide theoretical explanations as to why and how practice has become what it is in the context of the particular case study. Here theory is used in order to understand and explain the specific, rather than to produce generalizations. What we see here is a theoretical rationalization of the practice, and vice versa. If available theories do not provide convincing explanations, the epistemic outcome of the case study is theoretical problematization.

4.8 Summary and conclusions

This is the second of the two chapters that discuss the epistemic context of management accounting. As mentioned in the previous chapter, holding a dialectical connection between them, management accounting exists in two distinct forms: as a body of knowledge and as a set of practices. The epistemic context refers to the apparatuses which construct the dialectical connection between knowledge and practice. It is the context that makes each of them reproduce the other. Such apparatuses can broadly be classified into three interrelated epistemological processes or pillars: reflective practice, pedagogical reproduction, and academic theorization. The first two constitute the practicist epistemology of management accounting, and we discussed them in the previous chapter. The third one constitutes the scientific epistemology of management accounting – the focus of this chapter.

Professional knowledge constitutes three interrelated elements: skill and attitudinal components; applied science or engineering components; and discipline or basic science components. These components can be hierarchically arranged. Skill and attitudinal components are those that professional practitioners embody through their training and experiences, and they reflect their capacity to solve concrete organizational problems. Applied and engineering components represent various conceptual models, frameworks, and techniques that professional practitioners learn in their formal educational settings. These are the technical/managerial frameworks that they use to cognize, analyse, communicate, and regulate the organizational problems. These frameworks provide the necessary connection between the skill and attitudinal components, on the one hand, and the discipline or basic science components, on the other. Taken together, skill and attitudinal components and the applied science components constitute the technical rationality and the practicist epistemology that we discussed in the previous chapter. The third element – discipline or basic science components – constitutes the scientific rationality and the scientific epistemology.

The scientific epistemology mainly works from top to bottom – from abstract to concrete – providing the necessary scientific and theoretical justification for the lower-level components of professional knowledge. Nevertheless, there is a need to differentiate between mainstream theorization and critical theorization. As modes of theorizations, they operate on fundamentally different political logics. It is the mainstream theorization which is aimed at the 'justification' of established and institutionalized professional knowledge. To that end, mainstream theorization relies heavily on the neoclassical economic and systems theory rationalization of management accounting concepts, techniques, and ideologies.

Scientific justification of mainstream management accounting knowledge rests on two interrelated modes: rationalist justifications and empiricist justifications. Rationalist justification is rational and logical, embracing the idea that knowledge of a particular subject is underwritten by rational insight and logical reasoning and that the knowledge of a particular subject matter is innate. Rationalist justification relies upon the theoretical and scientific propositions already established in basic sciences or disciplines. In relation to management accounting, two distinct theoretical rationalizations can be seen: economic rationalization based on neoclassical economic theories and systems theory-based rationalizations. They provide different theoretical logics for management accounting and control practices and systems.

Empiricist rationalization offers empirical support for the theoretical conception and explanations of management accounting practices. Two distinct modes of providing such empirical support are important here. First, is the hypothetico-deductive testing of certain theoretical propositions. Contingency theory-based research in management accounting and control research are examples in this regard. Second, is the case study research in management accounting, which provides particular empirical narratives and stories regarding the way in which management accounting and control techniques are put into practice in particular organizational settings. Such case studies can take different forms.

Assignments

These assignments are meant to extend your knowledge beyond what you understand from this chapter. These are not simply revision questions. The content covered in this

96 *Liberal origins*

chapter is necessary but will not be sufficient in attempting these tasks. Therefore, you are required to do some extra reading in attempting these tasks.

1. **Thematic essay:**
   'Management accounting is indeed a branch of applied economics'. Do you agree?
   Write an essay, of approximately 3,000 words, on the above theme articulating how economic theories have influenced management accounting research and practice.

2. **Poster:**
   Draw a poster illustrating the 'scientific epistemology' of traditional management accounting. You need to pay special attention to rationalist and empiricist components of the scientific epistemology and the way in which economics, systems, and contingency logics frame the traditional understanding of management accounting and control.

3. **Presentation:**
   Prepare a set of PowerPoint slides, together with notes if necessary, for a 30-minute presentation explaining how structural functionalism underlies the systems theory-based theorization of management control.

4. **Extended bibliography:**
   Write an extended bibliography on the system theory-based analysis of management control. You may define and restrict the scope of your literature survey by concentrating on a particular management control issue such as strategy formulation and implementation, design of performance measurement and compensation systems, variance investigation procedures, or design of management information systems. Organize the bibliography into a table in the following format.

Bibliographic info	Nature of the paper/book chapter (e.g. conceptual/ theoretical, empirical, a response to a previous publication)	Major arguments, conclusions, and contributions

5. **Literature review:**
   Suppose you are writing a thesis/dissertation on management control dynamics of not-for-profit organizations. You intend to use systems theory in general and Simons' LOC framework in particular as your theoretical framework. Before launching into the empirical analysis, you wish to lay the theoretical foundations in a theory chapter. The aim of this chapter is to outline the theoretical notions which you will use to interpret the empirical data in your empirical chapters later on. You should aim to keep your theory chapter to a maximum of 5,000 words.
   You are required to do the necessary literature survey and write this chapter. You should research the academic journal databases for recent management accounting literature which draws on systems theory and, especially, Simons' LOC framework.

Note

1 Hybrid forms constitute a range of possibilities, such as long-term relationships between buyers and suppliers, joint ventures, business groups, informal networks, franchising, and so on, which have been increasingly popular in recent management accounting research.

Part II
Neoliberal trends

5 Neoliberalization of management accounting

5.1 A point of departure

Previous chapters discussed the political, institutional, and epistemological context of the conventional mode of management accounting. You will have realized now that it was the nineteenth-century evolution of liberalism, modernity, and industrial capitalism that gave rise to the political, institutional, and epistemological context for the formation of this type of management accounting. Its functionality was defined by the institutional necessities of structuring economic organizations into mechanisms of capital accumulation not only by controlling but also by 'disciplining' labour. Accounting provided the techno-rational means of this structuring: measures such as return on investment and practices such as budgeting and standard costing were the defining features of such structuring. Driven by the economic doctrines of mass production and economies of scale, these accounting technologies directed the managers to make 'efficient decisions' where efficiency was predominantly defined in terms of cost minimization through achieving economies of scale. The basic managerial decisions were to establish the optimum (i.e. profit maximizing) production mixes subject to resource constraints (i.e. availability of fixed and variable capital) and then to allocate resources and control their uses according to such optimization plans. The emphasis was on the creation of surplus value by disciplining labour within the factory and through creating a system of hierarchical surveillance. As such, this 'disciplinary form' of management accounting was rather factory-driven and inward looking under the condition or assumption that efficient production was sufficient for the realization of surplus value or profit. It was supply-driven economics conditioned by mass undifferentiated (and often protected) markets that were behind this form of management. The market was not perceived as the greatest challenge for profit. Markets were, by and large, taken for granted: 'Build a better mousetrap, and the world will beat a path to your door' had been a popular axiom of this liberal form of managing organizations. In popular management discourses this was understood as a product- and production-oriented management philosophy (Kotler and Keller 2016).

Management accounting's learning and pedagogical perspectives remained rooted in this conventional mode up until early the 1980s to portray the liberal origins of the firm, factory, and management hierarchy. Attention of the professionals, researchers, and consultants was on the 'scientific discovery' and popularization of sophisticated decision tools and assessing their efficacy in different organizational settings. Attempts were made to bring sophisticated statistical techniques (especially probability models to deal with risk and uncertainty inherent in managerial decision making) into, for example, production

100 *Neoliberal trends*

planning, investment decisions, and inventory control models. Attempts were also made to ascertain the efficacy of different types of control systems in terms of not only how they contribute to organizational productivity and profit but also employee motivation and morale.

However, since the late 1970s, we have seen a historical rupture in capitalism. We have seen significant changes not only in the macro spheres of political state, civil society, global markets, and economy but also in the micro spheres of organizational practices, including accounting. Sociologists, economists, and organizational theorists call this rupture 'neoliberalism' (Harvey 2005), 'a new spirit of capitalism' (Boltanski and Chiapello 2007; Du Gay and Morgan 2014), 'post-industrial society' (Touraine 1971), 'post-Fordism' (Amin 1994), 'liquid modernity' (Bauman 2000), 'empire' (Hardt and Negri 2000), and so on. They see capitalism entering a new phase of development encompassing: political-economic logics of neoliberalism; market dynamics of globalization; technological shifts of digitalization, networking, and virtualization; and consumerism-driven societal values. Such changes bring the old liberal spirit of capitalism into question at many frontiers, at the level of political ideology as well as in micro-organizational practices. As a result, liberalism has been critiqued, debated, and reformed into neoliberal forms, demanding management accounting to be self-evaluating and reconstructing. Management accounting is now being reconstructed in light of such changes: it has been redirected towards strategizing; scorecard-based balancing of conflicting systemic imperatives; managing activities and themes rather than departments and processes; creating strategic alliances and networks; continuous improvement of quality; managing risks and creating better systems of corporate governance; addressing issues of global sustainability and development agenda, and so on.

The overall aim of this chapter is to provide a conceptual outline of this neoliberal transformation. As such it sets the preface for second part of this book which articulates how neoliberalism is manifested in the changes to management accounting. Our line of argument constitutes the following elements:

(a) Neoliberal transformation consists of the transition from a disciplinary regime of governmentality to a biopolitical regime of governmentality. In the disciplinary regime confinement and disciplining were the focus whereas the circulation and construction of entrepreneurial selves has become the central focus of this new biopolitical governmentality. This has been effected in the realms of polity, society, and economy, constituting changes in governmental orientation, managerial focus, organization of objects, level of intervention, forms of intervention, type of normalization, and forms of subjectification. These aspects are discussed in Sections 5.2 and 5.3 together with the meaning of neoliberalism and the overall transformation that it brought about.

(b) The central element of this transition is nevertheless the transformation of markets into neoliberal forms where the market now plays a greater role of jurisdiction and veridiction. Section 5.4 explains this transformation in the markets and how a new neoliberal market logic is thus constructed to govern not only the economy but also polity and society. We see this transformation not only as a transformation in political ideology and macro-political apparatuses but also a techno-managerial reconstruction of the market. And we see the role that epistemic institutions play in these techno-managerial reconstructions of the market. We also discuss how the market now exists as an epistemic object on computer screens, databases, and various other digital platforms translating market into a powerful heterotopia – the market as a 'mirror-like' site in which all the other real sites are simultaneously represented, contested, and reinverted.

(c) Recent changes in management accounting technologies and practices then need to be seen through such biopolitical changes effected in the realm of economy, polity, and society. Economic and socio-political organizations effected the neoliberal transformation through (1) envisaging new external connections to facilitate the 'biopolitical circulation', and (2) envisaging internal reconfigurations. We discuss *external connections* in terms of *market and beyond the market connections*. We identify recent management accounting changes, especially the 'strategic turn' to cope with the changes in financial and output markets and 'network organization' to deal with the increasing complexities of factor markets. These are the techno-managerial organizational reinventions that deal with the new neoliberal market conditions. We also see recent attempts to 'strategize the state' and 'strategize civil society' through deploying so-called private-sector managerial tools and ideologies as instances of how management accounting is implicated in the neoliberal reconstruction of the political state and civil society. The second dimension of external connections – *beyond the market connections* – refers to the way in which neoliberal capitalism is driving economic enterprises to address certain socio-political, cultural, and environmental issues and themes that liberal capitalism often understands as 'externalities' or 'political issues' in which 'private capital' has no role to play. Three main issues or themes are salient here: governing corporations, greening the corporation, and accounting for global development. Section 5.5.1 discusses these elements of neoliberalizing social organizations and management accounting.

(d) The *internal reconfiguration* to cope with neoliberal transformations takes place, inter alia, under three main institutional themes: flexible manufacturing and manufacturing flexibility; construction of entrepreneurial selves within and outside economic enterprises; and the establishment of continuously performing and performance monitoring regimes. Section 5.5.2 discusses these themes.

None of these elements will be discussed in detail in this chapter, however. The aim is to provide just an overview so that this chapter works as a roadmap to the forthcoming chapters. This chapter therefore should provide you with a clear understanding of how the chapters in the rest of the book bind together to offer an overarching analysis of neoliberal trends of management accounting. After reading this chapter, you should understand the notion of neoliberalism and its rationale for being an overarching determinant in the postmodern world. Second, you will learn how neoliberalism has provided us with an alternative epistemology for unfolding the form of management accounting that is now 'becoming'. Third, you will understand the emerging substance of management accounting that reflects a neoliberal reconstruction. Finally, you will see how the rest of this book is organized and presented to unfold this emerging substance.

5.2 Neoliberal transformations

To begin with, we ask the question, 'What is neoliberalism?' This question can be approached in many ways. First, neoliberalism is a historical change that occurred in the ways in which we manage our economies and organizations. Mechanisms of this management relied on a particular new world order characterized by a free market

102 *Neoliberal trends*

economic theory embracing an intellectual commitment to the extension of the logics of markets and competitiveness, as Peck and Tickell (2002) observed. Then these intellectual and policy commitments were used to reorder the economic apparatuses, leading to aggressive forms of state downsizing, privatization, austerity financing, and public service reforms. And, in organizations, these market logics came to revitalize the rationalization of managerial thinking into a never-ending expectation mantra of 'competitive advantage' (Porter 1985). This historical change in both economic and organizational fronts, as we shall see later, has implications for the shifting of management accounting from its liberal foundations to a neoliberal form.

Second, neoliberalism is an ideological shift in a political sense. Previously, following the two World Wars, the world's dominant ideology was characterized by a Keynesian mode of thinking. The thought was that government must assume a greater welfare role in making lives easier, while the market was subject to government's regulations and intervention. Nevertheless, neoliberal economists, such as Milton Friedman and Friedrich Hayek, saw that the virtues of the Keynesian approach to political thinking could undervalue the merits of the market system and associated democratic institutions due to the state's bureaucratic orders, malfunctions, and widespread corruption. It was argued that the market solution, in contrast, could produce a fair distribution effect and efficient management of resources in the interests of the masses. It was emphasized that the market should even manage the state rather than the state managing the market. This is what David Harvey, a prominent critique of neoliberalism, captures when he defines neoliberalism as:

> A theory of political economic practices that proposes that human wellbeing can best be advanced by liberating individual entrepreneurial freedoms and skills within an institutional framework characterised by strong private property rights, free market, and free trade. The role of the state is to create and preserve an institutional framework appropriate to such practices.
>
> (Harvey 2005, 2)

Nevertheless, this was not something that was fundamentally different from the liberalist political ideology, which also assumed that the market should and would govern the economic activities of the people but may need to be regulated by the state to ensure the welfare of the masses. Indeed, neoliberalism further extends the fundamental liberal capitalist ideology that the market should govern. Neoliberalism also assumes that markets should be the ultimate mechanism of governance, but it may not be perfectly capable of doing so. The solution for this incapacity or imperfection of the market is, however, not the 'direct regulation of the market'[1] but the 'facilitation of the market'. This facilitation of the market is often realized in the form of various 'social engineering' programmes. This means that government intervention is more directed towards the social sphere (vis-à-vis the market) in order to promote and intensify market relations. Neoliberalism does not, therefore, mean less intervention by the state, but more. Miller (2010, 56) proposed that the 'grand contradiction of neo-liberalism was its passion for intervention in the name of non-intervention ... hailing freedom as a natural basis for life that could only function with the heavy hand of policing by government to administer property relations'. Neoliberalism requires continuous government intervention to transform social relations and culture into terms that are entirely mediated by the marketplace (see Munro 2012). In an overall sense, therefore, neoliberalism manifests a shift from a state-centric welfarist apparatus of governance to a market-centric apparatus of governance where market logic is to penetrate every aspect of economic, political, and social life. It is indeed a colonization of the social and the political by the economic.

Both as a historical change and as an ideological shift, neoliberalism now seems to be everywhere. From a utopian intellectual movement, it has grown into a dominant economic and political rationalization movement of globalization and changes in the work organization. This change has radicalized the mobilization of market logics, with an environment of less government and more performance in a regime of deregulation. Since the 1990s, neoliberalism has, however, been witnessing a 'rolling-out' of a new mode of social engineering within and outside the work organization. This development entails some aggressive re-regulation and more disciplines but in a context of 'deterritorialization' (Hardt and Negri 2000). Hence, neoliberalism is not a static mode of political ideology. It is out there, in the macro sphere, as a politico-ideological change signifying the markets as a mechanism of governance. But it is also in here, in the micro sphere, as a set of emerging processes and practices through which that political ideology is materialized within and outside economic enterprises. As such, it is in a continuous state of flux, recreating organizational practices in response to both local and global pressures and dynamics occurring in and outside work organizations. It is this very process in which we need to understand the reconstitution of management accounting.

5.3 Neoliberal effect

In chapter 1, we discussed how governmentality constituted the evolution of capitalism and management accounting. There we explained two modes of power – disciplinary and biopolitical that constituted governmentality. In its early phase of modernity and capitalism (i.e. its disciplinary phase of governmentality), until the emergence of neoliberalism, disciplinary power played a more significant role than biopolitical power. The focus was on the 'confinement' of individual bodies within the disciplinary spaces through the deployment of disciplinary principles and technologies, conventional management accounting being one of them. In contrast, neoliberalism brought about a different form of governmentality which we now call neoliberal governmentality. In this form of governmentality, biopolitics (vis-à-vis disciplinary power) plays a major role, and 'circulation' (instead of 'confinement') has become the modus operandi. This, however, does not mean that disciplinary power directed towards the 'anatomico-politics of the body' and 'disciplinary confinements' in disciplinary spaces like factories are no longer applicable. They are still in operation, perhaps more than ever, but they are being supplemented and to some extent supplanted by this new biopolitical apparatus directed towards the circulation of people and things. The control of flows has become more crucial than the discipline of bodies: appropriation of surplus value by circulation has become the focus rather than the creation of surplus value through disciplining. Table 5.1 summarizes this turn towards neoliberal governmentality.

How does this transformation take place? And how does this transformation influence management accounting technologies and practices? Indeed, these questions are very broad and complex. They encompass a wide spectrum of analyses ranging from ideological transformations in the political spheres to the changes in techno-managerial practices within various forms of social organizations. And underlining this transformation there are

104 *Neoliberal trends*

Table 5.1 From disciplinary governmentality to neoliberal governmentality

Dimension of comparison	Disciplinary governmentality (see Chapter 1, Section 1.3)	Neoliberal governmentality
Governmental orientation	Primarily towards the confinement of people and objects within disciplinary institutions to make them governable through disciplinary technologies and principles.	Primarily towards the circulation of people and objects through biopolitical construction (i.e. social engineering) of markets; facilitation of market logic to penetrate into other spheres of social and political life.
Managerial focus	Activities, budgets, processes, and bodies	Biopolitical themes and issues (e.g. sustainability, competitiveness, and competitive advantage, quality, (in)equality, (in)efficiency, (in)flexibility, etc.)
Organization of objects	Centripetal forces of discipline – enclosed sites, isolating and fixing bodies to particular disciplinary spaces.	Centrifugal forces of market – flexible networks for the circulation of capital, both in financial and human capital terms.
Level of intervention	The forces of the body, the individual, and micro-organizational spaces and technologies of discipline.	The population, the milieu in which decisions are made, setting the rules of the competitive game within which individuals become 'free' to compete.
Forms of intervention	Disciplining space (general confinement, partitioning, serialization, ranking); disciplining time; and disciplining bodies (hierarchical surveillance, normalizing sanctions, and examination).	Techniques for performance measurement, audit mechanisms, quasi-markets etc. that link individual performance with the wider circulating apparatuses of the markets.
Type of normalization	'Normalization' of individual bodies according to discourses that set standards and benchmarks to measure normality and abnormality (e.g. standard costing and variance analysis).	Normalization of population according to statistical norms.
Forms of subjectification	The docile, useful, normalized individual	Entrepreneur of one's self, competitive social relations, human capital

Source: adapted from (Munro 2012, 351).

certain epistemic, institutional, political-economic, and technological formations. One way or another, it is these questions that we will be dealing with in the forthcoming chapters. However, before we move onto these issues and chapters, it is important to lay down the broader conceptual framework – the neoliberal logic – that binds them together. And perhaps the focal point of that is the emergence of what we may call neoliberal market logic.

5.4 Neoliberal market logic

As we explained in the first chapter, the market, in its different modes, such as the final goods market, the capital market, the labour market and so on, has always been the core institution of capitalism. It is the means through which not only goods and services are exchanged but also the surplus value is valorized. Hence it operates as the principle means through which capital is accumulated in a capitalist social system. In neoclassical economic thought, market is often depicted as the site of interaction between the demand and supply to determine prices and quantities of what is being traded. And in both the liberal and neoliberal sense, the market is understood to be the coordinating mechanism of economic activities which ensures the efficient allocation of resources. Signifying the market as the most efficient mechanism of governance is, therefore, not necessarily something akin to neoliberalism only. It has long been a political axiom of liberal capitalism since its inception. Similarly, the notions of 'least or minimum government' and maximum market governance have been there since the early invention of 'political economics', and hence is not something specifically attributable to neoliberalism. Indeed, they are present as political axioms of liberalism. While such an economic understanding of the notion of market is to be emphasized, it is important to turn towards a Foucauldian interpretation of markets in order to explain their neoliberal transformations and to understand the way in which such transformations influenced management accounting technologies and practices.

For Foucault (2008), markets are more than sites of exchange. Qua being sites of exchanges, they become sites of *jurisdiction* and *veridiction*. As a site of jurisdiction or justice, the market is a social space in which certain political principles of justice are put into practice. This market deployment of political principles of justice appears in at least three ways, according to Foucault (2008, 30–31): regulation, the sanction of fraud, and the just price.

1. *Regulation*: Unregulated markets are a myth. They have always been invested with extremely prolific and strict regulations with regard to, for example, the definition of the products that can be sold in a particular market, their type of manufacture, their origin, the duties to be paid, the procedures of sales, terms of advertisements, and so on. To appreciate the fact that regulation is indeed a 'precondition' for the existence of markets, just think of the number of rules, laws, and regulations that the European Union has imposed on various product markets in terms of product, technological, sales, advertisement, health and safety, and many other aspects. Regulation is understood as a necessary precondition before the interaction of demand and supply can offer meaningful solutions to the problems of distribution and coordination. As a result, markets operate as a particular social space through which the state or similar political institutions can deploy their political principles of regulatory justice – a form of justice that ensures social actors participating in market exchanges are governed by a common set of regulatory and political principles.

2. *The sanction of fraud*: The market is inevitably a site of risk, not only in terms of the risk of making speculative losses but also the risk of fraud and crime. Hence, the regulation that we mentioned earlier must be further extended to the sanction of fraud. Hence a fine regulated market, whatever form the regulation may take, constitutes a social space where social actors can engage in 'fair and just deals' of economic value with a reasonable assurance that they are free of fraud and other malpractices. In this sense, the market represents (at least in its ideal form) a social space of justice for being reasonably free from risk of fraud.

3. *The just price*: The market is understood, both by economic theorists and policy practitioners, to be a site of justice because the price that the market determines is assumed to be, at any rate, a just price. In theoretical terms, market price is argued to be

106 *Neoliberal trends*

the 'fair value' that brings an equilibrium between the opposing social forces of consumer marginal utility and the producer marginal cost. Hence it is assumed to be the value that has a direct relationship between the capital invested in the product and the value offered to the final user of the product. In economic theory, market price brings a balance between consumer surplus and producer surplus. Even the generally accepted accounting principles and accounting standards (e.g. fair value accounting) have recognized this acceptance of market price as a just price and the market as a mechanism to establish a fair value for economic goods, including capital assets. This theoretical and practical acceptance of market price as a just price attributes the market with a particular notion of distributive justice. Market is discoursed as the most efficient and effective mechanism that would ensure a fair distribution of goods and services.

Veridiction here refers to the establishment of truth by the market and the way in which the market operates to establish the truth. Through the discourses of neoclassical economics and other adjacent social sciences, the market has become a 'natural order' and, hence, the price and quantities that it determines are considered to be a natural and superior truth. The market appears 'as something that obeyed and had to obey "natural," that is to say, spontaneous mechanisms' (Foucault 2008, 31, emphasis original) capable of revealing the truth. Nevertheless, this does not mean that the prices the market determines are, in the strict sense, true. Neither does it mean that there is a real dichotomy between true prices and false prices that really matters. Instead, what matters is that the market has the capacity to establish the truth – a sort of truth against which everything else is to be compared and judged. As Foucault (2008, 32) argues:

> It is the natural mechanism of the market and the formation of a natural price that enables us to falsify and verify governmental practice when, on the basis of these elements, we examine what government does, the measures it takes, and the rules it imposes. In this sense, inasmuch as it enables production, need, supply, demand, value, and price, etcetera, to be linked together through exchange, the market constitutes a site of veridiction, I mean a site of verification-falsification for governmental practice. Consequently, the market determines that good government is no longer simply government that functions according to justice. The market determines that a good government is no longer quite simply one that is just. The market now means that to be good government, government has to function according to truth [that the market establishes].

Neoliberalism involves a remarkable expansion of these jurisdictional, and especially verdictional, roles of markets. As Foucault (2008, 131) argues, the problem that neoliberalism tries to answer is 'how the overall exercise of political power can be modelled on the principles of a market economy ... how far and to what extent the formal principles of a market economy can index a general art of government'. This means that the principles of market economy are to be mobilized not only to govern and manage the 'economic enterprises' of private capital but all other social political institutions including the apparatuses of the government itself. Many other critics of neoliberalism, one way or the other, echo this theme. For example, critics like Fuchs (2008), Harvey (2005), Scholte (2005), argue that neoliberalism is an ideological imposition of an 'economically driven process that should proceed on first principles of private property and uninhibited market forces', and where 'other economic rules

Neoliberalization of management accounting   107

and institutions are reduced to a minimum' (Scholte 2005, 1; see also Flew 2012, 46). Critics like Dean (2008) and Brown (2005, 2006), while paying attention to the governmentality apparatuses of neoliberalism, argue that:

> [n]eoliberalism casts the political and social spheres both as appropriately dominated by market concerns and as themselves organized by market rationality ... the state itself must construct and construe itself in market terms, as well as develop policies and promulgate a political culture that figures citizens exhaustively as rational economic actors in every sphere of life.
>
> (Brown 2006, 694)

5.4.1 Techno-managerial reconstruction of neoliberal markets

This neoliberal indexing of governmentality on the basis of market principle is, however, not only an ideological and policy invention. It is true that neoliberal reinvention of the market was, on the one hand, a transformation in the political ideology and the political ontology of market (see Munro 2012). That is only one side of the story. The most important one for our analysis here is the other side – the techno-managerial transformation of the market into an epistemic site.

By the term epistemic site, what we mean is that the market has become the central element of producing the governing knowledge – a site of veridiction as we explained earlier. Since the 1960s, the advancement in information technology has enabled the market to perform this role of veridiction on a massive scale by continuously creating new markets for every aspect of our lives, continuously transforming them into market interactions. The market has become an accounting machine in itself. It continuously creates a massive amount of 'performance data' against which social actors can benchmark and assess their performance. In that sense, the market is not simply a site where demand and supply interact and market analyses are no more simply forecasting the potential demand for a product under different price offerings (i.e. estimating the demand curve). Instead, the market has become a massive 'informational grid' upon which the social actors' continuous gaze is placed, as a reference point to index their performance. Most importantly, through developments in information technology, the market has become 'visible' on a continuous basis making it a different ontological being. It exists as an 'epistemic object' (see Cetina and Bruegger 2000; Zwick and Dholakia 2006) often appearing on computer screens. As Zwick and Dholakia (2006, 48) explain:

> With the introduction of the market-on-screen, geographically remote and tech-nologically dispersed exchange relations were assembled and aggregated, making the market available and recognizable as a unique creature. The aesthetics of the screen turned the market into an entity in its own right for the first time by appresenting knowledge and information – prices, risks, ratios, interpretations, gains, and losses and other relevant information – in one place ... The boundaries of the screen configure a 'whole' market and an interactive market and most of all, a market that continually morphs, moves, and changes before one's own eyes.

Zwick and Dholakia here specifically talk about the stock markets, and the stock market is the 'epistemic object' par excellence. Nevertheless, this conception is equally

108 Neoliberal trends

applicable to other markets in their diverse forms as they now emerge with the inventions of various online market systems such as 'platform markets' and other information gateways that provide various forms of information on various products and industries. The neoliberal trend is that globally disorganized and isolated industries (Lash and Urry 1987) are aggregated onto online platforms so that they are visible and accessible on the screens at a distance. This visuality on the screen gives birth to new forms of markets as objects of information and knowledge, characterized by an ongoing cycle of revelation and discovery (Zwick and Dholakia 2006, 51). With an ever increasing technological ability to capture, store, and report every interaction in the market on a massive scale (e.g. think of Google Analytics) and, with the ability to analyse and provide more complex and sophisticated information on every aspect of market dynamics, the market 'becomes an ontologically open, question-generating, and complex entity, which has the capacity to continuously unfold, change, and morph into something else as new knowledge about the object is brought forth' (Zwick and Dholakia 2006, 51). In this way, the market has transformed itself into a site of continuous interaction, observation, consumption, production, examination, evaluation, and appropriation.

Epistemic institutions play a critical role in this neoliberal reconstruction of markets as epistemic sites. This is because, contrary to the neoclassical economic and liberal political ontology of the market, neoliberal markets have never been totally autonomous and independent entities. The liberal and neoclassical economic ontology of the market is that it is a natural phenomenon that could take care of itself if left alone. The neoliberal assertion, on the other hand, is that the 'rules of the game' must first be established and the market itself must be continually reinforced in order to perform its economic and epistemic functions (see Munro 2012). This continuous reinforcement, facilitation, and reconstruction of markets is nevertheless not a monopoly of the political state. While the political state itself plays a significant role, the functions have been distributed to various epistemic institutions.

Epistemic institutions here mean a range of organizations whose function is, inter alia, informational reconstruction and coordination of the markets. They can be pure epistemic organizations like universities and research institutions. Or they can be regulatory institutions such as the New York Stock Exchange (NYSE) and the National Association of Securities Dealers Automated Quotation System (NASDAQ). Or they can be international development funding agencies such as the World Bank, the IMF, and the OECD. Or they can even be profit-seeking corporations like Google, Facebook, Amazon, eBay or large consulting houses such as Boston Consultancy Group (BCG). And often it is the 'actor-networks' into which they themselves enrol which operate as the epistemic institutional setting behind the neoliberal reconstruction of markets (see Chapter 3 for a detailed discussion of how 'actor-networks' construct management accounting knowledge). After all, one way or another, they are all in the business of constructing neoliberal markets by developing and mobilizing technomanagerial systems and networks that enable neoliberal markets to come alive and penetrate every aspect of our lives.

The development of the Profit Impact of Market Strategy (PIMS) database provides a good example of the role of epistemic institutions in the evolution of data-driven or epistemic markets. PIMS was originally launched at General Electric in the mid-1960s and was then located at Harvard University between 1972 to 1974. In 1975 it was taken over by the Strategic Planning Institute (SPI), a not-for-profit organization specifically set up for the purpose of maintaining the database. PIMS is a comprehensive database which stores and analyses large numbers of descriptors of business strategy, market structure, and financial performance. It contains a massive set of data on products, customers, end users, marketing channels, and competitors etc. from strategic business units of 3000 US and European corporations. Enabling the corporate managers to carefully analyse how such descriptors would affect the financial performance of the corporations under different market conditions, PIMS brought the plurality of the market to a singular analytical platform so that the market is now conceived in terms of every possible biopolitical descriptor of the market (see Farris et al. 2004, for a collection of papers on PIMS). As such, corporate management and strategy become a concentrated attempt of reading and responding to the market, making it the most powerful point of reference in self-reforming corporate behaviour. PIMS represents one of the very early attempts at the neoliberal reconstruction of markets as epistemic sites. After all, markets are what such data sets reveal, and they now constitute the epistemic base of corporate strategic actions. Current 'big data' and 'analytics' movements of course are now taking forward this data-based reconstruction of the market.

5.4.2 Market as a heterotopia

Heterotopia is a useful concept here to explain the neoliberal market because the power of neoliberal markets to operate as sites of jurisdiction and veridiction also stems from its heterotopian character. Heterotopia is a particular theoretical notion that Foucault (1986) brought forward to explain how certain sites or spaces have a mirror-like relation to other sites and spaces. For Foucault (1986, 24), heterotopias are 'real places ... which are something like counter-sites, a kind of effectively enacted utopia in which ... all the other real sites that can be found within the culture, are simultaneously represented, contested, and inverted'. Markets, as they are today in databases and on screens averaging and aggregating as well as individualizing the performance of the market participants, are a placeless place which operates like a mirror, like Foucault's heterotopian mirror. The market is a subtle mixture of utopia and real – a subtle construction of a utopian view of ourselves through what is real in terms of data. Like a mirror, the market reflects a utopian view for the managers of what their corporation should be, what their performance ought to be, in comparison to the average and best performance indicators provided by the statistical grids that represent the market. As Foucault (1986, 24) writes:

> In the mirror, I see myself there where I am not, in an unreal, virtual space that opens up behind the surface; I am over there, there where I am not, a sort of shadow that gives my own visibility to myself, that enables me to see myself there where I am absent: such is the utopia of the mirror.

In the same manner, statistical grids and on-screen data that we now call the market enable managers to see themselves, their corporate performance, there where they are absent, in a particular ideal point in the market grid depending upon the reality that the data reveal. This may be, for example, as a dot in the top right corner of high–high quadrant of a two-dimensional strategic map or as a data point among the top 10% of the market league tables. So, market simultaneously realizes and idealizes performance.

110   *Neoliberal trends*

Because this idealization is not wholly utopian, it is driven by the reality – the reality that performance indicators reveal. Foucault (1986, 24) goes on to say that mirror is:

> [a]lso, a heterotopia in so far as the mirror does exist in reality, where it exerts a sort of counteraction on the position that I occupy. From the standpoint of the mirror I discover my absence from the place where I am since I see myself over there. Starting from this gaze that is, as it were, directed toward me, from the ground of this virtual space that is on the other side of the glass, I come back toward myself; I begin again to direct my eyes toward myself and to reconstitute myself there where I am. The mirror functions as a heterotopia in this respect: it makes this place that I occupy at the moment when I look at myself in the glass at once absolutely real, connected with all the space that surrounds it.

As such, the market enables the managers to direct their managerial attention towards themselves, their own performance and to reconstitute them, vis-à-vis the reality that the market projects upon them. Corporate performances become 'absolutely real' as far as they are being reflected through the performance of the statistical grids of the market project. The market tells the managers not only what their performance 'really' is but also who they should 'aspire to be' in terms of how they reflect themselves upon the market. It enables them to connect with all the spaces surrounding them – the population, demographic, technology, state, economy, polity, society, and so on – because neoliberal markets try to reflect them all through ever more sophisticated socio-economic and political analytics – or biopolitical accounting.

5.5 Neoliberal political logic

While markets have undergone dramatic transformations in these neoliberal times, political states and their governing ideologies have also seen dramatic shifts. In global policy circles, rather than the ultimate sovereign entity of governance, nation-states are now seen more or less as entities that play an intermediary role between the global political state (constituted by the World Bank, IMF, OECD, EU, and other supranational epistemic institutions including certain global consulting houses) and the populace that needs to be directed to 'perform' within and outside the markets. What is envisaged in global policy circles is not simply a law-abiding citizen with a cultural-historical sensitivity towards their own national circumstances, but rather a citizenship capable of 'performing' in the competitive market and competitive hierarchies (i.e. internal markets) including the nation-state itself. In that sense, the role of the nation-state is now seen as the provider of infrastructural and institutional arrangements necessary to ensure such 'competitive performance'. And the fundamental rules and the principles that govern this 'competitive performance' now come from the epistemic elements of the global state, World Bank, IMF, OECD, and the like.

This global state exists as a discourse, not apparently as an overarching dictatorial power dominating everything else (see chapters in Littoz-Monnet 2017). As we mentioned earlier, it operates in its pastoral mode, offering insight, advices, and financial support to 'emancipate' and 'develop' local populations. Nevertheless, there is an overarching political logic that it dictates: the axiom that it is the market that should govern everything, including the nation-state itself, and it is the market (vis-à-vis the government) which has the 'natural' capacity to coordinate individual and institutional actions towards enhancing the 'competitiveness', 'efficiency', and 'innovativeness', etc. which then drive nations, institutions, and individuals to solve all sorts of pathological problems – poverty, malnutrition, unemployment, discrimination, corruption, unsustainability, etc. The global state is thus biopolitical, meaning that it exists for the purpose of realizing biopolitical objectives (e.g. wealth, health, literacy, peace, order, etc.) through the deployment of pastoral or discursive powers (i.e. governmentality). It envisages and highlights a series of biopolitical issues as the prominent global issues towards which it should direct the nation-states. And the solution to such issues, it is discoursed, should and can only emanate from free market competition, if the market is properly facilitated and regulated.

Given the ever increasing jurisdictional and verdictional roles that the market now plays, and given its heterotopian character that posits the individual and institutions against the image that the market reflects back (see previous section), the market is now seen as the basis of global governance. The market is now reconceptualized and enacted as the 'completive terrain' that dictates and governs one's performance, success, and failure. One is judged on the basis of one's market performance, on the basis of one's location in performance grids aggregated and averaged from individual market performances. So, in this sense, the political logic of the global and nation-state is to connect the populace with the market, to make sure that, as global citizens, they are willing and capable of 'performing' in the markets. Hence, everyone is now expected to enhance their capacities to perform competitively.

It is the notion of strategy that captures one's capacity to perform competitively. Strategy is in fact the modus operandi of the competitive behaviour that neoliberalism envisages. It is the notion of 'competitive advantage' that solidifies the normative intention of neoliberal governmentality. This means that 'strategizing' has become the key element of the myriad programmes that neoliberal policy regimes have now enacted in the realms of not only economy, but also the polity and society. Hence, much of the neoliberal changes that we see in various sites is, one way or the other, connected to the agenda of strategizing.

5.6 Neoliberal reconstructions in management accounting

Both promoting 'market competition' as the modus operandi of enhancing economic efficiency and solving biopolitical problems that societies face today, this neoliberal market logic and political logic are imposing a necessity of *being strategic* in all realms of socio-economic activities. The notion of strategy has been one of the most prominent elements associated with the changes in managerial thought and process we are now undergoing. For the purpose of understanding the logic of the chapters in this second section of the book, we can see that the notion of strategy now influences not only the economic enterprises but also the polity and society. So, as illustrated in Figure 5.1, there are three interrelated strategic moves.

* Strategizing the firm
* Strategizing the state and civil society
* Strategizing biopolitical issues.

112   *Neoliberal trends*

5.6.1 Strategizing the firm

Taken together, these include the way in which new strategy discourses are mobilized to reorganize the economy, political state and civil society. When it comes to the theme of strategizing the firm, we discuss it in five interrelated chapters, separating it into four interrelated sub-themes of constructing a strategic organization.

Chapter 6 – Strategizing the firm: strategic discourses of competitive positioning. Here our attention is on the way in which recent strategic management discourses reconstruct the market as a 'strategic terrain' and how new sets of managerial intentions and technologies are constructed for 'strategic positioning' in that competitive terrain. With special reference to portfolio planning models and Porterian (i.e. associated with Michael Porter) discourses of strategy, we discuss here the implications of strategy discourses on management accounting.

Chapter 7 – Strategizing the firm: strategic discourses of organizational reconfiguration. While Chapter 6 concentrates on market positioning, this chapter's attention is on the way in which the internal structures and processes of the firm are reconfigured to meet the strategic imperatives brought about by neoliberal transformations. Here we first pay attention to *post-bureaucratic discourses* that aimed at reforming the internal configuration by correcting the dysfunctionalities of bureaucracy. Second, we deal with *postmodern discourses* that aimed at providing sociological interpretations of the wider cultural-political, economic, and technological transformations taking place within and beyond the organizational realms and how they were manifested within organizational practices and relations. Third, we explain how the *performance management discourses* of Kaplan and others attempted to strategize the internal managerial processes of the firm.

Chapter 8 – Strategizing the firm: strategic reconfiguration of the production systems – flexibility and quality. We identify three interrelated strategic imperatives towards which the firm's production system must now be reconfigured: flexibility, quality, and cost-efficiency. This chapter deals with the first two. Here we first discuss how the notion of 'flexibility' has gained its central role in the strategic management discourses of today and the different modes in which flexibility appears in the discourses. Accordingly, this chapter is organized into specific subsections that deal with the way in which flexibility is attributed to, and achieved through, different elements in capitalist systems ranging from the specific elements of the labour process (i.e. flexible machine, flexible labour, and flexible manufacturing systems) to macro-political (i.e. flexible specialization and flexible accumulation). Both managerial and sociological interpretations of flexibilization within and outside economic enterprises are discussed here. Second, we discuss the quality-based discourses of organizational reconfiguration, with special attention to the Japanization phenomena.

Chapter 9 – Strategizing cost management. Here we take the third strategic imperative of the internal processes – cost-efficiency – and discusses how the old paradigm of costing and cost accounting was reinvented as a 'surveillance assemblage' and a 'holistic programme' through a new set of cost management tools.

Chapter 10 – Strategizing interfirm relations. With circulation being the central proposition of neoliberal value creation, strategizing interfirm relationships, especially along the supply chain, has become one of the key elements in competitive success. The transformation of the organization forms from hierarchies to heterarchies is one of the key features of neoliberal transformations. This chapter unpacks this trajectory.

Neoliberalization of management accounting 113

5.6.2 Strategizing the state and civil society

We also need to acknowledge and discuss the wider political implications of the conceptual and institutional nexus between neoliberal market and strategy. In this respect we see the notions of markets, customer focus, and strategy have now made inroads into the management of public-sector organizations and civil society. In particular, the discourses of new public management (NPM), 'whole of government approaches' (see Patrick and Brown 2007), and the 'strategic state' (e.g. OECD 2015a) have brought market logic as an underlying doctrine of organizing the political state. This is the focus of *Chapter 11 – Strategizing the state and NPM agenda*. In Chapter 11, we will be specifically dealing with how management accounting technologies and practices are mobilized to transform public-sector organizations.

Since the late 1980s, we have witnessed a rapid growth of various civil society organizations in the form of non-governmental organizations and charities creating a complex network of accountabilities crossing the boundaries of political state, civil society, and the economy. One way or another, these manifest a social movement that attempts to mobilize the managerial apparatuses of the neoliberal market economy to organize civil society. What we see here is that the neoliberal market logic has been increasingly mobilized to transform convivial social relations in civil society into a set of relations through which neoliberal identities of 'entrepreneurial selves' are constructed. We call this institutional trajectory *strategizing civil society* and this will be discussed in Chapter 12.

5.6.3 Strategizing the biopolitical issues

Neoliberal capitalism has introduced, among many others of course, two major crises to the forefront of policy discussions. First, is the *crisis of corporate governance*, especially manifested by a series of financial crises that ended up in a massive programme of austerity across the globe, financial scandals, and corruption. Second, is the *crisis of sustainability* manifested not only by the issues pertaining to global warming and related ecological issues but also by the issues of growing poverty, underdevelopment, income disparity, and various modes of inequalities. These crises constitute an absence of meaningful connections that go beyond the market's relations – accountabilities that go beyond market mechanisms into polity, society, and ecology. Accounting has been central to these issues both as a problem and as a solution. On the one hand, the incapacity of the traditional liberal forms of accounting and accountability to deal with these issues has been acknowledged as one of the major causes of these crises. In particular, it has been often argued that the monologic and functional form of accountability and accounting, dominated by the liberal economic rationales of profit maximization, have not been that helpful in the fight against unsustainability and corporate corruption and abuses. Accounting and accountability, when transformed into dialogic and social forms, could be one of the major institutional mechanisms through which solutions to these issues can be found and institutionalized. It is not difficult to see, especially in the circles of critical accounting research, such issues of social, dialogic, and agonistic forms of accountability.

There is a particular feature of biopolitical or neoliberal governmentality that we have to stress here. As we mentioned earlier, disciplinary or liberal governmentality is oriented towards confinement of bodies within disciplinary spaces for the purposes of disciplinary

114   *Neoliberal trends*

control. There the managerial attention is on the disciplinary control and management of the labour process. In contrast, biopolitical governmentality takes the managerial and policy attention towards biopolitical themes – the political and social issues of the time. Hence neoliberal management is not simply management of organizations and markets; it takes the form of managing 'policy themes' – a form of theme-based-management (vis-à-vis activity or budget-based management). Salient examples include governing corporations, managing risk, alleviating poverty, managing sustainability, mitigating corruption, managing creativity, and so on. Both private- and public-sector organizations would be driven towards such themes reducing the ideological boundaries between the private vs the public. Both would be governed through market principles but addressing such biopolitical themes. Different forms of organizations, actor–networks, and coalitions would be formed to mobilize diverse social actors towards such issues. New managerial ideologies, technologies, and practices would be constructed and institutionalized to address such themes/issues.

In line with the dominating thematic issues that trouble current times, critical accounting researchers embarked on a broader debate about connecting wider socio-political, cultural, and environmental issues with accounting and accountability. Management accounting is no exception and now it is the right time to see how management accounting is implicated in such issues. For the purposes of this text, we have identified three major themes/issues that underlie the connections beyond the markets. They are (1) corporate governance and risk management, (2) accounting for sustainability, and (3) accounting for poverty alleviation and development. We have set aside three chapters to deal with these issues. *Chapter 13 – Neoliberalization of corporate governance* will deal with issues of corporate governance and risk management. *Chapter 14 – Greening the firm: environmental management accounting* then deals with the connection between sustainability and management accounting. *Chapter 15 – Strategizing development* will deal with development and accounting. In all these instances we will be discussing the accounting implications of these biopolitical themes.

5.7 Summary and conclusions

The aim of this chapter was to outline the neoliberal implications and their effect. In doing so, we first tried to explain the generic nature of neoliberalism. We then explained the 'neoliberal effect' paying special attention to how governmentality was transformed from a disciplinary governmentality to a neoliberal or biopolitical governmentality. We then moved on to further explain the political economic logic that neoliberalism brought about in terms of its market logic and political logic. We discussed how markets were transformed into sites of jurisdictions and veridictions, epistemic objects, and heterotopias, making them the central element of neoliberal governance not only of the economy but also the polity and society. Neoliberal political logic constitutes the emergence of the global epistemic state and its discursive apparatuses which promote free market competition as the modus operandi of growth and development, and the market-based governance and regulation as the modus operandi of control. Institutional implications of these neoliberal market and political logics was the necessity of 'strategizing' institutional apparatuses of not only the economy (i.e. the firms) but also society and the polity. This then also provided the roadmap for the forthcoming chapters, which is summarized in Figure 5.1.

Rectangular elements in Figure 5.1 denote the major contextual or structural transformations taking place. First, is the transformation taking place in the realm of market. The most critical transformation is that the 'biopolitical circulation' (rather than disciplinary confinement) has become the dominating mode of accumulation of capital. Neoliberalism

Neoliberalization of management accounting 115

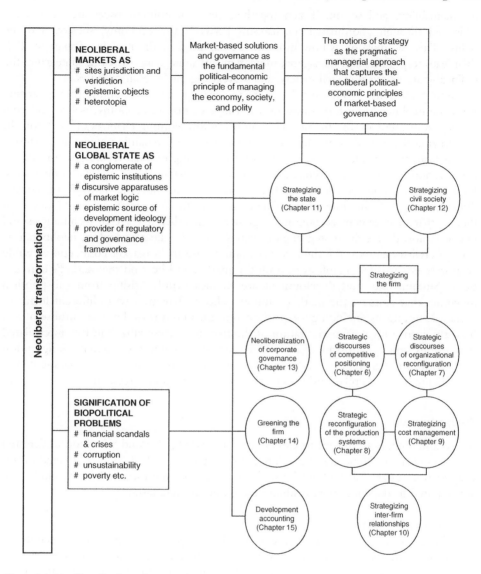

Figure 5.1 Neoliberalization of accounting: an overview

brought up the necessary political ideologies, policies, and institutional infrastructure by opening the national political economic boundaries to form global markets where the circulation of commodities, capital, and labour across nations, organizations, and networks can effectively take place. This emphasis in biopolitical circulation, together with accompanying advancements in information technologies that facilitated 'on-screen-gaze' on the market, transformed the markets into sites of jurisdiction, sites of veridiction, epistemic objects, and heterotopias. Second, is the transformation taking place in the realm of political state and civil society, both colonized by the logic of the market and now organized according to the political principles dictated by the markets. The third is the significance of a set of biopolitical issues such as global financial scandals, corruption, money laundering,

116   *Neoliberal trends*

unsustainability, and so on. Taken together, these biopolitical issues are now being addressed through coordinated mechanisms between the economy, society, and the polity. This coordination is now more or less captured by the notions of strategy. This then leads to political and managerial movements of strategizing the firm, strategizing the political state, strategizing civil society, and strategizing the biopolitical issues.

Circular elements in Figure 5.1 denote the management accounting themes arising from the neoliberal transformations in the realms of market economy, polity, and civil society. And these are the themes that constitute forthcoming chapters of the book. In recognizing these themes, we identify a particular set of dynamics: envisaging external connections that enable the 'circulation' and envisaging internal reconfiguration of the organizational structures, systems, and processes to enable those external connections. External connections constitute market connections and beyond. Though analytically distinct, they are highly interrelated. These connections give rise to different biopolitical themes that management accounting, together with other managerial technologies and practices, now deal with. Strategizing the firm, strategizing the state, and the neoliberalization of civil society are the themes that mainly arise from market connections, while corporate governance manifests in both the market and beyond the market's connections. Sustainability and development are themes mainly arising from the political dynamics that connect the market cultural-political dynamics with different forms of social organizations, including for-profit economic enterprises. For the purpose of this text, the institutional reconfiguration of the firm is conceptualized in five interrelated dimensions: strategic positioning in the market, strategizing the internal configuration of the firm, strategizing the production systems, strategizing the cost management, and strategizing interfirm relationships including supply chain management.

Assignments

These assignments are meant to extend your knowledge beyond what you understand from this chapter. These are not simply revision questions. The content covered in this chapter is necessary but will not be sufficient in attempting these tasks. Therefore, you are required to do some extra reading in attempting these tasks.

1. **Thematic essay:**
   'Since the late 1980s, we have evidenced a transition of management accounting from an internal-looking factory-driven set of practices to external market-oriented practices'.Discuss this statement with reference to the transition of governmentality from disciplinary confinement to biopolitical circulation.
2. **Poster:**
   Draw a poster illustrating how neoliberal reconstruction of markets resulted in a thematic revision of management accounting concerns.
3. **Presentation:**
   Prepare a set of PowerPoint slides, together with notes if necessary, for a 30-minute presentation on the following theme:'In neoliberal capitalism management accounting's primary role has shifted towards biopolitical circulation through external connections'.
4. **Extended bibliography:**
   Write an extended bibliography on the use of neoliberalism as an explanatory concept in accounting research. For this, you need to do a literature survey in

major accounting journals and edited books where critical accounting research is published. Organize the bibliography into a table in the following format.

Bibliographic info	Nature of the paper/book chapter (e.g. conceptual/theoretical, empirical, a response to a previous publication)	Major arguments, conclusions, and contributions

5. **Literature review:**

Review the following three papers and write an essay articulating the key elements of neoliberal changes in accounting and its political context.Chiapello, E. (2017). Critical accounting research and neoliberalism. *Critical Perspectives on Accounting*, 43(Supplement C), 47–64.Cooper, C. (2015). Entrepreneurs of the self: The development of management control since 1976. *Accounting, Organizations and Society*, 47, 14–24.Munro, I. (2012). The Management of Circulations: Biopolitical Variations after Foucault. *International Journal of Management Reviews*, 14(3), 345–362.

Note

1 Modes of direct interventions of the state in the market often include price controls, product or market specific taxes, import and export duties, product subsidies, etc.

6 Strategizing the firm
Strategic discourses of competitive positioning

6.1 Introduction

The previous chapter provided an overview of the 'neoliberal turn'. One of its managerial repercussions was the reinvention of the firm as a 'strategic entity'. Before this, as we noted in Chapter 4, based on neoclassical economic theories of the firm, traditional management accounting conceptualized the firm as an economic entity whose 'production function' was to be programmed and optimized in the light of market demand and the factor prices (i.e. costs). Market demand and production costs were the two main planning parameters for programming and optimization of production. The programming objective was profit maximization (or cost minimization). This optimization logic was firmly rooted in the neoclassical economic logic of 'economies of scale' and 'marginal analyses' where 'optimum' or 'equilibrium' point of production was sought through appropriate calculations (such as marginal revenue = marginal cost). The programming tools were budgeting and other related decision-making tools such as linear programming, inventory management, statistical demand forecasting, cost-volume-profit analysis, and so on. The neoliberal reinvention of the firm in fact turned this 'neat' economic programming logic upside down. It repositioned the central managerial attention from 'production optimization' to 'market positioning'. Rather than production and sales functions, the firm itself became the core managerial element that has to be positioned in a competitive structure: as a totality, as an image, as a brand, as a portfolio of strategic business units, and so on. Hence the invention of 'strategic management' and 'corporate planning' as the most critical managerial functions that consolidate everything else in the firm (see Knights and Morgan 1991; Levy et al. 2003). The notion of strategy thus became the overarching institutional logic of managing the neoliberal firm. In this context, what we mean by the term 'strategizing the firm' is the historical and discursive process of this managerial reconceptualization and reconstitution of the firm as a 'strategic entity' since the late 1980s.

So, the aim of this chapter is to explain how this happened and how certain management technologies were reinvented in this historical/discursive process. In doing so, we base our analysis on the popular managerial discourses pertaining to strategic management and how they brought up a different mode of calculative rationalities in conceptualizing and managing corporations. In a broader sense, in this book, we deal with 'strategizing the firm' based on three interlocking analytical pillars: (a) strategic reinvention of the market; (b) strategic reinvention of the organization; and (c) strategic reinvention of the factory. This chapter specifically deals with the first of these three themes, leaving the other two themes to the forthcoming chapters

Strategizing the firm 119

(especially Chapters 7, 8, and 9). The focus of this chapter is therefore specifically on the way in which a new set of managerial concepts and tools reconceptualized the market and industries as strategic terrains and how a new managerial paradigm was invented to position the firm in such strategic terrains. Accordingly, the chapter is structured into three main sections.

1. Section 6.2 deals with how a certain set of managerial models, especially 'portfolio planning models', brought about a new conception of a 'strategic terrain' – a competitive terrain in which the firm and its sub-units need to be strategically positioned to maximize corporate cash flow and return on investment. In this section, we will be discussing how a new stream of calculative rationalities and technologies came into being to cognize, communicate, and dominate in this strategic site. These calculative technologies constitute what came to be known as 'corporate planning models' or 'models of business portfolio analysis' that indeed initiated the historical process of neoliberalizing management.
2. While Section 6.2 concentrates on the managerial discourses on strategy emanating from management consultants (e.g. Boston Consultancy and General Electric), Section 6.3 takes your attention to the strategic discourses that industrial economics brought about. Here the attention is on Michael Porter's contribution to strategic management and how his models of competitive analysis reconstituted management accounting practices. Special attention is paid to the way in which discourses of competitive advantage and national competitiveness created a macro–micro link in the field of strategic management and how strategic management was lifted to a higher plane of analysing the development prospects of nations.
3. Section 6.4 explains the biopolitics of Porterian strategy discourses: how Porterian discourses reconstructed competitiveness as a biopolitical problem and the particular set of epistemological politics involved in this reconstruction.

6.2 Reinventing the strategic terrain

Despite its long history of use in military sciences, the term 'strategy' began to enter business management discourses strongly only in the 1980s. This 'strategic turn' in management can be linked to the open economic policies that emerged in the 1970s and the resulting growth of global competition which made business competition analogous with warfare: markets being the territories to capture; customers being the subjects to surrender; competitors being the enemies to defeat; the 4Ps[1] being the competitive weapons to use tactically; and strategy being the way in which 'business warfare' is thought out, led, and executed. Much of the credit for introducing the 'warfare' analogy to business competition and bringing the notion of strategy to the forefront of business analysis should go to Anglo-American management gurus. During the early 1980s, business school courses under the label of 'business policy' provided the initial pedagogical framework to capture the notion of strategy. However, initially it was only as an overarching organizational function that integrated and consolidated functional management areas. While functional disciplines such as accounting and finance, marketing, production, and human resource management dealt with their respective functional areas with clear-cut definitions and conceptual tools to partition them from each other, it was business policy that taught its students how to draw 'organizational' or 'corporate' (rather than 'functional' or 'departmental') policies to

120 *Neoliberal trends*

project the business enterprise as a single, unified entity to its stakeholders, especially to its shareholders. By definition, 'business policy' was an area of 'general managers' and 'directors' (rather than functional specialists) who led the business as a whole. It was this 'business policy' arena which provided the initial pedagogical framework to institutionalize militaristic notions of strategy within business discourse which later turned itself into the subject of 'strategic management'.

Business policy was more concerned with the issues of integrating and consolidating the internal functions through establishing overarching organizational objectives and policies. Its discursive transformation into strategic management was achieved by integrating certain economic and managerial reconceptualizations of the market and industry in industrial economics and management consultancy. Central to this transformation were the contributions by the Harvard industrial economics professor Michael E. Porter and management consultants, especially Boston Consultancy Group (BCG) and General Electric (GE). Their contributions were central to the discursive reconstruction of market and industry as a competitive terrain – a site in which the firm and its sub-units need to be strategically *positioned*. Taken together, they initiated a different set of calculative rationalities driven towards mapping and analysing the 'strategic terrains' in their competitive attributes to make sure that the company, and its sub-units, were positioned strategically. This means that the markets and industries were to be understood as competitive spaces embedding *opportunities* and *threats* and corporate entities as social units embedding *strengths* and *weaknesses* in terms of their potential for capitalizing on the opportunities provided by the competition. What were needed therefore were techniques of mapping the competitive terrain and a set of strategy prescriptions to make sure that the firm would win the competition by being strategically positioned in the competitive terrain.

6.2.1 Mapping the strategic terrain for strategy prescriptions

Diversification and the formation of multidivisional (M-form) businesses were the salient trend in the post-World War II period of Western industrial history (see Chandler 1977). Institutional economists, especially Chandler (1963, 1977) and Williamson (1975, 1988), argue that when firms get beyond a certain point, they shift from a unitary to multi-divisional structure. Firms organize their operations into a general corporate office and several product-based or regional-based divisions, each with its own functional departments. Each division would therefore operate as an independent business unit on its own and each division would encompass a unique competitive environment. Such divisions would therefore be identified as 'strategic business units' (SBUs). The general corporate office would be responsible for the resource allocation between divisions. This means that M-Form brought an institutional separation of the strategic and operational decisions between the divisions and the corporate centre, giving rise to what we now call 'corporate planning and control'. The general office is responsible for strategic decisions, and the divisions are responsible for operational decisions. Strategic decisions involve a choice of domain – decisions pertaining to the choice of market or industrial domains in which the firm's SBUs should operate. A further extension of the M-form is the conglomerate, a firm with unrelated divisions that span industry groups. Each division is treated as an investment centre, and the corporate planning office functions as an internal capital market encompassing a competitive flow of capital between different divisions. In the late 1960s, in an attempt to help clients to solve their problems with such strategic decisions, BCG conceived the growth-share matrix, whose power and reach over the next ten years would be unparalleled by any other device available to a diversified company's management (see Kiechel 2010).

As an analytical tool, the BCG growth–share matrix performs two interrelated analytical tasks. First, is mapping the strategic terrain into different categories so that each domain can be seen as investment worthy or not. In other words, it attempts to answer the fundamental strategic question: Is a particular market or industrial domain 'attractive' or 'strategic' enough for the firm's resources (i.e. an SBU) to be deployed? The criteria used to answer this question is the market growth rate so that the different market segments can be categorized in terms of having either a low or high market growth rate, high been attractive or strategic enough for the company to invest in. The second analytical task is to ascertain the relative strengths and weaknesses of each SBU. The criteria used for this purpose is the relative market share. It measures the market share of the business relative to the market share of the largest competitor. A relative market share more than 1 means that the business is the market leader. Yet again this provides a classification of the SBUs into high and low categories, high being strong enough to lead the market competition.

In this manner, as shown in Figure 6.1, the BCG matrix offers a conceptual map divided into four distinct arenas, each equating to different 'strategic positions'. Company SBUs are located across this map according to their relative market share and market growth rate. Each SBU is represented by a circle, the size of which is proportional to the sales volume. The result is that corporate managers are provided with a graphical overview of their business portfolio and the profit potential of their SBUs, from which they can recommend 'strategies' for each SBU in the portfolio. Like military strategists marshalling their troops, corporate managers are now provided with a map of where their troops (i.e. SBUs) are deployed so that they can make strategic decisions as to which troop should receive which command. For example, if an SBU is located in the quadrant of high market growth and high relative market share, then that SBU is identified as a 'star'. The 'strategic prescription' for a star is 'invest for growth' (see Figure 6.1 for a full description of classification and strategic prescriptions). This means that corporate leaders should love the business with a bright future and should invest in it to grow and expand. Thus, it should receive more funds from corporate head office for capacity expansion, new recruitment, research and development, market promotion, and so on.

General Electric's Portfolio Planning Model (see Figure 6.1), offers a further purification and extension of mapping the strategic terrain. The proponents of this model understand that market growth rate and relative market share alone cannot diagnose the strategic positions of SBUs. Thus, they use multiple criteria to measure 'market attractiveness' (which is measured only by market growth rate in the BCG matrix) and 'business strength' (which is measured only by relative market share in the BCG matrix). Furthermore, the strategic map is divided into nine areas, so that the marginal cases can be better analysed and a wider set of strategies can be recommended.

So, what is meant by corporate strategy as manifested in these portfolio planning models? Strategy is a set of resource allocation decisions among different businesses: deciding which businesses should receive more funds for growth, and which businesses those funds should be extracted from through 'milking' and 'divestments'. It offers an optimization logic aiming at maximizing future cash flows of the business portfolio by reallocating the capital according to the strategic positions of each element in the portfolio. The process of deciding strategies is rather analytical and rational: first diagnose the 'strategic position' of each SBU using an analytical tool and a 'strategic map' of where each SBU is located using two variables – 'market attractiveness' and 'business strength';

122 Neoliberal trends

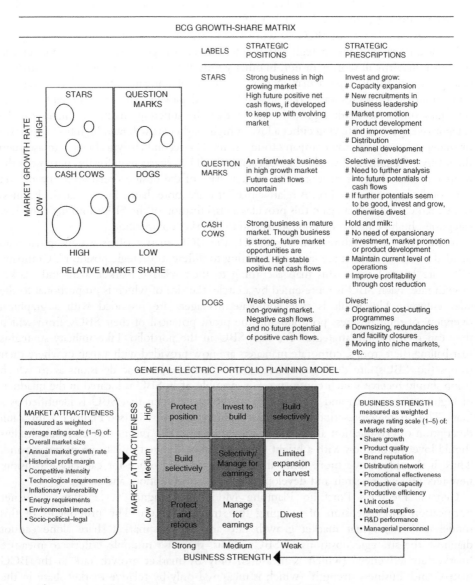

Figure 6.1 Corporate portfolio management: tools of strategic mapping

then prescribe the movement of capital from one SBU to another depending on their strategic positions on the map. In the BCG matrix, these are measured using a single measure (i.e. market growth rate for market attractiveness and relative market share for business strength) while in GE's Portfolio Planning Model they were represented by two 'composite indexes' each constituting many variables. Depending on its position on that map, each SBU is given a label (question mark, star, cash cow, or dog, in the case of the BCG matrix). For each label, there are ready-made 'strategic prescriptions'. Corporate managers' task made simple: use the tool, diagnose the strategic position, and then prescribe the strategy (e.g. invest, divest, selective growth, etc.).

Strategizing the firm 123

6.2.2 Neoliberal implications of portfolio planning models

In technical terms, business portfolio analyses have now grown much beyond these initial analytical models of BCG and GE. Currently Big Data Analytics has taken their place extending the meaning of the data as well as markets. Nevertheless, their basic neoliberal logic remains the same. As we discussed in the previous chapter, neoliberal transformation entails a signification of circulation (vis-à-vis confinement in the disciplinary spaces). It should create centrifugal forces of markets and flexible networks for the circulation of capital. This is exactly what these types of managerial technologies achieved. They transformed the organizational structures into internal capital markets through transforming corporate divisions into SBUs which then must compete within the parameters of corporate planning for corporate capital, in the form of investment and divestment decisions. In other words, the terminology of SBUs and business portfolio planning helped the managers to break up the corporations into circulatable entities that must be circulated from unfavourable positions (e.g. question marks and dogs) on the strategy map to favourable strategic positions (e.g. stars and cash cows). At the core of this managerial act of 'business repositioning' lies the perpetual circulation of capital to optimize future cash flows (i.e. capital accumulation). Strategic decision making within the parameters of the BCG matrix, the GE matrix, and other similar business portfolio assessment tools basically means enhancing the flow of capital between different SBUs, translating them into competing units of capital but within a hierarchical planning structure. A strong SBU operating in an attractive market would absorb capital from weak SBUs operating in non-attractive markets. Hence, portfolio planning models also facilitate capital circulation between different markets and industrial fields, yet achieving it through a visible hand of centralized planning rather than the so-called invisible hand of market forces. Rather than confining and specializing the capital in particular disciplinary spaces for economies of scale, these analytical techniques, therefore, enabled the circulation of capital between different business units as well as industrial fields or markets. This is indeed internalization of what Adam Smith used to call the invisible hand – the markets – into the organizational hierarchies, hence the 'visible hand', according to Chandler (1977).

In management accounting terms, information requirements of business portfolio and industry analysis models, however, extend beyond organizations to industry aggregates and trends. Computations of relative market share, market growth rate, and other indicators used in the GE matrix demand such industry data which are often beyond the domain of conventional internal-oriented management accounting. To attune with these strategic management tools, management accounting then acquires external orientation to collect market and industry information. In the absence of technological and managerial capacities of individual organizations, there emerged a new set of 'epistemic organizations' to cater for the necessity of circulating the strategic information. An early example is the PIMS database which we mentioned in the previous chapter. This is now pretty much manifested in the rapid growth of information platforms, software packages, and information warehouses aiming at Big Data Analytics (see Davenport 2014; Kitchin 2014).

6.3 Strategizing economics: Porter's strategy discourses

Michael Porter's work further extended this reconstruction of economic enterprises into strategic units which need to be 'strategically positioned' within the competitive terrains of market and industry. His contributions are indeed multiple and strongly

124 *Neoliberal trends*

reinforced certain neoliberal transformations that we discussed in the previous chapter (and which we will further elaborate here). Unlike the consultancy agenda associated with the development of corporate portfolio management tools (i.e. the BCG and GE matrices), Porter's contributions were theoretical as well as managerial, a feature that made his theories appealing to both academics and practitioners across many disciplines including economics, management, and accounting.

6.3.1 Structure-conduct-performance model

Porter's contributions revolve around his conceptions of competitive advantage, industry analysis, generic strategies, and value chain analysis. However, before appreciating how they strategize the industrial firms, it is important to briefly discuss a particular industrial economic framework which was popular before Porter. In fact, Porter's contributions started as a revision and extension of this framework in his attempts to link it with the field of business policy. This is the 'structure-conduct-performance framework' (see Figure 6.2 Panel A) initially popularized by industrial economists during the 1950s and 1960s (e.g. Joe S. Bain and Edward S. Mason). This framework asserts that a firm's performance depends critically on the characteristics of the industry environment in which it competes. Their argument was that the industry structure determines the behaviour or conduct of firms, whose joint conduct then determines the collective performance of the firms in the marketplace. Being industrial economists, their attention was not primarily on the notion of strategy but the industry or market efficiency (i.e. efficiency emanating from the firms' *collective* behaviour). They, therefore, defined performance broadly in the economist's sense of social performance, encompassing dimensions such as allocative efficiency (i.e. industry profitability), technical efficiency (i.e. cost minimization), and innovativeness. Industry structure was defined as the relatively stable economic and technical dimensions of an industry that provided the context in which competition occurred. The elements of the industrial structure included barriers to entry, the number and size distribution of firms, product differentiation, and the demand elasticity. Conduct was the firm's choice of key decision variables such as price, production quantities, production capacity, quality, etc. This is indeed the notion of strategy as it was conceptualized at that time.

A crucial aspect of this structure-conduct-performance framework was the view that one could effectively ignore conduct (i.e. strategy) and look directly at industry structure in *explaining* performance. In our current understanding of competitive strategy and business performance this is indeed a highly problematic understanding. However, industrial economists of the 1960s and 1950s held onto this assertion for two reasons, we believe:

1. The focal analytical attention of the industrial economists was not on the managerial problem of strategy or business policy but on explaining the industry or market performance. This means that they were primarily concerned about the structural conditions or characteristics under which allocative efficiency, technical efficiency, and innovativeness would be achieved.
2. This framework assumes a linear deterministic causality between structure, conduct, and performance in that structure determines the conduct and, in return, conduct determines the performance. Here, driven by the neoclassical economic doctrines that offer a superior deterministic power to the market structures, the conduct is simply assumed to be a passive response to the industry conditions (e.g. the firm as a price taker). Hence,

conduct merely reflects the industry condition at the firm's level, organizational management merely being a mediator between the structure and performance. So, after all, for industrial economists of the 1950s and 1960s, what determines performance is not the strategy but the structure. And, for them, what improves the performance is not the strategic or managerial actions at the level of firms but macro-economic policies that reshape the industrial structures, which then dictate the firm's actions.

The neoliberal implications of Porter's work stems from his reversal of this old industrial economic framework. Following some industrial economic studies in the 1970s and 1980s (e.g. Caves 1980; Caves and Murphy 1976; Caves et al. 1980; Comanor and Wilson 1974), and drawing from the theoretical and empirical developments in the field of business policy (e.g. Cyert and March 1963), Porter asserts that firms can, though not always, fundamentally change the structure of their industries through their strategic actions. Porter's emphasis was not on the linear deterministic relationship between the industry structure and the firms' conduct but the interplay between them. As shown in the dotted feedback arrow A in Figure 6.2 (Panel B), he recognizes that past performance affects the strategic options available to firms and, hence, it is not only the industry structure that determines the conduct but also the firm's own performance in the past. Similarly, for example, firms' innovations can enhance or diminish entry and mobility barriers, and thereby alter the industry structure further enhancing the firms' capacity to pursue unique strategies (see undotted feedback arrow B in the Figure 6.2, Panel B). As such, Porter's work started to offer a less structurally deterministic theorization of the firm, while still holding onto the significance of the influences of the industry/market structures. And it offered a certain degree of strategic agency to the corporate managers within the economic discourses, popularizing a new economic mode of 'strategic analysis' of the industrial firm's conduct. This indeed helped to fill the epistemic gap between neoclassical economics and business policy.

This reconceptualization of the interplay between the firm's conduct (i.e. strategy) and the industry structure concentrated on following interrelated concepts and analytical tools, which we will be discussing in the next few subsections:

- The notion of competitive advantage
- Generic strategies

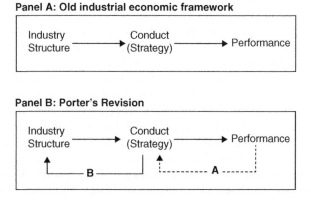

Figure 6.2 Porter's revision of structure-conduct-performance framework

126 *Neoliberal trends*

- The analysis of the competitive structure (five forces framework)
- Value chain analysis
- Competitor analysis (four corners framework).

6.3.2 Competitive advantage: from factor endowment to competitive positioning

In neoclassical economic discourses before Porterian times, theories of absolute advantage, comparative advantage, and factor endowment provided the major explanations as to why certain nations would dominate international trade in certain industries. In Porterian neoliberal discourses, such notions have now been replaced by the notion of competitive advantage. In a broader sense, competitive advantage refers to economic actors' (e.g. firms, nations, etc.) capacity to outperform their competitors for a sustainable period of time. Porter introduced this concept at two distinct but interrelated levels: national and organizational levels. However, for Porter (1990, 33) 'firms, not nations, compete in international markets'. Hence, Porter asserts that, while national factor conditions, demand conditions, and related and supporting industries play certain roles, 'firm strategies, structures and rivalry' play the most central role in determining the nations' competitive advantage. By articulating this centrality of the firms' strategies in the determining nations' competitive advantages, Porter helped create a neoliberal discourse whereby 'strategic management' became a significant epistemic element of the contemporary managerial-economic analyses. This discourse brought the firms' strategies to the forefront of economic analysis of industrial development, global competition, and national competitiveness, and it discursively constructed a hierarchical causality between the global competitiveness of nations and the firms' value creation processes (see Caves et al. 1980; Porter 1985, 1990, 2004). Figure 6.3 illustrates the Porterian epistemic connection between the firms' value creation processes, firms' strategies, and national competitiveness.

At the top of the strategic hierarchy we see the notion of 'competitive advantage of nations' (see Porter 1990). His famous 'diamond model' (the second layer of Figure 6.3) then articulates the factors that determine the competitive advantage of nations. Following the traditional neoclassical economic theories, Porter posits that factor conditions, demand conditions, related and supporting industries indeed play a certain role as mediated by government policy interventions and pure chance. However, departing from traditional economic theories, he stressed the strategic role that the 'firm strategy, structure and rivalry' play in determining nations' competitive advantage. As we have already noted, for him, it is not the nations that compete but the firms. Hence, he argues, it is not the macro-economic policies that primarily determine the competitive advantage of nations but the strategic analyses, decisions, and positioning that the individual firms carry out. By shifting this emphasis onto the firms' strategies, he not only brings the organizational-level managerial analysis to the forefront of the political-economic analyses and policy making but also discursively establishes the neoliberal development logic that it is the well-crafted strategies of the entities of private capital that drive nations' development. As such, the notion of competitive advantage has now become one of the most sought after normativities in economic and managerial discourses. Analyses and strategies are directed towards this normativity of competitive advantage.

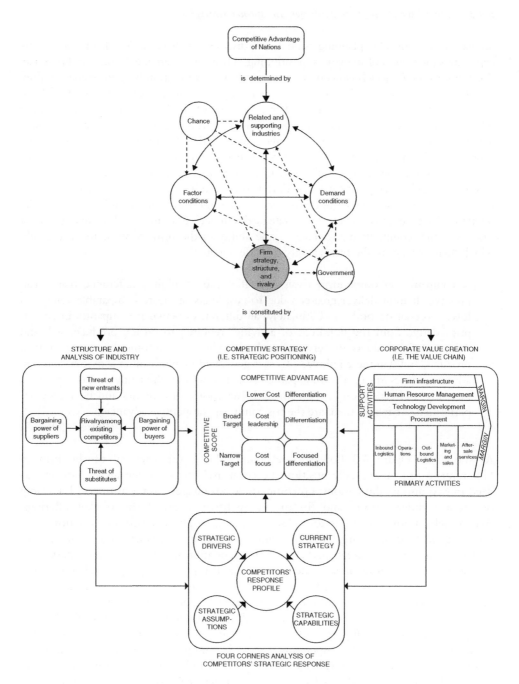

Figure 6.3 Epistemic location of firm strategy within national competitiveness

128   *Neoliberal trends*

6.3.3 Competitive strategy: towards generic market strategies

Similar to the portfolio planning models we discussed in Section 6.2, Porter also conceptualizes the notion of strategy as 'positioning'. However, there is a significant difference. Portfolio planning models concentrate on cash flow maximization by optimizing the flow of capital between SBUs. This is done by mapping the strategic position of each SBU in terms of industry attractiveness and relative strength of the SBU and then determining whether capital should be pumped into or withdrawn from a given SBU. Strategic choices are therefore mainly determining the investment or divestment strategies based on the 'strategic position' of the SBU on a strategic map conceptualized in terms of positional attractiveness and the strength of the SBU holding that position. As such, for portfolio planning models, strategy is financial. Porter, on the other hand, provides a much more nuanced market/customer/competition-driven definition of strategy and emphasizes the operational activities that can create a 'strategic difference'. For him the ultimate criterion of strategy is the 'competitive advantage' – the ability of the firm to outperform its rivals, which then stems from the firm's ability to 'differentiate':

> A company can outperform rivals only if it can establish a difference that it can preserve. It must deliver greater value to customers or create comparable value at a lower cost, or do both … Ultimately, all differences between companies in cost or price derive from the hundreds of activities required to create, produce, sell, and deliver their products or services, such as calling on customers, assembling final products, and training employees. Cost is generated by performing activities, and cost advantage arises from performing particular activities more efficiently than competitors. Similarly, differentiation arises from both the choice of activities and how they are performed. Activities, then, are the basic units of competitive advantage.
>
> (Porter 1996, 62)

As shown in Figure 6.3 (lower panel middle box), this capacity of the firm to 'differentiate' and strategically position the company's market offerings are conceptualized in two distinct dimensions: (a) competitive advantages arising from cost leadership or product differentiation and (b) the competitive scope of the market offerings. Accordingly, Porter identifies four distinct strategic options available to a firm: cost leadership in a broader target market, differentiation in a broader target market, cost leadership in a narrow target market, and differentiation in a narrow target market. In this sense, strategy now means the specific market positioning approaches that the companies would follow in order to achieve a sustainable competitive advantage. It involves demonstrating to a carefully chosen market segment (either narrow or broader) that the company's products are superior to those of their rivals in terms of either the cost or the product quality or both. The strategic choices so made would drive the companies to streamline their operational activities and processes so that the companies can sustain the lower cost advantage or the product differentiation advantage they are seeking. This means that Porter has initiated a particular managerial discourse in which the notion of strategy has now been connected with the firms' capacity to be efficient, effective, and innovative – something much more nuanced than the investment and divestment perspectives promoted by the portfolio planning models. This reinvention of strategic discourses has popularized three distinct but interrelated managerial analyses, which we will be discussing in the next section.

6.3.4 Strategic analyses

In a broader sense, strategic analysis refers to the managerial task of evaluating the internal and external factors that determine the company's strategic choices. Traditionally, SWOT (strengths, weaknesses, opportunities and threats) and PEST analyses (political, economic, social and technological) have been popular tools in this regard. While PEST analysis is exclusively an external environmental analysis, the SWOT analysis pays attention to both internal (i.e. strengths and weaknesses) and external (i.e. opportunities and threats) factors. In either case, the analytical aim is to match the company's strengths and weaknesses with the opportunities and threats stemming from the external environmental dynamics. Porter provides an analytical twist to this traditional mode of analysing the strategic conditions. He asserts that the strategic choices should stem from two types of analyses: industry/competition analysis (i.e. external) and value chain analysis (i.e. internal), enabling the companies to analyse and improve the internal processes and activities in the light of structural forces that determine the industry attractiveness.

Industry analysis: Akin to the portfolio planning models we discussed earlier, Porter asserts that 'the first fundamental determinant of a firm's profitability [and hence strategic choices] is industry attractiveness', and industry attractiveness is determined by five competitive forces: bargaining power of buyers, bargaining power of suppliers, threat of new entry, threat of substitutes, and rivalry among existing firms (see Figure 6.3 middle left-hand corner box). Porter's argument is that the collective strength of these five forces determines the rules of the competition that in turn determine the ability of a firm to earn an abnormal economic rate of return (i.e. a rate of return over and above the cost of capital). Hence, the ultimate aim of competitive strategy is to cope with and, ideally, to change those rules in the firm's favour (Porter 2008, 4). Porter's analysis here is not fundamentally or principally different from the portfolio planning models we discussed earlier. Both assert that competitive strategy must stem from an analysis of 'industry attractiveness' and the opportunities and threats imposed upon the firm by its external environment. For both approaches, strategic choices should lead to positioning the firm in markets/industries where it is possible and meaningful to gain a competitive advantage in the long run. However, Porter provides a more refined model of competitive structure that can accommodate many analytical variables under the five major headings of competitive forces. According to Porter, identification, classification, and analysis of such variables under these five broader headings should enable the strategic managers to identify:

- whether the industry structure necessitates and favours a cost leadership or product differentiation strategy and
- whether the firm should adopt a narrow or broader focus in offering either cost leadership or product differentiation.

Such decisions should stem from the way in which the firms are positioned in relation to those five competitive forces. However, it should also be noted that the firms are not conceived as mere passive actors (e.g. price takers) responding to pre-given competitive structure. Instead, Porter asserts that firms can indeed influence and alter the competitive structure in their favour through appropriate strategic choices and techno-managerial innovations. And the potential for such innovations then relates the strategy to internal processes or the value chain of the firm.

130   *Neoliberal trends*

Value chain analysis: Yet again, akin to other analytical models in the field of business policy, Porter identifies the second determinant of the strategic choices as the 'relative strength/weaknesses' of the business. In portfolio planning models, this is by and large conceptualized through the 'relative market share' and other similar variables that measure the market presence of the firm (see the BCG matrix in Figure 6.1). In that sense, these models pay little attention to the way in which the firm has organized its internal systems and processes. For Porter, however, the firm's capacity to follow a particular strategic posture to gain a competitive advantage stems not only from the imperatives of the competitive structure but also from the way in which business has organized its internal activities, processes, and their connections with the suppliers and buyers. This is the concept of 'value chain', which is depicted in the middle panel right-hand corner box of Figure 6.3. In this sense, a value chain analysis is imperative in choosing and implementing the appropriate strategic choices between differentiation and cost leadership.

In contrast to the traditional mode of internal analysis (i.e. analysing strength and weaknesses), which simply offers a 'resource-based' perspective on the company, the value chain analysis demands a 'process' perspective. This process perspective demands the managers reconceptualize their internal processes and activities in terms of their efficacy, efficiency, and effectiveness in delivering 'value to the customer' and, thereby, their capacity to create profits. This value needs to be understood in terms of the two fundamental strategic imperatives that Porter emphasizes: differentiation and cost leadership. In line with these strategic imperatives, then the analytical question is not so much as to whether the firm is strong or weak in terms of its resource (i.e. factor) endowments but whether the individual processes and activities that constitute the firm's value chain can deliver the intended strategic imperative – differentiation and cost leadership – better than its competitors do. In analytical terms this involves:

1. Conceptualizing firm activities in line with Porter's conceptual framework of value chain. This means that the firm's operations are classified into primary activities (i.e. inbound logistics, operations, outbound logistics, marketing and sales, and after-sales services) or support activities (e.g. procurement, technology development, etc.).
2. Analysing their criticalness in delivering the intended strategic imperatives: cost leadership and differentiation as well as their importance to other strategic parameters such as company mission and vision.
3. Assessing their efficiency and effectiveness in terms of various key performance indicators (KPIs) including various operational cost calculations.

Porter's writings indeed only provide a broader conceptual understanding of these analytical elements. They do not of course provide a clear set of calculative tools or procedures for doing these analytical tasks. Nevertheless, his conceptualization of the firm as a value chain and his emphasis on the importance of analysing and costing the activities in the value chain in determining the strategic choices, paved the way to significant managerial innovations in this neoliberal time, especially ABC and BSC (see Chapters 7 and 9).

Four corner analysis: This is Porter's third analytical model, which he proposed as a model of assessing what the competitor's strategies are likely to be in the medium-term future. Indeed, one can think of this model as a refined analysis of the competition. In contrast to the generic assessment of the competitive structure in the above-mentioned five forces model, it provides a much narrower and more focused analysis of the competitors' possible strategic actions in the medium-term future. Its explicit aim is to develop what Porter calls the 'competitor's response profile', which includes an assessment of four interrelated strategic elements underlying the competitor's future strategy (see Figure 6.3 bottom panel):

1. Strategic drivers – what drives the competitor? This includes an assessment of factors such as financial and non-financial goals; vision, mission and business philosophy; top management team and leadership; corporate culture; organizational structure; external and internal constraints.
2. Strategic assumptions held about itself and the industry – this dimension would include the competitor's perception of its strengths and weaknesses; cultural and value systems; perceived industry forces, etc.
3. Current strategy – what is the competitor currently doing and how is it currently competing? This dimension includes an assessment of the competitor's market positioning strategies (e.g. whether cost leadership or differentiation), its market scope, how it creates value, where it invests, and the relationships and networks the competitor has developed.
4. Capabilities – this includes an assessment of the strength and weaknesses of the competitor in terms of, for example, marketing skills, product and service quality, skills and training levels of the workforce, patents and copyrights, financial strength, leadership qualities of top management, etc.

According to Porter, an assessment of these 'four corners' should build the 'competitor's response profile' which answers the following questions (see Porter 2004, 49):

- Is the competitor satisfied with its current position?
- What likely moves or strategy shifts will the competitor make?
- Where is the competitor vulnerable?
- What will provoke the greatest and most effective retaliation by the competitor?

6.4 Biopolitics of Porterian strategy discourses

In the previous sections, we introduced the mainstream strategy discourses that have taken place since the late 1980s. There our attention was on the techno-managerial and economic elements that such discourses popularized. Now in this section, we aim to provide a biopolitical analysis and interpretation of these discourses. In doing so, we first need to look at some of the Foucauldian biopolitical themes we discussed in the previous chapters, especially in Chapters 1 and 5. As we discussed there, biopolitics involves the continuous reinvention of pathological issues at the level of macro categories such as population and economy, and then connecting them to anatomico politics at micro-organizational and cognitive levels. In other words, biopolitical accounting involves constructing the collective social bodies of population and economy as accounting entities. To this end, biopolitics invents 'technologies of regulation'. Population becomes a distinct social body through such technologies of regulation – biopolitical accounts, statistics, and narratives. Population and economy are accounted for as a political problem, as a problem that is at once scientific and political, as a social body that is at once present as a biological problem and a problem of power (see Foucault 2003, 245). Collectively, they create a numerical profile and a political narrative of the population and economy. They profile and narrate such macro entities as population, economy, and nation in terms of its pathological traits such as health, wealth, and literacy. It is the management of these pathological traits which then become the focus of regulation and management.

132   *Neoliberal trends*

6.4.1 Competitiveness as a biopolitical problem

In the early 1980s, strategic management discourses began with exactly such a problematization. In order to propagate themselves as solutions, Porterian and other strategic management discourses problematized the economy in a particular way. On the Anglo-American front in particular, a series of attempts to bring a new 'pathological problem' to the forefront of political discourse was started, which debated the lack or loss of competitiveness of the US and European economies. Perhaps more than health, poverty, education, welfare, and so on, the notion of competitiveness was reconstructed as one of the most significant political problems of our times. Competitiveness is accounted for as a political problem, as a problem that is at once scientific and political, as a pathological trait of the social body that at once presents as a biological problem and a problem of power (cf. Foucault 2003, 245). Most importantly, Porter and other Harvard academics have reconstructed the 'The Looming Challenge of Competitiveness' as the most important political criteria against which many other social and political elements of our societies should now be judged. In other words, the political efficacy of things like tax, education, democracy, employment rights and contracts, trade unions, political-administration and much more needs to be judged on the basis of their contribution to the global competitiveness of the nation's multinational firms. For example, Porter (2013), in his testimony to the US House of Representatives, argues that the 'challenge is competitiveness, not jobs per se'.

This message is often repeated and reemphasized, for example, in Harvard Business School's US Competitiveness project surveys. This project was initiated in 2011 and surveys Harvard Business School alumni and others to solicit views about the state of US competitiveness, 'as a multi-year, fact-based effort to understand the disappointing performance of the American economy, its causes, and steps needed by business and government' (Porter et al. 2016, 2). For example, in their 2016 survey, Porter et al. (2016, 2) argue that:

> U.S. competitiveness has been eroding since well before the Great Recession. America's economic challenges are structural, not cyclical. The weak recovery reflects the erosion of competitiveness, as well as the inability to take the steps necessary to address growing U.S. weaknesses ... Our failure to make progress reflects an unrealistic and ineffective national discourse on the reality of the challenges facing the U.S. economy and the steps needed to restore shared prosperity. Business has too often failed to play its part in recent decades, and a flawed U.S. political system has led to an absence of progress in government, especially in Washington.

The point here is not whether US competitiveness (or any other country for that matter) is actually eroding or not (which may or may not be the case), but the way in which a particular set of discourses constructs the 'competitiveness' as the greatest problem of this neoliberal time and the way in which strategic management is discursively articulated as the ultimate solution for the socio-economic and political problems of our times. As such, strategic management is propagated as a managerial technology not only for profit-seeking business enterprises but also for all the other socio-economic political entities including public-sector organizations, charities, and NGOs. In either case, competitiveness has been a central normative pillar upon which strategic management is legitimated as a valid and necessary body of knowledge. Disciplinary technologies and institutions exist to cure social

Strategizing the firm   133

ills. In a similar vein, medicine exists to cure ill-health, education for illiteracy, and jurisdiction for criminality. Now strategic management and other related fields such as management accounting have come to being a cure for a new pathological trait: the lack of competitiveness.

6.4.2 Epistemological politics of competitiveness

This construction of competitiveness as a biopolitical problem and strategic management as its solution involves epistemological politics. Here, in the context of discourses of competitiveness and strategy, by the term epistemological politics what we mean is the particular set of epistemic practices and institutions through which this biopolitical problematization is achieved. This invariably involves processes and institutions through which supposedly managerial and economic phenomena such as competitiveness and strategy are translated into normative and ideological elements within the realm of politics. And this also involves the politics through which supposedly 'non-political actors' such as management gurus, management professors, and management consultants have all gained an increasingly important role in the running of the state in the form of a 'shadow government' and 'consultocracy' (see Kantola and Seeck 2011; Saint-Martin 2000). Kantola and Seeck (2011, 26) explain the political implications involved in this biopoliticalization of competitiveness:

> In liberal market democracies, politics is a field of democratic and civic participation, discussion, disagreement and conflict ... However, management ideas, on the contrary, often suggest that there is one best practice for political problems and tend to play down opinionated political discussion and conflicts and replace them with a carefully packaged management scheme, which is presented as unquestionable expert knowledge. This worry has become all the more pervasive as the growing importance of management practices in the running of the state has been paralleled by a growing sense of politics as something that is opposite to management; something negative or even harmful.

In this sense, biopoliticalization involves a redefinition of political ideologies and thought processes in line with the evolving neoliberal market logic of governance and regulation where the competitiveness, both at macro national level and micro-organizational and personal levels, should be the defining criteria of social and political opportunities for the people. Distribution of resources, opportunities, and welfare are all to be determined by the competitiveness that the different social bodies (such as nations, industries, firms, and individuals) have factorized and embedded; being strategic is the way to make sure that such entities develop competitiveness. For us, this process of biopoliticalization, especially in relation to Porterian strategy discourses, involves following 'paradoxical' epistemic processes:

1. **Connecting macro with micro**: Porterian discourses of competitiveness and strategy is a well-packaged management scheme. Its capacity to penetrate into the realm of politics and to convert the 'non-political' into a disguised form of politics stems from the way in which it relates the notion of competitiveness and strategy to the macro-political and micro-organizational simultaneously. In Figure 6.3, we have already illustrated the way in which it conceptualizes the macro-micro

134 *Neoliberal trends*

connection. As explained there, at the macro-political level, in his theory of 'competitive advantage of a nation', Porter locates the notion of competitiveness and strategy in the realm of national politics. However, it should be noted that, even before Porter, competitiveness was one of the key parameters of economic development where attention has been on the factors affecting a given country's competitiveness. There were some classical economic theories in this regard (e.g. Ricardo's classical theory of competitive advantage and the Heckser-Olin Model). In the late 1970s, these classical models were challenged by Schumpeterian technology-driven competitiveness models (see Schumpeter 1934, 1947). Porter's innovation was that he combined the Schumpeterian technology driven model of competitiveness with the competitive analyses in strategic management to develop his diamond theory of competitiveness. This then connected to the micro-organizational level through industry analysis, value chain analysis, generic strategies, and competitor analysis at the level of individual market segments. This created a cascading causality between the macro and micro reinforcing the neoliberal political ideology that it is firms' competitiveness and strategic choices that would ultimately drive the competitiveness of the nation. Hence, for Porterians, there should be minimum political intervention by the state, and any intervention or regulation is permissible only to the extent that it enhances firms' competitiveness. This is because, for Porterians, it is firms not nations that compete; hence, by implication, they assert that politics is the opposite of management; something negative or even harmful.

2. **Using business elite as opinion leaders**: It seems that, for Porter and others, it is the business leaders' opinions which matter the most, and hence often, for justification and substantiation of their ideologies and policy recommendations, Porterians draw on these opinions. Here, Harvard Business School-led surveys (especially of Harvard Business School alumni) play a key role as the primary epistemic device in justifying and legitimating the competitiveness initiatives that Porterians propose. The political negativity we mentioned earlier is justified in that manner by drawing on the opinions of the business elites including Harvard alumni. For example, in proposing an 'economic strategy for Washington', Porter et al. (2016, 5) explain that:

> A large majority of HBS alumni believe the political system is obstructing U.S. economic growth and competitiveness. Many alumni who self-identified as Democrat or Republican blame the other party, but a sizable proportion also hold their own party responsible ... Overall, we believe that dysfunction in America's political system is now the single most important challenge to U.S. economic progress.

Inter alia, this political negativity is attributed to political states' unwillingness or inability to reform the US tax system in support of a lower corporate tax rate. So, Porter et al. (2016, 4–5) goes on to say:

> The top corporate tax problems, according to the surveyed business leaders, are the high corporate tax rate and the taxation of international income. Business leaders report overwhelming and bipartisan support (over 95%) for corporate tax reform. Consensus corporate tax reforms include reducing the statutory rate

Strategizing the firm 135

by at least 10 percentage points, moving to a territorial tax regime, and limiting the tax-free treatment of pass-through entities for business income. The transition to a territorial regime should be complete, not half-hearted via the inclusion of an alternative minimum tax on foreign income.

What we see in Porterian writings (and many other Harvard Business School writings) is the way in which business leaders are promoted as champions and opinion leaders of not only economic development but also democracy and social welfare. This is done by promoting the assertion that it is the businesses' leadership which would ultimately drive progressive social changes. Thereby, Porterian discourses of competitiveness and strategy create a particular knowledge-power regime in which (a) political processes and institutions are discredited as inefficient, out of date, and out of touch, and (b) business leaders are discursively reconstructed as anti-political figures but having a superior epistemic capacity and credibility than political leaders. Hence, they assert, we just need to follow what top corporate managers, especially Harvard Business School alumni, think about what is best for themselves, under the assertion that what is good for them is necessarily good for the public and nations.

3. **Consultocracy**: As we discussed in Chapter 1 of this book, before the neoliberal turn, the prototypical business enterprise was an industrial firm structured by and largely managed by a functionally differentiated bureaucracy. Managerial prerogatives and decision-making processes were structured on the basis of functional specialization and expertise. Hence, social, symbolic, cognitive-intellectual and emotional capital associated with deciding the way in which the firms should be governed and managed were by and large attributed to the 'expertise' of the functional managers which they had accumulated through the long association with the processes, systems, and institutions internal to the organization. Seeking the help from external advisors and consultants was quite rare and only sought in emergency or crisis situations. Much like doctors to whom they were compared (see Mckenna 2006, 330–331), external experts were called upon to care for 'sick firms' (Edersheim 2004, 204). Consultants of course played only a marginal role as hiring them signified 'bad' management and was not made public to protect the firm's reputation. Furthermore, compared to other specialists of corporate management, consultants were ranked low in status (Kipping 2011; Schmidt-Wellenburgh 2013).

However, since the 1980s, this has changed. Management consultancy has emerged as a very powerful epistemic force and an industry in its own right. The term 'consultocracy' manifests its significance in contemporary society. In its very generic meaning (vis-à-vis bureaucracy), it refers to the emergence of big consulting firms and their presence and influence in the strategic policy and operational decisions in private-sector companies as well as in public-sector and non-government organizations. Consultocracy has indeed become an institutional apparatus through which bureaucratic management becomes amenable to outside advice on a regular basis. Management consultancy has now become an indispensable part of the governance of the firm and the production of management knowledge and, as Schmidt-Wellenburgh (2013, 33) argues, it is a key *dispositif*[2] that creates and maintains the conditions under which firms can be managed along the lines of neoliberal ideals. As early as 1991, a United Nations (1993) survey on management consultancy estimated that the total world market on management consultancy was $25.3 billion (of which $6.4 billion was held by the big six at that time: Andersen

136 *Neoliberal trends*

Consulting, McKinsey & Co., Coopers & Lybrand, Mercer Consulting Group, Ernst & Young, and KPMG Peat Marwick). This stake of consultancy in the global market has grown even further in the recent past, concentrating most of the market share in the big four now, after a series of mergers and acquisitions. According to Consultancy.UK estimates (http://www.consultancy.uk/consulting-industry/global), the market size had grown to $251 billion by 2016. Of this, strategy consulting, operations consulting, and financial advisory collectively constitute $172 billion.

The development of consultocracy and the strategic turn in management are interlocking and reinforcing. Strategy discourses made the organizations amenable to external scrutiny and assessment. They provided the epistemic impetuses through which existing bureaucratic organizational forms were subjected to relentless critique. Porterian discourses of competitiveness, for example, provided the opportunity for external experts (mainly consultants and business school gurus) to create a narrative as to how the European and US businesses have lost their competitive advantages to especially Japanese and other East Asian companies. As we mentioned in the previous section, this narrative has brought a new biopolitical problem – losing competitiveness – a new 'epidemic' for which corporations should now seek external expert advice. Understanding strategic imperatives, diagnosing strategic issues, competitive analysis, defining corporate vision and missions, determining competitive strategies, and so on have emerged as new managerial themes that corporate managers can understand but with appropriate external consulting, training, and business school qualifications (especially executive MBAs).

These Porterian discourses are equally supplemented by another stream of strategic discourses which we call Peterian discourses of learning organizations: that is, discourses that began with Peters and Waterman's *In Search of Excellence* (Peters and Waterman 1982) and further expanded by Peter Senge's *Learning Organisation* (Senge 1990). While Porterian strategy discourses were by and large concentrated on market positioning, discourses of learning organizations (and other similar discourses on lean manufacturing and the lean firm) concentrated mainly on the internal reconfiguration of Western economic enterprises to enhance flexibility, innovativeness, and organizational learning. Here again this new strategic wisdom for change is to be gained from the new epistemic affiliations between business school professors and consulting firms. Collectively, these strategy discourses create a corporate mentality that they should create and maintain a sound affiliation with management gurus and consulting firms as a 'strategic necessity'.

'Action research' is one of the key epistemic practices through which this affiliation is built and maintained. The term action research is rather misleading and can connote so many different things in different fields (see Coghlan and Shani 2016). What we meant by 'action research' here in this discussion is the particular epistemic practice that especially US business school academics initiated in association with their consultancy projects (e.g. Argyris and Schön 1974, 1978). The notion of action research so developed, in a way, is an academic justification of university professors engaging in consultancy (vis-à-vis scientific research). On the other hand, they quickly grew into an 'acceptable' element of the 'practicist epistemology' (see Chapter 3) through which consulting university professors could develop some normative and positive theories about the way in which corporate managers make (or should make) operational and strategic decisions. Action research indeed operated as a mode of codification of practical experience and insight that the consulting professors gained through their consulting projects so that others in the corporate and academic worlds could learn from their 'intimate relations' with the corporations. *Harvard Business Review* articles and Harvard style case studies are the examples par excellence in this regard. They try to simulate real-world managerial problems so that students of executive MBAs and other corporate training programmes can reproduce management decision-making forums within the classroom. In this way they act as the tangible epistemic artefacts of the affiliation between the consulting professors, consulting firms, and corporations. Besides the money involved, they provide an 'epistemic reason' and forum for this neoliberal connection between academia, consulting firms, and corporations.

6.5 Summary and conclusions

This chapter discussed the first element of strategizing the firm: competitive positioning. This involves, first of all, reconceptualizing the organizational environment, especially its market and industry context, as a 'strategic terrain' – a terrain in which the firm and its sub-units need to be 'positioned' in terms of their relative strengths and weaknesses, on the one hand, and the attractiveness of the firm's location, on the other. Initially, this is achieved through portfolio planning models that consultancy firms popularized, notably the BCG Matrix and the GE Portfolio Planning Model. These models provide a strategic map of the competitive terrain in terms of attractiveness of the particular location or industry in which the firm operates and the relative strengths and weaknesses of the firm (or its sub-units). SBUs are given specific labels on the basis of their location on the map. Then such location/labelling are assigned a particular strategic prescription such as 'invest and grow', 'hold and milk', etc. In the light of such mapping techniques and strategic prescriptions, strategy making involves visualizing the corporation as a collection of competing SBUs and allocating resources between them in order to maximize the corporation's long-term cash flow. Neoliberal implications of these models is that they construct an intra-organizational managerial space (or an internal market for capital) to facilitate the circulation of capital between different markets and industrial fields. They achieve this through the visible hand of centralized planning rather than the invisible hand of market forces. Rather than confining and specializing the capital in particular disciplinary spaces for economies of scale, these analytical techniques enable the circulation of capital between different business units as well as industrial fields or markets. This is indeed the internalization of what Adam Smith used to call the invisible hand – the markets – in the organizational hierarchies, hence the 'visible hand', according to Chandler (1977).

Michael Porter's work further extends this reconstruction of the economic enterprise into strategic units, which need to be 'strategically positioned' within competitive terrains of market and industry. He provides an overarching framework in which the competitive advantage of a nation is discursively connected with the market positioning decisions that the individual firms make. His reconceptualization of industrial economics begins with revising the structure-conduct-performance model to emphasize the agential capacity of the individual firms. Porter asserts that firms can, though not always, fundamentally change the structure of their industries through their strategic actions: past performance affects the strategic options available to firms and, hence, it is not only the industry structure that determines the conduct but also the firm's own performance in the past. As such, the notion of strategy starts to gain an epistemic significance not only in business policy literature but also in economics.

138   *Neoliberal trends*

Central to Porterian discourses of strategy is the notion of competitive advantage – the capacity of the strategic unit (i.e. the firm or the nation) to outperform its competitors. The notion of competitive advantage is simultaneously related to both the nation and the firm, making a managerial and policy connection between the two. Porter's diamond model outlines the factors that determine the competitive advantage of a nation where, inter alia, 'firm strategy, structure, and rivalry' play a determining role in the nation's competitive advantage.

In comparison to portfolio planning models populated by BCG and GE, Porter provides a much more nuanced market/customer/competition driven definition of strategy and emphasizes the operational activities that can create a 'strategic difference' through either cost leadership or 'product differentiation' in either a broad or narrow market scope. This conception of strategy has popularized three distinct but interrelated managerial analyses. First, Porter's five forces model of the industry provides a framework to assess the attractiveness of the industry in which the firm operates. The attractiveness is determined by the rivalry among existing firms, the threat of new entrants, the threat of substitutes, the bargaining power of the buyers, and the bargaining power of the suppliers. Second, is the value chain analysis, which analyses the internal organizational factors with a view to ascertaining the distinct organizational features that would support the product differentiation or cost leadership. Third, is the four corner analysis aimed at assessing what the competitors' strategies are likely to be (or competitors' response profile) in the medium-term future.

Biopolitical implications of Porterian discourses of strategy were discussed in this chapter in terms of (a) the way in which they construct competitiveness as one of the key biopolitical problems in our time and (b) epistemological politics involved in that biopolitical construction. In relation to the construction of competitiveness as a biopolitical problem, strategic management discourses problematized the economy in a particular way, bringing the loss of competitiveness of the US and European economies to the political forefront as a problem that is at once scientific and political, as a pathological trait of the social body that at once presents as a biological problem and a problem of power (cf. Foucault 2003, 245). Most importantly, Porter and other Harvard academics have been able to reconstruct the 'The Looming Challenge of Competitiveness' as the most important political criteria against which many other social and political elements of our societies should now be judged. In relation to epistemological politics involved in this biopolitical construction, we emphasized three interlocking processes: connecting macro with micro; using business elites as opinion leaders; and consultocracy.

Assignments

These assignments are meant to extend your knowledge beyond what you understand from this chapter. These are not simply revision questions. The content covered in this chapter is necessary but will not be sufficient in attempting these tasks. Therefore, you are required to do some extra reading in attempting these tasks.

1. **Thematic essay:**
    'Strategy discourses have had a far-reaching impact on the way we manage not only micro-economic enterprises but also nations'.
    Discuss this statement with reference to the transition of governmentality from disciplinary confinement to biopolitical circulation.

2. **Poster:**
   Draw a poster illustrating how Porterian discourses of strategy change our conception of markets, corporate management, and national development.
3. **Presentation:**
   Prepare a set of PowerPoint slides, together with notes if necessary, for a 30-minute presentation on the following theme:
   'The neoliberal re-conception of industrial economics offers ontological and epistemological supremacy to the firm over the macro structures that conventionally draw the focal attention of industrial policy'.
4. **Extended bibliography:**
   Write an extended bibliography on the development of the concept of strategy as a positioning factor. For this, you need to do a literature survey of major accounting journals and edited books where critical accounting research is published. Organize the bibliography into a table in the following format.

Bibliographic info	Nature of the paper/book chapter (e.g. conceptual/ theoretical, empirical, a response to a previous publication)	Major arguments, conclusions, and contributions

5. **Literature review:**
   Suppose you are writing a thesis/dissertation on strategic management accounting. You intend to review the accounting and management literature in order to understand different approaches and perspectives on the concept of strategy and the strategy-making process. You are also thinking of the possibility of using 'biopolitics' as a theoretical framework to illustrate that recent developments in the field of strategy manifest a shift from a liberal to a neoliberal governance of firms and nations.

   You are required to do the necessary literature survey and write a chapter circa 5,000 words. You should search the academic journal databases for recent management and accounting literature on strategy as well as critical political assessments of the recent trends in management and accounting (e.g. Munro 2012).

Notes

1 Jerome McCarthy, in his 1960 marketing classic, *Basic Marketing: A Managerial Approach* first introduced the notion of the 4Ps (i.e. product, place or distribution, price, and promotion) as the four key competitive variables that marketers need to decide on in positioning their market offerings tactically.
2 The term *dispositif* is used here in a Foucauldian sense to mean 'a heterogeneous ensemble consisting of discourses, institutions, architectural forms, regulatory decisions, laws, administrative measures scientific statements, philosophical, moral and philanthropic propositions – in short, the said as much as the unsaid' (Foucault 1980, 194).

7 Strategizing the firm

Strategic discourses of organizational reconfiguration

7.1 Introduction

In the previous chapter, we mentioned that strategizing the firm includes changes to three interrelated and interlocking aspects: the strategic reinvention of the markets, organizational forms, and the production process (i.e. the factory). We explained how strategic discourses pertaining to portfolio planning (e.g. BCG's and GE's corporate planning models) and strategic positioning (i.e. Porterian strategy discourses) reinvented management thought as positioning the organization in the newly reinvented competitive terrains of market and industry. A new 'strategic rationality' was thereby invented to constitute: the notion of competitive advantage as the strategic normativity both in micro-organizational realms of management and macro-political realms of national policy planning; strategic analysis of competitiveness with a particular set of strategic tools (e.g. BCG's and GE's corporate planning models, Porter's five forces model of industry analysis and five corner analysis, Porter's diamond model of national competitiveness, the national competitiveness survey, and cluster analysis); and a particular set of managerial prescriptions to suit possible strategic scenarios that such strategic tools would reveal. Now in this chapter, we turn to the second theme – strategic reinvention of organizational forms. So, our focus here is the way in which the structural, relational, and processual elements of the firm are reinvented in the neoliberal managerial discourses.

The chapter is organized as follows:

1. Section 7.2 deals with *post-bureaucratic discourses*. Our attention here is particularly on various management discourses that are aimed at reinventing bureaucracy into a more efficient, flexible, and humanized system of control. Three important developments will be discussed. First (Section 7.2.1) is the job redesign movement which aimed to reinvent elements of 'scientific management' but with an appropriate balance between the technical efficiency imperatives of bureaucracy and the motivational imperatives of the human system. The second (Section 7.2.2) is the movement of management by objectives (MBO) of which the main concern is to enhance employee participation in the decision-making processes. The third (Section 7.3.3) is the discourse on post-bureaucratic ideal types or 'interactive types' (Heckscher 2012), which result from the attempts to implement Japanese management practices and ideologies in the West.

2. Section 7.3 concentrates on *postmodern discourses*. While the post-bureaucratic discourses are by and large concentrating on the intra-organizational dynamics of reinventing the firm, postmodern discourses take your attention to the wider

cultural-political, economic, and technological transformations taking place within and beyond the organizational realms and how they are manifested within organizational practices and relations. While the post-bureaucratic discourses are rather techno-managerial, the postmodern explanations are sociological. We deal with these postmodern explanations under four main themes: signification of simulacra and the movement from production to reproduction (Section 7.3.1); the entrepreneurialization of labour (Section 7.3.2); the immaterialization of labour (Section 7.3.3); the 'management by themes' (Section 7.2.4). These are social theory-based explanations of recent organizational and managerial changes which we broadly call neoliberal.

3. Section 7.4 concentrates more specifically on the transformations taking place in *performance management systems*, especially Kaplan and his colleagues' influences in this area. Here we explain the critiques that Kaplan and others have levelled against the traditional performance management systems (PMS), the key features of their proposed strategic performance management system (SPMS) – BSC, and how the BSC promotes and consolidates a particular managerial ideology that privileges shareholder wealth maximization by aligning other non-financial performance dimensions with it.

4. Finally, in Section 7.5, the chapter concludes with a summary.

7.2 Post-bureaucratic discourses: reinventing bureaucracy

The Japanese penetration and domination in the US and European markets created a 'cultural turn' in management. While Michael Porter and others emphasized the importance of 'strategic positioning' in the market, many other management gurus and consultants (e.g. Drucker 2011 [1977]; Peters and Waterman 1982; Senge 1990; Simons 1995) turn their attention to the cultural, leadership, and structural properties of Western corporations in order to understand why Western firms are losing competitiveness vis-à-vis their Japanese counterparts. Japanese success has often been perceived as 'cultural' and hence a 'cultural reform' within Western economic enterprises was sought. For them, the cultural and structural reconfiguration of the firm was as important as market positioning, because, after all, a firm's capacity to follow a particular strategy depends on its structural and cultural conditions. Hence, following Chandler's (1963) industrial economic argument, many argued that structure should follow the strategy. The result was the gradual emergence of what some scholars now call 'post-bureaucratic' (e.g. Heckscher 2012), 'postmodern organizational forms' (see Chia 1995; Featherstone 1988; Lyotard 1984), or 'post-mechanistic organizational forms' (Wickramasinghe and Alawattage 2007). The initial phase of this post-bureaucratic evolution started with a managerial and political critique of bureaucracy.

In Chapter 2, we discussed the emergence and growth of bureaucracy as the organizational apparatus of modernity. There we explained how bureaucracy encapsulated modernity in terms of: the disciplinary logic of compartmentalization and confining bodies in specific time-space localities for surveillance; the structural logic of specialization and division of work; the democratic logic of social mobility through meritocracy; and the economic logic of enhancing the efficiency with which economic activities are coordinated (see Chapter 2, Sections 2.4.1–2.4.4). For centuries, bureaucracy indeed provided the institutional apparatuses for the micro-organizational realization of liberal ideologies of modernity and accumulative imperatives of capitalism.

142   *Neoliberal trends*

However, since the late 1970s, management gurus and corporate leaders have started to question whether impersonal, rational-legal hierarchies were still the most appropriate organizational form, especially within the context of globalization and ever increasing competition.

Initially, this critique emerged as a problem of motivation, job satisfaction, and flexibility. Bureaucracy sought to improve organizational efficiency and efficacy through: dividing activities into specialized roles (i.e. specialization); laying down standard rules and procedures and the routinization of work (i.e. standardization); explaining processes in written instructions and procedures (i.e. formalization); placing decision-making authority at the top (i.e. centralization); and shaping organizational roles through chain of command, span of control, and specialized supporting functions (i.e. configuration) (see Pugh 1997, 18). Although these elements of bureaucracy improved the predictability and regularity of organizational activities, processes, and systems, they resulted in a great degree of job dissatisfaction among middle and lower level management, especially in relation to them being mere technocrats enjoying little power in decision making. During the 1960s and 1970s, there was a quite wide array of management research highlighting this managerial dissatisfaction. Boltanski and Chiapello (2007, 64), for example, cited Aumont (1963) and Bloch-Laine (1963) to exemplify how managers in bureaucratic organizations had a sense of embodying modernity, but felt cramped by centralized, quasi-autocratic managerial structures:

> Recognised in their role as technical relay; cadres [i.e. managers] demand much more … they feel unduly inserted into a rigid context; they feel that they are regimented and that they are suffocating … they often complain about the narrowness of their room for initiative; they find it difficult to tolerate not being extended broad trust.
>
> (Aumont 1963)

> Cadres aspire more to 'co-management' … They suffer from not 'knowing more about the situations on the basis of which objectives are fixed' and from not having 'more real contact with the employer' … They think that the authority of their (bosses) would remain intact and even be strengthened if, rather than operating mysteriously, they acted in such a way as to elicit from their subordinates the maximum number of voluntary acts conducive to the execution of decisions taken at the top.
>
> (Bloch-Laine 1963)

Such experiences of managers in centralized bureaucracies then resulted in a series of management discourses aiming at the decentralization of authority, the democratization of decision-making processes, and the empowerment of middle management and employees. The assumption was that efficiency requires bureaucracy, but bureaucracy impedes flexibility, managerial autonomy, and motivation. Hence, the managerial challenge was to find structures, relations, processes, and methods that could bring about a proper balance between these conflicting managerial imperatives. Since the early 1970s, a wide spectrum of management techniques and structural changes have been introduced by various management 'gurus', some of which indeed did not live long and were often considered to be fads and buzzwords (see Collins 2000). Nevertheless, they all, whether they were fads or not, manifested the emerging managerial discourses aiming at creating new organizational forms. They all, in one way or

Organizational reconfiguration 143

another, emphasized the necessity of reinventing bureaucracy so that it could be flexible, motivating, and empowering. This was highlighted in Kanter's (1990) words, the 'giants can dance' according to the changing tunes of the markets. Explained in the forthcoming sections are some noteworthy examples in this regard.

7.2.1 Job redesign movement: Taylorism humanized

Initially, attention was on job redesign with techniques of job rotation, job enlargement, and job enrichment. The aim was to enhance job autonomy, job satisfaction, flexibility, and creativity at the middle and the bottom of the organizational hierarchy, while holding onto the efficiency imperatives of their jobs. Adler (1993, 97), a Harvard management guru, highlights the possibilities of reinventing hierarchy through reinventing the time-and-motion studies:

> Standardization is the death of creativity. Time-and-motion regimentation prevents continuous improvement. Hierarchy suffocates learning. U.S. manufacturing is in the throes of revolution, and assumptions like these are becoming the new conventional wisdom about work. This new gospel sets up Frederick Winslow Taylor and his time-and-motion studies as the villain. It asserts that quality, productivity, and learning depend on management's ability to free workers from the coercive constraints of bureaucracy. It insists that detailed standards, implemented with great discipline in a hierarchical organization, will inevitably alienate employees, poison labour relations, stifle initiative and innovation, and hobble an organization's capacity to change and to learn.
>
> But what if, as I believe, this new creed is wrong? What if bureaucracy can actually be designed to encourage innovation and commitment? What if standardization, properly understood and practiced, should prove itself a wellspring of continuous learning and motivation?

Adler and his colleagues (see Adler 1993; Adler et al. 1999) provide a case example of how this balance between the technical efficiency imperatives of bureaucracy and the motivational imperatives of human systems have been achieved. They explain how a General Motors-Toyota joint venture called New United Motors Manufacturing Inc. (NUMMI) in Fremont, California, has succeeded in transforming the organizational structure and processes from what they called an 'idiot-proof bureaucracy' to a 'learning bureaucracy' through 'innovative use of Taylor's time-and-motion regimentation on the factory floor not only to create world class productivity and quality but also to increase worker motivation and satisfaction' (Adler 1993, 97). This 'innovative use of Taylor's time-and-motion regimentation' in NUMMI, explains Adler et al. (1999, see especially p. 50), constituted a deployment of four major job redesign concepts, which Japanese managers acculturated in the Californian plant:

1. Metaroutines: standardized procedures for changing existing routines and for creating new ones. This included standardization of problem solving in a six-step procedure, pilot teams relying on extensive documentation, a documented template for suppliers in model changeovers, and the standardization of the *hansei* (reflection-review) process.
2. Enrichment: adding non-routine tasks to routine production tasks. This included giving *kaizen* (continuous improvement) workers responsibility during the job design process, during regular production, and during acceleration.

144   *Neoliberal trends*

3. Switching: establishing separate times for routine and non-routine tasks and switching employees between them sequentially. This included conducting *kaizen* off-line in QC circles, production workers participating in *kaizen* activities during pilot runs, workers rotating through the pilot team, and suppliers polled for improvement ideas after each changeover project.
4. Partitioning: creating sub-units that specialized in routine or in non-routine tasks. This included creating a new partition for pilot teams, eliminating old partitioning where production workers were doing method engineering, the redistribution of responsibilities across existing partitions, and close and early mutual adjustments between design, engineering, manufacturing engineering, production management, and suppliers.

7.2.2 Management by objectives: participation in decision making and domesticating industrial relations

Management by objectives (MBO) was a quite popular discourse from the late 1950s until the mid-1990s. It emerged as a technique of enhancing the managerial autonomy at the middle and the bottom of the organizational hierarchy to avoid what Peter Drucker, the father of MBO, calls 'the problem of misdirection'[1] and to encourage the notion of 'self-control'. Here the notion of autonomy was conceptualized as the institutionalized opportunities of the subordinates to participate in deciding their own objectives and targets, rather than them being imposed by the superiors. As explained by its proponents, the mechanism of MBO was simple but effective and democratic. Manager and subordinate would meet periodically to collaborate, discuss, and agree upon the subordinate's performance goals. The manager would provide the organizational parameters (such as organizational and divisional objectives, policies, rules, and budget availabilities, etc.) within which the subordinate's objectives needed to be established. The subordinate was encouraged to propose the level of performance that s/he would be willing to achieve but within those organizational parameters. The manager's job was not commanding but exerting the willingness and commitment from the subordinate by collectively designing the appropriate reward-performance connection that would create a win-win situation. Subordinates would be given autonomy in deciding how to achieve these agreed upon objectives, resources would be allocated to them as agreed, and their performance would be monitored and assessed not on the basis of each individual decision they made but the degree to which they achieved the objectives they set for themselves in collaboration with management. Subordinates would retain the control and exercise self-control while committing to implementing the reforms deemed imperative by consultants and top management. As such, at least in its ideal form, the MBO would democratize bureaucracy, encourage the participation and commitments to decision making, enhance the level of job satisfaction, and, in turn, enhance the decision effectiveness because they were taken in close consultation with those concerned and affected by the decisions.

Empirical evidence for the successful implementation of MBO seems to be rather contingent, with mixed messages of partial success and diversity in implementation (e.g. Busch 1998; Covelski et al. 1998; Dirsmith et al. 1997; Dirsmith and Jablonsky 1979; Modell 2003). Yet, at least in its ideal form, as a powerful discourse led by a set of powerful management gurus in the 1960s and beyond, it inculcated a new spirt of capitalism. It was instrumental in institutionalizing the idea that 'self-control' and autonomy would work as far as people were ideologically connected and directed towards a common vision that top management could bring about to inspire the rest of the organization. It inculcated the managerial belief that this ideological connection would be possible through the individualized participation of subordinates in the organizational decision-making processes (Heckscher 2012).

The political significance of this arrangement becomes clearer when we locate it within the context of industrial relations in the 1950s and 1960s where employment contracts were primarily the result of trade union disputes and negotiations. MBO emerged against this highly unionized industrial context of collective bargaining; it emerged as a micro-organizational managerial alternative which was promising significant devolution of autonomy, a reduction in administrative tyranny, and a just system of performance management and reward.[2] In fact, it started to create a different hegemony[3] by individualizing and 'domesticating' (see Boltanski and Chiapello 2007, 66–67) the formal negotiations between capital and labour. Deciding the matters of pay and work were atomized within a dialogue between the manager and the subordinate. This means that it indeed provided the initial impetus for individualization of otherwise collective employment contracts by establishing an 'institutionalized dialogue' within the parameters of individualized agency between a manager and a subordinate.

7.2.3 The post–bureaucratic ideal: the interactive type

Structural, relational, and processual changes that MBO, the job redesign movement, and other managerial initiatives such as quality circles (which we will be discussing further in the next chapter) brought about created the desire for, and the possibilities of, a post-bureaucratic ideal type of organizational hierarchy. In a conventional bureaucratic organizational structure, as we mentioned earlier, bureaucracy sought to improve organizational efficiency and efficacy through specialization, standardization, formalization, centralization, and configuration (Pugh 1997). These processes of bureaucratization, nevertheless, led to an inherent and fundamental limitation: that is that people are responsible only for their own jobs, which Heckscher (2012, 98–99, italics original) explains as follows:

> [t]here is such an inherent and fundamental limitation of bureaucracy, one that derives from its very foundation in the specification of offices: That is that *people are responsible for their own jobs*. The point of the system is that it divides work up into chunks and holds individuals accountable for different pieces. If they move beyond their specific realms, or seek to communicate outside of the appropriate channels, they cause trouble: they confuse lines of responsibility and authority. The paradigm of a bureaucrat's attitude – a good one as well as a bad one – is, 'That's not my job'; and in the traditional organization, anyone who tries to break this bond will be *told*, 'That's not your job'.

The post-bureaucratic ideal type was proposed against this fundamental weakness (and other dysfunctionalities emanating from it). Its master concept, as Heckscher (2012, 101–102) puts it, was an organization in which everyone takes responsibility for the success of the whole; an organization in which people enter into relations that are determined by problems rather than predetermined by the structure; an organization in which organizational control centres on the management of relationships rather than the management of tasks; one in which politics are in the open, rather than being in the shadows. Heckscher (2012, 101–104) lists 12 key features of this ideal type, which he calls the 'interactive type' (see Table 7.1).

Table 7.1 Bureaucratic vs post-bureaucratic ideal types

	Comparative feature	Bureaucracy	Post-bureaucratic ideal (i.e. interactive type)
1	Creation of consensus	Through acquiescence to authority.	Through institutionalized dialogue.
2	Dialogue is defined by	Use of power, i.e. ability to command based on the official position.	Use of influence, i.e. ability to persuade based on such factors as knowledge of the issue, commitment to shared goals and collective wellbeing, and proven past experience.
3	Significance of trust	As interdependence and collectivity is mitigated through separation and compartmentalization of duties, trust plays a minimal role.	As interdependence, collectivity, and shared understanding of common goals and strategy are considered as a virtue, trust plays a significant role.
4	Emphasis on organizational mission	Weak: because the integration and coordination are based on job definitions and rules rather than on strategy and overarching values that emanate from the strategy.	Strong: mission plays a crucial integrating role in developing interdependency around the strategy.
5	Sharing of information of corporate strategy	Centralized and minimal: because strategy setting and implementation are assumed to be top managers' privileged and centralized role.	Widespread: in order to make individual contributions towards the corporate strategy clear, there is a widespread sharing of strategy information.
6	Guidelines for actions	Rules, procedures, and protocols imposed without explaining the principles behind them.	Take the form of abstract principles allowing flexibility and intelligent response to changing circumstances: people are asked to think about the reasons for constraints on their actions rather than rigidly following procedures.
7	Decision-making procedures and reference points for decision making	Fundamentally determined by the formal authority as specified by the organizational chart: 'who to go to' is directly to be read by the chart.	Processes are needed for *deciding how to decide* – what may be called meta decision-making mechanisms (cf. 'metaroutines' in Section 7.2.1) that help the frequent reconstruction of decision-making processes.
8	Information channels	Formalized and specialized to a higher degree: specific routes of information and advice seeking.	Open and temporary networks: it is possible for managers to put out a general message asking for help on a given project or to collect a list of people who have knowledge and experience in that area.
9	Performance evaluation	Formalized within a vertical/ hierarchical relationship.	Horizontal as well as vertical: open processes of association and peer evaluations so that people get a relatively detailed view of each other's strengths and weaknesses.

(Continued)

Organizational reconfiguration 147

Table 7.1 (Cont.)

	Comparative feature	Bureaucracy	Post-bureaucratic ideal (i.e. interactive type)
10	Organizational boundaries and career patterns	Relatively closed: less tolerance for outsiders coming in and insiders going out; seniority and job specific experiences are appreciated.	Open: no expectations that employees will spend their entire careers in one organization; far more tolerance of outsiders coming in and insiders going out.
11	Perception of equity	The main touchstone is always objectivity and equality of treatment and, hence, constant effort to devise rules for treatment of employees.	Increased pressure to reduce rules while recognizing the variety in individual performance; development of public standards of performance, openly discussed and often negotiated with individual employees.
12	The way time is structured	Review processes occur in regular intervals, usually annually in a budgeting process, as a way of checking that things are functioning as they should – but not with the anticipation of making fundamental changes.	Review processes are problems and issues/themes-driven; having expectations of constant change are built into the system; performance evaluations take place to enact changes.

7.3 Postmodern discourses: the emergence of a new cultural and informational social order

Our discussion in the previous section concentrated on the 'post-bureaucratic' discourses. Here our attention is on 'postmodern' discourses. In fact, these two concepts are interlocking and overlapping, often referring to the same organizational and historical dynamics but from different angles. For us, the difference is that post-bureaucratic mostly concentrates on the techno–managerial parameters of organizational structuring on their own. It is primarily about reforming the structural parameters of bureaucracy. Postmodern discourses, on the other hand, take our attention to a wider spectrum of changes taking place beyond the organization in the socio–cultural, ideological, and technological realms, how such changes complicate organizations to bring about new forms of organizations. As such, postmodern explanations are sociological. In other words, postmodernity and postmodernism manifest the political-economic thought and cultural movements that characterize contemporary neoliberal capitalism, while post-bureaucracy manifests the way in which postmodernity is implicated and manifested within organizational structures, relations, and practices.

In Chapter 1, we used the term modernity to mean the historical phase during which a new social order was established as the cultural and political base for capitalism. The term modernism was used there to mean the political economic thought and the cultural movements that characterized the modern epoch: the epistemological and the cultural that drew the world away from pre-modern feudalism towards modern capitalism. Postmodern is rather complicated and ambiguous. It necessarily means neither something that happens 'after' modernity nor something that supersedes and replaces modern liberal capitalism. However, it denotes a significant shift or rupture 'in the modern'. As

148   *Neoliberal trends*

Featherstone (1988, 198) explains, 'to speak of postmodernity is to suggest an epochal shift or break from modernity involving the emergence of a new social totality with its own distinct organizing principles'. In fact, what we mean by the set of terms that we use (postmodern, postmodernity, and postmodernism) is this 'shift' currently been enacted in various realms of our lives. It is the revision that the world is currently making in the modern, the change that is happening right now, not what it has become, but the process of becoming. And this shift is multi-layered and multi-faceted. For the purposes of this text, in order specially to understand the fundamental socio-technological and political drivers behind this shift, and to explain the new forms of organization that this shift has created, we concentrate on four key postmodern social dynamics: (1) the signification of simulacra and the movement from production to reproduction; (2) the entrepreneurialization of labour; (3) the immaterialization of labour; and (4) management by themes.

7.3.1 Signification of simulacra and the movement from production to reproduction

This shift manifests a movement towards a post-industrial and informational age, two concepts which are often widely used to characterize the postmodern changes now taking place. In a broader sense, these two terms, interconnectedly, mean two fundamental changes. First, technology expanding from *mechanization* to *digitalization* (a shift in the defining symbolic elements of technology from cog wheels, belts and wires, and machines to computer chips, cables, signals, and networks). Second, a shift from modes of production to modes of reproduction. And, they have interconnectedly brought about what we call the postmodern era.

Postmodern is an era in which digitalization has made the *virtualization* of production and distribution possible to an extent that pervades every realm of our social, economic, and political being. The political effect of virtualization technologies is the social signification of 'simulacra', a term that Baudrillard (1983) use to explain the postmodern. A simulacrum is any form of cultural-technical representation that 'simulates' reality, as in television, computer cyberspace, virtual reality, and so on. It is a sign, image, model, pretence, or a shadow likeness of something else (Macintosh et al. 2000, 14). This is an important concept to understand the way in which postmodern societies are organized.

As we have noted in our previous chapters, *modern* societies were organized around the production and consumption of commodities, and the social values and economic surpluses emanated from this production and consumption. Hence, mass production and mass consumption of material goods were the defining features of modern societies. Mechanization, Taylorism, the assembly line, industrial policies of regulation and deregulation, and so on were driven towards making the mass production and mass consumption of goods possible. In the modern industrial era, capital accumulation was closely associated with the capacity to produce, consume, and invest in material things (i.e. goods and services). Financial and material capital dominated the mode of production and appropriation of value. The socio-political realities of power and domination are constituted and manifested by the power to invest in and invent productive mechanisms. Companies like Ford, Toyota, General Motors, and General Electric were the symbolic manifestation of this modern 'mode of production'. The role of simulacrum in that modern period was a faithful and transparent representation of production: a sign is a reflection of a profound reality (Macintosh et al. 2000, 15; see also Graham 2008). Accounting appeared as an institutional apparatus of this mode of production, entrusted with the role of 'true and fair' representation, in financial terms, of the value of production, exchange, consumption, and investment. Accounting was the representational act associated with the material acts that created, appropriated, and distributed wealth in a modern mode of production.

In contrast, postmodern societies are increasingly organized around simulation into a mode of reproduction, a mode in which simulation of the 'real' creates more value and power than the production of 'real' itself.[4] As such, the capacity to simulate and reproduce through the language games, images, signs, codes, computer programs, and platforms etc. has become the defining feature of the social order. So, it is no more the production companies like Ford (which once defined industrial capitalism as the era of Fordism) that bear the signature of postmodern capitalism, but companies like Google, Facebook, Amazon, Microsoft, and Apple. It is true that companies like Ford and Toyota still carry a significant weight in the realm of production, but they have ceased to be the 'signature' or 'symbols' of postmodern capitalism. What these new signatory companies have produced, then, for which postmodern societies are rewarding them on a massive scale, are simulacra in which others can reproduce their material production, their identities, and their lives. They have made it possible for others to continually engage in what we now call 'hyperreal' and, thereby, to reproduce on a massive scale.

Unlike Mattessich's (2003) objectivist depiction of Baudrillard's conception of 'hyper-real' as 'unreal', we see 'hyperreal' as the postmodern condition that makes it possible to reproduce (and represent) the 'real' in a different vein. Then again, contrary to Macintosh et al.'s (2000, 14) conception of 'hyperreal' as a 'condition of postmodernity where simulacrum are [*sic*] no longer associated with any real referent and where signs, images, and models circulate, detached from any real material objects or romantic ideas', we see hyperreal as a condition where the simulacrum, as an object of reality in itself in the form of, say, software, cyberspace, a management model, an advertisement, or even a Harvard case study, has gained an agency to superimpose its vision as reality (or an ideal reality) over others. Hence, the simulacra continuously reproduce the other, rather than simply offering a faithful and transparent representation of the others. The association of hyperreal simulacra with other forms of real is this reproduction of them within the realm of hyperreal, making the hyperreal the basis upon which the others are reconstructed (rather than real being the basis for hyperreal as in modernity). This has provided the simulacrum with an ontological and epistemological superiority over the others, so that it appears to exist on its own. Postmodernity, in this sense, is the social order in which simulacra (which are often referred to as information capital, intellectual capital, and knowledge capital, etc. in the popular management press) has gained this agency, replacing traditional form of capital. For example, Amazon's Market Place, Google, and Facebook, as cyberspaces, do not simply offer a faithful representation of the markets, social networks, and social communication. Instead, they reconstruct them, offer a different identity to them and, thereby, offer possibilities for others to reproduce the real and appropriate value in many forms. Some would even call this tendency of economic capital being replaced by knowledge capital (i.e. simulacrum and capacity to reproduce through them) 'knowledge capitalism' (e.g. Burton-Jones 1999). We see this accumulative power of simulacra in new rich: in the new signatory companies we mentioned earlier, in epistemic institutions such as the Harvard Business School, and management gurus. Accounting tools such as ABC/M and the BSC do not simply offer a faithful representation of costs or performance. Instead, they impose a new vision of costs and performance along which we now reproduce our organizational lives.

150 *Neoliberal trends*

In these spaces of hyperreal, we see what Baudrillard (1994) calls 'implosion', which occurs when the boundaries between entities, concepts, and realms melt and collapse so that their differences start to disappear (see Graham 2008; Macintosh et al. 2000). We see this, for example, in the emergence of strategic management models and in matrix and project-based organizational structures, which melt the boundaries between traditional functional management areas. So, the differences between disciplinary fields which hitherto existed as neat and separate functional realms of operations management, marketing management, financial management, and human resource management etc. are now increasingly disappearing as strategic modelling of the firms has started to integrate them all. Interdisciplinarity has become a key managerial skill in the strategy-based management of corporations and new managerial pedagogies of 'integrated case studies' often attempt to inculcate this skill among the managers. We see this also in the implosion of boundaries between private and public forms of organizations (e.g. private public partnerships, NGOs, and charities), in the convergence of markets and hierarchies into network organizations and inter-organizational arrangements of supply chain management. The emergence of new public management (NPM) also sees the melting of conceptual boundaries between the management of private- and public-sector organizations.

In management accounting literature, this postmodern tendency of 'implosion' has often been explained by the notion of hybridity or hybridization. For example, Currie et al. (2015) use the notion of 'hybridization' to explain how neoliberal public-sector reforms co-opt professionals into hybrid managerial roles, which they call 'canny customers'. Boland et al. (2008) explain how rapid changes in the use of technologies, materials, and practices, through path creation and morphogenesis, lead high-stakes and high-risk enterprises that critically rely on their management control systems to produce hybrid forms of organizations and control systems. Kurunmaki (2004) explains how medical expertise in Finland was 'hybridized' through the willing adoption of management accounting techniques by medical professionals in the context of NPM reforms in Finland. Miller et al. (2008) explain how accounting is constantly engaged in a dual hybridization process, seeking to make visible and calculable the hybrids that it encounters, while at the same time hybridizing itself through encounters with a range of other disciplines.

7.3.2 Entrepreneurialization of labour

One of the important aspects of this 'implosion' is the gradual destruction of the boundary between labour and capital. In modernist and industrial capitalism, there was a clear demarcation between capital and labour and, hence, labour and management. This was very evident not only in the political ideologies of political parties (e.g. Labour vs Conservatives), and in the institutionalization of conflict between capital and labour in trade union and other institutional means of collective bargaining, but also in the particular organization of work at the point of production. As we explained in previous chapters, modernism and industrial capitalism evolved by constructing this duality between capital and labour in such a manner that planning and design of the work was taken over by the capital (i.e. the management) while the execution of the work was the labourer's job. This separation between management and execution of work was the core of Fordist and Taylorist developments of the capitalist mode of production, especially the deskilling of labour. The capital bought the labour time for which wages were paid while capital took the entrepreneurial risk of earning a profit (or making a loss). The managerial class was placed in between labour and management as the agent of capital, and management was by and large conceived as the institutionalized processes through which a 'negotiated order' between labour and capital was achieved in the realms of both the labour process and the industrial relations beyond the factory floors.

In postmodern neoliberal capitalism, this duality between labour and capital is increasingly disappearing or disguised, often as a capitalistic strategy for intensifying the possibilities for capital accumulation. At the macro-political level, we see this in the increasing convergence of political parties to the same neoliberal political ideologies of market-driven development and market-based governance and regulation. At the meso-institutional level, we see this in the rapid decline of unionized labour and the individualization of industrial relations. Nevertheless, the most prominent and fundamental occurrences of this 'implosion' take place at the micro-organizational level – in the way work is organized at the point of production (or rather the way in which the capitalist point of production is now been redistributed across other spheres of social life), and in the way in which new identities are attributed to labour in the emerging managerial discourses. It is at this level that labour is increasingly being reconfigured from being waged/salaried employees to 'entrepreneurs of the self', whom Cooper (2015, 14; see also Foucault 2008) explains as neoliberal subjects having a hyper individualized expectation placed upon them to maximize return on themselves. As Cooper (2015) explains, this hyper individualized expectation of becoming an entrepreneur, and thereby to maximize the return on themselves, is enacted, inter alia, through the neoliberal discourses of human capital, which especially started to gain ground since the early 1980s across many fields including management, education, and also development economics.

Underlying these neoliberal discourses of human capital, there is the projection of the economic simulacrum of capital to model the life of the labourer. In neoliberal economics and management discourses, the labourer is no longer projected simply as a mere factor of production, or an object of supply and demand, or a malleable agent subject to the continued control of a principal (as in agency theory). Instead, s/he is an active economic subject capable of realizing her/his own life dreams in corporate environments, which are often discoursed as providing the necessary infrastructure for entrepreneurial development. Accordingly, when it is reconceptualized as a form of capital – i.e. human capital – labour starts to see its worth not in terms of 'earning a living' but in terms of 'wealth' (i.e. sum total of all future benefits, as it is conceived in the model of enterprise). Cooper (2015, 15, emphasis in original), explains this new neoliberal logic of human capital as follows:

> Under neo-liberalism 'Capital' has come to mean a source of future income ... From the side of the worker, labour is not a commodity reduced by abstraction to the time which it is used. The neo-liberal understanding of a worker is a conception of capital-ability which, according to diverse variables, receives a certain income so that the worker appears as an enterprise for herself. Neo-liberal human capital includes both genetic and acquired elements. The genetic elements, akin to social Darwinism, are such that individuals achieve advantage over others as the result of genetic or biological superiority; the acquired elements include education

152　*Neoliberal trends*

and other investments in the self. Importantly, inequality, not equality, is the medium and relation of competing capitals. When we are configured as human capital, equality ceases to be our presumed natural relation with one another … Humans lose their standing as being simply valuable as humans.

Cooper (2015, 16) draws on Brown (2015) to further explain how the neoliberal notion of human capital transmogrifies labour:

> [h]uman capital's constant and ubiquitous aim, whether studying, interning, working, planning retirement … is to entrepreneurialize its endeavours, appreciate its value, and increase its rating or ranking. In this it mirrors the mandate for contemporary firms, countries, academic departments or journals, universities, media or websites: entrepreneurialize, enhance competitive positioning and value, maximize ratings or rankings.

Accordingly, new neoliberal organizational forms evolve in order to translate labour into human capital and to inculcate the wealth-maximizing 'entrepreneurial spirit' among employees. To this end, accounting and other managerial technologies need to be reinvented and redirected from being technologies of valuing and managing the production system in terms of inputs, processes, and outputs, to being capable of valuing, monitoring, rating, and motivating employees as income-maximizing entrepreneurial units of human capital. These new forms are enacted through various managerial and structural innovations that we discussed in the previous section (i.e. job-redesign, management by objectives, post-bureaucratic ideal types) and many other managerial practices such as the BSC, quality circles, succession planning, continuous professional development programmes, career development planning, and so on. Collectively, they play a role in producing an account of the value of our human capital, its ranking, position, and so on (see Cooper 2015, 16).

Management accounting, in this sense, is now enhancing its role and capacity. It is no more confined solely to financial quantification, costing, and providing decision-making, planning, and control tools. Instead, it moves into constructing narratives of human lives. For example, BSCs, especially in the collective process of preparing them, demand people not only quantify their past performance and compare them with standards but also actively construct a managerial narrative to justify their organizational existence: to explain how their life in the organization contributes to the organization's present and future, to explain how they see themselves within the grand scheme of the corporate strategy, and how they will realize their personal entrepreneurial goals through the opportunities that the corporation may throw at them (see Qu and Cooper 2011). In the ABM worksheets, employees are increasingly asked to construct a detailed narrative of how they 'spend their lives' in the organization that employs them (see Armstrong 2002; Drennan and Kelly 2002).

7.3.3 Immaterialization of labour

The origin of this entrepreneurial view of labour goes back to Joseph Schumpeter's conception of entrepreneurship. Here the notion of entrepreneurship is defined in terms of neither its 'risk-taking' qualities nor in the scientific discoveries and innovations. As Hardt and Negri (2017, 140) argue, the essence of this neoliberal

Organizational reconfiguration   153

entrepreneurship is to create *new combinations* among already existing workers, ideas, technologies, resources, and machines. And the essence of these new combinations is *cooperation* that enacts *immaterial labour.*

Immaterial labour exemplifies another form of postmodern 'implosion' between labour and capital. In the early phases of capitalism and modernism, labouring activities were radically heterogeneous. Tailoring and weaving, for example, involved incommensurable concrete actions. In computer-aided manufacturing and service production systems, this heterogeneity of labour is increasingly disappearing. The labour of computerized tailoring and the labour of computerized weaving involve exactly the same concrete practices – that is, the manipulation of symbols and information. This is a form of immaterialization of labour – labour now increasingly performing what is called *symbolic-analytical labour* of problem identifying, and problem solving (Hardt and Negri 2000, 292). Yet again, post-bureaucratic Toyotaist inventions such as quality circles enacted this form of immaterial labour.

The second form of the immaterialization of labour is the *communicative labour*: labour being engraved and enacted in computerized information networks where the labourer's job has now become mainly information processing and communication. As a result, the labour process has predominantly become informational and communicative. The majority of labourers in postmodern organizations are engaged in producing information for *abstract cooperation*, which is maintaining connections between deterritorialized organizations, production systems, and sites. They direct the production systems and the remaining material labour dispersed across geographically dispersed sites to produce goods and services according to the signals emanating from the markets.[5] As opposed to the old vertical industrial and corporate model, production now tends to be organized in horizontal network enterprises (Hardt and Negri 2000, 296) – outsourced, dispersed, deterritorialized systems coordinated through communicative labour. This is pretty much visible when we look at the global ordering of production – communicative and symbolic labour being concentrated at the communication and design centres in the developed West while the remaining deskilled material labour elements of production are distributed across modernist and Taylorist factories in peripheral countries such as China, Vietnam, Indonesia, Bangladesh, and India. Abstract cooperation between them is ensured through quasi-market information networks organized in the form of franchises, supply chains, joint ventures, etc. Hardt and Negri (2000, 297), explain this as follows:

> The decentralization and global dispersal of productive processes and sites, which is characteristic of the postmodernization or informatization of the economy, provokes a corresponding centralization of the control over production. The centrifugal movement of production is balanced by the centripetal trend of command. From the local perspective, the computer networks and communications technologies internal to production systems allow for more extensive monitoring of workers from a central, remote location. Control of labouring activity can potentially be individualized and continuous in the virtual panopticon of network production. The centralization of control, however, is even more clear from a global perspective. The geographical dispersal of manufacturing has created a demand for increasingly centralized management and planning, and also for a new centralization of specialized producer services, especially financial services. Financial and trade-related services in a few key cities (such as New York, London, and

154 *Neoliberal trends*

Tokyo) manage and direct the global networks of production. As a mass demographic shift, then, the decline and evacuation of industrial cities has corresponded to the rise of global cities, or really cities of control.

The third form of immaterialization is *affective labour*, which manifests as *kin work* and *caring labour* (Hardt 1999). As the organizations are increasingly becoming biopolitical sites (i.e. sites in which life itself has been put to work in the form of, for example, entrepreneurial human capital), they need to be sites of caring and love – sites in which not simply material production takes place but sites in which lives are spent meaningfully, safely, healthily, and not being subject to any form of harassment or discrimination. This demands all sorts of social, cultural, family, and welfare matters to be institutionalized within the organizational structures, processes, and practices. For example, physical and mental wellbeing and the welfare of organizational members, health and safety, equity and justice, customer care, and many other 'caring dimensions' should be formally recognized as structural elements of organizations. The structural implications of this increasingly important affective labour are discussed further in the next section.

7.3.4 Management by themes

The sign of a simulacrum, moving from modes of production to modes of reproduction, the entrepreneurialization of labour, and the immaterialization of labour, manifests itself in the ways in which organizations are transformed into biopolitical sites – sites in which life itself is put to work. As we noted earlier, life now has received neoliberal meaning within corporations – human capital with entrepreneurial ambitions of maximizing the accumulative potential of life. This means that the focal attention of management is no more on production per se but the reproduction of life according to the neoliberal logics of accumulation. The primacy is no more the efficient use of scarce resources (though it still holds true as a necessary condition of management) but the provision of a context within which lives can become productive and accumulative on their own. Labour is no more conceived simply as a mere resource but an enterprise in itself. The structural implication of this is that the organization itself has become a society on its own. Because, after all, it is the society in which lives can be reproduced, and, hence, organization needs to be managed as a society on its own. A biopolitical organization is one which is managed as a society, not purely as an economic enterprise.

So, as in the case of the biopolitical governance of society (i.e. governmentality), the organization needs to be reconceptualized in biopolitical themes (i.e. the pathological traits of the society). Management then becomes management by themes. During the last few decades, we have seen a dramatic shift in organizational structures, processes, and systems driven by this neoliberal thematization of management. Examples include quality, risk, health and safety, reputation, brand, diversity, gender equality, research and development, change, accreditation, certification, stress and mental health, customer care, and so on. Accordingly, we have seen numerous new managerial titles appearing: quality managers, health and safety managers, risk champions, change agents, accreditation managers, brand managers, social media managers, and so on. We have also seen numerous new structural elements such as committees, circles, forums, boards, etc. emerging to manage such themes (e.g. quality circles, health and safety

Organizational reconfiguration 155

forums and committees, risk management boards, etc.). Such themes are often conceived as interdisciplinary and cross-functional. Managers and workers, irrespective of their functional fields and rankings, are now required to actively learn skills and knowledge pertaining to such interdisciplinary and cross-functional themes. They are no more conceived as functional specialities but generic citizenship skills and knowledge that everyone in the new biopolitical organization (i.e. the micro society in which we reproduce our lives) should come to know, understand, and appreciate. They have now become the basic civic codes according to which we all are now told to reproduce our lives.

7.4 Strategic critique of performance management: Kaplanian influences

The discussion so far explains how organizations have been transformed into biopolitical sites in which life itself put to work. As we discussed in Section 7.2, the initial managerial impetus for this transformation stemmed from the post-bureaucratic discourses and transformations. Those post-bureaucratic discourses concentrated on the micro-managerial reforms driven to mitigate the behavioural and inflexibility issues in large bureaucratic structures. Nevertheless, such organizational reforms also had some sociological implications stemming from wider socio-technological changes that we broadly called postmodern transformations. We discussed this biopolitical transformation in terms of the signification of simulacrum and of reproduction, the entrepreneurialization of labour, and the immaterialization of labour. They all, in one way or another, contributed to making organizations postmodern and post-bureaucratic and, thereby, contributed to the historical process of strategizing organizational structures and processes.

However, perhaps the most pragmatic and programmatic critique of the traditional form of management accounting and its reforms towards a strategy-driven practice stemmed from a group of North American academic-consultants. We have already discussed some of these in the previous chapter under the theme 'strategizing the market'. In relation to the theme 'strategizing the firm', the 1980s and 1990s saw significantly influential managerial discourses, especially one in particular that originated from the Harvard Business School that offered a 'strategic critique' on the traditional form of management, especially performance management and costing. The most significant in this regard was the 'action research' by Robert Kaplan and his colleagues, especially around the development and implementing of two main management accounting tools: the BSC and ABC/ABM. The populist management research agenda at that time was about making the firms more flexible, market-responsive, innovative, and operationally efficient with a proper 'strategic focus' (e.g. Argyris and Schön 1978; Peters and Waterman 1982; Senge 1990). In line with this overall agenda of inventing post-bureaucratic management, Kaplan and others embarked on an action research programme based on their management consultancy projects to move 'beyond budgeting' (see Hope and Fraser 2003a, 2003b; Kaplan and Norton 1996a) and beyond traditional absorption costing (see Cooper and Kaplan 1988, 1991a, 1991b; Kaplan and Anderson 2007). The next section explains how Johnson and Kaplan's BSC discourses strategize the firm, while the strategic impact of ABC will be dealt with in the next chapter.

156 *Neoliberal trends*

7.4.1 Strategic linking and balancing: reinvention of performance management

The theoretical and conceptual parameters of performance management systems (PMS) stem from systems theory (see Chapter 4, Section 4.6). A PMS is generally understood as an organizational subsystem put in place to measure and communicate a set of indicators or measures which should accurately reflect 'critical success factors' – the factors which will determine the success of the company or its sub-units. Accordingly, elements of the PMS include: critical success factors or key performance indicators (KPIs) as they are now often labelled; methodologies adopted in measuring and communicating them; and the ways in which rewards and punishments are attached to the KPIs. These elements generally define the conception of organizational success and its management. In their traditional operational modes as well as contemporary strategic modes, PMS offer a toolset to conceive and manage organizations as machines, such as a car or an aeroplane. As it is often explained in the popular management accounting and management control textbooks, the managerial necessity of a PMS is that it offers a 'performance dash-board' based upon which managers can effectively drive their organizations towards the desired ends (see Anthony and Govindarajan 1998). In a sense, a PMS is a managerial simulacrum that represents and reproduces the organization in a particular manner, enforcing a particular view point and enabling a particular set of actions upon the organization, its sub-units, and individuals. In other words, as a simulacrum, a PMS has the epistemic capacity to reproduce the organization and change it into a different form. In this sense, the recent discourses that brought about new understandings of PMS show the organizational-level enactments of the neoliberal changes in organizational form. Such changes are often understood as a shift away from 'traditional PMS' to 'strategic PMS'. Hence, from the perspectives of corporate managers, the strategic transformation of organizations is driven by the reinvention of PMS.

Critiquing the traditional

Discursive reconstruction of management often begins with a critique of the existing or the traditional. In the early phase of management accounting, we see a particular set of managerial discourses directed against the traditional mode of accounting, costing, and performance measurement. One of the key milestones in this regard is the 'Relevance Lost' thesis that Johnson and Kaplan brought forward to argue and explain how management accounting, in its traditional form, is no longer relevant for globalized competitive settings. They went on to argue that:

> Today's management accounting systems provide a misleading target for managerial attention. They fail to provide the relevant set of measures that appropriately reflect the technology, products, processes, and competitive environment in which the organization operates. Originally designed earlier in this century to help coordinate the diverse activities of emerging vertically integrated enterprises, financial measures such as return on investment (ROI) have become for many organizations the only measure of success. Financial managers, relying exclusively on periodic financial statements for their view of the firm, get isolated from the real value-creating operations of the organization and fail to recognize when the accounting numbers are no longer providing relevant or appropriate measures of the organization's operations.
>
> (Johnson and Kaplan 1987a, 3; see also, 1987b, 22)

This 'relevance lost' argument is particularly directed towards traditional PMS on the basis that:

1. Their tendency to measure and manage performance is only on the basis of financial indicators. A traditional PMS is a collection of management accounting techniques and tools that provides segmented and detailed reports on various aspects of the company's financial performance. These techniques are mainly hinged upon the notion of responsibility accounting. Budgeting and variance analysis, divisional performance reporting and transfer pricing, and financial statement analysis (which mainly includes comparative financial statements, ratio analysis, and trend analysis) are the most popular. The key performance areas and indicators are often grouped under the financial dimensions of profitability, liquidity, efficiency, gearing, and investor attractiveness.

2. Their tendency is to disintegrate the organizational performance into a discrete set of responsibility centres. The basic principle of organizing a conventional PMS is the conceptual breakdown of overall business into a set of discrete operations, processes, and centres. For example, conventional budgeting compartmentalizes the overall business (represented by the master budget: i.e. the budgeted profit and loss account and balance sheet) into a set of related activities, such as sales, production, purchasing, labour usage, overhead expenses, etc. Targets and objectives are set by preparing budgets for each of these operations, processes, and centres. At the end of the budgetary period, these budgeted figures are flexed to reflect the actual level of operations, and variances are calculated and reported for the attention of management. The focus of a conventional PMS is on the contribution to return on investment (ROI). It provides cost, revenue, and profit indicators on how well resources are utilized within different divisions or departments, often called 'responsibility centres', which might be cost centres, profit centres, or investment centres. Thus, the main focus of a conventional PMS is to set budgetary targets in terms of revenue, costs, or profits for each responsibility centre, and then to measure how well each responsibility centre contributes to the overall organizational ROI by achieving those budgetary targets. This system, which prevailed for more than a century, was criticized for promoting organizational red-tapeism, budgetary slacks, disintegration, inflexibility, and short-termism (see Tangen 2004, 726–727).

3. They fail to link operations with the corporate strategies. Traditional budget-based PMS are argued to be inward looking and directed towards regulation of input, process, and output flows but only with reference to internal standards rather than the corporate strategies and external competitive benchmarks (see Berry et al. 2009).

Discoursing the new simulacrum: strategic performance management systems

The invention of strategic performance management systems (SPMS), especially the BSC, came about after the weaknesses of the traditional PMS became more evident. In an overall sense, the new systems are supposed to achieve two fundamental strategic functionalities: (a) *linking* the day-to-day operational activities with the long-term corporate vision, mission, and strategies; and (b) *balancing* the financial measures with the non-financial measures. As Chenhall (2005, 396) explains, SPMS are 'designed to

158 *Neoliberal trends*

present managers with financial and non-financial measures covering different perspectives which, in combination, provide a way of translating strategy into a coherent set of performance measures'. These measures have the potential to identify the cause-effect linkages that describe the way operations are related to the organization's strategy. For its proponents, the BSC:

> [p]rovides executives with a comprehensive framework that translates a company's strategic objectives into a coherent set of performance measures. Much more than a measurement exercise, the balanced scorecard is a management system that can motivate breakthrough improvements in such critical areas as product, process, customer, and market development.
>
> (Kaplan and Norton 1993, 134)

As this quote highlights, the BSC is marketed and popularized as a 'management system' that can solve the problems of the management orthodoxy and bring about breakthrough improvements in 'critical success areas'. In so doing, its proponents, adaptors, and adopters have discursively constructed a particular but powerful simulacrum of the postmodern or post-bureaucratic organization. As a simulacrum, it reproduces a particular neoliberal managerial ideology and a particular set of calculative tools and institutional practices driven towards that ideology. The BSC's simulation and reconstruction of strategic organizations is based on the following key elements (see Figure 7.1):

1. The critique: The BSC appears as a solution to an old problem. Hence it offers a discursive critique of the traditional PMS, especially budgeting, on the grounds that they are not making the firms competitive enough to face the globalized competition.
2. The binding principle: Strategy as the binding principle. BSC discourses propagate that a clear corporate strategy is necessary and critical for competitive success (a view that Kaplan and colleagues borrowed from other strategy thinkers like Porter), and everything else should be directed towards the strategy. The managerial rationale of everything else stems from their connection with the strategy. Hence an SPMS should be able to *link* operations with the strategy.
3. Operational principle: multiplicity of performance. Strategy needs to be expressed in four key performance perspectives: financial, customer, internal business processes, and learning and growth. Hence an SPMS should be able to provide a *balance* between financial and non-financial performance.
4. Causality: a particular causality (or rather 'finality', see later) is assumed across the four key dimensions of performance. The four key performance dimensions can be arranged in a 'strategic map' articulating how initiatives, programmes, targets, and actions in non-financial dimensions would eventually lead to financial success (as measured by ROI).
5. Cascading: The operational technique of *linking* operations with the strategy is cascading the strategic measures down the organizational hierarchy. This means that each layer of the organizational hierarchy would have strategic measures connecting that layer to those above and below.
6. Scorecards: the fundamental technical tool in linking and balancing is the scorecard. A scorecard would outline, depending upon the specific locality to which it is

Organizational reconfiguration 159

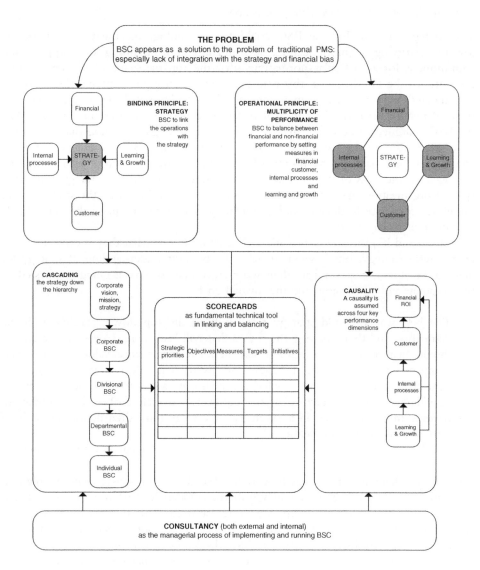

Figure 7.1 The BSC as a system of strategic performance management system

related, four elements that frame performance: objectives, measures, targets, and initiatives.
7. Consultancy: the managerial process of implementing and running BSCs is often conceived as a continuous 'project' involving both external and internal consultancy. External consultants are often brought in to facilitate the top-level strategic discussions and dialogues. In the process of cascading the implementation process downwards, top and middle managers (often together with external consultants) assume a consultancy role rather than a traditional managerial role. They often appear in the BSC forums as facilitators and trainers rather than managers and officials (see Qu and Cooper 2011).

160 *Neoliberal trends*

The BSC promotes top executive ideology as strategy

The strategy process that the BSC establishes is ideological:[6] the process is driven towards clarifying, communicating, legitimizing, and obtaining the support and commitment for a particular normativity that the top managers of the corporation promote. In the first instance, this is to be achieved through signifying the centrality of 'strategy' in performance management. The traditional PMS is critiqued and rejected mainly because of its incapacity to drive people towards the strategy. And the BSC is argued to be better mainly because it is strategic, meaning that it can link everything else to the corporate strategy. In this way, BSC discourses offer an ideological supremacy to the notion of strategy, and the efficacy of everything else is judged on the basis of their connection and contribution to the strategy. The ideal type of organization that BSC discourses conceive is one in which the strategy (and, therefore, corporate leadership and consultancy in defining it) plays the central role in corporate management.

Johnson and Kaplan do not provide a clear definition of what they specifically mean by the term strategy, but it seems to take the populist understanding of strategy for granted. For them, it seems from their writings, strategy is what is being manifested by the corporate vision, mission, and the 'overall goals':

> The best way to build strategy maps is from the top down, starting with the destination and then charting the routes that will lead there. Corporate executives should first review their mission statement and their core values – why their company exists and what it believes in. With that information, managers can develop a strategic vision, or what the company wants to become. This vision should create a clear picture of the company's overall goal – for example, to become the profit leader in an industry. A strategy must then define the logic of how to arrive at that destination.
>
> (Kaplan and Norton 2000, 6)

It is very clear here that the strategy process that BSC discourses envisage is necessarily top-to-bottom. The strategy necessarily stems from the visionary leadership at the top; it is their ideology and conception of the corporate future that need to be contextualized into vision and mission statements and overall goals. So, in so far as the notion of strategy is equated to the visionary leadership in this manner, BSC discourses situate the top executives and consultants as the most dominating element of the strategy-making and implementation process. Kaplan and Norton's (1996b) case example of a successful implementation of the BSC, where they present an ideal-type model/process of designing and implementing the BSC, exemplifies this top-down approach of strategy making and implementation.

Their model consists of ten basic steps that fundamentally rely upon the top executives' initiation and vision. The process begins (Step 1) with a newly formed top executive team. A corporate BSC is developed to translate the top executives' vision of the corporation into a strategy that can be communicated to the next layers of the corporation. Then, in order to communicate the strategy to middle managers (step 2), the top three layers of management (100 people) are brought together to learn about and discuss the new strategy by designing scorecards for these managers. Using the corporate scorecards as a template, each business unit translates its strategy into its own scorecard. This means the BSC is used as a communication vehicle of strategy from top

Organizational reconfiguration 161

to middle management. The corporate strategy is thereby translated into business unit scorecards.

Step 3 streamlines the investment portfolio and initiates the necessary cross-business change programmes. It is stated that the corporate scorecard, by clarifying strategic priorities, can identify many active programmes that are not contributing to the strategy and initiate cross-business change programmes. They are launched while the business units prepare their scorecards. Step 4 is to review the business unit scorecards. The CEO and the executive team review the individual business units' scorecards. The review permits the CEO to participate knowledgeably in shaping business unit strategy. In Step 5, top management (the executive team formed to design and implement the BSC) refine the vision: the review of business unit scorecards identifies several cross-business issues not included in the corporate strategy. The corporate scorecard is updated. Now the top management has an updated version of the corporate strategy and the BSC, which are ready to be communicated beyond the middle management to the whole company. In Step 6, the BSC is disseminated to the whole organization, and individual performance objectives are established: the top three layers of management link their individual objectives and incentive compensation to their scorecards. Step 7 is to link long-range plans and budgets to the BSC. Five-year goals are established for each measure. The investments required to meet those goals are identified and funded. The first year of the five-year plan becomes the annual budget.

Steps 8 and 9 are for periodic reviews. In Step 8, monthly and quarterly reviews begin. In Step 9, an annual strategy review is conducted. The executive committee lists ten strategic issues. Each business unit is asked to develop a position on each issue as a prelude to updating its strategy and scorecard. Finally, in Step 10, everyone's performance is linked to the BSC: all employees are asked to link their individual objectives to the BSC. In this way, it is stated, the entire organization's incentive compensation is linked to the corporate scorecard, and thereby to the corporate strategy.

The BSC's reconceptualization of the shareholder as the strategic ultimatum

One of the often-cited qualities of the BSC is that it 'balances' between financial and non-financial performance. This balancing aspect is pictorially presented in the famous 'five-boxes and arrows' illustration of the BSC where 'four perspectives' (i.e. financial, customer, internal business process, and learning and growth) are located around the central box of 'vision and strategy'. However, BSC materials also reveal how this 'balancing' idea has been quickly inverted into a particular pattern of 'causal connections' through the technique of strategy mapping (see Figure 7.1). In fact, strategy mapping provides a better understanding of what Johnson and Kaplan actually mean by the implementation of strategy through a BSC. According to the concept of a strategy map, in a pragmatic sense, it is the causality between the 'four perspectives' which ultimately constitutes the strategy as an action programme; and it is the programmatic construction of this assumed causal connection through scorecards that constitutes the strategy design and implementation process.

As shown in Figure 7.2, when the figure of balancing is translated into a figure of causality, the return on capital employed (i.e. the financial perspective) becomes the strategic ultimatum. The act of *balancing* then becomes an act of *aligning* the other perspectives towards shareholder wealth maximization. According to BSC terminology, the customer, internal business process, and learning and growth are 'drivers' that

162   *Neoliberal trends*

ultimately lead to the desired financial outcomes. As such, despite what its name implies (i.e. balanced), the BSC is a tool of alignment and integration of everything else towards the accumulation of capital. In fact, it does not offer a normative superiority to any of those perspectives other than the financial. Other perspectives are simply understood, appreciated, cognized, and communicated as necessary, and hence are critical for the attainment of shareholder wealth maximization. Still, it relies on the same old neoclassical economic logic of wealth maximization. It still draws on the neoclassical presumption that the legitimation of any organizational act stems from its capacity to contribute to the shareholder's wealth. Commitment and investment on other perspectives are justified on the basis that they have a causal connection to the return on capital employed. The role of scorecards is to construct and institutionalize a set of calculative practices through which this assumed causality is rationalized and legitimated.

Causal and finality relations in the BSC

The validity and plausibility of the causality that the BSC assumes between these four perspectives are debated in the accounting literature. For example, Norreklit (2000) argues that the BSC's cause-and-effect relationship is problematic mainly because a general law cannot be established from which this causal relation can be established. However, Norreklit (2000) also explains that the relationship that BSCs propagate between the perspectives can be more unambiguously seen as a 'finality relationship' rather than a 'causality'. That is because a finality relationship does not assume the existence of a general law from which it can be established that a particular action would lead to a good financial result. Instead, finality relations operate as in the case of 'wishful thinking' or 'ideal-type' connections (i.e. a form of normativity). As such, the connections that BSCs strategically map between the perspectives is not that which would necessarily happen (as in the case of causal relationships). Instead, it is a connection that managers try to establish through scorecards and various other forms of managerial techniques.

In our readings of various case studies that report 'successful implementation of BSCs', we see that the epistemic power of the BSC stems exactly from this finality relationship (though they seem to be often miscommunicated as causalities) because they form a 'normativity' and 'ideology' rather than a 'positive science'. Hence, what the BSC captures is not necessarily a valid and tested truth or science of what drives financial performance but a 'desire' and 'necessity' of investing in what comes to be generally understood as desirable and necessary elements in the post-bureaucratic and postmodern managerial discourses (which we discussed in the previous sections). This is the postmodern managerial desire and necessity to be post-bureaucratic, to go beyond the budgets, to enhance employee participation in deciding their own targets, and to rationalize one's own individual organizational circumstances as contributing to the big picture (which now is manifested as the strategy). In fact, what BSCs do is to provide a financial rationalization for all these post-bureaucratic and postmodern managerial desires by providing a rhetoric that connects them to the financial ultimatum – the return on capital employed. After all, what does a 'scorecard' do? Like any other management templates (e.g. budgets), it constructs a particular narrative or text (quantitative and otherwise) of such desires and necessities within a particular locality. However, the text or the narrative that a scorecard creates is more desirable than that of a traditional budget, not only because it is novel (and hence in itself signifies an improvement in management) but also because it indeed enhances the managerial dialogue, provides opportunities for employee participation in decision making,

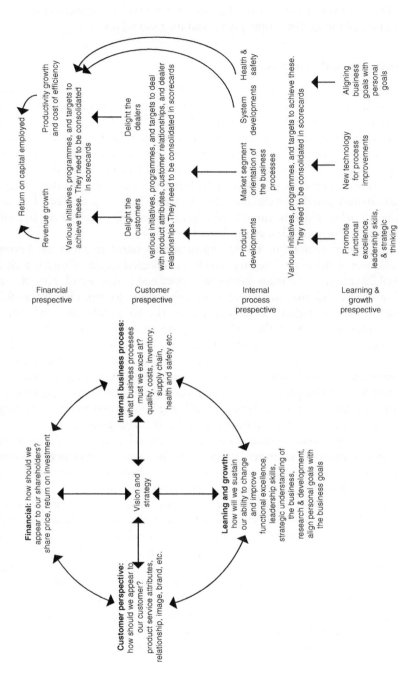

Figure 7.2 From balancing to causality in the BSC

164   *Neoliberal trends*

and also pushes people to think of the financial connection with the non-financial. In this sense, more than just providing a causal framework for understanding the non-financial drivers of financial performance, what the BSC does is to offer a financial rationalization for the non-financial things that people understand they should do.

7.5 Summary and conclusions

This chapter discussed the discourses pertaining to the second element of strategizing the firm – the postmodern and post-bureaucratic changes in the organizational form. We identified three interrelated and interlocking developments here: post-bureaucratic discourses, postmodern discourses, and discourses of strategic performance management. Post-bureaucratic discourses are aimed at incorporating a new set of techno-managerial elements that can address the issues of inflexibility, inefficiencies, job-dissatisfaction, and lack of workplace democracy associated with the modern type of bureaucracy. Three main techno-managerial movements were discussed here as providing the managerial approaches in achieving this: the job redesign movement, management by objectives, and the post-bureaucratic ideal of the 'interactive type'.

Postmodern explanations of recent organizational transformations go beyond such techno-managerial elements. They try to offer sociological explanations for such techno-managerial inventions. Four main themes were discussed in this regard. First, the signification of simulacra and the movement from production to reproduction explain how digitalization and networking technologies gave rise to a different socio-political and economic order in which simulacra played a significant political role in transforming the mode of production into the mode of reproduction. The second, entrepreneurialization of labour, connects this tendency of reproduction to the notions of entrepreneurship and human capital to explain how life itself is to be reproduced in the organization, transforming organizations into biopolitical sites of reproducing life. The immaterialization of labour argument takes this analysis a step further, articulating how techno-managerial changes now result in the workforces of postmodern organizations engaging in immaterial labour – symbolic-analytical labour, communicative labour, and affective labour. This immaterialization of labour argument is further reinforced by the structural tendency of 'management by themes'. The organizational processes and structures have been complicated by the ever increasing range of new theme management roles and structures.

The emergence of SPMS is the final element of strategizing the firm that we discussed in this chapter. Here the attention has been specifically on the strategic discourses pertaining to the BSC. As a SPMS, BSC discourses constitute seven fundamental elements: the *problematic* of traditional PMS; the *strategy as the binding principle* that demands linking operations with the strategy; the *multiplicity of performance dimensions* as the operational principle that demands balancing between the financial and the non-financial; the *causality* that connects non-financial to financial and, thereby, privileges the financial and rationalizes the non-financial; *cascading* that translates the strategy down through the organizational hierarchy; *scorecards* that translate the strategy into objectives, measures, targets, and initiatives; and *consultancy* that sets the managerial mode of implementation and control.

Assignments

These assignments are meant to extend your knowledge beyond what you understand from this chapter. These are not simply revision questions. The content covered in this

Organizational reconfiguration 165

chapter is necessary but will not be sufficient in attempting these tasks. Therefore, you are required to do some extra reading in attempting these tasks.

1. **Thematic essay:**
    'The postmodern evolution of management accounting is the result of a complex combination of techno-managerial and socio-cultural changes taking place within and beyond organizational boundaries'.
    Discuss this statement with reference to the techno-managerial and socio-cultural changes relevant to the recent transformations in the organizational form.
2. **Poster:**
    Draw a poster illustrating how post-bureaucratic, postmodern, and strategic performance management system discourses capture different aspects of neoliberal transformations of economic enterprises.
3. **Presentation:**
    Prepare a set of PowerPoint slides, together with notes if necessary, for a 30-minute presentation on the following theme:
    'Neoliberal transformations manifest a transition from mode of production to mode of reproduction'.
4. **Extended bibliography:**
    Write an extended bibliography on the development of the concept of strategic performance management systems. For this, you need to do a literature survey in major accounting journals and edited books where critical accounting research is published. Organize the bibliography into a table in the following format.

Bibliographic info	Nature of the paper/book chapter (e.g. conceptual/theoretical, empirical, a response to a previous publication)	Major arguments, conclusions, and contributions

5. **Literature review:**
    Suppose you are writing a thesis/dissertation on strategic management accounting. You intend to review the accounting and management literature in order to understand and theoretically explain the recent emergence and popularization of the BSC as the most dominant strategic management accounting tool. You are also thinking of the possibility of using theoretical notions pertaining to neoliberalism to illustrate this popularization of the BSC. You are required to do the necessary literature survey and write a chapter circa 5,000 words. You should search the academic journal databases for recent management and accounting literature on strategy as well as critical political assessments of the recent trends in management and accounting (e.g. Munro 2012).

Notes

1 Which Drucker (2011 [1977], 61) spells out as 'in the business enterprise managers are not automatically directed toward a common goal. On the contrary, business, by its very nature, contains three powerful factors of misdirection: in the specialized work of most managers; in the hierarchical structure of management; and in the differences in vision and work and the resultant insulation of various levels of management'

2 Just to contextualize the overall trend in industrial relations, according to the Trade Union Membership Bulletin of the Department of Business, Energy and Industrial Strategy (2017),

166 Neoliberal trends

around 6.2 million employees in the UK were trade union members in 2016 compared to 1979's 13 million. In 2016 itself, the level of overall union members decreased by 275,000 over the year from 2015 (a 4.2% decrease), the largest annual fall recorded since the series began in 1995. The union membership rate in the USA was just 10.7% in 2016 compared to 20.1% in 1983.

3 Following Gramsci, the term hegemony means here how fundamental social tensions (e.g. between labour and capital) are stabilized by fixing the meaning of social institutions and defining specific patterns of power relations within them. Hegemony is thus constructed by a particular organization of social institutions and power relations to ensure certain social categories dominate others but mostly by manufacturing consent rather than by coercion (see Burawoy 1979). Hence, hegemony is domination through cultural means.

4 Here the term 'real' provokes much debate (see Mattessich 2003). However, purely for the purpose of understanding postmodernity as a particular social era into which modern societies have now begun to enter, by the term real we here specifically refer to 'things' (such as goods, services, machineries, buildings, labour, capital, and so on) that we use to produce, exchange, invest in, and consume. This is in fact the so-called 'real economy'. And hence, socio-economic activities which are attributable to the production, exchange, investment, and consumption of such things constitute the 'real' in a modernist sense of mode of production. In other words, akin to the orthodox Marxist stance, our conception of 'real' here is understood in relation to the mode of 'production'.

5 In management accounting research, these aspects of 'abstract cooperation' have been explained differently with an emphasis on the techno-managerial and accounting developments in so-called 'horizontal organizations' (see Chenhall 2008). We will be dealing with these in the next chapter. Our attention here in this section is mainly on the 'sociological explanations' of postmodern organizations.

6 See Shrivastava (1986) for a splendid theoretical discussion on whether strategic management is ideological. He explains the ideological nature of strategic management research using Gidden (1979), namely: the factual underdetermination of action norms; the universalization of sectional interests; the denial of conflict and contradiction; the normative idealization of sectional goals; and the naturalization of the status quo. Accordingly, his conclusion is that strategic management is undeniably ideological.

8 Strategizing the firm

Strategic reconfiguration of the production systems – flexibility and quality

8.1 Introduction

In the previous two chapters, we discussed two aspects of strategizing the firm: strategic reinvention of the market through discourses of competitive positioning; and strategic reinvention of the organizational form through post-bureaucratic, postmodern, and strategic performance management discourses. Now, in this chapter, our attention is on the third dimension – strategizing the production systems and the role management accounting plays therein. Strategic management discourses aimed at 'strategizing the production' concentrate on three main managerial imperatives: flexibility, quality, and cost-efficiency. During the last few decades these three key themes have been identified as 'key success factors' or 'strategic imperatives' of the production system and, hence, much of the recent managerial discourse has been focused on how to improve the firm's performance in these areas. Accordingly, there have been a series of managerial innovations under the popular banners of flexible manufacturing, total quality management (TQM), just-in-time (JIT), and strategic cost management. In this chapter, our attention is mainly on the first two imperatives, namely flexibility and quality, and cost-efficiency will be dealt with in the next chapter.

The chapter is organized as follows:

1. Section 8.2 deals with *manufacturing flexibility*. Our attention here is particularly on various management discourses that aimed at reinventing production systems and processes to enhance their capacity to cater for changing markets and demand. Here we discuss how the notion of 'flexibility' has gained its central role in the strategic management discourses today and the different modes in which flexibility appears in those discourses. Accordingly, this section is organized into specific subsections that deal with the way in which flexibility is attributed to, and achieved through, different elements in the capitalist systems ranging from the specific elements of the labour process (i.e. flexible machine, flexible labour, and flexible manufacturing systems) to the macro-political (i.e. flexible specialization and flexible accumulation). Both managerial and sociological interpretations of flexibilization within and outside economic enterprises are discussed in this section.
2. Section 8.3 concentrates on *producing quality* and *leaning the production*. Here our attention is on how managerial discourses of quality and lean manufacturing have brought about a new set of managerial tool boxes to synchronize the factory floor with the market. Here we especially concentrate on: how quality has become a

168   *Neoliberal trends*

new managerial paradigm (Section 8.3.1), the economic or cost-based justification for TQM regimes (Section 8.3.2), and the quality-based discourses of organizational transformations, especially the Japanization phenomenon (Section 8.3.3).

3. Section 8.4 takes your attention to the disciplinary and biopolitical implications of TQM/JIT manufacturing systems. In this section, we revisit Foucauldian interpretations of organizations as disciplinary institutions, but with special focus on TQM/JIT to see how they have reinforced the disciplinary control of labour and how they have given rise to new forms of biopolitics.

4. Finally, in Section 8.5, the chapter concludes with a summary.

8.2 Manufacturing flexibility

From the discussions in the previous three chapters, we can state two important propositions about the neoliberal form of organizations, which form the basis for the discussions in this chapter. First, is that neoliberal organizations and neoliberal management thought take market dynamics so seriously that the market is seen as the source of every change. The market has become a referential point in the rationalization of everything we do in the name of management. Management has become the discursive and material act of building a dynamic and viable connection between what is happening in the market and what is happening within and between organizations. The corollary proposition of this market connection is that the firm needs to be so flexible in its structural, processual, and relational setup that it can adapt quickly to the changes taking place in the market realm. The notions of competitive advantage, competitive strategy, various post-bureaucratic organizational reforms, and strategic performance management systems are the conceptual parameters through which this market connection is institutionalized as a set of managerial doctrines and practices. The second proposition is that the neoliberal organizations are biopolitical sites in which life is reproduced. Moving beyond their disciplinary focus of confining bodies in specific time-space locations (which was the defining feature in liberal modernist organizations, as we discussed in Chapters 1 and 2), neoliberal organizations, on their own terms, have become societies in which life is reproduced as an enterprise in itself, moulding itself into the economic model of capital through the notions of human capital and entrepreneurship. Hence, the focus is on putting the lives into circulation through inculcating self-control and entrepreneurial ambitions to be realized through emerging biopolitical themes. As a result, neoliberal organizations are structured, organized, and managed by biopolitical themes. Coupled with the post-bureaucratic reforms and strategic performance management mentioned earlier, the entrepreneurialization and immaterialization of labour played critical roles in this transformation of organizations into biopolitical sites.

One of the key elements binding both these neoliberal propositions is the notion of flexibility. It has become one of the most sought-after characteristics of the post-bureaucratic organization. Basically, the populist argument in the mainstream management press is that the organization's competitiveness in a rather dynamic globalized market context is about its flexibility to cope with changes imposed by the market. Flexibility has often been populated as a critical element of competitive success (see Adler et al. 1999; Kanter 1990). In line with this centrality that the mainstream popular discourses attribute this to the notion of flexibility, even the critical sociological analyses have extensively used the term 'flexible' to characterize the postmodern post-Fordist transformations in production systems, as in the case of flexible manufacturing, flexible specialization, and flexible accumulation (see Gertler 1988; Harvey 1990). Either way, flexibility is a key byword to the changes that appear in the neoliberal transformations in the production systems. The term flexibility is used in a wide array of situations making its precise meaning rather obfuscated. However, our aim here is not to offer an overarching meaning for the term but to explain how different elements of flexibility are manifested in the post-Fordist systems of production and how management accounting is implicated differently in these various elements. These are:

- Flexible consumption
- Flexible machines
- Flexible labour
- Flexible manufacturing systems
- Flexible specialization and integration
- Flexible accumulation.

It is the totality of these elements that constitutes post-Fordism. These elements can indeed be hierarchically ordered, as summarized in Table 8.1 and explained in the forthcoming subsections.

8.2.1 Flexible consumption

One of the key economic trends in postmodern times is the emergence of what economists call buyers' markets: a segmented and fragmented market in which differences between buyers matter more than their similarities. Marking a rupture in 'monopoly capitalism' (a term that political economists like Braverman (1998 [1974]) used to characterize the Fordist mass production regime of capitalism), there was a significant power shift towards the buyers from the sellers. This means that the market is no longer conceived of as a homogeneous set of people whom firms can make happy by offering a standardized product. In other words, there is a growing understanding that, however good the product might be, the strategy of 'one good product for everybody' would not work in a highly competitive and segmented market. As we already discussed in Chapter 6, product differentiation on the basis of differences in customer needs becomes the cornerstone of marketing strategies. Underlying this trend, there is what we call 'flexible consumption' – the readiness and eagerness of firms, as a strategy, to offer the consumer variety and difference.

Table 8.1 The hierarchy of flexibility concepts

Flexibility concept	Realm of operation and scope of analysis
Flexible consumption	Market/consumer and consumer-firm connection
Flexible machines	Fixed capital – firm-level, technological
Flexible labour	Labour – firm-level, techno-managerial and political
Flexible manufacturing systems	Firm-level – techno-managerial
Flexible specialization and integration	Industry/meso level – interfirm coordination
Flexible accumulation	Total capitalist system, labour markets, capital markets

170   Neoliberal trends

It should be noted that the notion of 'flexible consumption' attempts not simply to capture the fact or the possibility that consumers now consume variety flexibly. More than the consumers' experience from their own point of view, what is the focus here is the strategic understanding, necessity, readiness, and capacity of the firm to offer flexibility to consumers. Hence, flexible consumption is a strategy emanating from the producer, though its outcome is that consumers may experience and enjoy the variety and flexibility. As a strategy and a managerial mentality, flexible consumption then demands and drives the firms to develop the organizational capacity to deliver it. This capacity rests on two interlocking and interrelated elements:

1. The capacity to produce flexibly. This is the capacity offered by flexible machines, flexible labour, flexible manufacturing systems, and flexible specialization and integration.
2. The information capacity across the markets, firms, and consumers in order to construct and maintain an effective network of communication between various elements of producing flexibly. As we will see later (especially in the discussion on flexible manufacturing systems and flexible specialization and integration), the capacity to produce flexibly cannot be reached by individual firms on their own. It is by no means firm-specific. Instead, it demands a high degree of interfirm (as well as intrafirm) coordination, spanning across industries and other regulatory and cultural fields. The rapid development of information technology during the last few decades has immensely facilitated this. For example, supply chain management platforms and software integrate various aspects of this connection, such as demand planning, import/export management, inventory and warehouse management, and transportation management and delivery tracking. In essence, this is what we called 'abstract cooperation' that the 'communicative labour' is dealing with (Hardt and Negri 2000) in the previous chapter (i.e. maintaining connections between deterritorialized organizations, production systems, and sites). This means that in this era of flexible consumption, management accounting information needs to be driven towards this type of cooperation – to abstract otherwise distant and deterritorialized organizational entities and consumers from their locality and to place them on integrated 'informational spaces' so that the different elements in manufacturing flexibly can be connected to each other.

8.2.2   Flexible machines

The second element of a flexible manufacturing system is flexible machines which, in a broader sense, refer to machines that can change what it produces at minimal cost and time involvement and that flexibility in production is no more prohibitive in terms of cost and extra investment needed. Examples include computerized numerically controlled (CNC) machines, robots, and 3D printers at the high-end spectrum of technology. At the low-end of the technical spectrum is one of the best and most easily understood examples, the printing/copying machine or multifunction device (MFD). They can change what they print and copy at almost no cost and time involvement in resetting the machine. To have a better idea, one can compare these machines with the old printing press machines which needed to be cleaned, have the typesetting and plates redone, be reinked, etc. in order to do a new printing or copying job. In a modern-day printing/copying machine, this is just a matter of replacing the original or resending another print command from the computer.

Reconfiguration of production systems   171

There is a specific management accounting logic in the way these machines facilitate flexible manufacturing. They influence the financial calculations and rationalization of the economic production quantity (EPQ). As you are aware from your intermediary management accounting courses, the EPQ calculation contains a particular optimization logic where the sum total of inventory holding costs and production setup costs is minimized. As shown in Figure 8.1, this optimum production size takes place when the total cost is minimized (i.e. when the holding cost and setup cost intersect). Setup cost is the cost needed to reset the machine from one production batch to another (i.e. the cost incurred for flexing the machine for another production run). Figure 8.1 illustrates a traditional mass production situation where the setup cost is relatively high (represented by curve SC1) for each possible order size. As a result of this relatively high setup cost, the economic order quantity remains higher (EOQ1 in Figure 8.1). The setup cost curve SC2 illustrates a situation of flexible machines where the setup cost is relatively low for all possible batch quantities. A downward shift in the setup cost manifests the shift in the production technology from non-flexible to flexible machines. Now, with this new setup cost, the EPQ has reduced to EPQ2, economically permitting a smaller batch size. In this manner, when the setup cost can be reduced

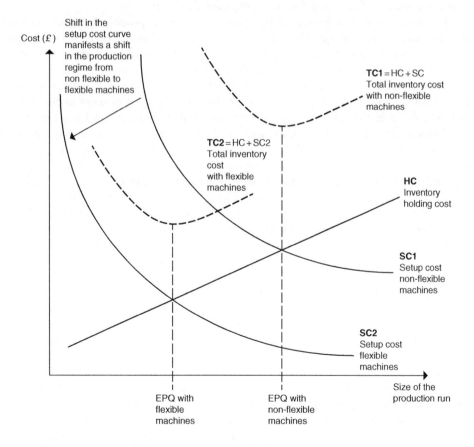

Figure 8.1 Reduction of production batch size due to flexible machines

172 *Neoliberal trends*

down to its absolute minimum, close to zero, the EPQ will reach 1 – a perfect mass customization production scenario – a situation where producing even one unit is still economically optimal.

In addition to this reduction in the EPQ, flexible machines will also have a significant impact on the longevity of the fixed capital. They obviate the need to scrap and replace existing fixed machines (i.e. fixed capital) when the company needs to replace its existing market offerings with new ones. Flexible machines can be reprogrammed, at minimal cost, extending their technical life. Hence the payback period of the investment on flexible machines can be longer, spanning a few product lifecycles.

8.2.3 Flexible labour

The third element of a flexible manufacturing system is flexible labour. In a broader sense, flexible labour means forms of labour that can be easily transferable across different jobs, different skill categories, different territorial sites of production, different time slots, and even be easily removed when no longer deemed necessary. In other words, rather than labour being a relatively fixed element, as in the case of permanent labour, flexible labour can be flexed according to the changing labour requirements imposed by flexible consumption and flexible machines. Two forms of flexibilization of labour are relevant here: skill flexibility and time flexibility.

The essence of skill or functional flexibility is to make it possible for firms to change the division of labour quickly without cost and to shift workers between tasks, positions, and workplaces (Standing 2011). Since the industrial revolution, the division of work has not been something specifically attributable to the qualities and skills of the labour force itself. Instead, it often stems from the techno-managerial apparatuses of the production system. It is the machinery itself that often triggers changes in the division of work. As such, the invention and reinvention of flexible machines has reconstructed the division of work and the type of labour it demands. As we discussed in the previous chapter, skill flexibility takes place within this immaterialization of labour: the emergence of *symbolic-analytical labour, communicative labour,* and *affective labour* (see Section 7.3.3) due to the techno-managerial inventions taking place within the realms of production and reproduction. As we noted in the previous chapter, in the early phases of capitalism and modernism, labouring activities were radically heterogeneous. Tailoring and weaving, for example, involved unique concrete actions by human beings. In production systems using flexible machines, this heterogeneity of labour increasingly disappears as labour involves exactly the same concrete practices, abstract labour – manipulation of symbols and information – abstract cooperation, and affective work. They are no longer the widely varying 'specialized' and 'deskilled' forms of labour common in Fordist factories – labour that performed unique concrete actions associated with a specialized machine. Hence, labour can easily be shifted from one flexible machine to another, because most of these machines would need more or less the same sort of symbolic-analytical and communicative actions. As far as the 'physicality' (that was part of labour in a conventional sense) is now carried out by machines and robot arms, and as far as labour now involves communication with the machine (and other co-workers), changing the division of labour and transferring labour to new jobs, new skill categories, new positions, and new sites has become relatively easy.

Time flexibility, on the other hand, is the enhanced discretion of management to move labour in a temporal manner. This includes the flexibility of labour between

Reconfiguration of production systems 173

different times including the extension of 'normal' work hours (vis-à-vis overtime) in terms of, for example, 24-hour machine shops and offices worked by shift workers. In an overall sense, this involves enhancing managerial discretion for hiring, firing, transferring, and stipulating the timing of the work. This is more political than techno-managerial and involves sweeping changes taking place in the context and content of industrial relations, within and beyond organizational boundaries. Some of the key political movements/trends in this regard include:

1. The discursive establishment of the economic policy idea that making it easier to fire workers is necessary to boost jobs. Transnational organizations such as the IMF, World Bank, and OECD were behind the spread of this neoliberal economic ideology (often as a conditionality of their loan and aid packages to countries). They often argue that loosening employment protection laws and regulations is necessary to attract foreign direct investment (Standing 2011, 31–32).
2. The global trend of out-sourcing labour contracts. Companies are contracting out much of their labour, only holding onto the core knowledge workers who carry out symbolic-analytical and communicative elements of labour (i.e. immaterial labour). Such outsourcing often takes place to developing countries where labour is abundant and hence cheap, and where the rather coercive regimes of labour controls can be deployed.
3. Coupled with the above two points, companies tend to increasingly use temporary labour rather than building a strong long-term permanent workforce. This has been the case even in Japan where lifetime employment was once a defining characteristic. Temporary labour has cost advantages: wages are lower, experience-rated pay is avoided, entitlement to enterprise benefits is less, and so on. Furthermore, there is less risk. Taking on somebody temporarily means not making a commitment that might be regretted, for whatever reason (Standing 2011, 32).
4. Growth of project-based hiring of employees. Work is often organized as short- or medium-term projects. Employment contracts have also followed this project-based organization of work.
5. These neoliberal changes in employment practices being made possible by the weakening presence of trade unions as a political institution in society. As we mentioned in the previous chapter, the proportion of unionized labour has drastically decreased during the last few decades. In addition, as a result of the relative absence of unionized labour to resist change, employers, together with right-wing governments supporting aggressive neoliberal reforms, are now capable of introducing rather more flexible labour contracts such as 'zero-hour contracts'.

8.2.4 Flexible manufacturing systems

The flexible manufacturing system (FMS) is the techno-managerial organization of the above three elements – flexible consumption, flexible machines, and flexible labour – to form a distinct mode of production. Flexible consumption constitutes its strategic intention while flexible machines and flexible labour provide the resources and competence or capacity to realize flexible manufacturing. An FMS is formed by combining a number of flexible machines into an integrated system usually linked

174   *Neoliberal trends*

together and coordinated by computers. Such an aggregation of flexible machines is often called a manufacturing cell. An FMS can either be a small manufacturing cell or a large cluster of manufacturing cells that form an 'assembly highway' (see Miller and O'Leary 1994).

The normative end of FMS is flexible consumption – offering customers the opportunity of meeting their differing and changing needs. In operational terms, this normativity is often captured by the concept of 'mass customization', which is the ability of the production system to customize its product offerings to meet differences and changes in demand patterns but with the same or a higher degree of production and cost-efficiency that a mass production facility can offer. In essence, an FMS should transform a mass production facility into a better one with the capacity to produce 'heterogeneity' rather 'homogeneity'. This is in fact a techno-managerial challenge because it demands that the same or a higher degree of 'economies' are achieved but with a smaller scale of production in terms of volume. In other words, the FMS is designed to integrate the flexibility of 'job shops' and the efficiency of 'mass production systems'. Traditionally, before the era of FMS, production of small quantities of different products was done in 'job shops' where multi-purpose machines and multi-skilled labour were occupied. However, relatively long setup times, large work-in-progress inventories, and delays in meeting customer demands were too common in job shop environments resulting in a relatively higher average cost of production. Conventionally, such inefficiencies were attributed to the lack of 'economies of scale', and scale of production volume was considered to be the primary driver of efficiency. On the other hand, producing large batches of identical products using specialized machines and labour in a high throughput plant layout created massive economies of scale and much lower average costs. But such mass production systems were not flexible enough to cater for the different and changing demand patterns. In essence, flexibility and efficiency were conventionally taken as the polar opposites of production programming. The FMS is indeed a negation of this opposition between flexibility and efficiency. With the advances in several fields of engineering and computer technology, the FMS makes efficient mass production of flexibility and difference possible with flexible labour, flexible multi-purpose machines with fast tool-changing capabilities, automated material handling systems, computer aided design and manufacturing, and digital communication networks that connect every aspect of production and distribution (Maleki 1991). How the FMS integrates job shops and mass production systems is summarized in Table 8.2.

System flexibilities

As mentioned earlier, the operational efficacy of an FMS is understood in terms of its capacity to produce and deliver customized products at lower costs and at high speed. In order to achieve this, an FMS needs to build and maintain different sorts of 'system flexibilities', which operational management literature (e.g. Maleki 1991) often categorizes into three main areas as follows:

1.   Basic or element flexibilities:

     (a)   Machine flexibility: how easily a machine can process various/different operations.

Reconfiguration of production systems 175

Table 8.2 FMS integration of efficiency with flexibility

Comparative dimension	Job shop production	Mass production	Flexible manufacturing systems
Strategic focus and intention	Quality, product variety, differentiation.	Cost-efficiency, speed of delivery and production.	Flexibility, quality and customization but with cost and time efficiency.
Core competence sought	Capacity to meet varieties in demand.	Capacity to produce a standardized product at a lower cost at high speed.	Customizability with lower cost and high-speed production and delivery.
Nature of the fixed capital	Multi-purpose machines capable of producing varieties but with high setup costs and greater time required for major retooling to cater for varying products.	Specialized machines, needing massive reinvestment to produce varieties.	Flexible machines capable of producing varieties with no major retooling, hence setup cost and time are very minimal.
Nature of the working capital			
Labour	Skilled jack-of-all-trades labour.	Deskilled, specialized in a single task/job.	Flexible immaterial labour mainly performing symbolic-analytical and communicative elements with automated machines.
Inventories	Large work-in-progress inventories	Large parts and raw material inventories.	Just-in-time.

    (b)   Labour flexibility: how easily labour can be moved and replaced across different jobs/operations in the system.

    (c)   Material handling flexibility: how easily different parts can be transported and properly positioned at the various machine tools in the system.

    (d)   Operation flexibility: how easily alternative operation sequences can be used for processing a product or part.

2.   System flexibilities:

    (a)   Volume flexibility: the system's capability to be operated profitably at different volumes of production.

    (b)   Expansion flexibility: the ability to expand the system incrementally.

    (c)   Routing flexibility: availability of alternative processing paths that throughput can effectively follow through a system.

    (d)   Process flexibility: number of different parts/product types that a system can produce without incurring any re-setup.

    (e)   Product flexibility: number of different parts/products types that a system can produce with minor re-setup.

3.   Aggregate flexibilities:

    (a)   Program flexibility: the ability of a system to run for reasonably long periods without external intervention.

176 *Neoliberal trends*

    (b)   Production flexibility: the ability of the system to produce a new product design without major investment in capital equipment.

    (c)   Market flexibility: the ability of a system to efficiently adapt to changing market conditions.

Accounting in FMS

Various forms of calculative practices, which we can broadly identify as emerging management accounting technologies, play a critical role in making flexible manufacturing regimes possible. In the forthcoming sections, we will be further elaborating on how recent accounting developments, in one way or another, were related to this flexibilization agenda. However, for the time being, it is important to note that the emerging role of 'new' accounting technologies (e.g. ABC and ERP) needed to be understood in terms of:

1. Their capacity to analyse the changing pattern in customer demands and preferences and to identify the strategic imperatives (e.g. new product attributes) emanating from such changes. To this end, companies are now increasingly using various techniques, software, and online platforms of market analytics coupled with 'big data' (see Davenport 2014; Kitchin 2014; Sathi 2014).
2. Their capacity to offer a financial insight into the value of differentiating 'tasks' or 'activities' that flexible machines and flexible labour carry out. In these new production environments, machine and labour cannot be meaningfully differentiated primarily based on their location (i.e. cost centres), as it used to be the case in a traditional absorption costing and budgeting environment. Their value is no more emanating from their location and the volume of output that their location collectively produces. Instead, their value stems from the specific 'differentiating' activities that they carry out. This means that flexible manufacturing demands managerial attention on the specific activities that the machines and labour carry out. This is because that in a flexible manufacturing setting, a given machine or labour would not carry out the same homogeneous activity during a given accounting period, but rather a heterogeneous set of activities, even though they were located in the same cost centre. In ABC terminology, this is captured in terms of 'activity cost drivers' and 'activity cost pools'. Proponents and adopters of ABC often argue that ABC would provide a better calculation of 'true' cost as it captures the variations in the activities that flexible machines and flexible labour carry out.
3. Their capacity to enhance *communication between different elements of the FMS* and, thereby, to integrate the elements into a holistic system. In this regard, *real-time information* provision is an essential condition, which traditional budgeting and standard costing systems would not be able to achieve. It is these most essential real-time information conditions that various computer-based and networked accounting software technologies (e.g. ERP and other supply chain management software) can achieve (see Wagner et al. 2011).
4. Their capacity to make detailed comparisons between the performance of their own units, machines, individuals, and those of their competitors. As Miller and O'Leary (1994) explain with empirical data from their Caterpillar case study, flexible manufacturing sometimes demands instilling a person-to-person sense of

competition, a situation where the individual and individual tasks are directly compared with their counterparts in competing firms. The calculative practices of competitor cost analysis were deployed as a way of making this detailed comparison possible (Miller and O'Leary 1994, 23)

8.2.5 Flexible specialization and integration

Flexible specialization (see Piore and Sabel 1984; Hirst and Zeitlin 1991) takes the notion of flexibility beyond the organizational boundaries of the FMS to the level of industrial regulation and industrial development. The argument here is that the organizational or production system level flexibility (i.e. FMS) cannot be achieved without a set of wider politico-institutional arrangements. Hence, the attention towards political institutional mechanisms through which the necessary integration beyond organizations is established to meet the flexibility demands of the postmodern organization. In other words, while FMS and post-Fordist interpretations of recent transformations in production regimes mainly concentrate techno-managerial apparatuses of the change, flexible specialization pays attention to the politics beyond the organizational level that make flexible manufacturing possible. For Hirst and Zeitlin (1991) the difference between post-Fordism and flexible specialization is that:

> Where post-Fordism sees productive systems as integrated and coherent totalities, flexible specialisation identifies complex and variable connections between technology, institutions and politics; where post-Fordism sees industrial change as a mechanical outcome of impersonal processes, flexible specialisation emphasizes contingency and the scope for strategic choice.

Hirst and Zeitlin (1991, 10) also argue that the post-Fordist concept of industrial change only pays 'little attention to the wide range of forms and hybrids of flexibly-specialized production and their social and institutional conditions'. This means that while post-Fordist explanations rely upon firm-initiated reactions to the collapse of mass markets, flexible specialization argues that the strategic turn towards flexible manufacturing means that 'not merely the firm but interfirm and collective regional and national patterns are crucial in the balancing of competition and co-operation necessary for their more progressive institutionalisation' (ibid.). For Piore and Sabel (1984), also, flexible specialization is not a phenomenon confined within the boundaries of individual organizations, but a result of micro regulations of innovative activities across industries. It is a matter of 'finding a compatible institutional answer to the problems of instigating and coordinating innovation, [because] competition of a wrong kind undermines the necessary coordination; misdirected coordination undermines competition' (Piore and Sabel 1984, 264–265). In other words, proponents of the flexible specialization hypothesis reckon on the importance of interfirm coordination through institutional mechanisms operating beyond the individual organizational settings or markets. A transition from mass production to flexible manufacturing thus requires an extra-organizational reconciliation of these apparently antagonistic principles of competition and coordination to facilitate financially viable innovations to ensure flexibility. According to Piore and Sabel (1984, 265–268), this reconciliation takes place in three different settings:

178 *Neoliberal trends*

1. **Regional conglomerations**. These are the specialized industrial districts composed of a core of more-or-less equal enterprises bound in a complex web of competition and coordination. These are established as 'strategic initiatives' to enhance industry and national competitiveness. A good example is Michael Porter's (1998) concept of 'industrial clusters', which he described as a new strategic arrangement to enhance national competitiveness. For him:

   > [c]lusters encompass an array of linked industries and other entities important to competition. They include, for example, suppliers of specialized inputs such as components, machinery, and services, and providers of specialized infrastructure. Clusters also often extend downstream to channels and customers and laterally to manufacturers of complementary products and to companies in industries related by skills, technologies, or common inputs. Finally, many clusters include governmental and other institutions – such as universities, standards-setting agencies, think tanks, vocational training providers, and trade associations-that provide specialized training, education, information, research, and technical support.

2. **Federated enterprises**. This refers to the pre-war Japanese *zaibatsu* and the looser post-war federations of Japanese enterprises which led industrial development in Japan towards flexible specialization. According to Miyajima (1994: 294):

   > [t]here are six corporate groups of this type in Japan. Three of them – Mitsu, Mitsubishi and Sumitomo – originated as pre-war zaibatsu and were organised as corporate groups in the early 1950s. The other three – Fuyo, Sanwa and Daiichi – originated as pre-war big banks and organised as corporate groups in the late 1960s.

   The salient characteristics of these federated enterprises or corporate groups were cross-shareholdings, a main bank system, an intermediary role for trading companies, presidents' clubs and cooperative investments of member companies, as well as the sharing of financial, marketing, and technological expertise between member corporations. However, according to Piore and Sabel (1984, 267), the group is not as integrated as the mass-production corporation, and member firms are not hierarchically arranged, but their sense of common identity is much sharper than that of firms in regional conglomerates or industrial clusters.

3. **Solar firms and workshop factories**. This type of coordination of innovative activities consists of 'firms with a solar-system model of orbiting suppliers and its close cousin the workshop factory' (Piore and Sabel 1984, 267). The link between the suppliers and the factory is not subordinate (as in the case of divisions of a multidivisional mass producer) but collaborative, and the solar firm depends on the subcontractors for advice in solving design and production problems. The example Piore and Sabel provide is the Boeing Company, which produces neither the engines nor much of the avionic equipment for its aeroplanes.

In essence, the flexible specialization thesis extends the evolution of flexible manufacturing beyond organizational boundaries to the sphere of interfirm coordination and competition. It emphasizes the significance of micro-regulatory institutional arrangements between firms and industries to reconcile competition and coordination – a necessary structural condition for the development of flexible manufacturing regimes.

8.2.6 Flexible accumulation

The concept of flexible accumulation takes the notion of flexibility a further step more into the global dynamics of capital and labour. Here the attention is on the 'new capitalism' that the micro-organizational changes in production systems, relations, and technologies have brought about. There is quite an array of terms that political-economists use to characterize this new form of capitalism; for example, 'the post-industrial paradigm' (Halal 1986), 'disorganised capitalism' (Lash and Urry 1987), and 'just-in-time capitalism' (Swyngedouw 1986). In essence, flexible accumulation captures everything we have discussed so far in Section 8.2 and then places it within the wider schema of transformed capitalism. For example, Swyngedouw (1986) explains this transformation in terms of the shifts that have taken place in the production processes, labour, industrial space, state, and ideology. Harvey (1989) explains flexible accumulation, inter alia, in terms of the transformation taking place in the pattern of international trade, business accumulation and profit rates, exchange rates, capacity utilization, the property boom, and the structure of labour markets. One way or another, they all connect flexible manufacturing with the macro dynamics of global capitalism. In this sense, flexible accumulation, in a broader sense, refers to post-Fordist capitalism in which the flexibilization of both capital and labour has been the central proposition of accumulation. Flexible accumulation provides a particular theorization of how circulation (through flexibilization) of labour and capital become more crucial than disciplinary confinement.

In order to identify neoliberalization elements (i.e. putting lives into circulation through biopolitics) of this transformation, we need to pay special attention to what has happened to labour markets in this flexible accumulation regime. As we discussed in previous chapters, a modern Fordist regime of production is characterized by a large blue-collar unskilled workforce often with long-term employment contracts and reasonable job security ensured through union negotiations with the employers. The majority of the labour force is therefore concentrated on the factory floor, constituting the 'core group' in the 'primary labour market'. As illustrated in Figure 8.2, and explained later, during the regime of flexible accumulation, this core was diluted and circulated into the periphery in different forms of labour contracts and labour market innovations so that the core element of labour was kept to its minimum. The condition of flexible labour was achieved through this circulation and peripheralization of labour.

The *core* is the steadily shrinking group of employees mainly engaging with what strategic management gurus would identify as those who deal with strategic or core competencies (Prahalad and Hamel 1990). This group of employees, often the top and middle management, are those who determine the strategic intent of the company, populate the company vision and mission, and then build collaborations in a wide array of partnerships and networks into which they have distributed most of their production and distribution activities. For example, Prahalad and Hamel (1990, 80) attributes NEC's business success to its organizational restructuring around this notion of 'core competencies':

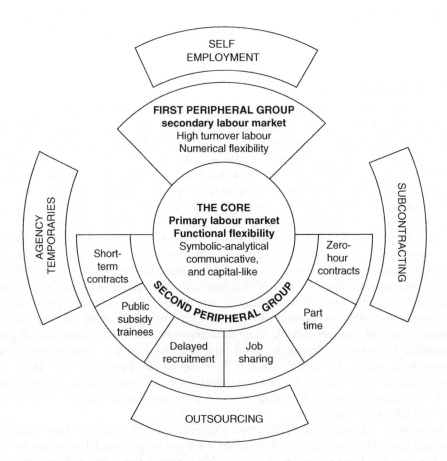

Figure 8.2 Circulation and peripheralization of labour
Source: adapted from Harvey (1990, 151).

NEC articulated a strategic intent to exploit the convergence of computing and communications, what it called 'C&C' ... adopted an appropriate 'strategic architecture' ... [which] constituted a 'C&C Committee' of top managers to oversee the development of core products and core competencies ... put in place coordination groups and committees that cut across the interests of individual businesses ... determined that semiconductors would be the company's most important 'core product' ... entered into myriad strategic alliances – over 100 as of 1987 – aimed at building competencies rapidly and at low cost ... almost all the collaborative arrangements in the semiconductor-component field were oriented towards technology access. As they entered collaborative arrangements, NEC's operating managers understood the rationale for these alliances and the goal of internalizing partner skills. NEC's director of research summed up its competence acquisition during the 1970s and 1980s this way: 'From an investment standpoint, it was much quicker and cheaper to use foreign technology. There wasn't a need for us to develop new ideas'.

By their very nature, their jobs are communicative and symbolic–analytical (i.e. immaterial labour) and often implode into the category of capital (rather than labour itself) in terms of intellectual or knowledge capital. They work more like dealers, networkers, collaborators, coordinators, and above all strategist, aiming at capitalizing on 'opportunities' that the others can bring them. And, for this particular reason, often like the owners of the capital (even though they have not invested a financial stake in the business), they claim a portion of profits through various forms of corporate performance-based (rather than individual performance) compensation schemes. They are employees with full-time, permanent status and are central to the long-term future of the organization, enjoying greater job security, good promotion and reskilling prospects, and relatively generous pension, insurance, and other fringe benefit rights. This core is nevertheless expected to be adaptable, flexible, and if necessary geographically mobile (Harvey 1989, 150).

While this core is increasingly acquiring the dominating features and capabilities of capital, the rest of the workforce is 'strategically' drawn to the *periphery* through 'myriad strategic alliances' (see above quote from Prahalad and Hamel 1990, 80). As Harvey (1989, 150) explains, this peripheralization involves creating two rather different sub-groups:

> The first consists of full-time employees with skills that are readily available in the labour market, such as clerical, secretarial, routine and lesser skilled manual work. With less access to career opportunities, this group tends to be characterized by high labour turnover which makes work force reductions relatively easy by natural wastage. The second peripheral group provides even greater numerical flexibility[1] and includes part-timers, casuals, fixed term contract staff, temporaries, sub-contractors and public subsidy trainees, with even less job security than the first peripheral group.

The 'appropriate strategic architecture' (see above quote from Prahalad and Hamel 1990, 80) that makes this peripheralization possible includes letting various previously internal functionalities of the corporation be outsourced. Experts who were hitherto managing support and service functions (e.g. security, labour contracting, research and development, training and development, process design, advertising, and even accounting and finance) would be 'encouraged' to setup their own enterprises and be self-employed to provide those support services as outsourcing companies. Different corporate functionalities are thus loosened from the core and are placed in quasi-market arrangements facilitating flexible labour and the circulation of both labour and capital.

8.3 Producing quality and leaning the production

Like flexibility, quality and lean production have also entered the managerial lexicon as defining elements of the post-Fordist organizational forms. They are often cited as 'critical or strategic success factors'. As Chenhall (1997) explains, the widespread adoption of total quality management (TQM) to compete in markets characterized by improved quality and service attributes, often at highly competitive prices, has elevated quality to a strategic competitive variable. At the same time, as TQM demands continuous process improvements of all aspects of production and distribution, especially in terms of significant reduction of wastages to offer quality at a low price, leaning

182 *Neoliberal trends*

the production processes has also become a central element of this new corporate strategic posture. Various structural, relational, processual and technological elements have been introduced to reorganize the firm to cater these two strategic imperatives. Like flexibility, quality and lean production have thus become key strategic themes around which the post-Fordist firm is reformed. They have indeed become 'higher order principles' (Boltanski and Thévenot 2006) towards which the other elements of organizations are now directed.

8.3.1 *Quality as a new managerial paradigm*

The discursive significance of quality stems from its capacity to reformulate managerial thought, structures, relations, processes, and practices. One of the key aspects in this regard is its capacity to 'customize' the organization. Here the notion of customization needs to be understood in two distinct, but interrelated and interlocking perspectives. First, as in our discussion in the previous section, we used the notion of customization to mean the capacity of the firm to 'customize its products' to meet different market segments and customer needs. Quality takes its *primary* meaning from this version of customization. Hence, quality is often defined as 'conformance to the requirements of the customer', or 'fitness for use' (Hill 1991, 400). This brings the customer to the forefront of the organizational purpose and design. Any pragmatic definition of quality, therefore, should begin with the specification that meets the needs of the customer not the producer. Product and organizational design, in that sense, mean making sure that the company understands, appreciates, and integrates customer requirements into the product's attributes and the production process. It is only when this primary definition of quality in terms of customer requirement is achieved that the *secondary* meaning of quality – quality as conformance to the design specifications – becomes operable and meaningful in the realm of market competition.

The second version of 'customization' is that the quality management discourses translate everyone, inside and outside the company, into customers. Quality demands treating the other elements and people in the organization that one interacts with as 'internal customers'. Hence, everyone now should receive a managerial redefinition as customers and, therefore, should be treated with the utmost care and consideration. This means that, while holding onto their other institutional imperatives, the internal hierarchy, structure, and processes are now to be reconceptualized as market relations. As a 'customer', every unit in the organization should conform to its own requirements, while as a supplier it has an obligation to conform to the requirements of others (Hill 1991, 400).

To take this customization beyond mere organizational rhetoric, new ideological, cultural, and structural rearrangements are required. These include quite a wide array of institutional rearrangements from the top of the organization to the bottom. Our aim here is not to provide a comprehensive discussion of these organizational reforms that quality discourses initiated and populated. Instead, we try here to articulate how quality as a strategic imperative influences management control and accounting thought and practices. In that sense, our attention is on:

1. How zero defects and the continuous regime of quality are justified through a particular accounting logic of optimization.
2. The way in which strategic attention on quality gives rise to a new set of structural, relational, and processual elements in organizations.

8.3.2 Economic justification of TQM: cost minimization logic of zero-defect rate and continuous improvements

A zero-defect rate is the operational and strategic doctrine of TQM, of which the best pragmatic realization is the 'six sigma' quality level denoting the possibility that only one out of a million products that the system produces would be defective (see chapters in Aized 2012). Continuous improvements are directed towards the strategic desire of zero defects not simply because of its ideological desirability but due to the newly established optimization logic that it is only at the zero-defect quality level that the total quality cost will be minimized and eventually reduced to zero. Explaining this optimization logic requires paying attention to the total quality cost function and its elements. Total quality cost has two main elements: the costs of non-conformance with quality standards and the costs of conformance with quality standards. The costs of non-conformance constitute *internal failure costs* and *external failure costs*. Internal failure costs are the costs associated with products being substandard but detected internally before they pass to the external customers (e.g. rework costs, scrap, disposal, etc.). External failure costs, on the other hand, are those associated with substandard products being passed to the external customers (e.g. replacements, guarantees, loss of goodwill, etc.). Costs of conformance can broadly be divided into two major elements: appraisal costs and prevention costs. The total qualify function, therefore, can be summarized as follows:

$$TQC = IFC + EFC + AC + PC$$

Where TQC is the total quality cost; IFC is the internal failure costs; EFC is the external failure cost; AC is the appraisal cost; and PC is the prevention cost.

For the purposes of explaining how these cost elements are related to the level of quality, quality is defined as:

$$Q = 1-\text{defective rate (i.e. the probability that the system}$$
$$\text{can produce effective products)}$$

Costs of conformance and non-conformance are supposed to be inversely related to the level of system quality. When the system reaches the zero-defects level, the cost of non-conformance should be zero while at higher levels of defects this cost should be higher. On the other hand, it is assumed that, generally, to reach a high level of quality, the company needs to spend more on appraisal and prevention costs. So, the higher the costs of conformance, the lower the costs of non-conformance. This inverse relationship of two quality cost elements to the quality level and the resulting optimization logic is illustrated in Figure 8.3.

Figure 8.3 illustrates that this paradigm dominated management thinking until the 1970s (and continues even now to a certain extent). Driven by the neoclassical economic logic of optimization, the zero-defect quality level is theorized as being 'too costly to be achieved' (i.e. lies beyond the optimum or cost-minimizing point). Hence, the theoretical assertion is that a certain level of defects should be acceptable as it is not economically optimum. In other words, the possibility of some customers receiving defective products needs to be tolerated as it is not economically optimum to make sure that every customer is satisfied (i.

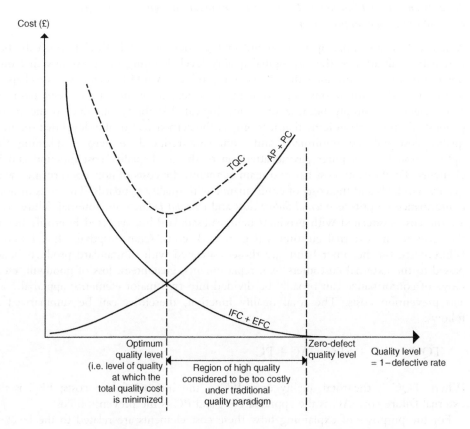

Figure 8.3 Quality cost optimization logic: traditional paradigm

e. the zero-defect quality). In fact, herein lies a particular cost-benefit analysis which negates the zero-defect quality as economical but not optimum. The classic example of this sort of managerial thinking and analysis was the Ford Pinto case. The Ford company launched some of its models in the 1970s with a defect in its fuel system which resulted in some cars exploding if hit behind at moderate speed. In subsequent lawsuits against the company, it was revealed that the company's management knew about this defect but decided to release the cars onto the market anyway with the defect on the basis of a cost-benefit analysis that it carried out. Not surprisingly, there was a great public outcry (see Ford Pinto case in Hoffman et al. 2014, 139–145)

The continuous improvement paradigm offers a rethink of this optimization logic by revising the fundamental assumptions behind the way in which appraisal and preventive costs of quality would behave beyond the level of quality. The new assertion is that, with continuous improvements, the cost of conformance (i.e. the sum of prevention and appraisal costs) would be at their maximum when the production system reached the zero-defect level of quality. This is because once it reaches that stage there would be no need to incur any more preventive and appraisal costs. This means that, as illustrated in Figure 8.4, the total quality cost would be minimized only when the production system reaches the zero-defect point. Not only that, with continuous improvements, in the long-run, the firm should be able to further reduce these costs (the downward shifts in quality cost curves in Figure 8.4), implying the possibility of, at least theoretically, achieving zero defects with no quality costs being incurred. Quality gurus' argument in this regard is that, through various continuous improvements to the production processes (e.g. the famous 5S quality control practices[2]), quality management should be so integrated into every activity that everyone in the firm carries it out and everyone would thereby become a quality manager. This means there would be no requirement for separate acts of prevention and appraisal independent of the very acts that people in the organizations already carry out. This is often manifested by the TQM slogan that quality is everywhere and everyone's job.

Quality costing: This understanding of quality cost behaviour and the justification for zero defects through optimization logic of minimizing quality costs has given rise to a set of calculative practices that we commonly call 'quality costing'. In essence, this includes the following steps:

1. Extracting quality cost information from the accounting system and classifying it into four categories of quality costs (i.e. costs associated with appraisal activities, preventive activities, internal failures, and external failures).

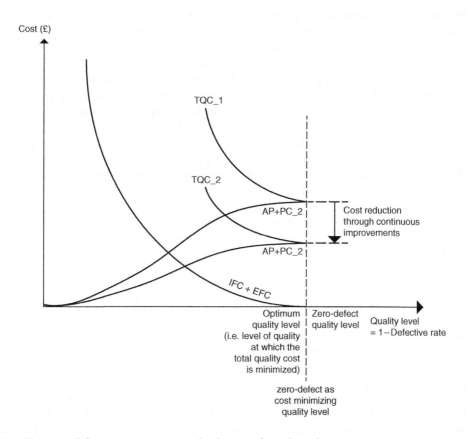

Figure 8.4 Zero-defects as cost optimum and reduction of cost through continuous improvement

186 *Neoliberal trends*

2. Comparing them with the relevant benchmarks which include prior year figures, industry averages, and also best competitor data. For the purposes of such comparison, the data may be analysed in line with specific production or quality management localities such as quality circles, departments, and committees.
3. Understanding and explaining the causalities between costs of conformance and non-conformance over time in order to see whether the quality management regime shows 'continuous improvements'. For example, in comparing the data with the previous year's figures, if management sees evidence that the appraisal and preventive activity costs have declined while external and internal failure costs have also declined, that would manifest a progressive continuous improvement scenario towards a zero-defect scenario with a downward shift in the costs of conformance.

8.3.3 Quality-based discourses of organizational transformation

When quality became a 'strategic imperative', firms needed to get behind this. The quality-based reformation of the organization introduced various 'new' post-Fordist organizational elements.

Incorporating quality into top management discourses and leadership

At the top managerial level, quality started to appear as a strong discourse that top management had to be committed to. This was manifested through incorporating quality as a strategic imperative across the communicative apparatuses of corporate strategy, such as the vision statement, the mission statement, and other strategic statements that top management made. Coupled with the notions of innovation, creativity, flexibility, and cost-efficiency, quality started to appear in corporate discourses to redefine organizational purpose and leadership. Top management's worth became a matter of their commitment to quality, and their capacity to articulate quality in the corporate strategy. This needed to be done not only in terms of product attributes and the capacity of the company's products to meet customer needs, but also in terms of how they organized and coordinated organizational units to achieve quality. Top management's commitment then had to go beyond such rhetoric into the relational and structural elements of the organization. Top management was expected to come out with quality improvement agendas. This was normally achieved through massive investment in specific quality improvement projects for which the expertise of external consultants was sought. To lead, coordinate, and monitor such projects, cross-functional steering committees of senior management were established. Such committees held the responsibility for the design and implementation of corporate quality improvement policies and projects, determining the procedures to be employed, and monitored outcomes (Hill 1991). They then established, monitored, and supervised the middle and lower level quality management arrangements (e.g. departmental or divisional quality management committees, quality circles, etc.).

Japanization of the organizational processes

In the 1980s and 1990s, Japan became the most critical reference point in Western managerial reformations. The quality, variety, flexibility, and cost-efficiency of Japanese firms posed an immense competitive pressure on Western companies. As Oliver and

Wilkinson (1992) survey on the Japanization of British industry reveals, the overwhelming majority of companies which underwent massive managerial reforms were for 'defensive' reasons – increasing competitiveness, the need to reduce cost, etc. so that they would be capable of facing the ever increasing competition from Japanese and other East Asian competitors. While Japanese firms posed a challenge and a threat, they were also seen as an opportunity – a source of wisdom to reform Western firms so that they could truly be flexible and capable of offering quality products and variety at a lower cost. Japanization is thus the historical account of the West importing Japanese organizational practices to reform Western firms with a view to enhancing their flexibility, cost-efficiency, quality, and variety.

In a broader sense, the Japanization of Western management involved institutionalizing the three strategic or critical success factors that we mentioned earlier (i.e. quality, flexibility, and cost). It involved the institutionalization of a certain set of practices and ideologies so that they would become innate assumptions and practices that people in the organization collectively held onto in deciding what would be best for them and their customers. These ideologies and practices, in one way or another, were all directed towards achieving quality, flexibility, and cost-efficiency. They constituted both 'hard' and 'soft' technologies of management. Here the hard technologies referred to those that involve the 'engineering elements' of improving quality, flexibility, and cost-efficiency. Examples are statistical process control techniques, technologies driven towards reductions in setup times, the mechanical and digital redesign of the factory, and the cellular design of manufacture through flexible machines (see the previous section). Soft technologies, on the other hand, emphasize the behavioural and cultural elements. Examples are quality circles, operator responsibility for quality, and Kanban material control.

Japanization in this sense is the particular managerial movement that we witnessed in the 1980s and 1990s that strategized the factory floor. Strategizing here basically means reforming the production processes so that they could now cater for these strategic success factors, namely quality, flexibility, and cost-efficiency. This was achieved through a particular set of managerial practices that integrated the firm's capacity to address these three issues. Some of these managerial reforms have already been discussed in the previous sections of this chapter. These 'new' practices are variably discussed in the literature with various overlapping, and hence, confusing terminology, including lean manufacturing, total quality management, and just-in-time manufacturing. These terms are often used interchangeably and in an overlapping sense to mean various managerial techniques, processes, and philosophies that Japanese firms (especially Toyota) introduced to the world. Hence, without drifting into a nuanced description of articulating the differences between the terminologies, in this section, we will concentrate on providing an overview of the Japanese production system.

In an overall sense, as Monden (1994) outlines, Japanese manufacturing is driven towards increasing profit in a 'slow growing economy'. When the market growth rate is at its minimum, in a slow growing economy, competition becomes intense and sales increments can only be achieved through offering a higher quality product at a lower cost than your competitors. There is only a very limited margin that a company can gain through rapid sales and market growth. This means that the profit increases need to come primarily through *cost reduction by eliminating waste*. Toyota's managerial revolution stemmed from its innovations in driving this cost reduction through the elimination of waste. Managerial terminology often associated with Japanese management (e.g. JIT, Kanban, TQM, quality circles, 'jidoka' and 'shojinka') are all elements that were invented as part of this cost reduction scheme. Figure 8.5 summarizes the

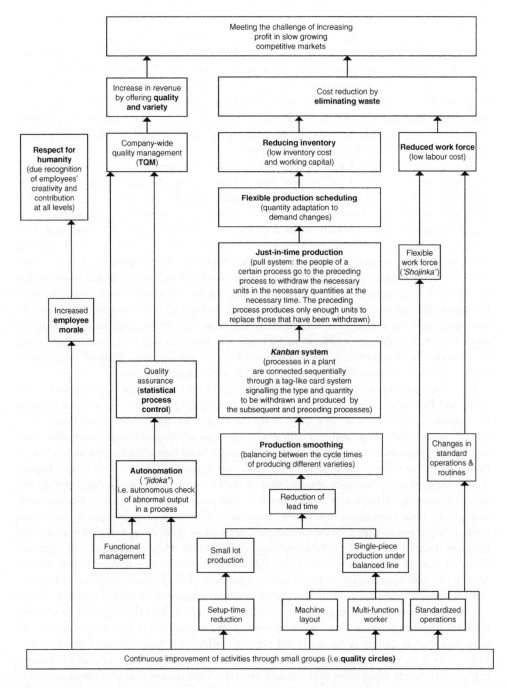

Figure 8.5 Elements of Japanese production system (using example of Toyota)
Source: adapted from (Monden 1994, 4).

main elements of Toyota's production system, which became the landmark of what we now call Japanese management. A brief description of the key elements is included in Figure 8.5, but readers are strongly advised to read other sources. Monden (1994) in particular provides a good techno-managerial discussion of Toyota's production and control system.

8.4 TQM and JIT as disciplinary and biopolitical regime

Our discussion so far has only provided a rather techno-managerial discussion on TQM/JIT. Now in this section we try to provide a brief note on their political implications. Generally, the techno-managerial literature we have used so far describes TQM/JIT-based managerial reforms as a rather progressive and strategically important evolution that first took place in Japanese firms and then in their Western counterparts. As we have already discussed, these quality-based managerial discourses signified the notions of flexibility, quality, and cost as strategic imperatives and provided a set of managerial tools and philosophies to meet those strategic imperatives. In fact, these managerial innovations marked a significant shift in managerial regimes, and their usefulness and efficacy as a set of managerial tools were not subject to too much criticism. With differences in the extent to which they were deployed and the degree of success in their implementation, the deployment of Japanese management processes in the West marked a 'new' regime of management which we generally now call post-Fordist, post-bureaucratic, or flexible manufacturing. Managerial literature in general feels quite comfortable with this attribution.

8.4.1 Disciplinary politics of TQM/JIT

However, some critical sociological *littérateurs* have brought different interpretations to the table. Some have seen this trajectory of Japanization as an extension of control through the intensification of disciplinary apparatuses. Sewell and Wilkinson (1992), for example, draw on Foucault's theory of discipline and punish to argue that TQM/JIT regimes create and demand systems of surveillance which improve on those previous factory regimes by instilling and thereby enhancing central control. Their argument is that Japanese management regimes, as they are deployed in the West, are premised on more direct and detailed control, or 'total control' (as in total quality management) and are characterized by a low degree of trust (despite popular managerial rhetoric to the opposite) and strong management discipline. The discipline is directed towards the establishment of a perfect symmetry between demand and supply, within and outside the factory, with no shortages, no costly stockpiles, and no waste (Sewell and Wilkinson 1992, 278). Inter alia, this discipline is achieved through the deliberate simplification and arrangement of workflow around products rather than management functions (work flow was primarily organized around functional management in bureaucratic Fordist organizational forms). In Japanized firms, 'Machines and people are grouped according to the product families they operate on rather than the specialist function they perform' (Sewell and Wilkinson 1992, 278–279). This has massively enhanced the 'visibility' and surveillance of the worker not only by their managers but also by their own peers. Two complementary disciplinary forces are in play here, according to Sewell and Wilkinson (1992). First, is the discipline which derives from the scrutiny of one's peers in a manufacturing cell, quality circle, etc. – a horizontal process of surveillance. The second is the discipline derived from the use of increasingly powerful

190   *Neoliberal trends*

management information systems and their associated assessment techniques (such as statistical process and quality control techniques) which provide an extensive shop floor surveillance – a vertical process of surveillance. With this subtle combination of vertical and horizontal surveillance, TQM/JIT, for Sewell and Wilkinson (1992), constitutes a system of surveillance which is more closely associated with the *panopticon* than traditional bureaucracy (see Chapter 2). They draw on Rule (1973) to explain the disciplinary effect of the total surveillance systems that an ideal type TQM/JIT would enact:

> Every action of every client would be scrutinized, recorded and evaluated both at the moment of occurrence and for ever afterwards. The system would collate all information at a single point, making it impossible for anyone to evade responsibility for his past by fleeing from the scene of earlier behaviour … Any sign of disobedience – present or anticipated – would result in corrective action … apprehension and sanction would occur immediately. By making detection and retaliation inevitable such a system would make disobedience almost unthinkable.
>
> (Rule 1973, 37)

What lies at the centre of this disciplinarity of TQM/JIT is making the defects and waste visible. In a Japanized workplace, abnormality or deficiency of labour is reconceptualized not in terms of labourers' generic subjective behavioural characteristics such as absenteeism, disobedience, incompetence, etc. but mainly in the production of defects and waste, which are then detected and analysed through objective measures and procedures such as statistical processes and quality control techniques. In other words, rather than making labour subject to the direct control and supervision of management, it is effectively associated with the notion of defects and waste, and hence labour becomes visible through these. The control in this sense is making the labour visible and directing it towards the continuous reduction of defects and waste through self-, peer-based, and informational control. The workflow and shop floor scheduling are so simplified and enhanced that the responsibility for defects and waste can more easily be pinpointed. Similarly stripping out inventory, especially work-in-progress between processes, reducing the size of the workforce and organizing the workforce around the products, reduces the scope for workers to hide any defective or poor quality goods, because detection and retaliation become quicker (Sewell and Wilkinson 1992).

8.4.2 Biopolitics of TQM/JIT

While the set of managerial techniques bundled into TQM/JIT reinvent and reinforce the disciplinary apparatuses of control, they also put labour into circulation in the form of the flexibilization of the labour force. As we discussed in the previous sections, in order to facilitate cellular flexible manufacturing, labour needs to be made flexible in terms of not only their capacity to adapt to changing manufacturing requirements but also in the ease of hiring and firing. So-called 'life-time employment' practices that characterized Japanese firms for so long have not passed to the West; neither indeed have they become part of the contemporary generation of Japanese firms. Instead, labour has become the entrepreneur on its own, forced to enhance its capacity by moving from one task to another within the same firm, or from one job to another between firms. In quality circles and other forms of 'devolved' decision making, labour has had to organize and manage itself by assuming the managerial functions that were hitherto carried out by managers. As Sewell and Wilkinson (1992) argue, TQM entails pushing managerial responsibility for quality, defect, waste, and flexibility downwards and flattening the organization. This is a form of 'devolutionism', where the decentralization of tactical responsibility occurs while strategic control is centralized. Responsibility and the decision-making authority are devolved only to the extent that there is strict monitoring of compliance with standards, which compliance is monitored by the workers themselves with the new 'cultural apparatuses' put in place through TQM. TQM was much celebrated and promoted in the name of job empowerment, decentralization, and the democratization of decision-making practices. We have already discussed the biopolitical implications of post-Fordist production systems in Section 8.2.

8.5 Summary and conclusions

Having discussed the way in which organizational forms were strategized in the previous chapter, this chapter moved to explain how strategic discourses in the last few decades have reconfigured production systems. These strategic discourses mainly concentrated on three interrelated strategic imperatives: flexibility, quality, and cost-efficiency. This chapter specifically concentrated on the first two, leaving the issues of cost-efficiency to the next chapter.

The issue of flexibility was discussed as a multi-faceted and multi-level phenomenon having a wider set of techno-managerial and cultural-political implications. At its first strategic front, organizations face flexibility in terms of *flexible consumption* – a managerial appreciation of the necessity of competitive companies to offer customers greater choice in terms of product variety and customization. Flexible consumption needs to be understood as a strategy and managerial philosophy. As such, flexible consumption then demands and drives the firms to develop the organizational capacity to deliver it. This capacity rests on two interlocking and interrelated elements. First, is the capacity to produce flexibly. The second is the information capacity across the markets and firms to construct and maintain an effective network of communication between the various elements of flexible production. This capacity is achieved through *flexible machines, flexible labour*, and their organization into *flexible manufacturing systems*. However, achieving flexibility is a strategic act that crosses organizational boundaries. It demands extra-organizational and inter-organizational coordination across various coordinating agencies to form strategic alliances between firms, such as regional conglomerations, federated enterprises, solar firms, and workshop factories. The concept of flexible accumulation takes the notion of flexibility one step further into the global dynamics of capital and labour. Here the attention is on the 'new capitalism' that the micro-organizational changes in production systems, relations, and technologies have brought about. There is a quite an array of terms that political-economists use to characterize this new form of capitalism: the post-industrial paradigm, disorganized capitalism, just-in-time capitalism, and so on. In essence, flexible accumulation captures everything we have discussed in the other sections – flexible consumption, flexible machines, flexible labour, flexible manufacturing systems, and flexible specialization. Flexible accumulation places them within the wider schema of capitalism transformed.

Quality as a strategic imperative enters management discourses as a result of the Western use of Japanese management systems and styles, which is often captured by the term *Japanization*. Quality in its primary meaning refers to the firm's capacity to meet customer requirements. When customer requirements are translated into a specific set of product attributes and quality standards, the secondary meaning of quality is derived as the conformance to standards. Zero-defect and six sigma quality are the competitive standards pertaining to quality in the contemporary world. This chapter mainly

192 *Neoliberal trends*

discussed how the zero-defect and continuous regime of quality was justified through a particular accounting logic of optimization and how strategic attention on quality gave rise to a new set of structural, relational, and processual elements in organizations. These new managerial elements involved incorporating top management discourses and leadership with attempts to bring various hard and soft elements of Japanese quality management into Western organizations. Japanization in fact constitutes a wide array of techno-managerial changes. Examples are statistical process control techniques, technologies driven towards setup time reduction, mechanical and digital redesign of the factory, and the cellular design of manufacturing using flexible machines. Soft technologies, on the other hand, emphasize the behavioural and cultural elements. Examples are quality circles, operator responsibility for quality, and Kanban material control.

Finally, the chapter also discussed the disciplinary and biopolitical implications of the Japanization project.

Assignments

These assignments are meant to extend your knowledge beyond what you understand from this chapter. These are not simply revision questions. The content covered in this chapter is necessary but will not be sufficient in attempting these tasks. Therefore, you are required to do some extra reading in attempting these tasks.

1. **Thematic essay:**
   'Flexibility, quality, and cost-efficiency have been the dominating institutional logics that have underlined the management transformations that have taken place since the late 1970s'.
   Discuss this statement with reference to the techno-managerial and political-economic changes relevant to the recent transformations in manufacturing systems.

2. **Poster:**
   Draw a poster illustrating how the notions of flexibility and quality were implicated in a wide array of changes within and outside economic enterprises. Pay attention to how these notions connect various ideological, institutional, organizational, and techno-managerial elements.

3. **Presentation:**
   Prepare a set of PowerPoint slides, together with notes if necessary, for a 30-minute presentation on the following theme:
   'Japanization involves reconceptualizing Western organizations in terms of not only flexibility and quality but also leaning the production system to eliminate all possible wastage'.

4. **Extended bibliography:**
   Write an extended bibliography on the topic 'Japanese management accounting practices'. For this, you need to do a literature survey of major accounting journals and edited books where critical accounting research is published. Organize the bibliography into a table in the following format.

Bibliographic info	Nature of the paper/book chapter (e.g. conceptual/theoretical, empirical, a response to a previous publication)	Major arguments, conclusions, and contributions

5. **Literature review:**

Suppose you are writing a thesis/dissertation on strategic management accounting. You intend to review critical accounting and management literature in order to explain the political-economic implications of the TQM/JIT-based reinvention of management. You are also thinking of the possibility of using a critical social theory (e.g. Foucault, Marx, institutional theory, etc.) in this respect. Your attention is mainly on how TQM/JIT gave rise to a new regime of labour control.

You are required to do the necessary literature survey and write a chapter circa 5,000 words. You should search the academic journal databases for recent management and accounting literature on strategy as well as critical political assessments of the recent trends in management and accounting (e.g. Munro 2012).

Notes

1 Here the term 'numerical flexibility' refers to the firm's capacity to contract or expand the workforce with ease, without incurring significant costs of hiring and firing.
2 The 5S management method, where 5S stands for *seri* (sort), *seiton* (set in order), *seiso* (shine), *seiketsu* (standardize), and *sitsuke* (sustain), was originally implemented by manufacturing enterprises in Japan. It was then introduced to various sectors in the West as one of the total quality management techniques (see Ishijima et al. 2016; Kanamori et al. 2015).

9 Strategizing cost management

9.1 Introduction

The previous chapter offered an analysis of how flexibility and quality became key pillars of strategizing the firm. The expositions of flexibility and quality were not just a discursive invention; they were problematizing how the old spirit of capitalism organized production and distribution. Rigid bureaucracies and the ethos of mass production started to become obsolete due to their incapacity to offer flexibility and quality in the context of intense global competition. The firm now needed to be reconfigured into a form that could respond to the neoliberal demands of flexibility, quality, and innovativeness. However, this is not possible if the firm is not competitive enough in terms of cost-efficiency. While flexibility and quality guarantee options and opportunities for customers to choose what they want, and for the firms to position themselves strategically in the competitive terrain, these choices are invariably governed by the possibilities that consumers have 'value for money' while capital earns a satisfactory return. Management accounting is thus implicated in helping the firm offer quality and flexibility but with a cost that can satisfy both the consumers and the producers. As such, cost management has become a strategic imperative.

Therefore, the notion of cost-efficiency must be unpacked to see how strategic imperatives of cost management created new forms of control in organizations. We need to understand the new demands that neoliberalism exerted on firms; how such demands problematized the traditional forms of cost accounting; how such demands were met by implementing new cost management programmes; and how such programmes reconfigured the firm. This chapter aims at answering these questions. To that end, the chapter is structured as follows:

1. Section 9.2 discusses the old spirit of cost management. Before moving into the neoliberal trajectory of its evolution, we will see how the old spirit of cost management evolved and operated. Here we pay attention to different theoretical and historical explanations of the evolution of costing and the role that costing played in the early phase (i.e. liberal phase) of capitalism until it was challenged by the neoliberal turn since the 1980s.

2. In Section 9.3 we problematize the old spirit. We move on to explain how and why traditional cost accounting was problematized in the face of an emerging set of neoliberal demands. Four aspects of problems will be emphasized in this discussion. They are: cost accounting's subservience to financial reporting; the abstract and economic theorizing which excluded practical complexities; the relative insignificance of overheads in old cost structures; and the lack of innovations in cost management ideas.

3. In Section 9.4 we discuss new cost management as a surveillance assemblage. This section will address an important theoretical perspective about ABC's implications for staff functions in the organization. Here, you will see what ABC has done to make the staff function, which was hitherto protected by the shelter of traditional cost allocation methods, visible for management control and accountability purposes. The notion of 'surveillance assemblage' will be used to explain this.

4. In Section 9.5 we look at cost management as a holistic programme. Here we will look at the pragmatic aspects of cost management. These show how reconfigured cost management has become amenable to four interrelated developments: controls beyond the shop-floor; the reinvention of the terrain of decision making; the bundling and hybridization of managerial practice; and the strategizing the cost objects.

5. Section 9.6 provides a summary and conclusions. We shall see how all these developments are implicated in the strategic intents and contents of the firm. This examination will enable us to see the extent to which management accounting is reimagined as a social and political practice that drives the neoliberal agenda. This will also enable us to explore whether or not this formation is homogenous across different social and political settings.

9.2 The old spirit of cost management

Cost management is a new term developed in the aftermath of Kaplan and Cooper's invention of ABC and ABM (see Jones and Dugdale 2002). Its predecessor was technically termed 'cost accounting' or just 'costing', connoting the role that it played under the old spirit of capitalism. This cost accounting phase of development was explored by many management accounting historians who provided some competing theoretical analyses surrounding the questions of when, why, and how costing emerged and evolved. Table 9.1. summarizes these analyses.

Works of researchers such as Edwards and Newell (1991), Fleischman and Parker (1991), and Pollard (1965) were central to the evolutionary economics approach to explaining the history of cost accounting. Their argument was that cost calculations emerged to control costs of production in order to ensure that the products were more competitive in the market and could offer a bigger profit margin. When the industrial revolution boosted mass production, competitive pressure became a governing principle. Costing was necessary not only to know the costs of production but also to put controls in place and to minimize inefficiencies such as waste and fraud. The idea was that controlled cost of production could foster a competitive business. This was premised on the assumption that managers are rational decision makers endowed with economic calculations to gauge what the optimal action should be, so that, in an evolutionary sense, the invention and growth of costing was an inevitable evolutionary outcome of becoming more capitalistically rational (cf. Carmona et al. 1997, Hopper and Armstrong 1991).

Alongside this, a complementary argument was put forward by Johnson and Kaplan (1987a, 1987b), whose primary concern was to explain the evolution of cost accounting through the theoretical lenses of 'transaction cost economics' (see Coase 1937; Williamson 1975, 1988), which saw hierarchies as an alternative coordinating mechanism to the markets. Postulating hierarchical coordination as an alternative to the market coordination of economic activities, the choice between the market and the hierarchy is determined

196 *Neoliberal trends*

Table 9.1 History of cost accounting: alternative explanations

Theoretical perspective	Thesis	Key authorities
Evolutionary economics	Cost accounting evolved to enhance efficiency and, thereby, to foster firms' competitiveness.	Edwards and Newell (1991), Fleischman and Parker (1991), Pollard (1965)
Transaction cost economics	Cost accounting evolved to facilitate the development of hierarchies as a more efficient mechanism of coordinating economic activities (vis-à-vis the market). Cost accounting makes sure that the transaction cost of coordinating economic activities within the hierarchy is smaller than that of market coordination.	Johnson (1975), Johnson and Kaplan (1987a, 1987b), Williamson (1975, 1988)
Labour process theory	Cost accounting was invented and developed to support capital's control and subordination of labour.	Clawson (1980), Hopper and Armstrong (1991), Littler (1982), Montgomery (1989)
Foucauldian approach	Evolution of cost accounting was part of the evolution of disciplinary institutions and societies. Cost accounting function as a 'disciplinary technology' (see Chapter 1).	Carmona et al. (1997), Hoskin and Macve (1986), Miller and O'Leary (1987)

by, as Williamson (1975, 1988) postulated, the ability to minimize transaction costs. Hierarchy exists because the transaction cost of coordinating certain transactions within the hierarchy is lower than that of the market coordination. As we all know, it is often argued that the coordinating decisions of economic activities need to be done in response to market signals. However, when economic activities are coordinated outside the market but within the hierarchy, then no such market signals (i.e. prices) exist. Hence, the need for cost accounting to proximate those lost market signals as a point of reference in making coordination decisions. For these neoclassical economic theorists, the evolution of cost accounting was the natural and progressive continuity of the social systems seeking to enhance the efficiency with which humans carry out their economic activities.

However, both the evolutionary model and the transaction cost argument were refuted by critical accounting researchers who drew upon Marxist and Foucauldian political economy. Marxists labour process theorists emphasized that the invention of cost accounting was driven by the historical necessity of finding new forms of control for capital to subsume labour, to better manage labour's resistance, and hence to achieve its accumulative imperatives. Hopper and Armstrong's (1991) critique of Johnson and Kaplan's (1987a) *Relevance Lost* thesis is the key publication here. Following the labour process writers (e.g. Braverman 1998 [1974]; Clawson 1980; Littler 1982; Montgomery 1989), they offered an alternative analysis of why cost accounting systems were invented in the USA. They characterized the theoretical properties of this approach to cost accounting history as follows:

> Thus a labour process approach, in contrast to one utilising transaction cost theory, stresses crisis rather than continuity; contradiction rather than internal consistency; social and political conflict rather than harmony; the monopoly power of corporations rather than self-equilibrating competitive markets; patterns of class formation

Strategizing cost management 197

in specific economies rather than an atomised view of the individual; and human agency in its cultural and institutional setting rather than economistic reductionism.

(Hopper and Armstrong 1991, 406)

When located within social contradictions, conflicts, monopoly powers, domination, and resistance, the evolution of cost accounting in the early phase of capitalism was not simply a natural efficiency-driven progressive continuity of social systems. Instead, it was a strategic invention by the capitalists to handle the crisis of control; to regain capital's capacity to control, command, and subordinate labour for its accumulative needs. They emphasized:

> Systems of control both entail costs and provoke characteristic forms of resistance which, under competitive conditions, render them increasingly ineffective as means of capital accumulation. These contradictions build into crises of control, especially in times of economic recession, and this leads to a search for new systems of controlling the labour process, either directly or through its immediate management ... key phases of innovation in cost and management accounting can be understood as part of this search for new methods of control. Thus, developments in accounting for direct labour costs were implicated both in the employer's liquidation of internal contract and in the curbing and focusing of the power of the salaried foremen who replaced them. Standard costing systems were pioneered as an aspect of the fragmentation and deskilling of craft labour, which had hitherto resisted employers' attempts at intensification through piecework payment systems.
>
> (Hopper and Armstrong 1991, 433)

One of the key points that Hopper and Armstrong's labour process argument highlights is that we need to locate cost accounting within the historical dynamics of capitalism in order to understand and appreciate their political implications.

Foucauldians also locate cost accounting in the historical dynamics of capitalism and modernity but stand beyond the class parameters of capitalism that the labour process theorists relied upon. They take a post-structuralist approach to explore the questions of why and how cost accounting systems were developed. Drawing on a historical case study of a Spanish Royal Tobacco Factory and the theory of power/knowledge relations espoused by Foucault (1980, 1995), Carmona et al. (1997), for example, provide an alternative critique of the evolutionary model and transaction cost economic approach to cost accounting history. Following other researchers who laid the foundation for this approach of deploying Foucault's notions of genealogy of knowledge/power to study the evolution of management accounting in the UK and the USA (e.g. Hoskin and Macve 1986; Loft 1995; Miller and O'Leary 1987), Carmona et al. illustrate that it was in the context of disciplinary surveillance that cost accounting systems evolved in the eighteenth century in Spain. They contended:

> We view accounting as a form of power/knowledge made up of regimes of calculation and associated discursive practices that operate as a scheme of surveillance. Accounting is able to establish new modes of accountability by rendering human activities visible, thereby promoting new areas of discourse, and enabling social fields to be represented as areas of rational economic action.
>
> (Carmona et al. 1997, 412)

198 Neoliberal trends

As we explained in detailed in Chapter 1, for Foucauldian accounting historians, accounting is a calculative technology through which disciplinary power is exercised. Foucauldian accounting historians provided detailed microscopic explanations, events, and incidents to illustrate how the invention and evolution of cost accounting techniques can be related to the institutionalization of disciplinary power and knowledge. Carmona et al. entertained this analysis by quoting Foucault in this way:

> Disciplinary power is exercised through its invisibility; at the same time, it imposes on those subjects a compulsory visibility. In discipline, it is the subjects who have to be seen. Their visibility assures the hold of the power that is exercised over them. It is the fact of being constantly seen that maintains the disciplined individual in his subjection.
>
> (Foucault 1995, 187; cited in Carmona et al. 1997, 443)

Despite their theoretical and ideological differences, in one way or another, all these explanations – whether they are neoclassical economic, Marxist, or Foucauldian – try to locate cost management within the historical dynamics of capitalism and modernity. Invariably, cost accounting emerged in the eighteenth and nineteenth centuries and evolved into the twentieth century along the lines of capitalistic developments in the West. In a way, the neoclassical economic arguments that it was the quest for efficiency and fostering competitiveness that underlined the development of cost accounting, have a point to sustain. However, there is no sufficient excuse for economic theorization to ignore the social and political underpinnings upon which this quest was carried out. We should not ignore the disciplinary and class implications of techno-managerial inventions that appear in purely economic logics. The alternative theorizations – both structuralist and post-structuralist, Marxist and Foucauldian – hold valid propositions in terms of connecting the notions of cost-efficiency with the dynamics of class struggle at the point of production and the disciplinary politics of modernity. From a structuralist perspective, cost accounting emerged to resolve the problem of control that emanated from the class politics and class struggles at the point of production. From a post-structuralist perspective, the institutional answer for this control problem was 'disciplining': the establishment of disciplinary institutions and technologies to materialize a set of disciplinary principles which we detailed in Chapters 1 and 2. Cost accounting was key to this disciplining. Whatever the argument, the fact remains undeniable: the development of cost accounting was a key part of the story of the old spirit of capitalism which evolved up until the 1980s, until the world was exposed to another historical rupture led by the ideological and economic imperatives of neoliberalism. With the emergence of the new neoliberal social order and a new set of managerial logics (such as strategy and governance), this old logic of cost accounting and control became problematic, being unable to help achieve strategic imperatives such as quality and flexibility. The transition of cost accounting and cost control to cost management through new accounting technologies such as ABC/ABM, beyond budgeting techniques, target costing, kaizen costing, etc. signifies this mismatch between the old tools of costing and cost control and the new neoliberal logics of strategy and governance. The transition was initiated by problematizing the old spirit of costing and cost control.

9.3 Problematizing the old spirit

Johnson and Kaplan, in their *Relevance Lost* thesis, observed that:

> By 1925 virtually all management accounting practices used today had been developed: cost accounts for labour, material and overheads; budgets for cash, income, and capital; flexible budgets, sales forecasts, standard costs, variance analysis, transfer prices, and divisional performance measures. These practices had evolved to serve the information and control needs of the managers of increasingly complex and diverse organisations. At that point the pace of innovation seemed to stop.
>
> (Johnson and Kaplan 1987a, 12)

It was not only management accounting but also all the other organizational practices and technologies, such as multidivisional organizational hierarchies, hierarchical management controls, production systems, and reporting and communication practices, that had been developed, established, and widely spread across the globe by the first half of the twentieth century. This all happened because capitalism spread across the world through, initially, colonialism and then post-colonial developments of the global economy. These included international trade and investment; the spread of Western professional accounting bodies throughout the world; the evolution and spread of the epistemic power of global educational institutions such as the Harvard Business School, the Chicago School of Economics and the London School of Economics; and also, the epistemic, fiscal, and administrative influences of the development of global funding institutions including the Bretton Woods twins of the World Bank and the International Monetary Fund (IMF). Collectively, they spread Taylor's scientific management, bureaucratic administration, and traditional cost and management accounting, especially budgeting and standard costing, as well as Western financial accounting standards and principles as the dominating form of management technologies across the world. This was the case even with the movement of 'embryonic socialism' around the world during the 1950s and 1960s. Especially after World War II, when the global political aim was to stabilize and regulate capitalism to make it a dependable and steady political regime, accounting and other managerial practices were solidified and established, rather than setting them in a continuous state of flux, change, and instability. As Hopper and Armstrong (1991) argued, this stabilization, solidification, and eventual stagnation of 'old' accounting and management techniques were further reinforced by the power of collective labour to resist any harsh and overly coercive imposition of new managerial techniques. The period that Johnson and Kaplan characterized as a period of 'stagnation' and 'lost relevance' was indeed monopoly capitalism arriving at its maturity and solidification, but also reaching its limits; liberal economic democracy moving itself into a crisis in terms of its capacity to further enhance capital accumulation.

There were two implications of these observations. One was that, as Johnson and Kaplan observed, there were virtually no significant developments after the 1920s despite the changes that happened in the broader economic and political landscapes, including a World War and the beginning of a dramatic move towards neoliberal open market economies and globalization in the 1970s. Another was that, on the other side of the coin, there was an increasingly felt need for alternative approaches to the way companies managed

200   *Neoliberal trends*

costs. This was critical because the new competitive environment pushed companies to conceive cost-efficiency as one of the most important strategic pillars upon which firms needed to be rebuilt.

Then came the 1980s. It was the time to revisit this liberal economic form of development, ideologically, intellectually, and institutionally. Policy makers, epistemic communities, and business leaders soon understood that the old logic of capitalism, including its managerial technologies, was no longer sufficiently effective to accelerate the rate of capital accumulation and economic growth. The world had to move to a new form of capitalism which we now generally call neoliberalism. As we discussed in the previous chapters, neoliberalism redefined everything. It brought in: acute competition through open market policies and globalization; a vast programme of financialization and privatization; global production networks and supply-chains; technological innovations that could accelerate everything corporations were doing on a massive scale; and a reterritorialized mode of global governance and regulation. There were implications of this phase of development on the reconfiguration of the firm searching for flexibility, quality, and cost-efficiency. These three were interrelated, and the attainment of cost-efficiency was considered to be difficult if there were no drastic changes in the way in which the costs of production were calculated. Kaplan and Cooper (1998, 1) observed this need as follows:

> Changes in business since the mid-1970s, triggered by global competition and technological innovations, have led to striking innovations in the use of financial and non-financial information in organizations. The new environment demands more relevant cost and performance information on the organisation's activities, processes, products, services and customers.

This observation led Kaplan and Cooper to reimagine cost accounting into cost management and promote a strategic view of cost management that accommodates the strategic changes taking place in the realms of production, distribution, consumption, and competition. This meant that a new form of costing and cost management were demanded to handle emerging strategic themes such as product and service redesign, business process reengineering, continuous improvement, and so on. Cost accounting, therefore, by transforming into cost management, was to be given new functionalities beyond its traditional role of estimating the cost of production and inventories for financial reporting purposes (see Figure 9.1).

In their *Relevance Lost* thesis, Johnson and Kaplan 1987a) accused the pre-1980s management accounting practice of not being able to handle these strategic imperatives because of certain inherent limitations in the conventional wisdom of costing. The four interrelated reasons for this inability (see Figure 9.2) of traditional cost accounting have now been well established in the management accounting literature (see Berliner and Brimson 1988; Bromwich and Bhimani 1989; Kaplan 1994; Roslender 1995, 1996; Shank and Govindarajan 1989). First, Johnson and Kaplan argued that cost management became *subservient to financial reporting* as the latter became more important due to regulatory pressures. As such, costing became primarily a task of inventory valuation and cost estimation for financial reporting to external parties rather than providing useful information for internal managerial decisions, management controls, and performance management. However, managers were neither worried nor affected too much by this negligence because the firms,

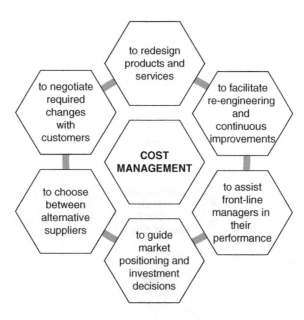

Figure 9.1 Cost management functionalities in a competitive edge

during the period from the 1920s to the 1980s, enjoyed a relative monopolistic power generated by the oligopolistic competition in protected markets through macro-economic policies (Chandler and Hikino 1994). This less intensive competitive environment was not too demanding of the accuracy, relevance, and sophistication of cost information.

Second, Johnson and Kaplan argued that there was a *lack of innovations* in cost management after the 1920s. This was because, they emphasized, that there happened to be a decoupling of accounting from industrial engineering and operations. In contrast to management accounting's golden period when management accounting innovations emanated from industrial engineering necessities and insights from the factory floor, in the period after the 1920s, accounting became idiosyncratic, inward looking, and self-serving of its own reporting needs. Innovations could have happened and cost-efficiency avenues could have been established, they argued, if the accounting practitioners were aware of the development of manufacturing technologies which resulted in higher productivity, enhanced quality, and expanded flexibility. However, accounting professionals were not interested in these as they thought that it was beyond the boundary of the discipline. Despite the technological changes that occurred in production processes and the structural changes taking place in the market place, old-fashioned costing techniques were only providing cost distortions rather than useful information for strategy-driven decisions, controls, and performance management. According to Johnson and Kaplan, accountants basically lacked the innovative spirit and drive towards evaluating the strategic needs of the firms and overemphasized the legal requirements of financial reporting.

Third, and related to the previous points, the pre-1980s witnessed an era of industrial society where technology was mechanistic, inflexible, and driven towards mass production, compared to today's industrial environment where production is facilitated by

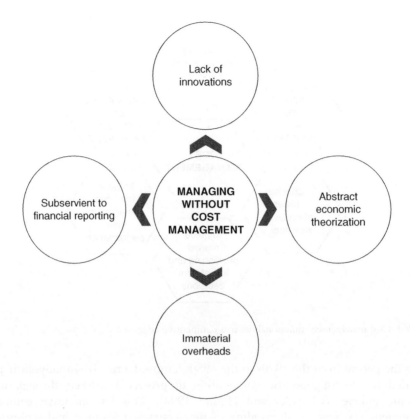

Figure 9.2 Problematizing the old spirit of cost accounting

flexible manufacturing technologies (see Chapter 8). One of the important comparisons here is that, in the pre-1980s' mass production environment, the significance of overhead costs was relatively small compared to direct costs, especially direct labour costs. The workforce was composed of a large proportion of blue-collar workers directly working on the products with a small proportion of service personnel (Piore and Sabel 1984). Hence, the accurate calculation of overhead costs was relatively immaterial as direct cost dominated total production costs. This provided a sufficient 'safe zone of calculations' for the cost accountants so that they could continue with arbitrary cost allocation methods based on 'unrelated' cost 'absorption bases' such as direct labour hours, machine hours, or direct production costs. Hence, costing was a ritualistic calculative practice (mainly driven towards providing calculations for financial reporting) without proper analyses of the impact of the costs and prices so calculated upon the firm's competitiveness in the market. As basic management textbook exercises of ABC today reveal, the traditional overhead absorption costing often resulted in over-costing and hence over-pricing. But such miscalculations continued because, on the one hand, such inaccuracies were not terminal in the face of the monopoly powers the firms enjoyed and, hence their capacity to shift the burdens of such inaccuracies to the customer. On the other hand, traditional absorption costing was so highly institutionalized that cost accountants were too blind to see their inappropriateness, or they felt that it was too radical and costly to initiate a change without understanding that not changing would be even costlier (see Roslender 1996). Consequently, traditional costing prevailed for a long period until there emerged an inescapable necessity to make a change – the neoliberal turn in which competition became so severe, and overheads became so important, that miscalculations of costs and the inability to keep these costs under control became strategically unforgiving.

Fourth, Johnson and Kapan criticized management accounting researchers of the kind of research they conducted, especially decision-making modelling based on neoclassical economic assumptions (see also Scapens 1994). This was mainly reflected in popular management accounting texts (e.g. books by Horngren and his colleagues; Shilliglow and his colleagues; and also Kaplan and Atkinson's *Advanced Management Accounting*) which promoted a techno-economic rationality of management accounting through articulating complex and sophisticated statistical tools and procedures in the areas of cost-volume-profit analysis, inventory management, cost allocation procedures, sales forecasting, transfer pricing scenarios, and interfirm relationships (see Amershi and Cheng 1990). Even after the 1980s (after the change in the economic landscape in the world), such technical frameworks governed research and the teaching of management accounting (for a critique, see Hopper et al. 1987). However, these textbook models neither captured the complexities and demands of the new neoliberal world, nor provided guides to gaining competitive advantage by exploring the venues of cost-efficiency. They simply complicated and abstracted the reality in epistemological terms. Consequently, cost accounting discourses before the 1980s were more or less a series of exercises with less reference to whether they could enhance the strategic imperatives such as flexibility, quality, and cost-efficiency.

9.4 New cost management: a surveillance assemblage

The problematizing project initiated by Johnson and Kaplan's *Relevance Lost* thesis was much more influential than expected. Despite critiques, it became a *bandwagon* for a whole host of new cost management ideas (Jones and Dugdale 2002). A number of techniques such as activity accounting, ABC, ABM, activity-based budgeting (ABB), and beyond budgeting came to populate management accounting texts. This list was further extended with other dimensions, namely strategic costing, target costing, time-driven costing, throughput costing, kaizen costing, customer profitability analysis, market segment analysis, etc. Cost management now bundled other rhetoric such as lean manufacturing and management, total quality management, business process re-engineering, and just-in-time management. What was behind this sudden burst in cost management techniques?

There are both pragmatic and theoretical explanations. The pragmatic one was manifested by the introduction of a new form of cost management, mainly thanks to the key proponents of ABC and ABM, Robert Kaplan and Robin Copper, and their epistemic power of being North American management gurus. They criticized the traditional absorption costing system for its distortion of 'true cost' and its misdirection of managers towards mispricing, wrong marketing strategies, and a misconceptualization of competitiveness. This criticism laid the groundwork for introducing ABC between 1988 and 1989. It was persuasively said that ABC could allocate overheads more 'accurately' to the cost objects on the basis of 'real cost drivers' rather than 'arbitrary overhead absorption bases'. This was started with the concept of a 'cost hierarchy' in which activities are identified, ordered, and organized into four levels: unit, batch,

204 *Neoliberal trends*

product-sustaining, and facility-sustaining. The aim was to attribute the first three types directly to the product, leaving the last to be left to the plant level. This translated much of the costs which traditionally were considered to be 'overheads' (and hence to be 'absorbed' on the basis of some arbitrary absorption bases) into directly attributable and variable costs. Technical procedures were established for this, which were published by Harvard Business School from 1988. The procedures were massively facilitated by the rapid development in information technologies, especially those associated with networking, real-time data processing, and expert-system integration with the transaction processing systems. Such developments were bundled into accounting and ERP packages. Many companies then installed ERP systems along with ABC modules (Jones and Dugdale 2002). There is a plethora of texts which explain the technicalities of implementing them (for example, the series of writings by Kaplan and Cooper, including their case studies published by Harvard Business School). Creating such packages and knowledge-bases and offering consultancy for their implementation became a multibillion business in itself (see Chapter 3, Section 3.2.4 and Chapter 6, Section 6.4.2).

The answer to the question of what actually happened beyond the technicalities has a fascinating theoretical and political explanation. Previously, cost allocation was linked mainly to labour hours, machine hours, or direct costs implying that overheads could be minimized by reducing labour and machine time spent on production. Whether this was managerially true or not, managers were under the impression that overheads could be controlled, managed, and reduced by controlling the blue-collar labour process (see Armstrong 2002). That said, the managerial problem of controlling overheads was reduced to the task of controlling direct labour spent on production under the calculative assumption that this was the reason for overheads. Conventional cost allocation systems operate to reveal how overhead facilities are consumed by labour hours and machine hours. Instead of revealing the true 'drivers' of the overheads, it 'black boxed' (see Chapter 3, note 1) the overheads, though it made the direct labour process visible for managerial controls. As such, the wages, working hours, and the production rates of direct labourers were the visible and controllable bases upon which cost was to be managed (Armstrong 2002). In effect, conventional absorption costing made the factory labour process visible and controllable at a distance but 'black boxed' the overheads.

This means that staff departments such as HR, Marketing, and Accounting were free from the accounting arrangements of surveillance. Such 'staff costs' were considered to be 'fixed' so there was no point in unfreezing this fixed cost for performance measurements and controls. It was fixed because, on the one hand, there were no meaningful costing techniques to link staff costs to cost objects (i.e. products and product lines). Hence, they were considered to be 'general administration costs' to be treated after the calculation of the direct costs of production. On the other hand, they were considered to be fixed in that staff enjoyed a 'hierarchical privilege' in the organization that protected their souls from the tyrannies of top management controls. Accountants established, without an in-depth articulation of the issue, that their costs were not determined by the *number of output units* (the basis upon which the variability and controllability of costs are understood traditionally), so that these costs had to go directly into the income statement, often implying that they were 'uncontrollable' and thereby releasing them from managerial scrutiny. Hiding behind the vagueness of financial reporting, these costs then remained naïve or undiscriminating. Armstrong (2002, 100) observed this: 'Employment in the staff department, on the other hand, remained relatively secure, depending on the abilities of

Strategizing cost management 205

its representatives to convince the rest of the management team of the importance of the services which it provided'.

This protection left the staff functions' real activities hidden and their cost implications were not accounted for. Mechanisms of standard costing acted as a way of imposing accountability among the production workers but left open the question of 'who controls the controllers'. However, the competitive pressures of neoliberal markets and the strategic necessity of becoming cost-efficient in every corner of the firm initiated a penetration into hitherto unchartered territories, including staff functions, to open up their *activities* (the basis upon which the variability and the controllability of costs are now understood after ABC) for managerial gaze and surveillance (cf. Armstrong 2002). As we highlighted in the preceding chapters, in the process of transforming everybody into 'entrepreneurs of the self' (see Cooper 2015), it provided a form of 'normative reasoning' (Brown 2005) to unpack such 'black boxes', to see how controls could be exerted, and how profitability could be maximized on every possible front. While this extension of surveillance to 'staff functions' had a number of theoretical precepts, Haggerty and Ericson (2000) used Deleuze and Guattari (1987) to describe this as a 'surveillance assemblage'. Haggerty and Ericson (2000, 608) observed:

> Deleuze and Guattari introduce a radical notion of multiplicity into phenomena which we traditionally approach as being discretely bounded, structured and stable. 'Assemblages' consist of a multiplicity of heterogenous objects, whose unity comes solely from the fact that these items function together, that they 'work' together as a functional entity ... They comprise discrete flows of an essentially limitless range of other phenomena such as people, signs, chemicals, knowledge, and institutions. To dig beneath the surface stability of any entity is to encounter a radical nature of this vision which becomes more apparent when one realises how any particular assemblage is itself composed of different discrete assemblages which are themselves multiple.

The case of the emergence of new cost management can be read in terms of this 'surveillance assemblage'. Cost management is an assemblage here because it encapsulates everything and encroaches on unchartered territories such as staff functions, public-sector management, and governments' fiscal discipline. While neoliberalism deployed a 'normative reasoning' of competition based on cost-efficiency, in order to bring everything under the rubric of this reasoning, all areas which had never been costed before now needed to be subject to cost management discourses. Accordingly, cost management now came to cost not only products and services (which had been the only 'cost objects' in a conventional sense) but also all functional entities including people, their knowledge and intellect, customers, market segments, relationships, environmental factors, and many more, often on the basis of reconstituting them as 'activities' that consume resources (whose financial value is the cost). New categories were identified as cost pools and activity pools; and they were interconnected through cost drivers. These interconnections became the bases for 'cost driver rates' through which staff time and activities could now be attributable to cost objects (Innes et al. 2000). This allowed managers to calculate 'true costs' and set the 'correct prices' for cost objects so that they could be 'strategically positioned' in the competitive markets.

However, creating the surveillance assemblage did more than simply correct the costs and prices. Activities that people carried out became visible through activity cost analysis, providing the opportunity for capital to maximize the efficacy of the labour

206   Neoliberal trends

time that it bought not only from the blue-collar workers but also from management. The managerial labour process, which was a black box under traditional cost accounting regimes, was now open to the perpetual scrutiny of the capital (see Armstrong 2002). It revealed the need for each staff function to be perpetually considered in terms of the validity of its 'value added' criteria. This resulted in the new managerial doctrine of justification: all staff costs must be justified in terms of their contribution to the value enhancement of the cost objects which would ultimately be positioned in the market; if not, the services provided by certain staff functions must be redundant. This was made possible by other rhetoric and practices such as business process re-engineering, total quality management, and lean manufacturing. On this point, Armstrong (2002, 102) made a vivid observation:

> In its prescription of multi-functional committees as means of implementation ... ABC promised the production function a major say in determining the services of which it bore the cost. As part of the same deal, the scrutiny of staff departments through which its activities were to be established could be used to reveal any which were 'non-value added', ... thus creating [a] respectable front for the productivist suspicion that quite a lot of staff activity is of no value at all. It is no accident that some of the most successful applications of ABC have been initiated by operational managers ... and also no accident that some applications have resulted in job losses in the staff departments ... In summary, ABC ... proposed that [the] staff department should be subjected to regimes of accountability similar to those already experienced by manufacturing.

ABC in effect started to dismantle the shelter provided for the staff functions with the traditional rhetoric of 'fixed costs'. This then was further intensified when Kaplan and Copper extended ABC to ABM. When ABC's narrow focus on overhead reallocation was critiqued (see Armstrong 2002; Drennan and Kelly 2002; Jones and Dugdale 2002), Kaplan and Cooper emphasized that their project was not about ABC only, it was about ABM which elaborated a broader view of encompassing cost management rather than cost accounting. ABM extended the 'vertical or cost assignment view' of ABC into 'horizontal or a process view' of cost management (see Figure 9.3). Hence, this was not a mere task of cost accounting – much work had to be done by industrial engineers, operations managers, and process managers, they argued.

ABM was then placed in the centre of the surveillance assemblage. Departing from the mere calculation of 'true' costs, ABM demanded that managers must pay attention to the 'strategic use of resources and time' by analysing activities and cost drivers, eliminating unnecessary costs, and revising the work processes continuously to establish competitiveness in the entire value chain. Hence, functional managers were now regarded not simply as 'cost centres' but as 'self-entrepreneurial consumers' of corporate resources (i.e. value creation-driven consumers or consumption for value creation). They needed to justify their consumption of resources, time, and their activities in terms of their capacity to 'add value', transforming themselves into a series of entrepreneurial and inventive acts of minimizing costs and creating value for those in the next element of the value chain, whose identity was now to be transformed into 'internal customers'. This transformed the organizational hierarchy into a system of social integration and surveillance through 'customizing' organizational relationships within and outside the markets. Again, Haggerty and Ericson (2000, 615) remarked:

Strategizing cost management 207

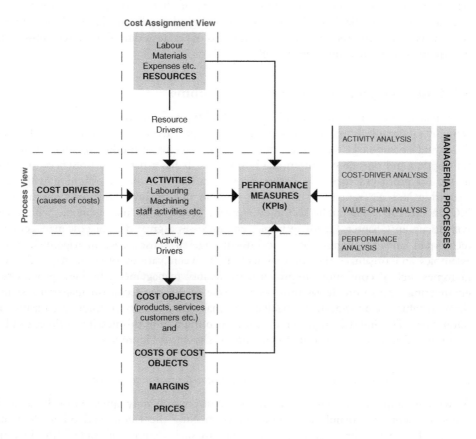

Figure 9.3 From ABC to ABM
Source: adapted from Miller (1996, 236).

[s]urveillance was a means to maintain a form of hierarchical social control. Foucault proposed that panoptic surveillance targeted the soul, disciplining the masses into a form of self-monitoring that was in harmony with the requirements of the developing factory system. However ... panopticism in contemporary society has been reduced in importance as a mechanism of social integration. Instead of being subject to disciplinary surveillance or simple repression, the population is increasingly constituted as consumers and seduced into the market economy.

Staff managers and their functions are now part of this wider mechanism of social integration through neoliberal entrepreneurial self and consumption, a mechanism through which 'biopolitical controls' (cf. Foucault 2008) are exercised within organizational boundaries, within the internal processes of the organization that have now been converted into market relations. ABM as a mode of surveillance is used to construct and monitor resource consumption patterns now conceived in terms of activities, activity drivers, cost drivers, resource drivers, and activity driver rates – to ensure that there is no non-value-added 'consumption' taking place within the organization, to ensure every

208   *Neoliberal trends*

activity is effectively adding to corporate profits. If their resource consumption and activities are not justifiable in the face of this neoliberal condition, that is, if the internal consumers cannot pay the required price in terms of 'value addition', resource consumers (i.e. the staff personnel) must be laid off.

9.5 Cost management as a holistic programme

Cost management is now established as a holistic programme encapsulating various elements of organizational practices and expanding its rhetoric beyond the firms' factory floors and operational domains to infrastructural elements of production and reproduction within and outside organizational boundaries. It has a pervasive presence not only in the for-profit enterprises as a strategic imperative of market positioning with cost leadership and differentiation but also in myriad not-for-profit organizations such as NGOs, charities, and public-sector enterprises. New public management, which we will discuss in Chapter 12, for example, encompasses a great deal of cost management techniques and ideologies. In a techno-managerial sense, cost management now assembles and organizes the interconnection between various other managerial programmes such as continuous improvements, quality management, business process re-engineering, and so on. It has thus become one of the key techno-managerial systems through which neoliberalism is enabled and enacted within and outside organizational boundaries. This holistic programme, as it is reconfigured in this neoliberal time, can be decomposed into four interrelated elements, as shown in Figure 9.4.

9.5.1 Cost controls beyond the shop-floor: new vistas for cost management

As we mentioned in Section 9.3, traditional cost controls only appeared in the area of shop-floor controls, mainly as a mode of controlling the labour and other elements associated with the direct cost of production. In such regimes of control, production workers became subservient to the process of controlling the direct costs of production through the use of standard costing and variance analysis (Hopper and Armstrong 1991; Wells 1977), or to the mere quantity control of production (Berry et al. 1985). In multidivisional 'M-form' organizational structures, such shop-floor controls were then connected to top management plans and objectives through a system of responsibility accounting where a hierarchical system of financial performance measures was constructed in such a manner that costs and revenues were ultimately connected to the return on investment. The DuPont system of ratio analysis is the classic example of this. Accordingly, top managers' plans were to be executed through a system of responsibility accounting in which costs were calculated based on traditional absorption techniques, and such cost-based performance was evaluated on variances. This tradition of management control became popular as responsibility accounting was propagated through textbooks, university education, and professional training programmes. This was top-down, bureaucratic, tedious, and directed towards confining the workers to the shop-floor while top managers exercised their managerial prerogatives over them. A pragmatic manifestation of such controls was traditionally seen in the mundane practices of physical supervision based on day-to-day accounting calculations aimed at attaining budget targets, which made the supervisors and lower-level managers responsible for avoiding possible variances (e.g. labour hour variances and labour efficiency variances), and producing variance reports to be discussed at management boards (see Hirst and

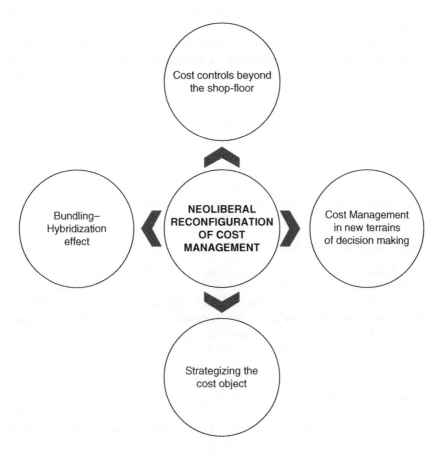

Figure 9.4 Neoliberal reconfiguration of cost management

Yetton 1999). In this system of making the shop-floor subservient to the monitoring by top managers, standard costing and absorption costing played a critical role (see Edwards et al. 2002; McLean and Tyson 2006).

The M-form model was amenable to this tradition of control by creating forms of decentralization (and centralization). This created decision-making centres across divisions and sub-divisions to which resources and targets were 'allocated' based on budgets. The actual costs of running these decision centres were then calculated through absorption costing systems, and performance was assessed by comparing the actuals with the budget and standards. Divisional managers were then given responsibilities to manage and control labour performance towards budget targets. Established textbooks (e.g. Anthony and Govindarajan 1998; Emmanuel et al. 2004; Merchant and van der Stede 2007) portrayed this as 'management control' and management control researchers (e.g. Hofstede 1981; Otley and Berry 1980) distinguished this 'surveillance assemblage' as a system of cybernetic control.

However, such systems of 'management control' became questionable with the arrival of neoliberal conditions, especially in terms of their inability to initiate and

210 *Neoliberal trends*

facilitate process changes towards flexibility, quality, and cost leadership. As Johnson and Kaplan argued, cost accounting 'lost its relevance' mainly because there emerged a gap between what was possible through existing accounting technologies and what was demanded under new neoliberal conditions. In particular, accounting's capacity to handle overhead expenses became strategically critical because the proportion of overhead in the total costs of production became quite significant in contemporary production and organizational configurations. So, the cost accounting practices underpinning the management control system had to be unpacked, disassembled, and re-assembled. This 'problematization' led Kaplan and his followers to introduce, propagate, and institutionalize a new assemblage of cost management.

In the process of reassembling, as outlined in Table 9.2, cost management was re-envisioned in two interrelated ways: (1) appreciating the programme beyond budgeting; and (2) accommodating operations management innovations.

1 The beyond budgeting movement

Following Johnson and Kaplan's initial critiques of traditional management accounting, the beyond budgeting (BB) movement also assumed the duty of raising concerns about the traditional mode of budgeting and offering alternatives to address those concerns. These concerns were listed as: traditional budgeting constrains responsiveness and flexibility; it is unnecessarily time consuming; it is rarely linked to strategy; it encourages perverse gaming behaviour; it does not reflect new forms of organizations; it produces long-term (more infrequent) budgets; it is prepared based on unsupported assumptions and guesswork; and it makes people feel under-valued (Marginson 2013). These concerns were not new – long ago Argyris (1952) began to raise such concerns and a tradition of budgeting research (e.g. Ansari 1979; Covaleski and Dirsmith 1988; Dunk and Nouri 1998; Hopwood 1972; Jensen 2003) propelled him to highlight specific issues. BB emerged to support this literature and to offer a pragmatic alternative to the traditional mode of budgeting, with Hope and Fraser's popular BB programme being largely implemented in Scandinavian countries (see Hope and Fraser 2003a).

Table 9.2 Re-envisioning of cost management

Aspects in question	Traditional budgeting	Beyond budgeting	Innovations in operations management
Focus	Top-down cost controls	Continuous cost reduction	Continuous process improvement
Methods adopted	Absorption costing and standard costing	Rolling forecasts; ABC, ABB, BSC	Lean management, ERP, functional analysis, target costing; continuous improvement and Kaizen costing
Organizational form and context	Hierarchical and command centred	Less heterarchical and participatory	Organizational flexibility and flexible manufacturing
Key research	Anthony (1965), Hofstede (2003 [1968])	Hope and Fraser (1997, 2000, 2001, 2003a, 2003b)	Davenport (1998), Imai (1986), Monden and Hamada (1991)

Strategizing cost management 211

BB's cost management rationale is that it focuses on continuous cost reduction by revising the decision scenarios through a process of rolling forecasts. The proponents of BB claim that it can accommodate contemporary developments in management accounting including BSC, ABM, and ABB. In particular, ABB is propagated as a control system based on ABC and ABM that guarantees both cost saving and better resource allocation. It also benefits from CAM-1 (Consortium of Advanced Manufacturing) which analyses the capacities of, and demands for, resources making ABB a closed-loop model (see Hansen 2010; Hansen and Torok 2004). This development, as proponents argue, if not embellish, not only eliminates the possibility of gaming the budget but also fosters a more responsive and meaningful budget that works much better in changing and dynamic environments. Consequently, it is argued that BB re-envisions cost management as a collaborative, decentralized, and participative phenomena.

Moreover, BB has exploited the opportunity for experimenting with some other popular practices such as: zero-based budgeting (see Wetherbe and Montanari 1981), which restarts the budget from a zero base for every budget period; value-based management, which promises shareholder value when undertaking project appraisal and valuation (see Neely et al. 2000); and profit planning, which assures both economic value and the necessary financial resources (Marginson 2013). These initiatives imply an elimination of undue delays and malfunctions in rigid hierarchical structures of traditional budgeting by introducing heterarchical planning arrangements which promote more flexibility, relationality, and organizational harmony. These initiatives also imply a 'bundling effect' (Modell 2009), constituting a 'surveillance assemblage' that we discussed earlier. In this assemblage, there are many ideas, practices, and initiatives: benchmarking, rolling forecasts, decentralization, and empowering managers and other employees, etc. This assemblage stands in stark contrast to conventional mono-logic control regimes where the 'fixed overhead shelter' was entertained only by staff managers. Now, it is much more egalitarian, heterogeneous, and cost-effective, and everyone is subjected to its surveillance. Proponents claim that this can generate enhanced competitiveness and flexibility, despite the critics who emphasized difficulties in implementation (Frow et al. 2010), concerns regarding the validity of the perceived problems of traditional budgeting (Dugdale and Lyne 2010), and some ambiguity of the soundness of the claim that more egalitarian approaches to budgeting do much better (Marginson and Ogden 2005). Hence, further research is still needed to explore whether BB is just a rhetoric with no basis for dismissing traditional budgeting and to consider how surveillance operates as a baggage of new ideas and practices that BB propagates.

2 Cost management innovations in operations management

The second programme that re-envisioned cost management, as we saw in Table 9.2, is operations management innovations. Its focus has been on continuous process improvement, with cost reduction as one of its key objectives. The production processes are re-engineered to eliminate waste, repetition, and even corruption and malpractices. During the 1980s and 1990s, production and manufacturing experts saw that traditional production systems in the West were full of inefficiencies that were passed onto customers resulting in a loss of customers and market share. Hence, they suggested that new ideas such as lean management, ERP, functional analysis, target costing, continuous improvement, and Kaizen costing could reinstate cost-efficiency together with quality and flexibility. For example, lean manufacturing is driven by the following seven principles that foster process effectiveness: (1) elimination of waste; (2) working

212   Neoliberal trends

for zero defects for JIT purposes; (3) producing for orders rather than forecasts; (4) employing multifunctional teams; (5) decentralization of responsibilities; (6) establishing an integrated information system by combining the vertical with the horizontal; and (7) engaging in a culture of continuous improvement (see Chapter 8). So, these principles were directly implicated in cost management in that all these could save enormous costs and generate cost-efficiency which would be reflected in enhanced competitiveness (see Mouritsen et al. 2009). For this to happen, some firms maintained Value Stream Maps (VSM) on a visual board communicating best standards to follow within a lean financial model. Consequently, at Toyota, production is defined as 'best quality – lowest cost – shortest lead time – best safety – high morale – through shortening the production flow by eliminating wastes' (Liker 2003). The consequential effects of this are then an effective and efficient form of cost management. Cost management innovations in operations management can be discussed under two headings: the ERP effect and the Japanese effect.

ERP effect

Behind this new assemblage of cost management, there were ICT enhancements. These occurred with the implementation of ERP systems which aimed at: integrating hitherto dispersed information systems; standardizing accounting and operational procedures; routinizing practices; and centralizing databases. This development became a global programme where cost management was technologically integrated with transaction processing systems, performance measurement systems, and logistic systems together with decision-support systems. Most firms are now adopting ERP systems for better cost and performance management (Scapens and Jazayeri 2003; Wagner et al. 2011). As a result, the role of management accountants has changed, people and things are effectively networked, everybody's actions are coordinated through computer networks, and individual actions become visible to one another in terms of the degree to which they perform the system-attributed functions (Hyvönen 2013). When we look more closely at the relationship between cost management and ERP, as Hyvönen (2013) observed, cost management now assumes a novel position. As you see in Figure 9.5, ERP has made cost management a technology, a body of knowledge (i.e. a discipline), a control structure, and a profession.

This means ERP has played a vital role in transforming cost accounting into cost management. Once performed through ERP, cost management is a hard technology because it encapsulates ICT into a system of management control and planning. It is a discipline because it is claimed that ERP-based cost management is about exercising knowledge and power at a mundane level on a daily basis. It is a control structure because it has redefined and re-enacted a set of structural relations through which everybody is known, planned, controlled, and integrated into a performance management system. And, it is a newly organized profession in that accountants as well as other professionals now claim their status of professional expertise in relation to their knowledge and experience of designing and operating in an ERP environment. These changes and transformations have been studied to report that the world of management accounting is now different, requiring drastic changes to training and education programmes to bring accountants into the field of surveillance that ERP-based cost management has enabled (Caglio 2003; Granlund and Malmi 2002; Hyvönen 2003). However, it does not mean that all this has happened without any issue: researchers have raised concerns about the shift in power from one category of personnel to another (Newman and Westrup 2005), about the

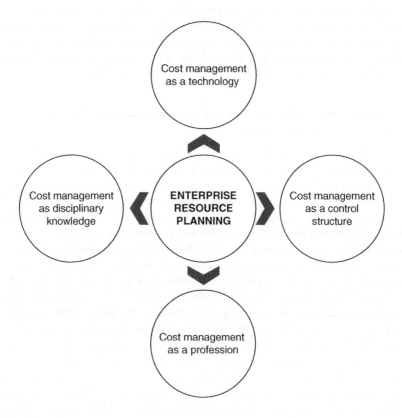

Figure 9.5 ERP in action

politics of visibility, homogeneity, and heterogeneity that ERP enables (see Quattrone and Hopper 2006), and about the multiplicity of information shifting panopticon controls to a kind of 'oligopticon' (Latour 2005).

The Japanese effect

In addition to ERP, there are other production technologies, mainly developed in Japanese manufacturing firms such as Toyota, which also reconfigured the way cost is managed. One salient development was the use of *cost tables through functional analyses*. These tables cost each and every tiny part of a product both at the design and finishing stages. Cost tables act as databases to derive detailed cost estimates before production takes place, which lead to better cost management during the process of actual production. Despite its simplicity as a concept, it provides details about everything so that there is little room for defects and malfunctions (see Yoshikawa and Innes 2013; Yoshikawa et al. 1995). Moreover, through integrating with target costing exercises (see Yoshikawa 1994, 2001) it accommodates both customer perspectives and market dynamics that guide the managers to analyse profitability. Alongside this practice in Toyota, some other Japanese companies (such as Daihatsu) have adopted a programme of continuous improvement, which they call Kaizen costing. The aim of this approach is also to reduce the cost of

214   *Neoliberal trends*

exiting products and services below the prevailing standard costs while giving priority to customers' expectations (see Yoshikawa 1994, 2001). Altogether, Japanese production systems operate in a cultural context in which people commit themselves to maintaining momentum, cost management has always been the centre of attention through which surveillance has been exercised differently (see Hopper et al. 1999).

9.5.2 Cost management in the new terrain of decision making: the theory of constraints and throughput accounting

Decision making has traditionally been associated with economic modelling, but new developments in cost management practices have created new areas of decision making. These developments have brought about not only new ideas and practices but also alternative theoretical explanations as to how cost management can be assimilated in new scenarios. To illustrate this, we shall look at two new interrelated developments: the Theory of Constraints (TOC) and Throughput Accounting (TA).

As an idea, TOC first appeared in a bestselling novel by Goldratt and Cox (1984). It was a story of a fictional manager who tried to save his plant. The manager was advised by a professor to recognize the plant as the bottleneck because it was the only limited resource he had to operate. He was then asked to identify the nature of this bottleneck and to exploit possibilities of improving throughput in the plant. This made him realize that the bottleneck can be broken by considering better throughput, which has become known as TA. Hence, TOC and TA go hand in hand with each other while corporate managers can maximize their performance by better materializing this connection.

The story of TOC and its associated practices of TA is about making decisions in relation to the constraints that managers face in optimizing their production plans. TOC offers a step-by-step process of decision making to address issues emanating from capacity constraints. As you see in Figure 9.6, the process includes: (1) identifying the constraint in the system; (2) finding a way of exploiting it; (3) subordinating and synchronizing everything else to the constraint; (4) elevating the performance of the constraint; and (5) going back to step 1 and repeating the cycle.

In fact, what TOC offers is a framework for perpetual reconsideration of shop-floor arrangements. If capacity is limited when compared to production needs, there is a constraint. Optimizing production around constraints is a cost management function which requires a perpetual cycle of calculations, observations, comparisons, and decisions. It starts with identifying the constraint by comparing available capacity with production/sales requirements. You then brainstorm how this constraint can be exploited. Managers may explore some fundamental questions: Is it about a better product mix? Are we using the facility's maximum capacity? Is that always possible to achieve? To address these questions, it is recommended that you first calculate the 'throughput' (= Revenue minus purchased materials and services) and determine the throughput per bottleneck minute. Prepare buffer stocks in front of the bottleneck and exploit the bottleneck when the facility is ready. You would then maximize your contribution by maximizing the throughput. However, this needs a careful coordination with non-bottleneck operations allowing the bottleneck to be exploited at its maximum level while the non-bottleneck facilities are given less priority as they can be used anytime once the bottleneck facilities have been exploited. This coordination is managed with the help of a scheduling technique called DBR (Drum-Buffer-Rope) which warrants that non-bottleneck operations can produce only the needs of the

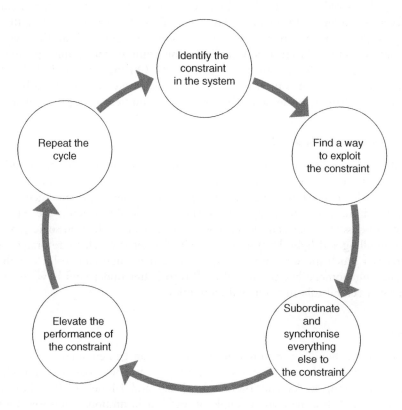

Figure 9.6 TOC and TA in action

bottleneck have been met. Once this kind of process has managed to break the bottleneck, you can go back to the first step to look for new constraints which need exploiting by adopting the same principles using the same techniques. Such a process then saves costs and maximizes profits by maximizing throughput. Hence, it is cost management by managing constraints.

TOC and TA have challenged the traditional overhead absorption costing. Early proponents, Goldratt and Cox (1984), considered traditional cost accounting as an 'enemy' because it treats the majority of facility or capacity costs as 'fixed', implying limited managerial discretion over them. Instead, from the cost management point of view that TOC propagates, it is operationally critical to identify the bottleneck versus the non-bottleneck facilities and to have buffer stock at its maximum level in case of bottlenecks so that any restrictions on sales and profitability can be avoided. TOC promoters also argue that even ABC is not helpful in realizing what Goldratt and Fox were aiming at. However, their attack on ABC has not been well received in the management accounting literature because ABC/M propose a long-term view of cost calculations whereas TOC and TA's emphasis is on short-term profitability (Dugdale 2013). Nevertheless, despite this conflict, TOC and TA have gained some popularity. Even when the constraints are multiple, TOC and TA can still be adopted in conjunction with linear programming and the use of MRP packages (Dugdale 2013).

216 *Neoliberal trends*

With regard to Goldratt and Fox's ambiguity about the use of ABC, some organizations have recently attempted to integrate ABC with TOC to exploit the strengths of both techniques (Kee and Schmidt 2000), but this is still doubtful in the eyes of the proponents of TOC. From a cost management point of view, this apparent rivalry needs handling carefully as both have equal merits. On the one hand, TOC is simple and pragmatic and, on the other, ABC/M is well established due to its global presence, so it is hard to deny its prominence and presence in numerous organizational settings.

9.5.3 Bundling: the hybridization effect

We will now discuss the effects of cost management on both organizations and society. We shall leave its effects on the organizational reconfigurations to the next chapter where we will discuss how cost management has facilitated the emergence of inter-organizational networks to manage cost, quality, and flexibility across the supply chain. Here, we discuss the important effects cost management has had on society, which we call the bundling and hybridization effects. The former is much more pragmatic while the latter is a much more theoretical explanation. It is important to look at these two interrelated phenomena because it will lead us to better understand how cost management plays a central role in neoliberal biopolitics.

Bundling

The notion of the bundling effect is developed in the management innovations literature. It has emphasized that when innovations occur, they get bundled together with other issues to eventually form, as Ax and Bjørnenak (2007) and Modell (2009) showed, 'new packages'. Behind this, there are a couple of social or institutional processes. First, is the effects of fads and fashions; second, is the institutionalization of new ideas at the organizational level. The effects of fads and fashion is when organizations embrace new ideas merely because of mere popularity among others, especially leading actors in the field. This is akin to what has been theorized by well-known institutional theory as institutional isomorphism (DiMaggio and Powell 1983); managers tend to think that 'we must also have it because others have it'. Because of this managerial psychology, Ax and Bjørnenak (2007) argue, organizations become attractive to new ideas emanating from powerful epistemic centres. Modell (2009; 61; see also Abrahamson 1991, 1996) summarized this literature thus:

> Drawing heavily on DiMaggio and Powell (1983), Abrahamson (1991) introduced the fad and fashion perspectives as complements to the efficient choice perspective, suggesting that adoption results from reasoned cost/benefit-centred decisions, and the forced selection perspective, according to which adoption is driven by the need to comply with regulatory powers. The fad and fashion perspectives differ, however, in that the former sees similar organisations within a particular group of adopters as the main source of imitation while paying little attention to the origins of innovations. On the other hand, the fashion perspective emphasises the active involvement of fashion-setters, such as influential consulting firms and other expert powers, typically located outside the group of adopting organisations in the creation of management fashions.

Because of this fad/fashion effect, firms tend to adopt a variety of practices together despite there probably not being significant differences between them. The similarities between such different practices may not be seen because managers become blinded by a passive isomorphism and may subconsciously ignore analysing their combined efficacy (DiMaggio and Powell 1983). Consequently, a company may adopt ABC, BB, BSC, lean management, TOC, TA together. Furthermore, ERP may facilitate this combination and re-combination technologically through specific 'modules' that can be added to the core programme.

However, we should not jump to the conclusion that all innovations and integrations are foolish and managers are necessarily blinded by forceful isomorphism. Instead, there are some possible 'rationalities' coupled with a process where the managers explore some 'serendipity' of success. Modell's (2009, 83–84) findings are important here:

> The notion of bundling may need to be re-conceptualised to illuminate how it is entangled with managerial and organisational learning processes. While fashionable innovations provide important inputs to such processes, our findings suggest that learning entails important elements of serendipity as well as 'rationality' as organisations experiment with various innovations. While the emerging literature on the bundling of management accounting and control innovations has ignored such processes ... it may be extended through integration with organisational learning theories recognising that bundling involves some balancing between goal-directed behaviour and less malleable experimenting ... Successful adjustments of innovations to a particular organisational context may require selective incorporation of design elements, emerging as particularly useful during the process of implementation but being mediated by repositories of organisational experience.

Innovations in cost management propelled other buddy practices such as ERP, BB, lean management, and TQM to produce some collective rationality and serendipity. Often a 'holistic approach' is envisaged which can bring different systems together to minimize inter-system conflicts. For example, Bjørnenak and Kaarbøe (2013, 172) were hopeful of a holistic costing and control package. They remarked:

> A control package, or a more holistic perspective, is also important for the design of costing systems. If you design an ad hoc ABC system in order to change your product portfolio, but have a sales budget and culture focusing on sales volume, the signals for the different systems maybe in conflict. The conflict should be addressed before the design of the system.

Hybridization

While the bundling perspective provides us with a pragmatic solution to the question of integrated cost management systems, the hybridization perspective offers a theoretical articulation of how hybridized practices burgeoned. Referring to the development of hybridized practice both in the organization and beyond its boundary, Miller et al. (2008, 944) observed the pervasiveness of the phenomenon and its social and organizational implications:

> The world is populated by hybrids or intermediaries that constantly mix up and link up apparently desperate and heterogeneous things ... Actors, entities, objects,

218   *Neoliberal trends*

practices, processes and bodies of expertise can all be regarded as hybrids ... Further, hybridization itself is a process, and assumes variable forms. Not all practices, processes, expertise hybridize with equal ease. Once formed, a hybrid may revert, as in the botanical world. Or the newly formed hybrid may stabilise for a sufficient period of time to be termed as an institution.

So, hybridization is a norm in today's economy and society. It becomes formed and reformed along with heterogeneous objects, practices, and processes. Cost management's hybridized outlook must be seen through these lenses; its unavoidable processes of hybridization imply this social reality. Miller et al. (2008) use this concept to discuss an unavoidable process of hybridization of risk management practices, but its application to cost management practices offers the same message: despite the politics of identity, hybridization occurs 'behind the scenes sometimes noisily and sometimes quietly' (Miller et al. 2008, 944).

Does this mean that cost management has been removed from the hands of the traditional management accountant? Has it been 'contaminated' with computer science, data analytics, organizational strategy, operations engineering, and so forth? As we said before, it is now a different profession and it is a hybridized one. As a result, like risk management and quality management, often under the slogan that 'it is everyone's job', cost management creates lateral information flows crossing the boundaries of different functional management areas. It accommodates a variety of issues to manage uncertainties across these lateral flows. It coordinates with other actors beyond the organization to address issues of cost-efficiencies in the interfirm production networks (Powell 1987, 1990). In doing so, as Powell (1987, 1990) pointed out, hybrids operate to generate reciprocal and mutual relationships because knowledge is now distributed, and competitive advantage is attained by exploiting this distributed form of intelligence. Cumulatively, cost management works with others and generates cost-efficiencies through the efficient functioning of other managerial processes and systems.

9.5.4 Strategizing the cost object

We have now reached a point where some deeper discussions can be carried out on the question of the cost object. Traditional cost accounting held out the image that the cost object was a more or less unproblematic notion in that overhead costs could be allocated to it with little concern for the rationale behind allocation procedures. For almost a century, this rationale was not subject to critical scrutiny either by management experts or factory accountants until, as we mentioned earlier, Johnson and Kaplan's (1987a) *Relevance Lost* thesis was put forward. As many commentators observed, the 1980s witnessed an escalation of debates about the relevance of cost allocation rationales and subsequent arguments about product cost distortions.

An interesting way to read this debate is through the notion of 'politics of the product' (Miller and O'Leary 1993). Miller and O'Leary argue that all the pitfalls of management and governance were linked to the notion of the 'product', into which all governance and management problems are ultimately connected to the extent that, for example, US products have lost its competitiveness in the global market. Miller and O'Leary remarked:

> This image of a lost competitiveness on the part of American industry is typically presented as much more than narrowly economic. Designers, engineers, and the

Strategizing cost management 219

research community are implicated in the downfall of American manufacturing. The education system is held significantly responsible for the absence of a properly educated workforce. And the capital markets are accused of being an important contributory factor in the move towards a financial structure more intent on short-run gain than sustainable excellence in production. The decline of American manufacturing is viewed as systemic and deeply rooted, its consequences economic, technological, sociological, and even moral.

(Miller and O'Leary 1993, 188)

This notion of 'politics of the product' is useful in understanding how cost management has become biopolitical – how a whole range of political actors and programmes are put into circulation in order to address the biopolitical problem of competitiveness; a problem which simultaneously relates to the macro-political phenomenon of the population, the nation, and the micro-organizational, or anatomico-politics of manufacturing (and hence costing). Multiple actors and practices were implicated in the problem of the loss of competitiveness of the product and hence the nation. The incapacity of 'our products' to compete in the global market is discursively projected as a problem of the firm and of the nation simultaneously. The solution to the problem thus cannot emanate only from micro-organizational actions such as cost management or product improvements. It requires a well-coordinated global agenda of enhancing competitiveness (see Chapters 5 and 6). Everything needs to be directed to 'add value to the product'. At the heart of neoliberalism is this globally coordinated competitiveness improvement programme in which strategic management and cost management play a vital role in directing everything else towards the cost-efficiency of producing and delivering the product. The politics of the product connects cost management and governance with epistemic innovations. This connection is depicted in Figure 9.7.

As we discussed in previous chapters (especially Chapters 5 and 6), biopolitics works through the perpetual reconstruction of biopolitical problems – creating pathological traits of the population. The 'politics of product' initiate biopolitical processes and assemblages by discursively reconstructing the biopolitical problem of the loss of competitiveness of the products and hence the nations to which the products are attributed. This then calls for various actors and assemblages to cooperate and coordinate to find solutions. This is in fact a construction of what we may call a 'programmatic domain of governance', a discursive site in which dialogues and debates are generated to explain the problem and to find solutions. It enrols multitudes in the project to enhance competitiveness, and things become fads and fashions in this site. It is in this site that various theories, concepts, technologies, and institutions are bundled and hybridized to form discursively (and hence biopolitically) powerful solutions, hybridized forms of cost management being one.

Nevertheless, in its enrolment of accounting in the biopolitical project, it creates a problematic image of accounting. Accounting has been regarded as a neutral and objective practice that can offer undeniable numbers for corporate managers to act upon. These numbers are considered to be 'facts' of an objective economic reality. The role of cost accounting has been to produce a 'realist' image of the economic processes and outcomes (Hopper and Powell 1985; Miller and O'Leary 1987). Given how this notion is taken for granted, management and governance systems are organized according to the 'facts' that accounting creates. And accounting thus encapsulates a biopolitical power of creating connections, programming biopolitical agendas, and coordinating assemblages. Miller and O'Leary (1993, 189) echoed this power of accounting:

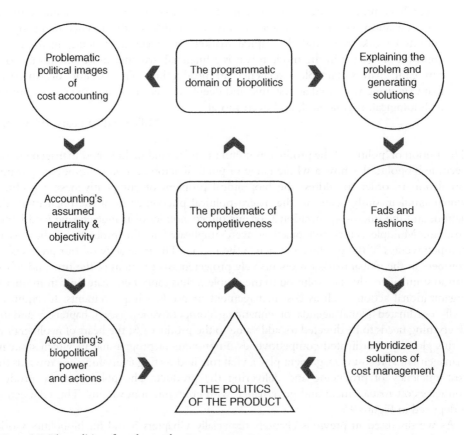

Figure 9.7 The politics of product and cost management

Across the present century this image has sustained the programmatic ambitions of accountancy in diverse domains. Calls to bring the facts of costing to light ... to link the corporation with capital markets ... to regulate management-labour relations ... to enable the pursuit of efficiency in the public sector ... and to enable the state to govern better both private enterprises as well as those entities formally tied to it ... have all appealed to the objectivity and neutrality of calculative expertise.

When a new set of neoliberal politics of the product started to emerge with a new biopolitical problem of the competitiveness of the product, this objectivity and neutrality of calculative expertise started to be challenged and problematized. Miller and O'Leary (1993) conceptualized this movement of problematization in two ways. First, entails discussions, arguments, and debates about the internal arrangement of the product: problematic alignment between the factory, the product, and accounting. Second, is the issue that Miller and O'Leary (1993) address, which has been cost accounting's operations in a context programmatic terrain. By this, they mean that (cost) accounting and its transformation are not simply an internal arrangement of production. Instead, they have become deeply rooted in an array of agency relationships (i.e. an assemblage) with consultants, professionals, academics, educationists, trainers, and so forth. The programmatic terrain, some elements of which we discussed differently as the practicist epistemology in Chapter 3, is the site in which new ideas and practices are programmed, promoted, diffused, and institutionalized.

As we mentioned at the start of this subsection, the politics of the product has strived towards 'strategizing the cost object', which is enhancing the competitiveness of the product in the market. It is a process of enabling the product to become operable in the context of acute competition. We generally understand that it is the firm which becomes strategized in the face of this competition. However, the way the idea of the politics of the product has been articulated has led us to think about this somewhat differently. It is the product indeed that needs to be placed in this competition for convincing the customer, for re-engineering the factory, for re-configuring the management, and, eventually, for devising a mode of new cost management. The task of strategizing then is about aligning all these together. The major concerns here are about exploring how the politics of the product render it operable in competition and how cost management is placed at the centre of this biopolitical process.

9.6 Summary and conclusions: neoliberal implications

This chapter aimed to offer a biopolitical explanation of recent developments in cost accounting and management with special reference to the issues of strategizing the firm. In doing so, we first examined how and why the predecessors of current cost management emerged, evolved, and were institutionalized as a calculative technology of the 'old spirit of capitalism'. Second, we explored how the neoliberal turn began to problematize the traditional wisdom of cost accounting. Third, we explained how this problematization provided a powerful and historical justification for the development, diffusion, and institutionalization of new cost management ideas from around the world. Fourth, the accounts of problematization gave rise to a surveillance assemblage consisting of moving multiple ideas into a single domain of management control through which everybody in the organization – including the administrative staff – were made amenable to surveillance. We explained how all the developments were articulated as a holistic programme of management control, giving new meanings to controls beyond the shop-floor, constituting bundling and hybridizing effects, and rallying the new techniques, processes, and practices around the themes of strategizing the product for it to be competitive.

These developments have implications for neoliberal forms of cost management. While neoliberalism offers a concrete form of governmentality by linking biopolitics to life processes, cost management and related managerial practices such as lean management, JIT, TQM, ERP, TOC, and TA have come to be the pragmatic tools through which the link between biopolitics and life processes are constructed. That said, while cost objects are being strategized through the 'politics of the product' we described, people's lives within and outside organizations are being organized, calculated, evaluated, and controlled in relation to certain biopolitical themes that characterize such macro-political categories as the population. As such, biopolitical notions such as 'national competitiveness' and cost–efficiency throughout the global supply chain have become policy themes that companies now need to address through the micro-organizational anatomico-politics of the body and space. This is the

222 *Neoliberal trends*

development of political power outside state apparatuses. Unlike under the regime of sovereign power, such practices now assume a novel form of administration at the level of the organization under neoliberalism, implying that, as Lemke (2011, 4) pronounced:

> [b]iopolitics is not the expression of a sovereign will but aims at the administration and regulation of life processes on the level of population. It focuses on living beings rather than on legal subjects – or, to be more precise, it deals with legal subjects that are at the same time living beings.

We have taken biopolitics repeatedly to comment on management accounting's transformation into a strategic form which we called strategizing. We have done the same here to buttress the argument we have made throughout. Like any other technology, cost management is also nicely implicated in biopolitics and its neoliberal governmentality. In the next chapter, we undertake a similar task to explore how neoliberal governmentality has blurred the boundaries of the organization, how biopolitics has lingered in its analytical scope from the level of organization to the level of inter-organizational relations or supply chains, and how management accounting is being implicated in such interfirm connections.

Assignments

These assignments are meant to extend your knowledge beyond what you understand from this chapter. These are not simply revision questions. The content covered in this chapter is necessary but will not be sufficient in attempting these tasks. Therefore, you are required to do some extra reading in attempting these tasks.

1. **Thematic essay:**
    'Cost management is a surveillance assemblage'.Write an essay, of approximately 3,000 words, on the above theme articulating how cost management can foster a holistic management control system.
2. **Poster:**
    Draw a poster showing how cost management's organizational and management position has shifted from an area of formality and objectivity to a movement of flexibility and domain-expansion, especially its novel function in the expanded labour process.
3. **Presentation:**
    Prepare a set of PowerPoint slides, together with notes if necessary, for a 30-minute presentation on the following theme:
    'ABC is not about just developing alternative cost allocation but about extending the controls from shop-floor to other areas of the organization'.
4. **Extended bibliography:**
    Write an extended bibliography on cost management focusing on sociological and critical theory analysis of the changes that occurred after the 1980s. For this, you should look for major accounting journals and edited books where critical accounting research is published. Organize the bibliography into a table in the following format.

Bibliographic info	Nature of the paper/book chapter (e.g. conceptual/theoretical, empirical, a response to a previous publication)	Major arguments, conclusions, and contributions

5. **Literature review:**
Write a literature review essay on the question of why and how cost accounting became a hybridized practice. In doing so, focus on the issues of the politics of bundling and the biopolitics of neoliberal governmentality.

10 Strategizing interfirm relations

10.1 Introduction

Preceding chapters discussed how management accounting is now trespassing its boundaries and exploring new vistas. Conventionally, we used to locate management accounting techniques, processes, and practices within the boundary of the organization and the hierarchical arrangement of accountability. But, we have now seen that, by trespassing beyond its boundaries, management accounting is invading new territories with new ideas and practices in which hierarchy is being replaced by heterarchical alternatives. The pragmatic outlook of this transformation is captured by the notions of interfirm relationships which have received various theoretical interpretations ranging from 'network analysis' to 'analyses of evaluative principles' of various heterarchical organizational forms. The purpose of this chapter is to discuss techno-managerial and socio-political elements of the recent transformations in interfirm relations and how these transformations point to a moment of strategizing the firm in terms of fostering competitive advantage through interfirm relationships. Then the chapter explores the role that management accounting plays in this regard and attempts to locate the transformation in the broader neoliberal schema of change.

The chapter is organized as follows.

1. In Section 10.2 you will understand how prolonged hierarchy has recently become problematic and how alternative heterarchical forms of accountability have been invented to handle strategic issues pertaining to old forms of hierarchical accountability. Such alternatives are implicated in supply chain management, characterizing the ways in which global production systems are now organized as networks and how new interfirm accountability relations are created to constitute lateral accountability as opposed to vertical accountability that characterized traditional hierarchical organizations for so long. To capture this development, this section will unpack the idea of heterarchy and will show how it has proliferated new organizational practices around the globe.
2. In Section 10.3 we will explore the form, process, and practice of management controls and performance management in the context of interfirm relations. Special attention will be paid to how new accountability systems emerge and establish heterarchical relations of accountability. This discussion will lead us to see how these emerging forms of control/performance management manifest neoliberalism and how these new forms differ from the interfirm relationships that conventional management accounting facilitated under the old spirit of capitalism.

3. Section 10.4 will expose you to accounting innovations that have occurred in the context of interfirm relations. Open-book accounting is one of the most important accounting innovations in this respect and we will be discussing that in this section. Here, you will see how intelligence is distributed and shared across networks and other heterarchical arrangements of production, distribution, and consumption through new technologies of information sharing and management for the purposes of enhancing competitiveness through interfirm relations. We will also be discussing how this has generated new management practices such as category management and supply chain performance measurement.

4. Section 10.5 discusses how all these emerging supply chain management technologies, ideologies, and concepts are hinged upon some social and institutional conditions surrounding the issues of trust and power. So, we will review the extant literature which has pointed to some interesting theoretical discussions about the nexus between accounting and trust and the empirical evidence as to how accounting and trust issues are linked to interfirm power relations and how heterarchy offers some possible solutions to these issues.

5. In Section 10.6 we pull together all these areas to synthesize an overarching theoretical argument on how the notions of neoliberalism and biopolitics are linked to the recent trends in managing interfirm relations and heterarchical tendencies.

10.2 Interfirm relations, supply chains, and heterarchy

The development of interfirm relations is a reaction to the problematic nature of traditional hierarchical organizational forms amid the neoliberal transformations taking place in the global market, and in political and technological contexts. The traditional hierarchical form of organizing economic enterprises has become problematic for several interrelated reasons. First, as they were fixed and rigid in their structures, they were not flexible enough to respond to the changing demands of customers. Market conditions have invariably become rather volatile as other competitors have taken strategic action to loosen established competitive advantages that firms had developed so far. Second, rigidly hierarchical organizations were not intelligent enough to be more creative in their actions, processes, and outcomes because their accountability relations were unvaryingly a commanding order leaving little discretion for new ideas emanating from the bottom of the organization where the real output as well as market encounters take place. Such commanding orders were imbedded in hierarchies with conventional managerial technologies such as management control and accounting, and they were conveniently driven towards regulation and maintenance of the status quo rather than inducing change. Last, because of bureaucratic properties that defined hierarchies, there were time-consuming, and hence inefficient, mechanisms of decision making. Most large organizational hierarchies in the West suffered from these limitations, losing their customers to their East Asian counterparts (Johnson and Kaplan 1987a). These conditions then compelled Western corporations to rethink their organizational structures and processes, which then led to the propagations of new organizational structures, relations, and practices including new interfirm heterarchical innovations. Accordingly, heterarchies are becoming a defining feature of neoliberal enterprises.

226   *Neoliberal trends*

Accordingly, interfirm relationships are now invariably seen as a set of new forms of business contracts moving beyond the idea that firms relate to one another necessarily through market transactions. In order to build better conditions to foster innovations and, thereby, competitive advantages through collaborations, firms are now seeking long-lasting organizational connections between firms. These include supply chain arrangements, joint ventures, outsourcing arrangements, and new public-sector initiatives such as public-private partnerships (PPPs). All these can have multitudes of relationships across the supply chain where autonomous parties become involved not only in demanding and supplying products and services but also in developing collaborative management and information-sharing platforms to coordinate activities between them. These new forms of collaboration then connote new organizational forms with diverse goals and strategic priorities, and they demand new management control systems and different roles for management accounting to play. In this section, we will explore the features of this new context of interfirm relations before we launch into a discussion on how management accounting is implicated therein in the following section.

We shall first look at this from a 'business contract perspective' in some detail. By the business contract perspective, we mean looking at the ways in which autonomous enterprises with different staratgic goals are coordinated. These are often situations where they come together to initiate new business ventures by establishing a form of network relationship. Castells' (2010) seminal work is important for us to explore this. Castells (2010, 187) defined this emerging form as a 'specific form of enterprise whose system of means is constituted by the intersection of autonomous systems of goals'. This intersection is a new site where a new form of enterprise is being developed. The salient factors such as globalization, technological advancement, and tendencies in deregulation have given rise to entrepreneurial motives for exploiting this site of intersection. And neoliberalism has provided an ideological and institutional prologue for this development in the sense that, in neoliberalism, putting lives and things into circulation has become more critical both in the creation and the valorization of surplus value (cf. Cooper 2015; Munro 2012). Hence, in order to manage the 'flow' of lives and things, to manage their circulation, new forms of coordination between firms beyond market transacting needed to be envisaged. This challenge is now well acknowledged, pervasive, and has become a norm in business organizations, government agencies, and NGOs. New terms such as Global Supply Chains (GSC), Business Processes Outsourcing (BPO), and Global Production Networks (GPN) embody this development.

While this is an unprecedented development, the vital managerial question here is how to 'organize' and 'manage' the enterprise through emerging forms of dynamic, fluid, and hence invariably risky, sets of interfirm relations. This point is vital because there is no strategic apex or hierarchical responsibility structure to guide and maintain these relations as in the case of orthodox hierarchical organizations. Mouritsen and Thrane (2006, 242) reflected on the vitality of this question arguing that interfirm relations constitute a fragile network:

> A network is a fragile accomplishment because its form, in principle, has no strategic apex and hierarchy, but this begs a series of questions. How does a network enterprise develop mechanisms that hold its elements together even if it does not have its own goal? And, how will a network enterprise develop

capabilities whose justification is collective or network-wide rather than firm specific?

Mouritsen and Thrane's questions direct us to think about the inappropriateness of orthodox hierarchy to run an enterprise within and between networks. They show how and why networked complementarity should be seen as an alternative form of organizational arrangement which demands new mechanisms (including new management accounting), capabilities, and justifications. As we said at the outset, this alternative is now conceptualized as heterarchy. Drawing on Boltanski and Thévenot (2006) and Callon (2003), Stark (2011) has provided an interesting conceptualization of heterarchy. He emphasized that, unlike in hierarchy where there is an overarching institutional framework to frame and evaluate everybody's involvement and accountability, heterarchy is characterized by an alternative organizational form where different parties' involvements are evaluated based on multiple evaluative principles. However, such principles can only be seen in frictions, which Stark (2011, 5–6) articulates in his 'sense of dissonance' as follows:

> Such organizations, we shall see, are not frictionless. But friction is not something to be avoided at all costs. We all prefer a smooth ride, but as you and your tire dealer know, when taking a sharp curve, we count on friction to keep us on course. Friction can be destructive. But, as the designers of the U.S. constitution well understood when they built the friction of checks and balances into our system of government, it can also be a principled component of a functioning system with productive outcomes. That is, having multiple performance criteria can produce a resourceful dissonance.

The friction that Stark highlights here is a disruption from a hierarchical perspective but a governing principle for the new forms of interfirm relations that the neoliberal world now seeks. Such relations, as Stark (2011, 19) explains, produce 'distributed intelligence coordinated through lateral accountability', which manifests the uncertainty of the environment and the necessity of heterarchical relations. This much is important for us to understand the transformation of the organization as a set of interfirm relations. We shall understand it comparatively with its predecessor – hierarchy.

10.2.1 Reorganization of accountability relations

How people in an organization are made accountable has been a prolonged question in the determination of an appropriate organizational structure. What is being organized in an organization is thus accountability – giving and demanding reasons for one's conduct (Roberts and Scapens 1985) and framing one's conduct through such reasoning. As such, it is through accountability that other things are organized. As has been summarized in Table 10.1, the pervasive hierarchical form is mostly characterized by top-down vertical relations of accountability where reasoning is directly connected to the command and positional authority or the legal-rational power. It is the 'superiors' who demand the reasons while the 'subordinates' respond to these demands in terms of providing the accounts/narratives for one's conduct and performance. This is a mode of justification of organizational actions by demonstrating their compliance with the demands stemming from the top of the command hierarchy. Accounting is central in

228 *Neoliberal trends*

Table 10.1 Hierarchy versus heterarchy

	Hierarchy	Heterarchy
Reorganization of accountability relations	Vertical, mostly top-down relationship with limited conception of autonomy, discretion, and local initiatives.	Lateral, mostly cross-cutting relationships, with more freedom for discretion but through network relations.
Organization of diversity	Derived from an ordered system of control in the face of predictable environmental conditions.	Derived from frictions leading to 'the sense of dissonance' in the face of unpredictable environmental conditions where different evaluative principles are adopted.

this hierarchical form of accountability. Hopwood (1996, 589) remarked on this organizational arrangement:

> Budgeting, planning, and performance evaluation are invariably seen in vertical terms. Whether it is concerned with bringing intelligence from the bottom of the organization to the top or putting down the intensions objectives of the top, accounting is centrally implicated in the mobilization of the organizational hierarchy.

Accounting here has a broader meaning. It is more than numbers being calculated; it connotes how people engage in accountability relations and how accountability demands are imposed upon people. Budgeting, for example, emerges from the top and creates contracts with subordinates to make them accountable for the tasks being planned and delegated through budgets. Because it is a top-down imposition, performance against the budget becomes a response to the demands imposed by the budget – a contractual arrangement between the budgeter and the budgetee. Budgeting thus creates an accountability relation upon which the hierarchy is rationalized and reproduced. In the context of this hierarchical arrangement, budgets then often become an unquestionable organizational proposition upon which the future is normatively seen and the present is objectively assessed against the normativity of the future. Uncertainties inevitably embedded in the construction of organizational propositions through budgets are handled, with partial success of course, by rolling forecast versions of short-term budgets, contingency plans, or practices of zero-based budgeting, etc. In this process, the budgetee has rather minimum autonomy to exercise her discretion and creativity to respond to the changing circumstances that she, in her locality, faces in her day-to-day operations. Insofar as the environment was relatively stable and the changes happening were not strategically significant, there was no political necessity to offer this autonomy to the budgetee. Hierarchical command worked relatively well, insofar as the environment was stable enough to be managed by it. However, the environmental and contextual dynamism that the 1980s brought about challenged this conventional hierarchical wisdom of accountability and responsibility (Hope and Fraser 2003b).

This problematization of hierarchy marked the tendency towards heterarchical forms. The growth of multinational firms, the advancement of information and networking

Strategizing interfirm relations 229

technologies, and, above all, the neoliberal epistemic justification of global networks as a fashionable and profitable postmodern form of enterprise have all contributed to the development of heterarchical alternatives. This development was then implicated in decreasing uses of traditional budgeting and decreasing dependency on the conventional arrangement of vertical accountability and communication. As you see in Table 10.1, this heterarchical arrangement is seen in the construction of cross-border relations, supplementing and replacing the existing vertical accountability with lateral account-ability forms in which multidisciplinary teams come to occupy knowledge-sharing endeavours. Rather than giving and demanding reasons for conduct on the basis of positional power-nexus, people in these new organizations, on the basis of their knowledge and information, debate the reasons and explore alternatives for enhancing efficiency, determining effectiveness, and combatting competition. Hopwood (1996, 589) continued to remark on this:

> Concerns with quality, cost and delivery are acted upon across supplier chains. Planning, budgeting and control processes flow from one organization into others, creating, as they do, a more explicit awareness of the interdependency of action and the role which joint action can play in organizational success.

Establishing and controlling regular flows of lateral information between firms have become critical in these new endeavours of network enterprising. Hence, lateral accountability relations should transcend the legal boundaries of the organizations to reproduce heterarchical accountability arrangements. This is a new social space in which intelligence is distributed in the service of this new type of accountability relations. While networking possibilities arising from new information technologies are invariably implicated in this transformation, the strategic necessities of interdepen-dent joint actions, the operational necessities of co-producing lateral informational flows, and the political-economic necessities of addressing the diversities arising from ever exploding organizational and national boundaries, make the heterarchical dimension of the organization more ubiquitous. We further elaborate this 'diversity' dimension of heterarchy in the next section.

10.2.2 Organization for diversity: basis of heterarchy

Traditional hierarchy has been a social space for imposing unitary goals that escort its members towards a common purpose – capital accumulation through mass production and mass consumption. The established industrial structures of mass production and mass markets neither found alternative purposes nor were challenged for a century or so (Chandler 1976). Corporate managers were blinded by this unitary culture for over 150 years since the industrial revolution until this form started to become problematic during the 1980s. Until then, the prevailing control systems, management accounting practices, and accountability relationships were driven towards mass production under the assumptions of competitive advantage through economies of scale and standardiza-tion. They neither saw a value in, nor were capable of handling organizational diversity and flexibility, which has only become strategically important since the mid-1980s. Neither did the prevailing hierarchical mode of management allow corporate managers to derail from the status quo of achieving economies of scale through rigid top-down hierarchical control and standardization of production. Unitary goals of mass production

230 Neoliberal trends

imposed through hierarchical control persisted to govern the organizations. Even the supply chain relations were often governed through absorbing the suppliers into the hierarchy through acquisitions and mergers (see Coase 1937; Williamson 1975, 1988, 1991) under the assumption that larger hierarchies are essentially more efficient and effective. This nevertheless restricted the possibilities for developing diversity and flexibility through friction.

Heterarchy, in contrast, negates the persistence of this unitary culture. Instead, it has now created a social space for organizing diversity and flexibility. The meaning of this term in this context is about conducting mundane managerial practices such as planning, decision making, controlling, and evaluating under the circumstances of friction. Rather than following the orders flowing down the hierarchy as they are, organizational members are now encouraged to be entrepreneurial to bring about unorthodox ideas and practices. For example, being inspired by Japanese practices of target costing, rather than imposing costs of production on customers, corporate managers now may go to the customer and ask at what cost they would buy and what features they would like in the product in question. This practice then takes the 'friction' between what the customers expect and what the company offers to the centre of the managerial decision-making processes, creating a managerial friction between engineers, marketers, and accountants, who operate with different and multiple evaluative criteria of success. Nevertheless, this also creates a social space for everybody to sit down together and address each other's concerns until they reach a 'sense of dissonance' through multiple evaluative criteria. (Stark 2011, 8) remarked:

> Within the same domain space, even within the same organization, diverse performance criteria are colliding and competing. Because there are multiple codes to evaluate performance, codified knowledge can be broken up and recoded. With analogy to genetics, think of the friction of rivalling principles as increasing the rate of mutation. But the dissonance of diverse evaluative frameworks does more than simply speed up the production of novelty.

The forms of interfirm relations we see today are a result of this increasing necessity for managing diversity and friction through incorporating multiple criteria of evaluative principles into the firm's control and governance structures and practices. In a sense, it is a natural evolution of hierarchy into heterarchy. Managers now increasingly find it so difficult to meet the diverse demands placed upon them within the managerial apparatuses of hierarchy that they need to invent heterarchical connections beyond the organizational hierarchies. In neoliberalism, diversity and friction are natural phenomena because globalized markets and firms bring about a collision between cultural and political differences. Heterarchical tendencies welcome these collisions because they create opportunities for value creation. Nevertheless, this demands careful organization and management of diversity. In an interfirm relational context, diversity allows and demands different firms with different organizational goals and strategies to develop lucrative contracts for everybody to be well off. Although this does not occur smoothly, partners in the contract debate each other's costs, revenues, and profits as well as technologies and practices. They reach a common ground where they can play the game of frictions; friction is the game and it is not merely winning the competition that creates value but running the competition and being in the competition. Competition is the value which needs to be 'fixed' through collaboration, the emerging neoliberal logic of interfirm relations.

As such, globalization, diversity, and friction have collectively become an important narrative in the postmodern world (see chapters in DiMaggio 2001). This is a narrative pronounced by multinational corporations, epistemic communities, professional bodies, and transnational organizations. Improvement of national competitiveness, gender equality, labour empowerment, participative planning and budgeting, and economic citizenship are related discourses that compose this narrative. Through this narrative, such issues then become the global biopolitical problems that are discoursed as issues that can only be solved through global networks. This narrative then lubricates the promotion of new forms of interfirm relations such as GSC, GPN, Foreign Direct Investments, Public-Private Partnership, and many other forms of 'global alliances'. These arrangements would not materialize unless they were so organized that they did not simply operate under frictions but rather exploited them.

10.3 New vistas of management accounting in interfirm relations

The above transition from hierarchies to heterarchies gives rise to a new form of management accounting, controls, and performance evaluation. We shall explore the vistas of this development along the themes outlined in Table 10.2.

As noted in Table 10.2, the change in management accounting can be seen in terms of three main themes: the control structure, mode of operation, and the methods of evaluation. These three interrelated dimensions point to a systemic shift away from management accounting's conventional hierarchical arrangement to a neoliberal heterarchical form. When we think about the control structures, as you see in Table 10.2, the responsibility accounting systems have been the cornerstone of conventional management accounting. They have been propagated by many textbooks, professional, and university programmes for the last century or so as the operational mode of directing and controlling the firm's operations towards the unitary goal of return on

Table 10.2 New vistas of management accounting in interfirm relations

Dimensions	Conventional arrangement (hierarchical)	Neoliberal accounting (heterarchical)
Control structure	Hierarchical responsibility accounting.	Boundary spanning sharing systems of accountability.
Mode of operation	Conventional management accounting techniques that operationalize hierarchical responsibility accounting. Production and distribution are the prominent objects for control – control is driven towards efficient use of production capacity.	A wide spectrum of new managerial technologies bundled into packages and platforms. Inter-organizational relations are the prominent objects for control – control is driven towards facilitation and enhancement of innovative collaborations and collaborative innovations.
Methods of evaluation	Single evaluative criterion, often financial criteria directed towards return on investment.	Multiple criteria, often articulated in terms of multiple stakeholder demands/expectations.

232 *Neoliberal trends*

investment. However, this has now become rather problematic. It is problematic because this system of responsibility accounting aims to maintain the hierarchical relations and the hegemony of the shareholder rather than addressing strategic imperatives pertaining value creation, in a pluralistic sense, for all its stakeholders. In other words, responsibility accounting, mainly framed by financial parameters of performance, is no more capable of addressing the diversity, pluralism, and frictions now placed upon companies by the neoliberal market and political contexts. As a result, firms are now forced to move beyond such hierarchically arranged responsibility accounting to systems of accounting that enable 'information sharing' (both financial and non-financial) within and between firms. Accounting information, in this respect, now has a different purpose. In responsibility accounting the purpose of information was predominantly to control. Hence, accounting information should enhance the visibility of control. In a heterarchical system, information is driven towards enabling innovative collaborations and collaborative innovations. As such, in the context of interfirm relations, accounting systems are now becoming sharing networks in which intelligence and other complementarities are distributed amid friction and debate. On this point, Mouritsen and Thrane (2006, 263) observe in their case studies:

> The network, which emerges as a topography of centres and peripheries, is an enterprise because it gradually defines its own objectives, proposing strategies that are 'larger' than the sum of the participating firms. In all three network enterprises, this 'larger' project concerned knowledge and complementarities in some form – the competitive advantages that the network provides the individual firm and which were distributed via management control technologies. Complementarities were found in relation to customers, marketing, and sourcing and learning.

So, the management control system in interfirm relations is a medium of knowledge distribution which aims not only to generate new ideas for creating value across the network but also to engage in a continuous assessment and reassessment of the firm's strategy. This engagement is often necessitated by what we may call 'coordinated competition', and by partners' demands for the realignment of the business and corporate strategy with one another. Such demands then refute the responsibility accounting systems (which basically operate in a form of top-down chain of command) by replacing them with a knowledge-sharing culture leading to a new vista of control configuration. The open-book accounting system, which we elaborate in the next section, is a good example of this new move.

The second dimension we mentioned in Table 10.2 is the mode of operation. As you know, mode of operation in a conventional hierarchical responsibility accounting system comprises established techniques and practices such as budgeting, standard costing, cost management, and various decision-making models (e.g. cost-volume-profit analysis, inventory planning models, etc. Here, techniques and practices are mobilized to maintain the operational efficiency of the production system with little attention to the possibilities of expanding the boundaries of the firm and identifying new strategic initiatives by networking with other firms across the supply chain. However, neoliberal moves into globalized supply chains made the conventional hierarchical arrangements ineffective and problematic. For example, conventional hierarchical budgeting cannot be used in the same manner when hierarchies become heterarchies where relations are lateral and boundary-crossing rather than top-down.

Hence, a new mode of operation has emerged in interfirm relations where we can now see the packaged deployment of new techniques and practices. Again, the transformation from hierarchical to heterarchical has problematized the usefulness of the old techniques and practices enforcing necessary replacements with new techniques. These include, for example, the bundled use of open-book accounting, ERP, target costing, functional analyses, etc. to manage inter-organizational relations – interfirm relations have become the prominent objects of control. Drawing on a set of case studies, Mouritsen et al. (2001, 240) illustrate this point:

> The cases illustrate that management controls weave in and out of translations. In both firms, inter-organizational relations were made prominent objects for control, and prompted important questions about centres and peripheries, or about who was able to act on others. Outsourcing implied that the two firms were partly divorced from insights into important business processes. Managers' intentions to act on these processes at a distance motivated the introduction of new managerial control, and they were justified by an 'information gap' which was found unacceptable. Hence, new management controls were an answer to the cry for insights and influence ... The new management controls could help translate the production and development processes at a distance by providing managers with information. Importantly, however, is that the controls did not only have an informing role in the two firms i.e. closing up an information gap. It also played a role in new re-presentations of the firms related to new translations of other aspects of organizational life in the two firms. These controls not only affected inter-organizational relations. They also had intra-organizational effects because they helped translate the firms' strategies, competencies, technologies and products.

Moreover, the new mode of control seeking to enable interfirm networking manifests a bundling effect where management accounting becomes bundled with other management practices such as JIT, Customer Relations Management (CRM), Vender Managed Inventory Systems (VMI), Electronic Data Interchange (EDI), and so forth (Håkansson and Lind 2006). The rationale of this bundling tendency, as Håkansson and Lind (2006) observe, is that interfirm relations require both financial and non-financial information as well as quantitative and qualitative data for them to integrate the interface of decision making between firms. Although the bundling effect has been a development in the context of intrafirm relations as well, the deployment and bundling of diverse techniques became more of a requirement in the context of interfirm relations where the managers operated so ambiguously that they adopted all possible tools to minimize any ensuing uncertainty.

The final dimension we itemized in Table 10.2 is methods of evaluation. As we have hinted upon previously, new methods of evaluation involving multiple evaluative criteria are emerging. Conventionally, firms adopted monologic financial criteria such as profitability and liquidity as the primary set of methods of evaluating their performance. But this is now problematic. Referring to a web design firm, Stark (2011, 106) underlined this problem:

> If the firm locked in to a single performance criterion, it would not be positioned to move with flexibility as the industry changed and the web evolved. Thus even the principle we have not yet mentioned – profitability – was not itself based on

234 *Neoliberal trends*

the ability to anticipate new developments and recognize new performance criteria for evaluating well-designed and well-functioning websites.

Multiple evaluative criteria emerge because different actors in the network of relations understand, and misunderstand, things differently. In a project, for example, actors in the network may get settled provisionally about what needs to be done. Stark calls this a 'pragmatic moment' in making performance evaluation. At the same time, this provisional settlement, in a heterarchical setting, is open to reinterpretation when they approach another moment of the project or a totally new project. This is called a 'discursive moment' which may produce different evaluative criteria. Hence, ongoing activities in a heterarchy point to multiple evaluative criteria. In short, the above 'settlement' is a pragmatic dimension which can produce an agreed set of evaluative criteria. When the managers come to reinterpret the information, there will then be a new set of evaluative criteria coming into play. In such circumstances, actors encounter 'boundary objects' (Star and Griesemer 1989) – objects such as maps, forms, and specimens. Star and Griesemer argue that these objects are recognized differently by various actors in the heterarchy depending upon their own circumstances and strategic aims. The point here is that boundary objects circulate 'misunderstanding' among the actors. Consequently, different actors come out with different justifications leading to multiple evaluative criteria. So, interfirm relations are representative of 'misunderstandings' and multiple evaluative criteria that they create, rather than a site of surrendering everyone into a monologic set of evaluative criteria and controls flowing down a hierarchy.

The above comparison points to a transformation of organizations as hierarchical spaces of top-down control and domination into a heterarchical site of struggles and change where actors try to settle the frictions. This is then a control structure that manifests a sharing system of accountability, modes of operations with bundles of techniques and practices, and adopting multiple evaluative criteria. Such a system values friction, through which both pragmatic settlements and discursive reinterpretations are materialized. Under such circumstances, actors in an interfirm relationship share the same boundary objects but these may lead to misunderstandings which are necessary for innovation. About this difference, Stark (2011, 21) commented:

> The situation in 'old' manufacturing sectors is scarcely different. Not so long ago, firms like General Motors (GM) were easily categorizable. Then, the major materials were steel, rubber, and plastic; the major costs were equipment and labour; and these firms made automobiles and other vehicles. Today, an automobile can be viewed as an entertainment system that we travel in; various computer components, taken together, account for the greatest share of the value of a car; financing contributes the greatest share of profits; and pension plans and medical insurance for retired employees are among the highest costs. GM, doubtless, makes automobiles. But it could well be seen as being in the computer business, the finance business, the insurance business, or even the entertainment business.

It is in this neoliberal reality in which new vistas of management accounting emerge. New forms of inter-organizational relationships give rise to heterarchical forms of management control. When neoliberalism aggravates its function globally, all firms will be characterized by these interfirm relations popularizing new vistas of management

Strategizing interfirm relations 235

accounting. The next section will elaborate a particular kind of management accounting characterizing this ensuing and inevitable development.

10.4 Open-book accounting and distributed intelligence

As we know, traditional management accounting has been occupied with an internal reporting function located in a closed organizational territory. Information provided was by and large concentrated on cost calculations, internal performance evaluations, demand forecasting, etc. Managers used this information for intrafirm purposes of decision making, corporate and operational planning, management control, and performance evaluation with little concern for exogenous repercussions. In short, management accounting's conventional outlook was a kind of closed-book accounting, available only to those involved in the intrafirm decision-making processes.

However, given the heterarchical tendencies that we experience today and the expansion of new management accounting technologies and practices such as BSC, ABC, and ERP, an open-book form of management accounting has emerged. So, what is open-book accounting (OBA)? The direct answer to this question is that it is more or less an intention and a partial reality. But, we can find some definitions as well. When the discussion about possibilities of OBA emerged in the 1990s, Carr and Ng (1995) defined OBA as an accounting technique where a company discloses detailed internal cost data to a particular external counterpart. However, when we say that it is about disclosing internal cost information to an external party, we have pragmatic questions beyond this intention such as: What cost data are they? And, how much disclosure? We can discuss these intentions in normative terms and their underlying realities in empirical terms. Whatever these normative and empirical conditions could be, we will be seeing that OBA is invariably a practice being developed and debated in the context of interfirm relations, but its development should equally be attributed to certain intrafirm conditions of information sharing (Mouritsen et al. 2001). In other words, this cannot be developed unless there is intrafirm support with a flexible mindset towards disclosing internal information to external parties.

In a context of expanding supply chains around the world, OBA emerged in the 1990s as a concept which described the practices of sharing cost information between suppliers and buyers in supply chain contexts. The initial intention was to share the supplier's cost information with the buyer and to maximize cost-efficiency against other supplier-buyer relationships (Kajüter and Kulmala 2005). This implies a deployment of distributed intelligence which we discussed earlier in the chapter, but it also shows how neoliberal conditions have pushed the partners in a supply chain to see themselves not simply as buyers and sellers but as entrepreneurial partners seeking collaborations for gaining competitive advantages through collaborative innovations. This cost information sharing initiative was pragmatically materialized through sharing information by firms, by discussing the contents at meetings, and by revisiting the cost structures as things changed with new scenarios (Agndal and Nilsson 2010). Later on, this was developed into an emerging set of inter-organizational cost management practices (Carr and Ng 1995; Kulmala et al. 2002). The fundamental properties of this emerging practice was embodied in three interrelated dimensions, as Windolph and Moeller (2012) outlined: the direction of the information exchange; the disclosure's degree and quality; and the boundaries to openness.

236 *Neoliberal trends*

The direction of the information exchange is a crucial factor in the success of OBA. In general terms, we can understand that in any business transaction, there can be some sort of information sharing between both parties. This may include prices, costs, and other relevant information for both parties to know before making a firm decision about the transaction. The information thus plays a role in developing the mindsets of the people involved in terms of clarifying what is to be bought and sold. In the context of a supply chain, this general market condition no longer served the purpose because it needed to expand beyond such a market-based transactional relationship to a long-lasting continuous and closer relationship that fosters collaborative innovations. Hence, information sharing needed to go beyond the mere transactional information necessary to secure a given spot-market transaction. This meant that parties were now seeking information upon which a sustainable relationship, competitiveness, and trustworthiness could be built. In this sense, OBA opened up a relational space for parties in the network to discuss and debate cost and other accounting information. Given that buyers seemed to dominate the supply chain, sharing cost data was initially unidirectional, information moving from the seller to the buyer. It was also reported that buyers tended to abuse this information (Hoffjan and Kruse 2006). Later, when competition increased, networks became more collaborative, and, despite their frictions and the possibility of misuse, a practice of bi-directional sharing developed where both parties began to exchange cost information. The outcome was more dependable, sustainable, and mutually beneficial supply chain relationships (Windolph and Moeller 2012).

The establishment of OBA was also determined by the degree and quality of disclosures (Mouritsen et al. 2001). By this, practitioners meant what details they shared and in what form. Details can be categories of costs in terms of different products and services or activity classifications. If the relationships have become more sustained and trustworthy, and the opportunities and benefits they can reap through information sharing are crucial, meaningful details can be exchanged. If the decisions the parties must make become crucial in terms of the competitive advantage they build up, other supplementary details such as sales forecasts in response to changing costs and prices and what-if analyses in relation to different levels of capacities can be exchanged. That said, the degree of detail and the quality of the data being disclosed depend on the nature of the relationship and the strategic imperatives of the parties involved. Axelsson et al. (2002) observe that if such strategically significant conditions and relations are realized, costs data would be transferred instantly as real-time information for parties to visualize what is going on. This is a kind of directness being developed as a governing principle of OBA intent, although the actual sustainability of such practices is not certain.

The phenomenon of openness is also an intention in OBA practices. By openness, we mean the tendency to share cost information beyond both unidirectional and bi-directional forms (i.e. in a supply chain's transactional conditions). Like 'open-source' software, openness here can mean the open sharing of information across global networks. Hence, information is available for many actors and intelligence is produced and distributed across a wider open network despite possible frictions. Technology is available for this distribution, and discussions can be had among partners in the network instantly to gather a pattern for gaining competitive advantage. In so doing, new technologies as well as practices are diffused among the partners in such networks. For example, as we will elaborate later in the chapter, supply chain relations are now being developed as wider networks through the practices of category management while cost

Strategizing interfirm relations 237

data sharing occurs based on the principle of openness and trustworthiness (Free 2008). In this way, OBA is sharing intelligence heterarchically.

Nevertheless, OBA, as we have seen so far, is more a statement of intent. It is because when the books are opened, parties in the network could abuse the opportunity for purposes that go beyond the mutually agreed aims. Hence, OBA has always been a risky attempt with some additional issues being encountered. These issues are diverse and the solutions to them can vary. Underlying issues of OBA practices are summarized in Table 10.3.

As the authors mentioned in Table 10.3 explain, OBA is more or less an ideal type and its practices are conditioned by certain managerial and organizational factors. As Seal et al. (1999) reveal, OBA has led to a situation where management accountants' roles have become rather dependent upon non-accountants' support and willingness to share information. Free (2008) illustrates that even with the declared support of others, the trustworthiness of both internal and external parties is an essential requirement for its success. However, trust cannot be delivered without appropriate managerial mechanisms, hence, for Håkansson and Lind (2006), other management practices must be coupled with OBA for its successful implementation. The need for trust is reinforced when buyers opportunistically abuse the cost data provided by the suppliers (Windolph and Moeller 2012). As Mouritsen et al. (2001) illustrate, for OBA to evolve and endure, supportive intra-organizational apparatuses should be there from the outset. The sample of this review thus provides us with evidence that OBA is more or less an idealistic type, manifesting intent rather than perfectly realized networking relationships. Nevertheless, this does not mean that OBA is a failure. If we take the views of heterarchical tendencies and the possibilities of innovations through friction and dissonance (Stark 2011), OBA seems to be an emerging phenomenon.

In this emerging sense, OBA's success is associated with a bundling effect. As we see in Figure 10.1, OBA is bundled with numerous other accounting companions. The intertwined use of these accounting technologies across supply chains, facilitating information sharing, more or less demonstrates a tendency towards OBA. In this sense, interfirm relations bring together different management accounting technologies, creating an assemblage of diverse practices aimed at connecting otherwise disconnected and dispersed organizational entities, managerial concepts, and organizational processes. To elaborate, we will now consider each of these practices and provide more details and some evidence.

Table 10.3 OBA practices and their underlying issues

Work	Focus	Managerial issue in OBA
Seal et al. (1999)	Role of management accounting	Need non-accountant's support.
Free (2008)	Category management	Need to enhance trust and trustworthiness.
Håkansson and Lind (2006)	Inter-organizational accounting	Need to couple with other related management practices.
Windolph and Moeller (2012)	Reasons for failures in OBA	Buyers may use the data opportunistically.
Mouritsen et al. (2001)	Inter-organizational controls	OBA cannot be sustained without intra-organizational backing.

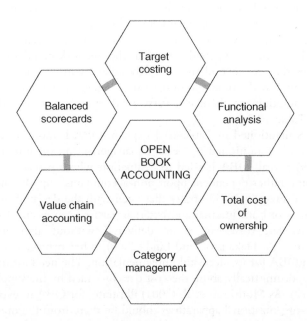

Figure 10.1 OBA's bundling effect

10.4.1 Target costing in interfirm relations

Target costing has long been discussed in the literature but in an intrafirm context. The same is now being adopted in an interfirm context where partners in the supply chain share target cost information, because they collectively need to achieve it in order to satisfy their customers. As Mouritsen et al. (2001) explain, target costing is implicated in a practice of openness or transparency in an interfirm context where costs of development, design, manufacturing, distribution, sales, and disposal targets are managed and controlled. This functional chain constitutes a network in interfirm relations and brings together partners to share targeted costs through an appropriate technological system such as an integrated ERP. Such practices were initially popularized in Japanese firms (see Monden and Sakurai 1998), but they are now common in interfirm relations around the globe (Cooper and Slagmulder 1997). What is salient here is that when the targets in target costing are shared, frictions develop, but when partners become open and transparent, agreements are reached through the different stages of friction and disagreement. These possibilities of improvement by resolving frictions and disagreements make the network a social space in which competitive advantages are explored and established collaboratively (Mouritsen et al. 2001).

10.4.2 Functional analysis in interfirm relations

Related to target costing in supply chains, functional analysis is about seeing the product in question in terms of a range of functionalities. As many Japanese firms do, these are divided into top and sub-functionalities allowing the customers to get involved in making design and development choices out of which target costs are determined (Kato 1993). In other words, customers choose product functions and related costs leaving management to make decisions about production and take necessary action to control the process of production. When this happens in an advanced information technology platform, the information about these choices and resultant designs are visible to all parties involved in the design, production, and distribution across the supply network. Functional analysis is an interesting cost management initiative because it creates a networked design and production space in which related parties contribute their views on the appearance of the final product as well as its delivery processes. This then also allows the design function to be outsourced so that enormous savings pertaining to costs of design can be achieved. Cooper and Slagmulder (1998) has observed that this development has led many Japanese firms to make their firms' operations much leaner allowing them to achieve massive cost reductions across the entire lifecycle of the products (Kato 1993). It has been found that functional analysis has been key to the development of leaner manufacturing across supply networks (Mouritsen et al. 2001).

10.4.3 The BSC in interfirm relations

BSC as a management accounting practice is now well known for its use in intrafirm performance management, but it has now also been embraced by the practitioners of OBA. Other than cost management information and practices, it has been observed that performance measurement is also an important aspect which needs to be shared between partners. In this regard, BSC has been seen as a useful accounting technique in generating KPIs by which partners' performance can be measured, made visible, and compared across the supply-network. Seal et al. (1999) have suggested that such a practice of performance measurement is important for establishing strategic partnerships. Heterarchical arrangements in interfirm relations and the use of OBA (along with BSC-like concepts) can reap the benefits for knowing what the others' capacities, targets, and achievements are. Salient here is that BSC has opened up a space for actors to process financial and non-financial measures and KPIs (Håkansson and Lind 2006). Non-financial measures such as yield, throughput time, capacity utilization, productivity, and so forth are derived from a BSC platform and these measures are translated into OBA practices so that partners can get together to discuss, organize, and maximize the potential of the interfirm relations (Anderson et al. 2000).

10.4.4 Value chain accounting in interfirm relations

By value chain accounting, practitioners mean a cost management model that combines ABC with value chain analysis (Anderson et al. 2000). Simply put, businesses in a supply chain network develop cost data for the entire value chain and initiate discussions for cost-reduction strategies. When this happens, partners in the value chain become aware of what activities are to be retained and what activities are to be eliminated in order to maximize the value delivered to the customer while cost is kept at a minimum level. This is materialized initially by sending a well-developed cost statement indicating the relevant costs of each stage in the process and by allowing the partners to discuss the matter in detail. As Håkansson and Lind (2006) see, this practice is also coupled with three types of analyses namely, benchmark analysis, strategic what-if analysis, and trend analysis. The point here is that everybody is informed of what is

240 Neoliberal trends

necessary for enhancing value in the value chain. This is seen as part of OBA because in an ideal type situation, parties in the network get serious about sharing correct information openly and take necessary actions. There is always the possibility that such open-book arrangements of value chain accounting could be detrimental to some parties but beneficial to the entire interfirm setting (Håkansson and Lind 2006).

10.4.5 Category management in interfirm relations

Category management has also come to be part of OBA. In a supply chain context, this practice focuses on integrating all activities and processes related to a product and sets out pricing, promotion, layout, and so forth based on product categories (Free 2008). A collection of management accounting practices and tools are included here as far as they are collectively driven towards the production, distribution, and marketing activities of a product category. Hence, category management can include cost management, performance measurements, risk analysis, forecasting, customer profitability analysis, formal profit sharing arrangements, and so forth. In a sense, the notion of category management is still more or less an intent, an emerging set of practices, rather than a well-solidified and concrete practice. The idea is that, when we organize an interfirm relation, we need to organize calculations, decisions, and actions for each product category. The hope is that the product category would provide the basis upon which the interfirm information sharing could be organized. It is an emerging system of 'fetish of calculations' – a system where (absent) things become material objects for calculations and then for evaluation (see Bloomfield 1991) and a way of distributing intelligence (Stark 2011) to cope with the complexities in the current landscape of competition that neoliberalism has introduced.

10.4.6 Total cost of ownership in interfirm relations

The last practice we have listed in Figure 10.1 is total cost of ownership (TCO). As Håkansson and Lind (2006) highlight, this is not a completely new practice, but it reinforces managers in charge of purchasing and outsourcing decisions. When they make purchasing decisions, they pay attention to the overall costs of the entire supply chain rather than just the cost of the item in question. This is also supported by ABC which emphasizes the overall costs of activities in the process of production. In this way, as Lamminmaki (2008) observe, managers are directed to use TCO as a proxy for transaction costs in making outsourcing and purchasing decisions. Managers pay attention to these because integrated information systems, EDI, and VMI make them aware of what is going on in the entire value chain. Nevertheless, these ideas, practices, technologies, and facilities cannot be the sole avenue by which interfirm relations are enacted and workable for all. It is trust and trustworthiness through which such things work. We will discuss the issues of trust and power in the next section.

10.5 Trust and power issues in interfirm relations

With emerging OBA technologies and practice, trust and power issues have become more critical in managing interfirm relations. Trust and power are non-technological soft resources that govern interfirm relations. They are non-technological and soft in

Strategizing interfirm relations 241

that their operational domain lies within people's behaviour, cognition, and behavioural propensities. Consequently, we turn to psychology and sociology to discern the meaning of trust and power and their consequences in the context of an interfirm relation. We turn first to look at the aspects of trust.

10.5.1 Trust as a social reality

Although trust is a fluid concept receiving its meanings from cultural and social settings, we may start with a definition drawn from a psychological perspective: Rousseau et al. (1998, 395) define it as a:

> [p]sychological state comprising intension to accept vulnerability based upon positive expectations of intensions or behaviour of the others.

This definition prompts us to think about trust as an interpersonal rather than inter-organizational matter. But this is the foundation for interfirm trust because the latter comprises invariably interpersonal affairs. The core element in this definition is the parties' readiness to accept others' vulnerability with a view to gaining competitive advantage from the relationship they enter into. Here, one party bears the other's vulnerability expecting s/he can deliver what has been promised. In this sense, trust is a medium by which one can depend on another in entering into a relationship of interdependency and mutual benefits.

This state of mind can be translated into an interfirm setting. Tomkins (2001) explores how trust can be fundamental in relation to the feasibility of interfirm relations, which are inevitably bounded by the future uncertainties of the parties' actions. He argues that, in order to be successful in interfirm relations, two important conditions must be met. One is holding a belief about others' actions without undue doubt or suspicion. It must be 'undue' here because it is hard to expect a certainty about future possibilities so that the parties involved need a freedom to 'break' trust under the due circumstances even though one does not expect that to happen. Second is that trust can be built upon in situations where there is a lack of detailed information: such information is not needed because the relationship is trustworthy. These two properties are held within social bonds between the parties involved. This means that trust is a phenomenon which operates not purely on psychological and cognitive conditions but within the social connections that parties build between them through pragmatic actions. Interfirm relations are built upon this sociological rather than psychological phenomenon (Luhmann 1979). In this sense, it is about one's confidence in the other's social actions and connections that help realize the expectations negotiated and agreed between the parties. That said, trust is a social reality to be achieved through necessary social actions that demonstrate one's commitment, capacity, resourcefulness, loyalty, and so on to the agreed upon collective aims and strategies (Lewis and Weigert 1985).

This social perspective on trust has implications for the state of accounting (see Tomkins 2001). Put simply, accounting and other forms of information are needed in a situation where trust is absent. Under such circumstances, forms of controls are imposed, and detailed accounting information is processed and used to take actions to mitigate possible issues arising from a lack of trust (this is often conceived as the

242 Neoliberal trends

agency problem in mainstream accounting research). However, if parties become involved to develop strong social bonds, then trust can be developed so that the costly dependence on accounting and other forms of information can be minimized; social bonds can replace the necessity for detailed accounting information. When accounting becomes complementary, parties may process accounting information to enhance the collective efficacy of decision making rather than for predominantly control purposes. This then would improve the possibilities for enhancing the sharing of accounting information among parties involved in interfirm relations. However, this cannot guarantee the total elimination or significant reduction of uncertainty with which decision making has to be carried out. When future expectations are uncertain, for example due to the unpredictability of market conditions, as Tomkins (2001) argues, replacing trust with accounting can bring in a further uncertainty, because decision makers may take the view that available accounting information has the power to mitigating uncertainty, which it cannot completely achieve (Feltham and Demski 1970). The message for us here is that trust can be an important resource which must be balanced with a suitable type of accounting information system depending upon the nature of future uncertainty in the network of interfirm relations. This understanding should have more implications for how we might design an accounting information system for interfirm relations. We look at this aspect now.

10.5.2 Trust as a basis for designing system interfirm relations

The social perspective on trust articulates it as a reciprocal system with dialectical connections between trust and the system; as a system of accounting and other forms of information where trust influences the system and system influences trust (Minnaar et al. 2017). It is this reciprocal relationship which leads practitioners to design a meaningful system of accounting gradually. It is a gradual process because the partners become acquainted with each other and build trust and design a suitable system as a result. In doing so, in an interfirm setting, partners realize what information is needed and what details are to be avoided in the design of an accounting system. Rather than using an available, non-customized accounting system, the one developed reciprocally in this way can be a lean and less red-taped system for the partners. If the system is packed with enormous information, contractual details, legal procedures, and so forth, as Minnaar et al. (2017) show, trust could be damaged. However, on the other hand, without those administrative, legal, and contractual complications, it is risky to develop relations because there would be ample opportunities for any partner to the interfirm relations to act opportunistically. Nevertheless, they argue, in the longer run, through experiences of not being opportunistic, partners can avoid details and rely upon trust. It is this process which develops a better system of accounting.

This reciprocity can be unpacked further in relation to the practices of management accounting systems within interfirm relations. As we have already seen, trust shapes a management accounting system. If the form of trust is 'thin', then the network would be inclined to rely on the practices' formal management accounting and controls (van der Kolk et al. 2015). These may include detailed budgets, scorecards, and incentive schemes. These practices may promote more rationalities, formalities, and procedures rather than healthy relations. In contrast, if the form of trust is 'thick', then the management accounting and control practices will be developed and institutionalized

Strategizing interfirm relations 243

interactively through a long process of mutual understanding. In this regard, although their primary focus is on an aspect of research methodology, Chua and Mahama (2012) highlight that such relationships are not linear and straightforward but develop through a complex and unpredictable process in which both human and non-human actors in a network setting interact and ensure the system is enacted by addressing issues and controversies that their relations bring about. Consequently, trust shapes the system of management accounting and vice versa.

There is another related dimension to this development. That is about how 'system trust' can be developed by the deployment of new ideas within an interfirm relationship. A good example of this is the deployment of category management, which we mentioned earlier in the chapter. By deploying this specific idea in a supply chain, as Free (2008) illustrates, suppliers are better organized, contracted, and established by activating the functions of 'category captains' and 'category managers' whose roles are dedicated to accounting calculations, relevant performance evaluations, and related cost management functions. Specific forms, data, numbers, directives, and instructions all act as boundary objects enhancing clarity and confidence among the partners in the network while the relationships are strengthened (Mouritsen et al. 2001). Giddens (1994) describes conditions similar to this possibility of system trust as a way of developing trust in the multiplicity of abstract systems where the things act at a distance rather though 'face work'. Eventually, what happens is that this kind of system trust leads to the development of personal trust among the partners allowing them to interactively finetune their management accounting system. What we see here is that in both stages (i.e. system trust development and personal trust development), trust is an 'actor' shaping management accounting practices in an interfirm setting (for empirical evidences see Free 2008; Minnaar et al. 2017; Mouritsen et al. 2001; Tomkins 2001; van der Kolk et al. 2015).

10.5.3 Power as an alternative to trust

Power is the ability to influence others despite their resistance and can be implicated in the nature of interfirm relations and the roles of management accounting therein (cf. Lukes 2005). This ability can be developed when one party in the network has more resources or capacities than the others. For example, most supermarkets in Europe exercise their domination over the suppliers (Seal et al. 1999). Such positions then allow the powerful partners in the network to coerce forms of management controls to others in the relationship. Formal management controls, centre-led performance measurements, and commanding cost management practices can be salient in these management control packages (Free 2008). If this is the case, the place for informal relationships in interfirm settings is limited. And, relational perspectives on trust can be defined while trust's ability to shape management accounting practices through reciprocal mechanisms is restricted by the power positions held by the dominant party. Hence, the thesis that trust is central to the design of an accounting system becomes debatable depending on the particular empirically observable power conditions in the supply chain network (cf. Minnaar et al. 2017).

If this is right, then power can be an alternative resource – alternative to the role of trust in interfirm relations (Free 2008; Jakobsen 2010; Kumar 2005). Powerful parties here exercise power, deploy mechanisms of controls, and, in turn, reduce uncertainty rather than waiting for trust to build up and accounting systems to be shaped and

244 *Neoliberal trends*

evolved through mutual social exchanges. When power becomes an alternative mechanism of control, sanctions rather than relationship, impositions rather than collaboration, and commanding rather than accommodation, may be the governing principles of interfirm relations (Hingley 2001). Consequently, controls can be developed faster than what trust can do in this regard. Perhaps, as some argue (e.g. Castells 2000; Sabel et al. 1987), this has become a necessary strategy in gaining competitive advantage before others when competitors exploit emerging opportunities. In contrast, trust can be time consuming and, as a result, some opportunities can be missed and the advantages lost to others who exercise power to reap the benefits from the opportunity in question. Even in situations where trust has been established but, later, has been breached by one of the parties involved, this will require power as an alternative strategy to get the momentum back on board (Uzzi 1997).

The power perspective we look at here is also invariably linked to the issue of governmentality, which we have also considered in preceding chapters. In relation to interfirm relations, it is now possible for us to view the issues of (mis)trust and control over supply chain networks as a biopolitical issue needing biopolitical governance (cf. Weiskopf and Munro 2012). As a biopolitical arrangement of governance, interfirm relations such as outsourcing contracts, business ventures, networked organizations, and interfirm relationship management now create surplus value through the 'circulation' of things, people, and information across networks. This is done through the emerging set of biopolitical technologies and techniques such as OBA, value chain accounting, category management, TCO, target costing. They are the mediating instruments in making the partners in the network visible to the 'network' and governable within the network by both confinement (to network rules, policies, and objectives, for example) and circulation across the network (cf. Seal et al. 1999). As such, interfirm networks now provide the disciplinary and biopolitical apparatuses for neoliberal governance. In this regard, governing partners exercise their biopolitical power, and management accounting practices mentioned in this chapter can play a constitutional role in mobilizing that power. Rather than following enclosure principles in a disciplinary control setting, those management accounting practices and related technologies act at a distance. They both supplement and substitute an ever increasing use of the notion of trust as a disciplinary tool in neoliberal times. In this sense, interfirm relations can be a manifestation of a society of control in which power is diffused through emerging ways of management accounting practices (cf. Hardt and Negri 2000).

10.6 Summary and conclusions

At the commencement of this chapter, we noted the problems of the prolonged hierarchy and showed that there is a heterarchical alternative emerging to alleviate these problems. Such alternatives are implicated in supply chain networks offering new forms for organizing GPNs. In this discussion, we also paid attention to how lateral accountability relationships are developed as opposed to vertical accountability relations institutionalized in the traditional hierarchy. We then looked at the properties of heterarchy as a philosophical foundation for us to understand the contemporary dynamics of interfirm relations. This foundational discussion led us to explore new vistas of management controls and performance evaluation. These new vistas have changed the way in which information is produced and shared and how controls are exercised within and between organizations in supply chain networks. We then looked at the specific literature on OBA see how intelligence is distributed and shared through the use of numerous management accounting and related practices. Here we saw how new jargons and discourses were bundled to characterize the emerging regimes of interfirm relations. Finally, we looked at how trust and power issues influenced these relationships. We explained how alternative accountability forms and shared management practices are being developed either though long-standing properties of trust or through the use of power to coerce particular forms of control and performance management by dominating parties in supply chain networks.

In conclusion, we can now see how neoliberal changes that we discussed in the previous chapters have given rise to different market conditions and hence new sets of strategic imperatives problematizing the properties of traditional hierarchical organizations. These emerging conditions have resulted in a demand for an alternative heterarchical organization of production and exchange, constituting various inventions in the realm of supply chain networking. Neoliberalism thus provides normative reasonings for the need for heterarchical forms, lateral accountability relations, and OBA practices which we outlined in the chapter. By so doing, neoliberalism has exposed the biopolitics of interfirm relations; biopolitical governmentality mechanisms centred on the management of the flow of circulation (rather than traditional disciplinary enclosure and confinement). Consequently, interfirm decisions and associated controls and governance become a matter of managing the design, production, distribution, costs, performance, and incentives throughout the lifecycle of a product. This means that now products and product categories need to be managed interconnectedly in every phase and site through which the product and product categories circulate. Hence, rather than considering solo-based single-site hierarchical management controls, neoliberal biopolitics demands management control and accounting techniques that criss-cross the organizational boundaries to integrate them into a single network, transforming individual organizations into what we now call 'networked organizations'. Partners in this network then have a number of discursive and techno-managerial tools and concepts which now seem to hold this network together as a biopolitical space for the global production of goods and services and thereby the reproduction of managerial and organizational practices. Consequential management practices such as OBA, category management, value chain costing, etc. have now become some attractive toolbox for global firms and global managers. This conclusion also has implications for providing a working definition for researchers who want to explore how interfirm relations are strategized. This neoliberal and biopolitical perspective will provide them with a tentative proposition that interfirm relations are strategized for sustaining their trust or maintaining their power relations for which the management accounting practices we have shown in the chapter play an animated role.

Assignments

These assignments are meant to extend your knowledge beyond what you understand from this chapter. These are not simply revision questions. The content covered in this chapter is necessary but will not be sufficient in attempting these tasks. Therefore, you are required to do some extra reading in attempting these tasks.

246   *Neoliberal trends*

1. **Thematic essay:**
    'Interfirm relations are a rather neoliberal space for doing management accounting differently'.
       Write an essay, of approximately 3,000 words, on the above theme articulating how interfirm relations are a product of neoliberalism.
2. **Poster:**
    Draw a poster showing open-book accounting's social and organizational roles in an interfirm-organizational setting. Pay special attention to both accounting technologies and managerial ideas/intentions that enmesh interfirm relations.
3. **Presentation:**
    Prepare a set of PowerPoint slides, together with notes if necessary, for a 30-minute presentation on the following theme:
       'Open-book accounting practices are an intention rather than a reality, and trust issues are amenable to making these practices a social reality'.
4. **Extended bibliography:**
    Write an extended bibliography on the development of a new form of management accounting in interfirm relations. For this, you need to do a literature survey in major accounting journals and edited books where critical accounting research is published. Organize the bibliography into a table in the following format.

Bibliographic info	Nature of the paper/book chapter (e.g. conceptual/theoretical, empirical, a response to a previous publication)	Major arguments, conclusions, and contributions

5. **Literature review:**
    Interfirm management accounting has explored few accounting technologies, but it has introduced doing management accounting differently along with other related management ideas and new arrangements of social bonds.
       Write a review essay elaborating this statement. Pay special attention to the debate about placing management accounting in the nexus of trust, trustworthiness, controls, and power relations.

11 Strategizing the state and NPM agenda

11.1 Setting the scene

As we discussed in the first two chapters, traditionally, management accounting was rooted in the principles of liberal-economic democracy where individuals celebrated their 'liberty to choose' in the political realm of parliamentary democracy and the economic realms of free markets. In this liberal regime of governance, governments were entrusted with the political function of looking after this liberty by implementing democracy through legislature and securing necessary welfare provisions. Welfare-economics then constituted the fundamental economic doctrines that provided the basis of liberal governments. There was a more or less clear demarcation of activities between the economy, society, and the political state, each operating with their own, relatively independent, 'higher order principles'. The performance of the political state was by and large measured through its political integrity (i.e. its adherence to the democratic principles), sovereignty (i.e. its capacity to 'rule' the society and the economy and to ensure the 'internal and external security' of the state itself), and its capacity to perform its welfare function (i.e. effective and efficient provision of public and political goods such as education, health, freedom of speech, justice, etc.). The Weberian model of legal-formal rationality was in operation for the maintenance of administrative structures implementing democracy, securing justice and fairness, and providing social welfare with a spirit of guaranteeing equality. Public-sector management is often considered as the 'civil service' directed towards administrative functionalities of securing the state's integrity, security, and public welfare.

In this context, governments' fiscal and tax systems prompted a definitive stream of revenues, budgetary allocation procedures managed resource allocation, and parliamentary oversight mechanisms provided the necessary integrity and counter checking of the use of public resources, and the Auditor General's department and other related public-sector accounting functionalities provided the conventional form of public-sector accounting mechanisms. Biopolitical accounting elements of this regime constituted two distinct elements: (a) public-sector accounting and auditing that ensured political, administrative, and financial integrity through making sure that conduct in the civil service was governed by the government's 'administrative codes' and 'financial codes', and (b) national accounting and statistics that collected performance data from various government and non-government agencies to produce 'national accounts and statistics' to assess the comparative performance of the nation's economy, its industrial sectors, and other welfare sectors. Agencies such as the Auditor General, the Department of Statistics, the Census and the central banks (e.g. the Bank of England and the US Federal Bank) play a central role in this regard.

248   *Neoliberal trends*

As we explained in the previous neoliberalization chapters, the neoliberal rupture included an implosion of hitherto established boundaries between the economy, society, and polity, all of which now had to be reorganized and governed based on market principles. This means that economic rationales of the market started to penetrate the state and civil society as governing principles. Neoliberalism rebelled against 'big governments'. Neoliberal prescriptions such as deregulation, privatization of public goods, and marketization of public spheres were at the heart of these rebellious acts of the economy against the political state. Propagators of neoliberalism started to critique and undermine the liberal and welfare-based doctrines of governance on the grounds of the 'economic inefficiency' of the liberal mode of governance. Government budget deficits and public debts were brought to the forefront of the political debates as symbols of gross inefficiencies in the liberal welfare-based models of government. The liberal model of government was subjected to severe political critiques for not facilitating self-help entrepreneurs of public goods and welfare provisions; for not promoting market-driven managerial practices in public institutions; and for not establishing postmodern managerial technologies in the use of public resources. State apparatuses were asked to reform and privatize not only its ownership but also managerial approaches in order to become entrepreneurial, market-driven, and market-governed. In short, the state was asked to neoliberalize itself.

Moreover, this movement was not just an economic reform of the public sector. It was indeed a pervasive agenda of cultural-political reforms spanning across every aspect of social life. As a form of new political rationality, neoliberalism forced everybody – be they a young job applicant who wanted to secure a better future; a poor rural woman trying to survive with micro-credits; or a firm which wanted to follow carbon foot-print regulations – to follow market principles and to reformulate their mundane practices based on the principles of capital accumulation. As a form of political rationality, neoliberalism transforms public goods and welfare provisions such as health, education, transportation, art, and even nature into consumer goods; seeking further opportunities of capital accumulation from things which were hitherto considered as 'public goods', 'welfare provisions', or even people's 'rights'. Their provisions now needed to be framed and governed, one way or another, as market transactions. It atomized collective notions such as 'public', 'communities', 'social', etc. into self-help entrepreneurs of providing and consuming such public goods and welfare on an individual basis. Margaret Thatcher, one of the key advocates of this neoliberalism, famously said: 'There is no such thing [as society], only individual men and women'.

However, it should be noted here that for so-called neoliberal market logic to become real, it must be translated into a mundane set of calculative practices in the realms of the political and social. As we noted previously, this is what accounting does; it materializes the political ideologies by translating them into a mundane set of practices by providing techniques and tools to structure the social actions and positions based on such calculations. In a capitalist society, accounting pragmatizes the ideology of capital accumulation. Thus, when civil society and polity need to be reorganized along the economic doctrines of efficiency and profits, and when the social actors in civil society and the political state are to be transformed into entrepreneurs of the self, for-profit sector accounting techniques should cross the border to civil society and the political state. New Public Management (NPM) discourses facilitated this importation of for-profit accounting to the public sector. NGO accountability, microfinance, etc. brought it to the civil society. Here in this chapter we concentrate on the management accounting reformation in the public sector while the next chapter will deal with its presence in civil society.

Strategizing the state and NPM agenda   249

As such, the aim of this chapter is to elaborate how management accounting is implicated in the neoliberal transformation of the public sector. The chapter will be structured as follows:

1. Section 11.2. In this section, we will explore the neoliberal transformations of the state. While this transformation can be articulated in terms of alternative frameworks, prominence will be given to the biopolitics of this transformation. We will seek to explain how (1) the state was 're-engineered'; (2) the state bureaucracy was subjected to a 'rightward' tilting; and (3) the penal wing of the state was elevated. By doing this, we will be able to locate the discourses of NPM in this changing context of the state.
2. Section 11.3. In this section, we will examine the NPM discourse in neoliberal terms and see how it was exerted to transform the state. Here we will explain how NPM operates as a 'deterministic embracement' and a 'critical encounter'.
3. In Section 11.4 we will discuss how management accounting is deployed in NPM. This will be done by concentrating on four key practices namely, cost management, strategic planning and performance measurements, new forms of budgeting, and new forms of public-sector accountability.
4. In Section 11.5 we summarize the contents of the chapter and conclude it with reference to the biopolitical implications of the NPM agenda. It will tease out three tenets of biopolitical effects: the construction of programmatic narratives in NPM; the accounting practices, processes, and tools in these programmatic narratives; and the issues of professional rivalries and boundary clashes.

11.2 Neoliberalism and the state transformation

As we explained from the Chapter 5 onwards, neoliberalism constitutes a historically critical signification of the market as a site of jurisdiction and veridiction (see Chapter 5). This means that the market became the basis upon which various social institutions and individuals must justify their existence, behaviour, and performance outcomes. One's market status was now the ultimate evaluative criterion of one's success. The managerial outcome of this was the corollary signification of the notion of 'strategy'. Organizations as well as individuals are now required to be strategic – capable of exploiting the 'opportunities' provided by the ever globalizing markets while mitigating the 'threats' that such globalizing markets simultaneously and perpetually bring about. To that end, everyone now needed to be entrepreneurial – capable of strategically positioning and circulating their life processes and outcomes in order to ensure a competitive advantage. Flexibility, quality, and cost-efficiency then had to become the defining factors that would determine one's strategic positioning and capacity to achieve a sustainable competitive advantage.

This neoliberal logic of doing everything to ensure one's market standing has now penetrated state apparatuses as well. Hence, the state must now strategize itself. When it comes to the issues of strategizing the state, neoliberalism should not be conceived only as a set of free market policies that privatized public services, abolished welfare states, and allowed people to be economically self-directed. It should also, as Brown (2006) argues, be conceived of as a political and social rationality that reorganizes the state. As Foucault (see, 'Politics and Reason' in Foucault and Kritzman 1988) explains it, neoliberalism should be understood as a normative political reason organizing the political sphere, governance practices, and citizenship. This political rationality is not

250   *Neoliberal trends*

merely a by-product of free market policies but a clear imposition of market rationality on the political and the social. This reconstructs the conducts, governance practices, and citizenship, and it rearticulates democracy differently. As a result, such conceptions developed in the eras of classical liberalism as public goods, citizens' rights, and democracy are now being transformed into opportunities of capital accumulation where citizens are now asked to exercise their entrepreneurial spirits. For example, as a public good, education becomes an individual investment decision rather than something the state must guarantee for citizens as one of their 'rights'. Hence, the market rationality is not simply leaking into the state. Instead, it has become a ubiquitous governing principle, rationality, and reality. It is the normativity of accelerating capital accumulation through transforming everything and everyone into an element of capital (i.e. entrepreneurship) that underlies this governmental rationality: capital (i.e. the 'empire', Hardt and Negri 2000) now expands not through the mere exploitation of labour but through transforming others into capital. As such, in the process of strategizing and neoliberalizing the state, the state itself becomes the capital by incorporating governing and managerial apparatuses of private capital and by conducting itself how private capital would behave.

This means that the state cannot be separated from the economic. Under the classical liberalism (as advocated by Adam Smith, David Ricardo, etc.), people exercised their free choice in the markets while the state governed the market in terms of democratic decisions in order to guarantee human liberty within and outside the markets. That was sustained over the last two centuries, producing a classical conception of the state and a clear distinction between the economy and the state. Now, this connection has been reversed: rather than the state governing the market, the market has come to govern the state. The state's *raison d'être* has now become the facilitating of the market to govern, providing the infrastructure for the market to be 'self-regulated'. The market has become the state to the extent that the state follows market principles; acts like a capitalist performing in the market; and becomes an actor in and for the market. In other words, the state is no more transcendental to the market economy to govern it as a 'sovereign body'. Instead, the market has encapsulated the state and the state has become one of its participants, one of its facilitators, and, above all, one of the elements in the market's 'self-regulation'. Given that neoliberalism promotes the self-regulation of the market by the market, the state's role in regulating the market is promoting this self-regulation by establishing and maintaining the necessary institutional and epistemic infrastructure for this. Hence, the regulatory role of the state is facilitating the market to govern (see Munro 2012). This state then guarantees, as Jessop (2002) emphasizes, the conditions for expanding the scope and reach of capital.

This implosion of state and the market, in one sense, is an ideological transformation (Harvey 2005). In another sense, it is an unavoidable programme of global governance (Newman 2014). Both these make the market transcendental to the polity and society. As an ideological transformation, as Hall (2011) and Massey (2011) emphasize, the notion of the market has been conceived as something 'outside' that cannot lie within the reach of politics so that the state has no other options but to follow market principles. As an unavoidable governance programme, the state has to think of a different form of governmentality which draws on market-driven managerial technologies, including NPM.

This submission of the liberal political rationality of the state to the neoliberal market rationality has created a different state. It now plays an active role in establishing, maintaining, and sustaining a 'society of entrepreneurs' which rationalizes its resource management in terms of the principles of competition (Morales et al. 2014a, 2014b). This role has been legitimized not only by the Thatcher government in the UK and

Strategizing the state and NPM agenda 251

Reagan's government in the USA, but also by transnational organizations such as the World Bank, IMF, WTO (formerly GATT), and of course, the European Union. Consequently, the state now is different. Brown (2006, 694) characterizes this vividly:

> That is, more than simply facilitating the economy, the state itself must construct and construe itself in market terms, as well as develop policies and promulgate a political culture that figures citizens exhaustively as rational economic actors in every sphere of life. Familiar here are the many privatization and outsourcing schemes for welfare, education, prisons, the police, and the military, but this aspect of neoliberalism also entails a host of policies that figure and produce citizens as individual entrepreneurs and consumers whose moral autonomy is measured by their capacity for 'self-care' – their ability to provide for their own needs and service their own ambitions, whether as welfare recipients, medical patients, consumers of pharmaceuticals, university students, or workers in ephemeral occupations.

This neoliberalization, nevertheless, does not mean that the state is shrinking. Instead, the state has become ever more important in propagating and maintaining neoliberalism. However, it needs to be reformed to embrace economic efficiency and market-drivenness as its governing principle, business-like discussions and reporting practices as its mechanism of accountability, and private-sector-like management practices such as corporate planning and balanced scorecards as its modus operandi. Wacquant (2012) explains this transformation in three interrelated theses: (1) that the state was subject to a re-engineering rather than a wholesale dismantling; (2) that the state bureaucracy was subject to a 'rightward' tilting; and (3) that the penal wing of the state is elevated.

11.2.1 The state is re-engineered

As we see around the world, the state has been neither dismantled nor reduced. It exists strongly but entrusted with a different political role articulated and justified by neoliberal reasoning, which we have already discussed. Wacquant (2012) argues that this existence is justified in three ways. First, it is characterized by robust machineries of political, legal, and administrative authorities (including old-fashioned state institutions) which guarantee the smooth functioning of market mechanisms. To this end, regulations, rules, and the necessary infrastructure are provided by the state. Second, as was demonstrated by social history and social theory, the state must protect the market by preventing all possible counteractions because social relations and cultural constructs are governed by market principles (and sanctions). Finally, following the 1930s economic crisis and the ideological critiques levelled against the Keynesian model of the state (which promotes welfare provisions and government interventions in the economy), a new political purpose was discovered to foster the market.

To this end, state needed to be re-engineered. This re-engineering manifested as a conscious and re-regulated state rather than a passive and de-regulated one. Wacquant (2010) characterizes this re-engineering project in four interrelated institutional logics: economic, social, penal, and cultural. In terms of the economic, state machineries are no more primarily for continuous maintenance of the 'constitutional order' but reforming itself into an efficiency-friendly, flexible, and market-responsive service provider (a seller in the market). New management and accounting ideas such as lean management, BPR, TQM, ABM, and BSC are all brought in for this reconfiguration. Around the world – both in

252 *Neoliberal trends*

advanced economies and less developed countries – the training institutes, consultants, and government departments are all brought into this re-engineering.

The social front in this re-engineering is that 'protective welfare' policies (which were the bedrock of the Keynesian welfare state) now shift to 'corrective workfare' policies. This is not only about dismantling welfare provisions but also providing individuals with a political reasoning to trust in their own capacity to determine their destinies. So, now they are forced to manage their own destinies in terms of ensuring themselves a proper education, job training, entrepreneurial development, flexible employment, and so on. The individuals have now become the centrepiece of social engineering programmes where individuals must be 'disciplined' to find 'self-help' rather than 'state-help' (Roy 2010). This is what lies underneath the creation of state-led self-help programmes such as microfinance, social bonds, self-employment, start-up capitals, etc. As we will see in Chapters 12 and 15, for example, microfinance has travelled into the lives of poor women in peripheral villages, supposedly enabling them to organize, construct, and conduct their own destinies with small loans, small 'self-help groups', and their own transformation of themselves into what have now come to be 'poor enterprising clients' (see Alawattage et al. forthcoming). Although the poor are still 'entrepreneurs-in-waiting' (Roy 2010), the 'workfare' strategy has been on the move as a powerful re-engineering programme of the state.

Re-engineering is also manifested in terms of an expansive 'penal policy' (Wacquant 2012). It is about managing population through surveillance (Wacquant 2012, 72) means to control social disorders generated by social insecurities. During the Keynesian liberal welfare state, the state concentrated on providing welfare and social security, but the neoliberal state does not guarantee this and has, instead, moved to various austerity measures to ensure the state's 'fiscal discipline'. The fiscal aims of reducing the budget deficit and government debts have become the dominating objective of the state across the world, under the conditions imposed by transnational agencies such as the World Bank and the IMF. As is quite obvious in the media, this has now resulted in social unrest, social insecurity, erosion of human rights, and an unprecedented level of income disparities (see Piketty 2014). The political outcome of all these is that the state is now entrusted with a new role – controlling social disorders through the new mechanisms of penal policies. This is understandable: the Keynesian state is being so eroded that new state-craft must be developed to minimize the issues of social insecurity, and its intended and unintended consequences must be managed in order for the market mechanism to function smoothly. This requires tougher controls through new forms of institutional and regulatory arrangements. For example, in advanced Western countries, there are new forms of judicial and legal arrangements brought to light through new technologies (such as CCTV cameras, DNA and other advanced autopsies, digital policing, anti-terrorism legislatures, and so on) allowing the prosecutors to take authoritative action. Mitchell (2001) calls these state transformations the 'post-justice city'. Peck (2003) remarks that this state restructuring is animated by an uneasy marriage between economic liberalization and authoritarian governance which developed from the former into the latter. And, the nature and degree of this restructuring is an empirical question leading to special and geopolitical analyses. Nevertheless, a widespread programme of punitive management and punitive regulations has become an unavoidable manifestation of the neoliberalization of the state.

To put all of these re-engineering scenarios together, there is a final one – the cultural one – which is the construction of individual responsibility. To adhere to efficiency principles in state agencies, to follow workfare rather than welfare orientations, and to control individuals with penal codes and regulations, now there is a need for a specific individual who can understand, hold, and maintain responsibility. It is, as Wacquant (2012, 72) argues, 'a motivating discourse and cultural glue' that can put all the state apparatuses together. This is the construction of the self which is responsible for all the above and is accountable to the rules and impositions stemming from the market sphere. This is not simply a release of a soft political rationality for individuals to be disciplined, but it is a hard form of governance of individuals making them governable and accountable. For example, in the case of the microfinance mentioned earlier, ideas have emerged to hold the individuals to account for what they do so that they must give an account to themselves about the delivery of this individual responsibility. This individual responsibility is, ironically, to 'self-help' in the absence of 'state help'.

11.2.2 Rightward orientation of state bureaucracy

The state is not a monolith and coherent form but a 'battlefield' in Bourdieu's (1990, 1998) terms. On the one hand, there has been a 'vertical battle' between the dominating state and the dominated populace. Backed by transnational development agencies such as the World Bank, the IMF, and the OECD, there is a quest for fiscal disciplining of the state that puts in place more and more austerity measures reducing public welfare and including a continuous fall in 'real wages'. That said, the neoliberal orientation of the state is a manifestation of a social crisis (rather than a solution) in that there emerges a policy debate about this 'tilting'; there is a political struggle between the extremely neoliberal and less neoliberal camps. This struggle in the policy arena is populated by various accounting and statistical analyses. There is a flood of alternative tools and discourses to legitimize this more or less neoliberalism in the state apparatuses and austerities in the fiscal domain. And it seems that the more neoliberalist and austerity camp is winning this debate in the policy arena supported by the epistemic power of the transnational development agencies we mentioned earlier. Beyond this policy arena, then there is a 'real political struggle' by people in the street and media around the world providing antagonistic reactions to these politics and their ideologies, leading people even to make somewhat 'unexplainable', politically emotional, mass decisions such as the election of Donald Trump, Brexit, and the Arab Spring.

On the other hand, there has been a horizontal battle between the 'left hand of the state' supporting political governance towards improving social and cultural capital and the 'right hand of the state' supporting market governance towards improving market-based economic capital. We can see these battles in parliamentary debates, media encounters, policy consultations, political party manifestos, and academic debates. Whether the state should favour the cultural capital of the 'big society' or the economic capital animated by market mechanisms has always been at the centre of politics, making it a field of struggle for gaining discursive advantages for those who sit at either of these extremes. Again, like in the vertical battle, various accounting and statistical tools, rhetoric, and jargon are used in these debates to articulate polity and economy as alternative governing mechanisms. The bigger policy question is then which should be given the priority over the other, the capacity to govern the other.

On both these fronts, the battle is an empirical issue of having different orientations in different spaces and times. As empirical evidence suggests, however, the state is now tilted towards neoliberalism governing everything by the market apparatuses and fiscal austerities; the 'right hand of the state' winning the horizontal battle (Hilgers 2012).

254 *Neoliberal trends*

However, this orientation is always in the making through discursive confrontations, as now seems to be the case empirically, between the far right and the middle right wings of the state. The specific neoliberal form that a given nation-state would take is spatially variable depending on the political confrontations underlying its making. Nevertheless, the confrontation is to find a form of state that can reconstruct the subjectivities and social relations necessary for the smooth functioning of the neoliberal markets and corporations. In other words, while state should secure competitive principles, the underlying principles and calculative technologies of the market should penetrate life-worlds, translating all social relations into market relations, so that market principles and calculative technologies govern them. This penetration needs to be supported by a strong form of state institutions which was, in practice, an arduous task.

This means that spatial variations in the neoliberal orientation of the state are an interesting field of empirical research. For example, reporting on the implementation experience around the world, Wacquant (2009) argues that the USA is still is a 'living laboratory of the neoliberal future' while, as Hilgers (2012) observes, developing countries face a wave of transformation with continual struggles and unintended agitations. In a similar fashion there is quite a long stream of accounting research that explores the accounting implications of neoliberal reforms of the public sector both in Western industrial economies (e.g. Craig and Amernic 2004, 2006, 2008; Crompton and Jupe 2002) and in less developed countries (e.g. Alawattage and Alsaid 2018; Uddin and Hopper 2001; Uddin and Tsamenyi 2005; Wickramasinghe et al. 2004). They collectively provide empirical evidence as to how accounting has been instrumental in realizing the neoliberalization agenda and how this has reformed accounting in the public sector.

11.2.3 Elevation of the penal scheme

Peck (2003) observes that neoliberal experiences created a necessity for institutionaliz-ing new forms of regulatory conventions while liberating market forces. The aim was not only to secure the 'market rule' in the functioning of the market but also to extend, maintain, and reproduce it in all realms of human life. This was complicated though because, on the one hand, there was a need to enforce deregulation, and, on the other, there was a need to introduce new regulations for managing the disastrous outcomes of deregulation and the imposition of market logic on non-market spheres. The latter included not only penal and social policies but also accounting and corporate govern-ance regulations (following several famous accounting scandals and frauds and the systemic crises of the financial markets – see Chapter 13).

Regulations are aimed at ensuring better labour controls for flexible accumulation (hence new labour regulations including legal provisions for zero-hour labour contracts), better social controls (hence new regulations for resolving social problems through PPP arrangements), and better management of social insecurity issues (hence, new forms of social security laws). This means that neoliberalism did not result in less regulation but more, bringing more regulation to ensure the smooth functioning of neoliberal markets. This in fact manifests as a process of 'carceralization' (McDowell 2001). As a result, the population is managed by categorizing people into new economic and social identities (e.g. young working class men, African-American women, the homeless, the disabled, etc.) bringing in new regulatory provisions to handle each of them distinctly. New programmes are now emerging, for example the rehabilitation of drug-addicted people; on-the-job training for the unemployed; and internet security and safety awareness programmes. By doing these, as Peck (2003, 227) comments, new state regulations aim to make people effectively individualized and allow them to understand, for example, 'the causes of and supposed remedies for unemployment, poverty and social breakdown'. In this way, these regulations reproduce the categories of population (in terms of gender, class, and ethnicity, for example) for them to realize the segmentation of the job market into which they fall. This 'regulated' process of individualization, though, often appears as facilitating the specific disadvantaged groups such as ethnic minorities and 'down-town people', forcing the population to either be punished or become self-managed. For example, punishments are on the rise and becoming a general phenomenon as a necessity in the ear of neoliberalism. Wacquant (2012, 75) summarizes this as follows:

> The relentless rise in [the] carceral population is moreover only one crude, surface manifestation of the expansion and exaltation of the penal state in the age of the triumphant market ... indicators include the aggressive deployment of police in and around neighbourhoods of relegation and the increased recourse to the courts to handle unruly behaviour and minor offenses; the widening [of] the judicial net through alternative sanctions, post-custodial schemes of control and the exponential development of digitalised justice data banks; the mushrooming of administrative retention centres to corral and expel migrants; the hyperactivity of legislatures on the criminal front ... and the boom of media sector trading on catastrophic images of criminal danger.

What we gather from this is that the neoliberal state is coming to be harsher in terms of penal procedures and more corrective in social engineering terms. It is associated with both a harsher system of crime control and a global social engineering programme of creating a society of control in which 'entrepreneurship' at all levels is promoted as the way to address all the socio-economic and political issues we face today. Penal institution then is only one fraction of this broader transformation of market-based reforms in the public sector. Empirical evidence in this regard proves that the more neoliberal initiatives are, the tougher the penal institution (see Lacey 2008; Young and Brown 1993). Hence, the building of penal institutions alongside the building of market apparatuses manifests a way of advancing the neoliberal state while controlling social consequences and crimes such as social insecurity, risk society, class inequality, ethnic violence, and so on that neoliberalism brings about.

11.3 NPM ideals

Neoliberalism and the subsequent transformation of the state were not enough to sustain the liberal ethos of public administration. Neoliberal advocates saw them as complex and ambiguous as well as excessively rule-based (Hood 1991). Taking a managerialist lens, they warned the practitioners, as O'Flynn (2007) puts it, that the public administration ethos underpinned by Weber's bureaucracy (see Weber 2009), Wilson's (1887) policy administration split, and Taylor's (1964 [1911]) scientific management ideals were no longer valid and useful because the context in which this ethos was rationalized, accepted, and implanted has now gone. Instead, new post-bureaucratic ideals of NPM were propagated. Hood (1991) saw these ideas in seven related themes: (1) hands-on professional management; (2) explicit standards and measures of performance; (3) greater emphasis on output controls; (4) disaggregation of

256   *Neoliberal trends*

units in the public sector; (5) greater competition in public agencies; (6) adaptation of private-sector-like management styles; and (7) enhanced discipline and parsimony in the management of resources. Others emphasized this as a new paradigm characterized by management rather than administrative principles, economic rather than democratic values, post-Fordist public management practices rather than conventional tedious processes of bureaucracy, and service-oriented rather than rule-based. Taking similar views, Dunleavy et al. (2006) discuss their themes to describe the practice of NPM, namely, disaggregation, competition, and incentivization. (Stoker 2006, 46) observes that NPM has come:

> [t]o dismantle the bureaucratic pillar of the Weberian model of traditional public administration. Out with large, multipurpose hierarchical bureaucracies, [NPM] proclaims, and in with the lean, flat, autonomous organizations drawn from the public and private sectors and steered by a tight central leadership corps. The idea of a public-sector ethos is rejected as simply a cover for inefficiency and empire building by bureaucrats.

This arrival of NPM tells us a story about reviving a set of functional theories such as public choice theory, agency theory, and transaction cost economics (see Davies and Thomas 2000), even though NPM has also been subject to critical academic scrutiny that revealed its intended and unintended consequences of varying practices in time and space. As such, research on NPM has documented pragmatic accounts from two dimensions: deterministic embracement and critical encounter.

11.3.1   NPM as a deterministic embracement

When NPM came to be active as an alternative paradigm in managing the state's institutions, management writers began to attach theoretical justifications for the management, accounting, and accountability practices that NPM brought about (see Diefenbach 2009; Gruening 2001; Hood 1991). They tried to map the practices (e.g. budget cuts, privatization, contracting out, accounting for performance, strategic planning, etc.) with neoclassical economics and a set of functional management theories. These included public-choice theory, agency theory, transaction costs theory, property rights, agency theory, etc. We do not intend to elaborate their theoretical assumptions, premises, and framings in detail as it is outside the scope of this chapter. Instead, we shall traverse some of fundamental embraces which have contributed to the project of neoliberalism in general and NPM in particular.

First, implying the principles of rational choice, these frameworks assumed a rational individual who takes the view that if anything is possible, a desirable and rational choice can be made, necessary plans can be devised and implemented with managerial tact, and outcomes can be measured and monitored. Accordingly, what was assumed to be necessary to enhance the efficiency and effectiveness of the public sector is a clear set of 'reform programmes' that can enhance the rationality of the decision makers (i.e. public-sector managers) and decision-making processes. For example, in the last several decades, most development schools in the UK maintained this assumption and promoted and sold reform ideas to countries around the world (Cooke 2004). These development gurus took a functionalist position and propagated that one can entertain this freedom of choice depending on the situations, conditions, and contingencies. They regarded their students (normally public/civil servants from developing countries) as such passive takers of their political views and policy recommendations who can, in turn, convey their messages to their fellow administrators in their home countries.

Second, these frameworks propagate normative modelling with linear relationships between 'relevant variables' and the 'efficiency/performance/effectiveness' of public-sector organizations. For example, proponents of rational public management theories would argue that a proper strategic mapping of the organizational visions and missions can lead to a better and achievable strategy (see Gruening 2001). This articulated the idea that crucial for public-sector reforms is nothing more than a set of managerial technologies (such as BSC and ABC) for strategic mapping, vision and mission setting, and evaluation of strategic outcomes. It is assumed that, once such managerial techniques are in place, relationships between strategy and performance outcomes should be linear, the processes of implementation should be smooth and functional, and the outcomes in the end should be definitely positive. In this way, as it is discoursed in the powerful epistemic centres in the West, NPM enjoys a certain discursive impact, creating a particular managerial language to cognize, communicate, and dominate public-sector management discourses.

Third, and related to the above two features, these frameworks are apolitical and ahistorical. In practical terms, NPM invariably operates in a highly contested, historically and spatially diverse, field of politics, debates, and conflicts. However, the normative modelling based on the assumptions of the universally rational individual can camouflage historical, political, and spatial variations. Despite reality representing politics and historical effects, jargons such as 'de-politicization' and accommodating 'local needs' tend to maintain this camouflaging project. Hence, public-sector administrators and managers attend conferences and workshops and discuss how to minimize politics and local cultural idiosyncrasies so that 'given' normative models and prescriptions can be successfully implemented. NPM is thus considered to be 'universal', which can be implemented in different localities, accommodating their specific requirements, resources, and governance systems. When things apparently fail and intended outcomes never realized, however, the reforms never stop. Instead, another wave of reforms comes, with the idea of correcting the mistakes in the previous attempts. New formulae are brought in with the rhetoric of 'learning the lessons' and enhancing local capacities for better implementation, reintegrating the decoupled system functionalities, adopting needs-based holism, digitalizing the system, and producing self-sustaining changes (Dunleavy et al. 2006).

That said, NPM discourses traverse nation-states, penetrate policy makers' and state bureaucrats' Keynesian world views, make changes in mundane practices, and construct new subjectivities, amid both agitated and silent resistance (Morales et al. 2014b; Newman 2014; Thomas and Davies 2005). This is in favour and a discursive expression of 'empire', which has now come to de-territorialize the nation-state and reinforce the discursive efforts of global players such as the OECD, World Bank, and IMF that propagate NPM (Hardt and Negri 2000). When penetration happens at the local level, there emerge successes as well as failures, support as well as opposition, different forms of neoliberal anthropologies, and unusual links between the state and the economy (Read 2009). These observations lead us to an examination of the critical encounters of the neoliberalization of the state through NPM.

258 *Neoliberal trends*

11.3.2 NPM as a critical encounter

While deterministic framing is dominant among NPM-friendly academics and global proponents, there are critical encounters at the bottom of agencies and organizations where NPM discourses encounter the life-world realities of people. To illustrate these critical encounters, we have chosen a few examples ranging from resistance to, and ambiguities, reimaginations and hybridization of, NPM discourses.

First, ambiguity is always a case of dispersing a discourse from the centre to the periphery (Giddens 1985). In the periphery, as Newman (2014) observed, the same neoliberalism would not be practised. She remarks:

> These do not all carry the same identification, or conduct the 'work' of neoliberalization in the same way. And each may draw on older subject positions, attempting to configure them within neoliberal projects … Such slips and slides may, in time, become appropriated in new phases of neoliberalization, but the outcome may be more ambiguous. Such ambiguities suggest the value of a conceptualisation of governmentalities as strategies or projects rather than outcomes.
>
> (Newman 2014, 3292)

Ambiguity is reflected in terms of the ways people understand NPM and the ways in which they organize the people into a network for embracing it differently or reject it altogether. They may produce new meanings and re-articulate the exiting systems into new configurations and assemblages. Reflecting these possibilities, researchers report on the 'landscape of antagonisms' (Newman 2014), 'gendered nature of re-structuring' (Davies and Thomas 2000), 'distinct spatiality of neoliberalism', (Andrew and Cahill 2017), and 'unrelenting expansions of neoliberalism' (Morales et al. 2014b). Hence, there is no one thing called NPM under neoliberalism. Instead, we see ambiguities that produce an incomplete version of neoliberalism, despite the pervasiveness of the 'governmentality effect' and the consequential 'normative reasoning' that those incomplete and diverse versions realize in different ways. Accounting researchers have made some attempts to report on such ambiguities, but much must be done in the future as the NPM agenda reproduces neoliberalism in different forms and in different subjectivities at the level of the organization (Andrew and Cahill 2017; Chiapello 2017).

Second, NPM produces new forms of management accounting through 'reimagining' the subjects into commercial-like categories. For example, as Thomas and Davies (2002) report, university students have now been 'reimagined' as customers so that the academics' role is to 'satisfy' them through performance measurement schemes such as student feedback arrangements, national level student surveys, and discussions in programme committee meetings. Similarly, patients, citizens, plaintiffs, and even prisoners become 'customers' and they are directed at 'measuring' their satisfaction using new forms of management accounting procedures and methods. This reimagination is not only a part of the discursive formation of neoliberalism as an ideological discourse but also a way of constructing and conducting the subject at the point of producing the government as a mundane set of service delivery practices. The conventional 'individuals' who were fitting into the Keynesian narratives of welfare economics are not appropriate now, hence the 'reimagination' into new neoliberal narratives of customers and entrepreneurs. This means that both the professionals working in public services and their service recipients are now being commodified and intensified through new neoliberal redefinitions of their identities, for which management accounting provides the necessary calculative technologies (Willmott 1995).

Third, related to the above developments, practitioners and professionals in public services are now hybridized. For example, in hospitals, medical practitioners are now learning costing and performance measurements in order to understand the 'cost effects of their operations' while accountants are learning clinical procedures in order to explain the 'operational' cost drivers and cost incidents underlying the hospital's cost of service delivery (Kurunmaki 2004). In universities and schools, similarly, teachers are carrying out various administrative procedures on top of their teaching and research duties while university managers closely scrutinize academic and exam matters in order to keep teaching costs to a minimum and to standardize the processes according to efficiency, effectiveness, quality assurance, and accreditation criteria. Accounting procedures and calculations make the necessary connection between these operational and cost management dimensions. In this way, management accounting becomes a lateral functionality rather than a hierarchical one causing the organizations to be much more lateral, flexible, and hybridized (Miller et al. 2008). There can be different ways of this happening, resulting in spatial variations in the way management accounting creates hybridized managers. The results can be both positive and negative leading to much more ambiguity and multiple realities (see Andrew and Cahill 2017).

Finally, this is linked to different forms of resistance. Rather than being passive recipients of neoliberal discourses, as researchers have reported on, organizational participants in public services have begun to exert some resistance. Nevertheless, as Thomas and Davies (2005) argue, this form of resistance is not leaner and simple as in the case of 'control and resistance' (Kondo 1990) or 'a response to repressive power' (McNay 2000). Rather, it is a subtle issue where resistance resides in identity reconstruction (or destruction) projects and in the process of 'adaptation, subversion, and re-inscription of dominant discourses' (Thomas and Davies 2005, 687). Stepping beyond the simple accounts of resistance, Thomas and Davies (2005) argue that resistance in the context of NPM can be complicated in that professional and managerial employees may engage in resistance at the level of their individualities (rather than collective resistance as in the case of trade union movements) with regard to new meanings and identities being created through NPM discourses. Accounting controls, performance measurements, continuous form filling, and various reviews may provoke them to take some agitative actions at the level of meaning and identity. That said, managerial and professional individuals confront the meanings presented by NPM measurements on a day-to-day basis at a very mundane level. For example, in universities, students are reimagined as customers but the teachers therein resist this idea and ask questions about the meanings of these reimaginations. Similarly, in a hospital context, in encountering the discourses of cost minimization, the medical practitioners' question of how far cost minimization would affect their priority of treating the patients appropriately is side-lined (Wickramasinghe 2015). Moreover, this leads to an identity crisis in these organizations in that traditional professional ethics, values, and morality might be discounted by these NPM-led initiatives pushing the professional to make compromises in their professional standards.

In this subsection, we paid attention to how neoliberal NPM discourses revitalize the state. We have seen that both deterministic embracement and critical encounters are inevitable outcomes of the NPM agenda. These opposing forces, in practice, may find a feasible space for them to co-exist with pragmatic solutions. Though such pragmatic solutions will always reveal some antagonism and cause uneasy relations between

260　*Neoliberal trends*

various parties, they can create a sort of tendency towards settled habits and can produce some durable institutions and practices of NPM. These would always be problematic, being in a continuous process of negotiation and reconstruction through coercive, normative, and cultural–cognitive institutions. Depending on the site-specific dialectics between the norms and values that NPM propagates and the cultural specificities of the local social actors, context-specific practices of NPM may get institutionalized. Research findings about what is actually going on in the NPM agenda is a clear indication of such pragmatic outcomes (see Andrew and Cahill 2017; Morales et al. 2014b; Wickramasinghe 2015).

11.4 Specific practices of NPM accounting (NPMA)

NPMA can vary from context to context and may attract diverse meanings and practices. For illustrative purposes, we have chosen five key areas of NPMA practices to trace their NPM ambitions and to reflect on their neoliberal manifestations. We use Table 11.1 as a roadmap for this illustrative discussion.

11.4.1 Cost management

The cost implications of managerial decisions and controls have been prominent management accounting considerations in manufacturing enterprises. This was never normal practice in the old-fashioned administration regimes in pre-NPM state bureaucracies. Decisions were predominantly driven towards compliance with rules, hierarchical commands, and authorizations with little attention given to the cost-efficiencies of doing so.

Table 11.1 NPM Accounting

Key NPMA initiatives	NPM ambitions	Neoliberal manifestation
Cost management	Unpacking the pooled, unidentified, and aggregated costs into meaningful and visible categories for management and accountability purposes.	Making agencies and individuals act upon costs, cost-drivers, cost-based analyses; framing policy discussions and debates (that lead to both ideological transformations and political struggles in the realm of politics and culture) on cost imperatives.
Strategic planning and performance measurements	Managing both financial and non-financial performance as a culture change programme.	Combining disciplinary controls with discursive framing of the organizational positioning in its competitive context.
New forms of budgeting	Devolved and flexible forms of budgeting that link mundane decoupled practices to central government's fiscal discipline.	Creation of a market inside public services, measuring the outcomes in terms of value for money ideals.
New form of accountability	Individualized forms of accountability having implications for self-governance and resource management aims.	Gathering, categorizing, and individualizing professionals and administrative personnel to be amenable to biopolitical purposes.

Strategizing the state and NPM agenda 261

Even when accounting calculations were used, they were not for enhancing cost-efficiency but to ensure compliance with bureaucratic rules and procedures. NPM questioned this fashion of administrative compliance for their gross cost inefficiencies and created a space in which new NPM ideals of cost management could be institutionalized. Accounting researchers have reported on such experiences and their intended and unintended consequences both in developed and developing countries (Alawattage and Alsaid 2018; Kurunmaki 1999b; Wickramasinghe 2015).

NPM's ambitions have been that services must be costed meaningfully, costs must be taken into managerial considerations seriously, and performance measurements and controls must be maintained in this spirit. As Wickramasinghe (2015) reports, this is a landmark event in the history of resource management within public services as, in pre-NPM regimes, costs were bluntly pooled in large financial accounting categories and aggregated only for reporting purposes rather than for management. Budget targets were provided mostly as maximum figures available for spending. While traditional public services never costed their deliveries effectively for managerial purposes, these NPM-inspired cost management initiatives (which drew on emerging costing techniques such as ABC) opened up these cost categories to comprehend their implications for cost reductions, cost savings, and even elimination of unnecessary cost drivers. On the one hand, this idea of cost management was a means of connecting public services to market competition and its veridiction roles, despite the process occurring outside a pure market condition (Broadbent et al. 1991; Kurunmaki 1999b). Hence, managers in the public sector have now started to be serious about cost management aims. For example, despite various resistances and shortcomings, Kurunmaki (1999b) reports that health care services in Finland have been trying to engender a transition from a planning allocation system to a competition-based resource allocation system. This idea seems to be implicated in a broader governance arrangement because some cost management projects aim to provide cost standards in terms of 'average costs' for varying units and operations. For example, Llewellyn and Northcott (2005) reports on how the UK government's National Reference Costing Exercise created benchmarks for all hospitals to follow as 'excellent' guides and how this exercise produced an 'average hospital' where cost calculations allowed hospital governing bodies to make their governing duties easy and efficient on the basis of this accounting construct of an 'average hospital'. Even in developing countries, such attempts are rehearsed, trying to act upon cost information which some say is 'evidenced-based' data (see Wickramasinghe 2015).

As a form of transformation, neoliberalism provides a narrative for embracing the importance of acting upon costs, cost savings, and cost management within and beyond organizational boundaries (i.e. policy circles and national debates). This manifests as both an ideological transformation of imputing a cost and efficiency consciousness and a set of mundane practices with new software, hardware, managerial protocols, and administrative positions and identities (such as cost managers, cost champions, cost controllers, etc.) in spaces where costs are in fact calculated, categorized, and managed in their day-to-day operations (Alawattage and Alsaid 2018; Gendron et al. 2007). As a form of struggle, these practices are implicated in: the changing roles of professionals, the challenges for traditional professional expertise, the reduction of material benefits and perks for public-sector managers, and the tensions between newly 'upgraded' expertise and 'conventional' expertise. For example, Kurunmaki (1999b, 122) reports that, as NPM provides a new form of rationality for government, there has been an attempt 'to diminish the occupational self-control of health care' having implications for

262   *Neoliberal trends*

power shifts from clinical experts to new health care financiers. Miller et al. (2008) term this a process of hybridization, but the intrusion of accounting is seen to be problematic due to the differences in pedagogic and institutional settings with regard to the legitimation of certain professions. Ashraf and Uddin (2016) rephrased this as 'regressive effects' in the context of developing counties. Hence, both transformational effects and the appearance of struggles tell us that NPM's cost management ambitions cannot be a mere panacea for the issues of traditional planning-based public administration but is also a programme of politics producing varying accounts of neoliberal effects in time and space (Newman 2014).

11.4.2 Strategic planning and performance measurements

NPM has also affected the regularization and legitimation of strategic intents for public services. Hood (1991) defines such processes and practices as Financial Management Initiatives (FMIs) through which NPM ideals were initially articulated (see also Richards 1987). In the UK, for example, a white paper appeared in 1982 entitled *Efficiency and Effectiveness in the Civil Service* and regularized that services must have 'a clear view of their objectives', 'best uses of resources', and a way to 'exercise ... responsibility effectively' (Laughlin et al. 1994). Based on these regulatory effects, UK schools and hospitals became sites for receiving conditions along with funding. For example, funds for these services were proffered on the condition of cash limits, defined accountability requirements, contractual relationships, and devolved budget allocations. Thus, strategic/corporate planning ideas were coercively imposed, performance requirements were deliberately attached to them, and value for money became a self-controllable narrative for the individuals in the agencies. For example, as summarized by Northcott and Llewellyn (2009), UK and New Zealand hospitals have now been coercively and normatively following BSC as a new form of performance measurement.

NPM's ambition on performance measurement was not confined to the boundaries of organizations. Other accounting technologies such as auditing and risk management were used to disperse the ideals of performance measurements across wider constituencies (Chang 2009; Modell 2014). This direction of NPM expansion pointed to various ways of influencing societies but with an inclination towards performance targets, measurements, and accountability promises. For example, as Watkins and Arrington (2007) and Chang (2009) reported, policy makers have now come to measure national performance based on accounting calculations. In terms of this development, there has been a particular proliferation of the involvement of accounting and auditing experts who exert their influence in determining the nature of performance, its credibility, and the consequences of reported deviations. For example, Power (1997) claims that state efficiency auditing has now been transformed into a new arena of expertise articulating that the government's 'efficiency' auditors must certify the 'value for money' in service delivery (see also Gendron et al. 2007). In this way, NPM has created a performance regime through regulatory impositions and through fostering an institutional environment where new accounting expertise is constructed. In the creation of this institutional environment, while regulative forces play a role to some extent, other mimetic and normative forces reproduce the performance measurements in varying constituencies.

In this way, public service units, and the national state as whole, have all become measurable entities. Managers and policy makers become embedded in a performance regime with continuous evaluations, reporting, meeting, and subsequent corrective actions.

For example, in universities, students' satisfaction on teaching and supervision is measured in terms of student feedback mechanisms. The data being collated from such exercises is fed into national and international ranking and accreditation regimes for linking the universities to a competitive configuration. This proceeds to a society-wide talk among potential students and their parents about the quality of universities based on rankings and accreditations. As we mentioned in the previous section, these students and parents are thus 'reimagined' as customers in a competitive market, 'choosing' the best product available to them. Research is judged in terms of journal ranking, impact cases, and citation indexes, creating a competitive mindset among researchers attempting to 'market' their academic work. This pushes them to invest themselves in fashionable and 'rich' fields of research, which, of course, mostly cater for the needs of the commercial world and the global neoliberal agenda. As such, the market operates as a 'regulator' of determining the investment flows in the field of research as well as privileging certain kinds of research over others. Consequently, neoliberal impulses would be translated into a landscape of antagonisms (Newman 2014) which point to some unintended regressions and outcomes (Ashraf and Uddin 2016). Such antagonisms do not mean, however, that government agencies would necessarily resist neoliberalism. Rather, these agencies may enact neoliberalism in multiple political projects, as we have already highlighted.

11.4.3 New forms of budgeting

Budgeting, as a practice of management accounting, entails the creation of systems engendering procedures for setting targets, allocating resources accordingly, and evaluating performance outcomes. Alongside these procedures, numerous regulations, white papers, and interventions are produced by public-sector agencies for making budgets a mechanism of 'expenditure authorization' for operational entities and individuals. In the public sector, they were governed, by and large, through financial codes, administrative codes, and relevant ministerial circulars including Treasury circulars. That was the pervasive fashion of the budgeting practice which became questionable upon the arrival of the NPM discourse. The key issue, from the lenses of neoliberal proponents, is that these conventional budgeting practices are predominantly control-driven – driven to prevent the abuse of power in public office. As such, they constrain the process of neoliberal reforms aimed at transforming public services into for-profit organization-like entities. They were deemed to be counterproductive for the inculcation of the entrepreneurial ethos. Hence, a new form of budgeting was now envisaged to transform the civil servant and administrator into enterprise managers.

Again, as with cost management, new forms of budgeting (often in the form of activity-based budgeting and project/programme budgeting) are being operated in the context of NPM reforms, making the public-sector agencies amenable to neoliberal ambitions. These budgeting initiatives are taking place not only as ways of allocating funds from central authorities to local operations but also as a way of the government economizing and reinforcing and revitalizing neoliberal ideals in the day-to-day running of the government. We know that, in traditional terms, budgets are financial planning practices aimed at creating budget targets for divisions and individuals and, in turn, creating a top-down, hierarchical form of accountability. However, new forms of budgeting practices are now becoming different in that they produce flexibility rather than uncompromising target and lateral heterarchies rather than vertical commands (Stark 2011). These forms of budgeting are thus 'mediating instruments' (Miller and O'Leary 2007) which lead to a new form of

264   Neoliberal trends

governmentality presented as an operating ensemble (Kurunmaki and Miller 2011). As a mediating instrument, these new forms of budget are now a manifestation of the new ways of intervention in terms of 'looking across rather than up and down' (Hopwood 1996). They represent a neoliberal narrative which may be translated into a local form in terms of the 'localized aspirations and activities of service providers' (Kurunmaki and Miller 2011, 237).

These new forms of budgeting, however, were not an immediate and instant development. They came to problematize the old systems of budgeting through a series of gradual, 'textual fabrications'. For example, Preston et al. (1992) illustrate how this fabrication has occurred in the context of the National Health Service (NHS) in the UK since the late 1970s. First, it was a moment of problematization through the production of documents which highlighted a new form of budgeting for the NHS which they called 'management budgeting'. The documents such as *Royal Commission on the NHS* (1979), *Griffith Report on NHS Management* (1983), *DHSS Interim Report on Management Budgeting* (1985), *DHSS Interim Report on Management Budgeting and Resource Management* (1986), and *Department of Health Proposals for Extending Resource Management 'Working for Patients'* (1989) constructed an 'NPM argument'. This was done by highlighting the conditions the NHS was under, by providing rhetoric and convincing arguments for linking budgets to resource management, and by signifying the importance of allocating resources based on resource management disciplines (Preston et al. 1992). The process of this fabrication was not easy. The national-level programmatic discourse of management budgeting in the NHS gradually produced a form of governmentality that influenced funding decisions, mode of management, and responsibilities of doctors and administrators. As Preston et al. (1992) argue, this was a difficult process as the old practices of budgeting opposed this new form of governmentality. However, the actors and mediators pushed through this difficult process until management budgeting became a 'matter of fact'. As Laughlin et al. (1994) later contend, this led to the development of a set of issues with a series of controversies, although new delineations about the use of budgets for 'resource allocation' were passed through doctors and administrators. Similar initiatives were embarked on around the world showing that these new forms of budgeting were becoming inevitable.

These illustrations reinforce our engagement with neoliberalism and its discursive effects on governments. As a mediating instrument, budgeting has become a mode of intervention in the construction of a neoliberal governmentality with new modes of governing principles, namely budgets must be devolved, their aims must be resource managed, their processes must create more flexible and lateral relationships, and their outcomes must be defined in terms of competitive financial performances. Hence, the neoliberal impulsion here is that budgets have been used for the creation of a market inside public services measuring the outcomes in terms of value for money ideals. This is like judging large corporations' performance in terms of 'shareholder value'. Introducing budgeting into public services is thus a way of transforming public service ideologies, inundated with far-reaching economic and rational properties that submit the state to market principles.

11.4.4 New form of accountability

NPM has created a broader space for policy makers, politicians, and professionals to realize a new domain of accounting, extending its scope to a wider terrain of accountability. In the context of NPM and as a necessary technology of modernizing the

Strategizing the state and NPM agenda   265

government, the accounting practices we outlined earlier (costing, strategic planning, performance measurements, and budgeting) are invariably linked to accountability – giving and demanding reasons for one's conduct (Roberts and Scapens 1985). NPMA is now coming to extend its scope in several forms of accountability, which we outline in this subsection.

First, the NPM agenda is now an appealing proposition for resource management. Through the process of cost calculations, through the functions of performance measurements, and through the rituals of budgeting, resource management has come to be a central focus of the NPM agenda. For example, Kurunmaki (1999a) illustrated that local governments in Finland are now following private-sector financial controls, including a shift from cash-based accounting practices to accrual-based accounting. The main difference now is that these controls are very much focused on effective and efficient resource management with reporting requirements that outcomes must be reported to respective authorities with a clear articulation of how such practices of resource management were achieved. Similarly, as Wickramasinghe (2015) analyses, cost-based decisions and subsequent cost-saving experiences are now discussed at wider decision-making circles beyond local administrative meetings. This extended discussion has created a new form of accountability which brings multiple stakeholders to the table. On the subject of the 'average hospital' we mentioned earlier, again this resource management task has been attached to UK hospitals, enabling them to make managerial decisions according to the 'averages' being imposed on them. NPM accounting is thus translated into a broader idea of resource management linking the outcomes to a new form of accountability.

Second, this form of accountability is linked to a transition from the established hierarchical form of accountability to an emerging heterarchical and flexible form. This is a 'regulatory hybrid' (Kurunmaki and Miller 2011) which demonstrates a different commitment towards the 'partners', who are now working with interdisciplinary groups of professionals expanding their traditional boundaries of professional work. This transition is also marked by an individualization of accountability because, despite these trans-professional connections, through new performance measurement systems, these professionals, as individuals, are made accountable to themselves about their engagement with others (Roberts 2009). Consequently, this creates an environment within public services for individuals to entertain a certain degree of internal flexibility for innovation and change. Kurunmaki and Miller (2011) nicely illustrate this transformation: individuals are now bound to the aims of delivering accountability based on the flexibility given. These possibilities for flexibility, as opposed to tedious processes of delays and red tape, are now operating in the context of inter-organizational relationships. Referring to a form of 'liquid modernity' (Bauman 2000) where society is becoming 'individualized', Wickramasinghe (2015) also echoes this development with some illustrations of constructing individuals in a hospital where cost-saving decisions are being entertained by individual nurses.

Third, also related to the above, this form of accountability is becoming a form of self-governance. The 'individualized individuals' are responsible not only for managing resources but also managing themselves, their territory, and their destiny. For example, in terms of a new regime of performance measurements, public universities are now creating individualized spaces for academics to further their career development prospects in terms of undertaking individualized tasks of publications and teaching and learning engagements (Brownlie 2009). Within this performance regime, academic performance is valued in terms of indicators superimposed upon the academic by various accreditation schemes, national performance frameworks, and emerging criteria which are now labelled as 'contribution to the enterprise'. Accordingly, her/his progress is defined as a self-governing accounting entity which is subject to periodical reviews and discussions with top managers. Similarly, in hospitals, clinical experts must now be engaged in decision making as self-governing entities with implications for their own resource uses and overall financial performance. For example, in the UK, GPs are entrusted with seeking locally determined solutions through the GP Contract which defines tight accountability with definable financial and other sanctions and rewards for 'good practice' (Broadbent and Laughlin 1998). Hence, the GP Contract is being redefined under neoliberal terms and makes GPs truly individual but tied into a tightly defined accountability which is to be delivered through a self-governing discipline. Most commentators (see van Helden and Uddin 2016) see this as erosion of professional autonomy, but neoliberalism narrates this as a way of improving accountability in public services (Kurunmaki et al. 2003).

11.5 Summary and conclusions

We can now conclude the aims of the chapter by returning to our biopolitical theorization. As we have already mentioned, NPMA focuses much on performance measurements linked to both cost management and new forms of budgeting, leading to new ways of thinking about accountability. As shown in Figure 11.1, NPM has orchestrated a new combination of these management ideas into a form of ultimate conception of accountability. This shows how biopolitical uses of management accounting can be highly visible while classical democratic values are being eroded.

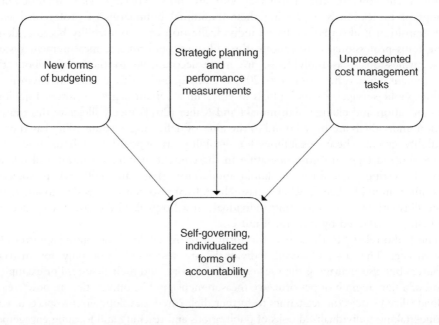

Figure 11.1 Neoliberal management accounting in the public sector

Strategizing the state and NPM agenda 267

What we see is that NPM's elaboration of neoliberalism has reimagined the state apparatuses and associated public services as a manageable space for governance, controls, and accountability. We thus see three interrelated themes which make NPM a biopolitical reconstruction of governance, controls, and accountability.

First, NPM has provided a specific book of narratives which emphasizes the significance of market signals that govern our everyday life, economy, and society. Consequently, policy makers and politicians together propagated this narrative in the form of reports, memos, meetings, negotiations, and regulations. Despite resistance, misunderstanding, and alternative views, this narrative became a programmatic discourse that spread worldwide and influenced policies and practices. In doing so, public-sector agencies and public services have been reimagined as a new governable space, characterizing it as a new pathological trait – inefficient and ineffective domains of public life that need to be reformed and subjected to the perpetual gaze of the market. Consequently, the nature of public services was rearticulated, the types of service deliveries were redesigned, and the public agencies were considered to be an object of cognizant calculations and interventions. While this is entirely a political project supported by conservative ideologies, its abstract nature of language and the development of narratives produced a generalized aspiration of normative reasoning for the identification of the state and associated agencies as sites for biopolitical management – a new era of governmentality.

Second, this form of biopolitical management necessitated certain tools, processes, and practices to enable and enact the neoliberal ideology of market governance of the public sphere. New cost management, strategic planning, performance measurements, and new forms of budgeting came to create a self-governing individualizing form of accountability. NPM accounting thus constitutes biopolitical reporting to facilitate political discussions, negotiations, and regulations. In other words, implementation of NPM means the use of terms such as costing, new forms of budgeting, strategic management tools at intra-organizational, inter-organizational, and policy levels. In the application of such managerial tools (which hitherto used to be in private-sector organizations), notions such as cost-efficiency, quality, differentiation, market positioning, etc. became not only rhetorical but also governing principles to which administrators, professionals, politicians, and beneficiaries of public services were subjugated. Their conventional political and civic logics of providing public services needed to be translated into a set of market-driven service delivery protocols. In this sense, as we mentioned earlier, these tools are mediating instruments. However, it does not mean that this resembles universally the practices in every geographical context and time. Researchers have pointed to the spatial and time variations of both intended and unintended consequences of NPM.

Last, this neoliberalization of public administration is truly political given that public services are made up of a number of varying professional enclosures (Kurunmaki and Miller 2011) which now are driven towards the biopolitical themes of economic efficiency through market-based regulations. In the transformation of public-sector accounting from a traditional administrative to a neoliberal market form, these distinct professional groups now must work with other professionals, crossing boundary lines but with many boundary clashes leading to sites of struggle and rivalry. Researchers have reported on these instances with numerous theoretical insights (see Kurunmaki 1999a; Kurunmaki and Miller 2011; Preston et al. 1992). They have pointed out that NPM transformation is an unfinished business so that making these narratives a final 'matter of fact' is beyond the destinies of realization. Controversy is not unusual in NPM accounting initiatives. They reproduce resistance

268 *Neoliberal trends*

and re-articulate alternatives highlighting the possibilities that biopolitics are problematic.

Neoliberal attempts at strategizing the state hence include a wide range of political, governance, managerial, and accounting initiatives aiming at normalizing a mode of normative reasoning that privileges 'market thinking'. Cost management, budgeting, strategic planning, performance measurement, accountability, etc. penetrate the local spaces as global imperatives, mainly pushed by the transnational development agencies such as the World Bank and the OECD. They all argue that governments should now have a clear strategic position that enacts and enables the market within the organizational programmes and a clever set of managerial tools to design and implement that strategic posture. Hence, the strategic management initiatives that we discussed in previous chapters in relation to private-sector corporations now increasingly penetrate public-sector organizations. In this agenda, management accounting now has new sites to perform its costing, decision making, and control functionalities. Strategizing the state and rationalizing the NPM agenda must be understood in these broader terms.

Assignments

These assignments are meant to extend your knowledge beyond what you understand from this chapter. These are not simply revision questions. The content covered in this chapter is necessary but will not be sufficient in attempting these tasks. Therefore, you are required to do some extra reading in attempting these tasks.

1. **Thematic essay:**
   'NPM accounting creates a site of struggle between competing professionals even though they are all aiming to realize one single vision'.
   Discuss this statement focusing on the issues of the biopolitical repercussions of NPM initiatives.
2. **Poster:**
   Elaborate Figure 11.1 illustrating not only the roles of management accounting under the NPM agenda but also the issues being created as a result of these interventions. In doing so, you may imagine a particular context you are familiar with.
3. **Presentation:**
   Prepare an adequate number of PowerPoint slides for you to use as visual aids for a presentation at a PhD colloquium where you are proposing a piece of potential research. In this regard, use the following working title:
   'What constitutes management accounting when it is seen in an NPM project?'
4. **Extended bibliography:**
   For the working title in question 1 above, explore the best ten journal articles published in accounting and management top-ranked journals. Reflect on them in terms of their (1) academic significance; (2) key contribution/s; and (3) remaining issues to be addressed. For this, use the following table to fill in those details:

Article	Significance	Key contribution/s	Remaining issues to be addressed

5. **Literature review:**

As was the case in the previous chapter, now produce a literature review based on the key articles you have chosen and other relevant ones you may discover. You may organize this as clear answers to these questions:

(a) What is the state-of-the art of this stream of research?
(b) What is it you want to propose?
(c) Why is it so important now?
(d) What are the key questions, and how are they considered to be novel?
(e) What aims do you want to achieve?

12 Strategizing civil society as a management accounting entity

12.1 Introduction

So far, you have been reading about how the neoliberalized order of the world is transforming the apparatuses of organizations and the state. You have seen that there is a change from a disciplinary control, which emphasizes confinement of bodies within disciplinary time-spaces for the creation of surplus value, to a biopolitical control, which emphasizes the creation of surplus values through the circulation of bodies across different sites. While the conventional organizations are now being internally transformed into strategic entities encompassing new structures, systems, and processes aimed at flexibility, quality, and cost-efficiency, this transformation also transpires to extra-organizational areas of operation. These include inter-organizational relations, reformation of the state with neoliberal technologies associated with NPM, and the neoliberalization of civil society. While Chapter 10 illustrates how this transformation is taking place in the inter-organizational context, and Chapter 11 dealt with that in the context of the state, this chapter examines how the same is occurring in the context of civil society.

Civil society is an intervening social space between the market and the state. It comprises not only people in families and communities but also their organizations, networks, institutions, or any other forms of civil associational engagements for the democratization of local developmental endeavours (Roy 2008). An organized civil society may consist of trade union movements and other political movements, NGOs, charities, media, and so on. Encompassing such institutional apparatuses, conventionally civil society has been understood as the counter-balancing force against the tyrannies of both the political state and the economy. Under this neoliberal regime, apparently, as the development literature sees it, civil society has come to be a primary focus for the re-embedding of the global ideas of democracy and civil rights principles in peripheral societies (Oommen 2003). In a conventional sense, civil society has been a site of little interest to management accounting. However, with the recent neoliberal discourses of reorganizing civil society as a force of development, especially through NGOs and other development discourses such as microfinance, the role of management accounting in civil society has now become an interesting accounting issue.

Given that neoliberalism's market logic is now exploding prevailing institutional boundaries, making uncharted territories amenable to market veridictions, civil society is being reinvented as a strategic entity. It is being targeted to give it new political-economic visions to achieve, organizational forms for it to get reorganized, managerial technologies to manage and evaluate its performance, and, thereby, to translate it into a competitive terrain. It is in this context that management accounting tools come to play both a disciplinary and a biopolitical role within civil society. For development scholars, this transformation is about both establishing good governance initiatives and introducing market logics that minimize the roles of the state (Roy 2008). Seen from a management accounting perspective, we discern that this development has produced unprecedented measurements, controls, and accountability forms (Apostol 2015). In this chapter, we will try to elaborate how civil society is being strategized, disciplined, and governed in the service of neoliberalism.

The chapter is structured as follows:

1. In Section 12.2 we will provide you with a working definition for the notion of civil society by which the chapter's analytical space is elucidated. As we have already mentioned, this analytical space can be found in the interface between where the private-sector and public-sector organizations such as NGOs, associations, voluntary organizations, and so forth, are located. In this section, this definition will be further elaborated to explore different organizational forms that characterize civil society and the different management control systems embedded therein. Moreover, this section outlines the historical phases of the evolution of civil society with special attention given to the transformation of management control and accounting.
2. Section 12.3 provides a biopolitical framework to analyse the transformations taking place in civil society. Special attention will be paid to the neoliberal purposes of emerging civil society organizations such as NGOs and charities. As we will explain, and in line with the governmentality themes that we have discussed in previous chapters, we will explain how such organizations are now subject to two interrelated forms of controls – disciplinary and biopolitical controls. In this section, you will see how management accounting performs these dual roles.
3. Section 12.4 will explore the process through which civil society organizations are transformed into strategic entities, attributing to them certain neoliberal functionalities that ensure the provision of infrastructural elements of capital accumulation. We pay special attention to how the neoliberal agenda of global development operates in the rural landscapes of peripheral countries, and we will explain how this strategizing is taking place based on four interrelated elements: corporatizing; incorporating ideologies and discourses; constructing individual selves; and adopting multiple evaluative criteria.
4. Section 12.5 summarizes and concludes the chapter with a reflection on how these management accounting practices are linked to new accountability forms evolving in the civil society context.

12.2 Civil society: meaning and transformation

12.2.1 Meaning

Before dealing with our overarching questions of how civil society is being strategized and how management accounting tools are mobilized for that, we shall define the term civil society. Although with certain vagueness, civil society has been conceived as 'a third sector', the state and the market being the other two sectors. As a third sector, civil society then plays the roles that the state and the market are not willing or fail to

272 *Neoliberal trends*

play. Between the state and the market, there are individuals who may want to become organized to achieve some other aims that neither the state nor the market contribute (Cohen and Arato 1992). These individuals may attempt to create a public space between the state and the individual. How can this be possible? These individuals are just a massive community if they stand alone as individuals. Such individuals may not speak about their rights in relation to the instances of some violation of such rights and they may not explore how such violations can be eliminated. In contrast, if these individuals interact with each other and become engaged in their community to talk about such violations and work collectively to address such issues, that association is conceived to be civil society, which is thus a public space which is organized and collective. Hence, civil society is represented by organizations such as voluntary organizations, grassroots organizations, NGOs, and charities They can also be very fixed organizations such as churches and universities or even international NGOs. They are all organizing individuals with a view to achieving a public purpose. It is these purposes which hold these organizations out as civil society organizations.

These purposes could be concerning public politics in general or particular kinds of issues such as education, the environment, or social welfare. Hence, civil society exists with a relatively more or less fixed purpose and is organized with routinized organizational characteristics. In a way, universities and religious institutions (e.g. churches) are fixed and well-organized civil society arms. But, at the same time, voluntary organizations such as environmental groups, neighbourhood organizations, supporters for women and children, organizations protecting animals' wellbeing, are also civil society elements which have relatively few fixed organizational characteristics. That said, a variant mixture of associations describes civil society (Hadenius and Uggla 1996). These associations and activities can be animated by ideological bases (political, social, or cultural) and the organizations can be large and formal or small and informal.

These organizations thus often represent the private interests of individuals but transformed into public or common interests. Private individual subjectivities and interests such as 'woman's escape from domestic violence' can become inter-subjective and transformed into what Habermas calls 'audience oriented' (Fernando 2011). Such inter-subjectivities, as advocates of civil society argue, provide moral support for self-interested individuals, rally them around a specific purpose, and intern formalized communities into organized modes of inter-subjectivities. Operating between the public and individuals, these organizations can make ineffective and inefficient public agencies and rogue private enterprises accountable to the public and, thereby, can reinvigorate social transformations. When societies are underdeveloped, economies are poor, and states are corrupt, the existence of a third sector can be regarded as a panacea for such public problems. However, some argue that such a justification for the existence of civil society would be problematic in that it can appeal to multitudes of ideological positions leaving disagreements about their purpose and debates about how they should operate (Ehrenberg 1999).

Hence, beyond such normative explanations about what we should mean by civil society, some have made attempts at asking a rather pragmatic question: why has civil society emerged? The broader answer to this question is that in a democratic capitalist system (which is the established and widely accepted form of capitalism), there should be both a well-balanced state and an autonomous civil society. This arrangement is, as Alexis de Tocqueville, Samuel Huntington, and Robert Putnam thought, undoubtedly a liberal one. As a social space between the state and the individual, civil society must entertain civil and political rights independently bound by a set of shared rules, while the state must be mobilizing an accountable government. Hence, as rights holders, civil society organizations ensure that governments mobilize democracy through good governance without exercising excessive power while the government as duty bearers must adhere to the principles of democracy and good governance. While these two complementary arms work separately, civil society has come to protect liberal capitalism. For example, when state power is excessively exercised over people and its activities become contradictory to the people's will, then civil society take actions to strengthen the state's capacity for good governance (Mercer 2003).

Hence, civil society is organized with resources, social networks, community-based activities, and principles of wider participation, pluralism, and decentralization (Roy 2008). Empirical studies have shown that both developed and developing countries have made substantive progress in mobilizing civil society organizations for development and good governance. For example, as Narayan and Pritchett (1999) report, in countries such as Egypt, El Salvador, India, Sri Lanka, Nepal, and Indonesia, civil society organizations not only deliver local services and facilities such as housing, education, and water supply with people's collective engagement, but also promote good governance and self-accountability in dealing with these projects. However, we should not just accept the idea that civil society is always effective in delivering services and establishing democratic principles such as good governance and accountability. The question of the effectiveness of civil society is to be addressed in relation to the historical context in which civil society organizations emerged and evolved.

12.2.2 Transformation: the case of developing countries

Civil society's purpose and the underlying definition above can be scrutinized through an examination of its historical transformations, especially in developing countries. Developing countries are important here in that it is these societies which suffer multitudes of social ills because their societies, governments, and markets have been reported as underdeveloped, ineffective, and, even, corrupt (Fernando 2011; Hopper et al. 2017). Hence, it is the civil society organizations which have been trying to fill the vacuum between these 'unsuccessful' states and markets in these countries while the 'rich' West is trying to provide the necessary financing to promote civil society as a mechanism for governing the economy and the political state. Hence, the West, through their international NGOs (INGOs) are mobilizing huge advocacy roles in developing countries with the funding in place to fill that vacuum (Chenhall et al. 2010). Fernando (2011, 2) argues that this mobilization has now created an ideology by constructing a hegemonic status in that:

> Hegemony involves the production, dissemination and legitimation of norms, values and practices that facilitate a social group's – or multiple social groups' view and understanding of the world. Ideology achieves hegemonic status when it becomes widely accepted as a description of the past, present and future and induces social agents to act in one manner rather than in another.

In filling this vacuum between 'unsuccessful' states and markets in developing countries, the involvement of NGOs as a hegemonic category has a transformative path. By looking at this transformation, we may gather some nuances about how NGOs have come to be in their present state in the peripheral countries. For this, as summarized in Table 12.1, we may periodize this transformation into three important historical phases: colonial, post-colonial and neoliberal (Fernando 2011; see also Hopper et al. 2009).

274 *Neoliberal trends*

Table 12.1 The transformation of civil society organizations in developing countries

Historical phase	Purpose	What is civil society?
Colonial phase	Regulating and controlling voluntary activities while establishing the nation-state.	The constitution of local societies regulated by the colonial government and the colonial church.
Post-colonial phase	Supporting the post-colonial independent nation-state building project.	Voluntary organizations to help people who were neglected by the colonial and post-colonial state.
Neoliberal phase	Engaging in self-funding developmental activities.	A third sector, mobilizing neoliberal ideas of development (e.g. empowerment, participatory development) while being financially self-funded.

As we see in Table 12.1, the colonial phase was not a time in which NGOs were propagated and established in the contemporary sense. The historical reasons in this period were propelled into another direction – the colonial governments operating in many parts of the world, especially in the nineteenth century – tried to establish their legitimacy while searching for efficient ways of conducting the colonial government. This was, indeed, the task of state formation in colonial spaces around the world rather than reorganizing economies from one regime to another. Referring to such tasks in Bangladesh and Sri Lanka, Fernando (2011, 43) remarked on this point:

> NGOism is an important part of nation building, particularly in terms of how the state mobilizes the nation and its history in order to concentrate and legitimise its power. Current controversies surrounding NGOs are not only about NGOs themselves, they also concern history, and how history informs a sense of belonging in multicultural states as they undergo capitalist development.

Hence, these countries tried to regulate and encourage public activities such as charities, fundraising, and promoting education and local developmental projects. Although they were in conflict with European ways of organizing local activities, such local associations followed European models to organize these activities. For example, as a result of these efforts, a number of religious organizations were established in India (in a region now known as Bangladesh), including the Hindu Orphan Relief Movement which was established in 1857 (Fernando 2011). Colonial government in India then provided an environment to grow such 'NGOs' (although they were not called NGOs at that time) as part of the task of nation-state building. Similar initiatives took place in Sri Lanka (then Ceylon), e.g. the establishment of the National Education Fund in 1882 to promote Buddhist schools (Burger 1992).

While we cannot find much about modern day practices of organizational controls in the colonial phase, we see a historical foundation for the development of formal associations in these countries. The post-colonial phase was built up with these inspirations. The task there was to concentrate on the areas that were neglected by both the colonial state and the newly established independent states. This kind of negligence occurred because newly elected governments in (mainly ex-British) post-colonial countries generally operated in metropolitan areas enjoying the infrastructure built by the colonial governments. As a result, remote, rural areas were largely neglected. For example, in Sri Lanka, the Sarvodaya Shramadana Movement (SSM) was instituted in 1958 as an important social movement to help disadvantageous people in rural Ceylon (see Ariyaratne 2001).

We shall elaborate this to some extent, so that we can see a particular historical context within which civil society, for example, evolved. This movement was based on Buddhist principles. It was possible for the leader of this campaign to go down this route because of the social conditions that were neglected as far as the rural poor and their indigenous ideologies were concerned by both colonial and the newly established post-colonial state. At this historical juncture, it should be noted that SSM did not evolve as an anti-state revolutionary movement but as a movement trying to support the post-colonial state in building an independent indigenous nation-state, which should include a strong civil society. This was done through gathering local people into associations and organizing them in terms of certain ideologies, political or religious, to 'perform' certain rural development activities (see Alawattage et al. 2015a, 2015b). Having seen that these civil associations were contributing a considerable amount of effort to national development, governments recognized their importance and provided the necessary resources for their further development. Later, circa the 1960s, these associations grew up and were supported by international funding agencies. For example, SSM in Sri Lanka had grown to organize 8000 villages in the 1960s and over 35 international organizations such as UNICEF, WHO, Oxfam, and the UK provided sufficient funding to establish and promote SSM's objectives. What happened though was that in the development of NGOs in developing countries (such as in Sri Lanka), global development capital was brought in and this justified the importance of interference in both providing funding and disciplining societies. In that sense, the post-colonial phases witnessed an era of disciplining developing societies through the mechanism of civil society strengthening programmes. A quite wide spectrum of NGOs, charities, and other voluntary clubs were promoted in peripheral countries by international donors.

However, the increasing involvement of international donor agencies in these organizations and the increasing dependency of such organizations on international donors created a tension between the accountability requirements of the donors and the socio-political and cultural intentions of the civil society organizations. With the arrival of neoliberal development discourses in the 1980s and later, in particular, this tension accelerated and most of the civil society organizations were forced to adopt market-driven accountability reforms if they were to continue with their international funding. This meant that these neoliberal circumstances led these NGOs to adopt more market-oriented principles in financing their activities and organizing their management functions (Sanders 2012). The adoption of market principles thus became an imperative manifesting a neocolonial phase in NGOs. Sanders (2012, 181) remarks, referring to the contemporary NGOs under neocolonialism:

> [n]on-profit organizations cannot function outside the realities of the market economies in which they pursue their work. Therefore, by independently and privately operating within a market economy to develop civil society and pursue the common good, non-profit organizations must organise their work around these competing and seemingly contradictory concerns.

276 *Neoliberal trends*

Hence, the neocolonial phase in the functioning of NGOs is an era of contradictions. Control systems in civil society organizations were a manifestation of these contradictions. On the one hand, they were driven towards protecting the populace, especially less powerful and suppressed elements of societies, from the power abuses by the political state and the economy. On the other, it was the same political state and the economy upon which they relied for funding and the managerial technologies to organize their own activities. That said, all artefacts such as performance measurements, budgetary controls, the mechanisms through which accountability is delivered, are a manifestation of this contradiction because the practices of these technologies are always intermingled with the purpose and the strategy of the organization in which such practice emerges, evolves, and is transformed. As we will be elaborating in the rest of the chapter, such practices, on the one hand, promote developmental discourses such as participatory development, participatory budgeting, empowerment, good governance, social auditing, and so forth (Hickey and Mohan 2004). On the other, NGOs consider these activities from a 'performance' perspective so that their efficiency is measured, reported, and discussed, and necessary actions and sanctions are taken in order to remedy any deficiency (Swanepoel 1992). Management accounting and controls play a more vital role in the latter than in the former.

This tension between the donor agencies' imposition of formal, for-profit-like accountabilities and the grassroots-level requirements of the civil society organizations has been often captured by the paradox between functional and social forms of accountability (see O'Dwyer and Unerman 2008). Functional, or top-down, accountability refers to the hierarchical accountabilities imposed by the donors and the state upon the civil society organizations. They demand civil society organizational activists produce various forms of formal and detailed accounts of how resources are to be deployed (e.g. project reports, feasibility studies, operational budgets, strategic plans, etc.), how efficiently and effectively resources are deployed (e.g. financial reporting and audits), and the effectiveness of their resource use (e.g. social impact reports, post-project surveys and reports, etc.). This type of accountability has often been initiated as a condition of funding. Social accountability, on the other hand, refers to the accountability that civil society organizations, their funding agencies, and also the facilitating governments should collectively hold towards the recipients of their services. This has become an important aspect of accountability because of the significant impact such civil society organizations, especially large INGOs, can have on the lives of the people in the peripheral societies. It is often argued that the functional form of accountability is dominating and so restricts the possibilities of social accountabilities (see Ebrahim 2003; Gray et al. 2006; O'Dwyer and Unerman 2008)

12.3 Biopolitics of civil society

We have briefly sketched the historical transformation of civil society organizations, especially in developing countries. It has been shown that civil society organizations' management structures evolved from an informal social gathering in the 1950s to hierarchical or functional forms, incorporating many management accounting and performance management techniques, processes, and structures from the 1980s.

The early post-colonial informal forms of civil society organizations (or rather movements) reminded us of village-based cultural practices where people gathered to work together towards developing local infrastructures (e.g. construction of local roads or bridges) or discussing an important social development matter (e.g. importance of using votes in elections). For this, a form of social management (social control) was established to serve the purpose: small informal meetings and gatherings with embedded social rituals, simple record keeping, informal cultural controls, and collective performance were salient characteristics. For example, SSM in Sri Lanka used mundane Buddhist cultural practices to gather, meet, work, and direct peoples' individual and collective performance towards developing a basic infrastructure in rural villages. The main thrust of this initial attempt was to establish disciplinary principles (based on Buddhist teachings), which then set the socio-cultural and institutional foundation for SSM to evolve into a large conglomerate of NGOs (Alawattage et al. 2015a, 2015b). Similar patterns of disciplinary practices (based on other religions) were also seen in other countries where seeds of NGOs were planted (see Hoque and Parker 2014; Kraus et al. 2017; O'Leary 2017). One salient feature of this inception was that they all maintained the simplicity, smallness, and self-discipline towards the original purpose.

This informal kind of disciplinary practice, which was operated as a mundane form of governance, was developed and evolved in its post-colonial phase, as we saw in the previous section. However, when they confronted the economic and political ramifications of the contemporary, neocolonial/neoliberal times, religiously articulated disciplinary practices were transformed into a formal-hierarchical type (Alawattage et al. 2015a, 2015b). Its operation was very large, its chain of command was now top-down, and its processes were rigid and tedious. In this setting, the control mechanisms were like those in a large corporation. Consequently, large formal meetings, formal budget cycles, routine performance reports, and external reporting requirements became part and parcel of the functioning of their disciplinary mechanism. The underlying control tools became unavoidable requirements because they were imposed by the INGOs who provided a huge amount of global funding for the sustenance of these NGOs.

This led these local NGOs to be 'self-contained places of confinement' (Macintosh 2002, 83), preoccupied with a series of rules, responsibilities, and calculations – so that these NGOs were made an 'analytical and useful space' by making them visible to transnational financial agencies (Fernando 2011). What we see here is that both liberal and neoliberal forms of the politics and the economics gave rise to a disciplinary power within the control practices of NGOs through the establishment of what Foucault (1995, 2000) calls the 'anatomico-politics of the human body'. The basic goal of this disciplinary power, as Foucault argues, is to increase the docility and utility of the elements of the system, thereby mastering the forces of the individual body and enabling more to be extracted from them to the satisfaction of capital, which is the funding provided by INGOs and other global financing institutions. Accordingly, the activists in the rural sites of less developed countries were expected to perform their operational activities in the manner that the INGOs and other funding bodies wanted them to be performed. This is the confinement of human actions in civil society to the standards and expectations of international development capital.

Despite the introduction of various control and accountability models for NGOs based on an array of disciplinary practices, most local NGOs failed to be accountable to those INGOs in terms of providing trustworthy reports. For example, as Perera (1995) wrote, SSM in Sri Lanka could not provide the necessary reports required by the international donors and led itself into an uncomfortable relationship with the donors. In return, the funding agencies were collectively organized to remedy the issue of non-

278 *Neoliberal trends*

compliance. The result was the development of an International Donor Consortium in 1986. Its purpose was to review the funding request and to evaluate the ways in which the fund was used. The Donor Consortium was highly critical of SSM's original Buddhist philosophy and demanded that they reform its mission and programmes more towards economic development initiatives rather than cultural and spiritual forms of development. For example, the Norwegian donor (NOVIB) insisted that they were not interested in philosophy because, for NOVIB, 'development is a business' as its Director at that time commented (see Perera 1995, 1997; Perera et al. 1992). As a result, SSM faced huge funding cuts leading to the problems of their continuity as a provider of common good. Eventually, in the 1990s, SSM decided to discontinue their 'unprofitable' programmes and concentrated much on 'profitable' ones, and now it is much more concentrated on 'profitable' microfinance businesses.

Thus, the imposition of disciplinary practices over peripheral NGOs by the global donors has become the norm. As such, NGOs and other civil society organizations, which came to be heavily dependent upon global development funders, were heavily structured by mechanisms of 'upward accountability' – various reports and accounts flowing from the bottom to satisfy the requirements of the donors. In effect, civil society activists had to spend much of their time in producing these accounts. In order to deliver such 'upward accountability', especially when the local NGOs became large conglomerates like Sri Lanka's SSM has now become, they maintained necessary disciplinary practices within their hierarchy. For the mobilization of a regime of control, such hierarchies used management accounting practices such as budgeting, performance measurements, and project management techniques to make the subordinates accountable to the superior at the top of the organization. From this stems the question as to whether there is any difference between the management controls in an NGO and those in a private-sector firm, beyond their explicit objectives of being not-for-profit. Addressing this question, researchers have identified some key differences in the practice of disciplinary controls in NGOs. For example, Kraus et al. (2017) illustrate with an Indian case study that organizational members' ideological positions are articulated with a formal management control system. They emphasized that 'ideological talk' has become the governing principle for accommodating the members into single organizational goals. These ideologies can either be rooted in religious, political, or any form of cultural and social agenda shaping organizational members' compliance, leadership, and involvement in the reproduction of an organizational hierarchy. Unlike in a private firm, NGOs then are vested with established ideologies so that the organizational members are ideologically controlled with little commands from the top management. Hence, members are empowered to realize their ideologically defined vision so that they are, in the same token, committed to lead, to comply, and to be involved, as Kraus et al. (2017) argue, in heading towards the materialization of their ideological vision.

However, as was hinted upon earlier in the chapter, there is a paradox between the NGOs' ideological positions and the INGOs' requirements towards delivering upward accountability. As we mentioned, this paradox has an implication for the shaping of hierarchical forms of management controls. The implication is that INGOs do not want to 'care' about the ideologies, which they call 'philosophies', but want to 'deliver' accounts showing how the NGOs create an economic and social 'impact' from the funders' money; and that 'impact' needs to be quantifiable. In the case of developing countries, development discourses are fortified by these impact policies and other

Strategizing civil society 279

ensuing ideas such as empowerment, participation, and good governance, but the funders want to have a clear quantitative assessment of how these discourses have been materialized in monetary terms because, as we mentioned earlier, they gauge development in business terms. It seems that, on the other hand, local NGOs may want to emphasize more on their cultural and political ideologies and ensuing practices, paying little attention to upward accountability. We shall get back to this accountability issue later in the chapter. For now, we see that this hierarchical arrangement and their underlying disciplinary mechanisms are shaped differently by the unique organizational characteristics of NGOs telling us an interesting story of a unique form of hierarchy which characterizes how ideology shapes hierarchy and hierarchy shapes ideology. In short, the materialization of disciplinary controls (which normally hinge upon 'accounting talks') within the intra-organizational apparatuses is constrained by concurrent ideological positions and vice versa (see Efferin and Hopper 2007).

The battle between the INGOs and local NGOs on this issue of contradiction came to be settled with the arrival of a biopolitical form of governmentality, which aggravated the neoliberal form of accounting with a nuanced view of economic efficiency as an evaluative criterion. This development has a transitional story. At the beginning, we saw that ideologies had a bigger role in shaping an informal type of organization, allowing the members to use more convivial types of controls and evaluations. We then saw that, when funding was needed for expansion and diversification, the organizations naturally sought private-sector types of controls but with continuous attempts to hold onto the original ideological foundations of the civil society organizations. This binary form of the organization faced an issue of delivering accounts upwards which created some uncomfortable relations between donors and civil society organizations. The inevitable consequence was funding cuts. Neoliberalism was indeed a further intensification of this funding regime as it created a global market for funding. Accordingly, peripheral civil society organizations now had to 'compete' for their funding in the charity and development funding markets, submitting competitive bids. In this market environment, now, the notions of quantifiable and assessable impact play a significant role in securing funding, demanding the peripheral NGOs to carefully think of their visions, missions, programme outcomes, and control systems. The NGOs' response to this 'marketization of civil society funding', then, is to reorganize their ideological positions in the light of neoliberal reasoning. That involves cutting out 'unprofitable' and 'difficult to measure outcomes' projects while showing how the rest can be profitable and sustainable. Referring to SSM, Fernando (2011, 131) reports on this issue:

> In response, SSM drastically restructured and reorganised, closing down several unprofitable programs and reducing its staff. Other NGOs did the same ... SSM demanded 'undated resignation letters' from its workers requiring that they state their willingness to resign voluntarily ... thereafter Sarvodaya progressively abandoned most of its social development programs in favour of commercial ventures.

This was how neoliberalism made drastic changes to the functioning of NGOs. Neoliberal reasoning, as was the case in other scenarios we illustrated in previous chapters, has washed away ideological positions, giving rise to commercial logic (Alawattage et al. 2015a, 2015b). On this point, referring to the situation in the early 1990s in the Bangladeshi case of the transformation of NGOs and their implications for gender relations, Feldman (1997, 64) concludes:

280   *Neoliberal trends*

> The growing significance of Jama'at-I-Islami under General Ershad and Khaleda Zia, renewed ties to Pakistan, and the decline in support for Awami League in the decade beginning in 1991, coupled with [the] neoliberal agenda of development assistance during this same period, drew our attention to the growing salience of NGO interests in the political discourse and practice of development in the country ... On the one hand, women signal the evils of westernization and the loss of the economic and political dominance of petty bourgeois rural interests; on the other hand, women have become the focus of NGO support, making process of commodification and new forms of market intervention possible.

Hence, despite what the NGO discourse of gender relation is, neoliberalism has provided strong impulses for its commodification in the service of global capitalism. Given this transformation is salient, management accounting and control mechanisms are now animated by this inevitable neoliberal reasoning. For example, in the context of microfinance projects, meetings with government agencies, compilation of macro-level data for poverty management purposes from micro-level surveys, form filling for micro-credit purposes, and the evaluation of the progress of women's microfinance-related projects, etc. now constitute various forms of biopolitical accounting.

In this biopolitical move, there is a subtle difference between disciplinary controls and biopolitical controls. In a regime of biopower, norms have an increasingly important role as was the case with disciplinary power. On the matter of disciplinary power, Foucault (2008) considers 'normalizing judgement' or normalization to be as important as surveillance and examination. The process of normalization involves the establishment of boundaries of accepted behaviour. A norm becomes a standard to which individuals are expected to conform. In disciplinary power, normalization functions by continuously setting standards to be accomplished and against which individuals are evaluated. The consequence is that individuals can be compared, with the aim of enhancing their utility as individuals, internalizing their own surveillance, and positioning them with others of a similar orientation. This process increases the efficiency of power, as individuals become self-disciplined and assume the responsibility for controlling their own selves. In contrast, in the context of biopolitics, as Foucault (1978, 144) considers, 'a normalizing society is the historical outcome of a technology of power centred on life'. As a technique of biopower, normalization arises from the socio-political authority of statistics such that 'the concept of healthy equilibrium and other associated norms became a regulative principle for the new science of political economy' (Munro 2012, 346). The regulation of population thus requires a series of mechanisms that 'qualify, measure, appraise, and hierarchize' (Foucault 1978, 144). In this way, biopower brings life and its mechanisms into explicit calculation and renders it subject to new forms of control and administration.

In this form of control and administration, in the case of microfinance, NGOs manage to make the productive surplus circulate through the immaterial labour. By immaterial labour, Hardt and Negri (2000) mean that labour can also be characterized with the workers' communicative, symbolic, and affective attachments. For example, in respect of a microfinance project in Sri Lanka, Alawattage et al. (forthcoming) show that there is a process of immaterialization of labour which displaces and distributes the primary functions of capital – the management of production while bearing the risk associated therein. As a result, the banker who provides funding for entrepreneurial engagement would not bear the risk or manage that enterprise. Instead, microfinance

Strategizing civil society 281

technologies operate as a biopolitical mechanism allowing the borrowers to be workers as well as entrepreneurs. Along with their immaterial labour, they bear the risk and manage the production on behalf of the capital owners, i.e. the global-level microfinance institutions. That said, microfinance enables us to have the capital's primary function distributed to these borrowers. Biopolitics thus decentralizes the controls by distributing the risks and return to labour, by immaterializing the labour in its affective, emotional, and communicative forms.

In this way, NGOs from the 1990s were now subject to biopolitical controls while disciplinary control practices continued alongside them. We have little evidence to suggest how these two forms of controls were articulated. Nevertheless, it is hard to conclude that biopolitical controls replaced disciplinary controls altogether. However, we can remark that normalizing technologies such as training, meeting, form filling, record-keeping, performance evaluation, physical supervision, collection of photographs, etc. are all playing a vital role in 'neoliberalized' NGOs (Feldman 1997), making them amenable to national level analyses and to the global purposes of the circulation of capital, despite them standing as 'contradictory enterprises' (Sanders 2012). However, it does not mean that the possible domination of biopolitical controls over disciplinary ones has been silently and unproblematically accepted by local NGOs. As reported on by Apostol (2015) with an in-depth case analysis of a Romanian scenario, there are counter-accounts – there are corners of resistance, critiques, and counter-arguments against the commodification of NGO services. By creating such counter-accounts, local activities hope that there can be implications for democratic changes in civil society and, in turn, NGOs can be emancipated in terms of their noble goals and visions. Whether management accounting plays a biopolitical role as Western donors expect, or whether the same can be influenced to achieve such emancipatory potential, is an issue waiting to be investigated.

12.4 The process of strategizing

Now, we have an important question. How should NGOs be strategized amid all these contradictions and counter-accounts? We may approach this question by referring to the term strategizing that we outlined in Chapter 5. By strategizing, we mean how organizations, communities, people, and even the state operate competitively by performing according to market principles. We have understood that this market is not just a place for exchanging values through the forces of demand and supply as envisaged by classical political economists. Instead, the neoliberal market operates like an epistemic site continuously creating ideas, products, patterns of consumption, and even ways of living. It also operates like a mirror through a sense of jurisdiction and veridiction, showing what should be done by managers in the light of indexes, benchmarks, and the volumes of statistics provided. In this sense, strategizing means making organizations competitive in the market (or market-like environment in which competition is enacted) by ensuring that they possess the necessary skills, resources, processes, and mindset to position themselves in relation to competitive forces. So, strategizing must occur by shaping performance and enacting behaviour according to this very principle of the neoliberal market.

Civil society, as it has evolved into the current form we outlined earlier, is now being transformed into a market, where various civil society organizations need to compete for their survival and success. This competition is enabled both (a) by possibility of funding civil society organizations and 'selling' their services, and (b) in

282 Neoliberal trends

the epistemic sense where civil society organization performances are now subject to perpetual comparison and disciplinary gaze within performance league tables and reported 'impact stories'. As an epistemic site, it enacts jurisdiction and veridiction roles through the discourses of development enabled through league tables and other comparative market performance indexes. Together with INGOs, transnational epistemic communities such as the WTO, World Bank, IMF, OECD, and UN promote and disseminate epistemic rationales and propagate the mechanisms of how civil society organizations must perform better and how they can strategically contribute to the global production of capitalism by being aligned to the aspirations of the neoliberal market (cf. Hopper et al. 2017). To this end, global epistemic and development funding institutions have promulgated a series of products such as best practices, models of well-functioning NGOs, myriads of performance measurement indicators, survey forms, audit protocols, reporting standards for NGOs, masses of training manuals, and so forth (Hickey and Mohan 2004). Strategizing means the deployment of these tools and enacting the conduct of civil society members' everyday behaviour towards the production and reproduction of global capital, which is the 'business of development' for some INGOs (Fernando 2011). To illustrating this notion of strategizing in some detail, Figure 12.1 elaborates four interrelated elements. Earlier in the chapter, we mentioned some of these roles in defining and characterizing the notion of civil society, but we revisit them here to articulate the notion of strategizing in the light of these four elements.

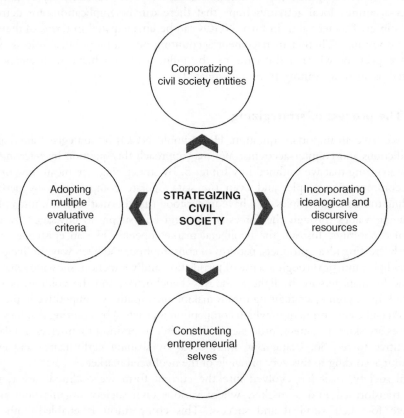

Figure 12.1 Strategizing civil society

12.4.1 Corporatizing civil society entities

We shall start with the notion that civil society is now being transformed into corporatized entities amenable to the processes of strategizing. We know that in a corporatized entity there are formal meetings where people discuss matters and make important decisions; there are reports and records that are used to provide justifications for what they do and for the reproduction of practices; there are office bearers who assume leadership roles to run the stipulated affairs; and there are relationships that are maintained with other apparatuses, e.g. state authorities on matters relating to regulation and compliance. Neoliberal civil society is operating in exactly the same manner, showing that it has now assumed the status of a corporate entity. In classical terms, civil society connects radical individualization with a rigorous collectivism, which Habermas (1989, 27) calls 'the sphere of private people com[ing] together as a public'. In neoliberal terms, this combined form of social setting has now been corporatized to formally connect individualism to the collectivism upon which a market is set up. As this market is an epistemic site for producing products, services, and consumption, this corporatizing tendency goes hand in hand with these neoliberal aims. For example, when civil society is organized as microfinance groups, the 'animator' (i.e. the bank employees who initiate and oversee microfinance 'self-help' groups) who goes into rural villages in less developed countries organizes the villagers in groups and then formalizes the groups into village-level societies where the members meet regularly and discuss matters of concern using books of accounts, minutes, and other records (Alawattage et al. forthcoming). In such meetings, people talk about their individual concerns, trajectories, and achievements, transforming those meetings into individualizing processes. At the same time, they discuss as a group what needs to be done to get the most out of ensuing opportunities in various realms of developments, enterprises, and innovations, thereby transforming their civic associations into a collectivizing and economizing process. Collectively, they corporatize their civil relationships.

As such, these attempts at corporatizing entail two types of interrelated mechanisms: a process of individualization and a process of collectivizing. On the question of the process of individualization, contemporary NGOs' activities are largely aimed at local-level capacity-building programmes (Fernando 2011). Under this, individuals are trained, changed, and disciplined for them to become effective and efficient participants of the neoliberal market. As we will see later, this transformation leads them to become more accountable for and to themselves through the ethos of market thinking, which is institutionalized not only in individuals' psyches but also in the immediate social settings in which they operate (e.g. microfinance self-help groups). In these developments, individuals are shown that they have rights, that these rights must be recognized, and that they must work according to these rights while exploring funding opportunities for enacting these rights through local projects (Apostol 2015; Gray et al. 2006). This is a learning programme for the individuals to improve their understanding of 'excelling in the market'. Lee and Cassell (2017) investigate how this can be made possible through trade union representatives in the UK context. In the context of microfinance in developing countries, these individuals are trained to know that they need an understanding of how finances can be supplied, used, and managed, and how families and lives surrounding these circumstances can be managed, produced, and reproduced – this leads them to manage their lives according to market rules (Hardt and Negri 2000).

284 *Neoliberal trends*

On the other hand, corporatizing occurs by forming and organizing collective groups, societies, and even partnering with private-sector organizations. This process of formalization has been a salient feature in the aggravation of civil society activities through the neoliberal strategies of making the collectives business-like entities entrusted with entrepreneurial engagements. For example, as Kaldor et al. (2012) note, there are NGOs which develop partnerships with private corporations and state apparatuses, become 'professionalized' by adopting management principles, and seek new forms of corporations in developmental projects and capacity-building trajectories. In microfinance projects, as Alawattage et al. (forthcoming) illustrate, villages are being accepting of the World Bank-sponsored state interventions to develop hierarchically organized village-based societies. Returning to the theme of strategizing, we can discern that, through these formalization processes, both as individuals and collectives, civil society is being configured as a network of organizations directed towards serving the neoliberal markets, translating members' engagements into ideas and products that can be sold for funding purposes. Such organizations are then able to continue their existence competitively because there is an 'industry' of NGOs (Gray et al. 2006).

12.4.2 Incorporating ideological and discursive resources

The above corporatizing agenda through the processes of individualization and collectivization is simultaneously rooted in a form of 'culture governance' (Dean 2003). It is about incorporating the individual to the collective through established cultural institutions such as religion, family, and any other local or indigenous institutions. It is to legitimize the functioning of civil society and to enhance its visibility to fundraising activities and related entrepreneurial engagements. We do not have the space to explore in detail the development of this agenda, but we can refer to some discussions about how these cultural institutions have become part and parcel of neoliberal governance that has led to the development of a strategizing trajectory. What has happened in the last few decades in this regard is that civil society organizations, on the one hand, have legitimized their presence by forming their activities around cultural, religious, and local ways of doing things. For example, Kraus et al. (2017) show that local religion was used to justify their existence and the continuation of their healthcare activities in rural India. They emphasized that healthcare organizations like these strategically combine formal management controls with these ideological foundations to eradicate the problems of resistance to formal controls and to maximize the rationale of its sustainability as a worthy civil society organization. Similarly, Joannides et al. (2015) illustrate how social work is articulated and justified on religious grounds while management accounting is implicated in mundane practices. Religion as a social institution is important here for the external legitimation of what people do, but at the same time, under neoliberalism, this legitimation is also translated into financial purposes.

While religion has given rise to such justifications and legitimations, local value systems rooted in family ties and local relationships have now been translated into a locally valuable social capital for the enactment of civil society activities (Chenhall et al. 2010). By social capital, as Woolcock and Narayan (2000) define, it is about the relationships rooted in norms and values that enable people to act collectively. Writing on the contributions of George Akerlof, Michael Spence, and Joseph Stiglitz Akerlof, the Nobel Laureate, Lofgren et al. (2002) observe that market failures can be eradicated by using social capital as a coping mechanism, because it can provide some tacit knowledge for people to work together. It can enhance management controls through a system of 'peer monitoring'. It can generate an alternative incentive system and a morale for people to work efficiently. Again, this has been exploited by microfinance programmes in developing countries where such social capital is more pervasive than their financial capital. Roy (2010) observes that social capital adds a new value to the work of credit associations through which members exploit their relations and improve their income levels. BRAC in Bangladesh invented the same in the name of 'process capital', which governs the ties between local women that ensure the success of the microfinance programmes (Abed and Matin 2007). All such accounts show that civil society is now a terrain of neoliberal experimental development with alternative forms of capital, as is much evidenced in the case of microfinance initiatives in developing counties. This is a strategic intent in that, when the markets fail, supplementary mechanisms are used to apply the same market principles albeit differently.

In addition, there are a number of discursive resources that provide extra ideological strength. For example, since the 1980s, the notion of good governance (in development) has been developed in parallel with the development of corporate governance ideas. UNDP (2007) provides clear guidance on understanding what we should mean by governance, which has three dimensions: economic (related to economic decision making), political (decision making relating to policy making), and administrative (the system of policy implementation). While this is akin to Solomon's (2007) ideas about corporate governance, good governance encompasses the processes and structures that guide political and socio-economic relationships. Consequently, UNDP has recognized that governance should have the following elements: (1) accountability; (2) transparency; (3) the rule of law; (4) participation; (5) responsiveness; (6) consensus orientation; (7) equity; (8) effectiveness and efficiency; and (9) strategic vision. Similarly, as Blair (2000) notes, the participative mantra has been a key component of development since the 1970s through which people's participation is valued and taken as a mechanism for implementing many projects. Participative budgeting, participative planning, social auditing, and so forth have become part and parcel of this broader agenda. Civil society organizations have exploited these ideas not only to justify what they do but also to create a market for generating the production, circulation, and consumption of capital through such ideas. Management accounting and control mechanisms have been very much interlinked with these discursive practices where the notion of participation has been used to produce planning and budgets, maintain control, and undertake performance evaluation tasks (see Rossmann and Shanahan 2012).

Returning to our strategizing theme, we see the above three interrelated elements (i.e. systems of economic decision making, systems of political decision making relating to policy making, and administrative systems of policy implementation), coupled with cultural, religious, and social ideologies, have become very powerful in reinventing the market and accommodating it for neoliberal governmentality. Economic, political, and administrative discourses and practices have been used not only to supplement the existing market and regulative mechanisms but also as an alternative way of conceiving the function of the market. As a result, as Easterly (2007) argues, the 'free market' would work for development, because the poor could now draw on the above 'cultural governance' to produce and reproduce in their own ways. He shows that, although the poor have no assets, this neoliberal move to the creation of a market in these ideas has made the poor an asset for the creation of wealth. The wealth so created is 'empowerment money' as Elyachar (2002) describe

286 *Neoliberal trends*

with reference to the context of Egypt. This is a novel way of strategizing when it comes to the notion of strategizing civil society.

12.4.3 Constructing entrepreneurial selves

On and off, we have pointed out that civil society is now making individuals entrepreneurial in the service of global capital and in the production of lives (Hardt and Negri 2000). This development is now being described as 'constructing entrepreneurial selves' (Alawattage et al. forthcoming). Through translating the developmental and political form of civil society to one that is governed by market logic, individuals therein are now reconstructing this logic. As the markets are functional on the individual body, and as the individuals are functional on market logic, the body and the market have become inseparable. Unlike the 'good old days' where people were engaged more in work for their own benefit within the 'self-sufficient' economy, individuals are now being trained to become standalone enterprises (Roy 2010).

However, this does not happen without some tension. On the one hand, these individuals wish to maintain their cultural and traditional modes of living. On the other, they cannot do this for its own sake because, in developing countries, they are now told (by international development agencies and local government which depends on their funding) that they cannot live without being entrepreneurial, without being funded by the international funding agencies. They would have been happy if either government jobs were offered or there were large-scale industrial developments to offer them stable employment opportunities (as was the case with Western industrial development in its early phases and even now). But the state is now being moved away from the welfare economy, and rural development based on large-scale industrial investments is in rapid decline. These industrial and welfare-based developments, where people are considered to be the material labour, are now considered to be out-of-date in the neoliberal regime where development is envisaged as transforming labourers into entrepreneurs. Hence, making entrepreneurs through civil society activities is inevitable and, as a strategy, is happening silently. Roy (2010, 73) describes this as follows:

> The great texts and voices of millennium development are deafeningly silent on the matter of production, converting the figure of the worker into that of heroic entrepreneur. It can be argued of course that in the millennial age, production itself is pure fiction, materializing only in the volatile circuits of finance capital rather than in the fields and factories.

That said, the individual so transformed into an entrepreneur, is now ready to produce to generate finance capital. Whatever s/he produces, that production is linked to this volatile circuit of finance capital because everybody must find finance for these entrepreneurial activities including whatever roles the NGOs play. Again, in the context of microfinance, individuals work to earn a return on the finance they consume so that it is a 'production' and, to the extent that these individuals earn that return, they are 'productive', as Shahe Emran et al. (2007) argue.

In order to produce for the global finance capital in this way, civil society activities have now been remodelled with the help of ideas labelled as 'capacity building programmes' (Fernando 2011). As we mentioned elsewhere in the chapter, these include training programmes for bookkeeping, marketing, business management, leadership, negotiation skills, and so forth. While these programmes are sponsored by transnational financial institutions such as the World Bank and the IMF, local and national government look after their modes operandi. NGOs then work for these governments achieving the aims of those international bodies. The individuals are very prepared to take risks and manage their finances on behalf of these financial agencies rather than these agencies themselves taking up that burden. Instead of just giving money away to be distributed as welfare packages, money is now made available for productive functions through NGOs' activities, disarticulating the rationale of constructing 'beneficiaries' in a welfare sense (cf. O'Leary 2017). Referring to the situation in India, Prahalad (2005, 1) argues that the NGOs and microfinance services are there to encourage the possibilities for production rather than delivering welfare. Hence, the time has now come to stop seeing these people 'as victims or as a burden for the government'. They are, instead, now resilient and creative entrepreneurs taking risks on behalf of finance capital. As a result, for governments, there are no political or social obligations. Instead, this a new move (through microfinance initiatives), and it is 'financially viable' (Roy 2010).

This transformation is part of the process of strategizing. It is strategic in that individuals are linked to a discursive formation of the financialization of the poor through the organizational mechanisms of civil society activities and the related programmes of NGOs. It is also strategic in that these individuals are now seeing their future in terms of their ability to make their loan repayments, complete their prolonged house-building projects, finance their children's education, and so forth. To that extent, they are 'strategically futuristic' and qualified as 'entrepreneurs in waiting' (Roy 2010). Although they do not become rich, the strategy still works as long as they can earn interest and repay their loans. When things are not going well, NGO activities will continue with their programmes to enhance the individuals' capacity to get them back on track over and over again. In this way, market failures are maintained along with the cultural governance mechanisms we discussed earlier, and the poor are eagerly and impatiently waiting to be rich. Management controls of NGOs, business plans of individuals, and individual and collective accounts of societies then become peculiar management accounting practices embedded in this system of civil society engagement.

12.4.4 Adopting multiple evaluative criteria

The final element in Figure 12.1 is the adoption of multiple evaluative criteria. By multiple criteria, we mean the actors' diverse and even conflicting ideas that are now mobilized in maintaining controls and delivering accountability on the matters of civil society engagements. This is an important strategic dimension because the notion of strategizing only occurs when intended (or unintended) compromises are materialized in decision making and in control areas. Compromises are crucial in the civil society sector because, as we saw in the chapter earlier, there are diverse aims and values which shape the nature of controls and accountability practices in these organizations (Chenhall et al. 2013; Hall and O'Dwyer 2017). We shall look at this phenomenon in some detail.

The ideological diversity, as we pointed out earlier, has always been a salient feature of these organizations. It encompasses at least two opposing objectives. On the one hand, there are social movements representing a number of social and cultural objectives such as human rights, gender balances, poverty alleviation, local

288 *Neoliberal trends*

developments, and so forth. When it comes to evaluating performance, civil society organizations focus on these social dimensions as the basis for developing evaluative criteria. These criteria aim to demonstrate the extent of the achievement of those social aims. Hence, measurements such as people's satisfaction levels of these activities, degree of progress made in the achievement of social goals, and the level of social solidarity guaranteed by local programmes, for example, are crucial in these evaluations. These can be 'expressive' criteria in qualitive details (Chenhall et al. 2017). Such details are needed to show the beneficiaries the extent to which civil society organizations achieve their social and cultural objectives. Otherwise it is hard to legitimize the existence of those organizations within the localities in which they operate. So, civil society is reconstructed as a space within which such information is created for legitimacy purposes and for delivering such information to the grassroots level. This form of accountability is now known as the social form of accountability (Hall and O'Dwyer 2017; O'Dwyer and Unerman 2008; Roberts 1991) or downward accountability (Ebrahim 2003).

However, such accounting practices are less meaningful to the donors who seek more transparency about civil society activities. Instead, they need objective rather than expressive accounts with credible evidence showing how funds are utilized and how the original aims of funding requirements match with this utilization. These accounts must be generated through formal organizational arrangements including a proper accounting system being embedded in the organizational hierarchy, what Roberts calls a hierarchical or functional form of accountability (Roberts 1991). Such 'functional' accountability is short term, essentially technical and rational, and concentrates on tangibles, like expended resources and immediate accomplishments. It is often driven by the concerns of donors and also governments and foundation trustees (O'Dwyer and Unerman 2008). When such upwards accounts are not delivered, or the details are not sufficiently justifiable, donors may enhance their mechanisms to remedy the accounts. For instance, as we mentioned early on in the chapter, INGOs now tend to set up a 'donor consortium' where both donors and local NGOs sit together to discuss funding requirements and the delivery of accounts (Fernando 2011). Seen through neoliberal lenses, NGO funding then forms part of the 'business' of development rather than ensuring rights-based accountability (O'Leary 2017). Nevertheless, this mechanism does not take away the tension. Instead, the tension is deployed so that civil society is considered a strategic unit.

The management of tension is now considered a strategic intent. Researchers are now beginning to establish the argument that such tensions can be useful because 'dissonance' can be organized for 'innovations' rather than disputes in the functioning of NGOs (Chenhall et al. 2013). Under such circumstances, multiple evaluative criteria – both functional and social dimensions – are used to construct compromises. In this way, civil society becomes a terrain of debate and a laboratory for innovations. Sanders (2012, 182) celebrates this phenomenon by encouraging practitioners to deploy such tension-led approaches. He writes:

[s]cholars can more successfully understand the organizing practices of non-profit work and make better sense of non-profit marketization. This theoretical move is made easier by the work of Trethewey and Ashcraft (2004), who have developed a framework for understanding the 'dilemmatic character of organizing' (p.81) as a normal outcome.

Strategizing civil society 289

This is not much different to what Stark (2011) describes as the 'sense of dissonance'. It is about doing things better, while frictions are accommodated in debates and disagreements are used to make better choices and produce more effective organizational outcomes. In civil society organizations, both social and functional accountability demands are then considered together to materialize a process towards making the organization much more pluralistic and democratic while giving due consideration to neoliberal aims.

This shows us how strategizing occurs in the context of the neoliberal civil society. As you can now see, there is an unavoidable but necessary tension here. Neoliberalism travels and imposes market principles whatever the terrain. It transforms unchartered territories by accommodating both the economic and the social. The non-economic dimensions such as social relations, cultural traditions, established values, and religious backgrounds are used for the very purposes of the economy, sometimes directly and explicitly, sometimes indirectly and implicitly. Management accounting and controls are used in whatever way for the purpose of materializing neoliberal aims. In such instances, both disciplinary mechanisms and biopolitical technologies are used. In short, strategizing civil society is about deploying such multiple evaluative criteria for managing tensions and exploiting frictions in the materialization of neoliberal aims.

12.5 Summary and conclusions: linking civil society accountability to management accounting

This chapter began by defining and describing what we mean by civil society. We understood that it lies between the state and the economy for getting individuals organized for collective purposes. We also understood that it has evolved into its current form where neoliberalism has shaped its position in the economy and society. This evolution has brought us a series of issues surrounding the matters of management accounting practices and accountability forms. They are matters of concern because civil society is, on the one hand, a social institution guaranteeing members' expectations about their welfare, rights, and development. On the other, it is an economic entity using others' funds and being entrusted with the production of efficiency in the light of market logic. Hence, civil society has become a problematic area for strategizing. We have seen that corporatizing efforts, entrepreneurial developments, promoting ideologies, and discourses are strategically deployed to make this organizational space a vibrant social setting in which to materialize these strategic intentions.

Management accounting thus becomes a matter of realizing accountability. As Roberts (1991) argues, accountability can take two complementary forms: the function/individualizing form and the socializing form. Under functional-individualizing accountability, the individual self (the administrator or the contractor in a local development context) is constructed as a 'subject' to be visualized by external parties on behalf of the members of the civil society. This visibility is created through which citizens (or media on their behalf) provide judgements, analyses, comparisons, and, even, exercise whistleblowing. By doing this, local NGOs are individualized, judged, and evaluated. In this way, the self (in NGOs) is seen through the lenses of citizens who point their fingers at 'individuals' for both their good and bad behaviours. Performance reports attested by the mechanisms of internal controls, internal audits, and face-to-face actions within NGOs become a 'powerful field of visibility' (Roberts 2001) for

290   *Neoliberal trends*

constructing these 'governable administrators who act upon accountability by providing "credible" stories of their governance affairs'. When things go wrong, citizens, media agencies, and whistleblowers may take the necessary actions to hold the individuals accountable.

The other process is the socialization process of accountability that good governance has embraced with the arrival of a new era in development since the 1990s. While the individualizing process of accountability operates remotely as a form of 'action at a distance', the socialization process of accountability operates on a face-to-face basis as a form of interdependent relationship. These are rather lateral, reciprocal, and intimate relations occurring in real time through the mundane processes which we highlighted before. This is a kind of construction of the self in relation to others – a form of good governance. For this purpose, the hierarchically concentrated administrative units must complement the lateral relations which NGOs have begun to cultivate. Hence, in its ideal form, citizens must be embedded in decision-making processes as observers (like having non-executive directors on corporate boards) who can oversee the processes in place and report to local communities.

The relationship between management accounting and accountability within civil society organizations is thus fiddly. In relation to functional accountability, management accounting has become an input providing the necessary environment for maintaining order through internal measurements and controls. In relation to social accountability, management accounting is often intermingled with the processes of social account-ability, and sometimes management accounting is an output of accountability because the latter plays a transcendental role showing what is worthy and what is not. Such dimensions are still waiting to be researched – an interesting area to explore (see Hall and O'Dwyer 2017).

Assignments

These assignments are meant to extend your knowledge beyond what you understand from this chapter. These are not simply revision questions. The content covered in this chapter is necessary but will not be sufficient in attempting these tasks. Therefore, you are required to do some extra reading in attempting these tasks.

1. **Thematic essay:**
   'Civil society has now passed from a site of development to a site of biopolitics'.
   Referring to recent developments of microfinance, write an essay, of approximately 3,000 words, on the above theme articulating how this transformation can be linked to neoliberalism.
2. **Poster:**
   Draw a poster showing how frictions play a role in relation to a different type of management accounting practice within a civil society organization. Give special reference to the ideas put forward by Sanders (2012) and Trethewey and Ashcraft (2004).
3. **Presentation:**
   Prepare a set of PowerPoint slides, together with notes if necessary, for a 30-minute presentation on the following theme:
   'Enmeshing management accounting with both disciplinary controls and biopolitical roles'.

Strategizing civil society 291

4. **Extended bibliography:**
   Write an extended bibliography on the development of a new form of management accounting in NGOs and civil society. For this, you need to do a literature survey in major accounting journals and edited books where critical accounting research is published. Organize the bibliography into a table in the following format.

Bibliographic info	Nature of the paper/book chapter (e.g. conceptual/theoretical, empirical, a response to a previous publication)	Major arguments, conclusions, and contributions

5. **Literature review:**

> We have elaborated on a number of key themes associated with control and accountability in NGOs and non-profits ... These comprise the connection between values and beliefs and control and accountability, the link between control, accountability and transformation, and the role of stakeholder engagement in control and accountability processes ... They have enabled us to propose future theoretical and empirical research directions which could enrich our knowledge of how accounting emerges and operates in diverse organizational contexts with significant societal impacts.
>
> (Hall and O'Dwyer 2017, 4)

Write a review essay elaborating this statement. Give due consideration to the importance of enhancing our understanding of management accounting operating in frictions and disagreements between organizational managers and other stakeholders.

13 Neoliberalization of corporate governance

13.1 Setting the scene

In the preceding chapters, we discussed how management accounting has changed its form in response to the problematic of neoliberalism which reassembled the terrains of the market, organization, and the factory. We explained that management accounting is now externalized, first by becoming market driven and, second, through policy debates of national and global competitiveness. This chapter explores this policy connection further by looking at how the agenda of corporate governance (CG) invades the territories of management accounting and shapes its orientation. Closely connected to other discourses such as strategy, sustainability, and accountability, CG has become an inescapable politico-managerial discourse challenging and changing management accounting's perceived epistemological rationales, mechanisms, practices, and processes. Accordingly, the chapter illustrates how political and epistemological effects of CG challenge management accounting's traditional scope, which is governed by the 'disciplinary controls' within the 'old spirit' of capitalism.

CG has now become ubiquitous and is a buzz word in business jargon. Its meaning and application is wide-ranging from attempts to assess the efficacy of corporate boards to the ways in which the political state needs to regulate corporations. It advocates a set of codes and practices (e.g. OECD 2015b; World Bank 2000; Financial Reporting Council 2012) and presents itself as a mode of: self-governance of corporate affairs; distribution of rights and responsibilities of stakeholders; mitigating social inequalities; balancing between competing interests of stakeholders; making firms accountable to society at large; and mitigating the agency problem between owners and managers (see Lemmon and Lins 2003). In the recent past, the sudden rise of CG discourses has been a political response, in the form of 'soft-regulation', to a 'systemic bubble' that burst in the heightened neoliberalization of corporate entities during the 1980s. The financial bubble, once celebrated as the triumph of financial capitalism, burst as the credit crunch took hold with disastrous consequences due to a series of corporate scandals such as the collapse of Enron and WorldCom in the USA and HIH in Australia. However, much before the credit crunch, the weaknesses governing neoliberal capitalism started to appear with the worldwide wave of privatizations, the takeover wave of the 1980s, the deregulation and integration of capital markets, and the 1997 East Asia financial crisis (Johnson et al. 2000; Lemmon and Lins 2003; The Tyson Task Force on the Recruitment and Development of Non-Executive Directors 2003). The politico-regulatory response was the promulgation of legal provisions such as the Sarbanes-Oxley Act of 2002 in the USA, reports recommending best practices such as the Cadbury Report (Cadbury Commission 1992) in the UK, and codes of practice

Neoliberalization of corporate governance 293

such as the Principles of Corporate Governance by the OECD (2015b). Those corporate collapses and resultant regulatory responses then formed an epistemological space for debating the problematic manner in which the world had become overly dependent upon the honesty, integrity, ethics, financial solvency, and capacity of their shareholders to monitor and govern the affairs of the corporate management of large profit-seeking economic enterprises. This created a whole new discursive regime of governance in which consultants, academics, professional bodies, transnational organizations (e.g. the World Bank, IMF, OECD), trans-governmental apparatuses (e.g. EU, ASEAN countries), national governments, and, of course, corporations, are all now engaged.

The CG discourse, on the one hand, has been presented as a form of legitimation through which confidence in the capital markets is to be rebuilt, advocates prescribing that the CG crisis must be addressed, weak forms of governance should be refurbished, and confidence in market signals should be restored (Rezaee 2009). On the other hand, individual firms see the importance of this discourse in terms of enhancing their capacity to further accumulate capital – a way of embracing external legitimation for the purposes of tightening internal controls (Stein 2008). This means that CG discourses have simultaneously received both an external focus on legitimation and governance and an internal focus on control and discipline. Strategies adopted between these two extremes of external legitimations and internal controls are now being converged to form a neoliberal rationality of CG based on a global policy agenda (see Aguilera and Cuervo-Cazurra 2004). Both external legitimations and internal controls are embedded in varying principles, processes, and mechanisms of CG. They all operate in the context of the politics of regulation and deregulation, socio-cultural contradictions, and (ir)rationalities of market forces.

The aim of this chapter is to unpack the discourses of CG in order to explain how they reconfigure the traditional boundaries of management accounting. Rather than a mere stock-taking of the literature in terms of how CG produces firm performance, as functionalists normally do (see Aguilera and Jackson 2003), our attempt here is to explore: (1) the epistemic politics of CG in which internal issues of control are connected to the external political problems of regulation and governance; (2) the processes of organizational enactments through which external enforcements are considered, incorporated, and legitimized; (3) the mechanisms of the biopolitical transformation of corporate controls which replace or supplement disciplinary controls; and (4) the reconfiguration of management accounting in the light of the neoliberal rationalities of governance and security. Hence, the chapter is structured in five main sections:

1. Section 13.2 articulates the neoclassical economic theorization of CG with reference to the so called 'agency problem' and then moves on to explain how and why this economic understanding of CG has now been extended to capture a wider set of socio-political issues beyond the agency problem between the shareholders and managers. Here, we draw on the CG literature and see what elements came to be prominent in the definition of CG and how CG then came to be a way of relating the organizational practices to issues beyond the owner-manager nexus.
2. Section 13.3 offers a biopolitical view on CG. Here we explain how a new regime of neoliberal governance and security emerged. We contrast this regime with its predecessor – the liberal disciplinary regime where the focus was on the state's territorial integrity. In the new neoliberal regime, we explain, instead of the state's territorial integrity, the security question is being redirected towards a doctrine that living populations and individuals ought to constitute the new object of security.

294 *Neoliberal trends*

Here we also explain the way in which this new regime of security and governance gave rise to a form of soft regulation structured around the apparatuses of the global political state.

3. Section 13.4 discusses the intra-organizational implications of neoliberal governance and security. Here our attention is specifically on the way in which neoliberal apparatuses of governance and security influence organizational legitimacy and accountability. Here we identify three distinct modes of accountabilities: individualizing, socializing, and the biopolitical.

4. Section 13.5 synthesizes the way in which neoliberal governance and security apparatuses penetrate into management accounting practices and rationalities. There our special attention is on the recursive layers through which macro-political elements of the neoliberal social order connect with the organizational practices of management accounting.

5. Section 13.6 concludes the chapter with a summary.

13.2 Neoclassical origin of corporate governance ideas and its neoliberal extensions

There is a managerial as well as political context for CG ideas to evolve. The managerial context has traditionally been well captured by the so-called 'agency problem' or the problem of stewardship in agency theory based on explanations of organizational control and governance. From an agency theory perspective, a corporation represents the separation of management from the owners. This then creates a situation in which the owners do not have full information and insight into what actually goes on in the firm and whether the managers are indeed acting to maximize the shareholders' wealth. This is the well-explained condition of information asymmetry which, when coupled with certain behavioural dispositions of the agents (such as opportunism, greed, risk, and work aversion), would eventually result in the agency problem – the possibility of a morally hazardous situation where the agents maximize their own interests but at the cost of their principals. Given that neoclassical economics always understands and measures the efficiency (and inefficiency) by the degree to which profit is maximized, agents maximizing their own interests is considered as a 'fundamental economic problem' of gross inefficiency. Therefore, the neoclassical economic argument is that specific mechanisms should be put in place to mitigate it. CG is the term that agency theorists commonly use to name such mechanisms that resolve the conflict of interests between the owners and the managers. This is the nucleus of the neoclassical economic rationalization of CG (see Baiman 1990, 2006). However, it should also be noted that agency theory is equally used to explain the intrafirm control issues, that is to explain the ways in which the agency problem between managers and their subordinates (vis-à-vis owners and managers or between majority shareholders and minority shareholders) is to be mitigated. Such intrafirm issues of information asymmetry, the agency problem, and moral hazard are often captured by the mainstream management accounting literature as a problem of management control (see Baiman 1990, 2006; and also Armstrong 1991).

This agency theory view of governance is still the pervasive, albeit implicit, ontological, and epistemological stance that regulators, law makers, accounting professional bodies, as well as international development organizations (such as the OECD and Word Bank) take. Following neoclassical economic interpretations, they always offer a political superiority to the shareholders and, hence, presume that the primary objective of CG is to safeguard the interests of the shareholders (vis-à-vis other stakeholders). For example, consider the following two definitions given by 'authoritative' bodies trying to define CG with 'legalistic' and 'regulatory' dispositions placed upon them:

> The role of corporate governance is to protect and advance interests of the shareholders through setting the strategic direction of a company and appointing and monitoring capable management to achieve this.
>
> (Walker Review 2009, 19)

The definition provided by the Financial Reporting Council (2012, 1) in the UK 'Corporate Governance Code' is a further extension and example of this agency theory view, which privileges shareholders over other stakeholders:

> Corporate governance is the system by which companies are directed and controlled. Boards of directors are responsible for the governance of their companies. The shareholders' role in governance is to appoint the directors and the auditors and to satisfy themselves that an appropriate governance structure is in place. The responsibilities of the board include setting the company's strategic aims, providing the leadership to put them into effect, supervising the management of the business and reporting to shareholders on their stewardship. The board's actions are subject to laws, regulations and the shareholders in general meeting.

In a broader sense, the agency theory-based legalistic/regulatory understanding of CG mainly relies on two interrelated mechanisms of CG: the board of directors and the audit function. The conflicting interests between the shareholders and the management, as well as between the majority and minority shareholders, are to be mitigated through: an 'appropriate' composition of the board of directors (e.g. the inclusion of independent directors), the clarification of the duties and functions of the board directors and its subcommittees (see Financial Reporting Council 2012), ensuring auditor independence, and the codification of board members' conduct so that it is principled. In other words, the assumption is that the conflicting interests can be sufficiently mitigated through a proper contractual and monitoring system between the management and the shareholders and a well-composed and codified board of directors. This would then minimize not only the information asymmetry between the management and the shareholders but also the economic inefficiencies arising from the agency problem. This means that 'the board' is conceived as the fundamental structural arrangement of governing the management. The board should operate as an internal government placed between the shareholders and the managers to ensure the maximization of shareholders' wealth, which is indeed the overarching normativity of capitalism. A typical arrangement of the board, its subcommittees, and the audit function as the primary mechanisms of governance, is illustrated in Figure 13.1. As Figure 13.1 illustrates, there are a number of checks and balances to ensure that shareholder interests are protected. This echoes the definition of CG provided by Parkinson (1993, 159): 'a process of supervision and control ... intended to ensure that the company's management acts in accordance with the interest of shareholders'.

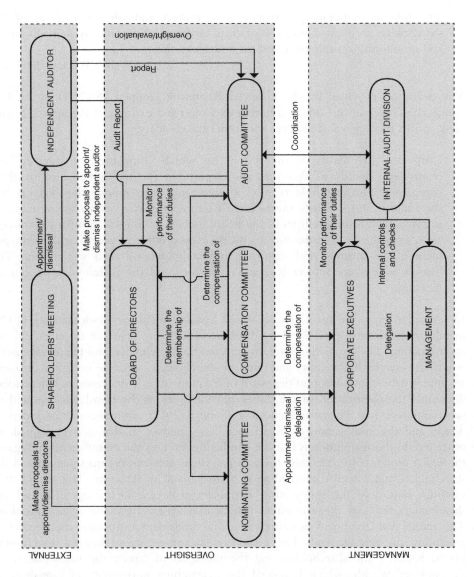

Figure 13.1 Corporate governance as an internal government

13.2.1 Neoliberal extensions

Despite the oversight of the corporate boards and audit functionalities illustrated in Figure 13.1, the passing of time has seen many scandals, corruptions, malpractices such as tax avoidance, environmental disasters, and even gross violations of human rights by large corporations. This was the case especially in the aftermath of the revitalization of neoliberal economic policies around the globe in the 1990s. Due to the sheer amount and severity of such instances of CG failures, and their impact on the economy, polity, and society, CG became one of the key global political issues which transnational agencies such as the World Bank, OECD, UN, as well as national governments had to take more seriously (Brennan and Solomon 2008). The reasons for such 'mega disasters' of CG were seen not only as ad hoc techno-managerial issues of accounting practices and the malfunctioning of the accounting profession but also a systemic crisis.

When taken as a systemic crisis, failures of CG become a threat to the survival of neoliberalism. Hence, there emerged a political rhetoric. As Conrad (2004) observes, the initial rhetorical response to the series of corporate scandals was to narrow it down to a 'temporary financial crisis', attracting some emotional rehabilitation with a view to postponing a public trial. Then, there came prescriptions to solve technical problems pertaining to the malfunctioning of accounting, auditing, and internal control mechanisms, demanding more rigid and tedious processes and protocols to be introduced. These rhetorical strategies derailed the discussions of systemic failures of neoliberalism (see Merino et al. 2010; Soederberg 2008). For example, regarding the widespread Enron saga, its audit committee was blamed:

> After all, Enron management wanted a blessing for every transaction during 2000 between the energy trading company and two partnerships run by then CFO Andrew Foster ... yet committee members, all of them outside directors, didn't challenge a single transaction, according to knowledgeable people and excerpts from [the] Feb 12 (2001) meeting's minutes. Their indifference wasn't a complete surprise....
>
> (Lublin 2002)

Then, the conceptions of CG expanded to include a wider set of constituencies taking a stakeholder perspective. Rather than focusing on a single shareholder's interest, CG ideas were evolved to aim to secure the interests of other stakeholders as well and to address the diversity and discrimination issues which became more politically sensitive. For example, the Tyson Report (2003) in the UK advocated boardroom diversity and inclusivity enabling the boards to comprise non-executive directors with diverse backgrounds (see Brennan and Solomon 2008). Similarly, in the recent past, we have seen the EU and the UK government highlighting the necessity to reform CG, especially the composition of boards, to create a gender balance. European politicians and media have also emphasized the necessity of addressing the increasing public outrage about top executive remuneration packages, especially those in banks rescued by tax-payers' money. What we indeed see here is the way in which the crisis of neoliberal capitalism has itself manifested in various ways, especially by bringing the disparities and inequalities that neoliberal economic policies have not been able to solve to the surface of the political debates. They are now increasingly being seen as the problematic of CG, perhaps side-lining the fundamental structural issues of neoliberal capitalism. Nevertheless, in a theoretical sense, this has allowed: (a) an epistemic space to offer a strong critique to the traditional agency theory-based understandings of CG,

298   *Neoliberal trends*

and (b) alternative theories such as stakeholder theory, legitimacy theory, and institutional theories to take some degree of prominence in redefining the CG discourse. So, CG has now been strongly connected to the notions of regulation and governance within and beyond the corporate boards, aiming at not only mitigating the 'agency problem' but broader issues of accountability and sustainability. Transnational organizations such as the Commonwealth Association for Corporate Governance (1999) and OECD (2015b) corroborated this development in their reports and meetings. Consequently, CG encompasses a broader definition such as the one provided by Solomon (2007, 14):

> [t]he system of checks and balances, both internal and external to companies, which ensures that companies discharge their accountability to all their stakeholders, and act in a socially responsible way in all areas of their business activities.

As such, what we see now is an implosion of CG into other techno-managerial and political notions such as strategy, accountability, social responsibility, and sustainability. As it should be, governance has now become a political issue extending its scope beyond the mitigation of the agency problem between shareholders and managers. The CG agenda has moved forward accommodating more ideas into the neoliberal reformation and regulation package. These include 'integrating' the conventional CG agenda with a wide range of emerging neoliberal managerial themes including: corporate social responsibility and sustainability, risk management initiatives, corporate philanthropy, human-rights and corruption issues, diversity and equality, as well as health and safety issues. This expansion to the CG agenda has now been, more or less, captured by various CG models and frameworks, which prescribe the functioning of all new corporate board committees and panels, policies, standards, and procedures (see Deloitte 2013; PriceWaterhouseCoopers 2010).

Academic research on CG has also widened its scope accordingly and has now started to see the CG issues from broader sociological and political perspectives than traditional neoclassical economic perspectives. Attention has now been paid to not only the 'formal' legal and administrative structures but also to cultural and behavioural structures and processes. Similarly, the inward-looking economic analysis of governance through the agency problem has now widened to an outward-looking analysis that attempts to capture legal accountabilities, social networks, and symbolic management. This expansion of academic perspectives on corporate governance is summarized in Table 13.1.

The broadening of CG can be understood as a form of the neoliberalization of organizations. As we discussed in previous chapters (especially Chapter 5, Section 5.2 and Chapter 6, Section 6.3.4), neoliberalization involves a reinvention around an ever emerging set of biopolitical themes of markets, economic enterprises, civil society, and the polity. In that sense, economic enterprises are more than economic units designed to discipline and control labour for profit maximization. The boundaries between the economic, social, and political are increasingly imploding. As a result, corporations are now evolving into socio-political and cultural entities driven towards actively managing a 'multitude' of biopolitical themes ranging from wealth maximization to themes such as sustainability, national competitiveness, economic, and other forms of risks, diversity, equality, democracy, anti-corruption, human rights, and so on. Their absence and/or lacking increasingly appear as 'crises of human civilization' more than ever before due to globalization and the neoliberalization of all spheres of social life. The security of the individual and the population is strongly attributed to our organizational capacity to address them. Hence, organizations are now asked not simply to follow the laws and

Table 13.1 Expanding scope of CG research

Analytical orientation	Analytical focus and managerial/policy intentions		
	Formal structures	Behavioural structures	Behavioural processes
Inward looking, intra-organizational	ECONOMIC: Designing optimal incentive structures and monitoring systems to mitigate the agency problem.	POWER: Understanding how positions affect power/ politics within the organization.	SOCIAL PSYCHOLOGY: Revealing how decision-making processes may be based on such factors as psychology of leadership and incentive packages.
Outward looking, extra-organizational	LEGAL: Creating and enforcing governance rules and regulations for social benefits and stakeholder legitimacy.	SOCIAL NETWORKS: Showing how power and information flow in inter-organizational networks.	SYMBOLIC MANAGEMENT: Understanding how symbolism and language can address normative compliance with society norms and values; impression management.

Source: based on Hambrick et al. (2008) and Zajac and Westphal (1998).

rules imposed upon them by the political state but to actively innovate and implement their own creative measures of handling these wider biopolitical themes. As we see it, CG has become the overarching managerial and politico-regulatory phenomenon which conceptually brings together all other biopolitical themes. Epistemic institutions such as consultancy firms (e.g. Deloitte 2013; PriceWaterhouseCoopers 2010), international development agencies (e.g. OECD 2015b) and regulatory bodies (e.g. Financial Reporting Council 2012) are now in the process of reinventing CG frameworks that are flexible enough to incorporate these emerging biopolitical themes. We will further elaborate the biopolitical implications of CG in the next few sections.

13.3 Corporate governance transformations: a biopolitical view

We see a clear shift of CG discourses from the narrow agency theory model, which describes CG as mechanisms that are designed to reduce the agency costs associated with the separation of ownership and control (see Fama 1980; Fama and Jensen 1983; Jensen and Meckling 1976), to a stakeholder model embracing a wider set of political issues beyond the agency problem between owners and managers (see Brennan and Solomon 2008; Solomon 2007; and also Section 13.4 below). This shift has been manifested in the recent discourses propagated by not only transnational organizations like the UN (e.g. UN Millennium Development Goals and Sustainability Goals), the OECD, and the World Bank but also the accounting and management consultants (e.g. Deloitte 2013; PriceWaterhouseCoopers 2010). They all want companies, in addition to making a sufficient profit for the investors, to embrace a wider business philosophy going beyond profit making to cater for various socio-cultural and political issues for which the political state has hitherto been held responsible. How can we explain this shift? What are the cultural-political reasons behind this shift? Foucauldian notions of neoliberalism and biopolitics, we reckon, can provide interesting explanations for this shift.

300   *Neoliberal trends*

A biopolitical explanation requires CG to be placed within the parameters of government, security, and regulation, which are three main conceptual notions that Foucauldians use to explain the evolution of the political state from a liberal to a neoliberal state. They are the notions through which, therefore, we can understand and explain how and why CG is now evolving into a wider apparatus of global governance beyond its conventional economic scope. We will do discuss this under two headings: (1) the problematic of security and the governmentality and (2) the problematic of regulation.

13.3.1 Corporate governance, security, and global governmentality

In Chapter 1 (especially in Section 1.3), we explained how governmentality, as a new rationality of government, emerged during modernity and reshaped the social order creating a whole spectrum of 'disciplinary institutions'. In the pre-neoliberal regimes, governmentality operated mainly through 'anatomico-politics of the human body' materialized through the application of disciplinary principles and technologies including scientific management. The primary disciplinary orientation was on the 'confinement' of the body in the disciplinary spaces and its synchronization with the productive machine so that the human body, the productive machine, and the disciplinary spaces all become efficient in terms of capital accumulation (see Foucault 1995; Hopper and Macintosh 1993). During this disciplinary regime, the political notion of 'security' was the 'security of the nation-state' – the defence of the state's territorial integrity. As Gros (2014, 21) explains:

> Here it is no longer a question of security as a spiritual condition, nor of the myth of an Empire of the last days. Instead, the goal is to think [of] the consistency of a nation-state in the midst of history. Security will be defined as the consistency of the state, which is simultaneously the consistency supplied by the state to the rights of its citizens and to the existence of its subjects, and the consistency that the state provides for itself as one political subject in relation to others. Indeed, the very meaning of the word 'security' is immediately divided into internal security and external security.

'Confinement' was the key mode of disciplining through which this notion of security was ensured. Two symbols of security were the prison, for internal security, and the border, for external security. When it came to external security, it was the establishment and effective imposition of the 'border' that constituted the principal apparatus of security, in terms of not only its physical apparatuses such as fences and walls but also administrative and trading apparatuses such as HM Customs & Excise, the Home Office, import/export duties, passports, visas, biometrics, and so on. When it comes to internal security it was the confinement of citizens within all sorts of disciplinary institutions that resembled prisons (see Chapter 1, Section 1.3 for a detailed discussion on this) which constituted the apparatuses of security.

The security of the nation-state has economic as well as political apparatuses. The protection of the border, war, peace, nuclear security, prevention of civil disobedience, and so on are all taken as political elements of security which, by and large, are concentrated in the hands of the political state and its administrative apparatuses. The economic apparatuses of security are related to the 'wealth of the nation', in Adam Smith's classical economics terms, and the 'competitive advantage of the nation', in

Porter's strategy discourses (see Chapter 5). In either case, economic security is ultimately seen as a matter of maximizing shareholders' wealth through enhancing the competitiveness of the nation's firms. The role of 'government' is therefore to make sure that necessary conditions are in place to enhance the firms' competitiveness and to safeguard the property rights of the shareholders, including their capacity to know what their managers do and achieve. Conventionally, the principal means of doing this were through the Companies Act and other related legislation. This 'governmental' role, when it is devolved and delegated to the firms themselves in the spirit of liberalism, becomes the notion of CG. So, in this 'liberal sense', CG is concerned about the shareholders' property and informational rights. The 'agency problem' was therefore conceived as the key danger for economic security which needed to be mitigated through CG. In that sense, traditional agency theory-based models (see Fama 1980; Fama and Jensen 1983; Jensen and Meckling 1976) of CG captured this political rationality. They were indeed valid, acceptable, and 'recommendable' (by relevant regulatory and epistemic institutions such as the Financial Reporting Council) when they were located within this political rationality of the 'economic security of the nation', which needed to be achieved through the profit-making capacity of the nation's firms. This is what it used to be until the neoliberal regime started to emerge.

Neoliberalism marks a rupture in this political rationality. It has changed the meaning of security and the purpose of government and governance. Instead of the state's territorial integrity, the doctrine of human security now proclaims insistently that living populations and individuals ought to constitute the new objects of security. Living populations and individuals are what must be protected. What is sacred is no longer the sovereignty of the state, but the 'life' of the individual (Gros 2014, 23), which needs to be protected from the tyrannies of 'rogue' political states as well as from other 'rogue' elements including 'rogue' corporations, into which any corporation can evolve if there is no 'proper' CG in place (such as Enron!). The symbolic-legal manifestation of this notion of security is the global-political doctrine which transnational institutions such as the UN define as 'responsibility to protect'.[1] The governance, whether it appears in the form of both 'good governance' and 'corporate governance', now need to encapsulate this notion of the security of 'life' in its all possible forms – the individual, the collective, and the natural. As we mentioned in previous chapters, the 'reproduction of life' and, hence, its protection, have become the fundamental doctrine of the neoliberal political economy (see Cooper 2015). Governance, therefore, needs to address any form of threats that endanger the 'life'. Gros (2014, 26, italicized emphasis and parenthesis ours) explains:

> What is indeed peculiar about this new doctrine is that it considers everything that might do harm to the living individual and to the good of civil populations as a threat. This new definition of security thus produces a continuous stream of threats, whether these are economic, climactic, social, ecological, political, hygienic, medical, or nutritional. Everything is part of one single continuum: natural disasters, epidemics, terrorist attacks, civil wars, rivalries between crime syndicates vying for the control of illicit trafficking in arms, drugs, people, climate change, poverty and unemployment, and so on. Today, all these threats are considered as risks to society understood in the broadest possible sense. In the interior of states, this continuum of threats is produced through the concept of 'global security' which stands to a given population as 'human security' stands to the whole of

302   *Neoliberal trends*

humanity, and which entails ... the fusion of all those institutional security authorities that had heretofore been separate. Today, it is commonly held that national, interior, medical, ecological, and other security departments ought to work together. The globalization of the world involves the abolition of the previous divisions between interior and exterior, criminal and enemy, the political and the natural. The biopolitical age of security has led to this great equivalence of all threats. This continuity and equalization entail the effacement of figures such as the worker, the citizen, the patriot, and so forth. All of them disappear for the benefit of the living individual whose vital nucleus must be secured, and nothing exists outside of the great community of living bodies, *the security of which will be the responsibility of private organisms acting with the blessing of the [global] state.*

As soon as the individual, rather than the state, becomes the sacred object of security, the nation-state becomes a paradoxical element in the neoliberal social order. On the one hand, it becomes a possible 'threat' against whose tyrannies the individual needs to be protected. On the other, it still needs to hold the legislative power and responsibility for protecting the individual. This paradox then necessitates apparatuses of global state and global governance, which constitute various forms of supranational institutions such as the UN, World Bank, OECD, International Accounting Standards Board, Global Reporting Initiative, and so on. They all, in one way or another, perform certain epistemic and regulatory functions of global governance. They have become the epistemic sources of new 'regulatory regimes' where the 'global codification' of 'good governance' and CG play a significant role. They are vocal of, inter alia, global issues of financial risks, regarding which, as they observe, CG can play a vital role. They have assumed multitudes of roles, depending on their institutional remits, driven towards mitigating various forms of insecurities. They have now become global institutions who: monitor and evaluate performance; set standards and behavioural codes for nation-states, multinational corporations and civil society organizations to follow; offer consultancy to nation-states and other global institutions; and thereby regulate behaviours and performance outcomes of others. For example, pertaining to CG specifically, the World Bank explores the ways in which shareholder confidence can be established, how ownership concentration can be minimized, how the structures of management committees and boards can be reassembled, and how the cross-holding of share ownership can be controlled (see World Bank 2000). The World Bank, together with other organizations, is working on a 'global consensus' of CG. OECD Guidelines, Cadbury, Hampel, and Greenbury Reports in the UK, the Bosh Report and also the Business Roundtable in Australia, and the Asian Roundtable on Corporate Governance echoed the same necessity for effective CG. For example, the 2014 OECD report *Improving Corporate Governance in India* proclaimed that:

> In a meeting held on 14-15 December 2011 in Mumbai, a number of areas for improvement were identified, and initial recommendations to support the policy design of reforms were provided. Discussions focused on the means to ... strengthen minority shareholder protection ... more active shareholder engagement, improved disclosure of company groups, and improved effectiveness of independent directors
>
> (OECD 2014, 4)

Neoliberalization of corporate governance 303

13.3.2 Neoliberal corporate governance as a form of soft regulation

As the problem of security is redirected from the state to security of the individual life, anything has the potential of becoming a security threat and, hence, becoming a biopolitical theme to be addressed through governance. This means that neoliberal governance is unpredictable and aleatory (Foucault 2003, 2008). Its modus operandi is the perpetual reinvention of biopolitical issues and solutions to them. This is a task which is now by and large entrusted to epistemic institutions such as the World Bank, IMF, global consultants, and so on. Their primary functionalities are to 'survey the world', highlight the biopolitical problems, propose solutions, and facilitate their implementations by nation-states, NGOs, and other social entities including corporations. Hence, for example, with every World Bank World Development Report we see a new biopolitical issue, or a new emphasis on an old biopolitical issue that the 'world' needs to address. Neoliberalism is also paradoxical in the sense that it creates a necessity to bring together apparently contradictory elements. Perhaps most critical in this respect is the 'paradox of market sovereignty'. As a political ethos, neoliberalism embraces the idea that market should govern 'lives' and that it should be given the freedom to do so. At the same time, in this neoliberal era, we have experienced the worst crises in the markets; the market's incapacity to govern is exemplified more than ever before. At the same time, neoliberalism does not trust the political state as a valid institution to regulate the market. For neoliberalism, the state itself should be driven by the market apparatuses of control and governance. This means that 'sovereignty' needs to be transferred from the political state to the market economy, which nevertheless cannot still operate as a state. Thus is the paradox of regulation vs market sovereignty.

The global governmental solution for this paradox is what we may call 'soft regulation', which is nothing else but an attempt to codify the market so that the actors in the market are told 'softly' (rather than imposing a binding law upon them, which is 'hard regulation') that it would be nice for them to comply with a particular code of conduct. So, compliance is voluntary and at its best amounts to 'comply or explain' (Financial Reporting Council 2012). Such requests of 'soft regulation' are to be made not by the nation-states but by the epistemic elements of the global state, which in turn should be backed up by the nation-states. Hence, the regulatory state of CG is global; the state apparatuses here are not necessarily the orthodox nation-states, whose support and acceptance are nevertheless critical. Regulation encompasses a series of 'soft' mechanisms of global governance promoted and executed by many 'non-state apparatuses' which introduce many 'best practices' (Djelic and Sahlin-Andersson 2006; Merino et al. 2010). Examples are the best practice guidelines and codes promoted by the World Bank, OECD, and International Organization of Corporate Governance. Some accounting and management consultants have also joined this circle of soft regulators by offering supporting 'managerial models' to comply with such codes and guidelines (see Deloitte 2013; PriceWaterhouseCoopers 2010). In this sense, the contemporary trajectory of CG regulation is a manifestation of a response to the perpetual crisis and paradox of neoliberal governance by soft regulating corporate behaviour which should be directed towards not only the interests of shareholders but also all other possible biopolitical threats that these epistemic and regulatory institutions identify and emphasize.

So, in an overall sense, with this biopolitical regime of security and governance, CG has become rather multi-faceted, no more just restricted to the mitigation of the agency problem. CG implodes various other notions of insecurity and risks. The functionalities and structures of CG, including the ever more complicated composition and functions of

304 Neoliberal trends

the board of directors, are being reinvented to encompass a range of issues pertaining to various stakeholders, all forms of risk management, sustainability and good citizenship, accountability and transparency, diversity and equality, etc. They all are now increasingly conceived as elements of corporate strategy. The terms strategy and governance are often used together as inseparable in corporate reporting. We will further elaborate on this 'pluralization' and 'multiplication' of CG in the next section where the attention is on the way in which organizational structures, relations, and practices are reconfigured to accommodate this new regime of security and global governance.

13.4 Neoliberal corporate governance in practice

We shall now see how the biopolitical dynamics of CG and regulations are being integrated into micro-organizational processes and practices. If you look at the web pages of large corporations such as Asda in the UK, Mitsubishi in Japan, Samsung in South Korea, or Walmart in the USA, they all demonstrate publicly that they are amenable to external pressures to adaptation their ensuing CG ideas, codes, and best practices. They all claim that their CG system is being amended and developed continuously in the light of changes taking place in the regulatory context and also the new 'biopolitical threats' they encounter in an ever evolving political economic landscape. They claim that they gain much from these developments in making them responsible and accountable to a wider spectrum of stakeholders. For example, Walmart proclaims:

> With continued advances in technology opening new growth opportunities in the retail sector, Walmart has developed a robust, flexible ethics and compliance program to keep pace with this evolving landscape. Around the world, online shopping continues to grow in popularity, complementing the traditional shopping experience. This dual setting online and in-store reaches more customers every day, making it an exciting time to be in the retail business, but it also presents its own compliance challenges. Our ethics and compliance program addresses 14 key areas of relevance to the changing retail sector . . . [which are of] critical importance to both our business and to our stakeholders.
>
> (https://corporate.walmart.com/2016grr/promoting-good-governance)

In a similar fashion, BHP Billiton conceptualizes its governance framework – 'operating with integrity' – in a very broad sense to include following elements:[2]

1. Working with integrity: This constitutes the 'codification' of individual and collective behaviour regarding operational matters of the company. The aim is to minimize illegal and unethical behaviours by the company employees and to ensure their health and safety at work. This aspect is formalized and communicated through BHP's Code of Business Conduct.
2. Anti-corruption compliance: Here the company declares its commitment to the 'global fight against corruption in the resources industry'. Anti-corruption risk assessments, anti-corruption training, independent monitoring and audit, confidential reporting and investigations, design and continuous improvement are listed as the key operational elements of this theme of CG.

Neoliberalization of corporate governance 305

3. Climate change portfolio analysis: Under this theme the company declares its commitment to the 2015 UN's Paris Agreement on the reduction of climate change. In its 2017 report, *Climate Change: Portfolio Analysis – Views after Paris*, the company explains how their strategic planning assumptions and processes are now being changed to accommodate climate change as a strategic imperative.
4. Closure planning: This element of BHP's CG attempts to address the potentially significant financial, environmental, and social risks associated with the future closure of mines. The company declares that 'Our governance framework for mine closure seeks to integrate resource planning and development; health; safety; environmental; community and social considerations; stakeholder engagement; risk; finance; and assurance in the operational design'.
5. Competition law compliance: This declares the company's commitment to ensure the competitive market practices by denouncing the following prohibitive practices: price fixing and bid-rigging; fixing other competitive terms, such as margins or rebates; limiting production, or agreeing to reduce or limit production capacity; allocating markets, customers, suppliers, or geographic territories; boycotting any customer or supplier. Competition law risk assessments, competition law training and awareness, confidential reporting, and investigations are listed as the operational methods of ensuring this element of governance.
6. Economic contribution reporting: This element of CG is to ensure compliance with tax regulations and laws. The report outlines the company payments to government by country.
7. Corporate responsibility forum: This is the form of 'social accountability' that the company envisages. It is in the form of a 'forum' that encourages a dialogue between the company and influential civil society organizations. As reported on the company's website, the forum is chaired by the company's CEO and 'the Forum meets to debate a broad range of topics including emerging global social and environmental trends; climate change scenarios and adaptation; issues facing indigenous peoples, including free, prior, and informed consent; sustainability reporting; and transparency'. Civil society members of the forum in 2017 included: Mick Dodson, National Centre for Indigenous Studies, ANU (Australia); Cristina Echavarria, Board Member, Alliance for Responsible Mining (Colombia); Don Henry, Public Policy Fellow – Environmentalism, University of Melbourne (Australia); Simon Longstaff, Executive Director, The Ethics Centre (Australia); Yaa Ntiamoa-Baidu, Centre for African Wetlands, University of Ghana (Ghana); Ray Offenheiser, President, Oxfam America (USA); Phil Vernon, Director of Programs, International Alert (UK); and Changhua Wu, Chair, China Redesign Hub (China).
8. Governance and transparency: This encompasses four 'good governance principles': responsibility, openness, fairness, and accessibility. Here the company declares its commitment to the Extractive Industries Transparency Initiative.
9. Indigenous peoples: Here the company declares its commitment to the traditional rights of Indigenous peoples and acknowledges their right to maintain their cultures, identities, traditions, and customs. BHP Indigenous Peoples Policy Statement, Indigenous People and Mining Position Statement, BHP Indigenous People Strategy, Reconciliation Action Plan 2017–2020 (Australia) are listed as the key operational elements of this dimension of CG.
10. Industry associations – BHP's approach: Here BHP articulates how it approaches its membership responsibilities in industry associations such as Minerals Council of

306 *Neoliberal trends*

Australia, Centre for Climate and Energy Solutions (C2ES), and International Council on Mining and Metals (ICMM). The company's approach is to publish a report *BHP Industry Association Review*, which outlines a list of the material differences between the positions BHP holds on climate and energy policy and the advocacy positions on climate and energy policy taken by industry associations to which BHP belongs. It also outlines the outcomes of BHP's current review of its membership of those industry associations.

11. Interaction with governments: This element emphasizes the company's commitment to maintaining ethical relationships with governments and their agencies, officials, and personnel. The 'Code of Business Conduct' and 'Our Charter' provide the necessary codification of behaviour in this regard.

12. Non-operated joint ventures: Here the company explains how it engages with its partners at non-operated joint ventures.

13. Product stewardship: This is the element where the company explains its responsibility regarding the safe, efficient, and reliable transportation, handling, and disposal of hazardous minerals including nuclear elements such as uranium. Here the company declares its commitment to the regulations and protocols issued by relevant authorities and regulators including the International Council of Mining and Metals Sustainable Development Framework, Steel Stewardship Forum, the European Copper Institute, the Australian Petroleum Production and Exploration Association, and the Australian Government through the Australian Safeguards and Non-Proliferation Office.

14. Respecting human rights and UK Modern Slavery Act statement: Here the company declares that its:

> [c]ommitment to operating to the highest standards of business integrity in relation to human rights and its strategy of focusing on the development of large, long-life operations bestows on us both an opportunity to make a positive contribution to the realisation of a wide range of human rights and a responsibility to respect human rights and mitigate human rights related risks.

15. Sustainable supply chain: This governance policy declares the company's commitment to safeguard various aspects of governance mentioned above throughout its supply chains as well.

What you see in these two examples (and many others which more or less resemble them) is the way that CG in practice has become very complex and wide ranging, pushing the companies to address myriad emerging biopolitical security themes. A multitude of biopolitical factors are presented as threats to the security of the life of the people around the world, and the companies seek (and are asked) to address them through various forms of regulatory compliance. Companies now need to show their global citizenship and 'character' by displaying their commitment to address these biopolitical issues. To that end, companies are now reinventing, from top to bottom, their governance structures, policies, practices, and relationships. Managers at all levels, across all managerial functions, are now facing the challenge of making sure that relevant governance policies are designed, put in place, well communicated, understood, and abided by, by every member of the organization. Organizing and directing people towards these ever emerging and changing biopolitical themes is the 'disciplinary challenge' that managers in neoliberal organizations now face. It is not simply controlling the labour towards creating a surplus value but towards mitigating all possible forms of insecurity pertaining to the reproduction of life. This happens in the form of micro-management of regulatory compliance. From a Foucauldian perspective, this is an alternative form of 'normalization' constructed through optimizing a combination of the regulatory regime of biopolitics with the disciplinary regime of anatomico-politics. This combination, Foucault argues, helps populations economize their duties towards the security of the individual life (whose reproduction accumulates the capital) while accelerating the accumulation of capital (Foucault 2003, 2008).

Accounting implications of this neoliberalization of CG can be discussed under two themes: legitimacy and accountability.

13.4.1 Neoliberalization of legitimacy

The neoliberal transformation of the security apparatuses of governmentality has created an important change in the way economic enterprises need to legitimize their operations. In a classical liberal world view until the early 1980s, where there was assumed to be a clear political and ideological demarcation between the economy, polity, and society, shareholders' wealth maximization operated as the higher order principle of legitimizing corporate affairs and rationalizing managerial decisions. Hence, on the grounds of this demarcation between the polity, economy, and society, in 1970, as an early proponent of neoliberal economics, Milton Friedman declared that 'the social responsibility of business is to increase its profits'. However, the subsequent implosion of economy, polity, and society during the 1990s and beyond has created a totally different rationale for legitimation. Legitimation now emanates from one's contribution towards the security of the individual life and one's capacity and willingness to fight against different forms of threats against it. However, it should be noted that as poverty is such a threat, the accumulation of wealth is still one of the dominant elements of the biopolitical notion of security. Nevertheless, the legitimation of even economic affairs has now become political and cultural. They cannot be legitimated and justified only through financial criteria. Legitimation now demands the display of 'good citizenship' and character as defined by myriad discourses on good governance, accountability, ethics, sustainability, etc. As exemplified by the examples provided in the previous section, compliance with a wide range of regulatory discourses of the global state is the key to this neoliberal legitimation of corporate affairs. To that end, corporations need to publish much more than their financial statements. For example, BHP, the example we discussed earlier, publishes more than 20 different reports on its website for public scrutiny, including certain internal documents on governance which were hitherto only for the employees.

13.4.2 Neoliberalization of accountability

CG ideas, as we now know, are aimed at holding corporate managers accountable for their behaviours, performance outcomes, and the impact that they make on the wider society and the environment. This process is called accountability – making corporate managers provide reasons for their conduct (Roberts 1991; Roberts and Scapens 1985), which is a form of legitimation. As Roberts (1991) argues, accountability processes can take two complementary forms: the individualizing form and the socializing form. This can then be extended to another form, which we call biopolitical accountability.

308 *Neoliberal trends*

Individualizing accountability in corporate governance

When operating in its individualizing form, accountability constructs individualized selves as 'subjects' to be visualized by others at a distant. This is done by confining the individuals and collectives within disciplinary spaces and connecting the performance of such spaces to the individuals and groups. Accounting technologies are used to create such spaces (e.g. investment centres, profit centres, cost centres, etc); to assign individuals to such spaces; to assess the performance of such productive cells and the people placed therein; and to justify, legitimate, and rationalize the managerial and political actions directed towards such spaces (see Miller and O'Leary 1994; Roberts 1991). This individualizing accountability is disciplinary because it operates on the basis of 'anatomico-politics of the body" (which we discussed earlier); it manifests essentially a form of panopticon like disciplinary controls through which people are 'compared, differentiated, hierarchized, homogenized, and excluded' (Roberts 2001, 1552). In this way, the self is seen and judged from the legitimating principles of the shareholders and other stakeholder groups who point their fingers at individuals (and distinctively identifiable groups) over their behaviours and performance outcomes. Neoliberal forms of CG accommodate disciplinary accounting for the purposes of ensuring that corporate managers act in the interests of shareholders and stakeholders. Accounting reports attested by the mechanisms of internal controls, internal audits, face-to-face actions within CG-led boards and committees, risk management apparatuses, and other related CG codes create a 'powerful field of visibility' (Roberts 2001) in which individuals become 'governable at a distance' by subjugating themselves to the disciplinary apparatuses (Miller and O'Leary 1987). Roberts (2001) cites Foucault (1979: 202–203) to highlight the nature of this 'field of visibility':

> He who is subject to a field of visibility, and who knows it, assumes responsibility for the constraints of power, he makes them play spontaneously upon himself. He inscribes in himself the power relation in which he simultaneously plays both roles.

CG reinforces the construction of this visibility; it constructs a form of accountability through which market principles of governance are localized and translated into 'mini regimes of truth' (Foucault 1995) where credibility and justification of individual actions are measured through compliance with the standards and the degree to which their performance reaches market expectations. In response, corporate managers, internal controllers, accountants, board members, and committees act upon accountability to ensure that the company complies with standards, achieves the market expectations, and provides 'credible' accounts of corporate affairs. When things go wrong, stakeholders, media agencies, whistleblowers, etc. provide counter-accounts to hold the relevant individuals and groups accountable. In short, governance reconfigures an individualization process of accountability.

Socializing accountability in corporate governance

While the individualizing process of accountability operates remotely as a form of 'action at a distance', the socialization process of accountability operates on a face-to-face basis as a form of interdependent social relation of convivial nature. These are rather lateral, reciprocal, and intimate relations occurring real time. This is the construction of the accountable self in

Neoliberalization of corporate governance 309

relation to the 'immediate others'. As Roberts (2001, 1558–1559) argues, the frequent face-to-face nature of board meetings should provide the opportunity for harnessing this kind of accountability and can 'generate a unique board culture out of the response, more or less shared, of individuals to external pressures and perceptions'. For example, when CG codes looked to introduce non-executives onto corporate boards, establish various committees, and separate the CEO from the chairman, the hierarchically concentrated organizations were gradually reassembled into lateral relations and hierarchical forms. Based on the possibilities of these two forms of accountability (i.e. individualizing and socializing effects of accountability), Roberts (2001) identifies four different forms of governance:

1. Individualized governance where individualizing effect is high but socializing effect is law.
2. Socialized governance where individualizing effect is low but socializing effect is high.
3. Sovereign governance where both individualizing and socializing effects are low.
4. Complementary governance where both individualizing and socializing effects are high

And the efficacy of the corporate boards as a mode of CG then depends upon the subtle interplay between these two forms of accountability. Roberts (2001, 1562–1563) goes on to explain:

> The play of individualizing and socializing forces within the board is empirically variable and depends upon the way that external pressures are mediated by board processes. Where the control role of non-executives reinforces external demands for shareholder value, there is always also the possibility of resistance by executives and the potential for a defensive dynamic of distrust. Conversely, there is empirical support for the conclusion that what agency theorists fear for its collusive potential – closeness between executive and non-executives – makes it much more possible for non-executives to contribute to firm performance through influencing strategic decision making. Here, the collective nature of the groups' formal responsibilities, the face-to-face structure of meetings and the relative balance of power between members can create a dynamic of openness and engagement.

Biopolitical accountability

The Roberts' analysis above is about the socio-interactional and techno-managerial processes of accountability and the forms that CG can take based upon accountability's individualizing and socializing effects. By the term biopolitical accountability, our attention is not necessarily on such socio-interactional and techno-managerial processes through which accountability is created but the nature of accounts and narratives that such processes produce.

As we noted earlier, the key feature of neoliberal CG is its orientation towards the new biopolitical security. This new *dispositif* [3] of security turns the individual, rather than the state, into a sacred object; the physical, economic, political, and cultural conditions of which then become the objective of neoliberal security and governance. In a rather globalized world where everything else is now increasingly imploding into markets, biopolitical security implies *flow control*: the control of movements and communications but in a decentralized fashion, depending on competing transnational

310 Neoliberal trends

networks that constitute the global state (Gros 2014). What is to be controlled is the 'minority flow' (Gros 2014) or what we may call the 'corruptive flow' owned and operated by the 'rogue' elements of the neoliberal systems, which may even include some elements of nation-states, multinational corporations, and NGOs. And there is always the perpetual threat that anybody can turn 'rogue' and engage in the corruptive flow either intentionally or unintentionally, knowingly or unknowingly.

This corruptive flow is manifested by, for example, money laundering, human trafficking, drug trafficking, data hacking, accounting scandals, international trade dumping, environmental pollution, human rights violations, and many other forms of corruption and malpractice. Controlling such corruptive elements has now evolved into specialized functions of certain associations and networks of the global state and civil society. Depending on their circumstances, corporations are now needed to be members of such associations and networks and to comply with the specific regulations that they impose upon the corporations. For example, consider the number of such associations that BHP Billiton (the example we provided in the previous section) is now dealing with through their CG systems and protocols. Corporate accountability now involves reporting to this ever growing network of associations that constitute the global state and civil society with the purpose of 'tracing' the corruptive flow or demonstrating that the company is not involved in this corruptive flow. The central problem of corporate accountability then becomes one of *traceability*: the ability to determine, at any given moment, what is moving, where it is coming from, where it is going, what it is doing in its current place, and if it actually has a right of access to the network in which it is moving, or if its use of the network is unauthorized (Gros 2014, 26). Accounting, in all its possible forms, then needs to provide the technical groundwork enabling these acts of tracking and tracing. This is the emerging form of biopolitical accountability – tracking and tracing the circulation of life and matters related to the security of life.

13.5 Management accounting and corporate governance

From a conventional point of view, management accounting is supposed to help corporate managers make better decisions and maintain effective controls. But the question here is what we mean by 'better' and 'effective'. From a neoclassical economic perspective, profit maximization is the criteria according to which the efficiency and effectiveness of managerial decisions should be assessed. Hence, management accounting was, and still is, by and large a set of technologies driven towards assessing the profitability of various decision scenarios and controlling the behaviour of social agents to make sure that they meet the profit targets. However, given the neoliberal transformations, these 'purely economic' arbitrations are no longer sufficient on their own, though they are necessary. Organizations are now judged by their contributions to the 'biopolitical criteria' of governance and security, i.e. mitigating threats to the reproduction of life in its social, cultural, and political as well as economic forms. Accordingly, the management accounting practices within organizations need to be reconfigured and reoriented. We see this happening through four forms of 'encounters' emanating from four distinct but interrelated and increasingly imploding spheres in the organizational context: market economy, global state, global civil society, and global ecology. Figure 13.2 illustrates the way in which this global context penetrates management accounting practices.

Neoliberalization of corporate governance 311

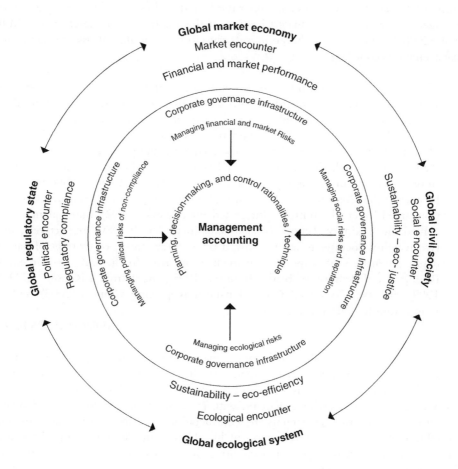

Figure 13.2 Management accounting encounters of biopolitical governance

Reading through Figure 13.2, the CG infrastructure is established to deal with four interrelated spheres in the organizational context, which places different biopolitical demands on corporations – financial and market performance, regulatory compliance, eco-justice aspects of sustainability, and eco-efficiency aspects of sustainability. The CG infrastructure, therefore, should address the biopolitical threats or insecurities associated with them – financial and market risks, social and reputational risks, ecological risks, and political risks. When management accounting is seen as a set of decision-making, planning, and control rationalities and techniques, the neoliberal transformation of management accounting involves transforming these rationalities and inventing new techniques to deal with them. Many of the discussions we had in previous chapters indeed explained how these neoliberal imperatives are incorporated into management accounting.

As a result, management accounting is pluralized to accommodate these encounters and regularizes a form of counterchecking between competing imperatives of the global political state, market economy, civil society, and the ecological system, so that different

312   *Neoliberal trends*

forms of insecurities are assessed, understood, and addressed. The discourses of risk management are indeed the materialization of this regime of counterchecking. Miller et al. (2008, 942) emphasize this point, referring to the centrality of risk management in management accounting:

> The management of organisations is rapidly being transformed into and formalised around the management of risk. This began in the early 1990s, and on both sides of the Atlantic. On the UK side, it can be identified by a seemingly unremarkable event – the publication of the Report of the Committee on the Financial Aspects of Corporate Governance (1992), produced by a body formed by the Financial Reporting Council, the London Stock Exchange and the accountancy profession. In the USA, and in the same year, there was a similar event – the publication of the Report of the Committee of Sponsoring Organisations of the Treadway Commission, titled 'Internal Control – Integrated Framework' (1992). Subsequently nicknamed the 'Cadbury Report' (after its Chairman) and 'COSO' respectively, these two weighty documents were followed by a steady stream of writings of variable depth on matters of corporate governance and risk. In the UK, the Greenbury Report (Confederation of British Industry, 1995), the Turnbull Report (ICAEW, 1999), and the Combined Code (Financial Reporting Council, 2003) built up momentum to address these issues.
>
> (Miller et al. 2008, 942)

If counterchecking is possible in this way, management accounting becomes a topography for the biopolitical management of the insecurities of life. Management accounting techniques such as BSC and ERP are now evolving, incorporating risk management as an overarching element, with extra dimensions, new key performance indicators, new planning constraints and considerations, etc. to accommodate emerging biopolitical threats to the reproduction of life. Hence, in addition to the disciplinary logic of confinement, management accounting should now be directed to optimize the flow, the circulation of life.

13.6 Summary and conclusions

This chapter sought to explore how neoliberalism transforms CG and how CG is linked to management accounting's transformation. Rather than showing that neoliberalism is problematic, its emerging rationales of security and governance provided a justification as to how a pluralistic model of CG started to emerge. Global debates, lobbying for new CG codes, and transnational institutional engagements for propagating CG made CG inevitable. Accordingly, discourses of CG now redefine the way in which corporations run their affairs.

In Section 13.2, we looked at how neoclassical economics framed the early shareholder wealth-maximization-driven understanding of CG and then how neoliberalism provided the political impetus to extend this view into a wider understanding of regulation and governance. Placed within and beyond the corporate boards, the new rationality of CG aims at not only mitigating the 'agency problem' but also addressing broader issues of corporate accountability and sustainability. Section 13.3 extended this understanding further into the biopolitical apparatuses of security and governance under neoliberalism. There we discussed how a new regime of neoliberal governance and

Neoliberalization of corporate governance 313

security emerged and how, in this regime, instead of the state's territorial integrity, which used to be higher order principle in the liberal regime of governance, the doctrine of human security now proclaims insistently that living populations and individuals ought to constitute the new objects of security. The regulatory implication of this new doctrine of security was the emergence of 'soft regulation' through the apparatuses of the global state. The CG implications of this new regime of biopolitical security and governance are discussed in Section 13.4 with special reference to legitimacy and accountability implications. Three modes of accountability – individualizing, socializing, and biopolitical – are identified and discussed. Finally, in Section 13.5 we synthesized how all those neoliberal developments in CG penetrate organizational spaces of management accounting.

Assignments

These assignments are meant to extend your knowledge beyond what you understand from this chapter. These are not simply revision questions. The content covered in this chapter is necessary but will not be sufficient in attempting these tasks. Therefore, you are required to do some extra reading in attempting these tasks.

1. **Thematic essay:**
   'Corporate governance is an organizational manifestation of how neoliberalism is justified, maintained, and redressed'.Discuss this statement focusing on the political economy of corporate governance discourse.
2. **Poster:**
   Illustrate in a poster how management accounting is reconfigured by the complex processes of debates, politics, and discursive formations of neoliberal corporate governance.
3. **Presentation:**
   Prepare an adequate number of PowerPoint slides for you to use as visual aids for a presentation at the PhD Colloquium where you are proposing a piece of potential research. In this regard, use the following working title:'What governs governance, and how does it evolve? Implications for management accounting in action'.
4. **Extended bibliography:**
   For the above working tile, explore the ten best journal articles published in accounting and management top-ranked journals. Reflect on them in terms of their (1) academic significance; (2) key contribution/s; and (3) remaining issues to be addressed. For this, use the following table for you to fill in those details:

Article	Significance	Key contribution/s	Remaining issues to be addressed

5. **Literature review:**
   Now that you have made some preliminary preparations, it is time to do a judicial review of the literature based on the key articles you have chosen and other relevant ones you may have discovered. You may organize this as clear answer to these questions:

314 *Neoliberal trends*

    (a)   What is the state-of-the art of this stream of research?

    (b)   What is it you want to propose?

    (c)   Why is it so important now?

    (d)   What are the key questions and how are they considered to be novel?

    (e)   What aims do you want to achieve?

Notes

1 The Responsibility to Protect (R2P or RtoP) is a global political commitment which was endorsed by all member states of the UN at the 2005 World Summit to prevent individuals and communities from various elements of tyrannies, especially of war.
2 This discussion is based on the information available on BHP Billiton's website, www.bhp. com/our-approach/operating-with-integrity. And we have of course taken the company's reported contents at face value.
3 Michel Foucault uses the term *dispositif* to mean the various institutional, physical, and administrative mechanisms and knowledge structures associated with the exercise of disciplinary power.

14 Greening the firm

Environmental management accounting

14.1 Introduction

For many years, and to a larger extent even now, social and environmental have been 'externalities' in neoclassical economic and accounting analyses of organizational practices and outcomes. Driven by the notions of the firm, the entity concepts, and money measurement concepts, accounting and economics have, for so long, ignored social and environmental consequences as they did not explicitly influence the firm's production, costs, revenue, and profit functions. However, since the mid-1970s, especially after the Brundtland Commission's report on the global environment and development in 1987, this 'ignorance' has been subjected to severe criticism both in academic and policy circles. Since then, despite the claims that 'sustainable growth when applied to the economy is a bad oxymoron – self-contradictory as prose, and un-evocative as poetry' (Daly 1993, 267) there has been a rapid increase in global awareness and the commitment to sustainability, making it a 'common sense' in our everyday lives. One way or another, for the good of all, the notion of sustainability has posed quite a critical and important array of questions as to how we conduct our organizational, social, economic, and personal affairs. It challenges us to rethink and redesign the way we make decisions, carry out our day-to-day affairs, and meet our accountabilities within and outside organizations.

Management accounting was no exception in this regard. Like many other academic and professional fields, management accounting has also now been challenged to change its ideologies, techniques, and practices to help achieve a sustainable world. The purpose of this chapter is to assess the extent to which management accounting has done this. In doing so we will:

1. First, in Section 14.2, articulate the meaning and elements of the notion of sustainability. Here the attention will be on the three interrelated dimensions of sustainability: economic, social, and ecological.
2. Second, in Section 14.3, we will explain sustainability's neoliberal logic. Here we begin our discussion with Friedman's and others' resistance to the early development of the sustainability agenda in the form of corporate social responsibility. We pay special attention to the neoclassical economic logic which questioned corporate engagement in corporate sustainability activities as an economic irrationality and an 'oxymoron'. We then provide a biopolitical explanation for the evolution of this so called 'oxymoron'.

316   *Neoliberal trends*

3. Then, in Section 14.4, we take the issue of how management accounting responded to the sustainability agenda. Here we provide a conceptual schema to understand management accounting's response to sustainability and provide a four-way analysis of how sustainability is incorporated into management discourses at the corporate apex: the corporate accountability reaction to sustainability; strategizing sustainability; envisioning sustainability; and sustainability as a postulate of strategic positioning.
4. Section 14.5 discusses the operational dimension of management accounting's response to sustainability. Here attention will be paid to: sustainability in capital investment decisions; sustainability in value chain analysis and competitive positioning; sustainability balanced scorecards; and cost accounting for sustainability, which explains how ABC, lifecycle costing, and whole life costing are used to manage the costs of corporate sustainability activities.
5. Finally, Section 14.5 concludes the chapter with a summary.

14.2 Sustainability: the basic concept and its components

Given the fact that 'sustainability' is a highly contested and debated concept, perhaps it is best to start with the Brundtland Commission's definition of sustainability, mainly because it is arguably the most influential point of reference, and the starting point of the contemporary debates on sustainability development. The Commission defines sustainability development as development that meets 'the needs of the present without compromising the ability of future generations to meet their own needs' (United Nations World Commission on Environment and Development (UNWCED) 1987, 8). At the outset, this definition captures the generational conflict between the present and the future; the condition that the way in which we exploit the globe's finite resources impacts upon the possibilities that the globe may become, at worst, uninhabitable in the future or, at best, the life standards of the future would not be as good as today. This early definition has indeed created an astonishing array of debate as to what should be the notion of sustainability, how, and also the possibilities of whether sustainability could be achieved within a capitalist political-economic framework (Bebbington 2001; Gladwin et al. 1995; Gray 2010; Thomson 2007). Nevertheless, 'there remains a widespread agreement that it involves the preservation and/or maintenance of a finite and crucial environment; and incurs some duty of social justice – between and within generations' (Gray 2010, 53). Also, there seems to be a general agreement that sustainability should pay attention to all three spheres that interconnectedly and interactively frame the possibilities of all forms of life, current and future:

1. Economic: This captures the challenges of ensuring sufficient growth in economic affairs in order to mitigate the problems of unemployment, poverty, economic insecurity, and capacity to feed an ever growing global population, and so on. This element of sustainability involves technological and organizational developments to ensure that the world is capable of producing income and resources to meet the needs of both the current and future generations. However, what is central to the notion of sustainability is that economic advancement should not be detrimental to social and environmental sustainability, which are often framed by the two concepts: eco-justice (social) and eco-efficiency (ecological).

2. Ecological: This eco-efficiency dimension concentrates on mitigating the environmental footprint; making sure that our economic and social activities are carried out with no harm to the ecological balance. Eco-efficiency has to be understood in relation to two other concepts: (1) biodiversity (human and other species) and (2) the carrying capacity of the planet and its stock of natural capital. In that sense, ideally speaking, eco-efficiency means that the manner in which we undertake our economic activities should deplete neither the biodiversity nor the stock of natural resources of the planet. It is exactly this notion of eco-efficiency that the Prince of Wales, as a key political proponent of the sustainability agenda, refers to when he writes:

> Since the industrial revolution we have achieved extraordinary prosperity: many people live longer, have access to universal education, better healthcare and the promise of pensions. However, on the debit [negative] side, we in the industrialised world have increased our consumption of the Earth's finite natural resources to such an extent that our collective demands now exceed the planet's capacity to renew itself by some twenty-five per cent annually. In other words, we are consuming Earth's capital as if it were income – and confusing capital for income is not sustainable in the long term.
>
> (HRH The Prince of Wales 2010, p. xiii)

Gray et al. (1996, 3) also echo this but in a different way:

> At minimum, a sustainable business is one which leaves the environment no worse off at the end of each accounting period than it was at the beginning of that accounting period. For a full sustainability, the sustainable business would also re-dress some of the excess of current un-sustainability and consider the intra-generational inequalities. It is perfectly clear that few, if any, businesses, especially in the developed economies, come anywhere near to anything that looks remotely like sustainability.

As Bebbington (2001, 137) argues, eco-efficiency, therefore, is compatible with the UNWCED definition of sustainability we mentioned earlier and is a necessary, but not sufficient, condition for achieving sustainable development. For example, if development was environmentally neutral but the benefits of that development were spread so unevenly that all people's needs were not met, then sustainable development would not be achieved. This is where the concept of eco-justice becomes relevant.

3. Social: This is the eco-justice dimension of sustainability where the attention should be on socio-political issues such as social justice, fairness, cultural diversity, equality, and so on. As such, this involves not only the *fair distribution* of benefits from development within the current generation (intra-generational equity) as well as between current and future generations (inter-generational equity) but also cultural and social struggles against the:

[i]ncreasing destruction of the world's diverse ecosystems, languages and cultures by the globalizing and ethnocentric forces of [predominately] Western consumer culture.

(www.ecojusticeeducation.com)

318   *Neoliberal trends*

In essence, these three dimensions reflect certain fundamental socio-political *contra-dictions* emanating from the way in which Western societies, and then rest of the world, started to organize their political economies since modernity and the scientific revolution. In effect, the contemporary problem of sustainability manifests the way in which our economic activities more or less have become destructive forces against the environment and socially. So, the sustainability agenda demands pervasive changes in all realms of our socio-political and economic activities from the ideological level to the day-to-day organizational practices.

14.3 Sustainability's neoliberal political logic

When it originally emerged in the form of the 'social responsibility of corporations' debate in the 1970s, in the circles of management and economics, the sustainability agenda was subjected to a stream of severe criticism from the proponents of neoliberal economics. At that time, corporations attempting to invest or spend on social responsibility and sustain-ability would be called 'unadulterated socialists undermining the basis of free societies'. Nobel Laureate economist Milton Friedman has been the most prominent in this regard. Writing an essay to *New York Times* magazine, titled 'The Social Responsibility of Business is to Increase its Profits' in the 1970s, he opened his essay declaring that:

> When I hear businessmen speak eloquently about the 'social responsibilities of business in a free-enterprise system,' I am reminded of the wonderful line about the Frenchman who discovered at the age of 70 that he had been speaking prose all his life. The businessmen believe that they are defending free enterprise when they declaim that business is not concerned 'merely' with profit but also with promoting desirable 'social' ends; that business has a 'social conscience' and takes seriously its responsibilities for providing employment, eliminating discrimination, avoiding pollution and whatever else may be the catchwords of the contemporary crop of reformers. In fact, they are − or would be if they or anyone else took them seriously − preaching pure and unadulterated socialism. Businessmen who talk this way are unwitting puppets of the intellectual forces that have been undermining the basis of a free society these past decades.

The reason for this rejection of corporate engagement in matters such as avoiding pollution, eliminating discrimination, etc. is based on the misguided idea of an 'artificial economic personality' − an idea that economic enterprises are, and should be, purely economic and hence cannot, and should not be, held responsible for social and political decisions. Friedman's conception is that, since economic enterprises are owned by shareholders, and since shareholders invest in firms purely for profit motives, and since corporate managers are agents of the shareholders and their ultimate responsibility is towards its shareholders, it is not politically correct for corporate managers to make decisions on social responsibility. Doing so, Friedman contends, would constitute corporate managers as exercising a political power of 'taxing' the owners, which should be in the realm of politics and government not corporations. Thus is the neoclassical economic ideology of the separation of politics and economics:

> This process raises political questions on two levels: principle and consequences. On the level of political principle, the imposition of taxes and the expenditure of

tax proceeds are governmental functions. We have established elaborate constitutional, parliamentary and judicial provisions to control these functions, to assure that taxes are imposed so far as possible in accordance with the preferences and desires of the public – after all, 'taxation without representation' was one of the battle cries of the American Revolution. We have a system of checks and balances to separate the legislative function of imposing taxes and enacting expenditures from the executive function of collecting taxes and administering expenditure programs and from the judicial function of mediating disputes and interpreting the law ... Here the businessman – self-selected or appointed directly or indirectly by stockholders – is to be simultaneously legislator, executive and jurist. He is to decide whom to tax by how much and for what purpose, and he is to spend the proceeds – all this guided only by general exhortations from on high to restrain inflation, improve the environment, fight poverty and so on and on.

(Friedman 1970)

Now, several decades later, the world has changed remarkably. It seems that the corporations have embarked on a drive towards a sustainable world, or at least are seen to give 'lip-service' to this future world. It has now become in fact a pervasive taken-for-granted understanding among large corporations, at least at the rhetorical level, that they should invest and spend on sustainability matters. And we see very little opposition from economists as well.

To the extent that Friedman (and others, e.g. Daly 1993) represents the principles of neoclassical and liberal economic governance, this dramatic change in the acceptance of sustainability as a corporate responsibility manifests a clear movement away from the neoclassical understanding of social responsibilities of economic enterprises. However, despite what neoliberal economists have been telling us regarding 'the nature of the firm', and despite their theories and ideologies being quite dominating and well accepted in the mainstream policy circles, the sociological and political-economic understanding (especially in the critical circles) about the political role of economic enterprises has been much more than just about this neoclassical economic conception. For example, as we already discussed in Chapter 1, since the invention of modernity, when governmentality came into being, certain jurisdictional and veridictional roles of the government have been played within the boundaries of economic enterprises and market apparatuses. Aa we explained in Chapter 1, from a Foucauldian perspective, for example, organizations like factories, schools, hospitals, and so on became their own miniature legal systems, relatively independent and separated from the state but capable of exercising their own judgements, punishments, and rewards on individuals. In that sense, normalizing sanctions within institutional spaces beyond the juridical processes of sovereign state were indeed an extension of the government into the 'normal' spaces of socio-economic life, but with a new disciplinary logic (i.e. governmentality): discipline and punishment now take place within these 'normal' private social spaces.

So, extending this view, one can see that corporations assuming responsibilities of sustainability beyond a mere profit motive are a further evolution of this governmentality; it now moves beyond the disciplinary politics (i.e. anatomico-politics of human body) of normalizing discipline and punishment, to the biopolitics of security. This is indeed neoliberal; extending and empowering the role of the market and private capital into what some might think that the state should be doing. Paradoxically and ironically, this is a process through which certain political and welfare functionalities that

320   *Neoliberal trends*

neoclassical economists like Friedman would see only in the hands of the sovereign state (because private capital paying them could be detrimental to capital accumulation, as they saw it) are now payed for by private capital. Not having a clear understanding or appreciation of this ever increasing governance role of private capital and market apparatuses, how they extend their power over every aspect of our lives, and how they absorb every aspect of political governance into it, Friedman and others initially saw this growth of social responsibility and sustainability as a threat to capital accumulation. And hence, as a threat to the 'freedom' which is conceived as the freedom to accumulate capital. So, they resisted. Nevertheless, their ignorant resistance did not matter, because capital was in the process of enhancing its capacity to accumulate in all its forms, economic, social, and political, translating itself into a much more powerful force of governance, which Hardt and Negri (2000) call the 'empire'. The capital itself is becoming the state, the sovereign, hence it needs to deal with all the matters that the political state hitherto dealt with. In the next few sections, we will explain how accounting researchers dealt with this rapid growth in the notion of sustainability into one of the key cross-disciplinary themes which many initially only understood as an 'oxymoron' (Daly 1993) or 'pure and unadulterated socialism' (Friedman 1970).

14.3.1 Rationalizing the oxymoron

Given the neoclassical economic proposition that an economically rational enterprise would only spend on those activities that would maximize shareholders' wealth, and for those whose analytical mind has been long framed by neoclassical economic logics of agency theory and transaction cost theory, the emergence and growth of the sustainability agenda was indeed an oxymoron, theoretically unexplainable. Yet, they empirically saw that the companies were indeed investing in such economically irrational activities, and corporate social responsibility has been taken very seriously by top managers of world-leading corporations. They saw that there was a measurable growth in sustainability activities, expenditure, and reporting content. For an economics-trained analytical mind, this meant that there was an ever growing dependent variable which needed to be explained. Given economics' ontological assumptions that company managers, being agents of capital, should spend only on those projects which can help contribute to the maximization of shareholders' wealth, this growth should then be related to its efficacy on company financial performance. So, they started to hypothesize that there should be a positive causality between corporate social responsibility (CSR, to also mean corporate sustainability reporting) and the financial performance in order for CSR to prevail and grow. So, the first phase of the academic rationalization of CSR was driven by the testing of this hypothesis and empirically justifying that there was a neoclassical economic rationality behind the growth of sustainability affairs in the corporate world. Al-Tuwaijri et al. (2004, 447), for example, justify their study as follows:

> As managers scramble to compete in the global economy, they must do so within societal constraints characterized by ever-increasing environmental accountability. This accountability includes heightened public scrutiny of both the firm's environmental performance and its public disclosure of that performance. These elements of corporate environmental accountability jointly impact the firm's profitability and the value of its common equity. This study provides

an integrated analysis of how management's overall strategy jointly affects (1) environmental disclosure, (2) environmental performance, and (3) economic performance. Understanding these interrelations is of increasing interest to both internal and external stakeholders in an era in which corporate environmental costs have become a significant business expense ... using a landfill to dump hazardous waste cost only $2.50 per ton in 1978, this charge rose to over $200 per ton by 1987 ... Between 1972 and 1992, total annualized environmental protection costs for US firms tripled as a percentage of Gross Domestic Product (GDP). Senior executives anticipate this trend to continue.

There were quite a large number of studies carried out with the intention of assessing whether 'it pays to be really good' in terms of CSR (e.g. Alexander and Buchholz 1978; Al-Tuwaijri et al. 2004; Artiach et al. 2010; Barnett and Salomon 2012). And they came out with a set of rather mixed research conclusions: some revealing positive while others revealing either negative or inconclusive connections between financial performance and CSR. However, what matters is not whether there is actually a positive or negative relationship, but rather the approach that they have taken and the normative political principles implicit in their approaches. One way or another, what they subsume is the idea that the 'economic' should have a political superiority over the social and environmental, so that the justification for being environmentally and socially sustainable and accountable comes from sustainability's contribution to financial performance, rather than considering that any economic profits calculated should be after considering the social and environmental protection first. In other words, in these approaches, it is still the economic criteria that operate as the higher order principles, or the moral philosophy, in determining whether one should act sustainably. Many economists and management consultants now tend to say that sustainability is good for companies, mainly because it can enhance company profits, either directly or indirectly; or at least it may help mitigate losses coming especially from the financial penalties of not doing so.

14.4 Management accounting's rationalization of sustainability

Mainstream management accounting's rationalization of sustainability also holds onto the same logic of the financial legitimation of sustainability. However, holding onto its prescriptive mode of providing strategic and operational frameworks to 'strategize' sustainability, they are more concerned not about whether there is actually a positive causality between financial performance and sustainability, but how to build a positive 'finality' (see Norreklit 2000) between sustainability and financial performance. This means that, at the outset, it seems that most of the management gurus have now accepted the necessity for corporations to address 'sustainability as a strategic imperative' (see Lubin and Esty 2010), and they are now concerned how sustainability can be incorporated into various management models that they have previously prescribed. Accordingly, what we can see in the recent past, is a series of attempts to modify and update models such as value chain analysis, balanced scorecards, and activity-based costing to address sustainability issues. From our reading of these 'popular' management discourses on sustainability and management accounting, we can outline a schema of incorporating sustainability into management accounting. This is illustrated in Figure 14.1.

The key elements illustrated in Figure 14.1 are discussed in the subsections below.

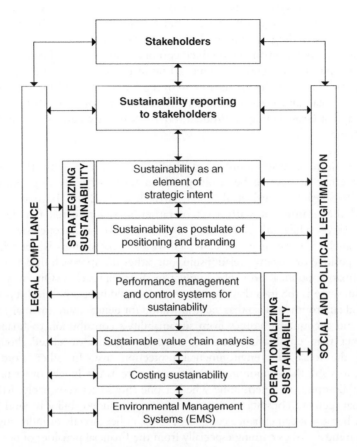

Figure 14.1 Management accounting's incorporation of sustainability

14.4.1 Corporate accountability and sustainability

Corporate engagement in sustainability demands communication with a wider spectrum of stakeholders for legitimation as well as for legal compliance. In the field of accounting, it was this reporting aspect of sustainability (vis-à-vis its institutionalization, strategizing, and operationalization) that became the popular and, hence, the most evolved. In fact, it was not an exaggeration to say that it was the requirement to report sustainability that created the managerial imperative of having internal sustainability management systems including the emerging tools of social and environmental management accounting. This means that sustainability started to penetrate the corporate world mainly as an 'accountability' requirement – as an externally imposed (though not legally imposing yet) demand to provide accounts regarding the environmental and social impact of corporate activities. When looked at it from this accountability angle, sustainability is an obligation imposed upon the companies by its external constituents to provide accounts as to what extent their profit-making operational activities impact upon the social and ecological environment.

The neoliberal transitions had a significant impact upon the way in which corporate accountabilities are conceived. In a sense, neoliberalization means unprecedented signification of the logic of the capital, of its individual entities (i.e. corporations), to reproduce the lives beyond the conventional boundaries of the firm. The economic logic of efficiency and capital accumulation started to penetrate the political state and civil society to reorganize society and polity according to the logic of capital accumulation. Capital itself became the empire, the master, dictating its terms to the world, demanding the world reorganize according to the terms that it imposes upon everyone and everything else (Cooper 2015; Hardt and Negri 2017; Harvey 2005). It is in this neoliberal period that the economic entities that we commonly call the 'firms' in fact became truly independent (and powerful) 'entities' to hold accounting's entity concept as politically true beyond its accounting logic. This means that capital, or its powerful entities such as multinational corporations, are no more 'owned' by someone else called the shareholders. Firms now exist on their own, as independent entities, dictating their terms even to the shareholders. Shareholders have just become not the owners in a true sense, but mere investors of their earnings, savings, and possessions in the capital market. Ownership has become just a legal rhetoric; ownership in itself is a commodity to be traded in the capital market. Investors earn their profit mostly by not actually 'owning' the firm but by trading their ownership in the stock market. The higher the frequency at which such trading of ownership is done, the greater the profit made (think of high frequency trading). In this sense, ownership in itself does not matter, but rather its circulation. The faster the circulation the greater the profits. In fact, in the case of corporate shareholdings, the notion of ownership has become less meaningful or even meaningless.

At the same time, corporations have become extremely big, powerful, and too critical in the global political-economic, cultural as well as ecological order. They have become too big to fail. Their failures are no longer just losses to its shareholders; their failures, either financial or otherwise, mean political-economic catastrophes. As such, corporations, while being the key to much of the progress that human civilization can make, has become the key source of insecurity and risk as well. Parallel to this, and as we have already discussed in Chapter 13 (see Section 13.3.1), neoliberalism has changed the meaning of security and the purpose of government and governance. We mentioned there that, instead of the state's territorial integrity, the doctrine of human security now proclaims insistently that living populations and individuals ought to constitute the new objects of security. Living populations and individuals are what must be protected. What is sacred is no longer the sovereignty of the state, but the 'life' of the individual (Gros 2014, 23) and the possibilities of reproducing that life profitably (see Cooper 2015). In this neoliberal context, therefore, corporations become paradoxical: on the one hand, they are the sites in which life can be reproduced profitably, and, on the other, they are the sites in which life (in its economic, social, cultural, as well as physical dimensions) is put in danger (often profitably), sometimes even resulting in its possible extinction as well.

This neoliberal implosion of ownership, and the paradoxical existence of the firm as a site of both reproducing and endangering life profitably, brought another concept to the forefront in redefining corporate accountability. This is the notion of 'stake' – the positive and negative impact that the firm can make on the collective and individual life. In accountability terms, perhaps for the first time in capitalistic history, the 'stake' has (or started to) become a more important concept than legal ownership. It should be noted that, in the popular management and accounting literature, especially in stakeholder theory, the notion of stake is defined as the capacity of so-called stakeholders to

324 *Neoliberal trends*

influence the firm. For us here, while their capacity to influence the firm is, in itself, important in realizing accountability, the opposite – the ways in which the firm influences the collective and individual life – is more apparent and useful in understanding the way in which accountability has been recently reconstructed as an element of biopolitical governance. This is especially important in the realization that multinational firms have become the most dominating force in determining the way in which we reproduce our lives. Because of this unprecedented capacity of these multinational firms to influence our individual and collective life, both positively and negatively, they have simultaneously become our enemy and our friend; the suspect and prospect; the protector and the danger.

The pluralization of corporate accountability today manifests this neoliberal paradox. Because of this dual existence of the firm in society as suspect and prospect, it needs to legitimize itself not only in its financial performance but on multiple fronts – in all possible realms in which it may pose a threat to the human life. Corporate accountability is this act of legitimation. It involves constructing corporate narratives explaining how corporations contribute to human prosperity and how they mitigate all possible threats that they can cause to human life. Sustainability reporting is the ultimate manifestation of this accountability of the firm towards mitigating all the possible threats that they can cause to human life, ranging from economic to eco-efficiency and eco-justice issues. Sustainability in effect captures this emerging doctrine of security; and sustainability reporting pragmatizes it as a particular set of communicative actions. The firms therefore now have to explain and justify not only how they would contribute to the accumulation of wealth through their financial statements but also how they pose no (or fewer) threats to human and non-human life within and around them. The latter element of this justification is now more or less achieved through sustainability reporting. When seen from this angle of neoliberal biopolitics and security, the rapid growth in corporate engagement with sustainability and its reporting in the recent past, which was once seen as an 'oxymoron' or 'pure and unadulterated socialism', is a particular biopolitical mechanism through which the neoliberal paradox of security associated with the very existence and growth of multinational corporations is attempting to be resolved, though with minimum success.

14.4.2 Strategizing sustainability

While sustainability reporting has been one of the legitimating strategies of corporations within the context of neoliberal accountability, and while such reporting may often count as 'greenwashing', at least some companies have started to take a strategic look at the problem of sustainability. They have recognized the necessity of considering sustainability as a strategic imperative – not only as a challenge posed upon them by the environment but also an opportunity which, if mobilized appropriately, can provide them with better ways to position the firm and its products in the competitive arena. This is what management gurus like Michael Porter have now started to discourse. For example, Porter and Kramer (2006, 2) argue:

> Governments, activists, and the media have become adept at holding the companies to account for the social consequences of their activities. Myriad organisations rank companies on the performance of their corporate social responsibility (CSR), and, despite sometimes questionable methodologies, these

rankings attract considerable publicity. As a result, CSR has emerged as an inescapable priority for business leaders in every country ... Many companies have already done much to improve the social and environmental consequences of their activities, yet these efforts have not been nearly as productive as they could be – for two reasons. First, they pit business against society, when clearly the two are interdependent. Second, they pressure companies to think of corporate social responsibility in generic ways instead of in the way most appropriate to each firm's strategy ... The fact is, the prevailing approaches to CSR are so fragmented and so disconnected from business and strategy as to obscure many of the greatest opportunities for companies to benefit society. If, instead, corporations were to analyse their prospects for social responsibility using the same frameworks that guide their core business choices, they would discover that CSR can be much more than a cost, a constraint, or a charitable deed – it can be a source of opportunity, innovation, and competitive advantage.

In a broader sense, managerial discourses of strategizing sustainability can broadly be categorized into three interrelated strategic moves:

1. Incorporating notions of sustainability in redefining the elements of organizational purpose such as corporate vision and mission.
2. Using sustainability as a postulate of strategic positioning for competitive advantage.
3. Integrating sustainability into the value chain.

14.4.3 Envisioning sustainability

What we mean by 'envisioning sustainability' here is the corporate attempts to incorporate certain sustainability definitions into the company's strategic intents, especially into the corporate vision and mission statements. Much of the top leadership commitment to sustainability is displayed in this way. Since the late 2000s, most of the large corporations who report on sustainability have indeed modified their vision and mission statements (and or other strategic intent statements such as the company credo) to manifest their commitment to sustainability. Figure 14.2 provides some examples in this regard.

One of the key drivers for corporations to redefine their vision and mission in terms of social and environmental sustainability is the reporting requirements of the accreditation bodies such as Global Reporting Initiative (GRI). They have very specifically set out that, in order to get their sustainability reporting accreditations, companies should display at their strategic level a clear commitment to sustainability. For example, GRI in its latest 2016 version of its reporting standards demands that the reporting organizations should include a statement from the most senior decision maker of the organization about the relevance of sustainability to the organization and its strategy for addressing sustainability. In doing so, GRI standards specify that, it should include:

- The overall vision and strategy for the short term, medium term, and long term, with respect to managing the significant economic, environmental, and social impacts that the organization causes, contributes to, or that are directly linked to

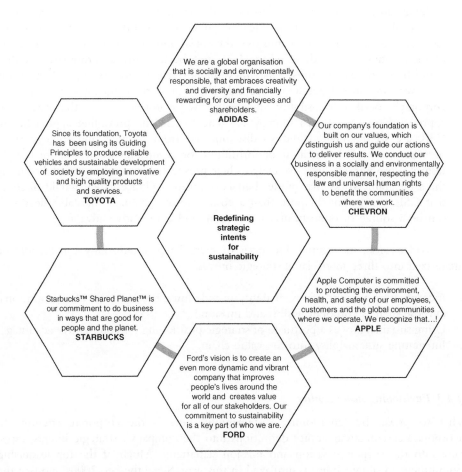

Figure 14.2 Redefining corporate strategic intents for sustainability

its activities, products, or services as a result of relationships with others (such as suppliers and persons or organizations in local communities).
- Strategic priorities and key topics for the short and medium term with respect to sustainability, including observance of internationally recognized standards and how such standards relate to long-term organizational strategy and success.
- Broader trends (such as macro-economic or political) affecting the organization and influencing its sustainability priorities.
- Key events, achievements, and failures during the reporting period.
- Views on performance with respect to targets.
- Outlook on the organization's main challenges and targets for the next year and goals for the coming 3–5 years.
- Other items pertaining to the organization's strategic approach.

When coupled with the companies' necessity for legitimating their actions through reporting (see Bebbington et al. 2008; Campbell 2000; Cho and Patten 2007), such standards provide the necessary institutional pressure for corporations to reform their strategic postures and operational outlook. It seems that companies do engage in the so-called 'rating game' – the companies' attempt at legitimating their operational presence through achieving a higher rating by global rating institutions such as GRI, ISO, the Dow Jones Sustainability Index and FTSE4Good Index (see Alawattage and Fernando 2017; Porter and Kramer 2006). In playing this rating game, the companies, especially those in the less developed countries, deploy a set of textual strategies – imitation, redefinition, innovation, and codification – to communicate the extent to which they are addressing sustainability issues (Alawattage and Fernando 2017). Accordingly, they need to match the communicative elements of their strategic posture with the reporting standards. Many of the changes in the vision and mission statements of the companies reflect this necessity of compliance, reporting, and accreditation.

14.4.4 Sustainability as postulate of strategic positioning

Due to social media as well as traditional media coverage of the instances of environmental pollution and social impact caused by industries, the recent past is characterized by an emergence of mass awareness, appreciation, and commitment towards the sustainability of the planet. In the realm of output markets, this has resulted in a greater demand in, and consumer readiness to pay a premium price for, sustainably produced products. For example, Nielson, a global measurement and data analytics company, in its publication, *Global Sustainability Report 2015: The Sustainability Imperative*, highlights the following key trends:

- Consumer brands that demonstrate commitment to sustainability outperform those that don't. In the past year alone, sales of consumer goods from brands with a demonstrated commitment to sustainability have grown more than 4% globally, while those without grew less than 1%.
- Sixty-six percent of consumers say they are willing to pay more for sustainable brands – up from 55% in 2014 and 50% in 2013.
- Social responsibility is a critical part of proactive reputation management. And companies with strong reputations outperform others when it comes to attracting top talent, investors, community partners, and most of all consumers.
- The following are identified as key purchasing drivers:
  - The products are made by a brand/company that I trust (62% of survey respondents rank this top)
  - The product is known for its health and wellness benefits (59%)
  - The product is made from fresh, natural, and/or organic ingredients (57%)
  - The product is from a company known for being environmentally friendly (45%)
  - The product is from a company known for its commitment to social values (43%)
  - The product's packaging is environmentally friendly (41%)
  - The product is from a company known for its commitment to my community (41%)

In response to such understanding and appreciation of the growing strategic importance of sustainability, especially the assessment that the consumers are ready to pay a

328 Neoliberal trends

premium for sustainably produced products and brands, companies have now embarked on various marketing ploys which are broadly aimed at scooping this market premium for sustainability. Nielsen's (2015, 11) global survey classifies marketing tactics that firm use in this regard into three categories:

1. Claim Only: brand directly indicates a connection to sustainability on a product's label or packaging.
2. Marketing Only: brand uses websites, news coverage, and other messaging vehicles to promote positive social and/or environmental impact in the local or global community.
3. Claim + Marketing: brand uses a product claim and also integrates sustainability into its marketing promotion.

In the global survey, Nielsen identifies that 65% of the companies engage in marketing only, 29% claim + marketing tactics, while only 2% are claim only.

14.5 Operationalizing sustainability

Operationalizing sustainability means corporate attempts to incorporate certain sustainability dimensions and criteria into their decision making, performance evaluation, transaction processing systems, and costing exercises. Accordingly, as illustrated in Figure 14.1, we identify five main elements here.

14.5.1 Sustainability in capital investment decisions

Even though there have not been significant technical breakthroughs in developing capital investment decisions models that can quantify and monetize how sustainability matters in investment decisions, there seems to be some willingness and readiness from corporate managers to 'consider' sustainability issues along with financial considerations in making investment decisions. In the absence of quantified and monetized information on the sustainability impact of investment proposals, managers seem to be increasingly ready to consider qualitative narratives and assessments, as far as they support and supplement the financial outcomes of the investment appraisal. This has been observed, for example, by a survey study that Vesty (2011) carried out in Australia. The survey concludes that:

- Desire to enhance corporate 'reputation' is a major contributing factor for companies to increasingly be positive about considering sustainability in relation to their capital investment decisions. The most prominent way of considering sustainability is to identify 'sustainability risks' in the investment appraisals. In addition, considerations are given to 'competitive advantage', 'community impacts' as well as actions that contribute to 'employee engagement'.
- Fifty-five per cent of CFO respondents claimed they did not downplay qualitative data in favour of quantitative analysis.
- The preference for qualitative data was more evident with social than environmental factors.
- Carbon and water accounting were the dominant sustainability themes that motivated financial capital appraisal experimentation.

Greening the firm 329

- Forty per cent of CFO respondents claimed they would not necessarily reject projects with negative net present values where sustainability benefits were identified.
- Sustainability managers are taking a lead role in capital investment appraisals. In general, they contribute with individual sustainability reports – a separated component of the appraisal process.
- In the case of 'direct' investments in sustainability projects that frequently required different appraisal techniques, the CFO and sustainability manager worked together on appraisal decisions.
- While sustainability impacts are being 'considered' in capital investment decisions, sustainability does not yet constitute the major decision criteria.

14.5.2 Sustainable value chain analysis and competitive position analysis

One of the key attempts to operationalize sustainability within the existing strategic analysis frameworks is the reconceptualization of Michael Porter's value chain analysis. This is a clear illustration of the way in which the global sustainability agenda compelled management gurus to rethink their managerial frameworks in terms of sustainability considerations, at least as a remarketing ploy in a changing epistemic market for managerial models. They argue that:

> When a company uses the value chain to chart all the social consequences of its activities, it has, in effect, created an inventory of problems and opportunities – mostly operational issues – that need to be investigated, prioritized, and addressed. In general, companies should attempt to clear away as many negative value-chain social impacts as possible. Some company activities will prove to offer opportunities for social and strategic distinction.
>
> (Porter and Kramer 2006, 5)

Porter and Kramer's (2006) epistemic strategy in this regard is to 'insert' specific examples of the ways in which sustainability can be 'considered' as an opportunity (rather than a constraint or a cost) for creating value across the value chain. Table 14.1 summarizes their illustrative prescriptions.

Porter and Kramer's (2006) next step is to offer similar 'insertions' into their famous 'diamond framework' of competitive context. As we discussed in Chapter 6, their diamond framework is used to analyse how conductive the national and industrial context is for firms to gain a competitive advantage. Accordingly, four main factors – context for firm strategy and rivalry, factor conditions, demand conditions, and related and supporting industries are to be analysed to see how they collectively create a competitive environment in which firms can excel and develop competitive advantage. We noted in Chapter 6 that this is the tool that Porter used to connect a firm's strategies with the nation's development policy and thereby to offer his theory of competitive advantage as being of political significance beyond the firm. Now, inserting 'sustainability' into this framework, Porter and Kramer try to further extend its political validity as a policy planning and analysis tool. Similar to an assessment of how the competitive environment is conductive to gaining a competitive advantage, now the same model is used to assess how conducive the environment is for firms to be sustainable. Table 14.2 summarizes their insertions into the model.

330 *Neoliberal trends*

Table 14.1 Inserting sustainability into value chain analysis

Value chain element	Examples of operational matters	Ways to consider sustainability: analyse and minimize
Inbound logistics	Incoming materials, storage, data, collection services, customer access.	Transportation impacts (e.g. emissions, congestion, logging roads).
Operations	Assembly, component fabrication, branch operations.	Emissions and waste; biodiversity and ecological impacts; energy and water usage; worker safety and labour relations; hazardous materials.
Outbound logistics	Order processing, warehousing, report preparation.	Packaging use and disposal; transportation impacts.
Marketing and sales	Sales force, promotion, advertising, proposal writing, website.	Marketing and advertising (e.g. truthful advertising, advertising to children); pricing practices (e.g. price discrimination among customers, anticompetitive pricing practices, pricing policy to the poor); consumer information; privacy.
After-sales service	Installation, customer support, complaint resolution, repair.	Disposal of obsolete products; handling of consumables (e.g. motor oil, printing ink); customer privacy.
Firm infrastructure	Financing, planning, investor relations.	Financial reporting practices; government practices; transparency; use of lobbying to promote sustainability.
Human resource management	Recruiting, training, compensation system.	Education and job training; safe working conditions; diversity and discrimination; health care and other benefits; compensation policies; layoff policies.
Technology development	Product design, testing, process design, material research, market research.	Relationships with universities; ethical research practices (e.g. animal testing, GMOs); product safety; conservation of raw materials; recycling.
Procurement	Components, machinery, advertising, services.	Procurement and supply chain practices (e.g. bribery, child labour, conflict diamonds, pricing to farmers); uses of particular inputs (e.g. animal fur); utilization of natural resources.

Source: Porter and Kramer (2006).

14.5.3 Sustainable balanced scorecards

The BSC has been a popular management accounting tool for decades now, and one of the key management accounting responses to the sustainability imperative was to think of ways in which the BSC could be adopted to operationalize sustainability. It seems that studies into the possibilities of sustainability through BSC deal with two major issues: (1) integration of sustainability into the BSC; and (2) establishing the causalities to the strategy and financial outcome measures.

1. First is the issue of integrating the sustainability issues into the strategic performance management systems that the BSC manifests. It is argued that the

Greening the firm   331

Table 14.2 Inserting sustainability into the framework of competitive advantage of a nation

Elements of the diamond framework	Definition of the element	Factors that enhance firms' collective capacity to be sustainable
Context for firm strategy and rivalry	The rules and incentives that govern competition.	Fair and open local competition (e.g. the absence of trade barriers, fair regulations); intellectual property protection; transparency (e.g. financial reporting, corruption: Extractive Industries Transparency Initiative); rule of law (e.g. security, protection of property, legal system); meritocratic incentive systems (e.g. antidiscrimination).
Local Demand Conditions	The nature and sophistication of local customer needs.	Sophistication of local demand (e.g. appeal of social value propositions: Whole Foods' customers); demanding regulatory standards (e.g. California Auto Emissions & Mileage Standards); unusual local needs that can be served nationally and globally (Urbi's housing financing; Unilever's 'bottom of the pyramid' strategy).
Related and Supporting Industries	The local availability of supporting industries.	Availability of local suppliers (Sysco's locally grown produce; Nestlé's milk collection dairies); access to firms in related fields; presence of clusters instead of isolated industries.
Factor (Input) Conditions	Presence of high quality, specialized inputs available to firms.	Availability of human resources (Marriott's job training); access to research institutions and universities (Microsoft's Working Connections); efficient physical infrastructure; efficient administrative infrastructure; availability of scientific and technological infrastructure (Nestlé's knowledge transfer to milk farmers); sustainable natural resources (GrupoNueva's water conservation); efficient access to capital.

Source: Porter and Kramer (2006).

BSC's hierarchical top-down structure of planning that supposedly deduces performance measures from the strategy would guarantee that all business activities, including those catering for environmental and social aspects, would be linked to the successful implementation of business strategy. As such, it is also understood that the relationship between the environmental, social, and economic performance of the firm can be explicitly taken into account in the management of corporate performance. Three possible approaches of integrating sustainability into the BSC are discussed in the literature (see Figge et al. 2002).

• *Integration of environmental and social aspects in the four BSC perspectives.* Here the understanding was that, like any other strategically important aspects, specific sustainability issues pertaining to each of the four BSC dimensions could be incorporated through augmenting the already existing BSC objectives, measures, indicators, and initiatives. This approach was more or less akin to the approach that Porter and Kramer (2006) suggest in relation to Porter's value

332 *Neoliberal trends*

chain analysis framework and diamond model of competitive advantage (discussed earlier). Managers would carefully take into account, for example, in relation to the dimension of internal processes, how these could be enhanced to address eco-justice and eco-efficiency issues such as mitigating gender and other forms of discrimination and reducing the carbon footprint associated with each element of the internal processes. Accordingly, Figge et al. (2002, 274) suppose that:

Environmental/social aspects consequently become an integral part of the conventional Scorecard and are automatically integrated in its cause–effect links and hierarchically orientated towards the financial perspective and a successful conversion of a business' strategy.

- *Introduction of an additional non-market perspective into the balanced BSC.* Here the assumption was that most of the eco-justice and eco-efficiency issues could not be incorporated into the existing scorecards because of the fact that they were not yet fully integrated into the market and institutional processes that the conventional BSC dimensions represent. This meant that an additional fifth dimension needed to be added to the BSC. This could be done, Figge et al. (2002, 274) argue, 'when environmental or social aspects that cannot be reflected according to their strategic relevance within the four standard BSC perspectives at the same time significantly influence the firm's success from outside the market system'. Once added, this additional fifth dimension would be considered as one that affects all other dimensions as well as the strategic core of the BSC.
- *Deduction of a derived environmental and social scorecard.* This approach *did not* mean that the company should develop a separate BSC parallel to the existing BSC. Instead, this was to be understood as an extension of the above two approaches. Here the focus is to 'derive' a BSC from the sustainability issues pertaining to the existing dimensions and the fifth sustainability dimension so that the conventional BSC could be augmented by this derived or extra sustainability BSC. Figge et al. (2002, 275) explain its logic as follows:

A derived scorecard as discussed in this section draws its contents from an existing BSC system and is thus predominantly used in order to coordinate, organize and further differentiate the environmental and social aspects, once their strategic relevance and position in the cause-and-effect chains have been identified by the two approaches presented above.

2. Second is the issue of establishing the causalities between sustainability, strategy, and other dimensions of the BSC. As we discussed in Chapter 7, the concept of the 'strategy map' has been used to articulate the causality (or finality) between key dimensions of the BSC in such a manner that all other dimensions would eventually result in better financial performance in terms of a higher return on investment (see Chapter 7, Section 7.4, especially Figure 7.2). Explaining the strategic causality of sustainability by integrating it into the BSC adopts the same methodology to see how various sustainability issues (such as child labour, the

example Figge et al. (2002) use in their illustrations) can be connected to the causality that sustainability holds within the BSC framework. So, the approach is quite akin to what Porter and Kramer (2006) did in the case of Porter's value chain and diamond model; to see the possibilities of inserting sustainability issues within the existing framework.

Privileging financial over sustainability

Such attempts at integrating sustainability into existing performance management and strategy frameworks would definitely bring some positive outcomes, not least in terms of the managerial acceptance and appreciation of the importance of sustainability issues. They would in fact bring out some KPIs that translate sustainability concerns into specific performance targets and, thereby, would enact some operational initiatives to deal with sustainability. However, such initiatives and enactments would be possible only to the extent that the management could effectively demonstrate a positive financial causality of such KPIs and initiatives. In other words, these attempts at integrating sustainability into the existing performance management and strategy framework limit the way in which we consider and prioritize sustainability. Sustainability is operationalized only if it can be established that there is a positive causality between financial performance and solving sustainability issues. This is because existing performance management and strategy frameworks, including BSC and value chain analysis, are too capitalistic and they assess managerial actions and initiatives only through their contributions towards shareholder wealth maximization. So, any attempt to integrate sustainability into such a framework would eventually surrender sustainability to the possibilities of profits and would only operate as a tool of 'financial legitimation of sustainability'. In effect, as our commonsense often tells us, many of the eco-justice and eco-efficiency issues would not have a direct demonstrable positive causality towards the return on investment. Perhaps the only financial causality would be the punitive cost effect (such as penalties, loss of reputation, loss of market share, etc.) that not attaining to eco-justice and eco-efficiency issues would create. This basically means the BSC and value chain analysis-based management of sustainability, as far as it is so far conceptualized, privileges the financial over sustainability.

14.5.4 Cost accounting for sustainability

Currently, we see two distinct cost accounting approaches to sustainability discussed in the literature: (1) the use of ABC to trace the cost of sustainability activities to the product costs, and (2) lifecycle costing. In either case, it should be noted that the existing approaches are more or less tilted towards tracing 'environmental' (more than social) elements of sustainability, especially accounting for greenhouse gas (GHG) emissions.

Use of ABC in sustainability costing

Here the assumption is that, similar to the way in which cost accounting systems trace and account for the 'financial effect' of organizational transactions and events, it is possible to accurately quantify environmental emissions – inventorying them over time (see Lemon and Pember 2014). To this end, then, ABC is understood to be an effective tool because it helps understand the 'drivers of resource consumption', which is an essential building

334 *Neoliberal trends*

block of understanding to what extent organizational activities lead to GHG emissions. In other words, ABC models resources that are consumed, why they are consumed, and who consumes them (see Lemon and Pember 2014). This means that ABC can also be used to understand and explain the extent of the organization's GHG emissions, why they are released, and who should be held accountable in the organization for these emissions.

There are of course numerous papers and texts that try to explain how corporations should go about accounting for environmental emissions, but two 'white papers' stand out in terms of not only their institutionalized epistemic power but also their comprehensiveness: 'Environmental Management Accounting: International Guidance Document' issued by the International Federation of Accountants (2005) and the 'Environmental Management Accounting Procedures and Principles' document issued by the United Nations Division for Sustainable Development (2001). The approach that both these white papers propagate can be understood more or less as a combination of 'natural capital inventory accounting' and 'input-output analysis' (for a detailed discussion of these approaches, see Gray and Bebbington 2001; Gray et al. 1993; Lamberton 2005). In a broader sense, this includes tracing the environmental impact of organizational activities by tracing the *physical flow* of inputs, processes, activities, and outputs and then *attributing monetary values* to such inputs, processes, activities, and outputs.

1. **Tracing the physical flows – materials flow accounting**: There is a systems theory assumption behind tracing the physical flow of the environmental impact such that all physical inputs must eventually become outputs – either physical products or waste and emissions – and the inputs and outputs must balance. This input-output balance needs to be accounted for in terms of physical resources such as energy, water, materials, and waste. This physical flow accounting is interchangeably called 'materials balance', 'input-output balance', 'mass balance', or 'eco-balance'. As International Federation of Accountants (2005, 30) prescribes:

   > [u]nder this physical accounting side of environmental management accounting, organizations should try to track all physical inputs and outputs and ensure that no significant amounts of energy, water or other materials are unaccounted for … Many organizations perform energy balances and water balances separately from other materials balances.

The 'accounting entity' for which this 'input-output balancing' is undertaken can be carried out at different levels: for the entire organization, for a particular manufacturing site or operational unit, a process, a machinery, product or a service line, or it can even be extended beyond the boundaries of the organization to include physical information from suppliers, customers, and other elements of the supply chain. When this is extended to such elements in the supply chain, then it is called Supply Chain Environmental Management. For this 'materials flow accounting' to offer a complete an integrated picture of 'eco-balance', International Federation of Accountants (2005, 31) prescribes that the details of materials flows must be traced through all the different organizational materials' management steps, such as materials procurement, delivery, inventory, internal distribution, product shipping, waste collection, and recycling, treatment, and disposal, etc. Such materials flow accounting should specifically account for:

- raw and auxiliary materials
- packaging materials

Greening the firm   335

- merchandize
- operating materials including energy
- waste water
- air emissions
- products, by produce and packaging
- solid waste and hazardous waste.

Accounting for the physical flow is important in two senses. First, it provides the physical activity basis upon which the cost accounting side of environmental management accounting can be designed and implemented. It provides a clear understanding of the particular activities that drive environmental costs. Second, and relatedly, physical flow accounting also provides the basis upon which certain *environmental performance indicators* (EPIs) can be established. Such EPIs can be either *absolute indicators* that measure the consumption of natural resources and the generation of waste and emissions, such as the total amount of fresh water consumed and the total amount of waste water generated for the accounting period. EPIs can also be *relative* or *normalized indicators* such as the amount of fresh water consumed per unit of output and the amount of waste water generated per unit of manufactured goods or services provided.

2. **Tracing the monetary flow – activity based costing of environmental impact**: Here the attempt is to trace the costs associated with environmental activities and then attribute them to the products (i.e. cost objects). United Nations Division of Sustainable Development (2001, 75) advocates that:

    > [w]henever possible, environment-driven costs should be allocated directly to the activity that causes the costs and to the respective cost centres and cost drivers. Consequently, the costs of treating, for example, the toxic waste arising from a product should directly and exclusively be allocated to that product.

In comparison to conventional absorption costing, ABC is said to be superior because it provides a better view of the 'cost incidents' or how resources are consumed by the organizational activities (including environmental activities) and, accordingly, how costs are generated by the activities. This means that it provides an analytical basis not only to measure the full cost of cost objects but also to set performance measures related to the activities. This dual usefulness of ABC is captured in the accounting textbooks by the terminology of 'cost assignment view' and 'process view'. This is summarized in Figure 14.3 in relation to environmental activities and costs.

Lifecycle costing (LCC) and whole life costing (WLC)

One of the key points to make about the costing sustainability that we have discussed so far is that physical flow accounting and monetary flow accounting based on ABC only consider the sustainability implications of capital investment decisions to the extent imputed in the depreciation of fixed assets. LCC and WLC, on the other hand, explicitly deal with large capital investment projects that have construction elements. It is often defined as a tool for assessing the total cost performance of an asset over its

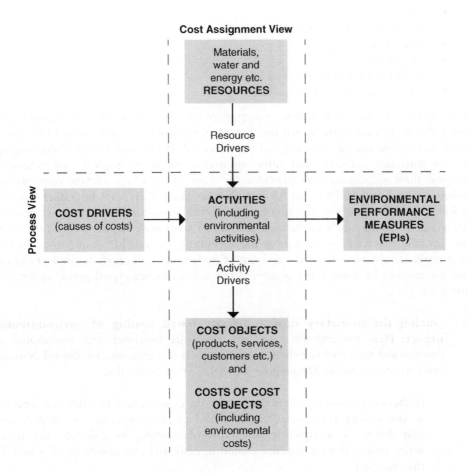

Figure 14.3 Environmental activity-based costing

lifecycle, including the acquisition, operating, maintenance, and disposal costs (Dragos and Neamtu 2013; Langdon 2007). This is an important tool of decision making in the construction industry, especially pertaining to the public procurement of capital assets and is covered by a set of international standards as well (e.g. BS/ISO15686-5).

Both LCC and WLC are based on the assumption that the purchase price of a capital asset alone does not reflect the financial and non-financial gains that an environmentally and socially preferable asset would offer, because such gains (and costs) accumulate throughout the lifecycle of the asset. This means that procurement decisions based on purchase price would favour economic efficiency but possibly at the expenses of environmental and social costs. LCC commonly considers four main cost categories, purely based on financial valuation: investment costs, operational costs, maintenance costs, and end-of-life disposal costs. When these basic cost categories are extended to incorporate 'externalities' associated with the work, service, or the product, then it becomes Environmental Life Cycle Costing (ELCC) which, for example, may measure the external costs of global warming contributions associated with the emissions of different GHGs, the amount of acidifications, eutrophication, or other measurable impacts (Dragos and Neamtu 2013).

WLC extends LCC. LCC focuses only on the construction, maintenance, operation, and disposal of the asset. WLC extends this into client and user costs, such as project financing, land, income, and external costs (those not borne by parties to the construction contract – such as tenants). So, LLC is in effect a subcategory of WLC. This difference is illustrated in Figure 14.4.

14.5.5 Environmental management systems

Environmental management systems (EMS) basically capture most of the elements we have discussed in this chapter. In a broader sense, EMS is the totality of the formal elements that the organization has put in place to decide, design, implement, manage, control, achieve, and report its environmental policies and objectives. As Gray and Bebbington (2001, 87) explain, EMS is the means by which the organizations' dispersed responses to environmental issues are systematically harmonized and integrated with the other management and accounting systems. The concept of EMS often works in a similar

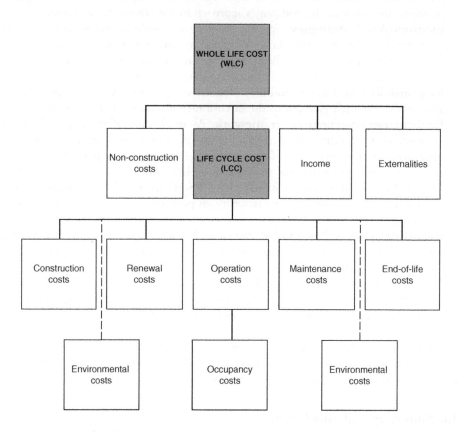

Figure 14.4 WLC and LLC costs
Source: Royal Institution of Chartered Surveyors (RICS) (2016, 5).

338   *Neoliberal trends*

way to total quality management (TQM) systems, aiming at 'integrating' the environmental quality into the operational processes and culture of the organization, and making it everyone's job and responsibility to minimize the environmental impact of the day-to-day operations of the firm. Of course, as in the case of quality management, the specific approaches that companies follow would differ depending on their specific circumstances. However, in a broader sense, we can outline the following key elements of EMS:

1. **Environmental audits, surveys, and assessments**: The organization should first carry out careful assessments of legislative, market, and industrial contexts in order to understand the legislative and other stakeholder pressures. This should then be combined with an internal assessment of the operations and processes in order to understand the nature of 'environmental impact' that the company is making and to determine the 'priorities' pertaining to mitigating this impact. Technical tools to be used for these assessments can include, for example, formal environmental audits, input-output analysis, lifecycle costing, value chain analysis, activity-based environmental analysis, etc.
2. **Environmental objectives and policies**: These include the policy framework that shows the company's (and its sub-units') overall normative approach to environmental issues. This specifies the level of corporate commitment to environmental issues, priority areas, necessities of legal and regulatory compliances, and the general principles upon which the company's approach to the environment is based.
3. **Environmental strategies**: Specific programmes, projects, and initiatives that the company is currently undertaking (or plans to undertake) in order to realize its environmental objectives and policies. And the ways in which the company's operational activities are to be redesigned and managed to make a positive environmental impact.
4. **Responsibility and accountability structure**: Specifying who is responsible and accountable for each element of the environmental management strategies.
5. **Performance management framework**: As an element of the responsibility and accountability structure, there need to be specific processes designed to ensure the operational implementation of environmental strategies, to periodically review their outcomes, and protocols to revise the plans and actions as necessary. Tools such as the BSC and budgets would play a significant role here in integrating the environmental elements into the mainstream performance management systems of the company.
6. **Reporting systems**: These include the establishment of transaction processing systems capable of accounting for the environmental impact of the day-to-day operations (e.g. recording travel mileages and physical consumption of energy) in a trustworthy manner (i.e. maintaining audit trails). This also includes establishing the systems through which such data are compiled into periodic reports and assessments including sustainability reports and environmental audits by internal and external parties.

Explaining these elements further is beyond the scope of this chapter. However, there are a number of good texts that provide a detailed discussion on these elements. One of the best to read in this regard is Bebbington (2001).

14.6 Summary and conclusions

The aim of this chapter was to discuss the way in which management accounting responded to the sustainability agenda. We started the discussion by explaining the financial, eco-efficiency, and eco-justice dimensions of sustainability. We then moved on to discuss the neoliberal political rationality of international organizations and corporations promoting the sustainability agenda. Initially, leading neoclassical economists like Friedman and Daly were opposed to the idea that private-sector organizations should engage in social responsibility activities. They saw corporate engagement in sustainability and corporate social responsibility as an 'oxymoron'. Nevertheless, despite such resistance from leading economists and policy gurus, the corporate social responsibility agenda grew significantly, in effect nullifying those neoclassical economic views. For neoclassical economics-based mainstream researchers, this was indeed a paradox to explain. Hence, their initial response was to hypothesize that there should be a positive correlation between corporations' sustainability engagements and shareholders' value. So, there emerged a series of studies attempting to empirically 'test' this hypothesis which, nevertheless, ended up with mixed conclusions, in effect failing to find a neoclassical economic explanation for the significant growth in the sustainability project.

Outside the mainstream neoclassical economics-based accounting studies, there emerged a strong stream of research which has now created what we broadly call sustainability accounting or social and environmental accounting. In this field of research, we see interesting and competing theorizations of corporations' engagement in sustainability activities. These include popular systems theory-based explanations extending to stakeholder theory and legitimacy theory, institutional explanations of isomorphism and institutional legitimation, as well as certain political-economic explanations. As these have been widely discussed in the field of sustainability accounting in general, we did not pay special attention to these theorizations of sustainability accounting. However, we provided a brief biopolitical explanation of the growth in the sustainability agenda. There we saw corporate engagement in sustainability as a neoliberal extension of governmentality – corporate capital assuming a greater role in social and political governance and corporate capital penetrating into the realm of politics.

The primary focus of this chapter was, however, the way in which management accounting responded to the sustainability agenda. We explained management accounting's response in a layered fashion, first, concentrating on the way in which strategic elements of management were reformed to incorporate sustainability and, second, to reveal how operational techniques were modified for that purpose. In the realm of corporate-level or strategic-level responses, we saw three distinct responses: (1) extending the corporate accountability beyond the shareholders; (2) recognizing the strategic significance of sustainability as a proposition of strategic positioning; and (3) envisioning sustainability through reforming corporate strategic statements such as the vision and mission statements.

In the realm of operationalizing sustainability through management accounting technologies and practices, we saw an emerging set of strategic management accounting tools being deployed to conceptualize and manage sustainability issues. We discussed them in four interrelated themes: (1) the way in which sustainability issues were incorporated into capital investment decisions; (2) the way in which Porterian strategy discourses, especially value chain analysis and competitive position analysis, were used in operationalizing sustainability; (3) the way in which BSC was mobilized to manage sustainability performance; and (4) the emergence of new cost accounting techniques for costing sustainability and managing sustainability costs. In respect of sustainability cost accounting, three important themes were discussed: the use of ABC, lifecycle costing, and whole life costing.

Finally, environmental management systems were discussed as the management framework that integrates much of the accounting and management techniques we discussed in the chapter.

340 *Neoliberal trends*

Assignments

These assignments are meant to extend your knowledge beyond what you understand from this chapter. These are not simply revision questions. The content covered in this chapter is necessary but will not be sufficient in attempting these tasks. Therefore, you are required to do some extra reading in attempting these tasks.

1. **Thematic essay:**

    > When I hear businessmen speak eloquently about the 'social responsibilities of business in a free-enterprise system,' I am reminded of the wonderful line about the Frenchman who discovered at the age of 70 that he had been speaking prose all his life. The businessmen believe that they are defending free enterprise when they declaim that business is not concerned 'merely' with profit but also with promoting desirable 'social' ends; that business has a 'social conscience' and takes seriously its responsibilities for providing employment, eliminating discrimination, avoiding pollution and whatever else may be the catchwords of the contemporary crop of reformers. In fact, they are – or would be if they or anyone else took them seriously – preaching pure and unadulterated socialism. Businessmen who talk this way are unwitting puppets of the intellectual forces that have been undermining the basis of a free society these past decades.
    >
    > (Milton Friedman 1970)

    Critically evaluate this statement. You should first articulate Friedman's economic arguments against the corporations engaging in sustainability and social responsibility related activities and then offer a critique drawing on alternative theoretical explanations of sustainability.

2. **Poster:**
    Draw a poster illustrating how management accounting has responded to emerging sustainability issues. Pay attention to both strategic and operational responses.

3. **Presentation:**
    Prepare a set of PowerPoint slides, together with notes if necessary, for a 30-minute presentation on the following theme:
    'Sustainability involves offering organizations a new set of strategic visions, competitive strategies, and operational tactics'.

4. **Extended bibliography:**
    Write an extended bibliography on the topic 'sustainability and management accounting'. For this, you need to do a literature survey in major accounting journals and edited books where critical accounting research is published. Organize the bibliography into a table in the following format.

Bibliographic info	Nature of the paper/book chapter (e.g. conceptual/ theoretical, empirical, a response to a previous publication)	Major arguments, conclusions, and contributions

Greening the firm 341

5. **Literature review:**
   Suppose you are writing a thesis/dissertation on strategic management accounting. You intend to review critical accounting and management literature in order to explain the biopolitical implications of the notions of sustainability. You intend to pay special attention to the way in which notions of sustainability demand that corporations extend their traditional management control systems and procedures to address an emerging set of biopolitical themes, and hence, assume a role of biopolitical accounting.

   You are required to do the necessary literature survey and write a chapter circa 5,000 words.

15 Strategizing development

15.1 Introduction

This chapter ends this book, but it also opens up a new domain for management accounting research. It invites you to recognize the development discourse as a managerial discourse which reproduces a unique set of management accounting practices – a set of calculative practices that subjugates nation-states and civil societies to a new regime of global governmentality which we may call 'developmentality' (see Ilcan and Phillips 2010). Operating within the biopolitical realms, these calculative practices set forth a new set of neoliberal ambitions not only for nation-states but also for all ranges of other organizations including multinational corporations, small and medium enterprises, NGOs, charities, etc. They bring all sorts of organizations and individuals under an overarching political-economic normativity which we now call 'development'. This normativity is discursive, calculative, and programmatic. Hence, the key terms to be elaborated in this chapter are thus development discourses, calculative practices, and development programmes and practices. This chapter will explore how these discourses have come about, how they are linked to a new set of biopolitical calculations, how development programmes are constructed and linked to those calculations, and how we can discern a form of management accounting[1] practice emanating from this neoliberal discourse of development. In doing so, the chapter will offer a framework for understanding how the notion of strategizing penetrates the realm of development with a new set of calculative practices, which we may call development accounting. This framework will, we hope, then be debated and used in future empirical research which is considering development as a domain of accounting analysis.

Even though the majority of the world's population lives in conditions of underdevelopment and poverty, accounting plays a crucial role in the reproduction of such exploitative conditions, and there is a possibility that accounting indeed can play a positive role in lessening such conditions. The notion of development has long been ignored in the accounting literature. However, the issues of development and accounting have been congenially used since the early 1990s when Professor Trevor Hopper at the University of Manchester, UK, promoted this agenda among some of his early PhD students, including one of the authors of this book. The trajectory has evolved since then producing a small flood of research (e.g. Alawattage et al. 2007; Hopper et al. 2009, 2017; Hoque and Hopper 1994; Uddin and Hopper 2001; Wickramasinghe et al. 2004). The agenda today is sparkling with: a growing number of PhD students looking into various connections between development issues and accounting, a new journal dedicated to this research (i.e. *Journal of Accounting and Finance in Emerging Economies*), an

Strategizing development 343

emerging research conference to showcase new ideas and frameworks, and enthusiastic research centres being established in Western universities. This chapter is built on these inspirations but with a framework strengthening the trajectory. The chapter is organized as follows.

1. Section 15.2. Here you will see development as a domain in which management accounting has started to play an important role, especially since the 1990s. It is what we call development accounting to connote that, on the one hand, development policies and programmes have now escaped their orthodox disciplinary parameters of economics and development geography and have invested heavily in accounting and other related managerial discourses to find a new neoliberal facet. The chapter then goes on to examine how accounting, on the other hand, is coming to be a forerunner in shaping those development programmes and practices, constituting new identities and roles. In short, we see accounting and development as reciprocal forces shaping each other's functions into different ones.

2. Section 15.3. In this section we articulate a biopolitical framework to understand development accounting. Here, we will be discussing how development discourses evolved in the West as a 'text' and then mobilized in the 'context' of the rest of the world. This discussion will then proceed to examine how development became a form of governmentality in the era of neoliberalism. It is this move in which we can see how management accounting plays a role in recognizing development as a 'strategic change'. This is in effect strategizing development.

3. Section 15.4. This section is about how global development funding institutions such as the World Bank and OECD have created a new set of calculative practices and deploy them to create a new biopolitical domain of governance and development. You will see that these practices – be they statistics, league tables, ranking and prioritizing certain programmes, or ideas – are textual technologies constituting a discursive assemblage of both quantitative and qualitative assessments, analyses, evaluations, as well as opinions. As a new form of accounting operating in the domain of development, these textual tactics and practices make development a powerful and influential discourse enabling governments, policy institutions, civil society organizations, multinational corporations, and various other institutions and individuals to embrace and participate in development in various ways.

4. Section 15.5 In this section, you will see whether and how local settings also become centres for creating new ideas of modifying existing practices in the light of embracing development discourses. This section will elaborate how such ideas and practices emerge due to local circumstances and how such developments are used to respond to the centre. One of the major ideas developed in the recent past has been the concept of microfinance. We will outline how the World Bank has taken steps to receive and promote it across less developed countries.

5. Section 15.6 concludes the chapter (and the whole book), showing how the liberal origins of management accounting have been transformed into a neoliberal origin and how management accounting is now different from its conventional wisdom. As will be concluded, the chapter as well as the book will be a space for future researchers to continue this examination with empirical evidence and theoretical modifications.

344 *Neoliberal trends*

15.2 Development and accounting: the connection

Development has been a contested term leading to debates and controversies both in academic and policy circles since the 1940s. From a development theory perspective, writers try to model development into scenarios of 'underdevelopment', mostly in terms of measuring the extent of the political-economic and social issues that former colonies confronted during their post-colonial regimes (Edwards 1989; Hunt 1989). By underdevelopment, they meant both economic and social 'backwardness' of developing countries in comparison to their developed counterparts, often measured in terms of a composite of 'development indicators' such as GDP growth rate, unemployment, income disparity, the human development index, and so on. They were worried about what development should be, how it should be measured, and how it can be better implemented (Crush 1995). As such, in the notions of development and under-development, there is an inevitable and inherent bipolarity between the North and the South, the so-called developed and the underdeveloped. These have always been understood in comparative terms between these two. From a critical-structuralist perspective, development was understood as a continuation of the North's imperialism on the South, which creates a world system of inequality (Cardoso and Faletto 1979; Frank 1979; Taylor 1979; Wallerstein 1974). For these writers, a developing country is only a site of the 'world system' which ensures the continuity of the accumulation of wealth by the rich West. It is in these sites that the Western centres, through various policy interventions, put their economic and epistemic power into practice to create both the ideological and material conditions of dependency and (under)development in order to continue the accumulation of capital in the West, often under the assumption that it was such accumulation which would eventually bring development to the periphery. Despite the criticisms levelled against this thesis (see Skocpol 1977), its theoretical premise generated a significant amount of attention from social scientists and explored the mechanisms by which this worldwide system of producing inequality was reproduced. From a Foucauldian governmentality perspective, development has been seen as a form of 'developmentality' which explores how power/knowledge relation-ships are established through various techno-managerial and policy discourses (Escobar 1995; Ferguson 2006; Ilcan and Phillips 2010; Tsing 2005). In either case, both structuralist and Foucauldians, in one way or the other, articulate centre-periphery dialectics of development where the centre's managerial and economic ideas are implemented in the periphery in the name of development, converting the peripheral economies into a set of perpetual sites of 'development experimentation', subjectiva-tion, and exploitation.

Other than this brief sketch, we do not attempt to define development in precise terms because it has now become a glossy term crossing a number of social science disciplines (see Crush 1995). However, we will consider development as a new epistemic terrain in which calculative practices play a performative role in linking the centre with the periphery, on the one hand, and in facilitating the periphery to respond to the centre with new forms of development ideologies, calculations, and justifications. In this reciprocity, various accounting programmes and technologies are initiated and promoted in the centre as elements of the neoliberal development package are disseminated to the developing world and are rooted in the periphery producing intended and unintended consequences. The unintended negative con-sequences, which indeed seem to be larger than the intended positive outcomes,

Strategizing development 345

then become the problems for the centre to re-resolve through continuous policy (and sometimes military) interventions (Hopper et al. 2009). In this problem-driven connection between the centre and the periphery, development discourses necessitate accounting as a technology of development. Accounting facilitates the legitimation and rationalization of development discourses. It is this dialectic nature of accounting's connection with development which we term 'development in accounting', and 'accounting in development' (Wickramasinghe 1996). And, it is this dual form which we call 'development accounting'. As we will discuss later in the chapter, development accounting plays a mediating role between the centre and the periphery, be this relationship a frictional (Tsing 2005) or a discursive encounter (Escobar 1995).

In this dialectical connection between the periphery and the centre, accounting can influence in two ways: 'development in accounting' and 'accounting in development'. By the term 'development in accounting', what we mean is the role that development discourses play in the reformation of accounting practices in the peripheral nations. In this regard, researchers have made a considerable effort to report on how development programmes are implicated in accounting reforms in less developed countries (Hopper et al. 2009, 2017). In other words, development discourses have interfered in the traditional forms of management accounting in discoursing accounting as a necessary and critical element of neoliberal development. In this signification of accounting as a development technology, management accounting is transformed into a new type. Researchers found that neoliberal development discourses and projects have transformed accounting practices from their colonial and post-colonial forms of being elements of the legal-rational bureaucracy and centralized planning, to neoliberal forms that can eliminate the pitfalls of centralized bureaucratic controls, the politicization of economic enterprises, and thereby enhance economic efficiency and profitability in private and public-sector organizations (see Uddin and Hopper 2001; Wickramasinghe and Hopper 2005; Wickramasinghe et al. 2004). The development discourses that enacted accounting as technology of development were, inter alia, structural adjustments, privatization programmes, liberalization policies, new public management, good governance, and sustainable development (for a review, see Hopper et al. 2009). These discourses have been entering the periphery through transnational development agencies such as the World Bank, IMF, OECD, and UN as well as through other epistemic communities such as consultants, management gurus, academic and professional programmes, and university programmes of development administration for the peripheral countries. Through such discourses, conventional accounting has now received a higher order purpose moving far beyond mere shareholder wealth maximization: it is now registered in the project of poverty alleviation, good governance, combatting corruption, and economic development.

For example, part of the Bangladeshi development agenda was its 1990s privatization programme. Its aim was to transfer the ownership of public enterprises to private owners. Prior to privatization, these enterprises' accounting systems were based on traditional bureaucratic procedures, often run on a conventional public-sector budgeting and cash-based accounting of transactions and events. Such accounting was not for decision making but primarily for financial reporting and national accounting. Imperatives for such accounting were regulatory and legal rather than strategic and managerial. Legal and regulatory compliance was the primary purpose rather than decision-usefulness. At their best, such accounting only legitimated the political decision making. With neoliberal reforms such as privatization, there were dramatic changes. Hopper et al. (2012) remarked on this:

346 *Neoliberal trends*

New owners computerised management accounting systems and linked market information to production schedules. Budget became centralised and market oriented, and all financial information became the preserve of the owning family.

(p. 213)

In Ghana['s] gold mine[s], greater private ownership brought updated Western management controls. The budgeting system was computerised, and an integrated accounting software package … and activity-based coting were introduced.

(p. 214)

[i]n the Sri Lankan telecommunications firm its post-privatisation Japanese chief executive exercised [a] direct but consultative style of management, worked within the prevailing trade union structure, and changed performance appraisal and reward to recognised achievement.

(p. 215)

Neoliberal reforms and modernization programmes in the 1990s brought new accounting practices through changing technical procedures and developing a culture of using accounting for mundane, operational purposes. Hence, the neoliberal development agenda became a vehicle for transforming the way in which accounting technologies were used. We will elaborate this point later in the chapter.

'Accounting in development' – the other side of the coin – came about with neoclassical economic justifications. While development became a vehicle for accounting transformations in less developed countries, accounting itself provided strands of justification in respect of development programmes propagated and institutionalized by the centre. Development agencies such as the World Bank, the IMF, and WTO assumed that accounting could enhance efficiency and resolve agency problems which were perennial in public-sector management (Hopper et al. 2009, 2012). In other words, the neoliberal rationale for privatization was based on 'management accounting' arguments derived from neoclassical economic theories. Hopper et al. (2012, 208) observed this:

> Frequently arguments for privatization rest on economic theories of productive and allocative efficiency that stress the micro-economic benefits of property rights and sound contractual relationships between agents and principals, and macro-economic benefits of private ownership and markets for public finances and capital investment.

Such neoclassical economic signification of efficient agency relationships was quite fashionable in the 1990s when neoliberalism started to promote the ideology that the private sector is the 'engine of growth and development'. The conventional wisdom of management accounting as a core technology of mitigating the agency problem in the private sector had already been developed in neoclassical economic terms by then (for a brief review, see Neimark and Tinker 1986). Hence, development gurus' formulation of privatization programmes was in effect a manifestation of that conventional wisdom of management accounting; an attempt to resolve the problem of public-sector inefficiencies through bringing in the technologies of mitigating the agency problem in property ownership. Although development economists did not explain this accounting connection explicitly, management accounting researchers discussed it in detail with a volume of rich case studies (for a review, see Hopper et al. 2009).

In explaining this connection between accounting and development discourses in the less developed countries, we need to understand the particular political-historical context within which this dialectical connection evolved. As we explained in Chapters 1 and 2, the historical evolution of management accounting in the Western centres was an intrinsic historical movement associated with the development of capitalism and modernity. This evolution was internal to the Western economies. In contrast, accounting developments in the peripheries had always been an imperialist project, superimposed upon them by the imperial centres. Initially, it was in the form of colonialism where development was then taking the form of 'civilizing' the rest of the world by the West. Accounting practices penetrated the non-Western countries thorough this imperial 'modernizing' and 'civilizing' project. These early accounting developments in the periphery have been well explained through imperial and post-colonial angles, articulating the idea that accounting has been a technology of imperialism and colonialism (see Annisette 1999, 2000). In such historical studies, the dialectical connection between accounting and imperialism has been well explained: the way in which imperialism necessitated accounting and the way in which accounting was instrumental in realizing the imperial project.

This dialectical connection between accounting and development took a new form in recent decades when neoliberalism penetrated the agenda of 'developing' (i.e. the post-colonial form of civilizing) the rest of the world. New forms of accounting were necessitated to facilitate the structural reforms driven by privatization and rural development, which were in turn driven by microfinance and its associated entrepreneurial development projects. International development funding agencies such as the World Bank and OECD initiated a massive programme of 'accounting development' across less developed countries. In the realms of industrial and commercial development, accounting reforms were introduced to modernize the management of privatized economic enterprises. The idea was to inculcate private-sector-like business practices and cultures within hitherto government-owned economic enterprises. New forms of cost management were introduced to the newly privatized economic enterprises in order to enhance their economic efficiency and profitability (see Alawattage and Alsaid 2018). Similarly, in the realm of rural development, accounting was introduced to the rural poor (especially women) to make them entrepreneurial through micro-credit programmes (Alawattage et al. forthcoming). We will discuss these accounting developments further in the forthcoming sections.

15.3 Developmentality and governmentality

15.3.1 Development discourse and its textual ramifications

Discourse analyses of development have drawn on Foucault's ideas (Bhabha 1990; Escobar 1995; Said 1978). Two main dimensions were salient in these discourse analyses of development: conditions of domination and conditions of possibility. Domination is about the imposition of Western power on the other parts of the world. This domination was inserted not only through the power of financial capital and technologies but also through their dominating ideas and concepts of development and progress, which constitute epistemic elements of global governance (Scholte 2002).

348 Neoliberal trends

Seeing the 'other world' as problematic and thus seeing opportunities for imposing Western solutions upon them meant that the peripheral nations gave rise to 'development as a possibility' through Western development discourses. This is to say that their economies are not like the West; their living conditions were miserable; and as people's life chances were restricted, so they needed interventions. Hence, some critical development researchers see development more as a Western discursive construct in which transnational institutions such as the World Bank played a crucial epistemic role (see Goldman 2005). This is the idea that 'development is a discourse', which Escobar (1995, 6) explains as follows:

> To see development as a historically developed discourse entails an examination of why so many countries started to see themselves as underdeveloped in the early post-World-War period, how 'to develop' become a fundamental problem for them, and how, finally, they embarked upon the task of 'un-underdeveloping' themselves by subjecting their societies to increasingly systematic, detailed, and comprehensive interventions. As Western experts and politicians started to see certain conditions in Asia, Africa and Latin America as a problem – mostly what was perceived as poverty and backwardness – a new domain of thought and experience, namely, development, came into being resulting in a new strategy for dealing with the alleged problem.

Reading through such critical writings, we can discern that development as a discourse involves three discursive strategies for policy (and sometimes even military) interventions by the West. First, is the construction of the rest of the world as a problem for which Western intervention is necessary. Second, is the perpetual construction of engagement strategies for development by proposing and implementing solutions such as structural adjustment, privatization, good governance, and new public management. Third, is the subjugation of the rest of the world to the epistemic power of seeing the world as such. This is done through subtle combinations of coercive elements (such as loan conditionalities) and 'disciplinary' elements which involve various 'scientific' articulations and calculations of the rest of the world as a biopolitical problem (e.g. through various global performance measures for nation-states).

As such, especially in this third element of development discourse, development becomes a text. Before development projects and practices came into being, the text of development was being written and disseminated. Powerful epistemic agencies such as the World Bank and OECD collectively wrote this development text, characterizing the globe through various statistical grids, articulating developed-underdeveloped dichotomies, hiding the possibilities that the West had been the reason for the problems of the rest of the world, explaining why and how the rest cannot have their own solutions to their problems, projecting the West as the solution to the problematic rest, and necessitating their perpetual intervention in the development of the rest. Although it would be misleading or controversial, the textualization of development was strategically imposed so it became globally powerful. Crush (1995, 5) writes thus:

> The text of development has always been avowedly and strategic and tactical – promoting, licencing, and justifying certain interventions and practices, delegitimizing

and excluding others. An interest in how the text of development writes and represents the world is therefore, by extension, an interest in how they interact with the strategies and tactics of their authors and of those who lend them authority.

Crush (1995) explains how these texts are written. He reminds us that the textualization of development as a discourse entails the making of certain objects including reports, plans, analyses, discussions, debates, presentations, papers, books, policies, evaluations, assessments, consultations, and so forth. As Alvares (1992) observed, these objects have come to be a powerful arena of knowledge which itself decides what knowledge is. This power is assumed in development texts because they are produced 'politically, sociologically, militarily, ideologically, scientifically, and imaginatively' (Said 1978, 3).

15.3.2 The development machine

These texts cannot be produced if there is not a specific material context. This should be in place in terms of a set of apparatuses of networks and agencies which Crush (1995) calls the 'development machine'. It is the machine through which these texts are circulated and enacted. The machine is used by development agencies who are continuously disseminating, de-disseminating, and reproducing the texts of development. For example, as one such agency, the World Bank conducts workshops for development practitioners who in turn disseminate the knowledge they gain in their home countries and generate suitable institutional arrangements to implement World Bank policy discourses. Goldman (2005, 4) reported on how this happened once when the World Bank conducted such a workshop on the theme of 'environmentally sustainable development':

> African professionals selected by the World Bank to carry out its mission enact their roles in diverse ways that defy simple categories. The only commonality is that they are rarely docile in their relationship with the Bank. People work for the Bank for many reasons, some very different from what the Bank might hope for. They may translate their assignment and improvise in ways that they do not follow the Bank's credo. Nonetheless, less than six years after this workshop, one of the Bank's earliest on 'environmentally sustainable development', the World Bank and its European-based aid partners have established more than fifty policy and training programs [which] are being taught by African professionals on themes ranging from environmental economics to water sector privatisation to making the WTO work in developing countries.

This does not mean that Western imperialism is always unidirectional and imposes ideas on the rest of the world with no reactions. Rather, development has to be materialized in the developing world either through manufacturing the consent of the locals and responding to the responses or concerns that the developing world subjects raise. That said, it is a naïve assumption that power emanates exclusively from one place to be directed to another (Fanon 1963). Reflecting on Fanon's observations, Crush (1995, 8) went on to say that:

> Development, for all its power to speak and to control the terms of speaking, has never been impervious to challenge and resistance, nor, in response, to formulating

350 *Neoliberal trends*

and change ... There is a great deal about the form and content of development that suggests that it is reactive as well as formative. As a set of ideas about the way the world works and should be ordered, understood and governed, development should also be glimpsed if not as 'creation of the Third World', then certainly as reflecting the responses, reactions and resistance of the people who are its object.

This means that development is enacted through the 'development machine' that the international development agencies such as the World Bank have institutionalized throughout the world. This machine creates the possibilities for collaborations between the West and the rest of the world and propagates the neoliberal development ideologies in such a manner that they have now increasingly become the ideologies of everyone in the dominating policy circles. Everyone seems to be participating in the machine in co-production of this ideology, which is then manifested in various development reports and statistics produced by this development machine. Calculations of 'development numbers' plays a significant role here.

15.3.3 Developmentality, governmentality, and calculative practices

The textual and material conditions discussed in the previous sections constitute a discursive formation of development leading to a form of governmentality which Ilcan and Phillips (2010) call 'developmentality'. It is about recasting biopolitical problems as problems of underdevelopment and hence offering a set of formulated solutions through the 'development machine' we mentioned earlier. Here, as in any case of biopolitics, a particular discourse operates as a rule aiming to connect the micro sites of governmentality (such as organizations, families, schools, etc.) with the global biopolitical issues. For this, the development advocates offer a wide range of programmes ranging from 'change management' and 'accountability reforms' in the micro-organizational sites to macro-policy formulations such as privatization. In this way they are aimed at organizing the population to embrace the neoliberal aims of development. As a neoliberal form of governmentality, such development programmes play three interrelated roles as Ilcan and Phillips (2010) argue. They are: (1) information profiling (for development); (2) responsibilization (assigning responsibility to development subjects); and (3) knowledge networking (approaching networks for development). By performing these roles, development can be institutionalized as a discourse and professionalized as a practice. Escobar (1995) calls these: (1) institutionalization and (2) professionalization of development. These interrelated processes accommodate varying forms of calculations, prioritizations, and rankings to maintain the notion of 'underdevelopment' as a strategic imperative for everybody.

Such functions manifest neoliberal governmentality, which promotes a market-driven and market-based development, the possibility of which is materialized by introducing and propagating global development programmes such as the privatization of state-owned enterprises, liberalization of trade, and the introduction of new public management to manage public-sector organizations. Simultaneously, discursive justifications of such programmes can mean certain ideas and goals are promoted and diffused. For example, Ilcan and Phillips (2010) illustrate that millennium development goals (MDG) have given prominence to the above roles of information profiling (for development); responsibilization (assigning responsibility to development subjects); and knowledge networking (creating networks for development). The ultimate purpose here is a 'goal directed' social transformation of the developing world – directing them towards an imagined set of status/conditions, the achievement of which is explicitly projected as the definite solution for the perennial socio-economic problems in the developing world. As such, not achieving them is conceived as underdevelopment.

Such neoliberal forms of solution cannot be offered unless all such justifications and arguments are supported by 'appropriate' calculations, analyses, and comparisons. Performing these epistemic acts of calculations, analyses, and comparisons are then the managerial functionality of global developmentality which should then be performed by 'appropriate' development professionals. This then leads to the institutionalization and professionalization of such practices, as Escobar (1995) observes. Hence, developmentality constitutes calculative practices – be they assessments, evaluations, ranking, prioritizing, and so forth. They have become central in the global programme of developmentality (cf. Walker et al. 2008). Focusing on their presence in the area of global governance, Ilcan and Phillips (2010, 867) reinforce the three centralities of calculative practices in performing the neoliberal functionalities of information, responsibility, and networking:

> [c]alculative practices that privilege conceptions of information, responsibility and networks as forces for social transformation, in what has been discursively framed as new era.

Hence, unlike in the past, neoliberal development – or developmentality – is about creating a new form of management accounting characterized by these three inter-related functions permeating managerial actions in every realm – a set of actions for the governance of populations and other performing entities (such as corporations, nations, civil societies, and individuals) where calculations of 'developmental performance' become pre-eminent. In understanding the emergence and popularization of this new form of accounting (i.e. accounting for development), we discern two interrelated accounting dynamics: accountingization of development and developmentalizing accounting. We discuss these in the next sections.

15.4 Accountingization of development: the case of World Bank Development Reporting

By accountingization of development, we mean how 'underdevelopment' is constructed based on certain calculations which we call 'development numbers'. In this section, we shall explore how the World Development Report (WDR) as a text can permeate a particular numerical shape of development. Here, we use much of Escobar's (1995) ideas to show how numbers were used to problematize the developing world's economic, political, and cultural order, and to create a particular 'scientific' and/or 'statistical' story of underdevelopment in the periphery. Through the process of creating this 'scientific' and 'statistical' image, development discourses also created a particular set of epistemic elites in the West who held the professional and institutional power to dictate underdevelopment as a 'scientific truth'. Escobar (1995) shows that these statistical stories represent the power of the West over the developing world – the West is rich and the developing world needs 'austerity measures' from global financial institutions such as the World Bank and the IMF. In the foregoing discussion, we showed how WDRs have become a means to propagate this discursive attempt through World Bank calculations which we call 'development numbers'.

352   *Neoliberal trends*

It would not be an overestimation to say that 'World Development Report has certainly been received more than any serial publication in the annals of development' (Yusuf et al. 2009, 1). Being the leading publication that reveals the beliefs and ideological leanings of the World Bank's management and its principal shareholders (Yusuf et al. 2009, 2), WDR has been shaping and reshaping development discourses since the late 1970s (for the list of such reports, see Table 15.1). Hence, an analysis of the history of WDR provides a meaningful neoliberal history of the calculative practices of development. We understand that the calculative practices of development have evolved over time, and we frame that evolution as having been from 'calculating (under)development' to 'managing (under)development'.

15.4.1 Calculating (under)development: the problematization phase

The first three issues of the WDR culminated in a long-evolving post-colonial tradition of 'calculating underdevelopment'. The focus was to provide a 'statistical capacity' to define underdevelopment through comparative statistics between developed and underdeveloped. The first three issues of WDR were driven towards the calculative establishment of the notion of 'absolute poverty' – the primary notion upon which the so-called Third World was created and objectified as a problematic entity needing the expertise and the 'long experience of the World Bank'. As such, the first WDR (World Bank 1978) claims:

> [a]bout 800 million people still live in absolute poverty. These are people living at the very margin of existence – with inadequate food, shelter, education, and health care. For many of them, there has been little improvement in the standard of living, and for some, there may have been a deterioration. Added to the sense of frustration at the size of the task ahead is an increasing awareness of how difficult it is to alter traditions and social rigidities, which often impede efforts to accelerate growth and to raise the living standards of the poor.
>
> (p. 1)

> [g]overnments have to act. They are faced with the necessity of daily decisions. And hence the quality of the information, and the range of available choices on which those decisions will have to be made become critically important ... That is why we have undertaken this analysis. *The World Bank, with its broad-based membership, its long experience, and its daily involvement with the development problems of its members is in a unique position to analyze the interrelationships between the principal components of the development process.* To the extent that these are more clearly understood, the institution itself, and all of its member governments individually, will be able to cooperate more effectively in accelerating economic growth, and reducing the intolerable deprivations of massive poverty.
>
> (p. iii, emphasis ours)

This analysis of the 'principal components of the (under)development process' was primarily calculative and had a clear but evolving structure of calculations. In its first phase of evolution, the calculative structure was idealized by demographics and economics of growth and driven towards the provision of what the World Bank called the 'statistical capacity' to buttress the development discourse. The discursive processes of problematization of the periphery as poor and the centre's self-

Strategizing development 353

acknowledgement of the responsibility to solve the problems of the periphery were started with Harry Truman's 1949 'Fair Deal' but were in need of a 'statistical justification' to create a 'numerical truth effect' around the development discourses. The first few issues of the WDR were quite successful in creating this much needed 'numerical truth effect' of underdevelopment and poverty. As Yusuf et al. (2009, 20) claim, WDR fundamentally 'thickened the empirical content of growth economics', and it:

> [m]ade poverty tangible by offering numerical information on the extent and depth of poverty. Poverty alleviation became a rallying cry for the Bank and for all those engaged in making development a meaningful objective. Vanquishing poverty gave the Bank a new focus and a credible mission, and it added moral underpinnings to the economic case for resource transfers from the rich to the developing nations. Moreover, growth economics, which was in danger of losing its purchase on reality, acquired a tangible purpose. With faster growth, a nation's domestic product would increase, and the incomes of the poor would be more likely to rise. Growth acquired a more human face.
>
> (p. 21)

The point here is that the discourses of modernity, including development discourses that tried to impose various forms of modernity into the non-Western periphery, needed some sort of calculative practices to transform them into a 'scientific' form of knowledge and thought[2] along which the hegemonic relations between the centre and the periphery were to be institutionalized and professionalized. It was a postcolonial historical necessity to construct an 'empirical science of development', a particular body of knowledge through which the historical and mutually interdependent processes of subjectivation (i.e. the centre becoming a legitimate subject for development discourses) and objectivation (i.e. the periphery becoming the object of development discourses) could be achieved. As such, calculating underdevelopment had its own historically specific discursive aims, and development discourses became calculations.

At its inception, at least until the early 1980s, as illustrated by the first few issues of WDR, such development numbers were driven by calculations of 'poverty' and 'growth', the primary components of the World Bank's development strategy at that time: poverty as the problem and economic growth as the solution. As such, development accounting at that time was primarily populated by statistical tables and figures that attempted to produce an empirical account to demonstrate the severity, extent, and depth of poverty and the necessity for Western intervention to accelerate the growth across the developing world. Such tables were meant to provide a 'positive' (vis-à-vis normative) account of the 'development experience and prospects' of the less developed countries and demonstrate a reasonable consistency in the format of presentation over time. As we have already mentioned, the measurement of the notion of 'absolute poverty' was the centrepiece of the analysis of the 'principal components of the (under) development process', and per capita income was drawn as the primary performance measurement indicator to which all other 'development indicators' were linked in a process of circular reasoning, both as the outcome of and the reason for the low income (see Figure 15.1 for an example of how WDR attempts to relate some of these poverty indicators to per capita income). As such, WDR tried to statistically conceptualize the

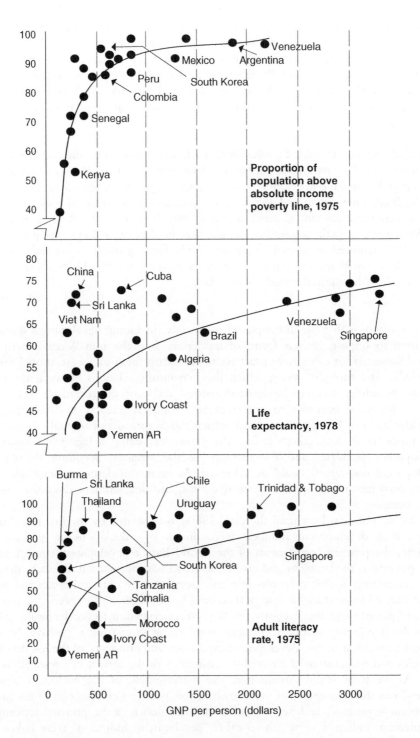

Figure 15.1 A calculative establishment of the interrelationships between the principal components of the development process

Source: WDR (1980, 36).

Strategizing development   355

'interrelationships between the principal components of the development process' as follows:

> Most poor people live in poor countries. Whether absolute poverty is measured by low income, low life expectancy or illiteracy, there is a strong correlation between the extent of poverty in a country and its GNP per person ... This suggests that the solution to poverty is economic growth .
>
> (World Bank 1980, 35)

The claim that 'the solution to poverty is economic growth' made measurement and explanation of the growth in per capita income terms the core of the development discourses. Despite all well-discussed and acknowledged limitations of per capita income as a measure of development and poverty, it has been a widely deployed and a discursively powerful number. Similar to the power of return on investment (ROI) as a unifying financial measure in corporate accounting (see Bryer 2006; Sloan 1964), per capita income was capable of providing a basis upon which all other development numbers were made meaningful and objective. First, it was not simply an economic objective but a political ideology capsulated in a number. When presented as an economic objective of development, the notion of per capita income was nothing else but the modernist ideology of progress through capital accumulation. Hence, imposing it as a development objective effectively fixed the Western ideology of growth and development into the economic and political apparatus of the post-colonial nation-states and such nation-states became the experimental objects of all forms of economic restructuring such as liberalization, nationalization, and privatization. Despite all claims and attempts at liberalizing the economies and providing the necessary 'freedom to private capital', post-colonial nations have become ever more dependent upon so-called 'development planning and funding' by the West. An independent path of national development, as in the case of the development of modernity in the West, has more than ever been impossible for these post-colonial nations.

Second, it not only measured the poverty and progress but defined them. Despite all other wider definitions that openly acknowledged the social and political characters of poverty and development, per capita income became the 'operational definition' of poverty and development. It was used single-handedly as the definitional criterion for placing national states on a classificatory schema of (under)development. This per capita income-based classification provided the bedrock for comparative accounts of development experiences that constituted the fundamental analytical framework. That is, a hegemonic dichotomy between the periphery and the centre was constructed so that, despite the socio-political and economic crises inherent in the Western forms of capitalism, the centre was always analysed and presented as the solution that the periphery should aim at. In other words, development discourses could not exist without such a dichotomy between developed and underdeveloped that placed the centre as the solution to the 'poverty' in the periphery. It needed a number based upon which such a dichotomy of developed and underdeveloped could be constructed and justified. The per capita income was that number, and once placed within this development dichotomy, the periphery was neither given nor acquired an opportunity to seek a solution beyond this development hegemony.

Third, and most importantly, by bringing the economics of growth and demography together, per capita income provided a conceptual framework for the WDR for its analysis and reporting. Implied in the overall reporting structure of the first few WDRs

356 *Neoliberal trends*

is a conceptual decomposition of the per capita income into what the WDR recognized as the 'principal components of the development process'. Figure 15.2 illustrates this conceptual decomposition of the per capita income and its resulting framework of analysis and reporting.

This was the calculative structure of development discourses of WDRs until at least the mid-1980s. We can call this phase of development discourse the 'problematization phase'. Here, the primary aim of development numbers was to problematize the periphery. This problematization had four interrelated aspects: creating a statistical

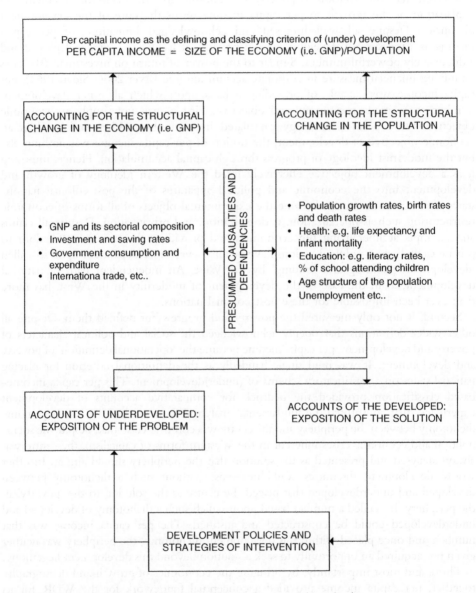

Figure 15.2 The calculative structure of development discourses: the early phase

Strategizing development 357

truth effect on the centre's claims on the 'poverty' of the periphery; implicating a presumed causality between so-called 'principal components of the development process'; implicating the centre as the only source of solutions to the problems of the periphery; and, after all, making the periphery blind to any possibilities of independent development (i.e. creating a discursive dependency of the periphery on the centre).

Problematization was one of the discursive outcomes of the development numbers. Underlying this problematization, there always was an 'institutionalization' process of such calculations. This is the process of establishing an institutional field in which, and from which, techniques of development numbers are produced, recorded, stabilized, modified, and put into operation (see Escobar 1988, 431). On the one hand, the field of development numbers constitutes a multitude of epistemic agencies ranging from international organizations such as the UN, World Bank, OECD, Asian Development Bank, CARE International, to national and regional agencies in the developing world (for example, central banks and governmental departments of census and statistics). These institutions are interrelated and interdependent in the production, exchange, and use of development numbers and, taken together, as an epistemic community, they form the 'order of development' (cf. Foucault 2005, 'order of things').

On the other hand, within this multitude of epistemic agencies, there is established a sort of 'transaction processing system', a system of information processing through which collections, compilations, calculations, analyses, and reporting of development numbers are routinized as day-to-day and periodic operations of specialized units of these agencies. For example, like in all other nations, we have seen that that Central Bank of Sri Lanka runs a research unit employing highly qualified economists, statisticians, and other social researchers whose full-time job is to produce the Annual Report, which analyses the macro-economic performance of the nation each year. The production of such annual reports being a statutory requirement, local governments have now institutionalized complex assemblages of accounting procedures, processes, and units to produce the necessary information for such reporting. This also includes 'whole of government accounts' systems. These local accounting systems then provide the basic data upon which the global development numbers (as those in the WDR) are produced. This is what we call institutionalization of development where we see a kind of 'automation of development calculations'. It is now 'automated' not only in terms of its systemic 'statistical capacity' to produce such reports periodically but also because this production of development numbers and their 'truth effect' have become unquestionable.

15.4.2 *Managing the underdeveloped and professionalization of development*

By the mid-1980s, development numbers had been so institutionalized that the annual production of world development indicators now have a life of their own. From 1986, WDR had hived off the section that reviewed the state of the world economy into a separate annual publication called the *Global Economic Prospects*. And, this has also been supplemented by the publication of World Development Indicators on a CD-ROM and on the web. At the outset, the production of World Development Indicators has become an automated system output, and development numbers have reached a status something akin to automated corporate transaction processing systems designed and routinized to generate predetermined financial figures, with a minimum of period-end adjustments and cosmetics to the final publications. With this achievement,

358 *Neoliberal trends*

development numbers have entered into a new phase of their own development – 'development management' as we call it, which is much evident in the contents and structure of WDRs in the 1990s and beyond.

The calculative problematization of the periphery still continues, but in a different mode. At the level of economic ideology and policy, policy focus has shifted away from macro-economic concerns and availability of development funding to rather micro-institutional and managerial issues of development. Development economics have emerged into what Cooke (2004) terms 'development administration and management'. Per capita income and other macro socio-economic development indicators have been pushed to the back in the appendixes, or are standalone statistical publications, CD-ROMs, and databases. They have evolved into some sort of 'taken-for-granted facts of underdevelopment' and the periodic production of them is no longer a 'development analysis' but a data-processing exercise. The analysis of underdevelopment is now thematized. Every WDR deals with a single thematic issue of underdevelopment that it acknowledges as a 'primary development challenge of our time' (see World Bank 2011, 1). Every year, a new theme of (under)development is identified and analysed or a previously visited theme would be given a revisit to provide a new thematic analysis. Themes of (under)development taken into account have been numerous and have ranged from predominantly economic issues such as 'Structural Change and Development Policy' and 'Agriculture and Economic Development' to rather socio-political and managerial issues such as 'The State in a Changing World', 'Knowledge for Development', 'Development and Climate Change', and 'Conflict, Security and Development' (See Table 15.1 for the full list of themes articulated by WDRs).

In line with these changes in the development discourses, the analytical and calculative structure of development has also changed. Now, the problematization of the periphery is rather thematic while the macro-economic data-based problematization still runs in the background as appendixes. Analyses are no longer concentrated on the measurement of various dimensions or aspects of poverty and underdevelopment, but on the analysis and resolution of socio-political processes that keep the periphery underdeveloped. So, development numbers are drawn from multiple sources to illustrate how such socio-political processes have evolved over time and space, how they now operate, and the potential impact of them on poverty and underdevelopment. Development numbers are now organized to tell a particular story or to illustrate a particular argument rather than to provide a comparison between the centre and the periphery. Also, numbers are now embedded in 'expert opinions' and 'case studies'. In other words, development numbers do not now stand as 'comparative statistics'. Instead, they are thematically organized and packed within illustrative case studies, expert opinions, and possible scenarios (often called 'boxes' or 'features') to demonstrate the impact of the selected socio-political or institutional processes on the lives of 'poor people'. Figure 15.3 shows an example of how development numbers are drawn for thematic problematization of the periphery. As such, development numbers are now doing a much more refined and focused role of micro-management of (under)development; they are now drawn not simply to calculate under-development but to manage: to identify and define problems, analyse the problems in terms of causes and impacts, to provide policy frameworks and solutions, and to assess the efficacy of previous solutions provided.

As such, the World Bank continues to furnish 'development numbers'. One of the salient features in its current shape is that the World Bank has now moved from the task of compiling case studies to producing league tables which rank the countries based on

Strategizing development 359

Table 15.1 List of themes articulated by World Development Reports: 1978–2018

Year	Title
1978	Prospects for Growth and Alleviation of Poverty
1979	Structural Change and Development Policy
1980	Poverty and Human Development
1981	National and International Adjustment
1982	Agriculture and Economic Development
1983	Management in Development
1984	Population Change and Development
1985	International Capital and Economic Development
1986	Trade and Pricing Policies in World Agriculture
1987	Industrialization and Foreign Trade
1988	Public Finance in Development
1989	Financial Systems and Development
1990	Poverty
1991	The Challenge of Development
1992	Development and the Environment
1993	Investing in Health
1994	Infrastructure for Development
1995	Workers in an Integrating World
1996	From Plan to Market
1997	The State in a Changing World
1998	Knowledge for Development
1999	Entering the 21st Century: The Changing Development Landscape
2000/01	Attacking Poverty
2002	Building Institutions for Markets
2003	Sustainable Development in a Dynamic World: Transforming Institutions, Growth, and Quality of Life
2004	Making Services Work for Poor People
2005	A Better Investment Climate for Everyone
2006	Equity and Development
2007	Development and the Next Generation
2008	Agriculture for Development
2009	Reshaping Economic Geography
2010	Development and Climate Change
2011	Conflict, Security, and Development
2012	Gender Equality and Development
2013	Jobs
2014	Risk and Opportunity: Managing Risk for Development
2015	Mind, Society, and Behavior
2016	Digital Dividends
2017	Governance and the Law
2018	Learning to Realize Education's Promise

their socio-economic and political capacities. A country can then be compared allowing the 'investors' to make informed decisions on lending, investing, and even maintaining diplomatic relations. The league table then acts as a screen reflecting market logics enabling the decision makers to judge the 'conditions of possibility': transnational agencies can now make those decisions in conjunction with the case studies we mentioned earlier. For example, as shown in Table 15.2, countries are ranked based on their 'entrepreneurial capacities' as envisaged by the World Bank.

360 Neoliberal trends

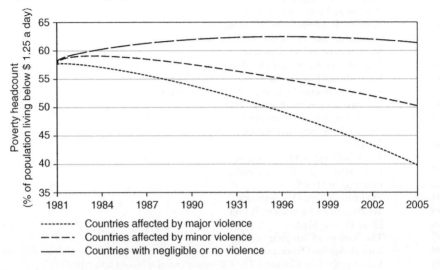

The gap in poverty is widening between countries affected by violence and others
New poverty data reveal that poverty is declining for much of the world, but countries affected by violence are lagging behind. For every three years a country is affected by major violence (battle deaths or excess deaths from homicides equivalent to a major war), poverty reduction lags behind 2.7 percentage points.

Figure 15.3 A thematic organization of development numbers
Source: WDR (2011, 4).

What we see on the website in the full table is that 190 world economies are ranked on their ease of doing business. In the table, first, it shows how these countries, for example in the South Asian region, are ranked against other countries in the world and derive their regional ranking accordingly. Then it goes on to show respective numbers for each of these 12 shown categories, giving an indicator as to how these countries can provide a 'conducive environment for doing business'. Following the weblink, you can browse such numerous rankings for different regions which can give you an impression as to how these numbers convert the countries into strategic units. In particular, as you will see that the league table thus mirrors the environment of those countries. By doing this, the World Bank assigns a 'market' logic to civic, political, legal, and governance aspects. As in the case of strategic management tools such as the BCG growth matrix, these league tables now provide a comparative market perspective based upon which strategic decisions on investing global funds should be made.

In this way, as we mentioned earlier, development numbers are accommodated into a process of strategizing development, which also entails an important discursive process, which Escobar labels as 'professionalization of development'. It is the process through which a politics of truth is created and maintained. Broadly speaking, the professionalization of development includes the creation and maintenance of a set of disciplinary techniques and practices through which the generation, diffusion, and validation of development knowledge is organized, managed, and controlled (Escobar 1988, 430). Calculative practices have always been intrinsic to this professionalization

Table 15.2 Selection of countries in a league table: 2017

Country	Ease of doing business	Filtered rank	Starting a business	Dealing with construction	Getting electricity	Registering property	Getting credit	Protecting minority	Paying taxes	Trading across borders	Enforcing contracts	Resolving insolvency
Bhutan	75	1	3	3	2	2	1	2	6	1	1	8
India	100	2	8	7	1	1	3	1	1	3	5	4
Nepal	105	3	5	6	4	4	2	3	4	4	3	1
Sri Lanka	111	4	2	2	3	3	4	6	3	6	6	3
Maldives	136	5	1	1	5	5	6	7	7	2	2	5
Pakistan	147	6	7	5	7	7	5	5	2	7	4	2
Bangladesh	**177**	**7**	**6**	**4**	**8**	**8**	**7**	**8**	**5**	**5**	**8**	**6**
Afghanistan	**183**	**8**	**4**	**8**	**6**	**6**	**8**	**4**	**8**	**8**	**7**	**7**

Source: see the World Bank site – www.doingbusiness.org/rankings?region=south-asia.

362 *Neoliberal trends*

process because their resulting development numbers are an essential element in creating *the* 'truth' of underdevelopment and of the efficacy of development planning. Even at its early stages, the development numbers have always been underlying the development discourses, but with a macro-economic outlook. However, since the late 2000s, techniques, practices, and ideologies of management consulting have increasingly been drawn as a 'tool kit' to professionalize development discourses, which have now converted the peripheral institutions and states into a set of clients and penetrated into:

- process consultation and organizational development for the prioritization of clients' needs and values
- organizational structures and processes through which plans are implemented and
- broader governance issues such as participation, accountability, transparency, responsiveness, and the role of the state (see Cooke 2004).

Replication, mimicking, and learning lessons from previous mistakes have become critical modes through which the generation, diffusion, and validation of development knowledge is organized, managed, and controlled. This is what the ever popular boxes and features in WDR do nowadays. In addition, similar to the field of management consulting, 'consulting personalities' have begun to emerge over and above the institutional identities which hitherto played a major role in development planning. In other words, the professionalization of development discourses has given rise to the emergence of 'professionals' within the institutional setup of development discourses. As such, WDR now contain 'reflections from advisory council members' as a mode of building credibility.

One interesting development is worth noting here. With the emergence of development consultants, one can see that development discourses which transformed development numbers into disciplinary techniques are now creating and increasingly relying on development 'figures' (i.e. development 'personalities'): a series of expert personalities hierarchically organized in the 'development field' by being attached to high-end development funding agencies such as the World Bank and to Western development schools, on the one hand, and to various governments and NGOs at the 'ground level', on the other. Those people at the bottom end of the consulting hierarchy take courses on Development Administration and Development in Western 'development schools' where they are introduced to a set of managerial techniques (such as quality management, HRM/HRD, MIS, Organizational Development, Development Finance, and even prototypical corporate accounting and governance). These development schools not only provide prototypical management ideologies and techniques to manage development but also create a set of 'bodies' through which 'management' is embodied into the 'field of development'. Upon return to their home countries, they boost their 'power of preaching development' through the newly acquired 'tools for better management of development' and become the 'local development agents', through whom the centre now ensures its persistent presence in the periphery. At the outset, these development agents are no longer politicians but apolitical professionals of development, often affiliated to NGOs with rather charitable and philanthropic missions. As such, NGOs are now increasingly becoming more powerful than government agencies in the implementation of development planning of, and feedback to, the centre – the professionalization of development at the periphery.

15.5 Developmentalization of accounting: the case of microfinance

While WDR provides an illustrative case example of how a new set of calculative practices have been invented to manage the discursive process of development, we can see how certain orthodox accounting tools are mobilized to recreate the peripheral social spaces as development spaces, translating social actors in such spaces into 'neoliberal entrepreneurs'. For this, we shall consider microfinance as a perfect illustration. We have already hinted upon this in Chapter 12 when we discussed how civil society has been strategized. We will have a slightly different discussion here to show how this development programme, which has been rooted in a developing country context (especially in Bangladesh), gets de-rooted from that context and discoursed as the prominent (and dominating) idea of rural development in neoliberal times. As Roy (2010) analysed this phenomenon, it is a 'bottom billion capitalism' materialized in a new global capital market.

15.5.1 Microfinance as a 'Holy Grail' of rural development

The initial idea of microfinance was a very fundamental human right. As was articulated by Muhammad Yunus, who invented the programme of microfinance in Bangladesh, it is premised that credit is a human right so that the poor must have this right to borrow on credit and develop. Based on this, starting with Grameen Bank in Bangladesh, microfinance grew exponentially. Development writers called this a powerful development programme with a great potential for poverty alleviation (see Hulme 2000). These positive accounts led the programme to become well rooted in Bangladesh and other developing countries across the world. As a result, microfinance was implicated in what (Roy 2010, 23) calls a 'democratization of capital and democratization of development'.

Taking Escobar's (1995) idea, we can say that microfinance was well institutionalized and professionalized as a social engineering programme. It was then allowed to develop and follow certain accounting and accountability practices. When microfinance is introduced into a village, it forms a network of women borrowers based on prevailing convivial and traditional social relations and organizes them into what is often called 'self-help groups'. These self-help groups, together with other institutional apparatuses put in place to monitor and manage them, produce a mundane set of accountability practices and mechanisms through which these women are motivated to take micro-credit, enabled to pay interest and repayment instalments, and monitored for their performance. These practices and mechanisms appear more informal and convivial in nature. And it is this informality and conviviality that have been the key features that has attracted the poor into microfinance around the world since the early 2000s. Within Bangladesh itself, there emerged the world's largest microfinance institutions such as Grameen Bank, Asha, and BRACK. In other developing countries, conventional banks and central banks assumed the role of popularizing microfinance as an important arm of their operations along with extra-microfinance services such as training and advocacy roles. Many NGOs have also now started to operate as microfinance providers or service providers for micro-credit providers.

15.5.2 Microfinance and accounting

This development programme was initially not considered as an area for the usual accounting, accountability, and control practices (Jacobs et al. 2012). It was because

364 *Neoliberal trends*

these programmes were not circumscribed by any requirement for formal financial reporting or stipulated governance and control practices. Jacobs et al summarize this accounting as:

> [t]he process and practices of control associated with microfinance is [that] institutions have rendered new groups visible and calculable ... This visibility and calculability occur through social and cultural process[es] of lending to and collecting from village-based groups and organizations. It could be argued that these more direct forms of visibility through the loan collectors and more indirect forms of collective visibility and control through group registration offer a substitutive to the relatively expensive ... process of accounting measurement and control.
>
> (p. 163)

Researchers explore such forms of accounting and report on how this emerging form of development programme permeated a new form of accounting knowledge (Dixon et al. 2007; Jacobs et al. 2012; Lisa et al. 2017). For example, Dixon et al. (2007), based on a field study, illustrate the functions of microfinance highlighting the roles of operational accountability at the mundane level and performance of microfinance institutes measured in terms of stipulated indicators. Now, originating more from neoliberal forms of social engineering embedded in microfinance, village-based practices create new forms of performance and accountability wherein informal types of accounts play both a disciplinary and biopolitical role to which we will return at the end of this chapter. These practices have presented a new financial language which is now being embedded in people's everyday lives.

15.5.3 Writing back to the World Bank: microfinance in the financial market

Microfinance is a compelling example of how a development idea has been infused in accounting generating a set of micro-level practices. The World Bank played a key role in this endeavour. They grabbed the idea of microfinance, had it institutionalized with an institutional arrangement, and professionalized certain practices. As a result, it was not the idea that Yunus developed in Bangladesh, but a different version that is ready for global circulation. The arrangement the World Bank had was the establishment of a donor consortium called Consultative Group to Assist the Poor (CGAP). Roy (2010, 26) says:

> It is thus the CGAP, a donor forum based at the World Bank, [that] has sought to construct a global microfinance industry integrated with financial markets. Such an approach breaks with the Grameen model of microfinance and its emphasis on human development.

Simultaneously, development writers promote the necessity of such an approach to microfinance. For example, Roy refers to Chu (2007) and Bruck (2006) to show how these texts promote and establish the idea of how poverty is connected to profits. It is about establishing microfinance as an industry which can generate high profits and can transform the lives of people. Human rights such as credit, education, health, etc. are the aims, but with these the poor must earn a profit by paying due interest.

Consequently, microfinance has come to be a pervasive financial instrument operating in the wider context of financialization, what Roy (2010) calls 'poverty capital'. It has permeated the mechanisms of connecting the local to the global through a global architecture of neoliberal governmentality that renders the poor governable. Roy (2010, 29) concludes:

> Microfinance then is a crucial part of a 'new development architecture', one where the poor are disciplined and appeased through 'novel experimentations' such as access to credit.

This transformation, then, would not be the version rooted in Bangladesh, but the one that the World Bank has now 'professionalized' through its institutional mechanisms. The resulting type of microfinance is truly neoliberal rather than developmental, and it aims at profit making on behalf of this financial architecture. Brett (2006) ironically wrote that in getting people to participate in this global machine, they would say 'We sacrifice and eat less'.

Two types of accounting can be developed from this global version of microfinance. On the one hand, there emerges a disciplinary form of accounting aimed at disciplining the poor to make savings, pay instalments, and get themselves organized and entrepreneurial (Jacobs et al. 2012; Weber 2002). As we mentioned in Chapter 12, training programmes, course manuals, group meetings, cashbooks are all in the toolkit of these disciplinary practices. Like a firm adopting various control mechanisms, rural villages are now fortified with these disciplinary mechanisms through the apparatuses of governmental agencies and NGO activities. This is an emerging area of research concerning how such disciplinary practices make these people bankable, accountable, and, eventually, governable in the service of global capital (Alawattage et al. forthcoming; Weber 2002, 2006). On the other hand, microfinance institutions, NGOs, and governmental agencies collect and collate data from these operations for macro-level purposes – the mission here is truly biopolitical. This is about an exercise in assessing poverty levels, evaluating their risk elements, and monitoring the diversity of poverty outreach and impact and about management of the population (Chua et al. 2000; Copestake et al. 2005). The accounting literature is still in its infancy in this area, but this trend of 'developmentalization of accounting' continues as a real and discursive programme. This points to tremendous potential for future management accounting research surrounding the issue of strategizing development. Ironically, even in mainstream strategic management, this has become an interesting issue, because Harvard gurus like Prahalad (2005) now see the potential of making 'fortunes at the bottom of the pyramid'. They now consult and encourage the multinational corporations to become involved in the 'business of development' because there is an opportunity for profit among the poorest in the world.

15.6 Summary and conclusions

We set out to deal with an important issue in this chapter – strategizing development. We first elaborated how development discourses reshape accounting practices and how accounting has become a central element of development discourses. We explained the way in which the development discourses set the pace for a set of new management accounting roles, especially since the 1990s, in the peripheral economies. There, especially in the context

366   *Neoliberal trends*

of structural reforms, accounting has been signified as a technology of development that can inculcate a private-sector market-driven enterprising culture in public-sector and civil society organizations. At the same time, accounting has also been playing a role in legitimizing the neoliberal agenda of development. Also, we saw, accounting is now playing a constitutive role shaping those development programmes and practices. This led on to us articulating the notion of developmentality as a form of governmentality. Here, we discussed how development can be considered as a discursive text enacting neoliberal global governance. The chapter's next task was to discuss two sides of the relationship between development discourse and accounting: 'accountingization of development' and 'developmentalization of accounting'. The former was about how the Western agencies such as the World Bank use calculative practices to discourse a particular vision of development, and the latter was about how accounting was mobilized to recreate entrepreneurial individuals in rural social settings. In this discussion, first, we saw how development is now articulated, presented, and disseminated in terms of statistics, league tables, or rankings and prioritize certain programmes or ideas. Second, in respect of the developmentalization of accounting, we saw how local settings create new ideas such as microfinance and how global forces grab them, modify its function, and disseminate the outcome as an alternative version of development where accounting and accountability play an imperative role.

This thus ends the book as well. We endeavoured to pass across an important message which is vital in our time – strategizing management accounting. The notion of strategizing has been employed to highlight two interrelated dimensions. First, is the way in which management accounting has transformed itself into a 'strategic' discourse encompassing all sorts of strategic analyses and functionalities. This is in response to the neoliberal demands placed upon it by the globalizing market and political contexts. The second is the way in which management accounting has been instrumental in strategizing various social and political phenomena in our times, including the markets, economic enterprises, political state, civil society, and also the global development discourses. Strategizing thus connotes a dynamic, complex, and globally programmed phenomenon that captures what is happening now in the name of transforming all elements of our socio-political and economic context and content. This duality between the stargazing face of management accounting and its role in strategizing other fields then connects the biopolitical of macro with the disciplinary politics of micro – the theoretical notion of governmentality that bound much of the analysis in this text.

Assignments

These assignments are meant to extend your knowledge beyond what you understand from this chapter. These are not simply revision questions. The content covered in this chapter is necessary but will not be sufficient in attempting these tasks. Therefore, you are required to do some extra reading in attempting these tasks.

1.   **Thematic essay:**
     'Development has accounting, and accounting has development'.
         Elaborate this statement to write an essay, of approximately 3,000 words, which articulates a possible reciprocity of accounting and development.
2.   **Poster:**
     Draw a poster showing how the roles of development accounting evolved from its formative phase to the contemporary neoliberal phase.

Strategizing development   367

3. **Presentation:**
    Prepare a set of PowerPoint slides, together with notes if necessary, for a 30-minute presentation on the following theme:
    'Development is both a discourse and text requiring the practices of management for its persistence and change'.
4. **Extended bibliography:**
    Write an extended bibliography on the development of a new form of management accounting in development discourse. For this, you need to do a literature survey in major accounting journals and edited books where critical accounting research is published. Organize the bibliography into a table in the following format.

Bibliographic info	Nature of the paper/book chapter (e.g. conceptual/theoretical, empirical, a response to a previous publication)	Major arguments, conclusions, and contributions

5. **Literature review:**
    'Development constructs the contemporary Third World, silently, without our noticing it. By means of this discourse, individuals, governments, communities are seen as "under developed" and treated as such' (Escobar 1995, 213).
    Write a review essay showing how a new form of management accounting plays a role in this construction. The review should end up with a set of key questions needing to be addressed in a potential research project.

Notes

1   It should be noted that, as we have done throughout this textbook, we take the notion of management accounting very broadly here to mean any sort of calculations and rationalizations driven towards managing. The form that management accounting can take thus varies on the basis of what it aims to manage. Thus, as we discussed in previous chapters, for example, calculative practices driven towards managing strategy is strategic management; such practices driven towards managing quality can be taken as quality costing; and so on. In the same vein, when the objects of management become the development programmes, processes, and practices, we can then discern development management accounting, though such calculations are not necessarily performed by 'accountants'. This widening of the scope of accounting beyond accountants is important to understand the neoliberal power (i.e. bio-power) of calculative practices, and how capitalist calculations are now much more than mere 'accounting calculations' (in a conventional sense) of profits and costs.
2   Foucault (1998, 459) defines thought as the act that posits a subject and an object, along with their possible relations. In this sense, development thought is the act that posits the Western centre and the underdeveloped periphery within a dichotomy of subject and object where the centre and the periphery assume the status of the subject and the object respectively.

References

Abed, F. H. & Matin, I. 2007. Beyond lending: How microfinance creates new forms of capital to fight poverty. *Innovations: Technology, Governance, Globalization*, 2, 3–17.

Abrahamson, E. 1991. Managerial fads and fashions: The diffusion and rejection of innovations. *Academy of Management. The Academy of Management Review*, 16, 586.

Abrahamson, E. 1996. Management fashion. *Academy of Management. The Academy of Management Review*, 21, 254.

Abrahamsson, G. & Gerdin, J. 2006. Exploiting institutional contradictions: The role of management accounting in continuous improvement implementation. *Qualitative Research in Accounting & Management*, 3(2), 126–44.

Adler, P. S. 1993. Time-and-motion regained. *Harvard Business Review*, 97–108.

Adler, P. S., Goldoftas, B., & Levine, D. I. 1999. Flexibility versus efficiency? A case study of model changeovers in the Toyota production system. *Organization Science*, 10, 43–68.

Agndal, H. & Nilsson, U. 2010. Different open book accounting practices for different purchasing strategies. *Management Accounting Research*, 21, 147–66.

Aguilera, R. V. & Cuervo-Cazurra, A. 2004. Codes of good governance worldwide: What is the trigger? *Organization Studies*, 25(3), 415–43.

Aguilera, R. V. & Jackson, G. 2003. The cross-national diversity of corporate governance: Dimensions and determinants. *Academy of Management Review*, 28, 447–65.

Aiken, M. & Hage, J. 1971. The organic organization and innovation. *Sociology*, 5(1), 63–82.

Aized, T. (ed.) 2012. *Total Quality Management and Six Sigma*, Online: InTech.

Alawattage, C. 2011. The calculative reproduction of social structures: The field of gem mining in Sri Lanka. *Critical Perspectives on Accounting*, 22, 1–19.

Alawattage, C. & Alsaid, L. A. 2018. Accounting and structural reforms: A case study of Egyptian electricity. *Critical Perspectives on Accounting*, 50, 15–35.

Alawattage, C. & Fernando, S. 2017. Postcoloniality in corporate social and environmental accountability. *Accounting, Organizations and Society*, 60, 1–20.

Alawattage, C., Graham, C., & Wickramasinghe, D. forthcoming. Microaccountability and biopolitics: Microfinance in a Sri Lankan village. *Accounting, Organizations and Society*.

Alawattage, C., Hopper, T., & Wickramasinghe, D. 2007. Introduction to management accounting in less developed countries. *Journal of Accounting & Organizational Change*, 3(3), 183–191.

Alawattage, C., Wickramasinghe, D., & Tennakoon, A. 2015a. Performing civil society. In: Hoque, Z. & Parker, L. (eds.) *Performance Management in Nonporoft Organizations: Global Perspectives*. London: Routledge.

Alawattage, C., Wickramasinghe, D., & Tennakoon, A. 2015b. Reading accountability with Boltanski and Thêvenot: Evidence from a Sri Lankan NGO. *Working paper presented at Interdisciplinary Perspectives on Accounting Conference, Stockholm*.

Alcouffe, S., Berland, N. & Levant, Y. 2008. Actor-networks and the diffusion of management accounting innovations: A comparative study. *Management Accounting Research*, 19(1), 1–17.

Alexander, G. J. & Buchholz, R. A. 1978. Corporate social responsibility and stock market performance. *The Academy of Management Journal*, 21, 479–86.

References 369

Al-Tuwaijri, S. A., Christensen, T. E., & Hughes, K. E. 2004. The relations among environmental disclosure, environmental performance, and economic performance: A simultaneous equations approach. *Accounting, Organizations and Society*, 29, 447–71.

Alvares, C. A. 1992. *Science, Development, and Violence: The Revolt against modernity/Claude Alvares*. New York: Oxford University Press.

Amershi, A. H. & Cheng, P. 1990. Intrafirm resource allocation: The economics of transfer pricing and cost allocations in accounting. *Contemporary Accounting Research*, 7, 61–99.

Amin, A. 1994. *Post-Fordism: A Reader*. Oxford, UK: Blackwell.

Anderson, S. W., Glenn, D., & Sedatole, K. L. 2000. Sourcing parts of complex products: Evidence on transactions costs, high-powered incentives and ex-post opportunism. *Accounting, Organizations and Society*, 25, 723–49.

Andrew, J. & Cahill, D. 2017. Rationalising and resisting neoliberalism: The uneven geography of costs. *Critical Perspectives on Accounting*, 45, 12–28.

Annisette, M. 1999. Importing accounting: The case of Trinidad and Tobago. *Accounting, Business & Financial History*, 9, 103–33.

Annisette, M. 2000. Imperialism and the professions: The education and certification of accountants in Trinidad and Tobago. *Accounting, Organizations and Society*, 25, 631–59.

Annisette, M. & Trivedi, V. U. 2013. Globalization, paradox and the (un)making of identities: Immigrant Chartered Accountants of India in Canada. *Accounting, Organizations and Society*, 38 (1), 1–29.

Ansari, S. L. 1979. Towards an open systems approach to budgeting. *Accounting, Organizations and Society*, 4, 149–61.

Anthony, R., Govindarajan, V., Hartmann, F., Kraus, K., & Nilsson, G. 2014. *Management Control Systems*. Maidenhead, UK: McGraw-Hill Education.

Anthony, R. N. 1965. *Planning and Control Systems: A Framework for Analysis*. Cambridge, MA: Division of Research, Graduate School of Business Administration, Harvard University.

Anthony, R. N. & Govindarajan, V. 1998. *Management Control Systems*. New York: Irwin McGraw-Hill.

Apostol, O. M. 2015. A project for Romania? The role of the civil society's counter-accounts in facilitating democratic change in society. *Accounting, Auditing & Accountability Journal*, 28, 210–41.

Argyris, C. 1952. *The Impact of Budgets on People*. New York: Controllership Foundation.

Argyris, C. & Schön, D. A. 1974. *Theory in Practice: Increasing Professional Effectiveness*. San Francisco, CA: Jossey-Bass Publishers.

Argyris, C. & Schön, D. A. 1978. *Organizational Learning: A Theory of Action Perspective*. Boston, MA: Addison-Wesley Pub. Co.

Ariyaratne, A. T. 2001. *Collected Works (Vol. 1-6)*. Rathmalana, Sri Lanka: Sarvodaya Vishva Lekha Press.

Armstrong, P. 1991. Contradiction and social dynamics in the capitalist agency relationship. *Accounting, Organizations and Society*, 16, 1–25.

Armstrong, P. 2002. The costs of activity-based management. *Accounting, Organizations and Society*, 27, 99–120.

Arnaboldi, M. & Azzone, G. 2010. Constructing performance measurement in the public sector. *Critical Perspectives on Accounting*, 21(4), 266–82.

Artiach, T., Lee, D., Nelson, D., & Walker, J. 2010. The determinants of corporate sustainability performance. *Accounting & Finance*, 50, 31–51.

Ashraf, J. & Uddin, S. 2016. New public management, cost savings and regressive effects: A case from a less developed country. *Critical Perspectives on Accounting*, 41, 18–33.

Ashton, D., Hopper, T. & Scapens, R. W. 1995. *Issues in Management Accounting*. 2nd ed. London: Prentice Hall.

Ax, C. & Bjørnenak, T. 2007. *Management Accounting Innovations: Origins and Diffusion. Issues in Management Accounting*. London: Financial Times/Prentice Hall.

Axelsson, B., Laage-Hellman, J., & Nilsson, U. 2002. Modern management accounting for modern purchasing. *European Journal of Purchasing & Supply Management*, 8, 53–62.

370   *References*

Baiman, S. 1990. Agency research in managerial accounting: A second look. *Accounting, Organizations and Society*, 15, 341–71.

Baiman, S. 2006. Contract theory analysis of management accounting issues. In: Bhimani, A. (ed.) *Contemporary Issues in Management Accounting*. Oxford, UK: Oxford University Press.

Bain, J. S. 1968. *Industrial Organization*. New York: John Wiley.

Barnett, M. L. & Salomon, R. M. 2012. Does it pay to be really good? addressing the shape of the relationship between social and financial performance. *Strategic Management Journal*, 33, 1304–20.

Baudrillard, J. 1983. *Simulations*. New York: Semiotext(e), Inc.

Baudrillard, J. 1994. *Simulacra and Simulation*. Ann Arbor, MI: University of Michigan Press.

Bauman, Z. 2000. *Liquid Modernity*. Cambridge, UK: Polity Press.

Baxter, J. & Chua, W. F. 2008. Be(com)ing the chief financial officer of an organisation: Experimenting with Bourdieu's practice theory. *Management Accounting Research*, 19, 212–30.

Bayou, M. E. 1993. Standardization issues in management accounting communication. *Accounting, Auditing & Accountability Journal*, 6(2), 32–51.

Bebbington, J. 2001. Sustainable development: A review of the international development, business and accounting literature. *Accounting Forum*, 25, 128–57.

Bebbington, J., Larrinaga-González, C., & Moneva-Abadía, J. M. 2008. Legitimating reputation/ the reputation of legitimacy theory. *Accounting, Auditing & Accountability Journal*, 21(3), 371–74.

Beer, S. 1972. *Brain of the Firm: The Managerial Cybernetics of Organization*. London: Allen Lane the Penguin Press.

Beer, S. 1994. *Decision and Control: The Meaning of Operational Research and Management Cybernetics*. London: John Wiley.

Berliner, C. & Brimson, J. A. 1988. *Cost Management for Today's Advanced Manufacturing: The CAM-I Conceptual Design*. Boston, MA: Harvard Business School Press.

Berry, A. J., Broadbent, J., & Otley, D. 2005. *Management Control: Theories, Issues and Performance*. Basingstoke, UK: Palgrave Macmillan.

Berry, A. J., Capps, T., Cooper, D., Ferguson, P., Hopper, T., & Lowe, E. A. 1985. Management control in an area of the NCB: Rationales of accounting practices in a public enterprise. *Accounting, Organizations and Society*, 10, 3–28.

Berry, A. J., Coad, A. F., Harris, E. P., Otley, D. T., & Stringer, C. 2009. Emerging themes in management control: A review of recent literature. *The British Accounting Review*, 41, 2–20.

Beynon, H. 1975. *Working for Ford*. Wakefield, UK: E.P. Publishing.

Bhabha, H. K. 1990. *Nation and Narration*. London: Routledge.

Bhimani, A. 2006. *Contemporary Issues in Management Accounting*. Oxford, UK: Oxford University Press.

Bijker, W. E., Hughes, T. P., & Pinch, T. J. 1987. *The Social Construction of Technological Systems: New Directions in the Sociology and History of Technology*. Cambridge, MA: MIT Press.

Bjørnenak, T. & Kaarbøe, K. 2013. The dynamics of management accounting and control systems. In: Mitchell, F., Norreklit, H., & Jakobsen, M. (eds.) *The Routledge Companion to Cost Management*. London: Routledge.

Blackburn, R. M. & Mann, M. 1979. *The Working Class in the Labour Market*. London: Macmillan.

Blair, H. 2000. Participation and accountability at the periphery: Democratic local governance in six countries. *World Development*, 28, 21–39.

Bloomfield, B. P. 1991. The role of information systems in the UK National Health Service: Action at a distance and the fetish of calculation. *Social Studies of Science*, 21, 701–34.

Boland Jr, R. J., Sharma, A. K., & Afonso, P. S. 2008. Designing management control in hybrid organizations: The role of path creation and morphogenesis. *Accounting, Organizations and Society*, 33, 899–914.

Boltanski, L. & Chiapello, E. 2007. *The New Spirit of Capitalism*. London: Verso.

Boltanski, L. & Thévenot, L. 2006. *On Justification: Economies of Worth*. Princeton, NJ: Princeton University Press.

Bourdieu, P. 1979. Symbolic power. *Critique of Anthropology*, 4, 77–85.

Bourdieu, P. 1986. The forms of capital. In: Richardson, J. G. (ed.) *Handbook of Theory and Research for the Sociology of Education*. New York: Greenwood Press.

Bourdieu, P. 1990. *The Logic of Practice*. Stanford, CA: Stanford University Press.

Bourdieu, P. 1993. *Sociology in Question*. London: Sage.

Bourdieu, P. 1998. *Practical Reason: On the Theory of Action*. Stanford, CA: Stanford University Press.

Bourdieu, P. & Passeron, J. C. 1990. *Reproduction in Education, Society and Culture*. London: Sage.

Braham, P., Allen, J., Lewis, P., & Hall, S. 1992. *Political and Economic Forms of Modernity: Understanding Modern Societies, Book II*. Cambridge, UK: Polity Press.

Braverman, H. 1998 [1974]. *Labor and Monopoly Capital: The Degradation of Work in the Twentieth Century*. New York: Monthly Review Press.

Brennan, N. M. & Solomon, J. 2008. Corporate governance, accountability and mechanisms of accountability: An overview. *Accounting Auditing and Accountability Journal*, 00021, 885–907.

Brett, J. A. 2006. 'We sacrifice and eat less': The structural complexities of microfinance participation. *Human Organization*, 65, 8–19.

Broadbent, J. & Laughlin, R. 1998. Resisting the 'new public management': Absorption and absorbing groups in schools and GP practices in the UK. *Accounting, Auditing & Accountability Journal*, 11(4), 403–35.

Broadbent, J., Laughlin, R., & Read, S. 1991. Recent financial and administrative changes in the NHS: A critical theory analysis. *Critical Perspectives on Accounting*, 2, 1–29.

Bromwich, M. & Bhimani, A. 1989. *Management Accounting: Evolution Not Revolution*. London: Chartered Institute of Management Accountants.

Bromwich, M. & Hopwood, T. 1986. *Research and Current Issues in Management Accounting*. London: Pitman.

Brown, W. 2005. *Edgework: Critical Essays on Knowledge and Politics*. Princeton, NJ: Princeton University Press.

Brown, W. 2006. American nightmare: Neoliberalism, neoconservatism, and de-democratization. *Political Theory*, 34, 690–714.

Brown, W. 2015. *Undoing the Demos: Neoliberalism's Stealth Revolution*. New York: Zone Books.

Brownell, P. 1981. Participation in budgeting, locus of control and organizational effectiveness. *The Accounting Review*, 56(4), 844–60.

Brownell, P. 1982. The role of accounting data in performance evaluation, budgetary participation, and organizational effectiveness. *Journal of Accounting Research*, 20(1), 12–27.

Brownell, P. 1983. Leadership style, budgetary participation and managerial behavior. *Accounting, Organizations and Society*, 8(4), 307–31.

Brownlie, J. 2009. Researching, not playing, in the public sphere. *Sociology*, 43, 699–716.

Bruck, C. 2006. Millions for millions. *The New Yorker*.

Bryer, R. 2006. Accounting and control of the labour process. *Critical Perspectives on Accounting*, 17, 551–98.

Bryer, R. A. 1993a. Double-entry bookkeeping and the birth of capitalism: Accounting for the commercial revolution in medieval Northern Italy. *Critical Perspectives on Accounting*, 4, 113–40.

Bryer, R. A. 1993b. The late nineteenth-century revolution in financial reporting: Accounting for the rise of investor or managerial capitalism? *Accounting, Organizations and Society*, 18, 649–90.

Bryer, R. A. 1994. Why Marx's labour theory is superior to the marginalist theory of value: The case from modern financial reporting. *Critical Perspectives on Accounting*, 5(4), 313–40.

Bryer, R. A. 1999. Marx and accounting. *Critical Perspectives on Accounting*, 10(5), 683–709.

Bryer, R. A. 2000a. The history of accounting and the transition to capitalism in England. Part one: Theory. *Accounting, Organizations and Society*, 25, 131–62.

Bryer, R. A. 2000b. The history of accounting and the transition to capitalism in England. Part two: Evidence. *Accounting, Organizations and Society*, 25, 327–81.

Burawoy, M. 1979. *Manufacturing Consent: Changes in the Labor Process under Monopoly Capitalism*. Chicago, IL: University of Chicago Press.

Burger, A. S. 1992. Changing civil-military relations in Sri Lanka. *Asian Survey*, 32, 744–56.

Burnett, R. D. & Hansen, D. R. 2008. Ecoefficiency: Defining a role for environmental cost management. *Accounting, Organizations and Society*, 33, 551–81.

Burns, J. & Baldvinsdottir, G. 2005. An institutional perspective of accountants' new roles – the interplay of contradictions and praxis. *European Accounting Review*, 14(4), 725–57.

372   References

Burns, T. & Stalker, G. M. 1961. *The Management of Innovations*. London: Tavistock.

Burrell, G. & Morgan, G. 1979. *Sociological Paradigms and Organisational Analysis: Elements of the Sociology of Corporate Life*. London: Heinemann.

Burton-Jones, A. 1999. *Knowledge Capitalism: Business, Work, and Learning in the New Economy*. Oxford, UK: Oxford University Press.

Busch, T. 1998. Attitudes towards management by objectives: An empirical investigation of self-efficacy and goal commitment. *Scandinavian Journal of Management*, 14, 289–99.

Cadbury Commission 1992. *The Report of the Commission on the Financial Aspects of Corporate Governance*. London: The Committee on the Financial Aspects of Corporate Governance.

Caglio, A. 2003. Enterprise resource planning systems and accountants: Towards hybridization? *European Accounting Review*, 12, 123–53.

Callon, M. 1991. Techno-economic networks and irreversibility. In: Law, J. (ed.) *A Sociology of Monsters: Essays on Power, Technology and Domination*. London: Routledge.

Callon, M. 2003. The increasing involvement of concerned groups in R&D policies: What lessons for public powers? In: Geuna, A., Salte, A. J., & Steinmuelle, W. E. (eds.) *Science and Innovation: Rethinking the Rationales for Funding and Governance*. Cheltenham, UK: Edward Elgar Publishing.

Calvert-Minor, C. 2012. The inescapability of theorizing practices within epistemology. *Kritike*, 6, 85–94.

Campbell, D. J. 2000. Legitimacy theory or managerial reality construction? Corporate social disclosure in Marks and Spencer plc corporate reports, 1969-1997. *Accounting Forum*, 24, 80–100.

Cardoso, F. H. & Faletto, E. 1979. *Dependency and Development in Latin America (Dependencia Y Desarrollo En América Latina, Engl.)*. Berkeley, CA: University of California Press.

Carmona, S., Ezzamel, M., & Gutierrez, F. 1997. Control and cost accounting practices in the Spanish Royal Tobacco Factory. *Accounting, Organizations and Society*, 22, 411–46.

Carr, C. & Ng, J. 1995. Total cost control: Nissan and its U.K. supplier partnerships. *Management Accounting Research*, 6, 347–65.

Castells, M. 2000. Toward a sociology of the network society. *Contemporary Sociology*, 29, 693–9.

Castells, M. 2010. *The Rise of the Network Society*. Chichester, UK: Wiley-Blackwell.

Caves, R. E. 1980. Industrial organization, corporate strategy and structure. *Journal of Economic Literature*, 18, 64–92.

Caves, R. E. & Murphy, W. F. 1976. Franchising: Firms, markets, and intangible assets. *Southern Economic Journal*, 42, 572–86.

Caves, R. E., Porter, M. E., Spence, A. M., & Scott, J. T. 1980. *Competition in the Open Economy: A Model Applied to Canada*. Cambridge, MA: Harvard University Press.

Cetina, K. K. & Bruegger, U. 2000. The market as an object of attachment: Exploring postsocial relations in financial markets. *The Canadian Journal of Sociology/Cahiers Canadiens De Sociologie*, 25, 141–68.

Chandler, A. D. 1962. *Strategy and Structure. Chapters in the History of the Industrial Enterprise*. Cambridge, MA: MIT Press.

Chandler, A. D. 1976. The development of modern management structure in the US and UK. In: Hannah, L. (ed.) *Management Strategy and Business Development: An Historical and Comparative Study*. London: Palgrave Macmillan UK.

Chandler, A. D. 1977. *The Visible Hand: The Managerial Revolution in American Business*. Cambridge, MA: Harvard University Press.

Chandler, A. D. & Hikino, T. 1994. *Scale and Scope*. Cambridge, MA: Harvard University Press.

Chang, L.-C. 2009. The impact of political interests upon the formulation of performance measurements: The NHS star rating system. *Financial Accountability & Management*, 25, 145–65.

Chapman, C. S. 1997. Reflections on a contingent view of accounting. *Accounting, Organizations and Society*, 22(2), 189–205.

Checkland, P. 1999. *Systems Thinking, Systems Practice*. London: John Wiley.

Chenhall, R. H. 1997. Reliance on manufacturing performance measures, total quality management and organizational performance. *Management Accounting Research*, 8, 187–206.

Chenhall, R. H. 2003. Management control systems design within its organizational context: Findings from contingency-based research and directions for the future. *Accounting, Organizations and Society*, 28(2–3), 127–68.

Chenhall, R. H. 2005. Integrative strategic performance measurement systems, strategic alignment of manufacturing, learning and strategic outcomes: An exploratory study. *Accounting, Organizations and Society*, 30, 395–422.

Chenhall, R. H. 2008. Accounting for the horizontal organization: A review essay. *Accounting, Organizations and Society*, 33, 517–50.

Chenhall, R. H. & Brownell, P. 1988. The effect of participative budgeting on job satisfaction and performance: Role ambiguity as an intervening variable. *Accounting, Organizations and Society*, 13 (3), 225–33.

Chenhall, R. H., Hall, M., & Smith, D. 2010. Social capital and management control systems: A study of a non-government organization. *Accounting, Organizations and Society*, 35, 737–56.

Chenhall, R. H., Hall, M., & Smith, D. 2013. Performance measurement, modes of evaluation and the development of compromising accounts. *Accounting, Organizations and Society*, 38, 268–87.

Chenhall, R. H., Hall, M., & Smith, D. 2017. The expressive role of performance measurement systems: A field study of a mental health development project. *Accounting, Organizations and Society*, 63, 60–75.

Chia, R. 1995. From modern to postmodern organizational analysis. *Organization Studies*, 16, 579–604.

Chiapello, E. 2007. Accounting and the birth of the notion of capitalism. *Critical Perspectives on Accounting*, 18, 263–96.

Chiapello, E. 2017. Critical accounting research and neoliberalism. *Critical Perspectives on Accounting*, 43, 47–64.

Child, J. 1972. Organizational structure, environment and performance: The role of strategic choice. *Sociology*, 6(1), 1–22.

Cho, C. H. & Patten, D. M. 2007. The role of environmental disclosures as tools of legitimacy: A research note. *Accounting, Organizations and Society*, 32, 639–47.

Chu, M. 2007. Microfinance: Business, profitability, and the creation of social value. In: Rangan, K., Quelch, J. A., Herrero, G., & Barton, B. (eds.) *Business Solutions for the Global Poor: Creating Social and Economic Value*. San Francisco, CA: John Wiley.

Chua, R. T., Mosley, G., Wright, A. N., & Zaman, H. 2000. *Microfinance, Risk Management, and Poverty: Assessing the Impact of Microenterprise Services (AIMS)*. Washington, DC: Management Systems International/USAID.

Chua, W. F. & Mahama, H. 2012. On theory as a 'deliverable' and its relevance in 'policy' arenas. *Critical Perspectives on Accounting*, 23, 78–82.

CIMA. 2005. *CIMA Official Terminology*. London: CIMA.

CIMA. 2008. *Qualification Structure and Syllabus: CIMA Chartered Management Accounting Qualification 2010*. London: CIMA.

CIMA. 2014. *2015 CIMA Professional Qualification Syllabus*. London: CIMA.

Clawson, D. 1980. *Bureaucracy and the Labor Process: The Transformation of U. S. Industry, 1860-1920*. New York: Monthly Review Press.

Clegg, S. 1990. *Modern Organizations*. London: Sage.

Clegg, S., Kornberger, M., & Pitsis, T. 2005. *Managing and Organizations: An Introduction to Theory and Practice*. London: Sage.

Coase, R. H. 1937. The nature of the firm. *Economica*, 4, 386–405.

Coase, R. H. 1988a. The nature of the firm: Influence. *Journal of Law, Economics, & Organization*, 4, 33–47.

Coase, R. H. 1988b. The nature of the firm: Meaning. *Journal of Law, Economics, & Organization*, 4, 19–32.

Coase, R. H. 1988c. The nature of the firm: Origin. *Journal of Law, Economics, & Organization*, 4, 3–17.

Coase, R. H. 1990. Accounting and the theory of the firm. *Journal of Accounting and Economics*, 12, 3–13.

Coase, R. H. 1992. The institutional structure of production. *The American Economic Review*, 82, 713–19.

374 *References*

Coase, R. H. 2000. The acquisition of fisher body by general motors. *The Journal of Law & Economics*, 43, 15–32.

Coghlan, D. & Shani, A. B. 2016. *Action Research in Business and Management*. London: Sage.

Cohen, J. & Arato, A. 1992. Politics and the reconstruction of the concept of civil society. In: Honneth, A., McCarthy, T., Offe, C., & Wellmer, A. (eds.) *Cultural-Political Interventions in the Unfinished Project of Enlightenment*. Cambridge, MA: MIT Press.

Collins, D. 2000. *Management Fads and Buzzwords: Critical-Practical Perspectives*. London: Routledge.

Colwyn Jones, T. & Dugdale, D. 2002. The ABC bandwagon and the juggernaut of modernity. *Accounting, Organizations and Society*, 27(1–2), 121–63.

Comanor, W. S. & Wilson, T. A. 1974. *Advertising and Market Power*. Cambridge, MA: Harvard University Press.

Commonwealth Association for Corporate Governance 1999. *CACG Guidelines - Principles for Corporate Governance in the Commonwealth: Towards Global Competitiveness and Economic Accountability*. Havelock, New Zealand: Commonwealth Association for Corporate Governance.

Confederation of British Industry. 1995. *Directors' Remuneration: Report of the Salary Group Chaired by Sir Richard Greenbury*. London: Gee Publishing.

Conrad, C. 2004. The illusion of reform: Corporate discourse and agenda denial in the 2002 'corporate meltdown'. *Rhetoric and Public Affairs*, 7, 311–38.

Cooke, B. 2004. The managing of the (third) world. *Organization*, 11, 603–29.

Cooper, C. 2002. Critical accounting in Scotland. *Critical Perspectives on Accounting*, 13, 451–62.

Cooper, C. 2015. Entrepreneurs of the self: The development of management control since 1976. *Accounting, Organizations and Society*, 47, 14–24.

Cooper, C., Coulson, A. & Taylor, P. 2011. Accounting for human rights: Doxic health and safety practices – The accounting lesson from ICL. *Critical Perspectives on Accounting*, 22(8), 738–58.

Cooper, D. J., Everett, J., & Neu, D. 2005. Financial scandals, accounting change and the role of accounting academics: A perspective from North America. *European Accounting Review*, 14, 373–82.

Cooper, D. J., Scapens, R. W., & Arnold, J. 1983. *Management Accounting: Research and Practice*. London: CIMA.

Cooper, R. & Kaplan, R. S. 1988. Measure costs right: Make the right decisions. *Harvard Business Review*, 1988, 96–103.

Cooper, R. & Kaplan, R. S. 1991a. *The Design of Cost Management Systems: Text, Cases, and Readings*. Upper Saddle River, NJ: Prentice Hall.

Cooper, R. & Kaplan, R. S. 1991b. Profit priorities from activity-based costing. *Harvard Business Review*, 1991, 130–135.

Cooper, R. & Slagmulder, R. 1997. *Target Costing and Value Engineering*. Portland, OR: Productivity Press.

Cooper, R. & Slagmulder, R. 1998. Extra-organizational cost analysis. *Management Accounting*, 80, 14–16.

Copestake, J., Dawson, P., Fanning, J. P., McKay, A., & Wright-Revolledo, K. 2005. Monitoring the diversity of the poverty outreach and impact of microfinance: A comparison of methods using data from Peru. *Development Policy Review*, 23, 703–23.

Covaleski, M. A. & Dirsmith, M. W. 1988. The use of budgetary symbols in the political arena: An historically informed field study. *Accounting, Organizations and Society*, 13, 1–24.

Covaleski, M. A., Dirsmith, M. W., Heian, J. B., & Samuel, S. 1998. The calculated and the avowed: Techniques of discipline and struggles over identity in big six public accounting firms. *Administrative Science Quarterly*, 43, 293–328.

Craig, R. & Amernic, J. 2004. The deployment of accounting-related rhetoric in the prelude to a privatization. *Accounting, Auditing & Accountability Journal*, 17(1), 41–58.

Craig, R. & Amernic, J. 2006. The mobilization of accounting in preening for privatization. *Accounting, Auditing & Accountability Journal*, 19(1), 82–95.

Craig, R. & Amernic, J. 2008. A privatization success story: Accounting and narrative expression over time. *Accounting Auditing and Accountability Journal*, 21, 1085–116.

References 375

Crompton, G. & Jupe, R. 2002. 'An awkward fence to cross': Railway capitalization in Britain in the inter-war years. *Accounting, Business & Financial History*, 12, 439–59.

Crush, J. 1995. *Power of Development*. London: Routledge.

Cuganesan, S. 2008. Calculating customer intimacy: accounting numbers in a sales and marketing department. *Accounting, Auditing & Accountability Journal*, 21(1), 78–103.

Currie, G., Tuck, P., & Morrell, K. 2015. How hybrid managers act as 'canny customers' to accelerate policy reform: A case study of regulator-regulatee relationships in the UK's tax agency. *Accounting, Auditing & Accountability Journal*, 28, 1291–309.

Cyert, R. M. & March, J. G. 1963. *A Behavioral Theory of the Firm [By] Richard M. Cyert [And] James G. March. With Contributions by G. P. E. Clarkson [And Others]*. Englewood Cliffs, NJ: Prentice-Hall.

Daly, H. E. 1993. Sustainable growth: An impossible theorem. In: Daly, H. E. & Townsend, K. N. (eds.) *Valuing the Earth: Economics, Ecology, Ethics*. Boston, MA: MIT Press.

Davenport, T. H. 1998. Putting the enterprise into the enterprise system. *Harvard Business Review*, 1998, 121–31.

Davenport, T. H. 2014. *Big Data at Work: Dispelling the Myths, Uncovering the Opportunities*. Boston, MA: Harvard Business Review Press.

Davies, A. & Thomas, R. 2000. Researching public sector change. *Public Management: An International Journal of Research and Theory*, 2, 547–54.

Dean, J. 2008. Enjoying neoliberalism. *Cultural Politics*, 4, 73–99.

Dean, M. 2003. Culture governance and individualisation. In: Bang, H. P. (ed.) *Governance as Social and Political Communication*. Manchester, UK: Manchester University Press.

Deleuze, G. & Guattari, F. 1987. *A Thousand Plateaus: Capitalism and Schizophrenia*. London: University of Minnesota Press.

Deloitte 2013. *Developing an Effective Governance Operating Model: A Guide for Financial Services Boards and Management Teams*. London: Deloitte.

Diefenbach, T. 2009. New public management in public sector organizations: The dark sides of managerialistic 'enlightenment'. *Public Administration*, 87, 892–909.

Dimaggio, P. 2001. *The Twenty-First-Century Firm: Changing Economic Organization in International Perspective*. Princeton, NJ: Princeton University Press.

Dimaggio, P. J. & Powell, W. W. 1983. The iron cage revisited: Institutional isomorphism and collective rationality in organizational fields. *American Sociological Review*, 48, 147–60.

Dirsmith, M. W., Heian, J. B., & Covaleski, M. A. 1997. Structure and agency in an institutionalized setting: The application and social transformation of control in the Big Six. *Accounting, Organizations and Society*, 22, 1–27.

Dirsmith, M. W. & Jablonsky, S. F. 1979. MBO, political rationality and information inductance. *Accounting, Organizations and Society*, 4, 39–52.

Dixon, R., Ritchie, J., & Siwale, J. 2007. Loan officers and loan 'delinquency' in microfinance: A Zambian case. *Accounting Forum*, 31, 47–71.

Djelic, M. L. & Sahlin-Andersson, K. 2006. *Transnational Governance: Institutional Dynamics of Regulation*. Cambridge, UK: Cambridge University Press.

Dragos, D. & Neamtu, B. 2013. Life Cycle Costing (LCC) in the new EU directive proposal. *Eppl*, 1, 19–30.

Drennan, L. & Kelly, M. 2002. Assessing an activity-based costing project. *Critical Perspectives on Accounting*, 13, 311–31.

Drucker, P. F. 2011 [1977]. *People and Performance: The Best of Peter Drucker on Management*. London: Routledge.

Du Gay, P. & Morgan, G. 2014. *New Spirits of Capitalism? Crises, Justifications, and Dynamics*. Oxford, UK: Oxford University Press.

Dugdale, D. 2013. The theory of constraints. In: Mitchell, F., Norreklit, H., & Jakobsen, M. (eds.) *The Routledge Companion to Cost Management*. London: Routledge.

Dugdale, D. & Lyne, S. 2010. *Budgeting Practice and Organisational Structure*. London: Elsevier Science.

376 References

Dunk, A. S. & Nouri, H. 1998. Antecedents of budgetary slack: A literature review and synthesis. *Journal of Accounting Literature*, 17, 72.

Dunleavy, P., Margetts, H., Bastow, S., & Tinkler, J. 2006. New public management is dead—long live digital-era governance. *Journal of Public Administration Research and Theory*, 16, 467–94.

Easterly, W. 2007. *The White Man's Burden: Why the West's Efforts to Aid the Rest Have Done So Much Ill and So Little Good*. Oxford, UK: Oxford University Press.

Ebrahim, A. 2003. Accountability in practice: Mechanisms for NGOs. *World Development*, 31, 813–29.

Edersheim, E. H. 2004. *McKinsey's Marvin Bower: Vision, Leadership, and the Creation of Management Consulting*. Hoboken, NJ: Wiley.

Edwards, J. R., Boyns, T., & Matthews, M. 2002. Standard costing and budgetary control in the British iron and steel industry: A study of accounting change. *Accounting, Auditing & Accountability Journal*, 15(1), 12–45.

Edwards, J. R. & Newell, E. 1991. The development of industrial cost and management accounting before 1850: A survey of the evidence. *Business History*, 33, 35–57.

Edwards, M. 1989. The irrelevance of development studies. *Third World Quarterly*, 11, 116–35.

Efferin, S. & Hopper, T. 2007. Management control, culture and ethnicity in a Chinese Indonesian company. *Accounting, Organizations and Society*, 32, 223–62.

Ehrenberg, J. R. 1999. *Civil Society: The Critical History of an Idea*. New York: NYU Press.

Elyachar, J. 2002. Empowerment money: The World Bank, non-governmental organizations, and the value of culture in Egypt. *Public Culture*, 14, 493–513.

Emmanuel, C., Otley, D., & Merchant, K. 2004. *Accounting for Management Control*. London: South-Western, Cengage Learning.

Escobar, A. 1988. Power and visibility: Development and the invention and management of the third world. *Cultural Anthropology*, 3, 428–43.

Escobar, A. 1995. *Encountering Development: The Making and Unmaking of the Third World*. Princeton, NJ: Princeton University Press.

Fama, E. F. 1980. Agency problems and the theory of the firm. *Journal of Political Economy*, 88, 288–307.

Fama, E. F. & Jensen, M. C. 1983. Separation of ownership and control. *The Journal of Law & Economics*, 26, 301–25.

Fanon, F. 1963. *The Wretched of the Earth*. New York: Grove Press.

Farris, P. W., Moore, M. J., & Buzzell, R. D. 2004. *The Profit Impact of Marketing Strategy Project: Retrospect and Prospects*. Cambridge, UK: Cambridge University Press.

Featherstone, M. 1988. In pursuit of the postmodern: An introduction. *Theory, Culture & Society*, 5, 195–215.

Feldman, S. 1997. NGOs and civil society: (Un)stated contradictions. *The Annals of the American Academy of Political and Social Science*, 554, 46–65.

Feltham, G. A. & Demski, J. S. 1970. The use of models in information evaluation. *The Accounting Review*, 45, 623–40.

Ferguson, J. 2006. *Global Shadows: Africa in the Neoliberal World Order*. Durham, NC: Duke University Press.

Fernando, J. L. 2011. *The Political Economy of NGOs State Formation in Sri Lanka and Bangladesh*. London: Pluto Press.

Ferreira, A. & Otley, D. 2009. The design and use of performance management systems: An extended framework for analysis. *Management Accounting Research*, 20, 263–82.

Figge, F., Hahn, T., Schaltegger, S., & Wagner, M. 2002. The sustainability balanced scorecard – Linking sustainability management to business strategy. *Business Strategy and the Environment*, 11, 269–84.

Financial Reporting Council. 2003. *The Combined Code on Corporate Governance*. London: Fianncial Reporting Council.

Financial Reporting Council. 2012. *The UK Corporate Governance Code*. London: Financial Reporting Council.

Fleischman, R. K. & Parker, L. D. 1991. British entrepreneurs and pre-industrial revolution evidence of cost management. *The Accounting Review*, 66, 361–75.

References 377

Flew, T. 2012. Michel Foucault's The Birth of Biopolitics and contemporary neo-liberalism debates. *Thesis Eleven*, 108, 44–65.

Foucault, M. 1978. *The History of Sexuality Volume I: An Introduction.* New York: Pantheon Books.

Foucault, M. 1979. *Discipline and Punish.* Harmondsworth, UK: Penguin.

Foucault, M. 1980. *Power/Knowledge: Selected Interviews and Other Writings, 1972/1977.* Brighton, UK: Harvester Press.

Foucault, M. 1986. Of other spaces. *Diacritics*, 16, 22–7.

Foucault, M. 1995. *Discipline and Punish: The Birth of the Prison.* New York: Vintage Books.

Foucault, M. 1998. *Aesthetics, Method and Epistemology: Essential Works of Foucault - Vol 2.* New York: The New Press.

Foucault, M. 2000. *Power: Essential Works of Foucault - Volume 3.* New York: New Press.

Foucault, M. 2003. *'Society Must Be Defended': Lectures at the College De France, 1975-76.* London: Allen Lane.

Foucault, M. 2005. *The Order of Things: An Archaeology of the Human Sciences.* London: Routledge.

Foucault, M. 2008. *The Birth of Biopolitics: Lectures at the College De France, 1978-79.* Basingstoke, UK: Palgrave Macmillan.

Foucault, M. & Kritzman, L. 1988. *Politics, Philosophy, Culture: Interviews and Other Writings, 1977-1984.* New York: Routledge.

Frank, A. G. 1967. *Capitalism and Underdevelopment in Latin America.* New York: Monthly Review Press.

Frank, A. G. 1979. *Sociology of Development and Underdevelopment of Sociology.* Lagos: Afrografika Publishers.

Free, C. 2008. Walking the talk? Supply chain accounting and trust among UK supermarkets and suppliers. *Accounting, Organizations and Society*, 33, 629–62.

Free, C. & Macintosh, N. B. 2009. Bourdieu's logic of practice theory: Possibilities for research on management accounting and control. *Queen's University School of Business Research Paper No. 02-09.* Ontario, Canada.

Friedman, M. 1970. The social responsibility of business is to increase its profits. *The New York Times Magazine.* New York: New York Times.

Frow, N., Marginson, D., & Ogden, S. 2010. 'Continuous' budgeting: Reconciling budget flexibility with budgetary control. *Accounting, Organizations and Society*, 35, 444–61.

Fuchs, C. 2008. *Internet and Society: Social Theory in the Information Age.* London: Routledge.

Galant, A. & Cadez, S. 2017. Corporate social responsibility and financial performance relationship: A review of measurement approaches. *Economic Research-Ekonomska Istraživanja*, 30, 676–93.

Galbraith, J. R. 1973. *Designing Complex Organizations.* Reading, MA: Addison-Wesley.

Gendron, Y., Cooper, D. J., & Townley, B. 2007. The construction of auditing expertise in measuring government performance. *Accounting, Organizations and Society*, 32, 101–29.

Gertler, M. S. 1988. The limits of flexibility: Comments on the post-Fordist vision of production and its geography. *Transactions of the Institute of British Geographers*, 13, 419–32.

Giddens, A. 1979. *Central Problems in Social Theory: Action, Structure and Contradiction in Social Analysis.* London: Macmillan.

Giddens, A. 1985. *The Nation-State and Violence.* Berkeley, CA: University of California Press.

Giddens, A. 1990. *The Consequences of Modernity.* Stanford, CA: Stanford University Press.

Giddens, A. 1994. Living in a post-traditional society. In: Beck, U., Lash, S., & Giddens, A. (eds.) *Reflexive Modernization: Politics, Tradition and Aesthetics in the Modern Social Order.* Cambridge, UK: Polity Press.

Gladwin, T. N., Krause, T.-S., & Kennelly, J. J. 1995. Beyond eco-efficiency: Towards socially sustainable business. *Sustainable Development*, 3, 35–43.

Goldman, M. 2005. *Imperial Nature: The World Bank and Struggles for Social Justice in the Age of Globalization.* New Haven, CT: Yale University Press.

Goldratt, E. M. & Cox, J. 1984. *The Goal: Excellence in Manufacturing.* New York: North River Press.

378   *References*

Govindarajan, V. 1984. Appropriateness of accounting data in performance evaluation: An empirical examination of environmental uncertainty as an intervening variable. *Accounting, Organizations and Society*, 9(2), 125–35.

Graham, C. 2008. Fearful asymmetry: The consumption of accounting signs in the Algoma Steel pension bailout. *Accounting, Organizations and Society*, 33, 756–82.

Granlund, M. & Malmi, T. 2002. Moderate impact of ERPS on management accounting: A lag or permanent outcome? *Management Accounting Research*, 13, 299–321.

Gray, R. 2010. Is accounting for sustainability actually accounting for sustainability…and how would we know? An exploration of narratives of organisations and the planet. *Accounting, Organizations and Society*, 35, 47–62.

Gray, R. & Bebbington, J. 2001. *Accounting for the Environment:. Second Edition*. London: Sage.

Gray, R., Bebbington, J., & Collison, D. 2006. NGOs, civil society and accountability: Making the people accountable to capital. *Accounting, Auditing & Accountability Journal*, 19, 319–48.

Gray, R., Bebbington, J., & Walters, D. 1993. *Accounting for the Environment*. London: Paul Chapman [for] ACCA, Chartered Association of Certified Accountants.

Gray, R., Owen, D., & Adams, C. 1996. *Accounting and Accountability*. London: FT Prentice Hall.

Gros, F. 2014. The fourth age of security. In: Lemm, V. & Vatter, M. (eds.) *The Government of Life: Foucault, Biopolitics, and Neoliberalism*. New York: Fordham University Press.

Gruber, J. 2011. *Public Finance and Public Policy*. New York: Worth Publishers.

Gruening, G. 2001. Origin and theoretical basis of New Public Management. *International Public Management Journal*, 4, 1–25.

Habermas, J. R. 1989. *Jürgen Habermas on Society and Politics: A Reader*. Boston, MA: Beacon Press.

Hadenius, A. & Uggla, F. 1996. Making civil society work, promoting democratic development: What can states and donors do? *World Development*, 24, 1621–39.

Hage, J. & Aiken, M. T. 1970. *Social Change in Complex Organizations*. New York: Random House.

Haggerty, K. D. & Ericson, R. V. 2000. The surveillant assemblage. *The British Journal of Sociology*, 51, 605–22.

Håkansson, H. & Lind, J. 2006. Accounting in an interorganizational setting. In: Chapman, C. S., Hopwood, A. G., & Shields, M. D. (eds.) *Handbooks of Management Accounting Research*. New York: Elsevier, vol 2, 885–902.

Halal, W. E. 1986. *The New Capitalism*. New York: Wiley.

Hall, M. & O'Dwyer, B. 2017. Accounting, non-governmental organizations and civil society: The importance of nonprofit organizations to understanding accounting, organizations and society. *Accounting, Organizations and Society*, 63, 1–5.

Hall, S. 2011. The neoliberal revolution. *Soundings*, 2011, 9–27.

Hall, S. & Gieben, B. 1993. *The Formations of Modernity: Understanding Modern Societies an Introduction*. Cambridge, UK: Polity Press.

Hall, S., Thompson, K., & Bocock, R. 1992. *Social and Cultural Forms of Modernity: Understanding Modern Societies*. Cambridge, UK: Polity Press.

Hambrick, D. C., Werder, A. V., & Zajac, E. J. 2008. New directions in corporate governance research. *Organization Science*, 19, 381–85.

Hamilton, G. & Ó hÓgartaigh, C. 2009. The third policeman: `The true and fair view', language and the habitus of accounting. *Critical Perspectives on Accounting*, 20, 910–20.

Hansen, E. G. & Schaltegger, S. 2017. Sustainability balanced scorecards and their architectures: Irrelevant or misunderstood? *Journal of Business Ethics*, 142(1): 1–16.

Hansen, S. C. 2010. A theoretical analysis of the impact of adopting rolling budgets, activity-based budgeting and beyond budgeting. *European Accounting Review*, 20, 289–319.

Hansen, S. C. & Torok, R. G. 2004. *The Closed Loop: Implementing Activity-Based Planning and Budgeting*. Fort Worth, TX: Bookman Publ.

Hardt, M. 1999. Affective labour. *Boundary 2*, 26, 89–100.

Hardt, M. & Negri, A. 2000. *Empire*. Cambridge, MA: Harvard University Press.

Hardt, M. & Negri, A. 2017. *Assembly*. Oxford, UK: Oxford University Press.

Harvey, D. 1989. *The Condition of Postmodernity: An Enquiry into the Origins of Cultural Change.* Oxford, UK: Basil Blackwell.

Harvey, D. 1990. Flexible accumulation through urbanization reflections on 'post-modernism' in the American city. *Perspecta*, 26, 251–72.

Harvey, D. 2005. *A Brief History of Neoliberalism.* Oxford, UK: Oxford University Press.

Heckscher, C. 2012. Defining the post-bureaucratic type. In: Godwyn, M. & Gittell, J. H. (eds.) *Sociology of Organizations: Structures and Relationships.* London: Sage.

Hickey, S. & Mohan, G. 2004. *Participation: From Tyranny to Transformation? Exploring New Approaches to Participation in Development.* London: Zed Books.

Hilgers, M. 2012. The historicity of the neoliberal state. *Social Anthropology*, 20, 80–94.

Hill, S. 1991. How do you manage a flexible firm? The total quality model. *Work Employment Society*, 5, 397–415.

Hingley, M. 2001. Relationship management in the supply chain. *The International Journal of Logistics Management*, 12, 57–71.

Hirst, M. K. & Yetton, P. W. 1999. The effects of budget goals and task interdependence on the level of and variance in performance: A research note. *Accounting, Organizations and Society*, 24, 205–16.

Hirst, P. & Zeitlin, J. 1991. Flexible specialization versus post-Fordism: Theory, evidence and policy implications. *Economy and Society*, 20, 5–9.

Hobsbawm, E. J. 1964. *Labouring Men: Studies in the History of Labour.* London: Weidenfeld & Nicolson.

Hoffjan, A. & Kruse, H. 2006. Open book accounting in supply chains – When and how is it used in practice? *Journal of Cost Management*, 20, 40–7.

Hoffman, W. M., Frederick, R., & Schwartz, M. S. 2014. *Business Ethics: Readings and Cases in Corporate Morality.* Chichester, UK: John Wiley.

Hofstede, G. 1981. Management control of public and not-for-profit activities. *Accounting, Organizations and Society*, 6, 193–211.

Hofstede, G. H. 2003 [1968]. *The Game of Budget Control.* Abingdon, UK: Routledge.

Hood, C. 1991. A public management for all seasons? *Public Administration*, 69, 3–19.

Hope, J. & Fraser, R. 1997. Beyond budgeting breaking through the barrier to the 'third wave'. *Management Accounting*, 75, 20–3.

Hope, J. & Fraser, R. 2000. Beyond budgeting. *Strategic Finance*, 82, 30–5.

Hope, J. & Fraser, R. 2001. *Beyond Budgeting: Questions and Answers.* Wincanton, UK: Dorset.

Hope, J. & Fraser, R. 2003a. *Beyond Budgeting: How Managers Can Break Free from the Annual Performance Trap.* Cambridge, MA: Harvard Business School Press.

Hope, J. & Fraser, R. 2003b. Who needs budgets? *Harvard Business Review*, 81, 108–15.

Hopper, T. 1999. Postcard from Japan: A management accounting view. *Accounting, Auditing & Accountability Journal*, 12(1), 58–68.

Hopper, T. & Armstrong, P. 1991. Cost accounting, controlling labour and the rise of conglomerates. *Accounting, Organizations and Society*, 16, 405–38.

Hopper, T., Koga, T., & Goto, J. 1999. Cost accounting in small and medium sized Japanese companies: An exploratory study. *Accounting and Business Research*, 30, 73–86.

Hopper, T., Lassou, P., & Soobaroyen, T. 2017. Globalisation, accounting and developing countries. *Critical Perspectives on Accounting*, 43, 125–48.

Hopper, T. & Macintosh, N. 1993. Management accounting as disciplinary practice: The case of ITT under Harold Geneen. *Management Accounting Research*, 4, 181–216.

Hopper, T. & Major, M. 2007. Extending institutional analysis through theoretical triangulation: Regulation and activity-based costing in Portuguese telecommunications. *European Accounting Review*, 16(1), 59–97.

Hopper, T. & Powell, A. 1985. Making sense of research into the organizational and social aspects of management accounting: A review of its underlying assumptions. *Journal of Management Studies*, 22, 429–65.

Hopper, T., Scapens, R. W. & Northcott, D. eds. 2007. *Issues in Management Accounting.* 3rd ed. Harlow, UK: Financial Times Prentice Hall.

380   References

Hopper, T., Storey, J., & Willmott, H. 1987. Accounting for accounting: Towards the development of a dialectical view. *Accounting, Organizations and Society*, 12, 437–56.

Hopper, T., Tsamenyi, M., Uddin, S., & Wickramasinghe, D. 2009. Management accounting in less developed countries: What is known and needs knowing. *Accounting, Auditing & Accountability Journal*, 22, 469–514.

Hopper, T., Tsamenyi, M., Uddin, S., & Wickramasinghe, D. 2012. Management control after privatization: Illustrations from less developed countries. In: Hopper, T., Tsamenyi, M., Uddin, S., & Wickramasinghe, D. (eds.) *Handbook of Accounting and Development*. Cheltenham, UK: Edward Elgar Publishing.

Hopwood, A. G. 1972. An empirical study of the role of accounting data in performance evaluation. *Journal of Accounting Research*, 10, 156–82.

Hopwood, A. G. 1987. The archaeology of accounting systems. *Accounting, Organizations and Society*, 12, 207–34.

Hopwood, A. G. 1996. Looking across rather than up and down: On the need to explore the lateral processing of information. *Accounting, Organizations and Society*, 21, 589–90.

Hopwood, A. G. & Miller, P. 1994. *Accounting as Social and Institutional Practice*. Cambridge, UK: Cambridge University Press.

Hoque, Z. & Hopper, T. 1994. Rationality, accounting and politics: A case study of management control in a Bangladeshi jute mill. *Management Accounting Research*, 5, 5–30.

Hoque, Z. & Parker, L. 2014. *Performance Management in Nonprofit Organizations: Global Perspectives*. New York: Routledge.

Hoskin, K. & Macve, R. 1994. Reappraising the genesis of managerialism: A re-examination of the role of accounting at the Springfield Armory, 1815-1845. *Accounting, Auditing & Accountability Journal*, 7(2), 4–29.

Hoskin, K. W. & Macve, R. H. 1986. Accounting and the examination: A genealogy of disciplinary power. *Accounting, Organizations and Society*, 11, 105–36.

Hoskin, K. W. & Macve, R. H. 1988. The genesis of accountability: The west point connections. *Accounting, Organizations and Society*, 13, 37–73.

HRH The Prince of Wales. 2010. Forward. In A. Hopwood, J. Unerman and J. Fries (eds.) *Accounting for Sustainability: Practical Insights*. London: Earthscan.

Hughes, T. P. 1988. The seamless web: Technology, science, et cetera, et cetera. In: Elliot, B. A. (ed.) *Technology and Social Process*. Edinburgh: Edinburgh University Press.

Hulme, D. 2000. Impact assessment methodologies for microfinance: Theory, experience and better practice. *World Development*, 28, 79–98.

Hunt, D. 1989. *Economic Theories of Development: An Analysis of Competing Paradigms*. Hemel Hempstead, UK: Harvester Wheatsheaf.

Hyvönen, T. 2003. Management accounting and information systems: ERP versus BoB. *European Accounting Review*, 12, 155–73.

Hyvönen, T. 2013. ICT systems and cost management. In: Mitchell, F., Norreklit, H., & Jakobsen, M. (eds.) *The Routledge Companion to Cost Management*. London: Routledge.

ICAEW. 1999. *Internal Control: Guidance for Directors on the Combined Code*. Turnball Report. London: ICAEW.

Ilcan, S. & Phillips, L. 2010. Developmentalities and calculative practices: The millennium development goals. *Antipode*, 42, 844–74.

Imai, M. 1986. *Kaizen: The Key to Japan's Competitive Success*. New York: McGraw-Hill Education.

Innes, J., Mitchell, F., & Sinclair, D. 2000. Activity-based costing in the U.K.'s largest companies: A comparison of 1994 and 1999 survey results. *Management Accounting Research*, 11, 349–62.

International Federation of Accountants 2005. *Environmental Management Accounting: International Guidance Document*. New York: International Federation of Accountants.

Ishijima, H., Eliakimu, E., & Mshana, J. M. 2016. The '5S' approach to improve a working environment can reduce waiting time: Findings from hospitals in Northern Tanzania. *The TQM Journal*, 28, 664–80.

Ivanova, G. M., Flath, C. A., & Raleigh, D. J. 2000. *Labor Camp Socialism: The Gulag in the Soviet Totalitarian System*. New York: M.E. Sharpe.

Jacobs, K., Habib, M., Musyoki, N., & Jubb, C. 2012. Empowering or oppressing: The case of microfinance institutions. In: Hopper, T., Tsamenyi, M., Uddin, S., & Wickramasinghe, D. (eds.) *Handbook of Accounting and Development*. Cheltenham, UK: Edward Elgar Publishing.

Jakobsen, M. 2010. Management accounting as the inter-organisational boundary. *Journal of Accounting and Organisational Change*, 6(1), 96–122.

Jensen, M. C. 2003. Paying people to lie: The truth about the budgeting process. *European Financial Management*, 9, 379–406.

Jensen, M. C. & Meckling, W. H. 1976. Theory of the firm: Managerial behavior, agency costs and ownership structure. *Journal of Financial Economics*, 3, 305–60.

Jessop, B. 2002. Liberalism, neoliberalism, and urban governance: A state–theoretical perspective. *Antipode*, 34, 452–72.

Joannides, V., Jaumier, S., & Hoque, Z. 2015. Patterns of boardroom discussions around the accountability process in a nonprofit organisation. In: Hoque, Z. & Parker, L. (eds.) *Performance Management in Nonprofit Organizations: Global Perspectives*. London: Routledge.

Johanson, U., Skoog, M., Backlund, A., & Almqvist, R. 2006. Balancing dilemmas of the balanced scorecard. *Accounting, Auditing & Accountability Journal*, 19(6), 842–57.

Johnson, H. T. 1975. Management accounting in an early integrated industrial: E. I. DuPont de Nemours Powder Company, 1903-1912. *The Business History Review*, 49, 184–204.

Johnson, H. T. & Kaplan, R. S. 1987a. *Relevance Lost: The Rise and Fall of Management Accounting*. Boston, MA: Harvard Business School Press.

Johnson, H. T. & Kaplan, R. S. 1987b. The rise and fall of management accounting. *Management Accounting*, 68, 22–9.

Johnson, S., Boone, P., Breach, A., & Friedman, E. 2000. Corporate governance in the Asian financial crisis. *Journal of Financial Economics*, 58, 141–86.

Jones, C. T. & Dugdale, D. 2002. The ABC bandwagon and the juggernaut of modernity. *Accounting, Organizations and Society*, 27, 121–63.

Justesen, L. & Mouritsen, J. 2011. Effects of actor-network theory in accounting research. *Accounting, Auditing and Accountability Journal*, 24(2), 161–94.

Kajüter, P. & Kulmala, H. I. 2005. Open-book accounting in networks: Potential achievements and reasons for failures. *Management Accounting Research*, 16, 179–204.

Kalagnanam, S. S. & Lindsay, R. M. 1999. The use of organic models of control in JIT firms: Generalising Woodward's findings to modern manufacturing practices. *Accounting, Organizations and Society*, 24(1), 1–30.

Kaldor, M., Moore, H. L., & Selchow, S. 2012. *Global Civil Society 2012: Ten Years of Critical Reflection*. Basingstoke, UK: Palgrave Macmillan.

Kanamori, S., Sow, S., Castro, M. C., Matsuno, R., Tsuru, A., & Jimba, M. 2015. Implementation of 5S management method for lean healthcare at a health center in Senegal: A qualitative study of staff perception. *Global Health Action*, 8, 27256.

Kanter, R. M. 1990. *When Giants Learn to Dance*. New York: Simon and Schuster.

Kantola, A. & Seeck, H. 2011. Dissemination of management into politics: Michael Porter and the political uses of management consulting. *Management Learning*, 42, 25–47.

Kaplan, R. S. 1984. The evolution of management accounting. *The Accounting Review*, 59, 390–418.

Kaplan, R. S. 1994. Management accounting (1984-1994): Development of new practice and theory. *Management Accounting Research*, 5, 247–60.

Kaplan, R. S. 2008. Conceptual foundations of the balanced scorecard. In: Christopher, S., Chapman, A. G. H., & Michael, D. S. (eds.) *Handbooks of Management Accounting Research*. New York: Elsevier.

Kaplan, R. S. & Anderson, S. R. 2007. *Time-Driven Activity-Based Costing: A Simpler and More Powerful Path to Higher Profits*. Boston, MA: Harvard Business Review Press.

Kaplan, R. S. & Cooper, R. 1998. *Cost & Effect: Using Integrated Cost Systems to Drive Profitability and Performance*. Boston, MA: Harvard Business School Press.

382 *References*

Kaplan, R. S. & Norton, D. P. 1993. Putting the balanced scorecard to work. *Harvard Business Review*, 1993, 134–47.

Kaplan, R. S. & Norton, D. P. 1996a. *The Balanced Scorecard: Translating Strategy into Action*. Boston, MA: Harvard Business School Press.

Kaplan, R. S. & Norton, D. P. 1996b. Using the balanced scorecard as a strategic management system. *Harvard Business Review*, 1996, 75–85.

Kaplan, R. S. & Norton, D. P. 2000. Having trouble with your strategy? Then map it. *Harvard Business Review*, 2000, 3–11.

Kato, Y. 1993. Target costing support systems: Lessons from leading Japanese companies. *Management Accounting Research*, 4, 33–47.

Kee, R. & Schmidt, C. 2000. A comparative analysis of utilizing activity-based costing and the theory of constraints for making product-mix decisions. *International Journal of Production Economics*, 63, 1–17.

Khandwalla, P.N. 1972. The effect of different types of competition on the use of management controls. *Journal of Accounting Research*, 10(2), 275–85.

Khandwalla, P. N. 1977. *The Design of Organizations*. New York: Harcourt Brace Jovanovich.

Kiechel, W. 2010. *The Lords of Strategy: The Secret Intellectual History of the New Corporate World*. Boston, MA: Harvard Business School Press.

Kinsella, E. A. 2009. Professional knowledge and the epistemology of reflective practice. *Nursing Philosophy*, 11, 3–14.

Kioupkiolis, A. & Katsambekis, G. 2014. *Radical Democracy and Collective Movements Today: The Biopolitics of the Multitude versus the Hegemony of the People*. Farnham, UK: Ashgate.

Kipping, M. 2011. Hollow from the start? Image professionalism in management consulting. *Current Sociology*, 59, 530–50.

Kitchin, R. A. 2014. *The Data Revolution: Big Data, Open Data, Data Infrastructures & Their Consequences*. London: Sage.

Knights, D. & Morgan, G. 1991. Corporate strategy, organizations, and subjectivity: A critique. *Organization Studies (Walter De Gruyter GmbH & Co. KG.)*, 12, 251–73.

Kondo, D. K. 1990. *Crafting Selves: Power, Gender, and Discourses of Identity in a Japanese Workplace*. Chicago, IL: University of Chicago Press.

Kotler, P. & Keller, K. L. 2016. *Marketing Management*. Boston, MA: Pearson.

Kraus, K., Kennergren, C., & Von Unge, A. 2017. The interplay between ideological control and formal management control systems – A case study of a non-governmental organisation. *Accounting, Organizations and Society*, 63, 42–59.

Kulmala, H. I., Paranko, J., & Uusi-Rauva, E. 2002. The role of cost management in network relationships. *International Journal of Production Economics*, 79, 33–43.

Kumar, N. 2005. The power of power in supplier–Retailer relationships. *Industrial Marketing Management*, 34, 863–6.

Kurunmaki, L. 1999a. Making an accounting entity: The case of the hospital in Finnish health care reforms. *European Accounting Review*, 8, 219–37.

Kurunmaki, L. 1999b. Professional vs financial capital in the field of health care–Struggles for the redistribution of power and control. *Accounting, Organizations and Society*, 24, 95–124.

Kurunmaki, L. 2004. A hybrid profession–The acquisition of management accounting expertise by medical professionals. *Accounting, Organizations and Society*, 29, 327–47.

Kurunmaki, L., Lapsley, I., & Melia, K. 2003. Accountingization v. legitimation: A comparative study of the use of accounting information in intensive care. *Management Accounting Research*, 14, 112–39.

Kurunmaki, L. & Miller, P. 2011. Regulatory hybrids: Partnerships, budgeting and modernising government. *Management Accounting Research*, 22, 220–41.

Lacey, N. 2008. *The Prisoners' Dilemma: Political Economy and Punishment in Contemporary Democracies*. Cambridge, UK: Cambridge University Press.

Lamberton, G. 2005. Sustainability accounting–A brief history and conceptual framework. *Accounting Forum*, 29, 7–26.

Lamminmaki, D. 2008. Accounting and the management of outsourcing: An empirical study in the hotel industry. *Management Accounting Research*, 19, 163–81.

Langdon, D. 2007. Life cycle costing (LCC) as a contribution to sustainable construction: Guidance on the use of the LCC methodology and its application in public procurement. Brussels: Davis Langdon Management Consulting.

Lash, S. & Urry, J. 1987. *The End of Organized Capitalism.* Cambridge, UK: Polity.

Latour, B. 2005. *Reassembling the Social: An Introduction to Actor-Network-Theory.* Oxford, UK: Oxford University Press.

Laughlin, R., Broadbent, J., & Willig-Atherton, H. 1994. Recent financial and administrative changes in GP practices in the UK: Initial experiences and effects. *Accounting, Auditing & Accountability Journal*, 7(3), 96–124.

Law, J. 1991. *A Sociology of Monsters: Essays on Power, Technology and Domination.* London: Routledge.

Law, J. & Hassard, J. 1999. *Actor Network Theory and After.* Oxford, UK: Blackwell.

Lawrence, P. R. & Lorsch, J. W. 1967. *Organization and Environment.* Boston, MA: Harvard Business School Press.

Lawrence, P. R. & Lorsch, J. W. 1986. *Organization and Environment: Managing Differentiation and Integration.* Boston, MA: Harvard Business School Press.

Lee, B. & Cassell, C. 2017. Facilitative reforms, democratic accountability, social accounting and learning representative initiatives. *Critical Perspectives on Accounting*, 46, 24–37.

Lemke, T. 2011. *Biopolitics: An Advanced Introduction.* New York: NYU Press.

Lemmon, M. L. & Lins, K. V. 2003. Ownership structure, corporate governance, and firm value: Evidence from the East Asian financial crisis. *The Journal of Finance*, 58, 1445–68.

Lemon, M. & Pember, A. 2014. *Environmental Sustainability: Activity-Based Costing/Management.* Toronto: Chartered Professional Accountants of Canada.

Levy, D. L., Alvesson, M., & Willmott, H. 2003. Critical approaches to strategic management. In: Alvesson, M. & Willmott, H. (eds.) *Studying Management Critically.* London: Sage.

Lewis, J. D. & Weigert, A. 1985. Trust as a social reality. *Social Forces*, 63, 967–85.

Liker, J. K. 2003. *The Toyota Way: 14 Management Principles from the World's Greatest Manufacturer.* New York: McGraw-Hill Education.

Lisa, M., Jane, A., & Sandra, V. D. L. 2017. Tools of accountability: Protecting microfinance clients in South Africa? *Accounting, Auditing & Accountability Journal*, 30, 1344–69.

Littler, C. R. 1982. *The Development of the Labour Process in Capitalist Societies: A Comparative Study of the Transformation of Work Organization in Britain, Japan and the USA.* London: Heinemann Educational.

Littoz-Monnet, A. 2017. *The Politics of Expertise in International Organizations: How International Bureaucracies Produce and Mobilize Knowledge.* London: Taylor & Francis.

Llewellyn, S. 1992. The role of case study methods in management accounting research: A comment. *The British Accounting Review*, 24, 17–31.

Llewellyn, S. & Northcott, D. 2005. The average hospital. *Accounting, Organizations and Society*, 30, 555–83.

Lockie, S. 2015. *Life Cycle Costing and Sustainability Assessments. Design Economics for the Built Environment.* Chichester, UK: John Wiley.

Lofgren, K. G., Persson, T., & Weibull, J. W. 2002. Markets with asymmetric information: The contributions of George Akerlof, Michael Spence and Joseph Stiglitz. *The Scandinavian Journal of Economics*, 104, 195–211.

Loft, A. 1995. *The History of Management Accounting: Relevance Found.* London: Prentice Hall.

Longworth, G. 2009. Rationalism and empiricism. In: Chapman, S. & Routledge, C. (eds.) *Key Ideas in Linguistics and the Philosophy of Language.* Edinburgh: Edinburgh University Press.

Lowe, E. A. 1971. On the idea of a management control system: Integrating accounting and management control. *Journal of Management Studies*, 8, 1–12.

Lubin, D. A. & Esty, D. C. 2010. The sustainability imperative. *Harvard Business Review*, 2010, 2–9.

Lublin, J. S. 2002. Enron audit panel is scrutinized for its cosy ties with the firm. *The Wall Street Journal*, 1st February 2002.

384 *References*

Luhmann, N. 1979. *Trust and Power.* Chichester, UK: John Wiley.

Lukes, S. 2005. Power and the battle for hearts and minds. *Millennium*, 33, 477–93.

Lukka, K. 2007. Management accounting change and stability: Loosely coupled rules and routines in action. *Management Accounting Research*, 18(1), 76–101.

Lyotard, J.-F. O. 1984. *The Postmodern Condition: A Report on Knowledge.* Manchester, UK: Manchester University Press.

Macintosh, N. 2002. *Accounting, Accountants and Accountability: Poststructuralist Positions.* London: Routledge.

Macintosh, N. B. & Quattrone, P. 2010. *Management Accounting and Control Systems: An Organizational and Sociological Approach.* 2nd ed. Chichester, UK: Wiley.

Macintosh, N. B., Shearer, T., Thornton, D. B., & Welker, M. 2000. Accounting as simulacrum and hyperreality: Perspectives on income and capital. *Accounting, Organizations and Society*, 25, 13–50.

Maleki, R. A. 1991. *Flexible Manufacturing Systems: The Technology and Management.* Englewood Cliffs, NJ: Prentice Hall.

Marginson, D. 2013. Budgetary control: What's been happening? In: Mitchell, F., Norreklit, H., & Jakobsen, M. (eds.) *The Routledge Companion to Cost Management.* London: Routledge.

Marginson, D. & Ogden, S. 2005. Coping with ambiguity through the budget: The positive effects of budgetary targets on managers' budgeting behaviours. *Accounting, Organizations and Society*, 30, 435–56.

Marx, K. 1990 [1867]. *Capital: A Critique of Political Economy, Volume One.* London: Penguin Books in association with New Left Review.

Massey, D. 2011. Ideology and economics in the present moment. *Soundings*, 2011, 29–39.

Mattessich, R. 2003. Accounting representation and the onion model of reality: A comparison with Baudrillard's orders of simulacra and his hyperreality. *Accounting, Organizations and Society*, 28, 443–70.

McDowell, L. 2001. Father and Ford revisited: Gender, class and employment change in the new millennium. *Transactions of the Institute of British Geographers*, 26, 448–64.

McKendrick, N. 1961. Josiah Wedgwood and factory discipline. *The Historical Journal*, 4, 30–55.

McKenna, C. D. 2006. *The World's Newest Profession: Management Consulting in the Twentieth Century.* Cambridge, UK: Cambridge University Press.

McKinlay, A., Carter, C., Pezet, E., & Clegg, S. 2010. Using Foucault to make strategy. *Accounting Auditing and Accountability Journal*, 23, 1012–32.

McNay, L. 2000. *Gender and Agency: Reconfiguring the Subject in Feminist and Social Theory.* London: Wiley.

Mercer, C. 2003. Performing partnership: Civil society and the illusions of good governance in Tanzania. *Political Geography*, 22, 741–63.

Merchant, K. A. & Van Der Stede, W. A. 2007. *Management Control Systems: Performance Measurement, Evaluation and Incentives.* Basingstoke, UK: Financial Times/Prentice Hall.

Merino, B. D., Mayper, A. G., & Tolleson, T. D. 2010. Neoliberalism, deregulation and Sarbanes-Oxley: The legitimation of a failed corporate governance model. *Accounting, Auditing & Accountability Journal*, 23, 774–92.

Mia, L. 1988. Managerial attitude, motivation and the effectiveness of budget participation. *Accounting, Organizations and Society*, 13, 465–75.

Mia, L. 1989. The impact of participation in budgeting and job difficulty on managerial performance and work motivation: A research note. *Accounting, Organizations and Society*, 14, 347–57.

Miyajima, H. 1994. The transformation of *zaibatsu* to postwar corporate groups: From hierarchically integrated groups to horizontally integrated groups. *Journal of the Japanese and International Economies*, 8(3), 293–328.

Miller, J. A. 1996. *Implementing Activity-Based Management in Daily Operations.* New York: John Wiley & Sons.

Miller, P. 2001. Governing by numbers: Why calculative practices matter. *Social Research*, 68, 379–96.

Miller, P., Kurunmaki, L., & O'Leary, T. 2008. Accounting, hybrids and the management of risk. *Accounting, Organizations and Society*, 33, 942–67.

Miller, P. & O'Leary, T. 1987. Accounting and the construction of the governable person. *Accounting, Organizations and Society*, 12, 235–65.

Miller, P. & O'Leary, T. 1993. Accounting expertise and the politics of the product: Economic citizenship and modes of corporate governance. *Accounting, Organizations and Society*, 18, 187–206.

Miller, P. & O'Leary, T. 1994. Accounting, 'economic citizenship' and the spatial reordering of manufacture. *Accounting, Organizations and Society*, 19, 15–43.

Miller, P. & O'Leary, T. 2007. Mediating instruments and making markets: Capital budgeting, science and the economy. *Accounting, Organizations and Society*, 32, 701–34.

Miller, T. 2010. Michel Foucault, The birth of biopolitics: Lectures at the Collège de France, 1978–79. *International Journal of Cultural Policy*, 16, 56–7.

Minnaar, R. A., Vosselman, E., Van Veen-Dirks, P. M. G., & Zahir-Ul-Hassan, M. K. 2017. A relational perspective on the contract-control-trust nexus in an interfirm relationship. *Management Accounting Research*, 34, 30–41.

Mistry, J. J. 2005. Supply chain management: A case study of an integrated lean and agile model. *Qualitative Research in Accounting & Management*, 2(2), 193–215.

Mitchell, D. 2001. Postmodern geographical praxis? The postmodern impulse and the war against homeless people in the 'post-justice' city. In: Minca, C. (ed.) *Postmodern Geography: Theory and Praxis*. London: Wiley.

Modell, S. 2001. Performance measurement and institutional processes: A study of managerial responses to public sector reform. *Management Accounting Research*, 12(4), 437–64.

Modell, S. 2003. Goals versus institutions: The development of performance measurement in the Swedish university sector. *Management Accounting Research*, 14, 333–59.

Modell, S. 2009. Bundling management control innovations: A field study of organisational experimenting with total quality management and the balanced scorecard. *Accounting, Auditing & Accountability Journal*, 22, 59–90.

Modell, S. 2014. The societal relevance of management accounting: An introduction to the special issue. *Accounting and Business Research*, 44, 83–103.

Modell, S. & Yang, C. in press. Financialisaton as a strategic action field: An historically informed field study of governance reforms in Chinese state-owned enterprises. *Critical Perspectives on Accounting*.

Monden, Y. 1994. *Toyota Production System: An Integrated Approach to Just-In-Time*. London: Chapman & Hall.

Monden, Y. & Hamada, K. 1991. Target costing and kaizen costing in Japanese automobile companies. *Journal of Management Accounting Research*, 3, 16–34.

Monden, Y. & Sakurai, M. 1998. *Japanese Management Accounting*. London: Taylor & Francis.

Montano, J. L. A., Donoso, J. A. Hassall, T. & Joyce, J. 2001. Vocational skills in the accounting professional profile: The Chartered Institute of Management Accountants (CIMA) employers' opinion. *Accounting Education*, 10(3), 299–313.

Montgomery, D. 1989. *The Fall of the House of Labor: The Workplace, the State, and American Labor Activism, 1865-1925*. Cambridge, UK: Cambridge University Press.

Moore, W. E. 1970. *The Professions: Roles and Rules*. New York: Russell Sage Foundation.

Morales, J., Gendron, Y., & Guénin-Paracini, H. 2014a. The construction of the risky individual and vigilant organization: A genealogy of the fraud triangle. *Accounting, Organizations and Society*, 39, 170–94.

Morales, J., Gendron, Y., & Guénin-Paracini, H. 2014b. State privatization and the unrelenting expansion of neoliberalism: The case of the Greek financial crisis. *Critical Perspectives on Accounting*, 25, 423–45.

Mouritsen, J., Hansen, A., & Hansen, C. Ø. 2001. Inter-organizational controls and organizational competencies: Episodes around target cost management/functional analysis and open book accounting. *Management Accounting Research*, 12, 221–44.

386   *References*

Mouritsen, J., Hansen, A., & Hansen, C. Ø. 2009. Short and long translations: Management accounting calculations and innovation management. *Accounting, Organizations and Society*, 34, 738–54.

Mouritsen, J. & Thrane, S. 2006. Accounting, network complementarities and the development of inter-organisational relations. *Accounting, Organizations and Society*, 31, 241–75.

Munro, I. 2012. The management of circulations: Biopolitical variations after Foucault. *International Journal of Management Reviews*, 14, 345–62.

Narayan, D. & Pritchett, L. 1999. Cents and sociability: Household income and social capital in rural Tanzania. *Economic Development and Cultural Change*, 47, 871–97.

Neely, A., Mills, J., Platts, K., Richards, H., Gregory, M., Bourne, M., & Kennerley, M. 2000. Performance measurement system design: Developing and testing a process-based approach. *International Journal of Operations & Production Management*, 20, 1119–45.

Neimark, M. & Tinker, T. 1986. The social construction of management control systems. *Accounting, Organizations and Society*, 11, 369–95.

Nelson, R. H. 2001. *Economics as Religion: From Samuelson to Chicago and Beyond*. Pittsburgh, PA: Pennsylvania State University Press.

Nelson, R. H. 2010. *New Holy Wars: Economic Religion versus Environmental Religion in Contemporary America*. Pittsburgh, PA: Pennsylvania State University Press.

Newman, J. 2014. Landscapes of antagonism: Local governance, neoliberalism and austerity. *Urban Studies*, 51, 3290–305.

Newman, M. & Westrup, C. 2005. Making ERPs work: Accountants and the introduction of ERP systems. *European Journal of Information Systems*, 14, 258–72.

Nielsen 2015. *The Sustainability Imperative: New Insights on Consumer Expectations*. London: Nielsen.

Norreklit, H. 2000. The balance on the balanced scorecard a critical analysis of some of its assumptions. *Management Accounting Research*, 11, 65–88.

Northcott, D. & Llewellyn, S. 2009. *The Balancing Act in Hospital Performance Measurement: A Comparison of UK and New Zealand Approaches*. London: CIMA.

Oakes, L. S., Townley, B., & Cooper, D. J. 1998. Business planning as pedagogy: Language and control in a changing institutional field. *Administrative Science Quarterly*, 43, 257–93.

O'Dwyer, B. & Unerman, J. 2008. The paradox of greater NGO accountability: A case study of Amnesty Ireland. *Accounting, Organizations and Society*, 33, 801–24.

OECD 2015a. *Hungary: towards a strategic state approach, OECD public governance reviews*, 10.1787/9789264213555-en. Paris: OECD.

OECD 2015b. *Principles of Corporate Governance*. Paris: OECD.

O'Flynn, J. 2007. From new public management to public value: Paradigmatic change and managerial implications. *Australian Journal of Public Administration*, 66, 353–66.

O'Leary, S. 2017. Grassroots accountability promises in rights-based approaches to development: The role of transformative monitoring and evaluation in NGOs. *Accounting, Organizations and Society*, 63, 21–41.

Oliver, N. & Wilkinson, B. 1992. *The Japanization of British Industry: New Developments in the 1990s*. Oxford, UK: Blackwell.

Oommen, T. K. 2003. Does civil society matter? Governance in contemporary India. In: Tandon, R. & Mohanty, R. (eds.) *Does Civil Society Matter? Governance in Contemporary India*. London: Sage.

Otley, D. 1999. Performance management: A framework for management control systems research. *Management Accounting Research*, 10, 363–82.

Otley, D. T. & Berry, A. J. 1980. Control, organisation and accounting. *Accounting, Organizations and Society*, 5, 231–44.

Parkinson, J. E. 1993. *Corporate Power and Responsibility: Issues in the Theory of Company Law*. Oxford, UK: Clarendon Press.

Parsons, T. & Smelser, N. 2005. *Economy and Society: A Study in the Integration of Economic and Social Theory*. London: Taylor & Francis.

Patrick, S. & Brown, K. 2007. *Greater than the Sum of Its Parts? Assessing 'Whole of Government' Approaches to Fragile States*. New York: International Peace Academy.

Peck, J. 2003. Geography and public policy: Mapping the penal state. *Progress in Human Geography*, 27, 222–32.

Peck, J. & Tickell, A. 2002. Neoliberalizing space. *Antipode*, 34, 380–404.

Perera, J. 1995. In unequal dialogue with donors: The experience of the Sarvodaya Shramadana movement. *Journal of International Development*, 7(6), 869–78.

Perera, J. 1997. unequal dialogue with donors: The experience of the Sarvodaya Shramadana movement. In: Hulme, D. & Edwards, M. (eds.) *NGOs, States and Donors: Too Closer for Comfort?* London: Macmillan Press Ltd.

Perera, J., Marasinghe, C., & Jayasekera, L. 1992. *A People's Movement under Siege*. Morotuwa, Sri Lanka: Sarvodaya Book Publication Services.

Perrow, C. 1970. *Organizational Analysis: A Sociological View*. London: Tavistock.

Peters, T. J. & Waterman, R. H. 1982. *Search of Excellence: Lessons from America's Best-Run Companies*. New York: Harper & Row.

Pfeffer, J. 1982. *Organizations and Organization Theory*. London: Pitman.

Pfeffer, J. 1997. *New Directions for Organization Theory: Problems and Prospects*. Oxford, UK: Oxford University Press.

Piketty, T. 2014. *Capital in the Twenty-First Century*. Boston, MA: Harvard University Press.

Piore, M. J. & Sabel, C. F. 1984. *The Second Industrial Divide: Possibilities for Prosperity*. New York: Basic Books.

Polanyi, K. 1944. *The Great Transformation: The Political and Economic Origins of Our Time*. Boston, MA: Beacon Press.

Pollard, S. 1965. *The Genesis of Modern Management: A Study of the Industrial Revolution in Great Britain*. London: E. Arnold.

Poovey, M. 1998. *A History of the Modern Fact: Problems of Knowledge in the Sciences of Wealth and Society*. Chicago, IL: University of Chicago Press.

Porter, M. E. 1985. *Competitive Advantage: Creating and Sustaining Superior Performance*. New York: Free Press.

Porter, M. E. 1990. *The Competitive Advantage of Nations*. New York: Free Press.

Porter, M. E. 1996. What is strategy? *Harvard Business Review*, 74(6), 61–78.

Porter, M. E. 1998. Clusters and the new economics of competition. *Harvard Business Review*, 1998, 77–90.

Porter, M. E. 2004. *The Competitive Strategy: Techniques for Analyzing Industries and Competitors*. London: Simon & Schuster.

Porter, M. E. 2008. *Competitive Advantage: Creating and Sustaining Superior Performance*. New York: Free Press.

Porter, M. E. 2013. *'Restoring U.S. Competitiveness' Testimony by Michael E. Porter, Bishop William Lawrence University Professor, Harvard Business School House Committee on Small Business, United States House of Representatives, July 9, 2013*. Representatives, H. C. O. S. B. U. S. H. O. (ed.). Washington, DC: House Committee on Small Business United States House of Representatives.

Porter, M. E. & Kramer, M. R. 2006. Strategy and society: The link between competitive advantage and corporate social responsibility. *Harvard Business Review*, 2006, [Reprint R0612D], 1–15.

Porter, M. E., Rivkin, J. W., Desai, M. A., & Eraman, M. 2016. *Problems Unsolved and a Nation Divided: The State of US Competitiveness 2016 Including Findings from Harvard Business School's Survey on US Competitiveness*. Boston, MA: Harvard Business School.

Powell, W. W. 1987. Hybrid organizational arrangements: New form or transitional development? *California Management Review*, 30, 67–87.

Powell, W. W. 1990. Neither market not hierarchy: Network forms of organization. *Research in Organizational Behavior*, 12, 295–336.

Power, M. 1997. *The Audit Society: Rituals of Verification*. Oxford, UK: Oxford University Press.

Prahalad, C. K. 2005. *The Fortune at the Bottom of the Pyramid: Eradicating Poverty through Profits, Enabling Dignity and Choice through Markets*. Pittsburgh, PA: Wharton School Publishing.

Prahalad, C. K. & Hamel, G. 1990. The core competence of the corporation. *Harvard Business Review*, 1990, 79–90.

388 *References*

Preston, A. M., Cooper, D. J., & Coombs, R. W. 1992. Fabricating budgets: A study of the production of management budgeting in the national health service. *Accounting, Organizations and Society*, 17, 561–93.

PriceWaterhouseCoopers 2010. *Corporate Governance Best Practice Reporting*. London: Price Waterhouse Coopers.

Pugh, D. S. 1997. *Organization Theory: Selected Readings*. London: Penguin.

Qu, S. Q. & Cooper, D. J. 2011. The role of inscriptions in producing a balanced scorecard. *Accounting, Organizations and Society*, 36, 344–62.

Quattrone, P. & Hopper, T. 2006. What is IT? SAP, accounting, and visibility in a multinational organisation. *Information and Organization*, 16, 212–50.

Raelin, J. A. 2007. Toward an epistemology of practice. *Academy of Management Learning & Education*, 6, 495–519.

Ramirez, C. 2013. 'We are being pilloried for something, we did not even know we had done wrong!' Quality control and orders of worth in the British audit profession. *Journal of Management Studies*, 50(5), 845–69.

Read, J. 2009. A genealogy of homo-economicus: Neoliberalism and the production of subjectivity. *Foucault Studies 2009*, 6(1), 25–36.

Reason, P. & Bradbury, H. 2013. *The SAGE Handbook of Action Research: Participative Inquiry and Practice*. London: Sage.

Rezaee, Z. 2009. *Corporate Governance and Ethics*. Hoboken, NJ: Wiley.

Richards, S. 1987. *The Financial Management Initiative*. In: Gretton, J. & Harrison, A. (eds.) *Reshaping Central Government*. New Brunswick, NJ: Transaction Publishers.

Roberts, J. 1991. The possibilities of accountability. *Accounting, Organizations and Society*, 16, 355–68.

Roberts, J. 2001. Trust and control in Anglo-American systems of corporate governance: The individualizing and socializing effects of processes of accountability. *Human Relations*, 54, 1547–72.

Roberts, J. 2009. No one is perfect: The limits of transparency and an ethic for 'intelligent' accountability. *Accounting, Organizations and Society*, 34, 957–70.

Roberts, J. & Scapens, R. 1985. Accounting systems and systems of accountability – Understanding accounting practices in their organisational contexts. *Accounting, Organizations and Society*, 10, 443–56.

Robins, N. 2006. *The Corporation that Changed the World: How the East India Company Shaped the Modern Multinational*. London: Pluto Press.

Rose, N. 1991. Governing by numbers: Figuring out democracy. *Accounting, Organizations and Society*, 16, 673–92.

Roslender, R. 1995. Accounting for strategic positioning: Responding to the crisis in management accounting. *British Journal of Management*, 6, 45–57.

Roslender, R. 1996. Relevance lost and found: Critical perspectives on the promise of management accounting. *Critical Perspectives on Accounting*, 7, 533–61.

Rossmann, D. & Shanahan, E. A. 2012. Defining and achieving normative democratic values in participatory budgeting processes. *Public Administration Review*, 72, 56–66.

Rousseau, D. M., Sitkin, S. B., Burt, R. S., & Camerer, C. 1998. Introduction to special topic forum: Not so different after all: A cross-discipline view of trust. *The Academy of Management Review*, 23, 393–404.

Roy, A. 2010. *Poverty Capital: Microfinance and the Making of Development*. London: Routledge.

Roy, I. 2008. Civil society and good governance: (Re-) conceptualizing the interface. *World Development*, 36, 677–705.

Royal Institution of Chartered Surveyors (RICS) 2016. *Life Cycle Costing RICS Guidance Note, UK*. London: Royal Institution of Chartered Surveyors (RICS).

Rule, J. B. 1973. *Private Lives and Public Surveillance*. London: Allen Lane.

Sabel, C. F., Herrigel, G., Kazis, R., & Deeg, R. 1987. How to keep mature industries innovative. *Technology Review*. Cambridge, UK: Technology Review, Inc.

Said, E. W. 1978. *Orientalism*. Harmondsworth, UK: Penguin, 1985.

Saint-Martin, D. 2000. *Building the New Managerialist State: Consultants and the Politics of Public Sector Reform in Comparative Perspective*. Oxford, UK: Oxford University Press.

Sanders, M. L. 2012. Theorizing nonprofit organizations as contradictory enterprises: Understanding the inherent tensions of nonprofit marketization. *Management Communication Quarterly*, 26, 179–85.

Sathi, A. 2014. *Engaging Customers Using Big Data: How Marketing Analytics are Transforming Business*. New York: Palgrave.

Scapens, R. W. 1990. Researching management accounting practice: The role of case study methods. *The British Accounting Review*, 22, 259–81.

Scapens, R. W. 1992. The role of case study methods in management accounting research: A personal reflection and reply. *The British Accounting Review*, 24, 369–83.

Scapens, R. W. 1994. Never mind the gap: Towards an institutional perspective on management accounting practice. *Management Accounting Research*, 5, 301–21.

Scapens, R. W. 2006. Understanding management accounting practices: A personal journey. *The British Accounting Review*, 38(1), 1–30.

Scapens, R. W. & Jazayeri, M. 2003. ERP systems and management accounting change: Opportunities or impacts? A research note. *European Accounting Review*, 12, 201–33.

Scapens, R. W. & Macintosh, N. B. 1996. Structure and agency in management accounting research: A response to Boland's interpretive act. *Accounting, Organizations and Society*, 21(7–8), 675–90.

Scarbrough, H. 1996. Commodifying professional expertise: IT in financial services. In H. Scarbrough (ed.) *The Management of Expertise*. Basingstoke, UK: Macmillan.

Schein, E. H. 1972. *Professional Education: Some New Directions*. New York: McGraw-Hill Book Co.

Schmidt-Wellenburgh, C. 2013. How the firm became consultable: Constructing governability in the field of management. *Economic Sociology, the European Electronic Newsletter*, 14, 32–8.

Scholte, J. A. 2002. Civil society and democracy in global governance. *Global Governance*, 8, 281–304.

Scholte, J. A. 2005. *The Sources of Neoliberal Globalization*. Geneva: United Nations Research Institute for Social Development.

Schon, D. A. 1991. *The Reflective Practitioner: How Professionals Think in Action*. Aldershot, UK: Ashgate.

Schumpeter, J. A. 1934. *The Theory of Economic Development: An Inquiry into Profits, Capital, Credit, Interest, and the Business Cycle*. New Brunswick, NJ: Transaction Books.

Schumpeter, J. A. 1947. *Capitalism, Socialism, and Democracy*. London: Harper Brothers.

Seal, W., Cullen, J., Dunlop, A., Berry, T., & Ahmed, M. 1999. Enacting a European supply chain: A case study on the role of management accounting. *Management Accounting Research*, 10, 303–22.

Senge, P. M. 1990. *The Fifth Discipline: The Art and Practice of the Learning Organization*. New York: Doubleday/Currency.

Sewell, G. & Wilkinson, B. 1992. 'Someone to watch over me': Surveillance, discipline and the just-in-time labour process. *Sociology*, 26, 271–89.

Shahe Emran, M., Morshed, A. K. M. M., & Stiglitz, J. E. 2007. *Microfinance and Missing Markets*. SSRN. http://dx.doi.org/10.2139/ssrn.1001309.

Shank, J. K. & Govindarajan, V. 1989. *Strategic Cost Analysis: The Evolution from Managerial to Strategic Accounting*. Homewood, IL: Richard D. Irwin.

Shenkin, M. & Coulson, A. B. 2007. Accountability through activism: Learning from Bourdieu. *Accounting, Auditing & Accountability Journal*, 20, 297–317.

Shrivastava, P. 1986. Is strategic management ideological? *Journal of Management*, 12, 363–77.

Simons, R. 1995. *Levers of Control: How Managers Use Innovative Control Systems to Drive Strategic Renewal*. Cambridge, MA: Harvard Business School Press.

Skocpol, T. 1977. Wallerstein's world capitalist system: A theoretical and historical critique. *American Journal of Sociology*, 82, 1075–90.

Sloan, A. P. 1964. *My Years with General Motors*. New York: Doubleday.

Smith, A. 2012 [1776]. *Wealth of Nations*. Ware, UK: Wordsworth.

390 References

Soederberg, S. 2008. A critique of the diagnosis and cure for 'enronitis': The Sarbanes-Oxley Act and neoliberal governance of corporate America. *Critical Sociology*, 34, 657–80.

Solomon, J. 2007. *Corporate Governance and Accountability*. Chichester, UK: Wiley.

Sowell, E. M. 1974. *The Evolution of the Theories and Techniques of Standard Costs*. Tuscaloosa, AL: University of Alabama Press.

Standing, G. 2011. *The Precariat: The New Dangerous Class*. London: Bloomsbury Academic.

Star, S. L. & Griesemer, J. R. 1989. Institutional ecology, 'translations' and boundary objects: Amateurs and professionals in Berkeley's museum of vertebrate zoology, 1907-39. *Social Studies of Science*, 19, 387–420.

Stark, D. 2011. *The Sense of Dissonance: Accounts of Worth in Economic Life*. Princeton, NJ: Princeton University Press.

Stein, M. J. 2008. Beyond the boardroom: Governmental perspectives on corporate governance. *Accounting Auditing and Accountability Journal*, 00021, 1001–26.

Stoker, G. 2006. Public value management: A new narrative for networked governance? *The American Review of Public Administration*, 36, 41–57.

Swanepoel, H. 1992. *Community Development: Putting Plans into Action*. Lansdowne, South Africa: Juta.

Sward, K. T. 1948. *The Legend of Henry Ford*. New York: Rinehart & Co.

Swartz, D. 1997. *Culture and Power: The Sociology of Pierre Bourdieu*. Chicago, IL: University of Chicago Press.

Swyngedouw, E. 1986. *The Socio-Spatial Implications of Innovations in Industrial Organisation: JIT Manufacturing and Regional Production Milieus. Working Paper, No.20, Johns Hopkins European Center For Regional Planning and Research*. Lille, France.

Tangen, S. 2004. Performance measurement: From philosophy to practice. *International Journal of Productivity and Performance Management*, 53, 726–37.

Taylor, F. W. 1964 [1911]. *Scientific Management. Comprising Shop Management, the Principles of Scientific Management, Testimony before the Special House Committee*. London: Harper & Row.

Taylor, F. W. 1967 [1911]. *The Principles of Scientific Management*. New York: Norton.

Taylor, J. G. 1979. *From Modernization to Modes of Production: A Critique of the Sociologies of Development and Underdevelopment*. Basingstoke, UK: Palgrave Macmillan.

Thomas, R. & Davies, A. 2002. Gender and new public management: Reconstituting academic subjectivities. *Gender, Work & Organization*, 9, 372–97.

Thomas, R. & Davies, A. 2005. Theorizing the micro-politics of resistance: New public management and managerial identities in the UK public services. *Organization Studies*, 26, 683–706.

Thompson, J. D. 1967. *Organizations in Action. Social Science Bases of Administrative Theory*. New York: McGraw-Hill Book Co.

Thomson, I. 2007. Mapping the terrain of sustainability accounting. In: Unerman, J., Bebbington, J., & O'Dwyer, B. (eds.) *Sustainability Accounting and Accountability*. London: Routledge.

Tinker, T. 1985. *Paper Prophets: A Social Critique of Accounting*. New York: Praeger.

Tomkins, C. 2001. Interdependencies, trust and information in relationships, alliances and networks. *Accounting, Organizations and Society*, 26, 161–91.

Touraine, A. 1971. *The Post-Industrial Society: Tomorrows Social History: Classes, Conflicts and Culture in the Programmed Society*. London: Wildwood House.

Trethewey, A. & Ashcraft, K. L. 2004. Special issue introduction. *Journal of Applied Communication Research*, 32, 81–8.

Tsing, A. L. 2005. *Friction: An Ethnography of Global Connection*. Pricneton, NJ: Princeton University Press.

The Tyson Task Force on the Recruitment and Development of Non-Executive Directors 2003. *The Tyson Report on the Recruitment and Development of Non-Executive Directors*. London: London Business School.

Uddin, S. & Hopper, T. 2001. A Bangladesh soap opera: Privatisation, accounting, and regimes of control in a less developed country. *Accounting, Organizations and Society*, 26, 643–72.

Uddin, S. & Tsamenyi, M. 2005. Public sector reforms and the public interest: A case study of accounting control changes and performance monitoring in a Ghanaian state-owned enterprise. *Accounting, Auditing & Accountability Journal*, 18(5), 648–74.

UNDP 2007. *Governance Indicators: A Users' Guide Second Edition Ed.* New York: UNDP.

United Nations 1993. *Management Consulting: A Survey of the Industry and Its Largest Firms.* Washington, DC: United Nations.

United Nations Division of Sustainable Development 2001. *Environmental Management Accounting Procedures and Principles.* New York: United Nations.

United Nations World Commission on Environment and Development 1987. *Our Common Future (The Brundtland Report).* Oxford, UK: Oxford University Press.

Uzzi, B. 1997. Social structure and competition in interfirm networks: The paradox of embeddedness. *Administrative Science Quarterly*, 42, 37–69.

Van der Kolk, B., Ter Bogt, H. J., & Van Veen-Dirks, P. M. G. 2015. Constraining and facilitating management control in times of austerity: Case studies in four municipal departments. *Accounting, Auditing & Accountability Journal*, 28, 934–65.

Van Helden, J. & Uddin, S. 2016. Public sector management accounting in emerging economies: A literature review. *Critical Perspectives on Accounting*, 41, 34–62.

Vesty, G. 2011. *The Influence and Impact of Sustainability Issues on Capital Investment Decisions.* Southbank, Victoria, Australia: CPA Australia.

Vollmer, H. 2009. Management accounting as normal social science. *Accounting, Organizations and Society*, 34(1), 141–50.

Wacquant, L. 2009. *Punishing the Poor: The Neoliberal Government of Social Insecurity.* Durham, NC: Duke University Press.

Wacquant, L. 2010. Crafting the neoliberal state: Workfare, prisonfare, and social insecurity. *Sociological Forum*, 25, 197–220.

Wacquant, L. 2012. Three steps to a historical anthropology of actually existing neoliberalism. *Social Anthropology*, 20, 66–79.

Wagner, E. L., Moll, J., & Newell, S. 2011. Accounting logics, reconfiguration of ERP systems and the emergence of new accounting practices: A sociomaterial perspective. *Management Accounting Research*, 22, 181–97.

Walker, M., Roberts, S. M., Jones, J. P., & Fröhling, O. 2008. Neoliberal development through technical assistance: Constructing communities of entrepreneurial subjects in Oaxaca, Mexico. *Geoforum*, 39, 527–42.

Walker Review. 2009. *A Review of Corporate Governance in UK Banks and Other Financial Industry Entities.* London: The Walker Review Secretariat.

Wallerstein, I. M. 1974. *Capitalist Agriculture and the Origins of the European World-Economy in the Sixteenth Century.* New York: Academic Press.

Watkins, A. L. & Arrington, C. E. 2007. Accounting, new public management and American politics: Theoretical insights into the national performance review. *Critical Perspectives on Accounting*, 18, 33–58.

Weber, H. 2002. The imposition of a global development architecture: The example of microcredit. *Review of International Studies*, 28, 537–55.

Weber, H. 2006. The global political economy of microfinance and poverty reduction: Locating local 'livelihoods' in political analysis. In: Fernando, J. L. (ed.) *Microfinance: Perils and Prospects.* London: Routledge.

Weber, M. 1978 [1968]. *Economy and Society: An Outline of Interpretive Sociology.* Berkeley, CA: University of California Press.

Weber, M. 2009. *From Max Weber: Essays in Sociology.* London: Routledge.

Wells, M. C. 1977. Some influences on the development of cost accounting. *The Accounting Historians Journal*, 4, 47–61.

Wetherbe, J. C. & Montanari, J. R. 1981. Zero based budgeting in the planning process. *Strategic Management Journal*, 2, 1–14.

Wickramasinghe, D. 2015. Getting management accounting off the ground: Post-colonial neoliberalism in healthcare budgets. *Accounting and Business Research*, 45, 323–55.

392   References

Wickramasinghe, D. & Alawattage, C. 2007. *Management Accounting Change: Approaches and Perspectives*. London: Routledge.

Wickramasinghe, D. & Hopper, T. 2005. A cultural political economy of management accounting controls: A case study of a textile Mill in a traditional Sinhalese village. *Critical Perspectives on Accounting*, 16, 473–503.

Wickramasinghe, D., Hopper, T., & Rathnasiri, C. 2004. Japanese cost management meets Sri Lankan politics: Disappearance and reappearance of bureaucratic management controls in a privatised utility. *Accounting, Auditing & Accountability Journal*, 17, 85–120.

Wickramasinghe, D. P. 1996. *Rationales of Accounting Control and Ownership Change in a Development Context: A Mode of Production Theory Analysis of Two Sri Lankan Case Studies*. PhD Thesis, University of Manchester, UK, Department of Accounting and Finance.

Wiener, N. 1988. *The Human Use of Human Beings: Cybernetics and Society*. Cambridge, MA: Da Capo Press, Incorporated.

Williamson, O. E. 1975. *Markets and Hierarchies: Analysis and Antitrust Implications - a Study in the Economics of Internal Organization*. New York: Free Press.

Williamson, O. E. 1988. The logic of economic organization. *Journal of Law, Economics, and Organization*, 4, 65–93.

Williamson, O. E. 1991a. Strategizing, economizing, and economic organization. *Strategic Management Journal*, 12, 75–94.

Williamson, O. E. 1991b. Comparative economic organization: the analysis of discrete structural alternatives. *Administrative Science Quarterly*, 36(2), 269–96.

Williamson, O. E. & Winter, S. G. 1988. Introduction. *Journal of Law, Economics & Organization*, 4, 1–2.

Willmott, H. 1995. Managing the academics: Commodification and control in the development of University Education in the U.K. *Human Relations*, 48, 993–1027.

Wilson, W. 1887. The Study of Administration. *Political Science Quarterly*, 2, 197–222.

Windolph, M. & Moeller, K. 2012. Open-book accounting: Reason for failure of inter-firm cooperation? *Management Accounting Research*, 23, 47–60.

Woolcock, M. & Narayan, D. 2000. Social capital: Implications for development theory research and policy. *The World Bank Research Observer*, 15, 225–49.

World Bank. 1978. *World Development Report 1978*. Washington, DC. © World Bank. https://openknowledge.worldbank.org/handle/10986/5961 License: CC BY 3.0 IGO.

World Bank. 1980. *World Development Report 1980*. New York: Oxford University Press. © World Bank. https://openknowledge.worldbank.org/handle/10986/5963 License: CC BY 3.0 IGO.

World Bank. 2000. *Corporate Governance: A Framework for Implementation*. Washington, DC: World Bank.

World Bank. 2011. *World Development Report 2011: Conflict, Security, and Development*. World Bank. © World Bank. https://openknowledge.worldbank.org/handle/10986/4389 License: CC BY 3.0 IGO.

Yoshikawa, T. 1994. Some aspects of the Japanese approach to management accounting. *Management Accounting Research*, 5, 279–87.

Yoshikawa, T. 2001. Cost accounting standard and cost accounting systems in Japan. Lessons from the past - recovering lost traditions. *Accounting, Business & Financial History*, 11, 269–81.

Yoshikawa, T. & Innes, J. 2013. Functional analysis. In: Mitchell, F., Norreklit, H., & Jakobsen, M. (eds.) *The Routledge Companion to Cost Management*. London: Routledge.

Yoshikawa, T., Innes, J., & Mitchell, F. 1995. A Japanese case study of functional cost analysis. *Management Accounting Research*, 6, 415–32.

Young, W. & Brown, M. 1993. Cross-national comparisons of imprisonment. *Crime and Justice*, 17, 1–49.

Yusuf, S., Deaton, A., Dervis, K., Easterly, W., Ito, T., & Stiglitz, J. E. 2009. *Development Economics through the Decades: A Critical Look at Thirty Years of the World Development Report*. Washington, DC: World Bank Publications.

Zajac, E. J. & Westphal, J. D. 1998. Toward a behavioural theory of the CEO-board relationship: How research can enhance our understanding of corporate governance practices. In: Hambrick, D. C., Nadler, D. A., & Tushman, M. L. (eds.) *Navigating Change: How CEOs, Top Teams, and Boards Steer Transformation*. Boston, MA: Harvard Business School Press.

Zwick, D. & Dholakia, N. 2006. Bringing the market to life: Screen aesthetics and the epistemic consumption object. *Marketing Theory*, 6, 41–62.

Index

Page numbers in *italics* refer to figures; page numbers in **bold** indicate tables.

AACU *see* Association of American Colleges and Universities
ABC (Activity-Based Costing) 53–4, 66, 203–8, 215, 216, 333–5
absorption costing 202–3, 204, 215
abstract cooperation 153, 170
academic performance 265–6
academic theorization 70–2
accountability: civil society 276, 288, 289–90; corporate 322–4; corporate governance 307–10; functional 288, 289, 290; hierarchical 224; interfirm relations 227–9; NPM 264–6; social 276, 290, 305; socialization process 290
accounting education xvi–xvii: *see also* pedagogy
accounting profession: chartered management accountants 56, 57; embodiment process 61–5
accounting technologies 77, 99, 176–7, 308
accumulation: capital accumulation 27–9, 248; flexible accumulation 179–81; markets 18–19
action research 51, 136–7, 155
Activity-Based Costing (ABC) 53–4, 66, 203–8, 215, 216, 333–5
actor-networks 52–4, 66; non-human actors 52, 53, 243
Adaptation, Goal attainment, Integration, Latency (AGIL) 86
Adler, P.S. 143
administrative hierarchies 40–3
Afghanistan **361**
agency theory 79–81, 294–5
AGIL (Adaptation, Goal attainment, Integration, Latency) 86
Alawattage, C. 275, 277, 284
Al-Tuwaijri, S.A. 320–1
alumni, Harvard Business School 132, 134
Alvares, C.A. 349
Amazon (company) 149
anatomico-politics 277
anti-corruption compliance 304

Apostol, O.M. 281
Armstrong, P. 197, 199, 204–5, 206
assembly-line production 36
Association of American Colleges and Universities (AACU) xvi
auditing 262, 338
austerity policies 252
Australia 328–9
autonomy, labour 32
avocation, profession comparison 49

Baiman, S. 80, 81
balanced scorecards (BSCs): balancing aspect of 161–2, *163*; cause-and-effect relationship of 162–4; environmental aspects of 331–2; interfirm relations 239; managerial narratives 152; non-market perspective 332; shareholder reconceptualization 161–2; social aspects of 331–2; strategic performance management systems 157–9, 164; sustainability 330–3; top executive ideology 160–1
Bangladesh: development agenda 345; microfinance 285, 363; nation-building 274; non-governmental organizations 279–80; World Bank league table **361**
Baudrillard, J. 148, 149, 150
Baxter, J. 64–5
BB *see* beyond budgeting
BCG *see* Boston Consulting Group
Bebbington, J. 317
Berry, A.J. 82–3, 84
beyond budgeting (BB) 210–11
BHP Billiton 304–6, 307, 310
Bhutan **361**
Big Data Analytics 123
biopolitics: accountability 309–10; biopolitical accounting 9; civil society 276–81; competitiveness 132–3; corporate governance 299–304, 310–12; 'corruptive flow' 310; cost management 219, 221–2; governance

299–304, 310–12; just-in-time production 189–91; neoliberal reconstruction of 113–14; New Public Management 266–8; Porterian strategy discourses 131–7, 138; total quality management 189–91
biopower 7, 8, 21, 280
black-boxing 54, 204
Blackburn, R.M. 32
bodily hexis, Bourdieu 63
body: anatomico-politics of 277; disciplined body 14–16
Boeing 178
Boltanski, L. 142
Boston Consulting Group (BCG) 120–2, 123, 137
'boundary objects' 234
Bourdieu, P.: bodily hexis 63; 'logic of the field' 61, 62; reflexive sociology 62, *63*, 64, 67; symbolic systems 55
brands, sustainability 327–8
Braverman, H. 35, 36
Brett, J.A. 365
Britain *see* United Kingdom
Brown, W. 107, 152, 249, 251
Brundtland Commission 316
Bryer, R.A. 19, 20, 29
BSCs *see* balanced scorecards
budgeting 228, 263–4
bundling effect: cost management 216–17; inter-firm relations 233; open-book accounting 237, *238*
bureaucracy 141–7; industrial relations 144–5; job redesign movement 143–4; management by objectives 144–5; political struggles 253–4; post-bureaucratic ideal types 145, **146–7**
Burns, T. 89–90, 92
business contract perspective 226
business elites 134

calculations 77, 176–7
Callon, M. 52
capital: accumulation of 27–9, 248; Bourdieu 64; circulation of 30; cultural capital 64; definitions of 44–5; human capital 151–2; investment, sustainability of 328–9; and labour 150–2; logic of 27; mode of operation 27; social capital 64, 284–5; socialization of 19–20, 24–9; transcendence of 26–7
capitalism: corporate capitalism 42–3; cost accounting 198, 199, 200; definition 5; factory system 33–40; free labour 19–20; governmentality 6–16; ideology 16–20; industrial capitalism 4; institutional context 24–45; liberal markets 17–19; and modernism 5–6; neoliberalism 100; political–economic context 3–23; production systems 30–40; socialization of capital 19–20, 24–9; transcendence of capital 26–7

'carceralization' process 254, 255
Carmona, S. 197, 198
Carr, C. 235
case studies 93–4
Castells, M. 226
category management 240
CEOs *see* Chief Executive Officers
CFOs *see* Chief Financial Officers
CG *see* corporate governance
CGAP *see* Consultative Group to Assist the Poor
Chandler, A.D. 123
chapter summaries xxviii–xxxi
charismatic authority 41
Charles, Prince of Wales 317
Chartered Institute of Management Accountants (CIMA) xviii, 56–61
chartered management accountants (CMAs) 56, 57
Chenhall, R.H. 157, 181, 288
Chiapello, E. 29, 142
Chief Executive Officers (CEOs) 161
Chief Financial Officers (CFOs) 64–5
Chua, W.F. 64–5
CIMA *see* Chartered Institute of Management Accountants
civil service 262
civil society 248, 270–91; accountability 276, 288, 289–90; biopolitics of 276–81; collectivization process 284; corporatized entities 283–4; definition 271–3; developing countries 273–81; discursive resources 284–6; emergence of 272–3; entrepreneurialism 286–7; evaluative criteria 287–9; ideological resources 284–6; individualization process 283; neoliberal reconstruction of 113; strategizing process 281–9
Clegg, S. 41
climate change 305
closure planning 305
CMAs *see* chartered management accountants
Coase, R.H. 74–5
collective labour *35*
colonial governments 274–5
commodification of labour 19
commodity circulation 18
communicative labour 153
companies *see* corporations; firms
company law 26
compensation contracts/schemes 81, 181
competencies xviii–xx, 58, **59–60**, 70–1, 179–80
competition 119, 230–1: *see also* competitiveness
competition law compliance 305
competitive advantage 126–7, 128, 130–1, 137–8, **331**
competitiveness: biopoliticalization of 133–7; as biopolitical problem 132–3; macro-micro connection 133–4; *see also* competition

396   *Index*

competitive positioning/strategy 118–39, 329; Porter's discourses 123–37; strategic terrain reinvention 119–23
compliance 191, 304, 305
conglomerates 120
conglomerations, regional 178
Conrad, C. 297
constraints, theory of 214–16
consultants 51, 120–2, 135–7, 362
Consultative Group to Assist the Poor (CGAP) 364
consultocracy 135–7
consumer brands, sustainability 327–8
consumption, flexible 169–70
contextualizing xxiii–xxiv, 3–5
contingency factors 90, *91*
contingency theory 89–92
continuous improvement 143, 144, 183–6
contractors 31, 32
contract theory *see* agency theory
control structures 231–2
Cooke, B. 358
cooperation, abstract 153, 170
Cooper, C. 151–2
Cooper, R. 200, 203, 206
corporate accountability 322–4
corporate capitalism 42–3
corporate governance (CG) 113, 292–314; academic perspectives 298, **299**; accountability 307–10; agency theory 294–5; BHP Billiton 304–6, 307, 310; biopolitics 299–310; definitions 295, 298; failures 297; 'field of visibility' 308; forms of governance 309; 'global consensus' 302; global context 310–12; global governmentality 300–2; as internal government *296*; intra-organizational processes 304–10; legitimacy 307; and management accounting 310–12; and neoclassical economics 294–6; neoliberal corporate governance 303–10; neoliberal extensions 297–9; regulation 303–4; research **299**; security 300–2; shareholders 293, 295, *296*, 297; socialization of accountability 308–9; soft regulation 303–4
corporate social responsibility (CSR) 320–1, 324–5
corporate strategy 121–2
corporations 25–9, 43; accumulation of capital 27–9; transcendence of capital 26–7; *see also* firms
corporatized entities 283–4
corrective training 14
corruption 304, 310
cost accounting *see* cost management
'cost driver rates' 205
'cost hierarchy' 203–4
cost management 38–40, 194–223; absorption costing 202–3, 204, 215; beyond budgeting 210–11; bundling effect 216–17; capitalism 198, 199, 200; constraints theory 214–16; 'cost driver rates' 205; 'cost hierarchy' 203–4; cost objects 218–21; evolution of 195–203; Foucauldian approach **196**, 197, 198; functionalities *201*; history of **196**; as holistic programme 208–21; hybridization 217–18; information technologies 212–13; innovations 201, 216–17; Japanese effect 213–14; labour process theory 196–7, 205–8; management control 208–10; Marxist approach 196; M-form model 208–9; NPM accounting 260–2; operations management 211–14; overhead costs 202, 203, 204, 215; 'politics of the product' 218–21; re-envisioning of **210**; 'Relevance Lost' thesis 199, 200–3; staff costs 204–5, 206–8; surveillance assemblage 203–8; sustainability 333–7; theory of constraints 214–16; throughput accounting 214–16; traditional costing 195–203; transaction cost economics 195–6
cost minimization 183–6
cost objects 218–21
cost optimization logic 183, *184*
Cox, J. 215, 216
craft production 32–3
crime risk 105
crises, neoliberal capitalism 113
critical success factors *see* key performance indicators
critical vs. mainstream theorizations 72, **73–4**
Crush, J. 349–50
CSR *see* corporate social responsibility
cultural capital 64
customization 174, 182
cybernetics 82–5
cyberspaces 149

Daly, H.E. 315, 339
Davies, A. 258, 259
DBR *see* Drum-Buffer-Rope
decision-making: economic logic of 75–9; participation in 144–5
Deleuze, G. 205
descriptive case studies 93–4
deskilled labour 153
detectors 84
developing countries 273–81, 344, 363
development 342–67; and accounting 344–7, 363–5, 366; 'accounting in development' 346–7; accountingization of 351–62; calculative interrelationships *354*; calculative practices/structure 344, 350–1, 355–7, 360–2; consultants 362; 'development in accounting' 345–6; 'developmentality' 344, 350–1; 'development machine' 349–50; development numbers 358–62; discourses 345–9;

Foucauldian perspective 344; funding agencies 347; governmentality 350–1; microfinance 363–5; neoliberalism 347; per capita income measure 355–6; problematization phase 356–7, 358; professionalization of 357–62; rural development 275, 277–8, 279, 363; schools 362; strategization of 360; textualization of 348–9; 'transaction processing system' 357; underdevelopment 352–62; Western domination 347–9
'developmentality' 344, 350–1
'devolutionism' 190–1
Dholakia, N. 107, 108
disciplinary accounting 11–16
disciplinary control/power 7–8, 21, 103, 113–14
disciplinary governmentality **104**
disciplinary knowledge 16
disciplinary politics 189–90
disciplined bodies 14–16
disciplined spaces 12–13
disciplined time 13–14
discourses *see* strategic discourses
distributed intelligence 235–40
Dixon, R. 364
doxa 63–4
dressage 14
Drucker, P. 144
Drum-Buffer-Rope (DBR) 214–15
Dugdale, D. 53, 54, 66
Dunleavy, P. 257
DuPont 28–9, 208

Easterly, W. 285
ecological sustainability 317
economic efficiency 77–8
economic–political context 3–23
economic production quantity (EPQ) 171–2
economic rationality 74–81; decision making 75–9; management control 79–81
economic security 301
economic structures 16–20
economic sustainability 316
economy, biopolitical accounting 9
education xvi–xviii, 250, 259, 263, 265–6; *see also* pedagogy
efficiency of firms 77–8
efficient body principle 13
Ehrenberg, J.R. 272
ELCC *see* environmental life cycle costing
elites 134
embodiment process 61–5
empiricist epistemology 89–94, 95; case studies 93–4; contingency testing 89–92
employment protection 173
EMS *see* environmental management systems
enclosures, disciplined spaces 12
England, social medicine 10; *see also* United Kingdom

Enron 297
enterprise resource planning (ERP) systems 54, 56, 204, 212–13
entity concept 323
entrepreneurialism: civil society 286–7; labour 150–2; neoliberal entrepreneurship 152–3
environmental audits 338
environmental life cycle costing (ELCC) 336–7
environmental management accounting *see* sustainability
environmental management systems (EMS) 337–8
environmental performance indicators (EPIs) 335
environmental strategies 338
EPIs *see* environmental performance indicators
epistemic context: competitiveness 133–7; knowledge apparatuses 4; practicist epistemology 46–68; scientific epistemology 69–96
epistemic institutions 108, 110
EPQ *see* economic production quantity
Ericson, R.V. 205, 206–7
ERP *see* enterprise resource planning
Escobar, A. 348, 351
European Union (EU) 105
evaluation criteria/methods: civil society 287–9; interfirm relations 233–5
examinations 15–16, 58
experimental case studies 94
expert systems 53–4
explanatory case studies 94
exploratory case studies 94
external failure costs 183
extra-organizational epistemic practices 50–2

Facebook 149
factor endowment 126–7
factories 12–13, 33–40, 43, 178
failure costs 183
fair price 105–6
Featherstone, M. 148
federated enterprises 178
Feldman, S. 279–80, 281
Fernando, J.L. 273, 277, 279, 282, 283
fieldwork 93
Figge, F. 332
financial analysis systems 28–9
financial bubbles 292
Financial Management Initiatives (FMIs) 262
financial markets 364
financial privileging 333
financial reporting 200, 201, 295, 303
Financial Reporting Council 295, 303
Finland 150, 261, 265
firms: bureaucracy 141–7; competitive advantage 126–7; competitive positioning/strategy 118–39; economic efficiency 77–8; entity concept 323; environmental management

398 *Index*

accounting 315–41; flexibility 168–81, 191; industrial relations 144–5; interfirm relations 224–46; neoliberal reconstruction of 112; organizational reconfiguration 140–66; ownership of 323; production systems 167–93; solar firms 178; stakeholders 323–4; structure-conduct-performance model 124–6; structuring of 28–9, 76–7; sustainability 315–41; transaction costs 76; *see also* corporations
five forces model, Porter 126, *127*, 138
flexibility 168–81, 191; accumulation 179–81; concepts **169**; consumption 169–70; integration **175**, 177–9; labour 172–3, 179, *180*, 181; machines 170–2; specialization 177–9; systems 174–6; time 172–3
flexible manufacturing systems (FMS) 173–7; accounting in 176–7; efficiency integration **175**; system flexibilities 174–6
FMIs *see* Financial Management Initiatives
FMS *see* flexible manufacturing systems
Ford, Henry 36
Ford Motor Company 36–7, 149, 184
Foucault, M.: anatomico-politics 277; cost accounting **196**, 197, 198; developmentality 344; disciplined spaces 12; disciplined time 13; 'field of visibility' 308; governmentality 6, 11, 17; heteropias 109, 110; markets 105–6; normalization process 280; normalizing sanctions 15; population 7; social medicine 9–10; the state 249
four corner analysis, Porter 130–1
fragmentation, labour 35
fraud risk 105
Free, C. 237, 243
'free capital' 20
freedom 17, 18
free labour 19–20
Friedman, M. 318–20, 339
functional analysis, interfirm relations 238–9
functional-individualizing accountability 289
functionalist discipline, management accounting as xx–xxi
funding agencies 347

General Electric (GE) 121–2, 123, 137
General Motors (GM) 143, 234
general practitioners (GPs) 266
general systems theory (GST) 82
Germany 9–10
Ghana 346
Giddens, A. 53
global governmentality 300–2
Global Reporting Initiative (GRI) 325–6, 327
global state 110–11
GM (General Motors) 143, 234
Goldman, M. 349
Goldratt, E.M. 215, 216

Google 149
governance: biopolitical governance 310–12; civil society 285; neoliberal governance 244; self-governance 265–6; *see also* corporate governance
governmentality 6–16, 17, 21, 244, 300–2; development 350–1; neoliberal governmentality 103, **104**, 113–14
GPs (general practitioners) 266
Gray, R. 284, 316, 317
greening of firms *see* sustainability
GRI *see* Global Reporting Initiative
Griesemer, J.R. 234
Gros, F. 300, 301–2, 310
growth-share matrix 120–2, 123, 137
GST *see* general systems theory
Guattari, F. 205

Habermas, J.R. 283
habitus 62–3
Haggerty, K.D. 205, 206–7
Håkansson, H. 237, 239–40
Hambrick, D.C. **299**
Hamel, G. 179–80
Hardt, M. 152–4
Harvard Business Review 51
Harvard Business School 132, 134
Harvey, D. 102, 179, *180*, 181
hazardous minerals 306
healthcare sector 10, 259, 261–2, 265, 266, 284
Heckscher, C. 145
heterarchies 225–31, **228**, 229–31, 234
heteropias 109–10
hierarchies: accountability 224; 'cost hierarchy' 203–4; managerial hierarchies 40–4; organizational hierarchies 225, 227–30, 234; surveillance 15; versus heterarchies **228**
Hilgers, M. 254
Hill, S. 182
Hingley, M. 244
Hirst, P. 177
historicizing xxiv–xxv
Hobsbawm, E.J. 31
Hofstede, G. 84–5
Hood, C. 255, 262
Hopper, T. 197, 199, 342, 345–6
Hopwood, A.G. xxii, 228, 229
hospitals 259, 261, 262, 265, 266
human capital 151–2
human nature 79
human rights 306
hybridization: cost management 217–18; New Public Management 259
'hyperreal' 149–50

ideology: capitalism 16–20; civil society 284–6; top executive ideology 160–1

Ilcan, S. 350, 351
illusio 62
illustrative case studies 94
'implosion' 150, 153
India: corporate governance 302; healthcare 284; nation-building 274; non-governmental organizations 274, 278, 287; World Bank league table **361**
indigenous peoples 305
individualization process 283, 308
individualized labour *35*
individual responsibility 252–3
industrial capitalism 4
industrial clusters 178
industrial relations 144–5, 173
industry analysis 129
industry associations 305–6
information asymmetry 80
information-sharing 232, 236–7
information technologies 107, 204, 212–13; *see also* accounting technologies
informed practice *47*
INGOs *see* international non-governmental organizations
innovations, cost management 201, 211–14, 216–17
'input–output balancing' 334
institutional context 4, 24–45
integration, flexible 177–9
intelligence, distributed 235–40
interactive types 145, **146–7**
interfirm relations 224–46; accountability 227–9; balanced scorecards 239; 'boundary objects' 234; budgeting 228; bundling effect 233; business contract perspective 226; category management 240; competition 230–1; control structures 231–2; distributed intelligence 235–40; evaluation methods 233–5; friction 230–1; functional analysis 238–9; heterarchies 225–31, 234; information-sharing 232, 236–7; knowledge-sharing culture 232; misunderstandings 234; mode of operation 232–3; neo-liberalism 226, 231–5, 245; networks 229; open-book accounting 235–40, 245; power issues 240–3; responsibility accounting 232; supply chains 225–31; 'system trust' 242–3; target costing 230, 238; total cost of ownership 240; trust issues 237, 240–3; value chain accounting 239–40
intermediaries 52–3
internal failure costs 183
International Donor Consortium 278
International Federation of Accountants 334
international non-governmental organizations (INGOs) 273, 276, 277–82, 288
intra-organizational epistemic practices 50
investment, sustainability of 328–9

Jacobs, K. 363, 364
Japanese management/production system 141, 143–4, 178, 186–91, 213–14
Japanization 186–9, 192
Jessop, B. 250
JIT (just-in-time) production 189–91
job autonomy 32
job redesign movement 143–4
job shop production **175**
Johnson, H.T. 38, 72, 156, 160, 195, 199, 200–3, 210
Jones, C.T. 53, 54, 66
journals 50–1
justice, markets 105–6
just-in-time (JIT) production 189–91
just price 105–6

kaizen (continuous improvement) 143, 144
Kaldor, M. 284
Kanter, R.M. 143
Kantola, A. 133
Kaplan, R.S.: Activity-Based Costing 52, 53, 72; cost management 38, 195, 199, 200–3, 206, 210; performance management 155–64
Kato, Y. 239
key performance indicators (KPIs) 156, 239
knowledge: apparatuses of 4; body of knowledge xviii; disciplinary knowledge 16; examinations 16; knowledge-sharing culture 232; professional knowledge 49, 56–61, 70, 95; rationalist justification of 72–4, 95; systematization of 34–5; validation of 52; vertical and horizontal ordering of **59–60**
KPIs *see* key performance indicators
Kramer, M.R. 324–5, 329–30, **331**
Kraus, K. 278, 284
Kurunmaki, L. 150, 259, 261–2, 265

labour: autonomy of 32; collective vs. individualized labour *35*; commodification of 19; communicative labour 153; deskilled labour 153; entrepreneurialization of 150–2; flexible labour 172–3, 179, *180*, 181; fragmentation of 35; free labour 19–20; immaterialization of 152–4, 280–1; medical care 10; out-sourcing of 173; peripheralization of *180*, 181; rationalization of work 34–6; regimentation of 36–7; relational aspects 32; social medicine 10; symbolic-analytical labour 153; temporary labour 173; unionized labour 173
labour process theory 196–7, 205–8
Latour, B. 52
Laughlin, R. 264
LCC *see* lifecycle costing
leaders/leadership 134, 160, 186
lean production 181–9
learning organizations 136

400   *Index*

legitimacy, neoliberalization of 307
Lemke, T. 222
levers of control (LOC) 87–9
liberal education xvi–xviii
liberalism 17–18, 100, 102, 248, 250
lifecycle costing (LCC) 335–7
Liker, J.K. 212
Lind, J. 237, 239–40
linear programming 77
Littler, C.R. 31, 32
LOC *see* levers of control
'logic of the field', Bourdieu 61, 62, 65
Lublin, J.S. 297

McDowell, L. 254
machines, flexible 170–2
magazines 50–1
mainstream vs. critical theorizations 72, **73**–4
Maldives **361**
Maleki, R.A. 174
management accounting: definition xviii; as a
    social science xvii; vocational tradition xvii
management by objectives (MBO) 144–5
management by themes 154–5
management consultants 51, 120–2, 135–7
management control: cybernetics 82–5;
    definition 86; economic rationality of 79–81;
    Hofstede's typology 84–5; structural function-
    alism 86–9
management control systems (MCSs) xx, 92
managerial hierarchies 40–4; *see also* top
    management
managerial interpretations xx
managerial titles 154
Mann, M. 32
manufacturing 30–1, 153, 168–81, 191, 218–19;
    see also production
mapping, strategic terrains 120–2
markets: accumulative markets 18–19; competi-
    tive positioning/strategy 118–39; coordination
    of 108; crime risk 105; dynamics of xxvii–xviii;
    fair price 105–6; fraud risk 105; as heteropias
    109–10; and hierarchies 42–3; just price
    105–6; liberal markets 17–18; microfinance
    364; neoliberalism 102, 104–10, 250; political
    logic 110–11; regulation of 105; roles of 22;
    as sites of jurisdiction 195; as sites of veridiction
    105; and the state 250; strategies 128; techno-
    managerial reconstruction of 107–9; and truth
    106
Marxist approach: cost accounting 196, 198;
    production theory 31
Marx, K. 18, 19, 58
mass production 36, 171, 174, **175**, 201–2
materials flow accounting 334–5
Mattessich, R. 149
MBO *see* management by objectives

M-C-M *see* money-commodity-money
    circulation
MCSs *see* management control systems
MDGs *see* millennium development goals
measurement of systems 84
mechanization of production 34
medicine 9–11
meetings 65
mercantilism 9, 25–6
Mercer, C. 273
MFD *see* multifunction devices
M-form (multidivisional) businesses 120, 208–9
microfinance 280–1, 283–7, 363–5
micro-management, governmentality 11–16
millennium development goals (MDGs) 350
Miller, J.A. *207*
Miller, P. xxii, 39, 102, 176, 217–21, 312
Mill, J.S. xv
Minnaar, R.A. 242
misunderstandings, interfirm relations 234
Modell, S. 216, 217
modernism 5–6
modernity 5, 20, 53, 353
Monden, Y. 187–9
monetary flows, environmental impact costing
    335, *336*
money-commodity-money (M-C-M)
    circulation 18
monopolies 25–6
Moore, W.E. 49, 51
Mouritsen, J. 226–7, 232, 233, 237
multidivisional (M-form) businesses 120, 208–9
multifunction devices (MFD) 170
multiple evaluative criteria 287–9
Munro, I. **104**, 107, 280

National Health Service (NHS) 264
National Reference Costing Exercise, hospitals
    261
nation-states *see* the state
NEC Corporation 179–80
Negri, A. 152–4
Nelson, R.H. 75
neoclassical economics 294–6, 318–20
neocolonialism 275–6
neoliberalism/neoliberalization 99–117;
    accounting, neoliberalization of *115*;
    corporate governance 292–314; cost account-
    ing/management 200, 209–10, 221–2; critics
    of 106–7; definition 102; development 347;
    flexibility 168–81; governance 244; govern-
    mentality 103, **104**, 113–14; human capital
    151–2; individual responsibility 252–3;
    interfirm relations 226, 231–5, 245; labour and
    capital 151; legitimacy 307; markets 102,
    104–10, 250; neoliberal effect 103–4;
    neoliberal reconstructions 111–14; neoliberal

transformations 101–3, 114–16; New Public Management 255–68; ownership 323; political logic 110–11; portfolio planning models 123; privatization 345–6; public administration 255–68; regulation 254–5; resistance to 259; security 301; and the state 102, 107, 110–11, 113, 247–69; strategic moves 111–14

Nepal **361**

networks: actor-networks 52–4, 66; interfirm relations 229; 'networked organizations' 245; social networks 64, 86, 149

Newman, J. 258

New Public Management (NPM) 150, 248, 255–68; accountability 264–6; ambiguities of 258; biopolitical theorization 266–8; budgeting 263–4; commercial-like categories 258; cost management 260–2; as critical encounter 258–60; as deterministic embracement 256–7; hybridization 259; NPM accounting 260–6; performance measurement 262–3; resistance to 259; resource management 265; self-governance 265–6; strategic planning 262–3; 'universality' of 257

New United Motors Manufacturing Inc. (NUMMI) 143

Ng, J. 235

NGOs *see* non-governmental organizations

NHS *see* National Health Service

Nielson (data analytics company) 327, 328

non-governmental organizations (NGOs) 273–83, 287, 288, 289–90, 362

normalization process 280

normalizing sanctions 15

Norreklit, H. 162

Norton, D.P. 158, 160

Norwegian donor (NOVIB) 278

NPM *see* New Public Management

NUMMI *see* New United Motors Manufacturing Inc.

OBA *see* open-book accounting

objectivation 7–8

occupation, profession comparison 49

OECD (Organisation for Economic Co-operation and Development) 302, 303

official publications 51

O'Leary, T. 39, 176, 218–21

Oommen, T.K. 270

open-book accounting (OBA) 235–40, 245; bundling effect 237, *238*; issues **237**

operations management 211–14

opinion leaders 134

Organisation for Economic Co-operation and Development (OECD) 302, 303

organizational hierarchies 225, 227–30, 234

organizational memory 50

organizational processes, Japanization of 186–9

organizational reconfiguration 140–66; bureaucracy 141–7; performance management 155–64; postmodern discourses 147–55

organizational structures *see* interfirm relations

organizational systems xx

Otley, D.T. 82–3, 84

out-sourcing of labour 173

overhead costs 202, 203, 204, 215; *see also* Activity-Based Costing

ownership of firms 323

Pakistan **361**

Parkinson, J.E. 295

Parsons, T. 86

Peck, J. 252, 254, 255

pedagogy 55–65; CIMA qualification structure 56–61; embodiment process 61–5; pedagogic acts **61**; as symbolic system 55–6

penal scheme 254–5

Perera, J. 277

performance contracts 81

performance management 155–64, 338

performance management systems (PMS) 156, 157, 158, 160, 164

performance measurement 262–3

performance, time-defined 13–14

PEST (political, economic, social and technological) analysis 129

Peters, T.J. 136

Pfeffer, J. 90

Phillips, L. 350, 351

physical flows accounting 334–5

PIMS *see* Profit Impact of Market Strategy database

Piore, M.J. 177–8

PMS *see* performance management systems

Polanyi, K. 6

political–economic context 3–23

political, economic, social and technological (PEST) analysis 129

political logic, neoliberal 110–11

political perspective xxi–xxvii

'politics of the product' 218–21

politics, state bureaucracy 253–4; *see also* biopolitics

population 7, 9–11

Porter, M.E.: competitive advantage 126–7, 128, 130–1, 137–8, **331**; corporate social responsibility 324–5; five forces model 126, *127*, 138; four corner analysis 130–1; industrial clusters 178; strategy discourses 123–37, 138; structure-conduct-performance model *125*; value chain analysis 329–30

portfolio planning models 121–2, 128, 137

positioning, sustainability 327–8

post-bureaucratic discourses 141–7

post-bureaucratic ideal types 145, **146–7**

402 Index

post-Fordism 169, 177
postmodern discourses 147–55, 164;
  entrepreneurialization of labour 150–2;
  immaterialization of labour 152–4;
  management by themes 154–5; production
  to reproduction shift 148–50; simulacra
  148–50
poverty 352, 353, 355, *360*
Powell, W.W. 218
power 7–8, 21, 240–3, 280
Power, M. 262
practicist epistemology 46–68; actor-networks
  52–4, 66; elements of 48–9; extra-organizational practices 50–2; intra-organizational
  practices 50; pedagogical reproduction 55–65;
  reflective practice 48–54; standardization of
  practice 49–50
Prahalad, C.K. 179–80, 287, 365
predictive models, cybernetics 84
Preston, A.M. 264
Prince of Wales 317
printing/copying machines 170
privatization 345–6
production 30–40, 167–93; cost accounting
  38–40; flexibility 168–81, 191; immaterialization of labour 153–4; just-in-time production
  189–91; lean production 181–9; Marxist
  theory 31; mechanization of 34; pre-factory
  systems 30–3; production to reproduction shift
  148–50; quality 181–9; regimentation of
  labour 36–7
product stewardship 306
professional interpretations xx
professional knowledge 49, 56–61, 70, 95
professional magazines/journals 50–1
profession, avocation comparison 49
profit 19, 30, 99
Profit Impact of Market Strategy (PIMS) database
  108, 109
public administration *see* New Public
  Management
public health 10; *see also* healthcare sector
punishment 254–5
putting-out systems 30–1

qualification structures 56–61
quality 181–9, 191–2; cost optimization logic
  183, *184*; discourses 186–9; as managerial
  paradigm 182; quality circles 190; quality
  costing 185–6

rational choice 256
rationalism 5
rationalist approach 72–4, 95
reflective practice 48–54, 66
reflexive sociology 62, *63*, 64, 67
regional conglomerations 178

regulation: corporate governance 303–4; markets
  105; and neoliberalism 254–5
'Relevance Lost' thesis (Johnson and Kaplan)
  156–7, 199, 200–3
religion 284
reporting systems, environmental impacts 338
research, action 51, 136–7, 155
resource management 265
responsibility accounting 28, 77, 232
responsibility centres 77
retail sector 304
return on investment (ROI) 156, 157
Rezaee, Z. 293
RICS *see* Royal Institution of Chartered
  Surveyors
risk management 312
risk, markets 105
Roberts, J. 265, 288, 289, 307, 308, 309
ROI *see* return on investment
Rousseau, D.M. 241
Roy, A. 252, 270, 271, 285, 286, 287, 363, 364,
  365
Royal Institution of Chartered Surveyors (RICS)
  337
Rule, J.B. 190
rural development 275, 277–8, 279, 363

Sabel, C.F. 177–8
sanctions, normalizing 15
Sanders, M.L. 275, 288
Sarvodaya Shramadana Movement (SSM) 275,
  277–8, 279
SBUs *see* strategic business units
Scapens, R.W. 93–4
Scarbrough, H. 54
Schmidt-Wellenburgh, C. 135
Scholte, J.A. 347
schools, development 362
scientific epistemology 69–96; academic
  theorization 70–2; critical vs. mainstream
  theorizations 72, **73–4**; economic rationality
  74–81; empiricist epistemology 89–94;
  purpose of 71; rationalist justification of
  knowledge 72–4; systems rationality 81–9
Scientific Management Movement 14, 34, 36
scientific rationality/reasoning 6, 52, 72
scorecards *see* balanced scorecards
security: corporate governance 300–2; flow control 309–10
Seeck, H. 133
self-governance 265–6
self-interest 80
Senge, P. 136
setup costs 171–2
Sewell, G. 189–91
shareholders 161–2, 293, 295, *296*, 297, 323
Simons, R. 87–9

Index   403

simulacra 148–50
skilled labour 32
Smith, A. 18
Smith, Ralph 64–5
social accountability 276, 305
social bodies 9
social capital 64, 284–5
social fields 62
socialization: accountability 290, 308–9; of capital 19–20, 24–9
social medicine 9–11
social mobility 41–2
social networks 64, 86, 149
social progress 5–6
social responsibility 318, 327
social science approach xxi–xxvii
social structures 86
social sustainability 317
social work 284
sociological perspective xxi–xxvii
software, enterprise resource planning 54, 56, 204, 212–13
solar firms 178
Solomon, J. 298
sovereignty 6, 7, 21, 247, 303
spaces, disciplined 12–13
Spain 197
specialization 40–1, 177–9
SPI see Strategic Planning Institute
SPMS see strategic performance management systems
Sri Lanka: Annual Report 357; microfinance 280; non-governmental organizations 274; privatization 346; rural development 275, 277–8, 279; World Bank league table **361**
SSM see Sarvodaya Shramadana Movement
staff costs 204–5, 206–8
stakeholders 323–4
Stalker, G.M. 89–90, 92
standardization 35, 49–50, 143
Standing, G. 172
Stark, D. 227, 230, 233–4, 289
Star, S.L. 234
the state: bureaucracy 253–4; competitive advantage 126–7, **331**; medicine 9–10; neoliberalism 102, 107, 110–11, 113, 247–69; penal scheme 254–5; re-engineering of 251–3; security 300–2; sovereignty 6, 7, 21, 247, 303
stock markets 107
Stoker, G. 256
strategic analyses 129–31
strategic business units (SBUs) 120, 121, 123, 128, 137
strategic discourses: competitive positioning 118–39; development 345–9; organizational reconfiguration 140–66; Porter's discourses 123–37; post-bureaucratic discourses 141–7;

postmodern discourses 147–55, 164; production systems 167–93; quality-based discourses 186–9
strategic mapping 120–2
strategic performance management systems (SPMS) 157–9, 164
strategic planning 262–3
Strategic Planning Institute (SPI) 108–9
strategic positioning, sustainability 327–8
strategic terrains 119–23
strategic units 123
strengths, weaknesses, opportunities and threats (SWOT) analysis 129
structural contingencies 90, *91*
structural dimensions 90
structural functionalism 86–9; Parsons' structural functionalism **87**; Simons' levers of control 87–9
structure-conduct-performance model 124–6
structuring of firms 28–9, 76–7
student feedback 263
subcontractors 31, 32
subjectivation 7–8
supply chains 170, 225–31
surplus value 19, 30, 99
surveillance 15, 190, 197, 203–8, 280
sustainability 315–41; balanced scorecards 330–3; capital investment decisions 328–9; competitive advantage **331**; competitive position analysis 329; concept/components of 316–18; consumer brands 327–8; corporate accountability 322–4; corporate strategic intents for *326*; cost accounting for 333–7; crisis of 113; definition 316; ecological sustainability 317; economic sustainability 316; envisioning of 325–7; financial privileging over 333; Friedman's conception 318–20; neoliberal political logic 318–21; operationalization of 328–38, 339; rationalization of 321–8; reporting 324, 327; social sustainability 317; strategic causality of 332–3; strategic positioning 327–8; strategizing of 324–5; surrendering of 333; sustainable products 327–8; value chain analysis 329, **330**
Swanepoel, H. 276
Swartz, D. 61
SWOT (strengths, weaknesses, opportunities and threats) analysis 129
Swyngedouw, E. 179
symbolic-analytical labour 153
symbolic capital 64–5, 66–7
symbolic systems 55–6
systematization, knowledge 34–5
system dynamics 90
system flexibilities 174–6
systems measurement 84
systems rationality 81–9; cybernetics 82–5; structural functionalism 86–9
'system trust' 242–3

404 *Index*

TA *see* throughput accounting
target costing 230, 238
taxation 134–5
Taylor, F.W. 143–4
TCE *see* transaction cost economics
TCO *see* total cost of ownership
teaching *see* pedagogy
technical competence xviii–xx
technical rationality 71
technology, flexible machines 170–2; *see also*
    accounting technologies; information
    technologies
techno-organizational dynamics xxviii
temporary labour 173
testing of contingencies 89–92
textbooks 56
textualization of practice 49–50
themes, management by 154–5
theoretical logics xxv–xxvii
theory of constraints (TOC) 214–16
Thomas, R. 258, 259
Thrane, S. 226–7, 232
throughput accounting (TA) 214–16
time: disciplined time 13–14; flexibility 172–3
time and motion studies 14, 143
timetabling 14
Tinker, T. xxii
TOC *see* theory of constraints
Tomkins, C. 241, 242
top management: ideology 160–1; quality-based
    discourses 186
total cost of ownership (TCO) 240
total quality cost 183
total quality management (TQM): biopolitical
    regime 189–91; economic justification of
    183–6; lean production 181
Toyota 143, 149, 187–9, 212, 213
TQM *see* total quality management
trade magazines 50–1
traditional accounting 156–7
traditional authority 41
transaction cost economics (TCE) 42, 75–6,
    195–6
transaction cost minimization 76
trust 237, 240–3
truth, and markets 106
Tyson Report 297

UN *see* United Nations
underdevelopment 352–62
UNDP (United Nations Development
    Programme) 285
unionized labour 173
United Kingdom (UK): civil service 262;
    corporate governance 295, 297; health sector
    10, 261, 264, 265, 266; Japanization of British
    industry 187

United Nations Development Programme
    (UNDP) 285
United Nations (UN), management consultancy
    survey 135–6
United States (US): competitiveness project
    surveys 132; manufacturing 218–19; tax
    system 134–5
universities 263
urban medicine 10
US *see* United States
Uzzi, B. 244

value chain accounting 239–40
value chain analysis 130, 329, **330**
Value Stream Maps (VSM) 212
Vesty, G. 328–9
violence *360*
virtualization technologies 148
visionary leadership 160
vocationalism xvi–xxi
Vollmer, H. xxii–xxiii
VSM *see* Value Stream Maps

Wacquant, L. 251–5
Wales, Prince of 317
Walker Review 295
Walmart 304
waste disposal/minimization 189, 190, 306
Waterman, R.H. 136
WDRs *see* World Development Reports
Weber, M. 41, 42, 49, 93
Wedgwood, Josiah 33, 39
welfare policies/provision 248, 252
Western management, Japanization of 187
Westphal, J.D. **299**
whole life costing (WLC) 335–7
Wickramasinghe, D. 261, 265, 345
Wiener, N. 82
Wilkinson, B. 189–91
Williamson, O.E. 42, 195, 196
WLC *see* whole life costing
work, rationalization of 34–6; *see also* labour
workshop factories 178
World Bank: corporate governance 302;
    country league tables 358–9, **361**; develop-
    ment 348, 349, 351–62; microfinance
    364–5
World Development Indicators 357
World Development Reports (WDRs) 303,
    351–62

Yusuf, S. 352, 353

Zajac, E.J. **299**
Zeitlin, J. 177
zero-defect rate 183–6, 191–2
Zwick, D. 107, 108